The Original Analects

D1055962

TRANSLATIONS FROM THE ASIAN CLASSICS

Translations from the Asian Classics

論語辨

The Original Analects

Sayings of Confucius and His Successors

A New Translation and Commentary by
白牧之
E. Bruce Brooks

and

白妙子
A. Taeko Brooks

Columbia University Press

New York

Library of Congress Cataloging-in-Publication Data

Confucius.
    [Lun yü. English]
    The original Analects : sayings of Confucius and his successors,
0479-0249 / a new translation and commentary by E. Bruce Brooks and
A. Taeko Brooks = [Lun yü pien / Pai Mu-chih, Pai Miao-tzu].
        p.   cm. — (Translations from the Asian classics)
    Parallel title in Chinese characters: translators' names also in
Chinese characters.
    Includes bibliographical references and index.
    ISBN 978-0-231-10431-9 (paper)

    I. Brooks, E. Bruce, 1936–   II. Brooks, A. Taeko.   III. Title.
IV. Series.
PL2478.L33   1997
181'.112—dc21
                                         97-25748

To

Tswēi Shù 崔述 (1740–1816)

述而不作

Preface

Chinese wisdom is known to the West chiefly in its escapist mode. But since China, alone among the great civilizations, has maintained a continuous political identity for more than two thousand years, its *practical* aspect also invites attention, on the chance that there may, after all, be more to life than the retreat from life.

Those who choose to pursue this possibility do encounter suggestive contrasts. Many Western thinkers posit an essential antagonism between a state and its people, with government little more than an armed truce between them, whereas one strand of Chinese thought holds that state and society complete each other; that they do not ultimately conflict; that rule is beneficial. There are also negative views, less novel to Westerners, which find the state to be hostile to the aspirations of its people, or aspiration itself to be absurd. These streams of thought and their variants meet and interact to form the rich tradition of Chinese philosophy.

The Analects dates from the beginning of the period when these philosophical traditions were beginning to be articulated. It seems to consist of disconnected sayings or conversations between Confucius and his followers, among which will be found striking remarks about social mutuality and governmental responsibility, but also much less obviously relevant material, and an apparent lack of overall plan. It is at this point that the search for an alternate political theory tends to peter out. According to our researches, which are briefly summarized in the Appendices, the Analects does have a rationale, but a developmental rather than an integral one. We find that the work contains only a core of sayings by the historical Confucius, to which were added layers of attributed sayings and conversations invented by his successors to update their heritage, and to address the new needs of changing times. Understood in this way, the Analects sayings do indeed document the historical Confucius, as tradition has always held, but they also reflect the changing concerns of his later followers, including their disputes with rival points of view, over a period of 230 years from his death in 0479 until the extinction of his state, Lǔ, and with it the Confucian school of Lǔ, in 0249.

This span encompasses all but the last 20 years of the period known as the Warring States, the classic period of Chinese thought, which ended in the political unity imposed by the Chín conquest of 0221. Thus was established the first of the Chinese empires, for which the Warring States centuries seem in retrospect to have been a period of preparation. Besides the frequent wars for which they are named, these were also the centuries which witnessed the growth of trade, the spread of writing, the rise of bureaucracy, the elaboration of ritual, the growth of technology, the invention of myth, and the rise of the "little" people as a factor in great affairs. This social and intellectual tumult, which is only dimly visible in the extant texts, profoundly shaped the development of Chinese thought.

To assist the reader in perceiving the Analects in this way, the present translation departs from all previous ones in presenting the material *in historical order*. The old numbering of passages has been retained, to facilitate scholarly reference and maintain convertibility with other translations, but the sayings themselves have been arranged, as nearly as possible, in the order in which they were added to the text. Behind the Analects as thus ordered, the reader may for the first time discern the great events of the age, the rival thinkers with whom Confucius's successors kept up a sometimes acrimonious debate, and, alone at the beginning, Confucius himself, the intensely dedicated if unsuccessful courtier who speaks to us in the core sayings.

A few conventions have been adopted to make the commentary more accessible for readers new to antiquity or things Chinese. The culturally intrusive abbreviation BC in dates is replaced by a prefixed zero (as, 0221 = 221 BC), and Chinese words have been spelled by a convention more intuitively obvious than the standard systems to readers with established English-alphabet reflexes. These devices (for details, see the Introduction) are commended herewith to other writers on these subjects. On the other hand, the specific thought and syntax of the text, and the form of some of its idioms, have as far as possible been preserved, drawing for the purpose on the wide resources of literary English, rather than adjusted to the supposed predispositions of readers, in the conviction that the value of a translation lies in conveying to its readers something that they did not already possess.

It may not be a coincidence that most previous English translations of the Analects have been made for a British audience, since the feudal heritage of Britain helps make the postfeudal world of the Analects more intelligible. To annex this advantage for American readers, occasional European references have been made. It is hoped that any European readers will look on these touches with an indulgent and forgiving eye. Another motif in the commentary is a running discussion with Arthur Waley, to our mind the most probing of Analects translators, to remind the student of the existence of other opinions, and also for what Bernhard Karlgren once felicitously called "the pleasure of crossing swords with him."

Specialists may skip the commentaries after each passage, which are set in smaller type to facilitate that process. Generalists will find in them a modest sample of what a learned commentary might contain. Another part of their purpose for the general reader is simply to slow the general reader down. The Analects is not a unitary treatise, to be skimmed in half an hour, but a corpus of insights, each to be pondered before going on to the next. Its gnomic sayings by their nature invite, and indeed require, the reader's mental participation in order to extract their meaning and develop their value.

The intent of these sayings is at bottom ethical: to guide Confucius's hearers (and their successors) by strengthening resolve, shaping conduct, and preparing for the crises of practical life. Over the centuries, they have proved highly effective for that purpose. They convey, not less strikingly because discontinuously, a vivid sense of the importance of holding to right principles, doing the honorable thing, and working toward the ideal, the humane, public outcome. Confucius was himself a political failure, and many of these sayings also provide psychological support for the principled individual *in adversity*, and have helped such individuals not only to survive, but to preserve their capacity to contribute to society. Still other sayings constitute a different resource: a plan for society itself, in which ruler and ruled interact on a less adverse basis. This not quite lost tradition may prove to be of value for the long future of China; it may also conceivably become a suggestive addition to the heritage of other nations.

Readers of this Analects are thus invited to join earlier readers in many centuries and indeed in many languages, who have found in this text a faithful companion on our common, ongoing journey.

E. Bruce Brooks
A. Taeko Brooks

22 November 1997

Contents

Bronze Terminal Ornament

Length 25·5 cm (10 in). 04c/03c. Courtesy Freer Gallery of Art (32·14)

Introduction

This translation seeks to make available to readers our finding that the Analects (Lún Yǔ 論語; LY) is not one text but *a series of texts* of different date, containing a few sayings that may go back to the historical Confucius, along with many others that were added in the next two centuries by his successors in what gradually became the Confucian school of Lǔ.[1] While thus preserving (as tradition has always held) an authentic glimpse of the historical Confucius, the Analects on this view acquires additional interest as a consecutive record of the progressive elaboration of Confucius's thought, and its interaction with other modes of thought, from the time of his death to shortly before the founding of the Chín Empire. Under the form of a set of sayings ascribed to Confucius, the Analects emerges instead as a *history of early Confucianism*, compiled from year to year by the Confucians of Lǔ. Approaching the text in this way permits the reader to follow the school's changing philosophical emphases, and, to a certain extent, to see how they may have related to the changing social and intellectual context of the Warring States period.

To make this new view of the work fully apparent, it is necessary to present the material in what we find to be *the order of its composition*. This entails some rearrangement of chapters (LY 1–3 were all preposed at different times during the course of the work, whereas LY 4–20 were added in that order), and of individual sayings (a quarter of which we find to be interpolations).[2] Such a rearrangement has thus been made the basis for the present version. At the same time, for the convenience of new and experienced readers alike, it has been thought well to maintain contact with the traditional sequence of the text, represented by the classic translation of James Legge,[3] which also contains a complete Chinese character text. The following conventions have been adopted to facilitate reader cross-consultation of that text: (1) The chapter numbers are retained, so that the nucleus of genuine Confucian sayings, which might logically be labeled as "LY 1," still appears here as "LY 4." (2) Readers who expect LY 1 at the beginning of this book and find LY 4 instead are directed (by a note in the righthand running head) to the pages on which LY 1, as well as LY 2–3, begin. (3) Passages, like chapters, have not been renumbered; nonconsecutive passage numbers, such as LY 4:16 directly following LY 4:14, will show that an interpolation (LY 4:15) has been removed. A full list of the interpolated passages, and the locations to which they have been reassigned, is given on page 329. (4) The Legge numbering is added in brackets at the end of all translated passages, whether interpolated or not, which are differently numbered in the present version.[4]

---

[1] For an introduction to the general Warring States text researches of which this finding is a part, see Brooks **Prospects** (these and other short citation forms are expanded in the list of Works Cited, at the end of the book). A schematic idea of the larger argument will be given later in this Introduction.

[2] The scholarly reader may wish to detour at this point to Appendices 1–3, where this view of the text is derived and illustrated in more detail.

[3] For this towering Sinological figure, see Ride **Biographical**. We are pleased to be informed that a full biography, by Norman Giradot and L. Pfister, is in preparation.

[4] Readers consulting other versions, including Legge's, are cautioned that most texts and translations vary slightly from each other in the division, and thus in the numbering, of passages. The present version follows the numbering of the 1929 concordance.

Notes following an Analects passage are cited by a suffixed n (as 9:5n), and the Reflections at the end of chapters by a suffixed r (as 9r). Interpolated passages are marked by a prefixed asterisk (as *9:1), and by a suffixed superscript number for the chapter to which they have been appended (as *9:1¹¹, indicating that, in our best judgement, *9:1 was composed shortly before or after the main body of chapter 11). The latter feature serves also as an approximate cross-reference, and should spare the reader constant recourse to the finding list of interpolations on page 329.

Citations, in both text and notes, are given in short form (Author Surname followed by **Title Keyword**). Some short forms will themselves be recognizable to scholars, thus making unnecessary a reference to the final listing of Works Cited on page 315, in which all short citations have been bibliographically expanded.

Form. The pairing of sayings, an important feature of the original, is indicated in the translation by symbols prefixed to the reference code: ⌐ for the first of a pair, ∟ for the second, and ⊨ for the unpaired final saying, or envoi, in some sections. Pairing is an aid in the identification of interpolations, which often interrupt the original pairing pattern. It also assists interpretation, by letting each of two paired sayings serve as a microcontext for the other. Some cryptic Analects sayings have been rendered even more obscure by the passage of time, but the Analects in its fully-interpolated form is made *needlessly baffling* by the loss of these pairing clues. Removing the interpolations thus makes the original Analects sayings less opaque. It also reveals a hitherto unsuspected formal beauty in some of the chapter layouts.

Dates. The culturally parochial abbreviations BC and its variant BCE are here replaced by prefixed zero: 0479 is "479 BC" (479 = AD 479). A prefixed c ("circa") means a *most likely* year, whether or not its name ends in a zero, 04c means "04th [pronounced oh-fourth] century," 0548–0479 is the *span* from 0548 to 0479 inclusive, and 0315/0305 is a *range of possible dates*, also inclusive.[5]

Chinese Words are here spelled for maximum "guessability" by readers with English-alphabet reflexes. The rule is "consonants as in English, vowels as in Italian," with a few special conventions, such as v (an analogue of the linguist's *inverted* ʌ) for the central vowel of "gut," plus æ as in "cat," r as in "fur," z as in "adz," and yw (after l or n, simply w) for "umlaut u." Tones are given as contours: hīgh, rísing, lŏw, or fàlling. This system is compatible with the unproblematic one long established for Japanese; it is hoped that its use will help to dispel the "Oriental mystique" which several aggressively nonphonetic Chinese spelling systems have helped to promote.[6] An equivalence table for the systems most often encountered begins on page 325. The pronunciation represented is that of standard scholarly Mandarin, except that a few words which through sound change are now identical in Mandarin are distinguished by restoring lost consonants, among them the states Wèi 衛 and [Ng]wèi 魏, both now pronounced "Wèi." Coordinate compounds are here distinguished from subordinating compounds by a slash rather than a hyphen joining their romanized forms, for example Chūn/Chyōu = Spring *and* Autumn, yīn/yáng = yīn *and* yáng, and Dàu/Dv́ Jīng = The Book of Dàu *and* Dv́.

---

[5]Unless otherwise noted, our authority for historical dates is Chyén **Kǎu**.

[6]We join the plea of Boodberg **Comments** 23 for a system more accessible to generalists, and that of Kennedy **Biographies** 499f for one less hampering for scholars. The sense that one is unavoidably pronouncing the words wrong inhibits students in survey courses, and also tends to discourage dialogue between experts in different fields.

The Spring and Autumn Background

When we meet Confucius in LY 4, his values are obviously under attack, but it is less obvious exactly what his values *are*. We must infer them from LY 4 and from whatever can be known of his own period, the end of the Spring and Autumn era. Our primary source for this period is the Lǔ court chronicle after which it is named, covering the years 0721–0479. It tells us something of ritual, diplomacy, and war, but tantalizingly little of anything else. Supplemented by archaeology, it suggests the following picture of the world out of which Confucius emerged.

Lǔ had been founded by the Jōu rulers as a buffer state west of Sùng, the home of a remnant of the Shāng people, whom the Jōu had replaced as the dominant force in the middle Yellow River valley. After one Shāng rebellion, Lǔ was relocated *east* of Sùng, strategically outflanking future revolts, and imposing a top layer on the indigenous population.[7] The Jōu lost power in 0771, and moved their capital eastward to a new site on the Lwò River. Thereafter, Lǔ took charge of its own affairs, including the keeping of its own chronicle, the building of its own palace, and the gradual accumulation of divination expertise and a series of state rituals.[8] It grew from a series of strongpoints to a continuous domain, control of which came to be disputed between the hereditary Prince[9] and the three collateral clans. Communications with other post-Jōu states were improved. Farming was extended at the expense of tree cover, and double-cropping further increased the food supply; hunting was gradually confined to forest preserves, and became an elite monopoly.

The core of this society was a warrior elite whose weapons were the compound bow and the horse-drawn chariot. They lived on separate farmholds and assembled for campaigns at the order of the Prince, but seem to have themselves controlled the perhaps indigenous people on their holdings.[10] They were trained in martial skills and a service ethic based on ideals of duty, courage, selflessness, and comradeship. Traces of such a heritage may be detected in Confucius's own value system.

Iron was known from at least 0493; its first effect was probably an increase in agricultural production. A shift in the relation of the state to its military elite, and (apparently from 0490) the direct taxation of their lands, undermined the old feudal-service pattern. The new bureaucracy was staffed in part by artisans and other palace-connected individuals with a profit rather than a service ethic. Thus began the merging of the lower order with the old elite.[11] It is this crass "lower" culture that we seem to see in the early Analects, as a resented rival of the older values.

---

[7]Jōu-style graves are found side by side with different-style graves (presumably those of the local population) throughout the archaeological history of Lǔ; Zhang **Lu** 58. For the later military suppression of the indigenous Rúng peoples, see Brooks **Point**.

[8]For the post-0771 palace, see Zhang **Lu**; for the ritual cycle, see Brooks **Divination**.

[9]Legge has accustomed English readers to the translation "duke" for gūng 公, here rendered "prince," and to overly hierarchical treatment of other Spring and Autumn titles. Kennedy **Butterfly** 312–319 has exposed the latter fallacy. We here use, as more responsive to the early Chinese common-language usage of these terms, the equivalents gūng 公 / prince, hóu 侯 / lord, bwó 伯 / elder, dž 子 / master, and nán 男 / chieftain.

[10]This *indirect* or *nontransitive sovereignty* seems to us the most fruitful definition of the vexed term "feudal." We adopt it here, following the discussion in Strayer **Idea** 4–5.

[11]For a brief summary of Warring States changes, see Bodde **Feudalism** 66–67.

Sources of Warring States Thought

Warring States thought is preserved for us in some three dozen received texts, including the Analects, all of more or less disputed date. It is a matter of some urgency to re-examine this corpus, and to resolve the uncertainties as far as possible.

As a sample[12] of this process, consider six well-known texts: the Gwǎndž (GZ), Mwòdž (MZ), Analects (Lún Yw̌; LY), Mencius (MC), Lǎudž or Dàu/Dv́ Jīng (DDJ), and Jwāngdž (JZ). Each is associated with, and most are named for, an individual: (1) the Chí minister Gwǎn Jùng (died 0645), (2) Mwò Dí, thought to be a generation after Confucius; (3) Confucius (died 0479); (4) Mencius, whose public career began in c0320; (5) Lǎudž, claimed as an older contemporary of Confucius; and (6) Jwāngdž, a supposed contemporary of Mencius. If we begin by attributing these texts wholly to these figures, and plot them on a scale from the 0771 fall of Jōu to a point (0100) in early Hàn, with divisions at the 0479 death of Confucius (which we take as the beginning of the Warring States period)[13] and the 0221 Chín political unification (which ends it), we get the following picture:

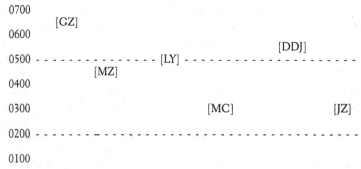

```
0700
         [GZ]
0600
                                                        [DDJ]
0500 - - - - - - - - - - - - - [LY] - - - - - - - - - - - - - - - - - - -
                   [MZ]
0400

0300                         [MC]                    [JZ]

0200 - - - - - - - - - - - - - - - - - - - - - - - - - - - - - - - - - - -

0100
```

Critical scholars now reject the connection of the GZ with Gwǎn Jùng; Rickett dates its parts to a range from the 04c to early Hàn.[14] A wide range of dates in the MZ is also now recognized,[15] and many scholars would assign the DDJ to the 03c rather than the 06c.[16] The JZ is self-labeled as having "inner/outer/miscellaneous" strata; the latest seem to be from Hàn.[17] The drift of these opinions is (1) to reject some claims associating certain texts with early historical figures, and (2) to date those texts later than those associations would imply, sometimes to a *span* of dates rather than one single compositional date. The concept of a span of dates differs from that of a unitary text *composed at one time*, and implies a different process.

---

[12]From a lecture at the University of North Carolina in 1993. We are grateful to host Eric Henry and to members of the audience for their comments on that occasion. A more detailed overview of selected results can be found in Brooks **Prospects**.

[13]Lawton **Art** 9–10 surveys various endpoints assigned to the Warring States period; we here use 0479–0221 (and, for Spring and Autumn, 0771–0479).

[14]Rickett **Guanzi** 1/3, 14–15; Rickett **Guanzi Xuekan** 201–204.

[15]Graham **Later** 3, Graham **Mo Tzu** 337–338; see also Loewe **Crisis** 108.

[16]The trend to the later date can be observed in motion from Hu **Recent** (1933) through Chan **Way** (1963) 61–63 to Boltz **Lau Tzu** (1993) 269–271.

[17]Watson **Chuang** 13–17; Roth **Chuang Tzu** 56–57.

Freed of the association with their authenticating *historical figures*, these accumulations of material then present, *as texts*, the following picture:

```
0700

0600

0500 - - - - - - - - - - - - - - - [LY] - - - - - - - - - - - - - - - - - - - -

0400              MZ
         GZ       MZ
0300     GZ       MZ              [MC]                    JZ
         GZ       MZ                        [DDJ]         JZ
0200 - - -GZ - - - MZ - - - - - - - - - - - - - - - - - - -JZ - - - -
         GZ       MZ                                     JZ
0100
```

We note that two of the integral texts *are Confucian*, and that the accumulating texts cease with the Hàn establishment of Confucianism as the state ideology in 0136. Are the Confucian texts merely immune from critical scholarship which operates more freely on extinct-school texts?[18] Inconsistencies in LY and MC *do* imply an accretion process, as do those of the DDJ. Arguing thus, we arrive at:

```
0700

0600

0500 - - - - - - - - - - - - - - - LY - - - - - - - - - - - - - - - - - - - -
                                   LY
0400              MZ               LY
         GZ       MZ               LY                DDJ
0300     GZ       MZ               LY      MC        DDJ
         GZ       MZ               LY      MC        DDJ        JZ
0200 - - -GZ - - - MZ - - - - - - - - - - - - - - - - - - - - -JZ - - -
         GZ       MZ                                           JZ
0100
```

in which another cutoff date emerges: the Lǔ texts LY, MC, and (surprisingly) DDJ all cease being compiled in 0249, the date of the Lǔ conquest. We infer that these *cumulative texts* were in the care of groups with an *ongoing advocational unity*, each continually updating its position as time passed, and ceasing when the military situation (in 0249) or the political climate (in 0136) became inhospitable.

So much for the *dating* of the texts. The next step is to *take the dates seriously*, by not treating an 04c and later text like the GZ as a primary source for the 07c. This second step has proved to be by far the more difficult for later investigators.[19]

[18]So Gù Jyé-gāng on Tswēi Shù: Gù **Lùn Gǔ Shř** 1/59 (Gù **Ancient** #192).

[19]The implications of text dates are sometimes evaded by assuming oral transmission from earlier centuries. Studies of oral praxis (Ong **Orality** 34, 57–68; WSWG Q20, and letter from Walter J. Ong to the authors, 20 June 96) do not support such assumptions. The Confucian *school* did preserve its text intact in memory from 0249 to the end of the 0213-0191 Chín/Hàn ban on Confucian texts, but that interval is only two generations, and that degree of advocacy-group organization did not obtain in earlier periods.

The World of Thought

The hint of different viewpoints contained in the above illustration can be expanded here, as an orientation to the opinion-context of the Analects.

Confucianism. As noted above, the root ideas of Confucius, and thus the starting-point of Confucianism, came out of the Spring and Autumn warrior ethos that was already obsolescent at his death in 0479. The Analects apparently preserves some actual sayings of Confucius, and many more by successive heads of the school which was founded after his death, and continued active until the conquest of Lǔ in 0249. This is the core tradition within the larger Confucian heritage. Confucians also established themselves in Wèi (and its geographic successor Ngwèi) and Chí. At the Chí court they produced in c0312 a work called the Dzwǒ Jwàn, ostensibly a commentary on the Lǔ chronicle Spring and Autumn, but in fact a prediction of, and a blueprint for, Chí domination of the other states. Mencius, a student in the Lǔ school, left Lǔ in 0320 for a career advising contemporary rulers in Ngwèi, Chí, and some lesser states. He founded his own school of Confucian thought (which later split into two subschools, both of which are represented in the present Mencius text). Still later, and wholly within the 03c, comes Sywndz, probably educated by the Confucians of Ngwèi, briefly prominent in Chí, but for much of his philosophical life employed as the civil administrator of conquered Lǔ, where he had his own influential school (documents of which survive as the Sywndz text). His Confucianism replaced other forms in the 03c, and remained dominant into the Hàn dynasty. It is much more compatible than other forms of Confucianism with the autocratic, divine-ruler, universal empire established by Chín in 0221.

Micianism. Also Anglicized as Mohism; this is apparently the ideology of a group at a lower social level than the Confucians, whose founder was the unknown Mwò Dí. It had become an organized movement by the early 04c, and competed successfully with the Confucians for positions at the Lǔ court, where its adherents compiled a sort of counter-Analects, now preserved as MZ 46–50 (see Appendix 3). The core of the Mwòdz is its ethical teachings; there are also sections on defensive warfare and logic. The Micians are the technocrats among the schools, and show a seemingly mercantile influence in their touchstone concept of profit or benefit,[20] which was highly offensive to the more aristocratic, more selfless, Confucians.

Legalism. This is the term conventionally applied to a range of thinkers whose only surviving early text is the Gwǎndz. They took a managerial approach, and worked to elaborate the ideal form of the new bureaucratic state and its economic and social structures, the whole being conceived largely in productive terms. This early Chí Legalism differs somewhat from the later and more draconic Chín version, which was less explained in texts than adumbrated in practice, and which contributed much to the final form of the universal Chinese state founded by Chín in 0221 and resumed, with variations, by the Hàn after 0206. The development of this western form of Legalism falls within a later time-frame than the Analects, and we shall not be much concerned with it in the present work. A Chín-sponsored encyclopedic compendium, the Lw̌-shr̀ Chūn/Chyōu (LSCC) of 0239, with its two later strata, does preserve some useful information about earlier schools of thought.

---

[20]Graham **Later** 4–8; compare, with reservations, Jàu **Tān** 131–134.

Dàuism. The Dàuists do not form a *philosophical* group in this period; the root insight of many who later came to be included in that rubric is the technique of meditation, which was apparently known in Lǔ (and probably Chí) by the 05c. Its first textual representative is the Dàu/Dv́ Jīng (DDJ), a Lǔ work compiled over the period c0340–0250. Like the Micians, the DDJ group competed successfully with the Confucians at the Lǔ court; the later DDJ reflects their theories of statecraft. In the 03c, stimulated by the traumatic 0286 obliteration of Sùng by Chí, there arose a number of groups advocating lifestyles ranging from the primitivist through the transcendental. Some writings of these groups are preserved in the Jwāngdž. Their oerall tone is anti-governmental, and their dialogue with the Analects group, who stoutly defend a more positive view of government service, is predictably bitter.

Military Writers. The defensive skills of the Micians were honed in symbiosis with those of the generals proper. The Sūndž Bīng-fǎ, or simply the Sūndž, a Lǔ or perhaps Chí work which accumulated over the latter part of the 04c, represents this vital expertise, which unsurprisingly also exerted its influence at the Lǔ court. The policy differences leading to the loss of Confucian court influence in c0302 seem to have been largely over the Lǔ state's military ambitions.

The Cosmologists. Another strand of thought, which became prominent in the last quarter of the 04c, was a philosophy of nature which related human institutions to a permanent, objective reality, especially astronomical and calendrical reality. The theories of yīn and yáng as constitutive forces, the associated Five Planets or wǔ-syíng 五行 theory of successive astral domination in terrestrial affairs, and above all the fascination with the predictability of astronomical phenomena, and the mapping of mundane phenomena on each other in numerical sets, offered an optimistic if also rigid view of an intelligible and controllable world. Dzōu Yĕn of Chí is usually regarded as the leading figure in this line of thought, which is unfortunately not represented by surviving early texts, and must be glimpsed indirectly in other writings (both the yīn/yáng and astral correspondence theories are already reflected in the c0312 Chí text Dzwŏ Jwàn); see also Sivin **Naturalists**. Their contribution to the eventual theory of the autocratic state was profound.

The Logicians. The logical portions of the Mwòdž are the largest surviving trace of a late 04c and 03c interest in words and referents, the validity of statements and of chains of propositions, the technique of definition, and the art of verbal argument in general. Several rival schools of debate also existed. Concern for the reliability of statements underlay what Waley has called the "language crisis" of the late 04c.

The Warring Classics. One of the most effective stratagems in what is often called the Hundred Schools debate turned out to be not argument, but something that could silence argument: ancient authority. The false attribution of several texts, noted above, was undoubtedly motivated by the desire of rival schools to claim greater antiquity than that of the Confucians. Such competition led in the late 04c to widespread forgery of authenticating texts. The Confucians, not to be outflanked, also embodied their ideas in purportedly pre-Confucian texts. The first of these was the Shī, or Classic of Poetry, which had been begun already in the 05c; its progress to completion in c0325 is mirrored in the Analects. First heard from in the mid 04c, and part of the new rivalry, are several Shū, or Documents (purported speeches by ancient kings) and the Yì, or Changes, a divination text which is still a cult classic. In Ngwèi, a similar mania led to the forging of a chronicle, the Bamboo Annals, linking that state to the earliest of the mythical rulers, the so-called Yellow Emperor, who was also claimed as a progenitor by the ruling house of Chí.

A Checklist of Texts

The texts mentioned above, and others which will be referred to in the notes to the translation, are here listed in the order of their short-citation codes. A list will also be found in the Works Cited section at the end of the book.

• **BA** (Bamboo Annals). A spurious Ngwèi chronicle composed in imitation of the CC but annexing all of Jōu and pre-Jōu history as well (the earliest portions claim to come from a time before writing was known in this part of the world); completed, by its own account, in 0299. Its 04c portions, being recent as of the time of compilation, are more accurate than such later sources as the SJ; they have been used by scholars to correct errors in the SJ. Translated in Legge **Shoo**.

• **CC** (Chūn/Chyōu, "Spring and Autumn"). The genuine court chronicle of Lǔ, covering the years 0721–0479. Translated in Legge **Ch'un**.

• **DDJ** (Dàu/Dv́ Jīng). The text of a Lǔ meditation group from c0350 on, later influential in Lǔ politics; its latter portion, DDJ 38–81, is especially rich in this "purposive" material. Translated from the oldest (Chín) version in Henricks **Te** and Mair **Tao**, and from the standard text in Waley **Way** and many others.

• **DJ** (Dzwǒ Jwàn). A supplement to the CC, begun in Lǔ in c0350; the present text is a Chín-adapted expansion of c0312. Gives a retrospective picture of Spring and Autumn life, apparently blended with details from the late 04c. Justly esteemed as a narrative, but must be used cautiously as a source. Translated in Legge **Ch'un**.

• **GY** (Gwó Yw̌). A c0306 imitation of the DJ: a set of stories without the CC framework (and with an emphasis on Jìn), and sometimes at odds with the DJ. There is at present no English translation; we have used Henry **Summaries**.

• **GZ** (Gwǎndž). A compendium of the writings of several governmental theorists and advisors in Chí (including one strand which has a Mician character) and their successors from the early 04c to Hàn. Translated in Rickett **Guanzi**.

• **HNZ** (Hwái-nándž). An eclectic Dàuist work of early Hàn, commissioned and overseen by the Hàn king Lyóu Ān, and completed in its present form by 0139. Excerpts are translated in Morgan **Tao**, Major **Heaven**, and Ames **Rulership**.

• **HS** (Hàn Shū). A history of the Hàn dynasty, completed c90. Esteemed by later scholars for its stylistic elegance, but later than, and in parallel chapters never preferable to, the earlier SJ. Partially translated in Dubs **Han**.

• **JGT** (Jàn-Gwó Tsv̀; "Stratagems of the Warring States"). A Hàn conflation of six collections of tales, some wholly fictional but others apparently preserving a memory of Warring States events or conditions. Translated in Crump **Ts'e**.

• **JY** (Jūng Yūng; the "Doctrine of the Mean"). An 03c treatise with affinities to Mencius and echoes in the Analects. Translated in Legge **Analects**.

• **JZ** (Jwāngdž). A collection of Dàuist material of diverse viewpoints from several states, ranging in date from the early 03c to Hàn. Philosophically nihilistic and anti-governmental, but stylistically brilliant, and of enormous literary influence. Translated in Watson **Chuang** and in Mair **Wandering**.

• **KZJY** (Kǔngdž Jyā-yw̌; "Family Traditions of Confucius"). A late text with some early material which may go back to an 04c Kǔng tradition. These portions, though mythologically elaborated, are in parts useful for Confucius's early life and personal circle. Ten later chapters are translated in Kramers **Chia Yü**.

• **LJ** (Lǐ Jì). A Hàn compilation of texts relating to ritual (including JY), some of them reflecting pre-Hàn traditions which may go back to the late 04c, and others being little more than schematic fantasizing. Translated in Legge **Li**.

• **LSCC** (Lǔ-shř Chūn/Chyōu). An eclectic compendium of 0239 and later, commissioned by the Chín statesman Lǔ Bù-wéi. It is apparently an attempt to synthesize major Warring States schools of thought as a basis for the universal state. An English translation by Jeffrey Riegel and John Knoblock is in preparation.

• **LY** (Lún Yǔ; the Analects). Sayings of Confucius and his successors in the school of Lǔ, 0479–0249. Translated below; the standard English version of the traditional neo-Confucian interpretation remains Legge **Analects**. Waley **Analects** attempts to get behind this "scriptural" reading to an earlier, Hàn-dynasty one.

• **MC** (Mencius). Mencius's interviews with rulers from 0320 on make up part of MC 1; the rest is of 03c date, and stems from the activity of two posthumous schools: a politically focused southern one, and an ethically focused northern one. Translated in Legge **Mencius**, Lau **Mencius**, and other versions.

• **MTJ** (Mù Tyēndž Jwàn). A spurious record of the western travels of the 010c King Mù of Jōu, composed in Ngwèi c0310 and reflecting a late 04c interest in foreign peoples and distant travels. Translated in Cheng **Mu** and Mathieu **Mu**.

• **MZ** (Mwòdž). The text of an 04c–02c school which claimed as its founder the unknown figure Mwò Dí. It seems to reflect the interests of small property-owners and entrepreneurs; its key concept is profit, and its cultural agenda emphasizes utility and social consistency. The ethical and anecdotal portions are translated in Mei **Ethical**; the logical ones in Graham **Later**.

• **SBF** (Sūndž Bīng-fǎ, or Sūndž's Art of War). A treatise on the 04c art of war, written during c0345–c0272. Considered the greatest of the early military treatises. Translated in Griffith **Sun** and, with other military texts, in Sawyer **Seven**.

• **Shř** (The [Classic of] Poetry). Compiled (and, we argue, mostly written) from the middle 05c to the late 04c; one can watch from the evolving Analects as it reaches its final 305-poem size. Translated in Legge **She** and Waley **Songs**.

• **Shū** (The [Classic of] Documents). Purported speeches of ancient rulers, the earliest written in the middle 04c by the Micians and other rivals of the Confucians. The extant Shū contains the Confucian school documents plus later forgeries of the lost Mician ones. Translated in Legge **Shoo**; for numbering, see Brooks **Shū**.

• **SJ** (Shř Jì). A history of China through early Hàn, largely complete by c090. Its use is unavoidable but problematic, since it is a synthesis of pre-Imperial thought traditions which are not otherwise preserved. Partly translated in Watson **Records**; a complete translation, Nienhauser **Records**, is currently in progress.

• **SSSY** (Shř-shwō Syīn Yǔ; "New Stories of the Age"). Anecdotes illustrating the style and character of noted Six Dynasties personalities; compiled c430. Shows the place of the Analects in the post-Hàn high culture. Translated in Mather **Yü**.

• **SZ** (Sywndž). As Director of Chǔ-occupied Lǔ from 0254, Sywndž had power over contemporary Lǔ thought; his influence may be detected in late layers of the Analects and Mencius. These school writings are translated in Knoblock **Xunzi**.

• **Yì** (The [Classic of] Changes), a divination text not referred to, and probably not written, before the middle 04c. Translated from the oldest (Chín) version in Shaughnessy **I**, and from the received text in Wilhelm **I** and many others.

Prolegomena to LY 4

We here provide, for readers about to encounter Confucius in LY 4, what we feel can be plausibly deduced from early sources about his life and career.[21]

Family. Confucius's father Shú (or Shúlyáng) Hv̀ was descended from Kǔng Fáng-shú, a warrior refugee from Sùng who had settled to the east of the Lǔ capital after a Sùng military defeat under Hwà Ywǽn in 0607. Fáng-shú and his son had no great success in Lǔ (Hwà Ywǽn remained prominent in Sùng, and twice visited Lǔ in later years). His grandson Hv̀, born c0592, abandoned the surname Kǔng and moved to Dzōu, south of the capital, to seek a better fortune. He distinguished himself in a battle of 0563, and led a raid in 0556, probably receiving a capital-area farmhold for the latter service.[22] In c0552 he married Yén Jv̄ng-dzài, daughter of a family that may have been involved in trade.[23] A first son was born crippled, and the couple prayed at Ní Mountain, southeast of the capital, for the health of the second. That second son, Chyōu ("Hill"), or Jùng-ní (from "Ní Mountain"), born in 0549, was the future Confucius.

Confucius. Chyōu's father died when he was three. He grew up in poverty, doing low-level jobs that were not the ordinary lot of an heir to a military holding. He probably retained from this period an emphasis on will and self-improvement, and a willingness to learn from low as well as high. Early hardship accelerated his maturity (he married at nineteen in c0531; his son Lǐ "Carp" or Bwó-yv̄, "Fish," was born in c0530) but delayed his career cycle. It may not have been until he was thirty, in c0518, that he entered on his military service. Jāu-gūng, the reigning Lǔ Prince, attempted to overthrow the rival Jì clan in 0517, and, failing, went into exile that fall, quite possibly with Confucius in his military escort, wandering from Chí on the north to Jìn on the west; he died there in 0510. His brother (Dìng-gūng) was allowed to rule in Lǔ, but those like Confucius who had supported Jāu-gūng were initially excluded from court. We may see here the root of Confucius's legitimist political position, and his personal resentment. With the 0494 accession of Āi-gūng, who took a bolder line against the Jì, Confucius may have received a modest post at court; it was perhaps then that he resumed the surname Kǔng. He last attended court in 0481; his withdrawal may have been occasioned by the death of his son Bwó-yv̄, who was then in his fiftieth year. Bwó-yv̄'s death may have had other consequences: the process of the creation of deities in Chinese popular religion can begin with the lack of an heir to perform the ancestral rites for a deceased man, and thus the formation of a cult to permit veneration of him by non-kin outsiders.[24] Confucius himself died in the fourth month of 0479, in his seventieth year.

---

[21]For a more detailed discussion of Confucius and his circle, see Appendix 4.

[22]As an example of how newcomers make their way in a hereditary military tradition, we note that some WW2 German generals were descended from centuries-old Prussian military-nobility families (Barnett **Generals** 175 [von Rundstedt], 422 [von Manteuffel]); others received an endowment as a reward for outstanding service during the war itself (Barnett 216 [von Reichenau]).

[23]The word yén 顔 means "face" or "complexion," and might be the occupational surname of a cosmetics preparer or purveyor. There is also a phonetically compatible Syūngnú word for "rouge" (Boodberg **Sino-Altaica III** 144–146).

[24]Suggested by Alvin P. Cohen, 25 January 1996; see further Cohen **Coercing** 257f. For the mythic implications of Confucius's fatherlessness, see Jensen **Wise**.

Confucius's Circle. These were, properly speaking, his official protégés (the term "disciples" implies a relationship which arose only later, as the Confucian school became more organized): young men whom he had been guiding in the early years of a civilian court career. There may have been a secondary relationship with the relatives of these protégés, or with others for whom Confucius may have functioned as a social conduit (see Appendix 4); there are, for example, besides the well-known protégé Yén Hwéi, a veritable cloud of other, unknown Yéns, all presumably Confucius's maternal relatives. Confucius probably began to function as a mentor for those entering on court careers late in the reign of Dǐng-gūng, with enhanced visibility from 0494 on under the new regime of Aī-gūng. Some of his protégés were of good social or economic background (they are distinguished in the text by the Dž- or "Young Master" prefix in their personal names); others were obscure. Members of both groups seem to have held or been offered responsible positions. The general impression is one of genuine opportunity, in which ability, apart from status, counted for something.

The early Analects sayings imply tensions within the group, largely due to political differences: several of the earliest and most promising protégés took service under the illegitimate Jì clan, while others, on the average less successful, were like Confucius firmly loyal to the princely line. Another type of tension which can be seen in the early Analects layers is that between the old warrior elite, who had once monopolized most court positions, whose social ideal was the jyūndž 君子 or "gentleman," the code of those who were born to rule others, and what the text calls the syǎu-rýn 小人 or "little people," newcomers of artisan or entrepreneurial origin, with the value system of those who survive by wit rather than force: know-how, personal charm, ingratiating speech, avoiding rather than facing danger, and a keen eye for the bottom line. Their managerial skills probably helped them to compete with the warrior elite for positions at the court or with the clans. The position of the warrior elite was that, while still called on for military *service* (even the new-style mass army of the 04c would need a large number of chariot officers), they apparently had to rely for *income* on civil posts in the emerging new bureaucracy; that is, they were subject to an ethos that no longer guaranteed them a livelihood.[25] The Prince underwent a comparable evolution: having been in Spring and Autumn a remote feudal overlord, he evolved in the 05c into something like a head of state; the ruler not of the land, but of the people.

LY 4 Itself

The reader may now turn to LY 4. It has been customary to regard all of the Analects as reflecting Confucius, yet its inconsistencies, of which even a beginning reader soon becomes aware, tend to undermine one's confidence in its authenticity. Some recent scholars have doubted that *any* of the book can be said to reflect Confucius. If our theory is correct, however, the LY 4 sayings *are* literally authentic sayings of Confucius, transcribed after his death, preserving something like his actual voice, and embodying the austere code of the warrior, adjusted but not bent to the different needs of the new-society courtier.

---

[25]Lattimore **Frontiers** 397–399 rightly locates Confucius at the end of feudalism, but, by combining *all* the Analects sayings, sees him also as a prophet of postfeudal society. The LY 4 sayings, undiluted, tend to show that Confucius *detested* postfeudal society.

Bronze Sword with Gold Inscription
Length 55 cm (21·7 in). Early 05c. Courtesy Freer Gallery of Art (29·19)

4
c0479

Young men entering court service presumably needed the guidance of a mentor. From the beginning of the reign of the Lǔ Prince Aī-gūng in 0494, Confucius had been mentor to a series of such hopefuls, some of good family, some humbler. The last of these protégés, left stranded at his death in 0479, may have continued as a group. It was perhaps Dž-gùng (for a later tale of his prominence among the disciples at this time, see MC 3A4) who compiled this set of remembered sayingss. They preserve the voice of a disappointed but dedicated officer, hoping for the return of authority to the Lǔ Prince, but scornful of the culture of self-interest to which the Prince's new society had opened the gates. Confucius urges a more spartan service ethic, in descriptions of the ideal gentleman officer (the "he" of the typical Analects saying).

These sayings, as remembered, were no more than a wisdom repository, but here, written down and arranged thematically, they imply a conscious philosophy: the first of many that were to come under the label "Confucian."

Thematic sections are not marked in the original; headings are supplied [in brackets] for the convenience of readers. The pairing of sayings, also implicit in the original, is marked by half brackets: ⌐ for the first and ∟ for the second, of a pair; any unpaired section-final sayings are indicated with ⌐. For an explanation of the accretion theory of the Analects, see Appendix 1.

The numbering of passages is identical in the Legge text.

[A. The Cardinal Virtue Rŕn 仁]

⌐ 4:1. The Master said, It is best to dwell in rŕn. If he choose not to abide in rŕn, how will he get to be known?

Court officers were chosen by personal acquaintance, hence being known for the right qualities was the only route to advancement. The theme of the ruler who recognizes talent remained important in later ages; see Henry **Motif**.

∟ 4:2. The Master said, He who is not rŕn cannot for long abide in privation; cannot forever abide in happiness. The rŕn are content with rŕn; the knowing turn rŕn to their advantage.

Most Analects translations argue for a single English equivalent for "rŕn," but its meaning changes within the text, and the original term can better take on these various nuances. We here learn that, as a career asset, it may be paraded by the ambitious. You need to have your qualities observed by others (4:1), though as a matter of good form you cannot display them yourself (4:2). We also discover that rŕn is steadfast in adversity and success. The crass new value lì 利 "advantage, profit" is here the causative verb "take advantage of."

⌐ 4:3. The Master said, It is only the rŕn who can like others; who can hate others.

Rŕn is not niceness, though it evolves in that direction. It confers a capacity to judge others (William James saw this as the end of education; Kallen **James** 287). Enthusiasm for right implies antagonism (hatred, wù 惡) for its opposite. Right is not only *different* from wrong, it is *better* than wrong.

if my heart is completely devoted to

he will have no room for hatred

L 4:4. The Master said, If once he sets his mind on rv́n, he will have no hatred.

The putative verb wù 惡 "regard as evil, hate" is also read as ỳ 惡 "evil," but the juxtaposition with 4:3 makes 4:4 a mitigation of that saying. Taking them together: the rv́n person knows how to hate (4:3) but is without malice (4:4). The first word in this saying (gǒu 苟 "if") is sarcastic: "if only; if contrary to expectation." One can imagine Confucius rebuking an eager young man who had pointed out a deficiency of rv́n in a colleague. The previous pair of sayings described candidates; the present 4:3/4 seem to focus instead on junior officers.

4:5. The Master said, Wealth and honor: these are what everyone desires, but if he cannot do so in accordance with his principles he will not abide in them. Poverty and lowliness: these are what everyone hates, but if he cannot do so in accordance with his principles, he will not avoid them. If the gentleman avoid rv́n, how shall he make his name? A gentleman does not for the space of a meal depart from rv́n. In direst straits he cleaves to it; in deepest distress he cleaves to it.

This eloquent saying, with its sonorous courtly parallel diction, suggests that Confucius had, not without emotional difficulty, come through such a trial by distress, and had kept his principles (dàu 道, his "way") intact. Rv́n is an at-large virtue; only an individual commitment to it makes it a personal dàu, or principle, for that person. The steadfastness of 4:2 is prominent here as well; rv́n evidently requires not only stability, but courage. Note the implication that honor (social position) as well as wealth *can be sought*: this is a fluid society.

L 4:6. The Master said, For my part, I have never seen anyone who loved rv́n and hated the not-rv́n. One who loved rv́n would put nothing else above it. One who hated the not-rv́n would himself be rv́n; he would not let the not-rv́n come near his person. Is there anyone who for a single day has put forth all his strength on rv́n? For my part, I have never seen anyone whose *strength* was not sufficient for it. There may be some, but, for my part, I have never seen one.

The contrastive "I" (wǒ 我 "as for me; for my part," analogous to the French exposed pronoun in "*Moi*, je dis que les bonbons . . ."), rather than the neutral pronoun wú 吾, gives this saying sarcastic emphasis. The length of 4:6, like that of 4:5, conveys conviction. The identity of rv́n with the hatred of its opposite helps further explain 4:6. The final idea of will faltering before strength fails recurs in 5:10b and 6:12. We here discover that rv́n requires more than assent, and more even than dedication: it exacts a strenuous and continual exertion. It is not yet the incessant self-cultivation found in subsequent chapters (8:3), but a continual readiness to prove equal to the challenge of the moment.

L 4:7. The Master said, In making mistakes, people stay true to type. If you observe their mistakes, you will be able to tell what sort of rv́n they have.

This unpaired saying returns to the idea of judging others (4:3) without malice (4:4), using mistakes to detect positive capacities. The idea that human beings are of different types (dǎng 黨; the "association" group of 6:5), with general virtues like rv́n taking a different form in different types, gives us an insight into the basis of the personal judgements expected of 05c officers of the court. The theme of judging subordinates completes the progression from the unknown youth of 4:1/2, whose capacity is judged by others, to the junior of 4:3/4, the experienced officer of 4:5/6, and the selector of talent who is implied by 4:7.

Court service had probably been a monopoly of the chariot-driving elite. Their military values are here civilianized, but retain links to a military ethos. The rvn man has the traits of an ideal comrade-at-arms: strength, courage, steadfastness in crisis, consideration for others, capacity for self-sacrifice. If rvn 仁 (homophonous with rvn 人 "man") was originally "manliness" (strength, courage; Lin **Evolution** 181), then the derived civilian rvn makes easier sense. It may help to remember the connotations of the Western term "honor."

[B. The Public Context: Dàu 道]

4:8. The Master said, If one morning he should hear of the Way, and that evening he should die, it is enough.

Besides the personal "way" of 4:5, there must be a context for those principles: a public Way (Mao **Suggestions** 284; compare 4:8An). The 05c Princes of Lǔ had lost their power to the Jì clan. Confucius was loyal to the legitimate line, but did not live to see a restored political Way; the Lǔ Prince of his last years, Āi-gūng, died in 0468, on the road to Ywè in search of support against the Jì.

4:9. The Master said, If an officer is dedicated to the Way, but is ashamed of having bad clothes or bad food, he is not worth taking counsel with.

The Way here is shared principles, rather than political legitimacy. The disdain for sartorial elegance contrasts with the emphasis on exquisitely balanced color combinations which comes up in the later Analects (see especially 10:5a).

4:10. The Master said, The gentleman's relation to the world is thus: he has no predilections or prohibitions. When he regards something as right, he sides with it.

Yì 義 "right" is here the putative "regard as right." Confucius's feudal world (tyēn-syà 天下 "what is under heaven," for a more transcendent sense see 3:11) is in a sense personalistic, but here is the universal in the feudal: a standard of right determined *objectively*, and not given by prior personal commitment.

[C. The Gentleman and His Opposite]

4:11. The Master said, The gentleman likes virtue; the little man likes partiality. The gentleman likes justice; the little man likes mercy.

Between gentleman (jywŭndž 君子) and common folk (mín 民; see 6:22) come the "little people," the mobile middle group of artisans and traders. Like the mín, their values are based on self-interest; unlike them, they turn up at court, competing with the jywŭndž elite for position. Thus arises the problem of public officials who retain a preference for local favoritism and special exemptions.

4:12. The Master said, Those who act with a view to their own personal advantage will arouse much resentment.

Rvn is a value that must be *general* to be *viable*; supporting your comrades in battle is mere suicide unless they support you in turn. In civilian life also, selfishness or nonreciprocal behavior makes an interactive system untenable for generosity (Gosse **Son** 191f). At a higher level probably not envisioned here (but explicit in MC 1A1, c0320), a policy of selfishness is seen as undermining the general acceptance of all policy, and ultimately all government.

└ 4:13. The Master said, If you *can* run the country with courtesy and deference, what is the obstacle? But if you *cannot* run it with courtesy and deference, what good is courtesy?

The only LY 4 mention of lǐ 禮 "ritual propriety; courtesy" (and the only 05c instance of ràng 讓 "yield to others," Emerson **Fugitive** 868 "postpone oneself") which becomes dominant in later chapters. The debate on whether rv́n or lǐ is central to Confucianism is thus solved: rv́n is central to *Confucius*, whereas lǐ is central to *Confucianism*. But courtesy, putting others first, *is* one of Confucius's values, and he will not accept a merely symbolic place for it. Either it works or it does not, and if it does not, he has no use for it at all.

[D. Preparation for Office]

┌ 4:14. The Master said, He does not worry that he has no position; he worries about whether he is qualified to hold one. He does not worry that no one recognizes his worth; he seeks to become worthy to be recognized.

Here is the essence of feudal, one-way obligations. There may be injustice in your being passed over for office, but that injustice *is not your concern*; it is a mistake, but one which it is not your business to correct. The feudal courtier (as *14:26a[15b] will later say) never acts, or thinks, above his station.

└ 4:16. The Master said, The gentleman concentrates on right; the little man concentrates on advantage.   *(handwritten: Commitment = desire)*

You are *not concerned* with career calculations; your career is in the hands of others. The gentleman, born to rule, is contrasted with the little man, trying to get ahead and bringing the profit culture with him. For a sympathetic glimpse of the "little man" profit culture in recent times, see Zhang **Lives** 3f.

The interpolated 4:15 has been relocated after LY 1. Such interpolations are cited as *4:15[1], the asterisk indicating an interpolation, and the superscript giving the present chapter location. See also Interpolations, below.

└ 4:17. The Master said, When he sees a worthy man, let him think how he might come up to him; when he sees an unworthy man, let him examine within himself.

This saying shows a process of self-training by observation, judgement, and the imitation of virtues and avoidance of faults. As of 0479, with Confucius gone and no book texts in existence, such self-training would have been important to the former protégés. Hence, perhaps, the climactic final placement of 4:17.

Syén 賢 "worthy" was originally "able, doughty" (compare dv́ 德 "virtue," originally "character, force, effectiveness," Waley **Way** 31f). "With him" renders final yén 焉, a contraction of the coverb phrase yu 於 "in" + an 安 "it," whence early phonetic yan, corresponding to modern yén (Kennedy **Yen**).

It will be seen that the four sections of the text are not devoted to parallel "virtues," but to different concerns of Confucius; this is a *philosophy*, but not a philosophical *system*. The only value seen as thematic by the compiler is rv́n.

Interpolations

For a complete finding list of interpolated passages, see page 329.

仁者，美德於天氣也

The Original LY 4:1-5

The first five LY 4 sayings are presented here to show their parallel structures.
Bold syllables are assumed to have most stress, and *italicized* ones least.

民之仰仁
而居

4:1.

里	仁	爲	美
lǐ	**rv́n**	wéi	**měi**.
To dwell in	rv́n	is	best.

擇	不處	仁	焉	得	知
dzv́	bùchǔ	**rv́n**,	yēn	dv́	**jī**?
If he choose	not to abide in	rv́n,	how	can he	become known?

不居而已处仁者之里，
不得为有知

4:2.

不仁者
bùrv́n jv̌:
He who is not rv́n:

不可以	久	處	約
bùkv̌yǐ	**jyǒu**	chǔ	**ywē**,
cannot	long	abide in	privation,

不可以	長	處	樂
bùkv̌ yǐ	**cháng**	chǔ	**lv̀**.
cannot	forever	abide in	happiness.

仁者	安	仁
rv́n jv̌	ān	**rv́n**,
The rv́n	are content with	rv́n.

知者	利	仁
jī jv̌	lì	**rv́n**.
The knowing	take advantage of	rv́n.

4:3.

唯	仁者
wéi	**rv́n** jv̌
It is only	the rv́n

能	好	人
nv́ng	**hàu**	rv́n,
who can	like	others,

能	惡	人
nv́ng	**wù**	rv́n.
who can	hate	others.

4:4.

苟	志於	仁矣	無	惡也
gǒu	jī ywv̌	**rv́n** yǐ,	wú	**wù** yě.
If once	he sets his mind on	rv́n,	he will be without	hatred.

富　　與　　貴
4:5.　fù　　yw̌　　gwèi,
　　　Wealth and honor,

是　　　人之所　　欲也
shr̆　　rv́n jr̄ swǒ　yẁ yě:
these are　what men　desire;

不以　　其道　得之　　不處也
bùyĭ　　chí dàu　dv́ jr̄,　bùchǔ yě.
if not by　his way　he do so,　he will not abide in them.

貧　　與　　賤
pín　　yw̌　　jyèn,
Poverty and lowliness,

是　　　人之所　　惡也
shr̆　　rv́n jr̄ swǒ　wù yě;
these are　what men　hate;

不以　　其道　得之　　不去也
bùyĭ　　chí dàu　dv́ jr̄,　bùchyẁ yě.
if not by　his way　he do so,　he will not avoid them.

君子　　　　去　　仁
jyw̄ndž　　chyẁ　rv́n,
If a gentleman　avoid　rv́n,

惡乎　　　成　　　名
wūhū　　　chv́ng　míng?
how shall　he make　a name?

君子　　無　　終食之間　　　　違　　仁
jyw̄ndž　wú　jūng-shŕ jr̄ jyēn　wéi　rv́n.
A gentleman does not　for the space of a meal　depart from　rv́n.

造次　　　必　　於　　是
dzàu-tsž　bì　yẃ　shr̀.
In direst straits　he will　cleave to　this.

顛沛　　　必　　於　　是
dyēn-pèı　bì　yẃ　shr̀.
In deepest distress　he will　cleave to　this.

The parallels in these sayings are mostly simple pairs, but the first sentences in 4:5 are more complex: one three-element structure balances another. This complexity, besides its length and the identically repeated predicate at the end, give 4:5 a special intensity. Parallelism in general, as in the Biblical Proverbs, lets a saying stand free of other context, giving it a feeling of universality and rhetorical force, and making it at once more impressive and more memorable.

Reflections

Before proceeding to the next chapter, and thus time period, it will be useful to pause to acquire a vivid sense of *this* chapter and time period, which means a sense of Confucius. The LY 4 sayings lack several motifs prominent in the later image of Confucius: there is no mention of filial piety or Heaven, and no hint of an organized "school." These gaps are later filled (the school appears in LY 5, and the supernatural in LY 7; ritual emerges in the early, and domestic virtue in the late, 04c), but as of LY 4 they should be seen as genuine absences in the range of Confucius's concerns, rather than as mere omissions on the part of the compiler. In the text of LY 4 as we now possess it, these omissions have been partly made good by 04c interpolations, which devote a section to filial piety, and portray the disciples not only as interpreting the thought of Confucius, but as teaching in their own right.

The chapter seems to hint, tantalizingly but vividly, at Confucius's early experiences. There are what look like echoes of early hardship (4:5, 4:9), career opposition (4:3), and unrewarded loyalty (4:8). At the end of that life, we feel in LY 4 the final Confucius: sonorous, steadfast, consistent in his values, but unconcerned for logical rigor (in deference to the later taste for consistency, a grand unifying maxim will eventually be supplied by an interpolated *4:15[1]). He is *himself* a locus of authority, and never cites texts, traditions, or models ancient or modern. As is said of Jesus in Mark 1:22, the Confucius of LY 4 invariably speaks in his own voice. His influence over his protégés thus derived from his direct personal authority, and not from mastery of earlier traditions. The Confucius we meet in LY 4 is above all immediate: here and now.

The "profit" value scorned in LY 4 seems to be typical of the "little people." Confucius's counterpart value, the mysterious rv́n, is translated by Waley as "Goodness" (with an intentional capital "G"). This interpretation owes more to 04c reformulations (see, for example, 12:22) than to LY 4. The sense of "good" that fits the military ethos is being "good at" the warrior's specific skills. See Parker **Rachel** 164–168, **Place** 61, and **Early** 114 and 99, where "good" means "skilled at hand-to-hand fighting." An ethos in which violence is perceived as the only "good" on which its sharers can rely, and dependability, keeping your word to others, is a central requirement, is found in Western chivalry (Stephenson **Mediaeval** 50–53, compare Emerson **English** 594f), and can be observed in nonchivalric context in Parker **Early** 176, **Taming** 227, **Rachel** 193, and **Ceremony** 136. On the LY 4 reluctance to explain this ethos, or even speak of it, note the diffident mention of "honor" (Parker **Land** 95) and the taciturn English school code (Orwell **Such** 33 "Buck up"). For these values in their original military setting, see Parker **Rachel** 44–45, Orwell **Such** 41–42, and Barnett **Generals** 23 "self-abnegation" (von Fritsch), 260 "a gentleman" (von Kleist), and 376 "duty and honor" (von Senger und Etterlin). These descriptions reach an emotional peak in von Manstein's formal eulogy of his son Gero, who was killed in action in 1942: "He had no thought for himself, but knew only comradeship and charity" (von Manstein **Lost** 271).

If sought here, and not in the distractingly civilized revaluations of the later Analects layers, or in the systematic structures of Imperial philosophies, the mystery of Confucius's central but elusive rv́n, in all its austere otherness, is perhaps after all not so very mysterious.

Gold Inlaid Bronze Vessel (see LY 5:4)
Width 18·7 cm (7·4 in). Early 05c. Courtesy Freer Gallery of Art (39·41)

5
c0470

The six-year Dž-gùng hiatus after the death of Confucius (the factual core behind the 03c legend represented in MC 3A4) ended in 0473. What seems to have happened next is the emergence of an organized Confucian school, under a new "Master," perhaps Confucius's early protégé Dž-yóu. As his name implies (the prefix Dž- "Young Master" seems to have been reserved for the socially advantaged), he had the appropriate background for a court career. According to LY 6:14 (and 17:3) he had been Steward of Wǔ-chv́ng, the Prince of Lǔ's stronghold city at the southern edge of Lǔ. On his return to the capital from Wǔ-chv́ng, he seems to have taken charge, not of an informal group of individual protégés, but of a *body of students*, preparing for public office in a new and more collective way. The sayings of LY 4 seem to have been spoken on isolated occasions, to an individual. The sayings of LY 5 were in many cases obviously said in the hearing of more than one person. No feature of this chapter stands out more strongly than the rivalry among these young hopefuls. LY 5 is the prototypical Confucian schoolroom.

Prominent among the hopefuls is the previous leader Dž-gùng, who is here pictured as once again under Confucius's tutelage. He is repeatedly (if also encouragingly) chided for his pretensions to virtue, and unfavorably compared with Confucius's poor relative Yén Hwéi.

None of the LY 5 sayings can safely be attributed to the actual Confucius, but Dž-yóu as an early follower may have possessed a fund of family lore that was of interest to the new students in the LY 5 school who had never known Confucius. Besides these recollections, which are grouped in section A, most of LY 5 is devoted to the theme of judging men; in that sense it develops 4:3. It is divided into sections according to the status of those judged: (B) the Confucian protégés or (C) earlier historical figures. Section D, on the theme of striving for perfection, is a structural echo of the final section of LY 4.

Formally, Dž-yóu shows himself a master of the parallel-saying structure. Each saying in sections B and C is linked to both the preceding and following saying. These linkages are shown by the usual ⌐ and ∟ marks at the beginnings of sayings, and by complementary ¬ and ⌐ at their ends. For a schematic overview of these structures, see page 29.

Reference numbers to Legge are given at the end of each passage.

[A. Confucius's Family and Rival Mentors]

⌐ 5:1. The Master said of Gūngyě Cháng, He is marriageable. Though he has been in durance, it was not his fault. And he gave him his daughter to wife. [5:1a]

The surname Gūngyě 公冶 "Palace Smith" implies a court-artisan family. The warrior/artisan mix is similar to that inferred (p10) for Confucius's own parents; this particular match seems to have been a modest one. Notice the narrative context provided in the last line. This is a device first encountered in LY 5.

Léı-syè 縲 絏 is literally "binding" (said by commentators to be with black ropes; perhaps part of branding or marking?), but "durance" or incarceration may already have been used as a punishment in this early period.

∟ 5:2. The Master said of Nán Rúng, When the state has the Way, he will not be cast aside; when the state has not the Way, he will keep clear of penalties and punishments. And he gave him his elder brother's daughter to wife. [5:1b]

> Another modest marriage, though later tradition identifies Nán Rúng with a more elegant figure (see 11:6). Kǔng family lore, plausibly, makes the brother a cripple, which explains Confucius's role in arranging this marriage also.

⊦ 5:3. The Master said of Dž-jyèn, A gentleman indeed is this man! If Lǔ indeed had no gentleman, where did he get *that* from? [5:2]

> Less literally: if there were no model gentleman, how did he learn to be one? The implication is that the way to become a gentleman is to imitate one (the LY 4 sayings show Confucius *functioning* as a model). Since Confucius will hardly have been praising himself, Dž-jyèn must have had a different mentor. In defiance of this, later tradition makes him Confucius's own protégé.

[B. The Original Protégés]

┌ 5:4. Dž-gùng asked, What is Sž? The Master said, You are a vessel. He said, What kind of vessel? He said, An ornamented vessel. [5:3]

> Those of high status in this period had two names, a personal míng 名 used in self-reference, and a semantically related, more formal dž 字. This interchange puns on Dž-gùng's names Sž 賜 "gift" and Gùng 貢 "offering" by alluding to a ritual offering vessel, criticizing him as a mere container rather than a leader; it is the first of three evenly spaced sayings in this section criticizing him. This suggests tension between him and Dž-yóu, his successor as head of the group. The seemingly consoling reference to the ornate decoration of certain vessels (p20) may in fact be a poke at Dž-gùng's wealth (later proverbial; see 11:18b).

∟ 5:5. Someone said, Yúng is rv́n but not eloquent. The Master said, Why should he be eloquent? If he answers others with verbal intricacies, he will often be disliked by them. I don't know if he is rv́n, but why should he be eloquent? [5:4] ┐

> Like the paired 5:4, this saying deprecates outward polish, which, however much the warrior ethos might disapprove of it (warriors are doers, not sayers), proved to be vital in an open society; later sayings accept the need for it. There is in this section a second level of pairing of passages, here indicated by half brackets at the ends as well as at the beginnings of sayings. The primary pairing 5:4/5 focuses on speciousness; the secondary pairing 5:5/6 is a modest estimate of the official capacity of one of the humbler protégés.

┌ 5:6. The Master gave Chīdyāu Kāi permission to take office. He answered, I am not yet able to be faithful enough for that. The Master was pleased. [5:5] ┘

> Chīdyāu 漆雕 "Lacquer Carver" Kāi, like Rǎn 冉 "Dyer" Yúng in 5:5, seems to be of an artisan family. Note the "able to be" rather than simply "am not" – virtue in this chapter is not something you *are*, it is something you *get better at*. Like rv́n, fidelity (syìn 信 "keeping one's word") may have had a military origin; it is often paired with jūng 忠 "loyal." It has a different scope in these sayings than it does in later ones. Note that it lay with the mentor, in this highly organized operation, whether or not the protégé took office. The school head is no longer a mere personal advisor; he has become a purveyor of civic talent.

└ 5:8. Mv̀ng Wŭ-bwó asked, Is Dž-lù rv́n? The Master said, I don't know. He asked again. The Master said, As for Yóu, in a state of a thousand chariots he could be employed to take charge of collecting taxes; I don't know if he is rv́n. [He asked] What about Chyóu? The Master said, As for Chyóu, in a town of a thousand families, or a state of a hundred chariots, he could be employed as a steward; I don't know if he is rv́n. [He asked] What about Chr̀? The Master said, As for Chr̀, girt with a sash and standing in court, he could be employed to speak with guests and visitors; I don't know if he is rv́n. [5:7] ┐

> One pairing (5:6/8) is about protégés taking office; the other (5:8/9) focuses on negatives, denying rv́n in 5:8 and intellect in 5:9. Those mentioned have two names (Dž-lù 路 "road" / Yóu 由 "follow," Răn Yŏu 有 "have" / Chyóu 求 "seek," Gūngsyī Hwá 華 "flower" / Chr̀ 赤 "red") and are thus of some status; all are elsewhere criticized as more or less wealthy. "Confucius" acknowledges their skills but not their ethics (note the offer from the rival Mv̀ng clan). The jobs listed suggest the skills (toughness, accountancy, and protocol expertise) favored by the new society. Such jobworthiness has nothing to do with rv́n.

┌ 5:9. The Master said to Dž-gùng, Of you and Hwéı who is the abler? He answered, How dare Sž even look at Hwéı! If Hwéı hears one thing, he can find out ten; if Sž hears one thing, he can find out two. The Master said, Not as good as him: you and me *both* are not as good as him. [5:8] ┘

> The "him" is contained in the negative fút 弗, a contraction of bù 不 and a preposed object jr̄ 之 (Boodberg **Morphology** 430f) . This second criticism of Dž-gùng (see 5:4n) takes note of his limits but also ends with a consolation: "Confucius" too is not as good as Hwéı. One of the riddles of the Analects is the nature of Hwéı's superiority. Something more than skill in inference may be involved, perhaps the inner discipline of meditation (see 6:23).

└ 5:10a. Dzǎı Yẃ slept in the daytime. The Master said, Rotten wood cannot be carved; a wall of dung cannot be decorated. What is there in Yẃ for me to reprove? [5:9a] ┐

> The primary link is a judgement of unfitness; the secondary one (5:9/10) is Dzǎı Yẃ. Dzǎı 宰 (sty-ward "Butcher" > "Steward") is an artisan surname; for the linked personal names Yẃ/Wŏ (both "I," the latter, in ancient times, had an initial ng-), see 7:23. The point of the saying is the shaping of character; the 5:4 image of the ornamented vessel here recurs as carving and decorating. With no *basis* for improvement, one cannot complain of *lack* of improvement.

┌ 5:10b. The Master said, At first, my way with others was to listen to their words and trust their actions. Now, my way with others is to listen to their words and watch their actions. It was after my dealings with Yẃ that I made this change. [5:9b] ┘

> This saying completes the preceding one, and explains that it was through a presumption of virtue, not by a failure of insight, that Confucius misjudged Dzǎı Yẃ. The judging of others in 4:7 presupposed similar background values; but with a more socially diverse talent pool, those expectations can no longer be relied on. This passage admits that social change. The virtue of living up to one's word, which is never mentioned in LY 4, is repeatedly stressed in LY 5. Unlike the comradely virtue rv́n, the accountable virtue syìn seems to have been perfectly viable as a quality for members of the emerging bureaucracy.

└ 5:11. The Master said, I have never seen one who was firm. Someone answered, Shv̄n Chv́ng. The Master said, Chv́ng is subject to desire; how could *he* be firm? [5:10] ┐

> Shv̄n 申 (near modern Nán-yáng), 75 km south of the old site of Lǔ (modern Lǔ-shān), was conquered by Chǔ in 0688; some refugees may have fled to Lǔ at that time (see Appendix 4). Of this most obscure of protégés, we know only that he was obsessive rather than steadfast. Desire is not steadfastness.
>
> Unlike those in LY 4, this saying implies a *group* of hearers, and a collective context for LY 5 sayings generally. Confucius's remark was rhetorically meant to provoke a response in that context, hence the "answered" (對曰) in the text.

Ŀ 5:12. Dž-gùng said, If I do not wish others to do something to me, I wish not to do it to them. The Master said, Sz̀, this is not what you can come up to. [5:11] ┘

> This unpaired envoi to the 5B section is secondarily paired with 5:11 as a denial of claimed virtue. It is the third and last derogation of Dž-gùng, who is told that the maxim by which he claims to live is in fact far beyond his ability.
>
> 5:12 is the oldest appearance of the "Golden Rule" in world literature. Allinson **Golden** labors to excuse its negative form, but most ethical principles are negative: most freedoms are freedoms *from* something. Nivison **Golden** 19, following Fingarette **Sacred**, notes an echo in the mutual yielding of court courtesy, and concludes that this is the basic moral precept, "the very ground of community." It is notable as *not* a saying of Confucius. Its laterality (there are no sacred or other vertical sanctions), and its basis in desire (the appeal is exclusively to feelings; compare 5:11), imply an origin outside the Analects itself, perhaps among the Mician or some other segment of the "little people" (for several of these points, compare Roetz **Axial** 133–148).
>
> There is a later and terser restatement of the principle in 12:2.

[C. Exemplary Personages]

┌ 5:15. Dž-gùng asked, Why was Kǔng Wv́ndž called Wv́n? The Master said, He was quick and loved learning, and was not ashamed to inquire of those below him. For these reasons they called him Wv́n. [5:14]

> This is a paradox: wv́n 文 means "cultured," hence presumably of *high* status. Posthumous epithets usually characterized the deceased as cultural paradigms, but some were euphemisms (Wv́ndž, died c0480, was a bad Wèi statesman), hence the possibility of an opposite meaning. "Confucius" uses the inquiry to comment on culture, not as something you *have*, but as something you *do*: curiosity plus a willingness to inquire in humble places. Such practicality was important to Confucius, given his early poverty. For sywé 學 "learn," see 5:28.

└ 5:17. The Master said, Yèn Píng-jùng was good at associating with others. Even after a long time, he would still treat them with respect. [5:16] ┐

> We expect acquaintance to lead to informality, but "Confucius" respects the difference between association and friendship (on the avoidance of favoritism, compare 4:11). Yèn Píng-jùng (Yèndž) was a Chì minister of c0500, and like Kǔng Wv́ndž was a contemporary of Confucius. Anecdotes were collected under his name in c0300 as the Yèndž Chūn/Chyōu, which is still extant.

⌐ 5:18. The Master said, Dzàng Wv́n-jùng had a Tsàı tortoise in his house; he had
mountain rafters and waterweed beams. So how good was his knowledge? [5:17] ⌐

> Such decorations were reserved for the ruler. The 07c minister Wv́n-jùng thus
> knew architecture, but not propriety (compare Gwǎn Jùng in 3:21). His clan
> founder is said to have had the *personal* name Dzàng 藏 "storehouse." If so, we
> do not have here an *occupational* surname with a later rise in social status.
>
> The tortoises used in state divination came from the south; Tsàı (often
> bracketed with Chv́n) was on Lǔ's trade route south to the Yángdž delta (Tom
> **Communications** fp172, fp212). Commentators take jyw̄ Tsàı 居蔡 as in the
> translation, but the interpretation "dwelt in Tsàı" is also possible. If Wv́n-jùng
> was a trade representative of Lǔ in Tsàı, it might account for his great wealth
> at this early period. Tortoise divination is first mentioned in the CC under
> 0629, and may have been new in Lǔ at that time. It had long been known in
> Sùng, whose ancient divination records are the famous "Shāng oracle bones."

∟ 5:19a. Dž-jāng asked, Director Intendant Dž-wv́n thrice took office as Director
Intendant without showing pleasure, and thrice left it without showing resentment;
of the former Director Intendant's acts he would always inform the new Director
Intendant. What would you say about that? The Master said, He was loyal. He said,
Was he rv́n? He said, I don't know; where would he qualify as rv́n? [5:18a] ⌐

> For the militarily able, politically adroit 07c Chǔ minister Dž-wv́n (his name
> in the Chǔ language was "Suckled by a Tiger"), see Blakeley **King** 5–13. The
> title Director Intendant (Lìng-yǐn 令尹) is typical of Chǔ, which pioneered the
> use of functional titles. Uncertainty over what qualifies as rv́n implies that this
> concept, central in LY 4, is obscure for the protégés of LY 5; Dž-jāng's effort to
> meet its code-of-honor demands by citing *bureaucratically* exemplary conduct
> merely dramatizes the change in values in the generation after Confucius.
>
> Dž-jāng is the perfect Analects questioner, a virtual bystander who does not
> interact with the other disciples. He is said to have been from Chv́n, a state
> absorbed by Chǔ in 0479 (see p12), and may in that year have fled to the Lǔ
> border fortress Wǔ-chv́ng, where he could have met its Steward, Dž-yóu. We
> infer that he was a protégé of Dž-yóu, who brought him to the capital in c0473
> to become a bright, if seemingly also deferential, student in Dž-yóu's school.

⌐ 5:19b. Master Tswēı assassinated the ruler of Chí. Chv́n Wv́ndž had horses for
ten chariots, but he abandoned them and left him. Reaching another state, he said,
They are as bad as our great officer Master Tswēı, and left them. Arriving at yet
another state, he again said, They are as bad as our great officer Master Tswēı, and
left them. What about that? The Master said, He was uncompromising. He said,
Was he rv́n? He said, I don't know; where would he qualify as rv́n? [5:18b] ⌐

> Dž-jāng drops his example of imperturbability and offers one of intransigence.
> It probably evoked for him the furious integrity of LY 4, but it also asserts an
> unfeudal right to judge one's own superiors. Though *psychologically* parallel
> (see 5:11), it uses a different energy, and inhabits a different world, from rv́n.
>
> Notice the southern focus of these sayings, and the Chǔ affinities of the
> earliest figures mentioned in this section. Early Lǔ communications did look
> largely southward: the Lǔ Prince personally visited Chǔ in 0545, whereas Yēn,
> the gateway to the northern steppe, is mentioned only rarely in the CC.

└ 5:20. Jì Wv́ndž would think thrice and then act. The Master heard of it, and said, Twice would be enough. [5:19] ┐

> The calculating and unscrupulous Wv́ndž, an officer of Lǔ, appears in the DJ (Wv́n 6, 0621) as associated with Dzàng Wv́n-jùng (5:18), at the period when the Jì clan were beginning to usurp power from the Lǔ Prince.

> A second thought can prevent impulsiveness; a third is vacillation. Chv́n Wv́ndž's fastidiousness is not rv́n; Jì Wv́ndž's circumspection is not caution.

┌ 5:21. The Master said, Níng Wǔdž: when the state possessed the Way, he was wise; when the state lost the Way, he was stupid. His wisdom can be equaled, but his stupidity cannot be equaled. [5:20] ┘

> Níng Wǔdž of Wèi (07c), who at great risk gave aid to his imprisoned Prince, came to symbolize principle in adversity, and the word "stupid" (yǔ 愚) in the sense "heedless of self in the discharge of duty" acquired a cult status, most famously exemplified by the Táng poet-official Lyǒu Dzūng-ywǽn (773–819), an associate of Hán Yù and one of the first scholars to approach the Analects in a spirit of independent inquiry. His "Stupid River" poems and preface of c810, written in his southern exile under the guise of rueful self-criticism, affirm an unshakable devotion to right principles despite living in wrong times.

└ 5:23. The Master said, Bwó-yí and Shú-chí did not dwell on old hatreds; if they felt any resentment, it was surely very slight. [5:22] ┐

> Bwó-yí and Shú-chí, subjects of the evil Shāng who refused to side with the conquering Jōu and forfeited their positions as local rulers (in later legend, they starved to death rather than eat the food of Jōu; see 16:12), here match the inexpedient loyalty of Níng Wǔdž. They did what was right regardless of the cost to themselves, and did not invalidate their sacrifice by feeling resentment (some commentators read this as "arousing" resentment, but compare *7:15[14]).

├ 5:24. The Master said, Who says that Wèishv̄ng Gāu is upright? When someone begged vinegar of him, he begged it of his neighbor and then gave it. [5:23] ┘

> Wèishv̄ng Gāu gives borrowed goods as his own gift, and belies his reputation for honesty. The 5C section includes early 05c figures (5:15/17), but as Waley notes, Gāu seems to be a paradigmatic rather than a contemporary persona; the comment here might refer to an exemplary tale told of him. 5:24 is the envoi for the 5C section, most of whose judgements are negative; it implies that consistency in virtue (see 5:6) is rare. This moral pessimism is not the last word on the subject, but the background for the moral resolve in the next section.

[D. Confucius on Self-Improvement]

┌ 5:25. The Master said, Artful words, impressive appearance, specious respect: Dzwǒchyōu Míng was ashamed of them, and Chyōu is also ashamed of them. To hide resentment and befriend a man: Dzwǒchyōu Míng was ashamed of it, and Chyōu is also ashamed of it. [5:24]

> These vices (compare 5:5) amount to various kinds of insincerity. Dzwǒchyōu Míng, later claimed as a disciple and the transmitter of the Dzwǒ Jwàn (DJ), is evidently an older contemporary admired by Confucius ("Chyōu"). Note the use of the sense of shame as an inner moral compass in self-improvement.

L 5:27. The Master said, It is all over. I have never seen one who could see his faults and inwardly accuse himself. [5:26]

> This was probably intended by Dž-yóu to stimulate his protégés to disprove "Confucius's" judgement. The metaphor of the lawsuit, with 5:1/2, is the first reference to legal institutions in the text, but the context here is the interior accusation of a "shame" culture, where the motivation of individual conduct is desire to meet a social standard. The idea of a conscience, a social standard so fully internalized that it operates as the inner prompting of an individual, will not become important until Mencius, more than a century in the future.

Ŀ 5:28. The Master said, In any town of ten households, there will surely be someone as loyal and faithful as Chyōu, but he will not be equal to Chyōu in love of learning. [5:27]

> And here, as a counterpart, "Confucius" offers himself as an ethical example, not of *virtue*, but of *effort in its acquisition*. 5:28 echoes 4:17, and creates a resonance between the ends of the two chapters (as they existed at this time). Sywé 學 "learn" (pronounced syàu in the sense "imitate," see 5:15) is learning by imitation; it does not yet (compare 1:1) have the sense "book learning."

Interpolations

For a complete finding list of interpolated passages, see page 329.

Reflections

LY 5 implies an actual school, with a head other than Confucius, and with model personages besides Confucius. In contrast to LY 4, where rv́n is a given, only the mentor here understands it, thus implying an obsolescent value. The 5C judgements are also obsolescent, criticizing those adept in war and policy, and praising the inexpedient but honorable. The Kŭng family lore in 5A may be the new mentor's way of claiming direct acquaintance. In 5:25 and 5:28 (where personal aspirations are highlighted), it is emphasized that "Confucius" is the speaker by using his personal name "Chyōu" (Confucius in LY 4 always refers to himself as "I"). There is thus no doubt that these sayings "of the Master" were offered to students *as from Confucius*, not from Dž-yóu as the current "Master." As for the protégés of LY 5B, we should not imagine them as literally present, but as contemporaries who are often criticized. Dž-gùng, on our view the leader of the interim group, comes in for special attack: he has less capacity for office than he thinks (5:4; metaphor of the vessel), is not as quick as he imagines (5:9; the Yén Hwéi comparison), and is not as ethically independent as he claims (5:12; the Golden Rule). The praise of Confucius's relative Yén Hwéi may imply that he was still in contact with the LY 5 group. The later students thus might have known him (see the LY 7 Reflections, 7r).

There are also continuities with LY 4, one of which is that there is still no mention of texts as sources of learning. The official lore tradition implied in 5C need rest on nothing more than common knowledge. The only thing like an oral text is the Golden Rule maxim of 5:12. It is clear that this is an *outside* maxim, and it is possible to read 5:12 as subtly disapproving of it. Beyond this, the only source of self-improvement in LY 5 is seeing and hearing.

A point of historical importance is the way in which the structural divisions in LY 5 permit us to draw conclusions about the original protégés, these being distinguished by being mentioned in section 5B. This evidence is earlier than anything else we possess, and lets us correct several lists found in later tradition, such as the one in KZJY 38, which is in turn the basis for the 77-name roster of SJ 67. The Analects evidence forces us to dissent from some familiar details of KZJY 38, such as its inclusion of the contemporary nondisciple Dž-jyèn (5:3). But it also shows that KZJY 38, which it would be easy to reject as later myth, does go back to something. The key fact is that the name Shv̄n Chv́ng, variously mistranscribed and thus not copied from the Analects, can be found in both KZJY 38 and its SJ 47 transform. Shv̄n Chv́ng is absent from the later Analects and later lore generally: he has no mythic value for posterity. His inclusion in KZJY 38 must thus imply a factual basis for that list. Identifying the original protégés in turn helps to determine the extent of Confucius's reputation in his lifetime. The summary of his life in the Introduction is based on such inferences; for an outline of the argument on these and other points, see Appendix 4.

Within the protégé circle, we seem to find a contrast between an older, socially higher, subgroup, established in office as of LY 5 (Dž-lù, Rǎn Chyóu, Gūngsyī Hwá), and humbler aspirants still approaching their first possible job opening (Rǎn Yūng, Chīdyāu Kāi). The latter are treated more supportively than the former; it would seem that job placement was one of Dž-yóu's chief concerns. One feels that Confucius the courtier, as glimpsed in LY 4, counseled his protégés (so to speak) from behind, whereas Dž-yóu the officer is here managing his students' careers from in front.

LY 5 has 24 sayings, as against the 16 of LY 4. Whatever the symbolism of this, if any, the 24-saying model established by LY 5 became standard for later Analects chapters. Later in the history of the text (see p114), more sayings were added to LY 4 to bring it up to this length (for their effect, see Appendix 5).

Finally, there is at work in LY 5 a conspicuous aesthetic sensibility, shown in frequent references to contemporary decorative arts (5:4, 5:10), and the elaborate interlocking symmetry of the chapter design itself. This must be due to Dž-yóu, and shows him to be a person of taste and ability, a combination perhaps surprising to modern readers, but made plausible by the testimony of archaeologically recovered evidence of Warring States elite life. One element in the chapter design is the number of passages in each section, which makes the satisfying palindromic pattern 3-9-9-3 (this seemingly intentional design is one piece of evidence for deciding where 5C ends and 5D begins, and for the identification of 5:26 as an interpolation; another is the first appearance of Confucius as a commentator on himself rather than on others). Another design element is the double pairing of passages in the inner two sections by two mutually offset series of verbal and conceptual linkages. Though they never became regular features, the traits of double pairing and palindromic form do recur in later chapters, including the subtly complex LY 1, and it thus seems that LY 5 was continually available as a style model for later Analects writers. This in turn implies that earlier parts of the text were still read in later times, a fact which underlies the logic of the later interpolations in these chapters.

The in-and-out pairing pattern found in the middle sections of LY 5 is shown schematically in the diagram opposite.

[A. Confucius's Family and Rival Mentors]

Gūngyĕ Cháng	1	⌈	**is unlucky but blameless**
Nán Rúng	2	⌊	**is curcumspect but worthy**
Dž-jyèn	3	⌶	**is cultivated**

[B. The Original Protégés]

Dž-gùng	4	⌈	**is at least elegant**
Rǎn Yūng, though **not rv́n enough** ⌉	5	⌊	**is at least straightforward**
Chīdyāu Kāi, though **not syìn enough** ⌏	6	⌈	**is allowed to take office**
Dž-lù, though **said not to be rv́n** ⌉	8	⌊	**is recommended for office**
Dž-gùng is **said not to be quick** ⌏	9	⌈	**and implicitly scolded**
Indolent **Dzǎi Yv́** ⌉	10a	⌊	**is not worth scolding**
Specious **Dzǎi Yv́** ⌏	10b	⌈	**did not live up to his promise**
Shv̄n Chv́ng is **claimed to be steadfast** ⌉	11	⌊	**but does not live up to reputation**
Dž-gùng is **vain of his empathy** ⌏	12	⌶	**and cannot live up to his ideal**

[C. Exemplary Personages]

Kŭng Wv́ndž is cultured	15	⌈	**despite** vulgar experience
Yèn Píng-**jùng** is punctilious ⌉	17	⌊	**despite** long acquaintance
Dzàng Wv́n-**jùng**'s knowledge ⌏	18	⌈	**does not guarantee** propriety
[**Triple**] detachment ⌉	19a	⌊	**does not attest** rv́n
[**Triple**] departure ⌏	19b	⌈	does not qualify Chv́n **Wv́ndž**
Excessive circumspection ⌉	20	⌊	does not avail Jì **Wv́ndž**
Foolish fidelity ⌏	21	⌈	is shown in **extreme crisis**
Proverbial loyalty ⌉	23	⌊	is shown in **ultimate suffering**
Proverbial honesty ⌏	24	⌶	is not after all flawless

[D. Confucius on Self-Improvement]

Confucius emulates	25	⌈	**others' virtues**
Confucius finds none correcting	27	⌊	**their own faults**
Confucius is eminent	28	⌶	only in self-improvement

LY 5 Formal Overview

Bronze Gū (see LY 6:25)

Height 33 cm (13 in). 011c. Courtesy Freer Gallery of Art (51·18)

6
c0460

LY 5 echoed with the schoolroom, but LY 6 reflects the issues of actual office. It seems that some of Dž-yóu's LY 5 protégés have risen high by c0460.

Of two persons called "Master" (-dž) in the Analects, Dzv̄ngdž, seen on his deathbed in LY 8, was probably head as of LY 7. The other, Yǒudž, may have been the compiler of LY 6. The DJ shows Yǒudž on campaign near Wǔ-chv́ng in 0487; he might have met Dž-yóu and been referred by him to Confucius, later succeeding Dž-yóu as head. In MC 3A4 (mid 03c) Dž-yóu supports Yǒudž but Dzv̄ngdž attacks him; his headship may thus have been short and troubled. It may be no coincidence that the "Confucius" of LY 6 (unlike the strong persona present in LY 5) seems to have so little influence over his followers.

Reference numbers to Legge are given at the end of each passage.

[A. Fitness for High Office]

⌐ 6:1. The Master said, Yūng might be made to face south. [6:1a]

Yūng is Rǎn Yūng (see 5:5). The Chinese ruler faced south; the phrase here must imply a position of responsibility under the ruler's authority. 6:1 does not say what earned Yūng this praise; its original hearers presumably knew.

∟ 6:2. Jùng-gūng asked about Dž-sāng Bwódž. The Master said, He would do; he is easy. Jùng-gūng said, If he is assiduous in person and easy in deed, as he oversees his people, would that not indeed do? But if he is easy in person and easy in deed, is that not *too* easy? The Master said, What Yūng says is true. [6:1b]

Jùng-gūng, the Rǎn Yūng of 6:1, asks about a colleague (although no later protégé list includes Bwódž) to hear further praise of himself. Bwódž seems to have been neglectful (jyěn 簡), but Confucius contrives to praise this bad trait as a rebuke to Jùng-gūng, who then counters with the standard idea that the gentleman ask much of himself and little of others. The point of historical interest here is the approval of an administration that is "easy" on the people; compare Confucius's own disapproval of easements and exemptions in 4:11.

This is one of four places in the text where a protégé has the last word in discussion with Confucius; see 201n1 for Jv̀ng Sywǽn's possible use of this fact.

⌐ 6:3. Aī-gūng asked which of the disciples loved learning. Confucius replied, There was Yén Hwéi who loved learning: he did not transfer his anger; he did not repeat a fault. Unfortunately his allotted span was short, and he has died. Now there are none, nor have I *heard* of any, who love learning. [6:2]

Aī-gūng's posthumous epithet dates this passage after 0469. In his presence, Confucius is called Kǔngdž ("Master Kǔng"), not simply Dž ("The Master"). Learning (sywé 學) is still self-cultivation: not being angry at the unoffending, learning from your mistakes. Hwéi, alive in 5:9, seems recently dead as of 6:3; he might have died in c0470. Early myth (9:21–22, 11:8–11) claims that he had predeceased Confucius, thus depriving Confucius of a worthy successor. The last line (contra Mao **Suggestions** 284) means "there are none in the group, nor have I heard of any elsewhere" (for other groups, see 5:3).

[B. Judgements In and Out of Office]

⌐ 6:4. Dž-hwá went on a mission to Chí. Master Răn requested a grain allowance for his mother. The Master said, Give her a fù 釜. He said, I request more. He said, give her a yǔ 庾. Master Răn gave her five *loads*. The master said, When Chì went to Chí, he drove sleek horses and wore light furs. I have heard that the gentleman relieves the needy, but does not enrich the wealthy. [6:3a]

> It is claimed that Dž-hwá went to Chí *for Confucius*, but only in myth did Confucius have his own foreign policy and granary; Dž-hwá and Răn Chyóu may have been in the service of the Mvng (see 5:8). The title "Master Răn" (Răndž) shows that Răn Chyóu himself had the authority to set the allotment, and is merely consulting Confucius ("requested" is here the incipient aspect "was about to request"). The trip to Chí took half a month. Confucius first suggests provision for Dž-hwá's mother for that time; 64 handfuls or shvng 升 (the daily ration was probably 4 handfuls or 800 cc of millet; compare the Greek khoiniks χοῖνιξ; Palmer **Rations** 121f), making this a 16-day allowance. His second suggestion (160 handfuls; 40 person/days), would have provided for mother, wife, and child (or servant), supporting Dž-hwá's entire household in his absence and making his salary a bonus, but staying *conceptually* within the subsistence ethic. Master Răn gives her five carry-loads (bǐng 秉, 1,000 handfuls; 250 person/days), *six times more* than the subsistence requirement. This yields an excess of 525%, and puts Dž-hwá's mission on the probable profit level of a commercial venture; the LY 4 culture clash now includes the disciples in the profit sector. LY 6:4/5 insist that salaries should be functional, and that the economic gap between high and low should not be widened.

⌊ 6:5. Ywæn Sž was their Steward. They gave him nine hundred of grain, but he declined. The Master said, Was there no way you could give it to the neighboring households or the county association? [6:3b]

> "Their," as in 6:4, may have been the Mvng clan; "gave" is the incipient aspect "offered to give." Nine hundred ("nine hundred *what*" cries the frustrated metrologist) must be the salary and household allowance for an official family; like the rates in 6:4, it probably has a subsistence basis. Sž can afford to decline this, and expects praise for avoiding the fault criticized in 6:4. The "Master" instead regrets the loss of food that others (including the rural self-government council) could have used. In terms of 6:4, Sž avoids the superfluity it censures but misses the charity it enjoins. 6:4/5 are a stand against the new society's abuses. With central taxation replacing the levies of a resident warrior-magnate, there is a danger of concentrated palace luxury based on remote rural hardship.

⌐ 6:6. The Master said of Jùng-gūng, If the calf of a plow-ox is plain-colored and has horns, even though one might prefer not to use it, are the hills and streams going to reject it? [6:4].

> Plain-colored oxen were apparently required for sacrifice, and parti-colored ones were limited to work-animal status; hence the curious if standard gloss "spotted" for lí 犁 "plow." This amounts to a plea for social mobility: if a son measures up to proper standards, his parents' low social status should not preclude his being "used" (sacrificially; compare "eaten" in 17:6) in office. For the humble but worthy junior protégé Răn Yūng, see also 5:5 and 6:1/2.

˪ 6:7. The Master said, Hwéı: he could go three months without in his heart departing from rv́n. The others: they can manage it for a day or a month, but that is all. [6:5].

> The superiority of Hwéı, which was relative in 5:9, has since his death become absolute (see 6:3). "Hwéı" and "The others" are grammatical topics (hence the colons); floating noun phrases on which the predicates comment, not close grammatical subjects in the usual sense (in which case we would have simply "Hwéı could . . ."). It is hard to render this in English without a vernacular tinge, as above, or the awkward "as for" and its equivalents (see 4:6c). The subject/topic difference is relevant to style, and sometimes also to meaning.

┌ 6:8. Jì Kāngdž asked, Could Jùng Yóu be used in government? The Master said, Yóu is decisive; why could he not be used in government? He asked, Could Sž be used in government? The Master said, Sž is experienced; why could he not be used in government? He asked, Could Chyóu be used in government? He said, Chyóu is skilled; why could he not be used in government? [6:6]

> The Jì held the real power in Lǔ, and were the chief enemy of the legitimist party. It is therefore strange to hear Confucius recommending Dž-lù, Dž-gùng, and Rǎn Chyóu (Dž-gùng, of whom we have not heard since LY 5, here replaces Gūngsyī Hwá in the unprincipled trio of 5:8). Subtlety is probably involved: it is not specified whose "administration" these people would be serving, and "Confucius" mentions in his response only what he would himself have regarded as trifling virtues. The paired saying 6:9 will make things clearer.

˪ 6:9. The Jì were intending to employ Mǐn Dž-chyēn as the Steward of Bì. Mǐn Dž-chyēn said, Make some plausible excuse for me. If they should come back to me, then I will have to go live north of the Wv̀n. [6:7]

> The Wv̀n River was the northwest boundary of Lǔ. Once safely in the next state, Dž-chyēn would be beyond the reach of this tempting but politically unwelcome offer to manage the illegitimate Jì clan's stronghold of Bì.

┌ 6:10. Bwó-nyóu was ill. The Master went to inquire after him. Grasping his hand through the window, he said, Would it were not so! It is surely fate. Such a man, and to have such a disease! Such a man, and to have such a disease! [6:8]

> Bwó-nyóu is Rǎn Gv̄ng. The name links Nyóu/Ox and Gv̄ng/Plow seem to prove the use of oxen for plowing in 05c Lǔ. Confucius's not entering the house, and deploring the disease, suggests leprosy. "Would it were not so!" is usually construed as spoken to the others ("We have as good as lost him"), but after the handclasp, one expects, if not a second-person remark, at least one that includes the dying man, and we so render it here. Fate in this passage is simply the unpredictable, not, as in later chapters, the cosmically intended.

˪ 6:11. The Master said, Worthy indeed was Hwéı! One dish of food, one dipper of drink, living in a narrow alley – others could not have borne their sorrow, but Hwéı did not waver in his happiness. Worthy indeed was Hwéı! [6:9]

> This immortal passage has given solace to uncounted impoverished scholars in later centuries. We need hardly add that Hwéı's happiness was not a delight in hardship, but obliviousness to hardship in the the pursuit of virtue. Such lyrical detachment will in later chapters be ascribed to Confucius himself.

⌐ 6:12. Răn Chyóu said, It is not that I do not take delight in the Master's Way, but that my strength is not sufficient. The Master said, One whose strength is not sufficient gives out along the way, but you are drawing the line. [6:10]

> The word "way" (dàu 道) has the primary sense "roadway," whence "course of travel" and "way of doing things, code, principles." Răn Chyóu here defends his failure to follow the Master's principles. The Master crisply retorts that, not having tried and failed, Chyóu has no idea if his *strength* is sufficient; his *will* is weak (for a wider consideration of this concept, see Nivison **Weakness**). Will and strength are important features of the old ethos. The obligation to use oneself up in pursuit of a goal (compare 4:6) is typical of 05c moral extremism; it will be mitigated in the 04c (see 11:16) by a concept of the moral middle.

∟ 6:13. The Master said to Dž-syà, You should work on the rú of the gentleman, not the rú of the little people. [6:11]

> Rú 儒, in the 03c already a label for "Confucianist," is here "learning" or cultural tradition: Dž-syà is being told to concentrate on elite culture, and avoid folkways. In later tradition, Dž-syà is named as a transmitter of the Shr̄ or Classic of Poetry, the first half of which (the Fv̄ng or "Airs" section) purports to be folksongs reflecting the ethos of the various states. When we meet Dž-syà in the later 3:8, he will be discussing with Confucius the deep meaning of one such song: Shr̄ 57, from the "Airs" of Wèi. That he received the Shr̄ from Confucius to transmit to later ages is unlikely, since Confucius in the early LY gives no sign that he is aware of any fixed texts whatever. 6:13 seems to catch Dž-syà in the act of himself compiling its folk or "little people" section. This is startling, but later Analects mentions of the Shr̄ seem to attest later stages in the compilation process, ending (in 13:5, c0322) with the 300-poem anthology which, or a version of which, we now possess (see page 255)
>
> The pairing of 6:12/13 shows two kinds of failure (indolence in 6:12 and vulgarity in 6:13) to follow the proper way (political in 6:12 and cultural in 6:13). This does not enforce, but it does allow, our reading of 6:13.

∟ 6:14. Dž-yóu was Steward of Wŭ-chv̆ng. The Master said, Have you found any men there? He said, There is Tántái Myè-míng; when he walks he does not take shortcuts, and except on state business he has never come to Yĕn's chamber. [6:12]

> For a suggestion that the odd name Tántái Myè-míng refers to Dzv̄ngdž, a native of Wŭ-chv̆ng, see page 280. What he is here praised for is the refusal to shortcut procedures or to use his personal influence on public business. This is more momentous than it may seem. We are here in the middle of an evolution from what had once been the Prince's business (gūng-shr̄ 公事) but has now become "state business" or "public business" – the more direct relation between the ruler and the people is giving rise to the idea of the state not as the possession of the ruler, but as a thing in itself, subsisting apart from the ruler. The term "gūng" will continue to evolve, in the 03c, from "public" to "fair, equitable," the evenhandedness that *should* characterize the state, investing the new political entity with moral obligations of its own.
>
> Besides being a concluding tribute to Dž-yóu, 6:14 concludes the LY 6B section theme by identifying the great task of the new bureaucracy: to find the right men. Since the LY 6 compiler Yŏudž (or so we argue) was himself one of Dž-yóu's finds, 6:14 would have the function of validating him as well.

[C. The Balance of Qualities]

6:16. The Master said, Unless one has Invocator Twó's suavity, and Sùng Jāu's beauty, he will have difficulty keeping out of trouble in these times. [6:14]

This violates 4:9 and directly reverses 5:25. Such contrasts strongly suggest that LY 5 and 6 are not by the same hand. At least the reversal is announced with ruefulness: not urged as a good, but admitted as a necessity. Twó was from Wèi, and Sùng Jāu ("Jāu of Sùng") was from Sùng. Commentaries supply some details; fortunately, their metaphorical import in 6:16 is obvious without them.

6:18. The Master said, When substance predominates over style, it is crude; when style predominates over substance, it is pedantic. When style and substance are in balance, then you have the gentleman. [6:16]

As often in paired sayings, 6:18 mitigates the preceding 6:16 – surface qualities, though necessary, must be balanced by inner principles. Style (wv́n 文, "ornament") refers to the decorations on bronze vessels (p20), the carving of panels, the painting of walls (5:10a), and much else. It may here already have the sense of literary style; 6:18 is constantly cited (Brooks **Geometry** 142) in later discussions of literary art. Here is a harbinger of the idea of balance (compare 6:12n) that will be important in the 04c Analects.

6:19. The Master said, A man's life is uprightness, and if he does not have that, he will be lucky if he even *escapes* with his life. [6:17]

This section envoi further qualifies 6:16, and repeats its image of "escaping." It makes inner principle not equal to (as in 6:18), but more fundamental than, external graces. One hesitates to speculate on the minds of Analects authors, but 6:16–19 read like a statement of, and then a hasty retreat from, a new idea. The importance of charisma (Snow **Government** 6, 57 "mana") is granted by modern analysts, but seems to have been hard for the Confucians to accept.

[D. Acquiring the Qualities of the Gentleman]

6:20. The Master said, Knowing it is not as good as loving it; loving it is not as good as taking delight in it. [6:18]

The section begins with the idea, present in 6:11–12, of the love of virtue as a condition for the acquisition of virtue. Awareness, even desire, is not enough. This may be compared with the 4:2 contrast between sincere and expedient rv́n (and with the 4:3/4 association of rv́n with the ability to love and hate wisely). 6:20 differs in that the inner impulse toward virtue is primary. This *internalized* virtue, derived from feelings, is different from the exterior, exemplary virtue which was characteristic of the feudal world; it will recur in the 04c Analects, and thereafter in Mencius. The shame culture is yielding to the desire culture.

6:21. The Master said, To those above the middle level, one can speak of something higher. To those below the middle level, one cannot speak of anything higher. [6:19]

There is a cutoff point (notwithstanding the quibble of Mao **Suggestions** 285) in the capacity for virtue, below which it is useless to urge virtue. Humanity spirals either up or down. Here, as in 5:10a/b, speaks the discouraged teacher.

⌐ 6:22. Fán Chŕ asked about knowledge. The Master said, Concern yourself with what is rightful for the people; be assiduous toward the ghosts and spirits so as to keep them at a distance – this can be called knowledge. He asked about rýn. He said, First it is difficult, and only afterward do you have success – this can be called rýn. [6:20]

> "Knowledge" here is know-how: providing for the needs and exorcisms of the subject populace (mín 民). This is the first hint of a concept of popular right, a prelegal social expectation amounting to a social obligation. Rýn, by contrast, is described obscurely, and in terms of the process by which it is cultivated. The phrase can also be read as "focus on the effort and not the outcome."

ᒪ 6:23. The Master said, The knowing take delight in rivers; the rýn take delight in mountains. The knowing move; the rýn are still. The knowing are happy; the rýn live long. [6:21]

> A yet more cryptic contrast between knowledge and rýn. It is easy to grasp the knowledge half: activity leading to happiness. It is the mountainous stillness of the rýn half that seems mystical (Waley **Analects** 120n4 finds it "distorted by quietist influences"). Possibly rýn here *is* mystical (a contrast between action and stillness is common in meditational writings), and the initial difficulties and later success of 6:22, above, describe an inward meditation process and its sudden breakthrough, beyond conventional "happiness."
>
> We now note 5:9 (Yén Hwéı's superior mental powers), 6:7 (protracted mental concentration on rýn), and 6:11 (happiness amid austerities). Hwéı is always a mysterious figure, never narratively present (as Răn Gývng in 6:10, though he never speaks, *is* vividly present), or doing a describable deed (in 6:3 he instead *refrains* from deeds). All this suggests the meditation adept. The point of ethical interest is that Hwéı has gradually appropriated as his own the virtue rýn, undefined in LY 4, puzzling in LY 5, and in LY 6:19 replaced in its original sense by another term altogether. Rýn is here still opposed to knowing, but now in the sense of being a higher *kind* of knowing.
>
> These maxims yield a commonsense meaning also, but we suggest that 6:23 is an esoteric pairing of Knowing and (in the adept sense) Unknowing.

⌐ 6:25. The Master said, A gū not used as a gū. What a gū! What a gū! [6:23]

> The gū 觚 (p30), the most beautiful of Shāng bronze vessels, ceased to be made from Jōu onward (Willetts **Art** 148). A Warring States viewer might see one in a collection, but not in use. There may be a pun (see 6:26) on gū 孤 "lonely" in the sense "discontexted." Might this ancient and disused entity be rýn itself?

ᒪ 6:26. Dzăı Wŏ said, The rýn man: if you just told him, "The well has rýn in it," I suppose he would go and jump into it. The Master said, Why should that be so? A gentleman can be misled but not trapped; can be lured but not netted. [6:24]

> This second pun (rýn 仁 is homophonous with rýn 人 "man") derides the rýn man as idealistic but naive in his ceaseless quest for further perfection in rýn. The reply is that though he may be initially deceived, he will discover his error.

ᒪ 6:27. The Master said, If a gentleman learns widely in culture but limits it by propriety, he will surely manage not to overstep its proper boundary. [6:25]

> A summary saying on the reasonable balance between different positive values.

Interpolations

For a complete finding list of interpolated passages, see page 329.

Reflections

Waley **Analects** 20 notes that Yŏudž, as a foot soldier, cannot be of the high-chariot elite. Though his honorific -dž *suffix*, as argued above, implies status within the school, he lacks the honorific Dž- *prefix* that Dž-gùng and others have; a fact that supports Waley's inference. After presentable Dž-yòu, his headship may have been a problem for the group, which would explain his near-eclipse in the later Analects, and the hostile tales about him in later lore.

It would also explain a curious feature of LY 6: the lowliness of its angle of vision. It is the most *outdoor* of Analects chapters (note the calf of 6:6 and the mountains of 6:23). It knows that you have to be plausible to get by (6:16), and that there are bad diseases (6:10). It cares how much people get to eat, from the lyrical Yén Hwéi (6:11) to the unregarded neighbors of Ywæn Sž (6:5).

Yén Hwéi's "narrow alley" (6:11) marks him as a man of the city, and probably of its artisan sector. The Lŭ capital had two gates in its formal south wall, opposite the palace, but three each on the other sides, near to the areas where the artisans lived and worked (Li **Eastern** 141–142, Zhang **Lu** 54–56), perhaps because there were no large goods-transporting roads *within* the city.

Apart from such shocking innovations as 6:16, LY 6 depends doctrinally on LY 5. It is an interesting project to map the two chapters against each other (to begin with, we might have 6:3 < 5:28, 6:8 < 5:8, 6:9 < 5:5, and 6:16 < 5:25, which have a rather strikingly limited distribution within LY 5), to see what is derivative and what is new. A series of such overlap charts is a good way to become aware of the ideological drift in the text. In such comparisons, one must allow for the tendency of the text to repeat old ideas alongside new ones, perhaps as a way of acclimatizing the new ones.

A key aspect of Yŏudž's lowliness is his vulgarity: his acceptance of salary in 6:5, of adroitness in 6:16, and of style in 6:18 on a par with all the older traits (the solid "substance") of the classic feudal gentleman.

Formally, LY 6 is considerably more relaxed than LY 5. The four divisions with their 3-11-3-7 sayings are not only nonpalindromic but nonsymmetrical. On the other hand, there is a break that tends to mark off the last 3 sayings of LY 6D, as though they were a vestige of Dž-yóu's final 5D section, also with 3 sayings. It is the same with pairing: there is no conspicuous double-stitch pattern like that of the LY 5 middle sections, but there are traces of what might be a secondary pairing in 6:11/12 (on the theme of happiness). On the whole, we might conclude that Dž-yóu's formal elaborateness is not entirely without its faint analogues in the looser form of Yŏudž's LY 6.

The enigma of the chapter is Yén Hwéi, proclaimed in the esoteric material of 6C, and especially in a trio of evenly spaced sayings (6:3, 6:7, 6:11), which, though not as adroitly placed, seem to be an LY 6 formal counterpart of the Dž-gùng triad in LY 5 (5:4, 5:9, 5:12). The focus on the internally motivated, indeed mystical, Yén Hwéi in LY 6 shows replacement of an external warrior ethic by an internal personal ethic, an esoteric counterpart of the desire culture which had been deplored by Confucius in LY 4.

Bronze Snaffle Bit (see LY 7:12)
Length 22·2 cm (8·7 in). 05c/04c. Courtesy Freer Gallery of Art (79·9)

7
c0450

Dzŭng Shvm (to be distinguished from his second son Dzŭng Shvn), known in the Analects as Dzvngdž "Master Dzvng," is shown in LY 8 as on his deathbed surrounded by disciples. This suggests that he was alive, and head of the school of Lŭ, as of the preceding LY 7, a possibility supported by thematic usages common to the LY 8 Dzvngdž sayings and parts of LY 7.

Dzvngdž was from the fortress town of Wŭ-chvng in southern Lŭ, and despite later tradition seems not to have been one of the original protégés. He was probably noticed as a promising officer by Dž-yóu when he was Steward of Wŭ-chvng, and came north sometime after Dž-yóu himself, in c0473. As the first *outside* school head, he will have needed something to tell his students about a Confucius whom he had never known. LY 7 may be the result.

It continues the aestheticism of LY 5, while at the same time extending the lowliness noted in LY 6. It is a portrait of Confucius, and many features of that portrait are new. It defines him in terms of the sage (shvng), a word absent from earlier chapters, and makes him a transmitter of antiquity, not an inculcator of more recent feudal-military values. Other elements of the LY 7 portrait (such as personal invulnerability) were not incorporated in the final Confucius myth, but the idea of a sage conveying ancient wisdom has proved to be enduring.

Reference numbers to Legge are given at the end of each passage.

[A. Personal Character]

⌐ 7:1. The Master said, In handing on and not inventing, in being faithful to and loving antiquity, I might be compared to our old Pvng. [7:1]

Confucius's actual Spring and Autumn feudal-warrior ethos seems, on the evidence of LY 4, to have been outmoded at the end of his life. His stance as a teacher in LY 4 involved no references to antiquity or to any other authority. These traits have been generally preserved in LY 5–6, composed within living memory of Confucius. This saying is the first to link him to antiquity as such. Who "old Pvng" may have been at this early period is difficult to say.

∟ 7:2. To be silent and understand, to study and not tire of it, to encourage others and not grow weary in so doing: what problem do these present for me? [7:2]

This rhetorically modest claim (compare 7:34) is outrageous in wider context: it makes Confucius himself, not merely Yén Hwéi, a meditational adept. Structurally, the "self-improvement" theme which has figured at the end of each chapter since the authentic LY 4, turns up *at the beginning* of LY 7. This not only emphasizes pedagogy in general, it highlights the meditationist theme (the mystical element of 7:2 joins the mysterious motif of antiquity, in 7:1), and adds it to the other arts of the teacher. For Dzvngdž as a teacher and an interpreter of Confucius, see the Reflections (7r), following.

Anxiousness over the adequacy of teaching is also new. In his own closed society, Confucius's position itself made him an authority. The impatience of 5:10a/b and 6:21 is here, in 7:2, replaced by solicitousness; it has now become the *teacher* who must put energy into the situation. See also 7:7 below.

⌐ 7:3. The Master said, My character not being cultivated, my studies not being pursued, hearing the right and not able to follow it, being not good and unable to change it: these are my anxieties. [7:3]

> This saying reverts from mysticism to ordinary self-improvement (as in LY 4–6), and from the claimed successes of 7:1/2 to the confessed shortcomings of 7:3/5.

└ 7:5. The Master said, Extreme has been my decline; long has it been since last I dreamed of Jōu-gūng! [7:5]

> For the emphatic inverted predicate, compare 6:11. Jōu-gūng, the "Prince of Jōu," brother of the Jōu founder and first holder of the fief of Lǔ (see page 3), was the regent and thus the preserver of Jōu in the minority of the second Jōu king. If we fold the 7:3/5 pair back over 7:1/2, then 7:5 (the first Lǔ Prince) will match 7:1 (Confucius as continuous with the past); 7:5 thus *explicates* 7:1. Though here recollected in age, the dream itself – the sense of continuity with the Jōu – would presumably have belonged to the youth of "Confucius."

⊢ 7:6. The Master said, Intent upon the Way, based on virtue, close to rýn, and acquainted with the arts. [7:6]

> These parallel clauses may be advisory ("Be . . . ") or descriptive ("I am . . . "); the best reading may be a general description ("He [the gentleman] is . . . "). If so, it fits the LY 7 portrait by epitomizing Confucius's behavioral ideal.
>
> "Intent upon the Way" (compare 4:9) implies initial commitment. Virtue (dý 德), a goal in 7:3, is here a resource (see 7:23); rýn, a mainstay in 4:5, is now an ideal to be approached. The arts (yì 藝), except as "accomplishments" for Rǎn Chyóu in 6:8, are new: it seems (from the verb yóu 游 "travel, wander," here "acquainted with") that they serve as relaxation after the hard ethical work (compare 9:2). With this hint, we may take the phrases as a sequence (and 7:6 as a precursor of the ethical progress passage 2:4): initial determination on the right path, reliance on virtue for further progress, homing on rýn as a beacon in the last stages, and seemly personal accomplishments at the end.

[B. Early Teaching]

⌐ 7:7. The Master said, From those who have brought a bundle of dried meat on up, I have never been without a lesson to give them. [7:7]

> The point is Confucius's welcome to sincere students whatever their wealth. 7:7 attests the use of tuition payments (structured, in this society, as gifts) in the school of Lǔ. Dried meat (see 10:6c) has humble associations, implying that "Confucius" had meaningful things to say to pupils who were not in line for palace positions. The social broadening since LY 4–5 is enormous.

└ 7:8. The Master said, If they are not eager, I don't expound. If they are not urgent, I don't explain. If I give out one corner and they don't come back with three corners, then I don't go on. [7:8]

> Discipline, balancing the acceptance of 7:7 (Grafflin **Form:** "open admissions but post-matriculation screening"). A new idea (like that in 7:3) is often paired with an older idea. "Corners" suggest carpentry: given one right angle, a novice should be able to make the other corners square. What Confucius wants is the ability to infer the next step (see 5:9). For the desire to learn, see 6:21.

⌐ 7:12. If wealth could be had for the seeking, though it were only as some officer who holds the whip, I too would do it. But if it cannot be had, I will follow what I love. [7:11]

> "Wealth" (see 4:5) is temptation to wrongful office; for a tragic overtone, see Durrant **Mirror** 23. "If," usually rú 如, is here ár 而, seemingly a (dialectal?) shift in the syllabicity of medial -i- (nyu/niw). There is a similar interplay in the text between standard rǔ 汝 and variant ǎr 爾, both "you."
>
> Waley makes "officer" (shr̀ 士) ironic for "groom," but driving was an elite skill, and here, at least, rank and salary would seem to attend it. It may attest the decreasing prestige of horsemanship as such (compare again 9:2).

└ 7:14. When the Master was living in Chí he heard the Sháu; for three months he did not know the taste of meat. He said, I did not imagine that making music could reach to this. [7:13]

> The Sháu ("Summons") was a dance with orchestral accompaniment. Warring States orchestras, flutes ornamenting bells and chimes and supported by drums, were (to judge from the related Japanese gagaku) capable of impressive effects.
>
> The aesthetic rapture of 7:14 pairs it with the "love" of virtue in 7:12. There is a reverse or palindromic (ABBA) secondary pairing of 7:12/14 with 7:7/8 (compare 7:5). The reader may wish to search for further examples of ABBA.
>
> The implication is that these performances were not known in Lǔ at this date; the Chí contact may also suggest a shift northward from Lǔ's heretofore predominantly southern trade focus (see 5:18n, 5:19bn). For the possibility that 7:14 preserves a memory of Confucius's actual travels, see page 271.

⌐ 7:16. The Master said, Eating coarse food, drinking water, crooking one's arm and pillowing upon it – happiness may be found also in these circumstances. To be unrighteous and so become wealthy and even honored – to me this is like a drifting cloud. [7:15]

> An echo of 6:11 and 7:12. The drifting cloud symbolizes indifference.

└ 7:17. The Master said, Give me several more years; with fifty to study, I too might come to be without major faults. [7:16]

> "Too" (yì 亦) is the Lǔ reading (**Shr̀-wv́n** 51; not in Mǎ **Shr̀ Jīng**), which with most critical scholars (Waley; Mao **Suggestions** 286) we prefer to the Gǔ text's homophonous Yì 易, the Changes; the sentence pause is affected, and in such matters oral tradition is safer. Despite the identity of the phrase "major faults" (dà gwò 大過) with the name of Hexagram 28, it is doubtful (Dubs **Changes**) that Confucius studied, or knew, the Yì. The theme of lifelong ethical striving is echoed poetically in Dzv̄ngdž's last words, 8:3 below.

Ŀ 7:19. The Prince of Shv̀ asked Dž-lù about Confucius. Dž-lù did not reply. The Master said, Why did you not say, "This is the kind of man he is: in his enthusiasm he forgets to eat; in his happiness he forgets his sorrows; he is not even aware that old age will soon be at hand." [7:18]

> The "Prince" was a local rebel; Confucius (in the presence of a ruler called Kǔngdž; compare 6:3) hints that employment could be declined if offered (compare the temptations of 7:12 and 7:16). For his "happiness," see again 7:12 and 7:16; Confucius (compare 7:2) is here taking on *another* trait of Yén Hwéɪ.

[C. Late Teaching]

⌐ 7:20. The Master said, I am not one who knows things from birth. I am one who loves antiquity and seeks after it with diligence. [7:19]

> In this second half of the chapter, we return to the antiquity theme of 7:1. The denial of inborn knowledge, like the frequent denial of sagely or supernatural insight, has in the end the reverse effect, probably intended, of suggesting that Confucius was himself a sage. The "ritual modesty" theory of the orthodox commentators (Waley **Analects** 74) may have its beginnings in this LY 7 motif.

∟ 7:22. The Master said, When I am walking in a group of three people, there will surely be a teacher for me among them. I pick out the good parts and follow them; the bad parts, and change them. [7:21]

> This, balancing the probably esoteric claim of 7:20, returns to the empirical ethics with which we have been familiar since 4:17, and gives it its most striking formulation in the Analects (compare the ten households of 5:28). The experienced reader will no longer require the gloss "change them [in myself]." The Lǔ text (**Shr̀-wv́n** 52; not in Mǎ **Shŕ Jīng**) adds an explicit "I" (wǒ 我) to the first line, making clear that Confucius is himself one of the "three men."

⌐ 7:23. The Master said, Heaven begat virtue in me. What does Hwán Twéi expect to do to me? [7:22]

> Hwán Twéi was a minister of Sùng by whom Confucius is supposed to have been threatened. The implication of travel to other states, and thus a reputation beyond Lǔ (compare 7:14), also appears for the first time in LY 7. Even stronger is the claim of supernatural invulnerability, based on a charge from Heaven, and relating to the Jōu connection which is asserted in 7:5.
>
> This passage has an aberrant pronoun (yv́ 予, ancient initial y-, in place of the standard wǒ 我, ancient initial ng-), here found for the first of many times in the text. It is merely a plural in the Shāng oracle bones (information from David N. Keightley), but in the Warring States, when it was known only from ritual inscriptions, it was invested with something like a sacral nuance; hence its use in this "Heaven" context (Alvin P. Cohen notes that a similar association of yv́ with oaths obtains in the Dzwǒ Jwàn). The idea of divine protection is novel in LY 7, and part of Dzv̄ngdž's contribution to what, on the model of "Christology," we might call "Confucianology." Such theories may be typical of successors who lack direct acquaintance with the founder of a movement.

∟ 7:24. The Master said, Do you disciples take me as concealing something? There is nothing I conceal from you; I never act but that I share it with you. This is Chyōu. [7:23]

> Again the disclaimer (despite the sincere "Chyōu," and the direct address to "[you] two or three [young] masters" 二 三 子) fails to convince. The idea of a secret teaching is part of this revisionist portrait of Confucius. It explains to Dzv̄ngdž's hearers the lack of support for the LY 7 portrait in earlier chapters, and lets Dzv̄ngdž the latecomer monopolize the interpretation of Confucius as he could not have done otherwise. It may be relevant that in the interpolated *4:15¹, Dzv̄ngdž appears in exactly this light: explaining the secret meaning of an otherwise cryptic saying of Confucius. For secret *actions*, see 7:29, below.

⌐ 7:26a. The Master said, A *sagely* man, I have not managed to find; if I could find a *gentleman*, it would be enough. [7:25a]

> The new concept of the Sage is treated as remote from all possible experience (dv́ ár 得而 "contrive to" is more emphatic than dv́ "get to"). Confucius would gladly be content with the traditional jyw̄ndž ideal, if (see 5:3) he could get it.

∟ 7:26b. [The Master said,] A *good* man, I have not been able to find; if I could find a *constant* man, it would be enough. But when lacking seems having, empty seems full, and privation seems opulence, it will be hard to find constancy. [7:25b]

> The term "good (shàn 善) man" suggests the later Micians. With the 5:12 Golden Rule, this is the second time that a seemingly popular ideal is accepted by "Confucius" as worthy but difficult to attain. Such receptivity implies that the Micians were yet not a competitive threat; this will change in the 04c.
>
> As for steadfastness, the *concept* is compatible with earlier ideas, but the *term* (hv́ng 恆) is new; besides 7:26b, it recurs only in *13:22[14] as the "stabilizing" of omens. In 7:26b it is rather "candor," nondissimulation. Note the esoteric, positive value of "lacking, empty, privation," associated in 6:11 with mystical insight: see 5:11 for "firmness" (gāng 剛) and desirelessness, and 6:23 for rv́n and stillness. We might paraphrase: It is hard to detect one of mystical insight behind the facade of conventional success.
>
> It may then be (note the pairing with the "sage" in 7:26a) that we have here a concept of a "sage" whose special insight rests on meditation techniques.

⌐ 7:28. The Master said, To be sure, there are those who can originate something of which they did not previously know. I myself have no such capacity. But to hear much and pick out the good so as to follow it, and to see much and remember it, is the next-best kind of knowing. [7:27]

> This is the method of experiential gradualism (7:22), not (wǒ 我 "me" is the contrastive "I") the new inspiration technique, the old Confucius sharing the chapter with, and preparing reader acceptance for, the new. For a disclaimer of inborn knowledge, see 7:20; for transmission versus innovation, see 7:1.
>
> Mao **Suggestions** 286 regards "pick out . . ." as a false repeat due to a broken bamboo slip at 7:22. But breaks lead to *displacement*, not *duplication*. The line as we have it is meaningful: one is selective with things heard, but accepting of things seen. Experience is primary over advice. The contrast between oral and written advice has not yet emerged (compare 9:24).

∟ 7:29. In Hù County it was hard to find anyone to talk with. A youth presented himself. The disciples had their doubts, but the Master said, We are involved with his coming forward, but not with his going away. Why be so fastidious? If someone purifies himself and comes to us, we accept his purification; we do not guarantee his future conduct. [7:28]

> It would appear that Confucius and his disciples are traveling about the country, proselytizing any who will receive them. We may then notice that there is in LY 7 no mention of government service or policy (compare LY 6); instead, Confucius appears as a knower and a teacher, working in the byways with inferior material (compare 7:26a/b). It may be that 7:26a–7:29 express, among other things, a concern with transmitting the school leadership.

⌊ 7:30. The Master said, Is rýn really far away? If I want rýn, then rýn is already there. [7:29]

Here is the instantaneous-attainment method applied to rýn (compare 6:22–23 and 7:2). The superficial point is that will is not only necessary but sufficient for the attainment of virtue. The emphasis on willingness over experience also tends to validate the sort of leader that Dzvngdž was: not knowing Confucius, but by an inner effort directly intuiting the essence of his teachings.

[D. Retrospection and Death]

⌈ 7:33. The Master said, As for culture, I am no worse than anybody else. But as for personally carrying out the role of a gentleman, I have never had the opportunity to do it. [7:32]

This refers to Confucius's career failure, already implied in LY 4. It shows how faithfully, despite his association in LY 7 with supernatural contacts (7:5) and protections (7:23), the historic fact of the failed Confucius is still respected.

⌊ 7:34. The Master said, If it is a matter of a Sage or of rýn, how dare I presume? But if one looks to acting for others without tiring of it, or teaching others without growing weary in so doing, perhaps something might be said. Gūngsyī Hwá said, The only problem is that the disciples cannot learn. [7:33]

The 7:33 career failure is neatly balanced by this second failure to pass on wisdom to others. It evokes the idealistic teacher of 7:2 (minus its meditational component), and the strict one of 7:8. After all, nothing has been transmitted.

⌊ 7:35. The Master was very ill. Dž-lù asked to offer a prayer. The Master said, Is this done? Dž-lù replied, It is. The Elegy says, "We prayed for you to the higher and lower divinities." The Master said, Chyōu's praying was done long ago. [7:34]

Confucius's self-reference by his personal name Chyōu tends to occur in expressions of emphatic sincerity; compare 5:28 and 7:24. This passage also reflects the LY 7 sensitivity to ritual (compare 7:14). Following the 5:12 maxim and the 6:13 hint of the Shī, this is the third reference to a non-Analects text.

It is very moving, is it not? The Master patiently lets Dž-lù instruct him in ritual propriety, notwithstanding the fact (or what the hearer of this saying may be presumed to have regarded as a fact) that he knows much more about it than Dž-lù. He then rejects the suggested intercession with the deities. Instead, he offers his whole life as the secular equivalent of a prayer: devoted to the pursuit and dissemination of virtue, fulfilling his early aspirations (7:1–6), though without temporal rewards (7:33) or conspicuous educational results (7:34; this biographical element seems already present in 5:27). All this is borne with an unconcern fully worthy of the feudal resignation enjoined in 4:14. Confucius has done his part.

And his uncomprehending direct disciples have done their part too. Being unworthy to succeed him, they have left the door open for Dzvngdž.

Interpolations

For a complete finding list of interpolated passages, see page 329.

Reflections

Dzv̄ngdž as a writer in LY 7, like Yŏudž in LY 6, is less formally elaborate than Dž-yóu in LY 5. He does, however, in 7:6 and 7:14, reveal a certain aesthetic sensibility. In this sense he ranks with Dž-yóu, and this may help explain why, despite a period of hostility which we shall encounter LY 11, he survives in the Analects record, not only along with Dž-yóu but eclipsing him as a figure in the history of the school. Refinement was increasingly important to the school as it evolved toward a more ritual-based definition of itself.

In content, he continues the LY 6 trend toward lowliness (most clearly in the countryside encounter of 7:29), and toward a mystical/meditational layer of discourse (7:2, 7:30). The next few layers of the Analects will see a swing back to a more courtly focus, but the combination of lowliness and mysticism will recur in the late 04c, reaching a climax with Mencius and his successors in their own separate school of Confucianism.

The conjunction of Dàu "Way" and Dv́ "Virtue" in 7:6 may suggest to readers not only the Dàu/Dv́ Jīng text (DDJ), but the tradition that its alleged author, Lǎudž, was an older contemporary and teacher of Confucius. Though the hints of meditationism in the early LY help explain the genesis of this story, there are no echoes of the DDJ *text* in the Analects until the middle 04c.

The parallel between accretion processes in the Analects and the Biblical New Testament offers some points of interest. The earliest NT writings were the letters of Paul, which aimed to clarify the heritage of the deceased founder for different times and places (Goodspeed **Story** 1–7). They correspond roughly to the adaptive LY 5–6. It was not until the death of Peter, the last follower who had directly known the founder, that a consecutive portrait or history of the founder was felt necessary, an early example being the Gospel of Mark (Goodspeed **Story** 49–53). What are assumed to have existed in the NT case, namely collections of sayings such as the Gospel of Thomas, are actually preserved in the Analects case as the LY 4 nucleus. And the incomprehension or wrongdoing of the original disciples of Jesus in the crucifixion narratives (like that of Confucius's disciples in 7:35) tends to validate the leadership of those who were known to have been outside the original disciple circle.

One of Dzv̄ngdž's authorial tactics is to eliminate disciple anecdotes; only two disciples, Dž-lù and Gūngsyī Hwá, are mentioned in LY 7. Another is to calm the political animosities that were evident in the transitional LY 5–6; neither Dž-lù nor Gūngsyī Hwá is politically faulted, and both are instead portrayed as earnest if imperceptive. A third is to reconceive Confucius along novel lines, giving him a Jōu cultural continuity and a special relationship with Heaven. Confucius also acquires traits earlier seen in the Yén Hwéi persona, most importantly his meditation skill. This esoteric aspect of earlier chapters has thus as of LY 7 begun to affect the Confucius persona, where it joins other, new esoteric aspects such as his sponsorship by Heaven.

LY 7 is not the last Confucian gospel. LY 9 is something like a revision of it, and LY 10 and 11, especially the latter, contribute their share to the image of the founder and his circle. What is important about LY 7 is that with it we seem to be out of the period when Confucius and his circle were still directly remembered, and into a period of mythic adaptation, in which they are defined, indeed enshrined, for a socially wider and more permanent posterity.

Bronze Figure of a Commoner (see LY 7:29 and 8:6n)

Height 9·1 cm (3·6 in). 05c. Courtesy Freer Gallery of Art (51·7, detail)

8
c0436

Dzv̄ngdž's death, portrayed in LY 8:3 (and in the more elaborate and thus probably later *8:4[16]) is traditionally assigned to 0436. This becomes our date for what appears to be a memorial compilation of four Dzv̄ngdž sayings (perhaps a gesture of respect to the four *sections* of the Confucius memorial). They are the only subset which can be firmly attributed to a known figure.

The LY 8 core sayings have the distinctive pronoun and other usages which were noted in LY 7. One of them, the sacral pronoun yẃ 予, seems rather subject-related than dialectically conditioned (Dzv̄ngdž was from Wŭ-chv́ng in southern Lŭ), but the continuity of theme is still striking. They occur also in LY 9, at points clearly a reworking of LY 7. The simplest assumption is that Dzv̄ngdž's elder son Dzv̄ng Ywǽn, his chief mourner and thus the likeliest compiler of LY 8, also succeeded him as school head, in which role he would be the presumptive compiler of LY 9 as well.

The numbering of passages is identical in the Legge text.

⌐ 8:3. When Dzv̄ngdž fell ill, he summoned the disciples at his gate, and said, Uncover my feet; uncover my hands. The poem says:

> Tremblingly and full of fear,
> As though I verged the deep abyss,
> As though I trod the thinnest ice –

but now and hereafter, I know I have come through safely, my little ones.

Disciples "at the gate" imply a gate and thus a residential center, whereas the "Confucius" of LY 5–7 is never observed at home, but always elsewhere.

Dzv̄ngdž (who in the presence of death uses the sacral "I," see 7:23) need not worry about assuming a ritually improper posture in his dying moments: he has safely negotiated the perils of life. Confucius in LY 4 spoke of a constant need for improvement; here is a strenuous anxiety to avoid wrongdoing. The eloquence of Dzv̄ngdž's negative claim echoes Paul's farewell (2 Timothy 4:7), "I have fought a good fight, I have finished the race, I have kept the faith."

Dzv̄ngdž here sounds the note he ascribed to "Confucius" in 7:35. It is not the ritual (the prayer of 7:35, or the posture of the corpse in 8:3) that counts: the dying man's previous life has been one long prayer, one continuous effort.

The lines quoted here are identical with lines in Shī 195 (a political lament that the ruler follows bad advice). The *force* of the quote is however closer to Shī 196 (containing three *near*-identical lines), on measuring up to an exacting standard of conduct; the lines are thus a likely ancestor of *both* poems. LY 6:13 implied the Fv̄ng section of the Shī early in its compilation process; 8:3 may show the Yǎ or courtly section of the Shī (presumably the highbrow alternative that was commended to Dž-syà in 6:13) in a similarly fluid state.

The different functions of the texts quoted at these deaths is noteworthy: "Confucius" in 7:35 had rejected the model and instead instanced his life; Dzv̄ngdž accepts the model and fulfils it with his life. Life and art converge.

└ 8:5. Dzv̄ngdž said, Able, yet inquiring of the less able; versatile, yet inquiring of the limited; having, yet seeming to lack; full, yet seeming empty; wronged, yet not retaliating – long ago, a friend of mine used to devote himself to these.

> One can only agree with the commentators that the friend was Yén Hwéɪ, here described in terms taken from earlier passages. One strand is courtly modesty; the willingness to learn from inferiors, praised by or attributed to Confucius (4:17, 5:15, 5:28, nothing in LY 6, 7:22, 7:28). Another is the speciousness faulted in 7:26b, transformed into paradoxical praise of the meditation adept (for "empty" as a codeword see LaFargue **Tao** 210–211). A third is humility, the suppression of anger or resentment, implied by the Golden Rule of 5:12 and associated with Yén Hwéɪ in 6:3 and 6:11. It is notable that Confucius is never mentioned in LY 8; his virtues are here blended with Hwéɪ's. This agrees with our inferences that Hwéɪ survived Confucius and that Dzv̄ngdž was a latecomer to the circle. His feeling for Hwéɪ is then more than friendship: Hwéɪ was Dzv̄ngdž's point of contact with Confucius.

┌ 8:6. Dzv̄ngdž said, He can be entrusted with a six-span orphan, he can be sent on a hundred-league mission, having charge in a crisis he cannot be overwhelmed – is he a gentleman? He is a gentleman.

> A span (chř 尺) was 23 cm or 9 in (Dubs **Han** 1/279; Reifler **Span**); a six-span orphan stood 138 cm or 54 in: below adult size and needing custodianship. "Gentleman" (usually jyw̄ndž) has an added rv́n "man" (jyw̄ndž-rv́n), as in modern colloquial. The first two clauses are parallel, based on the measures span and league (lĭ 里, about 0.5 km); the third is cadential. In the family, civil, or military spheres, a gentleman is one who can take responsibility, not one of a certain social status (compare 6:6). Unlike Confucius in 4:11 and 4:16 (or Yŏudž in 6:13), Dzv̄ngdž never defines the jyw̄ndž ("gentleman") in opposition to the syău-rv́n ("little man"), or uses the latter term at all. The inclusion of family leadership in this functional definition makes it applicable also to those of modest status. Here, then, may be a Confucian movement in the direction of making cultural common cause with the lower-status group.

└ 8:7. Dzv̄ngdž said, An officer cannot but be broad and resolute, for his burden is heavy and his road is far. Rv́n makes up his burden; is that not indeed heavy? Only with death is he done; is that not indeed far?

> Here again is the onerousness seen in 8:3. It is a favorite quotation of teachers, and is alluded to at the beginning of the primer Hán Shř Wàɪ-jwàn (HSWJ 1:1, Hightower **Wai** 11; compare Brooks **Prospects** 3f) to motivate a young king.
>
> The personal motif in 8:3 and 8:7 give these sayings an ABBA double pairing format, like 7:1–5 and 7:12–17. The compiler may thus have preserved not only Dzv̄ngdž's words, but his proclivities of form. In his use of secondary pairing, Dzv̄ngdž resembles Dž-yòu (LY 5) and not Yŏudž (LY 6). The same *resumed* affinity, with Dž-yòu and Dzv̄ngdž sharing a trait that Yŏudž lacks, appears in the theme of learning from inferiors (see 8:5n) and in the avoidance of the derogatory term syău-rv́n (see 8:6n).

Interpolations

For a complete finding list of interpolated passages, see page 329.

Reflections

Quite apart from the striking similarity in their final utterances (8:3n), it seems that Dzv̄ngdž has, in Confucianism, very much the position occupied by Paul in the history of Christianity – that of a latecomer, who had never known the founder, but becomes a strong and indeed constitutive leader of the movement. They are intense, making up in energy for lack of authenticity; original, taking the movement into new areas; and, most importantly, political, imposing new discipline and reconciling old enmities.

Like zeal and originality, which are almost required of a latecomer by his lack of continuity with the founder, harmonizing may also be inherent in such situations. One who had known Confucius can claim to be speaking for him in disputes among the followers, as Dž-yóu (LY 5) and Yŏudž (LY 6), with their praise and blame of disciples, repeatedly do. Dzv̄ngdž's LY 7 is by contrast a zone of reconciliation. It praises Yén Hwéı, but it also lets Gūngsyī Hwá (corrupt in 6:4) make a supportive remark in 7:34, and gives Dž-lù (associated with Gūngsyī Hwá in the negative 5:8) a role as a spokesman at the hour of Confucius's death in 7:35. It is noteworthy that the text's earlier disapproval of Dž-lù is made up only in the final period of Confucius's life (assuming LY 7 to be chronologically arranged), but the point is that it *is* made up. In venturing into the new sociological and ideological directions implied by LY 7–8, Dzv̄ngdž seems to have chosen to redefine the past as a heritage of peace.

Dzv̄ngdž's distinctive traits include his mystical propensity, centering on Yén Hwéı, the cognate qualities of meekness and interest in the lower orders, and his own mixture of austerity and aesthetic sensitivity. He shows a keen interest in stewardship (8:6; compare 7:5), as befits his headship, and a strong sense of effort (8:7; not courage) and indeed of wayfaring, implying nonmilitary origin (compare MC 4B31). All the early Analects chapters are quotable, but each has its own flavor. The "stupid" Níng Wŭdž of 5:21 will later appeal to the bold Lyŏu Dzūng-ywǣn (773–819); the humble Yén Hwéı of 6:11 will be evoked by the reticent Wáng Wéı (699–759). If there is such a salient passage in LY 7, it is perhaps the equally striking but less strained "three men" image of 7:22. Its simple interactive humanity, its random but sufficient conjunction, have a different charm. If there is a moment in the Analects when three moral agents can safely take a ten-minute break, this is surely it. Here the sometimes cosmic Dzv̄ngdž of LY 7 approaches the direct laterality of the Golden Rule, which was only *quoted*, from afar and perhaps disapprovingly, in 5:12.

Differences between works ascribed to a single author, such as Homer, are often explained as reflecting the difference between youth and age. If our inferences above are sound, we have in LY 7–8 a real case of early and late statements by one person. It is a complication that the LY 7 sayings purport to represent Confucius, whereas the LY 8 ones are openly attributed to Dzv̄ngdž and may represent him more directly. With that qualification, it is still useful to analyze the LY 8 sayings down to the last detail, and then see how much of LY 7 reflects the same personality. This is parallel to, but independent of, the investigation of linguistic similarities and differences between the two chapters. A more advanced exercise of this sort is to get an impression of Dž-gùng from LY 5, and then try to remove that component from LY 4. The result should be Confucius without the Dž-gùng filter, or as near as we can get to it.

Jade Carving (see LY 9:13)

Width 9 cm (3·5 in). 04c/03c. Courtesy Freer Gallery of Art (39·30)

9

c0405

Chí attacked Lǔ border territory in 0412, 0411, and 0408, undoubtedly creating a sense of diplomatic urgency. LY 9:15 shows a shift in cultural affinity from Chí to Wèi, which may imply a political shift in the same direction. If an alliance with Wèi was explored in 0408 and concluded in 0406, the situation of LY 9 might have obtained by 0405. We date it to that year.

LY 9 shows traces of the same usages as LY 7–8, implying that Dzēngdž's line continued in charge of the Analects school; his likeliest successor in any case will have been his elder son, Dzēng Ywǽn. A younger son, Dzēng Shēn, is listed after Dž-syà in a later transmission genealogy of the Shr̄, and probably contributed to the formation of that text, a process visible in 9:15. LY 9 has a greater interest in political and governmental matters, including the intrigue of practical politics, but its focus is largely that of LY 7–8: pedagogy, values, the acquisition of virtue. The LY 7–8 interest in culture persists. As in LY 7, polity is defined as culture, specifically Jōu culture. This chapter incidentally but unmistakably documents contemporary economic and material progress, and the parallel growth of the government bureaucracy.

Reference numbers to Legge are given at the end of each passage.

[A. On Culture]

⌐ 9:2. A man of Dá-syàng Association said, Great indeed is Confucius! He has learned a lot, but has nothing to base a reputation on! The Master heard of it, and said to the disciples at his gate, What shall I take up? Shall I take up chariot driving? Shall I take up archery? I shall take up chariot driving! [9:2]

The issue here is general versus specialized knowledge, a new form of the jyūndž/syǎu-rýn contrast first mentioned by Confucius in 4:11 and 4:16. The artisans had always been specialized; what Confucius here resists (needless to say, he does not really intend to hone his skills as a stock-car race driver; the exchange is sarcastic) is the new presumption that the elite are also specialists. The "association" (dǎng 黨; compare 6:5) seems to have been some sort of neighborhood organization. This one ("Through Lane") probably comprised the residents of some narrow but not dead-end way in the city (see 6r).

∟ 9:3. The Master said, The hemp cap has been customary, but now silk is cheaper. I follow the majority. To bow below is customary, but now they bow above. It is presumptuous, and though I differ from the majority, I follow the "below." [9:3]

The point of etiquette is whether to bow before, or after, ascending the raised platform on which the ruler sits (the "below" option implies *asking* permission to ascend; the "above" *presumes* it). The cap example, in which an intent of courtesy (lǐ 禮) is not involved, but simply a question of practicality, shows that "Confucius," the self-image of the school, is not averse to mere change as such.

That silk now is cheaper than the older hemp-fiber cloth is full of political meaning. Silk is labor-intensive, monopolizing rural women at weaving time and rural families at silkworm-tending time; it implies an above-subsistence agriculture and a systematic platooning of the rural populace.

└ 9:5. The Master was threatened in Kwáng. He said, Since King Wýn passed away, does not culture survive here? If Heaven were going to destroy this culture, no one of later date could have managed to take part in this culture. And if Heaven is *not* going to destroy this culture, what can the men of Kwáng do to me? [9:5]

The final "me" is yẃ 予, noted in 7:23n as sacral. 9:5 also develops the 7:23 invulnerability motif: Heaven protects Confucius as conveying the Jōu past to a Lǔ future. The contact in 7:5 (to Jōu-gūng, the *Lǔ* founder) is here upgraded to King Wýn, the *Jōu* founder, Jōu being seen as a nexus of cultural values. The Jōu having fallen in 0771, that heritage can now validly pass to Lǔ. The Lǔ legitimism of 4:8, centering on the Prince, here aims at the legitimacy of Lǔ itself. The thrice-repeated phrase sž wýn 斯 文 "this culture" (Bol **Culture** 1) retains its magic in later ages; in Wáng Syì-jī's Orchid Pavilion Preface of 353 it evokes the flow of cultural continuity as giving meaning to life itself.

[B. Confucius's Life and Teaching]

┌ 9:6. The Grand Steward asked Dž-gùng, Your master is a sage, is he not? Why does he have these many skills? Dž-gùng said, Surely Heaven will let him be a sage, and he also has these many skills. The Master heard of it, and said, Does the Grand Steward perhaps know me? When I was young I was poor, so I became skilled in many mean matters. Does a *gentleman* have so many of them? He does not. [9:6a]

The specialization issue (compare 9:2) arises again, and Dž-gùng is at a loss how to handle it (he will do better later, in 19:22). The Master simply admits the criticism (accepting the embarrassment of his impoverished early years) and thus keeps the basic principle intact: gentlemen are not technicians.

└ 9:7. Láu says that the Master said, I was not given a chance, therefore I have all these accomplishments. [9:6b]

This explicit variant of 9:6 shows that the LY 9 compiler did not rely solely on his own authority. Given its fit with the probable facts of Confucius's life, this story may have been handed down in the school (Láu is identified with a Chín Jāng 琴張 who is mentioned in the DJ, but does not recur in the Analects). Though we reject the theory that the entire Analects was culled from a parallel oral tradition (the signs of development in the sayings point to evolution rather than memory), here is one hint of its existence. Note that 9:7 is simpler, and less compromised by later concepts, than the perhaps expanded version in 9:6. These are the first uses of gù 故 "so, therefore" in the text. For later stages in the development of implicative or analytical thinking, see 11:16, 3:4, and 3:9

┌ 9:8. The Master said, Do I have wisdom? I do not. But if some common fellow should ask a question of me, in a simpleminded way, I knock at it from both ends and squeeze something out of it. [9:7]

A denial of "sagely" wisdom, and a claim (made earlier for Yén Hwéi; new for "Confucius") to get answers by inspection. We take 空 空 如 as 悾悾 如 (the "simpleminded" of *8:16[14]), describing the questioner's untutored sincerity. The metaphor is obscure (broaching a two-ended container? Dwān 端 "end" is a fixed point for measurement in Mician logic; 兩 端 are the two ends of a pole or arrow in Mician tactics). For the 05c art of induction, see 5:9 and 7:8.

└ 9:11. Yén Ywǣn sighed deeply and said, I look up at it and find it lofty, I bore into it and find it hard; I behold it in front of me, and then suddenly it is behind. Our Master in his solicitude is good at guiding people. He broadens me with culture; he limits me with propriety. I want to desist, but I cannot, and when I have utterly exhausted my capacity, it still seems that there is something there, towering up majestically, and though I want to go toward it, there is no path to follow. [9:10]

The elusive goal of this metaphorical ascent seems mystical rather than intellectual; 9:11 balances and corrects 9:8 by attributing mystical expertise to Confucius (not Yén Hwéi; compare Hwéi's superiority to Confucius in 5:9). It appropriates and expands on 6:12, by showing what it is like (there in political, here in mystical terms) to have one's strength give out on the way. With LY 9, it seems that mystical elements begin to take a more central position.

The verb ywē 約 ("limits"), which means stringency in 4:2 and 4:23, and abstract limitation in 6:27 and 7:26, here makes (except for a quotation of 6:27 in 12:15) its last Analects appearance. The limit concept helped the austerity ethos to control the new luxury "culture" – these pleasures are all very well, but they must be appropriately restrained. The next stage, with propriety *including* the splendors of court and supermarket, will arrive in the 04c, with LY 10.

Older ideas will continue to be expressed along with the new, in the ongoing synthesis which each Analects chapter readjusts for its own time.

┌ 9:12. The Master was very ill, and Dž-lù had the disciples act as attendants. When the illness moderated, he said, Of long standing indeed are Yóu's dissemblings. I have no attendants, but you act as though I had attendants. Who will I deceive? Will I deceive Heaven? And besides, for my own part, than die in the arms of attendants, would I not rather die in the arms of you disciples? And even if I *cannot* have a grand funeral; will I be dying by the roadside? [9:11]

Yw 予 as a contrastive pronoun ("for my own part") and thereafter as a subject (previous sentences use standard wú 吾) seems to reflect the presence of death (compare 8:3, which uses it; the source for the situation of 9:12 is 7:35, which does not). The translation respects the Chinese usage of níng 寧 "rather" by locating it, climactically, in the second clause of a "than . . . rather . . ." sequence. The "attendants" were slaves in great households; the disciples are ashamed that their Master is dying in humble circumstances. "Confucius" insists on his low rank, with devoted disciples and not sullen lackeys at his gate. Even a modern reader can hardly miss the note of intense, reproving affection. By LY 11, Confucius will have become a much more consequential figure.

└ 9:13. Dž-gùng said, I have a beautiful jade here. Shall I wrap it up in its box and keep it, or shall I look for a good price and sell it? The Master said, Sell it! Sell it! I am just waiting for a buyer! [9:12]

The jade metaphor (see page 50, and compare 9:11) attests a money economy. Dž-gùng chides a reluctant Confucius to realize his value as an officer by "selling" himself to a ruler, and Confucius nominally agrees, while still waiting for the *right* ruler. The crass metaphor (not to speak of the crass advice) would have scandalized the actual Confucius (4:2) or even the late Dzvngdž (7:12). It implies that virtue has become just one more saleable commodity.

The pairing is based on lack of, and hope for, high office.

⌐ 9:15. The Master said, When I returned from Wèi to Lǔ, only then did the music get put right, and the Yǎ and Sùng find their proper places. [9:14]

> This saying updates 7:14 in substituting Wèi for Chí as the source of court ceremonies in Lǔ (implying the political shift conjectured above), and in hinting at a later stage in the evolution of the Shī or Poetry text. 9:15 by itself does not prove that the Yǎ (Court Odes) and Sùng (Sacrificial Hymns) "found their places" in an anthology which combined Dzūngdž's court lament (8:3) with Dž-syà's folk pieces (6:13), but 9:27, below, provides additional evidence. We infer that Dž-syà and his project, though scorned in 6:13, are now accepted by the school. For the later development of the Shī, see further 3:2 and 3:8.

L 9:16. The Master said, Outside, he serves Prince and nobles; inside, he serves father and elders. In funeral services he does not dare to be remiss; he does not get in trouble over wine. What difficulty has this for me? [9:15]

> The term chīng 卿 "nobles" occurs in the Analects only in this passage. In the CC it refers to court figures like the husbands of the Prince's daughters, who seem to have occupied an honorary position. These chīng are still associated with the palace, but they evidently have a genuine governmental function.

> Relying on hv yǒu 何有 ("what is there" or "what is the problem?" in 4:13, 6:8, and 7:2), we take 9:16 as listing minor obligations which the gentleman can easily meet (a ritual-modesty interpretation is also possible). 9:15/16 then pair as higher and lower duties. They are, with 9:3, an indication of a rising standard of living; more elaborate rituals and wider beverage options (compare 10:6c; this saying generally foreshadows LY 10) require new rules of propriety. The model citizen now has both court and domestic duties. It may be that the new industrial progress has helped to create a sphere of private life.

> From LY 4 we know that Confucius never served Prince and nobles in *any* major capacity; from tradition, that his father died when he was three, so that he never fulfilled *any* obligations to him; from 5:2 that he had to assume extra responsibility because of his brother's incapacity; and from 9:6 that these humble circumstances were still remembered in LY 9. The "Confucius" of this passage must thus be fictive, and *seen at the time* as fictive; a constructed rather than a remembered figure. The myth grows side by side in these chapters with passages preserving the very memory that the myth functionally replaces.

[C. The Pursuit of Virtue]

⌐ 9:17. The Master, standing by a stream, said, Its passing by is like this – it does not cease by day or night. [9:16]

> This cryptic line is variously explained. The paired 9:18, if it is meant to explain rather than qualify 9:17, makes them both comments on the continual effort needed in self-improvement. Interpreters cite MC 4B18, which however merely quotes the image as the text for a different sermon. One must recognize that the Mencius is much more than a commentary on the Analects.

L 9:18. The Master said, I have never seen anyone who loves virtue the way he loves beauty. [9:17]

> The need for passion in the pursuit of virtue (under whatever name) has been emphasized before; see 4:6, 6:12, 8:7, and now also 9:17.

⌐ 9:19. The Master said, I compare it to making a mound: though he is only one basketful short of completion, if he stops, I stop. I compare it to leveling ground: though he has only dumped one basketful, if he has started, I go to join him. [9:18]

> Neighborhood earthmoving projects (tomb making, field leveling) as similes for a teacher who assists, but does not replace, a student's effort (cf 7:8).

∟ 9:20. The Master said, One to whom I could talk without his growing weary; that would be Hwéı, would it not? [9:19]

> This continues the praise of Yén Hwéı in 6:7; the gnomic Confucius of LY 4 (or 7:8) might have been surprised at the garrulousness of this "Confucius." This pair of sayings, on students, is parallel *as a set* to 9:17/18, on teachers.

⌐ 9:21. The Master said of Yén Hwéı, Alas! I saw him start, but I did not see him finish. [9:20]

> The metaphor is exactly that of 9:19, above. This and the next develop the theme of the departed Yén Hwéı as the perfect student.

∟ 9:22. The Master said, Those who sprout but do not flower; truly there are such! Those who flower but do not fruit; truly there are such! [9:21]

> Unusually for paired Analects sayings on the same subject, the mysterious 9:22 with its orchard metaphor here *follows* the completely explicit 9:21.

> It is hard for modern readers to bear with this continual praise of Yén Hwéı, but if they can somehow hold out through LY 11, they will have the satisfaction of seeing the ancients weary of him too. There are only eighty years to go.

⌐ 9:23. The Master said, The young are to be held in awe. How do we know that what is to come will not surpass the present? If someone is forty or fifty and nothing has been heard from him, then he indeed is not worthy to be held in awe. [9:22]

> This is an utterly revolutionary comment. In the old society of fixed position, age determined respect (or fear; "awe"). In the new society of opportunity (which is to say, of performance), this respect-order is reversed. It is now the young with their potential who deserve at least provisional respect, and the mature nonachievers whose age only makes them more valid objects of scorn.

∟ 9:24. The Master said, The words of the Model Maxims: can one not assent to them? But the point is to *change*. The words of the Select Advices: can one not delight in them? But the point is to *progress*. Those who delight but do not progress, who assent but do not change – I don't know what is to be done with them! [9:23]

> As 6:12 and 6:20 had already emphasized, inner assent is worthless (for a repetition of the last line, see 15:16) if it does not issue in change of conduct, and worse still if it insulates the assenter from the *need* for change. Note the relation with the preceding, paired saying, which also emphasizes progress. Waley has noticed that Fǎ Yw̌ 法語 and Sywěn Jyw̌ 選舉 are titles, evidently of maxim collections not unlike the Analects itself. Here again (compare 5:12, 6:13, 7:35, 8:3) we sense the presence of other texts existing, or coming to exist, in the world surrounding the Analects. As in some previous cases, an outside text or maxim, though clearly not attributed to Confucius, is accepted as a valid guideline by the Confucians. Opposing schools of thought, insofar as they exist, are not yet as sharply differentiated as they will later be in the 04c (see 11:19a), and an easier, more casually accepting atmosphere (compare 5:3) still obtains.

⌐ 9:25. The Master said, Emphasize loyalty and fidelity, do not befriend those who are not your equal, and if you make a mistake, do not hesitate to change it. [9:24]

> The "it" of "change *it*" is embedded in a contraction: a negative verb "do not" plus the initial sound of an unstressed and preposed object pronoun "it." In archaizing pronunciation, the equation is vú 毋 "don't" + dī 之 "it" > vùt 勿. This saying concludes the inner cultivation maxims with a career maxim, within the ethos of LY 4; its emphasis on right acquaintance echoes 4:2. The last line of 9:25 was the occasion of a hilarious misunderstanding when it was alluded to, if perhaps a bit obscurely, by the Japanese court lady Sei Shōnagon (Waley **Pillow** 65); see under 1:8.

∟ 9:27. The Master said, Wearing a tattered robe and standing by those wearing fox and badger, but not being embarrassed: this would be Yóu, would it not?

> Not hostile, and not covetous,
> What is there that one could but praise?

Dž-lù recited this endlessly. The Master said, What is there to praise in *this* behavior? [9:26]

> Dž-lù, disapproved in LY 5–6, is now the well-intentioned follower who always gets things just a little wrong (an ethical direction opposite to that of 9:25, hence the pairing); this is the pedagogically useful *schoolroom* Dž-lù persona. The quote from Shī 33 helps gloss 9:15. It completes the 4:9 type behavior here attributed to Dž-lù. His pleasure on being said to exemplify one original saying (in wording that evokes another saying, 4:12) may readily be imagined. He then proceeds to fall foul of a third, 4:14, by his too public self-satisfaction.

[D. Intrigues in Office]

⌐ 9:28. The Master said, When the year grows cold, only then do we discover that the pine and cypress are the last to fade. [9:27]

> This beautiful image, reinforced by 9:29, is a metaphor of personal integrity revealed under adversity, wryly suggesting the vicissitudes of court politics. The Hàn historian Sžmǎ Chyēn, despairing of a larger rationale in history, ended with this passage (Durrant **Mirror** 23f). Later Confucians have left an eloquent record of *personal* integrity, but the problem of *social* integrity remains open.

∟ 9:29. The Master said, The wise have no doubts, the rýn have no anxieties, the brave have no fears. [9:28]

> It is left to the reader to supply the qualifications: the *truly* wise, rýn, and brave; this nuance links 9:29 with 9:28. Doubts, anxieties, and fears are vacillations that negate virtues. Note that beside the old virtues courage and rýn, we now have wisdom, which in earlier chapters was denigrated as mere "knowledge."

∟ 9:30a. The Master said, One who can be studied with cannot be journeyed with. One who can be journeyed with cannot be taken stand with. One who can be taken stand with cannot be conferred with. [9:29]

> Readers will supply "*necessarily*" after each "cannot." Not all talents operate at the next higher level; balancing 9:28, one may need to change associates at the chief career transitions: from qualification to employment to policy-making (chywǽn 權 "discretion," the exercise of judgement; the planning level).

Interpolations

For a complete finding list of interpolated passages, see page 329.

Reflections

Along with the interest in private life (9:16n), an interest in individual death emerges in LY 7–9. There is no dying testament of Confucius in LY 4. His comments from life are vividly expressed, but his death does not register. LY 5 apparently speaks only of the living. Two disciple deaths (probably recent, though reported as taking place earlier) are noted in LY 6. Confucius's death is imagined in LY 7; Dzv̄ngdž's is witnessed in LY 8. The importance of death in a culture may reflect the degree of individuality which that culture supports. This series suggests an increasing development in that direction.

A major political development in this period is the tripartition of Jìn 晉, the successor states Jàu 趙, Hán 韓, and Ngwèi 魏 being recognized as separate by the Jōu court in 0403. Some references to Wèi 衛 in the Analects may actually have in mind Ngwèi 魏, whose capital was a focus of Confucian influence by the late 04c (Dzv̄ng Ywæn's brother, Dzv̄ng Shv̄n, is reputed to have taken the Shī text to Ngwèi; 9:15 seems to echo that tradition). In the late 05c, however, the nearest of the three was Hán, which in 0408 attacked Chí's defensive western wall (for the BA record, representing a supposed chronicle of Ngwèi, see Legge **Shoo** Prolegomena 169; for the victory inscription of the Hán general, see Karlgren **Piao**). This sally might be a response to a military appeal from Lǔ, and part of the alliance process which is here conjectured for c0406.

LY 7 and 9 are easily compared, since they are on the same literary level (being cast as sayings by Confucius). One may start by eliminating points of obvious indebtedness (such as the Confucius death scenes, 9:12 < 7:35), and studying the rest as Dzv̄ng Ywæn's contribution. One trait of LY 9 is an interest in government, perhaps reflecting an upturn in the school's political fortunes.

Readers with access to a concordance (which can be used very easily by those knowing no Chinese but possessing the Legge or Lau bilingual texts) can do chapter comparisons in great detail, provided they beware of interpolations. One striking development that has been pointed out in the notes is the transition from a Confucius who is never seen at home in the earliest chapters LY 4–6, to references to a gate, and disciples (dìdž 弟子) at that gate, in the next phase of the text, LY 7–9. This almost certainly reflects the establishment of a residential school. It need not yet be the palatial mansion, adjoining the Prince's own palace, in the wall of which, when it was torn down in c0154, the manuscript of the Analects is said to have been discovered, but it is evidently a substantial affair (for architectural aggrandizement, see "Confucius's House" in Appendix 2). In this context we can best understand the pedagogical emphases of these three chapters. One point worthy of notice and reflection is the relation between grander premises and wider-spectrum recruitment.

The material growth indicated in the chapter implies a more organized government, and a new art of working in government. To appreciate the more developed theories of power which we shall meet in later chapters, the reader may pause to extract and ponder the implied political philosophy of LY 4–9. This exercise may usefully be repeated with each later chapter in turn.

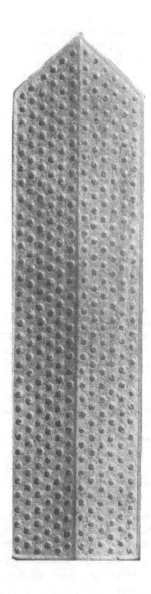

Jade Scepter (see LY 10:4)
Length 27·2 cm (10·7 in). 03c. Courtesy Freer Gallery of Art (14·496)

10

c0380

It may have been the Dzvngs (LY 7–9) who founded the Confucian mansion, but it was the Kǔngs (LY 10f) who dwelt in it. The SJ 47 list of Kǔng successors is too short (at 25 years per birth generation) to reach back to Confucius; it suggests that the first Kǔng head of the school, Dž-sž, began his term in c0400, just after the date we have assigned to LY 9. This would imply a transfer of power from the Dzvngs to the intrinsically more authoritative Kǔng lineage. The Kǔng phase of the text lasts to the end of Lǔ, and of the Analects, in 0249.

This first Kǔng chapter, LY 10, expanding on the social need already seen in 9:16, contains dress and behavior prescriptions for the gentleman courtier and householder (jywndž). At some later point, they were partly relabeled as descriptions of "Confucius" (Kǔngdž; see Waley **Analects** 146n1, 147n3), thus transforming the chapter into a biographical sketch, in the tradition of LY 7 and LY 9. As an arbitrary code of behavior, LY 10 is fascinating if not always intelligible to modern readers; it was presumably a useful guide for newcomers to official life. Once it came to be viewed as an intimate portrait of Confucius, it exerted a considerable influence on his perceived historical persona.

As to ethical teachings, there are none. LY 10 fits much more smoothly into the school's increasing preoccupation with ritual and propriety in general. Beginning with the LY 10 first precepts of behavior, a new ritualist agenda quickly unfolds in succeeding Analects chapters.

Reference numbers to Legge are given at the end of each saying.

[A. Public Occasions]

⌐ 10:1a. In the county association he is hesitant, as though unable to speak; in the ancestral temple or at the court, he is forthcoming, but circumspect. [10:1]

Kǔngdž 孔子 "Confucius" was later supplied as the subject of this sentence, one of the few instances where we must assume a change in the *old* text, as distinct from the interpolation of a *new* text. The stances and movements of the LY 10 persona, presumably the gentleman, are here, as often, described by reduplicative expressions whose meaning is sometimes unclear or contextually determined (see *7:4[10], below) ; interpretations thus vary widely. We gather that officers of this period regularly attended local occasions (see 10:7b; for "county association" see 6:5 and 9:2). The elite are now taking closer notice of local structures than in 6:5, and the novel practice requires a new rule.

One might have expected greater volubility in the *county* than at court. Perhaps the reservations of 6:13 about popular culture still obtain. Perhaps also it is the *unobviousness* of the rule that makes it necessary, here, to *state* the rule.

L 10:1b. When at court, speaking with the lesser dignitaries, he is unassuming; when speaking with the greater dignitaries, he is formal. When the ruler is present, he is deferential; he is open. [10:2]

It is officious to be stiff with lower-ranking colleagues, pushy to be casual with higher-ranking ones, and disrespectful to seem withdrawn before the Prince.

⌐ 10:2. When the ruler summons him to accompany a visitor, his demeanor is severe and his strides are low. In genuflecting to those with whom he is to take his stand, he extends his hands left and right, letting his garment touch the ground before and behind; he is imposing. When he hastens forward it is as though he were on wings. When the visitor has withdrawn, he must return his charge, saying, The visitor is no longer looking back. [10:3]

> Bwò 勃 [-rú] "severe" is followed in 10:4 and in MC 5B9 by predicates like "changed expression"; some commentators assign this meaning to bwò itself, which from context must here be a predicate meaning "alert and serious." Jywé 躩 [-rú] elsewhere implies, not small steps, as in some commentaries, but long striding ones. A modern English businessman approaching his sovereign to be knighted uses this same "glide" motion (Barrie **Twelve** 44–46).
>
> Lyóu Bǎu-nán (**Jvng-yì** 198) argues that the real diplomatic power in Confucius's day lay with the Jì, and that Confucius, as a loyalist, thus could not have had charge of palace diplomatic functions. Since the chapter originally *did not refer* to Confucius, this argument fails. We must suppose that by the time LY 10 was thought of as describing Confucius (which we put at c0370; see under Interpolations, below), the Jì threat was sufficiently far in the past that the Analects proprietors were not conscious of an anachronism.

∟ 10:3. When approaching the Prince's gate, he bends his body low, as though it will not admit him; he does not resume an upright posture within the gateway, nor step on the sill. When passing by the Place, his expression becomes severe and his strides become slow; his words seem insufficient. When gathering his skirt to ascend the hall, he bends his body low, and holds his breath as though he were not breathing at all. When he emerges, as soon as he has descended one step, he relaxes his expression and appears more at ease. When he reaches the bottom of the stairs, he hastens forward as though he were on wings. On returning to his place, he shuffles restlessly. [10:4]

> The incipient aspect of rù 入 "enter" (hence "*about* to enter; approach") is implied by later clauses. The capitalization of "Place" is meant to suggest the *ruler's* place (not his "throne," since chairs were unknown in this period). The final predicate tsù-jí 踧踖 "fidget, shuffle" seems inappropriate, hence Legge "respectful uneasiness," Lau, Dawson, and Huang "respectful." Waley has "*resumes* his attitude of wariness and hesitation," but 10:3 is a contrast of demeanor before and after an audience, hence "resumes" seems unjustified.

∟ 10:4. When he holds the scepter, he bends his body low, as though he cannot support its weight. He ascends as though genuflecting; descends as though presenting. He is severe, with an anxious look. His feet move shufflingly as though there were something he was following. At a presentation ceremony, he has an open expression. At a private viewing, he appears animated. [10:5]

> The gwèi 圭 is the minister's authority symbol. The verbs in the second sentence (shàng/syà 上 / 下) are usually interpreted "holds it no higher/lower than" (Legge, Waley) or "at the top/bottom end" (Lau). The reader can see from p58 that there is little latitude in grasping the gwèi; there was probably also a correct height (chest-high) at which to carry it. The style of walking described later, which prevents bobbing, may help to maintain this altitude.

This unpaired saying shows the courtier rising above his status to carry a symbol of the ruler's authority delegated to him. That authority does not affect his own bearing, which instead expresses anxious stewardship. The courtier does not acquire, with delegated authority, the bearing of its original possessor. This distinction between delegatable and intrinsic authority suggests a nascent "constitutional" concept of the ruler in the new state.

[B. Clothing and Food]

┌ 10:5a. The gentleman does not use violet or puce as accents, nor are red or purple worn as casual dress. During the hot season his unlined garment is of hemp or linen, but always as an outer layer. With a black garment he wears a fleece mantle, with a plain garment a fawn mantle, and with a yellow garment a fox mantle. [10:6a]

> Deep blue-violets need room, and do not work as touches on something else; reds and purples are too strong for casual statement. An open-weave robe needs an under-robe for modesty. The color combinations black/oyster, ivory/taupe, and beige/brown commend themselves without comment. Note the expressed subject "gentleman," originally if implicitly that of the whole chapter.

└ 10:5b. His casual robe is long, with a short right sleeve; he always has his sleeping garments longer by half than his body. The thicker furs of fox and badger he uses at home. When out of mourning, there is no sash ornament he may not wear. Except for ceremonial ones, his lower garments are always tailored. [10:6b]

> If Waley is right about the short right sleeve as facilitating swordsmanship, 10:5a is early evidence for the sword (not the bow) as the standard sidearm, a cultural change which required a new practice. Too short nightclothes ride up during sleep. This and the home use of heavy furs suggest unheated houses. Ritual conservatism seems to preclude newfangled tailoring (compare *5:22[11]).

┌ 10:5c. He does not visit the bereaved in fleece robe or dark cap. On auspicious days, he always attends court in his court dress. When fasting, he always has clean clothes, and of linen. [10:6c–7a]

> 10:5c on appropriate clothing pairs with 10:6a on appropriate food. Fasting for purification requires freshly laundered, light-colored clothing made of a traditional fiber (not newfangled silk; compare 9:3).
>
> "Auspicious" days were new-moon days, when court was held. Since the Spring and Autumn period, one function of the court had been to determine the beginning of the seasons, and to locate the extra or intercalary months which were needed to keep the lunar and solar calendars coordinated.

└ 10:6a. When fasting, he always uses different food, and when resting, he always moves his seat to a different place. His food he does not mind being of choice quality; his mincemeat he does not mind being cut fine. [10:7b–8a]

> The point of fasting (selective rather than total abstinence; see further 10:6b/c). is its abnormality, hence the use of nonroutine foods and seating locations. There is at this period apparently no requirement that such food as the observer may eat should be literally coarse or ill-prepared.

⌐ 10:6b. If food has gotten damp and is spoiled, if fish has softened and its flesh has gone bad, he does not eat it. If the color is bad, he does not eat it. If the smell is bad, he does not eat it. If it is incompletely cooked, he does not eat it. If it is out of season, he does not eat it. If it is not cut straight across, he does not eat it. If it does not have the appropriate condiment, he does not eat it. [10:8b]

> "Food" (sż 食, deverbal of shŕ "eat") means the basic grain food (Legge "rice," but the staple grain at this time was millet). Grain keeps only if stored dry. These rules, including seasonability, seem meant to avoid illness or discomfort from eating. Cutting across the grain reveals hidden defects, and condiments (jyàng 醬) help by making the safe but probably rather bland fare palatable.
>
> Plant foods attested in the CC include winter wheat, winter barley, plums, soybeans (following the 0663 conquest of the Mountain Rúng people, and the adoption of this important vegetable), and millet. Early LY mentions add vinegar (5:24, attesting the use of fermentation and pickling), dried meat (7:7), plus, in 9:3, hemp and the mulberry tree implied by the mention of silk cloth. So far the 05c. The LY 10 range (from the early 04c), as we see, is much wider.

∟ 10:6c Even if meat is plentiful, he does not let it overpower the food. It is only with wine that there is no set limit, but he does not drink to the point of confusion. Bought wine or market jerky he does not eat. He does not disdain food with ginger. He does not eat to excess. [10:8c]

> The economy provides larger supplies of meat, but the gentleman, respectful of tradition, still treats it as a garnish on the basic grain food. There are urban markets (their first mention in the text), but the gentleman supplies fermented wine and cured meat (compare 7:7, and note the low social status of dried meat) from his own farmstead in the hinterland. Ginger as a spice for meat (unmentioned in the contemporary but archaizing Shŕ) is a novelty which seems welcome even in this generally traditional household.
>
> Waley's reading of these rules as preparatory to sacrifice seems sometimes forced; some of them suggest mere dietary snobbery like the modern disdain, in country-club circles, for canned food (Cleary **Henshaw** 49, 67).

⌐ 10:6d. After sacrificing with the Prince, he does not keep the meat overnight. With other sacrificial meat, he does not go beyond three days. If it is more than three days old, he will no longer eat it. [10:8d]

> The flesh of ceremonially sacrificed animals was distributed to higher officials as a mark of favor. Being unpreserved, it could not be kept long. Meat from sacrifices was probably eaten the same day in order to avoid the implications of storing it (using it as mere food rather than as a mark of ceremonial honor). The safe keep limit on fresh meat was obviously the three days here insisted on.

∟ 10:6e–7a. He does not converse at meals. He does not talk in bed. Even with a meal of coarse food and vegetable broth or melons, in making an offering from it he is always solemn. If his mat is not straight, he will not sit on it. [10:8e–9a]

> This is not a regimen for handling sacrificial food (though Waley ingeniously so argues), but the influence of sacrificial decorum on nonsacrificial manners. An increasing richness of elite-level domestic life is implied, as is a solemn manner for the official personality even in his domestic aspect.

[C. Visits and Gifts]

⌐ 10:7b. When the country folk are drinking wine and the elders have left, he also takes his leave. [10:10a]

> Evidently a low-society festive and social occasion at which the gentleman is present ex officio (see again the note to 10:1a). He puts in his appearance, and withdraws before the proceedings degenerate to the level of mere merriment. For the limited interpenetration of the two social orders, compare next.

└ 10:8. When the country folk are performing an exorcism, he takes his stand in his court dress on the formal stairs. [10:10b]

> The exorcism was a driving away of evil spirits; a ceremonial and religious occasion which the gentleman (compare 10:7b) attends in an official capacity. The gentleman is not a priest, or technician of the unseen (for thaumaturges in early China, see Mair *M'ag), but knows how to behave *in the presence of the unseen.* It seems (pace Waley) that the people perform the ceremony, with the gentleman as an official onlooker. The ruler/ruled architectural axis is north and south, but there was also a reception-of-guest entrance and stairway on the east side of the larger buildings. The gentleman occupies this position, as a sort of envoy from the higher culture.

⌐ 10:12a. When the ruler makes a gift of food, he must sit straight on his mat and first taste it. If the ruler makes a gift of sacrificial flesh, he must heat it and make an offering from it. If the ruler makes a gift of a live animal, he must rear it. [10:13a]

> Later "tribute missions" concealed trade between peoples, and these supposed sacrificial sharings may amount functionally to salary, or a salary bonus. The respectful treatment accorded gifts from the palace avoids acknowledgement of this more crass meaning. Society appears to be outgrowing a sacrificial bond between ruler and henchmen, and replacing it with a secular ceremonial one.

└ 10:12b. When he is attending at a meal in the ruler's palace, what the ruler sacrifices he is the first to make a meal of. [10:13b]

> The seeming lowly attendant actually occupies a place of honor; he stands by the ruler when the ruler is discharging his formal or sacrificial functions. Hence his precedence at the meal (the verb is fǎn 飯 "make a meal of," not, as many commentators wish it were, cháng 嘗 "taste") following the sacrifice.

⌐ 10:13. When he is ill and the ruler comes to see him, he places his head to the east, covers himself with his court robe, and spreads out his sash. [10:13c]

> Even a sick man must receive his ruler in a prone equivalent of court dress. Note the alignment on the east/west "guest" axis, as in 10:8.

└ 10:14. When the ruler's command summons him, he does not wait for the horses to be yoked, but simply goes. [10:13d]

> In the old days, when the feudal warriors resided on their farmsteads, they responded to the ruler's summons by mustering with their chariots and arms. With the advent of urban residences for their more civilized descendants (see again the implication of a grand official residence in 8:3, and its departure from the implied domicile of Confucius in the earlier LY 5–7), it is faster and thus more respectful to simply walk across to the palace.

[D. Private Behavior]

⌐ 10:16a. When a friend dies, and there is nowhere else to turn, he says, Bury him at my expense. [10:15a]

> Perhaps a holdover from the obligations of feudal warriors to fallen comrades (yẃ 於 can here *almost* be construed as an archaic full verb "it lies with me"), and perhaps an indication of the rising complexity, and thus cost, of funerals.

∟ 10:16b. When a friend sends a gift, even a carriage and horses, unless it be sacrificial meat, he does not bow before it. [10:15b]

> Another cultural adjustment, probably designed to insulate the genuinely sacral occasions from the homogenization of manners. Even the most lavish gifts, if not from the court/sacrificial context, should not be accorded the respect which is properly reserved for that context. The money value of this gift between friends is staggering, and again implies a society of widespread wealth.
>
> The pairing (as in several previous sayings) is based on a giving/receiving (or going/staying) contrast. Note the new attention given to the protocol of lateral relations, as distinct from the older vertical or hierarchical ones.

⌐ 10:17. When asleep, he does not assume the posture of a corpse. When at ease, he does not adopt formal demeanor. [10:16a]

> The first clause seems merely superstitious, and may have been so in origin, but combined with the second it is a barrier to the spread of sacral paradigms into the whole of life. The more relaxed moments have their own propriety.

∟ 10:18. On seeing one fasting or in mourning, even if it is an intimate, he changes expression. On seeing an officiant or blind man, even if it is an acquaintance, he assumes the proper attitude. Those in ill-omened garb he bows to; he bows to one carrying planks. When there are piles of delicacies, he changes expression and rises. On hearing thunder, or if the wind gusts, he changes countenance. [10:16d]

> Another distinction between sacral and everyday realms, in which ceremonial roles ("blind men" are court musicians) supersede personal acquaintance in determining behavior. There is a constant respect for death (garb of "ill omen" is a circumlocution for funeral dress, and planks are used to make coffins), higher powers (in their weather aspect), and the unknown generally.
>
> The "piles of delicacies" have presumably been previously offered to the spirit of the departed, hence the gentleman rises (dzwò 作) in respect when they are served. Waley suggests an analogy with a modern banquet guest saluting the arrival of a new dish; the mourning context seems to forbid this.

∟ 10:19. When getting into his chariot, he must stand squarely, holding the guide rope. Once in his chariot, he does not look back. He does not speak hurriedly, and does not point at individuals. [10:17]

> The chariot is a power symbol, and must be approached with the straight, respectful stance with which power symbols (such as gifts of sacrificial food) are treated elsewhere in LY 10. Casualness and uncertainty are disrespectful, and they also undermine the social basis of the power (Orwell **Shooting** 158–159). Hurried speech and individual pointing can be threatening when combined, as they here seem to be, with a power position in the chariot.

Interpolations

As Waley notes, LY 10 was originally a description of the private and public conduct of the ideal gentleman, and was only at some later point partially relabeled as a description of the historical Confucius. The pattern of chapters and interpolations as a whole suggests that this point came after LY 10 itself (c0380) but before LY 11 (c0360), and thus, as a first approximation, in c0370. It was inevitable that, once appended to the previous series of Confucian teachings, this extended description of the protocol-perfect gentleman should have been assumed to have been true of Confucius as well, and that the literal Confucius profiles in LY 7 and LY 9 should thenceforth have been read from the viewpoint of, or so to speak through the filer of, the LY 10 prescriptions. The next step was to regard LY 10 itself not as a Confucian primer but as itself a third Confucius profile, and it is this change of view which the relabeling noted by Waley makes explicit. Having textually adjusted LY 10 to fit this new presumption, the next logical step was to touch up LY 7 and 9 also, to bring them closer to the kind of Confucius that was being perceived through LY 10. This was accomplished by adding some descriptive statements of the very distinctive LY 10 type to those chapters, thus providing similar information at those points, and homogenizing the three Confucius "portraits" stylistically. Apart from the retrospective adjustment to LY 10 itself, these homogenizing additions to LY 7 and 9 were the earliest use of the interpolation device as a way of maintaining consistency in a text which up until that point had simply accumulated, any internal conflicts being allowed to stand. A desire for internal consistency would seem to be intelligible as part of the ritual interest of the new Kǔng family heads, since ritual itself tends to emphasize both canonicity and repeatability, and since their interest as a new leadership group was to minimize any perceived differences between their own teachings and the accumulated doctrinal pronouncements of the 05c series of disciple heads. These older chapters seem to have constituted a heritage that both defined them as successors, and challenged them as interlopers.

Below we present the material which we identify as having been added to LY 7 and LY 9 at this slightly later date. It is modest, even innocuous, in both extent and character. It will however be followed, in LY 11 (c0360), by a much bolder attempt to revise and reshape, not merely to retouch, the entire previous tradition of the school.

For a complete finding list of interpolated passages, see page 329.

Added to LY 7

*7:4. When the Master was at leisure, he was easy; he was open. [7:4]

It would be hard to imagine a more modest example of so sinister a process as interpolation. It describes demeanor with the kind of reduplicative expressions (shvnshvn-rú 申申如 "easy," yāuyāu-rú 夭夭如 "open," both unique in the text) that are repeatedly used in LY 10 (see the note to 10:1a). The meaning of these expressions often has only a tenuous relation with the meaning of the single character (respectively, "stretch out" and "youthful"), and must be inferred situationally (for this principle, see Kennedy **Ode**). Such precise specification of casual behavior shows how serious were the early 04c cataloguers of ritual.

г *7:9. When the Master was eating beside someone who was observing mourning, he would never eat his fill. [7:9a]

He respects, by meeting it partway, the restraint that is obligatory on the mourner (*full* compliance would usurp the mourner's own position; compare Maugham **Cakes** 239). It was presumably at court banquets after a sacrifice that the courtier might find himself seated beside someone in mourning (the mourner would normally remain at home, but a palace summons had to be answered). Kennedy **Ode** explores the disorderly revelry that might eventuate on these occasions. Rowdy behavior in an ostensibly formal context is also encountered in Western postfeudal societies (Wodehouse **Option** 301–302).

This interpolation covers a situation not dealt with in 10:18. Why was it not simply added to LY 10 itself? Such questions are unanswerable, but perhaps, beside the above-mentioned desire for canonical homogeneity, LY 10 was too recently issued, or too fondly regarded by its author, to be thus disfigured.

L *7:10. If the Master had wailed on some day, then he would not sing. [7:9b]

Wailing (kū 哭) is a stylized lamenting conventional at funerals. The principle of ritual propinquity (see *7:9 above, with which *7:10 is in effect paired) applies to one visiting the bereaved on a given day, but not himself in mourning for the *remainder* of that day. Here, the grief is the gentleman's own. Weeping and singing flow from different feelings, and emotional sincerity is inconsistent with too rapid a change of feeling. The idea of a human-feeling basis for ritual will be much further elaborated in LY 3.

*7:27. The Master angled but did not net; shot, but not at perching birds. [7:26]

Hunting was increasingly obsolete in these days of intensive agriculture, but the small angling and birding of this passage is quite plausible for the 04c. Hunting with line or bow is unfair unless it gives the prey a chance; it is not victory, but rather skill and courage that count. On postfeudal sportsmanship see also 3:7 and 3:16, and compare Wodehouse **Bludleigh** 204–209.

*7:32. When the Master was singing with others and liked the song, he always let it come round again, and only then harmonized with it. [7:31]

As in *7:9, above, the point is to avoid intrusiveness while giving scope to pleasure. Hv̀ 和 "harmonize with" may imply adding a countermelody rather than simply joining in; if so, awaiting the next repetition of the song makes all the more sense. For further, albeit enigmatic, evidence on singing in the partly contemporary Shī, see Waley **Songs** #15–16, #210.

Added to LY 9

*9:10. When the Master saw one who was wearing mourning, one who was dressed in full court costume, or one who was blind, as soon as he caught sight of them, even though they were younger, he would always rise; on passing by them, he would always hurry. [9:9]

A similarity in the ritual treatment of the bereaved, the consecrated, and the disabled. Rising in another's presence symbolizes solicitous attention; hurrying when passing in front of someone symbolizes the minimizing of obstruction. For further details on the protocol of blindness, see the later 15:42.

Reflections

The bafflement of English-language Analects commentators at the ethical desert of LY 10 is echoed in that of English-language Bible explicators at having to deal with Leviticus (**Interpreter's** 2/4). With LY 10, a new ritual emphasis enters Confucianism. Ethics reappears in the Analects from LY 11 on, but the tone of Confucianism is permanently altered in a ritual direction. It is with LY 10 that the later emphasis on lǐ 禮 ("ritual, propriety, procedure") takes over from the earlier emphasis on rv́n 仁. Modern commentators differ in how they handle the result: Fingarette **Sacred** expounds the entire text from the lǐ viewpoint toward which its later layers indeed tend; Roetz **Axial** 119–148 detects the early rv́n beneath the later overlay of lǐ. Following LY 10, later lǐ chapters were not only added (LY 11), but preposed (LY 3), and individual lǐ sayings were interpolated within the older sequence of rv́n chapters, LY 4-9, thus giving lǐ a longer pedigree in the writings of the Confucian school.

To put the ritual interpretation in perspective, the reader may usefully contrast LY 10 and Leviticus in extenso, noting especially how different the respective background assumptions are. Waley's comparison (**Analects** 59) with the Indian householder text Āpastamba Dharma Sūtra seems to be more to the point: domestic conventions may well *take account* of the otherworldly, but they are not themselves seen as *grounded in* a view of the otherworld.

Many of the LY 10 prescriptions have more elaborate and systematic counterparts in the documents constituting the Lǐ Jì; this fact is one reason for believing the Lǐ Jì to be of late date. LY 10 itself does not so much codify elite behavior as constitute a primer of it for the non-elite novice. It has the socially homogenizing mission of the English "public" school (Orwell **England** 272; "an aristocracy constantly recruited from parvenus"). Nor is it anomalous that such outsiders should become arbiters of elite taste (Wodehouse **Bingo** 342). This social fluidity is a central, and apparently recent, fact of the 04c.

As a corrective to the sacrificial tone of LY 10, we note Waley's remark on the prestige value of clothing in the Shī: "a girl in a garrison town turning down one lover in preference for another who has more stripes on his sleeve" (**Songs** 16–17). Rank and status are certainly the point of many of these rules, as they are in the courtship songs of the Shī (some of which may have been composed at just this period). But there are other aspects too. On the value of "dress and address" to the gentleman, see Hazlitt **Life** 200; the aesthetic aspect denied by Waley also peeps through in such details as the color combinations of 10:5a. Agricultural production (see 9:3n) has long been above subsistence level, and there seems to have been a proportionately abundant *urban* surplus. The arts of the enjoyment of life thus begin to loom large in the text.

The "Reflections" on LY 7 (7r) compared that chapter and LY 9, and to a lesser extent LY 10–11, with the Christian Gospel portraits of that movement's founder. We now see that LY 10 began by describing an ideal gentleman, and only later acquired a "Confucius" biographical label. The original LY 10 had therefore *turned away* from the persona of the founder to the content of the ideology. Later chapters add other details to the Confucian persona, but there are no more full-length portraits. In LY 10, ideology first freed itself from the Confucius persona. In the later Analects elaboration of that persona, it seems to be evolving ideology, more than evolving myth *as such*, that drives the text.

Bronze Axle Cap and Linchpin (see LY 11:8)
Length 8·1 cm (3·2 in). 05c. Courtesy Freer Gallery of Art (79·13)

11
c0360

LY 10 only gradually became a portrait of Confucius, but LY 11 was from the first intended as a definitive, and balancing, repository of disciple lore; the key passage is 11:3. Some lore preserved in KZJY 38, including 11:3 itself, goes back to this period. Dzv̄ngdž, whose line the Kŭngs had replaced in c0400, fares badly, but many disciples criticized in LY 5–6 are rehabilitated. As noted in 11:7, the 05c danger of usurpation by the Jì clan must have receded; from here on, political philosophy develops not as a legitimacy question, but as a set of function and policy questions, and Lŭ state policy begins to come into focus.

LY 11 seems to have been written sometime in the headship of Dž-shàng, of whom we firmly know from SJ 47 only that he died at the age of 47.

Reference numbers to Legge are given at the end of each passage.

[A. The Disciple Pantheon]

┌ 11:1. The Master said, Those who first advanced were rustics in ritual and music; those who later advanced were gentlemen in ritual and music. If I were employing anyone, I would go with the "first advanced." [11:1]

> In terms of the later, ritualized Confucianism, this seeming preference for the yě-rv́n 野人 ("rustics") over ritual experts is astonishing; a nice conundrum for the commentators. Waley takes the first sentence as a quote, "Only common people wait till they are advanced in ritual and music [before taking office]," of which the last line disapproves, giving a consistently ritualistic Confucius. Legge takes the contrast as historical: the ancients knew less ritual than the moderns. This requires punctuating after jìn 進 "came forward" (which is awkward; the concordance punctuates after lǐ/ywè 禮 樂 "ritual and music"). Lau accepts the awkwardness, but takes 11:1 as about early and late disciples. What to do?

└ 11:2. The Master said, Of those who followed me in Chv́n and Tsàı, none now approach my gate. [11:2a]

> This too worries commentators: exactly what are these followers accused of? They are clearly being singled out from others, and a time lapse is involved. Thus there is a contrast of earlier and later disciples, supporting Lau in 11:1.
>
> 11:2 marks a further growth (see 9:15) of the myth of the international Confucius, who travels to foreign states. The Chv́n/Tsàı story is one of the central features of this myth. In 15:2 we find Dž-lù hard-pressed in Chv́n; other late traditions include Yén Hwéı as well. Why, in 11:2, do they not come to Confucius's gate? In 6:3 it is claimed that Yén Hwéı predeceased Confucius; this chapter (11:13b) for the first time says the same of Dž-lù. Perhaps, then, they do not come *because they are viewed by the narrator as having died?*
>
> These two sayings then tell us, of the early disciples, that though worthy of office they were not expert in ritual (11:1), that they shared hardships with Confucius in Chv́n, and died early (11:2). By implication, the later disciples were "gentlemen" skilled in ritual, who survived the Master and were thus the ones who founded the posthumous school. We are now ready for 11:3.

⌊ 11:3. Virtuous conduct: Yén Ywǣn, Mǐn Dž-chyēn, Rǎn Bwó-nyóu, Jùng-gūng. Language: Dzǎɪ Wǒ, Dž-gùng. Administration: Rǎn Yǒu, Jì-lù. Culture: Dž-yóu, Dž-syà. [11:2b]

> This important passage, not offered as a quotation from Confucius but asserted as a statement, lists disciples by area of distinction. It is often at variance with the opinion of earlier chapters; for example, it is odd not to find Dž-yóu, Steward of Wǔ-chv́ng, under Administration. Even where the *area* of expertise is familiar, its *value* may not be: the lowbrow Dž-syà of 6:13 (see further 3:8), appears under Culture; the punster Dzǎɪ Wǒ of 6:26 is in Language. These figures have been either mythologized or deeply reconsidered. The tendency is to accept disciples disapproved of in LY 5–6, while eliminating Dzv̄ngdž, whose territory is LY 7–8. The 11:1/2 praise of early rather than late disciples could in this light be interpreted as chiefly aimed at Dzv̄ngdž.

> 11:3 was authoritative for the later body of disciple lore; it formed the nucleus of the KZJY 38 disciple list. With the establishment of Confucianism by Hàn Wǔ-dì in 0136, every officeholder had to present himself as a votary of Confucius. In this context, the emblematic influence of LY 11:3 became enormous. Its rubrics were used as titles for the first four chapters of the SSSY collection (Mather **Yü** 3, 25, 81, 92), typifying Six Dynasties elite qualities. They also figured in the Táng official evaluation system (Bol **Culture** 15–16).

[B. Praise of Disciples: Yén Hwéɪ]

⌐ 11:4. The Master said, Hwéɪ: he was not one who helped me. In all that I said, there was nothing he did not take pleasure in. [11:3]

> The underlying idea here is that the teacher only learns from his mistakes, such as when a remark addressed to a protégé fails to produce the desired effect. Hwéɪ is so quick that he sees at once the point of even an imperfect maxim. This wry but extravagant praise is a development of 9:20; compare 9:11.

⌊ 11:5. The Master said, Filial indeed was Mǐn Dž-chyēn! Others did not disagree with the comments of his father and mother, his elder and younger brothers. [11:4]

> Their praise might be biased, but is confirmed by the judgements of others (note the subtle parallel 11:4/5 based on "disagreeing"). The public virtue of Dž-chyēn in 6:9 (retained in 11:14) is here domesticated, a trend we shall find several times exemplified in LY 11. 11:4/5 gloss the first two names in 11:3.

⌐ 11:6. Nán Rúng thrice repeated the White Scepter. Confucius gave him his elder brother's daughter to wife. [11:5]

> The White Scepter refers to Shī 256E. The image is polishing away a scratch on a piece of white jade, whereas an indiscreet word can never be retrieved. This elegant characterization upgrades the grudging view of Nán Rúng in 5:2. Later tradition seems to be sensitive to slurs on the Kǔng bloodline.

⌊ 11:7. Jì Kāngdž asked, Of the disciples, who loves learning? Confucius replied, There was Yén Hwéɪ who loved learning. Unfortunately, his allotted span was short, and he has died. Now there are none. [11:6]

> This cut-down version of 6:3 has Jì Kāngdž as questioner, perhaps reflecting a lessening of 05c political tensions with the Jì; see 10:2n and compare 11:23.

⌐ 11:8. When Yén Ywǽn died, Yén Lù asked for the Master's carriage in order to make him an enclosure. The Master said, Talented or not talented, let us each speak of his son. When Lǐ died, he had a coffin but no enclosure. I did not go on foot in order to make him an enclosure. Because I follow the Great Dignitaries, I cannot go on foot. [11:7]

> Hwéɪ's father Yén Lù figures on the KZJY 38 list as himself a disciple, a mythical extension. Chariots in Warring States graves are usually intact, with horses slaughtered between the shafts, and proclaim the power and wealth of the deceased; chariot axle caps (see page 68) also occur as a symbolic variant. The chariot here seems intended as an outer coffin. Confucius's ceremonial duties are part of the myth of his official importance. Waley suggests that he was shǐ-shī 士 師 "Leader of the Officers" (see *18:2[18] and 19:19). In CC times, the Prince of Lǔ or a relative had led the warriors himself; the delegation of military leadership is a sign of evolution from a feudal to a functional state.
>
> This is the first we hear of Confucius's son Lǐ "Carp" (or Bwó-yẃ "Elder Brother Fish"). According to KZJY 39, Lǐ was born in his father's 20th year, and died in his own 50th year, giving the span c0530–c0481/0480. Yén Hwéɪ's death *after* Bwó-yẃ would barely fit into Confucius's lifespan (0549–0479). The point of these traditions is their concern with the *succession* of Confucius; they are in a sense the authority myth of the Kǔng family school heads.

└ 11:9. When Yén Ywǽn died, the Master said, Ah! Heaven is destroying me! Heaven is destroying me! [11:8]

> The reiteration conveys intense sincerity; the use of yẃ 予 for "me" reflects the presence of death and the reference to Heaven (see 9:12n). The basis of the pairing with 11:8 is the loss of physical and intellectual heirs (compare 11:2).

⌐ 11:10. When Yén Ywǽn died, the Master wailed for him movedly. His followers said, The Master is moved. He said, Am I moved? If for such a man I am not moved, then for whom? [9:14]

> Ritual lamentation ("wailing," see 7:10[10]) was a duty, but heartfelt emotion (tùng 慟 "be moved," requiring a neologism in the translation for its adverb use) was apparently reserved for one's own kin. Yén Hwéɪ may have been a cousin; he is here almost a son, worthy of Confucius as his own son and other followers were not (compare the dismissive treatment of Dzv̄ngdž in 11:18a).
>
> Later tradition (SJ 47, 4/1946–1947) would deny that there had been any disciple heads at all, by representing the first Kǔng head, Dž-sz̄, as Lǐ's son. We have not yet reached that stage. The more modest aim of LY 11 is to discredit what was still acknowledged to have been the century of disciple headship.

└ 11:11. When Yén Ywǽn died, the school wanted to bury him lavishly. The Master said, It cannot be done. The school buried him lavishly. The Master said, Hwéɪ looked on me as a father, but I have not been able to look on him as a son. It is not me; it is you disciples. [11:10]

> For the son's burial, see 11:8; for the use of yẃ 予 "I" see 11:9. False splendor (as in 9:12) spoils the validity of a modest burial. The disciples ignoring Confucius's wishes, and the "sonship" of Yén Hwéɪ, may be a Kǔng family claim to have restored the true tradition after a century of disciple headship.
>
> Note the litany effect of the recurring initial phrase in sayings 11:8–11.

[C. Praise and Blame of Disciples: Dž-lù]

⌐ 11:13a. Mǐn Dž-chyēn, attending by his side, was formal; Dž-lù was energetic;
Rǎn Yǒu and Dž-gùng were unassuming. The Master was pleased. [11:12a]

> The first and third of these reduplicative predicates occur in 10:1b, where they
> characterize behavior toward upper and lower dignitaries, respectively. For the
> Mǐndž "Master Mǐn" of the present text, we adopt the variant given, as
> agreeing with the form of the other disciple names. We have here a formal,
> even courtly, situation (see 11:15), with Confucius portrayed almost as a ruler,
> and his disciples flanking him as virtual ministers. It seems (compare 10:1b)
> that Mǐn Dž-chyēn's stance to those approaching Confucius was less lofty
> than that of Rǎn Yǒu and calmer than that of Dž-lù. All are clearly acceptable.
> For Dž-lù's swashbuckling and early death, see next.

L 11:13b. As for Yóu, he will not reach his death. [11:12b]

> The informal name marks this passage off from the preceding (with which it
> is now combined: a "Master said" phrase presumably dropped out of the text
> at some point in its history), but where the narrator's "Dž-lù" is used instead.
> 11:13b also contrasts with 11:13a in being hostile to Dž-lù, who, because of his
> martial forwardness, will not die his fated, natural death (this common phrase
> occurs in the later DDJ 42), but end violently. This expands the subtle 11:13a
> characterization of Dž-lù, making it explicit that Confucius thinks him rash.
> DJ (sv Aī 15 = 0480; Legge Ch'un 843b) narrates the violent end of Dž-lù,
> where he dies sword in hand, defending the Wèi Prince, and Confucius on
> hearing of it makes a remark similar to 11:13b. That does not mean that the
> story existed at this time; 11:13b is a step leading to the story. The truth of the
> matter (implied by Dzv̄ngdž's apparently having known him) is that Dž-lù died
> after Confucius (SJ, amusingly, preserves both versions in different chapters).
> Such romanticizing of the past (as in the DJ) shows that a psychological
> watershed has been reached. As of LY 11, the feudal past is in fact the past.

⌐ 11:14. The men of Lǔ were going to undertake work on the Long Treasury. Mǐn
Dž-chyēn said, How would it be to keep to the old lines? What need is there to
build it anew? The Master said, That man does not talk, but when he does talk, he
is sure to hit the mark. [11:14]

> Note the contrastive "does" ("He does not talk much, but when exceptionally
> he talks . . . "), with its disapproval of glibness. The issue is whether to repair
> the building on its old foundation, retaining its feudal function, or enlarge it,
> recognizing the need of a salary-based bureaucracy for more grain storage.
> Confucius does not want the new social basis architecturally acknowledged.

L 11:15. The Master said, Yóu's cithern: what is it doing at Chyōu's gate? The
school then ceased to respect Dž-lù. The Master said, Yóu has ascended to the hall,
but not yet entered into the chamber. [11:14]

> A severe remark is mitigated by a milder one. The narrative transition "The
> school then . . . " links what would otherwise be two separate sayings. We may
> note the grand house of Confucius, with its public hall (táng 堂) and private
> chamber (shǐ 室). The seven-string cithern chín 琴, with its long horizontal
> sounding board, is held on the lap of the seated player. The musical prowess
> here attributed to the disciples implies greatly increased leisure in 04c culture.

⌐ 11:16. Dž-gùng asked, Of Shr̄ and Shāng, which is worthier? The Master said, Shr̄ goes too far, Shāng does not go far enough. He said, If so, then Shr̄ is better, is he not? The Master said, To go too far is as bad as not to go far enough. [11:15]

> We here take up Shr̄ (Dž-jāng) and Shāng (Dž-syà). The latter, praised in 11:3, is here censured (notice yóu 猶 "as bad as," versus rú 如 "as good as"). 11:16 rests on a new idea: deeds are mapped on a line between too much and too little, with *the right amount in the middle.* This is puzzling to those with the 6:12 idea of a line running from not enough to enough, where *more is better.* The contrast is between perfection in meeting an ideal, and an equilibrium between imperfect extremes. The former suits the feudal obligation culture (can one ever be brave or faithful enough?); the latter better fits the postfeudal compromise culture, with its more diverse society. The idea of an ethical mean was developed in the 03c text Jūng Yūng. This and 11:21 are the first Analects instances of rán dzv̌ 然則 "if so, then," signaling a stage in the development of propositional logic. The earliest Mician cases are in MZ 8 (Mei **Ethical** 30 "therefore," 31–32 "hence"), contemporary with LY 11. Near approaches to a *two-step* argument are 16:1 (c0285, "if all is thus") and 17:13 (c0270); for the Syẃndzian multi-step or chain argument, see the interpolated *13:3[19] (c0253).

└ 11:17. The Jì were wealthier than Jōu-gūng, but Chyóu collected and gathered for them, and still further enriched them. The Master said, He is not my follower. Little ones, you may sound the drum and denounce him. [11:16].

> The dislike of acquired wealth (compare the contempt of the British clergy for trade; Maugham **Cakes** 103) is a feudal survival; the act of public dissociation implies the existence *of a public,* and thus more directly attests the new society (for the tradition implied by the drum, see Arbuckle **Metaphor**); the almost contemporary MZ 18 (Mei **Ethical** 106) quotes proverbial sayings as ethical authorities. For Rǎn Chyóu's association with the Jì, see 6:8. 11:17, which Mencius would have known as a student in Lǔ, is expanded in MC 4A15.

⌐ 11:18a. Chái is stupid, Shv̄m is dull, Shr̄ is vulgar, Yóu is commonplace. [11:17]

> Those here disparaged are Gāu Chái, Dzv̄ngdž, Dž-jāng, and Dž-lù. Chái's only other Analects appearance is in 11:23; he is probably not invented (see page 294), but he is unreported in earlier chapters. Dzv̄ngdž is the great figure of 05c Confucianism; to ridicule him is to reject the whole drift of the 05c school. Dž-jāng is positively treated in the 05c but, like Dzv̄ngdž, is criticized here and excluded from 11:3. Dž-lù is currently undergoing image evolution.

└ 11:18b. The Master said, Hwéi is almost there, is he not? He is often empty. Sz̀ does not accept his fate, and has traded to advantage. If we reckon up his results, then he is often on the mark. [11:18]

> Hwéi"s "empty" (kūng 空) rhymes with Dž-gùng's "on the mark" (jūng 中 ; the verbal *"hit the mark"* is read jùng). For "empty" as a metaphor of meditation, see 8:5n. From about this date, a meditation group seems to have existed in Lǔ. The group's text was the Dàu/Dv́ Jīng (DDJ), whose oldest chapter, DDJ 14 (LaFargue **Tao** 422–423), expresses the mysteriousness of the meditative vision. Dž-gùng's wealth through trade is a sign of the newly commercial times.
>
> Hwéi accepts poverty, turning inward to emptiness; Dž-gùng rebels, turning outward to commerce. Hwéi meditates; Sz̀ calculates. Both succeed.

[D. Self-Cultivation]

⌐ 11:19a. Dž-jāng asked about the Way of the Good. The Master said, If you don't tread in the tracks, you cannot enter into the chamber. [11:19]

> The "Way of the Good" (shàn-rńn 善人; compare the harbinger 7:26b) is here almost certainly the Mician Way, which in the populist and meritocratic 04c was gaining ground as a public philosophy. Its rejection here (compare the tolerance of 9:24) implies that it was now successful enough to count as a rival.

∟ 11:19b. The Master said, If his talk is sound, he is all right, is he not? But is he a gentleman, or is he one of impressive appearance? [11:20]

> Just as there are two roads to virtue in 11:19a, one of them leading wrong, so there are two kinds of impressive talkers, one of them false. There may again be an allusion to the Micians, with their interest in rhetoric and argument.

⊾ 11:21. The Master was alarmed in Kwáng. Yén Ywēn fell behind. The Master said, I thought you were dead. He said, While the Master is alive, how dare Hwéi die? [11:22]

> Invented (after 9:5) or not, this is very sweet. It may be here to conclude the section with positive advice: the proper course is following Confucius all one's life, and thus having a duty to prolong one's life so as to continue learning. What this adds to the devotion of 9:11, keeping it vivid after 2,400 years, is the personal affection (typical of emerging 04c individualism) which it implies.

[E. Envoi: Final Denunciations]

⌐ 11:22. Jì Dž-rán asked, Can Jùng-yóu and Rǎn Chyóu be called great ministers? The Master said, I thought you were going to put some unusual question, but it is only a question about Yóu and Chyóu. Those whom one calls great ministers serve their ruler according to the Way, and when they can do so no longer, they stop. Now, as for Yóu and Chyóu, they are utility ministers. He said, If so, then they would just go along with him? The Master said, If it came to killing father or ruler, even they would not go along. [11:23]

> Greatness lies not in obedience, but in integrity, having things *you will not do*. Yóu and Chyóu have their limits, but limits located far north of where a principled minister would draw them. For the idiom "if so" see 11:16n.

∟ 11:23. Dž-lù got Dž-gāu employed as Steward of Bì. The Master said, You are making a thief out of another man's son. Dž-lù said, The people are involved, the altars of grain and the soil are involved; why must one qualify as learned only after reading books? The Master said, It is for just this reason that I hate glibness. [11:24]

> Bì was the stronghold of the Jì family, once the villains of Lǔ politics. Some of that emblematic value lingers here (and in 11:7, where Confucius does not recommend any *living* disciple to Jì Kāngdž). The other issue is the readiness of Dž-gāu (Gāu Chái) for office, without which he is a thief of office. Dž-lù relies on the principle of 6:8 and 6:22, that low-level ability is enough to hold office; Confucius, irked, reiterates his disapproval of glibness from 5:5 and 5:8. It is a sign of the times that the *higher* qualification for office, which in 6:22 was rńn (imitation leading to self-improvement), is now literal book learning.

Interpolations

The school's hostile attitude toward its 05c disciple century (see 11:8–11) is manifest in this chapter, and to its period we also date some doctrinal revisions interpolated in earlier chapters, notably the notorious crux *9:1. The LY 11 concentration on disciples makes it plausible that disciple-anecdote passages added to LY 10 (and possibly also the Confucius-anecdote ones in LY 10) are of about this date. All are appended below.

For a complete finding list of interpolated passages, see page 329.

Added to LY 5

*5:7. The Master said, The Way does not progress; I shall board a raft and drift out to sea. The one who would follow me would be Yóu, would it not? Dž-lù heard of this, and was delighted. The Master said, Yóu loves daring more than I do. I don't have any material that I can use. [5:6]

> This is on a par with the LY 11 use of narrative transition (11:15) and its image of rash Dž-lù (11:13a; compare *7:11[14], from c0310). Dž-lù's love of daring disqualifies him as "material" for what the Master is trying to build, namely his movement (Leys **Analects** 138f proposes, and Huang **Analects** 73 rejects, the idea that the "material" is for the raft; this literary non sequitur ignores the affinity of *5:7 with other Analects criticisms of Dž-lù, and its sarcastic tone).
>
> For intimations of wealth and trade, and foreign contacts, see 11:17–18b (Dž-gùng in 11:18b is traditionally associated with Chí). The wealth of Chí in this period rested in part on its seacoast salt monopoly. It seems that Lǔ, in CC times cut off from it by various warlike peoples, had now also reached the sea. Coastal sailing rafts would have allowed a heavier trade with the Yángdž delta than the old route by skiff, drifting down, and rowing back up, the Sž River.

*5:14. When Dž-lù heard something, and had not yet been able to put it into practice, his only fear was that he might hear something else. [5:13]

> This comically highlights Dž-lù's intense energy and narrowness of focus: the acceptance of one task shuts him off from awareness of any other. This explains the *5:7[11] criticism that he is "not the right material" for the 04c Confucius. His bravery is too risky, and his intellectual grasp is too linear, for the new age.

*5:22. The Master was in Chýn, and said, Should we go back? Should we go back? The little ones of our group are running wild; they are producing all that elegance, but don't know what to cut out of it. [5:21]

> The image is of fine figured silk being woven without knowledge of what clothes it is to be tailored into. It apparently refers to the ritual expertise of the younger disciples (11:1), which, with the Master himself away (compare 11:2), they are unable to apply to the proper purpose.
>
> Trade with the steppe was important at this time, such objects as bronzes in the hunting style being produced specifically for export (So **Traders** 58, 69; for the currency used in the Lǔ trading bloc, see Li **Eastern** 387–393). The steppe peoples hunted on horseback, and the astride position required tailored clothes, rather than Chinese-style robes. The implication of the metaphor is that Lǔ, like Chí and Yēn, was engaged in this export industry.

Added to LY 6

*6:15. The Master said, Mv̀ng Jī-fǎn did not brag. When they fled, he served as the rear guard. When they were about to enter the gate, he whipped up his horses, and said, It is not that I dared to remain behind; my horses would not go forward. [6:13]

> This battle was fought with an invading Chí force outside the Lǔ capital in 0484. According to the later and more consecutive narrative in the DJ (Aī 11, Legge **Ch'un** 824–825), another squad in the same retreating army lost their lives in this sort of rearguard duty. The immediate ethical point is the chivalric code of modesty, a somewhat romanticized view of Spring and Autumn times which is also developed in the DJ. The old code required selfless courage, which in a ritually modest form (approaching self-denial) is here approved of. Compare the disapproval of conspicuous courage in *5:7, above.

*6:17. The Master said, Who can go out but by the door? Why is it that no one follows this Way? [6:15]

> Analogous to *5:7, above, in despairing that none follow the Master's Way. In the original 6:12, Rǎn Chyóu (who also figures in the battle of 0484; see above) gives an excuse for not following the Master's Way, but this failure is wider. It may relate to an LY 11 claim that Confucius's Way was lost in his own time, and only revived in the Kǔng century.

Added to LY 9

*9:1. The Master seldom spoke of profit and fate and rv́n. [9:1]

> A large exegetic literature has grown up around this problematic saying (see Bodde **Perplexing**, Laufer **Lun Yü**, Chan **Jen** 296–297, Chan **Source** 34–35, Malmqvist **What**, Bodde **Introduction** 27–29, and Boltz **Word**) which seeks to neutralize its outrageous claim by giving the "and" (yw̌ 與) a meaning that will separate the often-mentioned virtue rv́n from one or both of the others. The accretional theory of the text obviates such ingenuity by noting that rv́n is common in the 05c layers but *vanishes from LY 10–11.* *9:1 thus says what it *seems* to say (as most translators have held from Legge 1892 through Soothill 1911, Wilhelm 1921, Waley 1938, Lau 1983, Dawson 1993, and Leys 1997, along with commentators from Lyóu 1866 to Nán 1990), and is an attempt by the LY 11 people (for whom rv́n was obsolete) to protect their lǐ-based theory of Confucianism by denying the rv́n basis of the original school.

Added to LY 10

*10:9. When he is sending someone to make inquiries in another country, he bows twice in sending them on their way. [10:11a]

> A bit of diplomatic courtesy is here appropriated to Confucius, implying private contacts between Confucians in, say, Lǔ and Chí (which did exist; see LY 12).

*10:10. When Kāngdž bestowed a gift of medicine, he bowed in receiving it. He said, Chyōu is not versed in these matters, and does not dare to take it. [10:11b]

> He does not decline the Jì-clan gift, which would be disrespectful, but he also does not take ("taste," cháng 嘗) the medicine, which might be imprudent.

*10:11. The stables burned down. When the Master returned from court, he said, Did it injure anyone? He did not ask about the horses. [10:12]

> The stables of Lǔ (see Shř 297; Waley **Songs** #252) bred horses for the state's military expansion program. The refusal to ask about the horses is always taken as showing Confucius's human focus; in SSSY 24:11 (Mather **Yü** 396), the phrase has simply entered the language, and is used to excuse the ignorance of a cavalry officer. *10:11 in its own time was probably antimilitary, typical of Kǔng Confucianism but at odds with the code of warrior comradeship (rvn). The negative image of Dž-lù is probably a Kǔng satire on the military virtues.

*10:20. At an expression, it rose up; it soared and then flocked. [10:18a]

> Apparently describing a bird, and probably associated with the next.

*10:21. He said, Pheasant on the mountain ridge / Timely indeed, timely indeed. Dž-lù clasped his hands to it. It sniffed thrice and arose. [10:18b]

> Bamboo slips at the ends of rolls are liable to breaking, and these two passages seem to be fragments of an anecdote about Dž-lù and a bird, perhaps, with Waley **Analects** 152n1, an allegory of the Jì clan's offer of reconciliation with Confucius (see *10:10 above). Clasping one's own hands and bowing is a gesture of respectful recognition, analogous to Western handshaking.

Reflections

LY 11 and its interpolations give us an idea of early Kǔng Confucianism. It continued to exaggerate Confucius's rank and influence in the state. Though concerned with ritual, it did not equate ritual propriety with political virtue; the relation between them is discussed in the chapter. It had distanced itself from the military tone of original Confucianism (Dž-lù is the chief symbol of the old values), including the obsolete rvn, which it sought, by inserting *9:1, to negate in the 05c part of the text. It was not concerned with Lǔ legitimacy, but had a theory of school legitimacy, in which the 05c disciple heads were an aberration within a clan succession. They were especially hostile to Dzvngdž, the most important disciple head. The revisionist 11:3–4 pantheon of disciples and their accomplishments deeply influenced all later Confucian tradition.

LY 11 deprecates economic progress (the 11:18b praise of Dž-gùng's enterprise is surely not the equal of its praise of Yén Hwéi's inner success), from the export silk trade to the leisure craft of medicine (*10:10). Markets, first mentioned in 10:6c, imply not merely urbanization but urban consumerism. Readers may list the items that LY 10–11 show were available in such markets, and ponder the degree of social specialization which they imply.

Even more than trade, LY 11 opposes the military revolution which had abandoned the limited warfare of the old elite chariot host for the inclusive war of mass armies. A parallel protest against the disruptions of the new warfare was made by the Micians, whose first preserved tract (MZ 17, probably by the movement founder Mwò Dí) is the first of three against war. It is thus quite on schedule that this new movement is reflected, and opposed as a rival, in 11:19a.

The observation in 11:13bn is more widely applicable: in mediaeval sacred paintings, the members of the Holy Family are depicted wearing contemporary (mediaeval) clothing; Renaissance treatments aim instead at historic authenticity. There comes a moment when the past is suddenly recognized *as being the past*.

Jade Figure of a Dancer (see LY 3:1)
Height 9·7 cm (3·82 in). 03c. Courtesy Freer Gallery of Art (30·43)

3

c0342

Ritual can give antique dignity to an innovating state, and psychological continuity to a changing society. LY 3, the most unified Analects chapter, is on this theme of ritual. It has the form of an intentionally consecutive treatise, except that the form is interrupted by some sayings (3:1–3, 6, 10, 22, 26) which express indignation at a usurpation of royal forms. Ostensibly criticisms of the Jì clan, these seem to refer to the Chí ruler's adopting the title "King" in 0342, the year after his defeat of Ngwèi in the battle of Mǎ-líng. These topical sayings complete, but also interrupt, the design of the original treatise (which had begun with 3:4). The present chapter thus has two not quite compatible layers.

LY 3 is the first chapter to have been *preposed:* placed in front of older chapters. Its front position tended to increase its visibility, highlighting the protest component, and to give the whole text the character of a ritual treatise. The LY 3 theory of ritual goes beyond the description of propriety in LY 10 to include state sacrifices. It was probably by Dž-jyā, who may have succeeded Dž-shàng in c0355. By Hàn times (in the early 02c), little was left of Lǔ Confucianism but this ritual focus (see the story of Shúsūn Tūng, SJ 99, and the SJ 121 remark on Lǔ and Chí; Watson **Records** 1/295, 2/397).

Pairing of sayings is shown by the usual ⌐ and └ brackets, at the left of the saying numbers, and section-final unpaired sayings by the usual ⊢ bracket. Pairing of sayings in the proto-chapter that was interrupted by the c0342 protest addenda is shown by ⌐ and ⌐ brackets at the ends of passages. The interruptive sayings themselves are marked by an arrow > with, or in place of, a bracket.

The numbering of passages is identical in the Legge text.

[Prologue: The Usurpation of Ritual]

>⌐ 3:1. The Master said of the head of the Jì, Eight rows of dancers performing in his courtyard: if this can be borne, what cannot be borne?

Later ritual texts specify a descending order of grandeur for ceremonies at different levels. One may wonder how far this reflects early practice rather than systematizing fantasy, but some usurpation *is* implied. For contemporary concern in other states about excessive expenditure as a burden on society, see MZ 21 (Mei **Ethical** 120) and GZ 3:6 (Rickett **Guanzi** 92).

>└ 3:2. The Three Families exited to the Yūng. The Master said,

> Assisting Princes standing by,
> And Heaven's Son in majesty –

where in the halls of the Three Families was *this* drawn from?

The Three Families (Jì, Mvng, Shú) were the rival Lǔ clans. Here and in 3:1, they symbolize the Chí ruler, who in 0342 proclaimed himself King, assuming in the east the position still held by the Jōu King in the west (compare 17:4). The Yūng is Shr̄ 282, from the Hymns of Jōu. The two preceding lines in the stanza are "Slow and solemn they draw nigh / til all are ranged in panoply." As a recessional hymn, it was most probably sung by a chorus, who narrated, as though it were happening, the sacrifice that had just been concluded.

> ⌐ 3:3. The Master said, A man, but not rv́n, what has he to do with ritual? A man, but not rv́n, what has he to do with music?

In 3:1/2 context, this pun (人 "man" and 仁 [the virtue], both pronounced rv́n) articulates the principle that music and ritual cannot validate an unworthy ruler. The old term rv́n, absent in LY 10–11, here recurs in a new sense, as a quality not of the officer but of the ruler. This amounts to including the ruler in an ethical context which had previously defined only the elite warrior. Rv́n here shifts its meaning from "manly" to "humane," anticipating by 25 years the later Mencian "rv́n [compassionate] government" 仁政 theory of MC 1A5.

[A. Basic Principles of Ritual]

⌐ 3:4. Lín Fàng asked about the basis of ritual. The Master said, Great indeed is this question! In ceremonies: than lavish, be rather sparing. In funerals: than detached, be rather moved.⌐

For the handling of the Chinese idiom "rather than," see 9:12. This passage seems to have been the intended beginning of the chapter (note the secondary pairings, which are assumed to be those of the original draft). It is the first appearance in the text of the analytical concept bvn 本 "basis, fundament," and itself states two principles for ritual practice. For a slightly later Mician protest against lavish funerals, see MZ 25 (Mei **Ethical** 123f; two earlier tracts on this theme are lost). 3:4 also recommends frugality and genuineness of feeling. Ceremonies are made valid by sincerity; they are not efficacious *in themselves*.

Lín Fàng was not a disciple (not even the SJ 67 list includes him); his question here may imply that Confucius was not seen in this period as a teacher of only his own disciples, but, consistent with the high rank which 3:1 pictures him as holding, as an advisor-at-large to Lǔ court and society.

> ⌐ 3:6. The Jì were going to sacrifice to Mount Tài. The Master said to Rǎn Yǒu, Can you not save the situation? He replied, I cannot. The Master said, Alas! Who will say that Mount Tài is not as good as Lín Fàng!

The object of "save" is an "it" which appears, preposed and contracted, in the compound negative fú, early pronunciation fút 弗 "not . . . it" (see 9:25n). The idiom "not as good as" (bù-rú 不如) is context-sensitive; here, it implies "not as perceptive [of ritual nuances] as." The mountain knows the ritual, and will reject a sacrifice offered by the wrong person (compare the mountain sacrifices of 6:6). The superficial pairing based on the name Lín Fàng may have been a device to justify the intrusion of 3:6; the original pairing was 3:4/7.

⌐ 3:7. The Master said, "Gentlemen never compete." Surely the exception will be in archery? But they bow and defer as they ascend, and drink a toast as they descend: in their competing, they show themselves gentlemen.⌐

The crossbow had been known in Chǔ since the 05c; in Chí and Lǔ the chariot warrior's longbow was still in use. The archery contest (Shŕ 11 and 25) was thus not a mere ceremony; it was probably still functional militarily.

In the original 3:4/7 pairing, this is a second, lateral principle to match the vertical or sacrificial one of 3:4. The 3:7/8 juxtaposition enforced by the later intrusion of 3:6 has no obvious link beyond the general chapter theme of ritual.

∟ 3:8. Dž-syà asked,

> The artful smile so charming, ah,
> The lovely eyes so sparkling, ah,
> *The plain on which to make the painting, ah –*

what does it mean? The Master said, The painting comes *after* the plain. He said, Does ritual then come afterward? The Master said, The one who takes my hint is Shāng; he begins to be talkable-to about the Poetry.⌉

The first two lines are from Shī 57; the third, a rhyming commentary, refers to the lady's decorated robe, and hints that true beauty lies beneath cosmetically enhanced lips and eyes. After a further hint ("corner," see 7:8), Dž-syà extracts from this analogy one about ritual; the point, as often in LY 3, is that emotion underlies ceremony. The use of the yẃ 予 "my" (compare 9:12, 11:9) suggests that Confucius's former political mission (4:8), later replaced by a Jōu cultural mission (9:5), is now a personal interpretative mission (compare *15:3[15a]).

For Dž-syà's role in the Shī, see 6:13n. Notice the link between his two names, Shāng and Syà, the dynasties that are supposed to have preceded Jōu. On the ritual traditions of those dynasties, see 3:9.

The first two Fēng sections, Jōu-nán and Shàu-nán, refer to Lǔ and Yēn as the domains (nán 南 "south," the direction in which the ruler faced) of their founders, Jōu-gūng and Shàu-gūng. The titles emphasize the ancient lineage of those states, perhaps to contrast them with Chí, ruled by Tyén clan usurpers since 0375. The implied friendly relations between Lǔ and Yēn, the border gateway state, tend to suggest Lǔ contact with the 04c northern border trade.

[B. Explanations of Ritual Traditions]

⌈ 3:9. The Master said, The ceremonies of Syà: I could discuss them, but Kǐ has not enough evidence. The ceremonies of Yīn: I could discuss them, but Sùng has not enough evidence. The reason is that the writings and worthies are not enough. If they *were* enough, I could then give evidence for them.⌐

This is the first mention of Syà and Yīn (Shāng) in the text. Experts may have been combing old lore to devise ceremonies for royal Chí; perhaps a like effort was made in Lǔ, for a cultural hegemony which the Chí usurpation forestalled.

Kǐ 杞 (modern pronunciation "Chǐ") had in earlier centuries occupied several sites northeast of Lǔ. It is said to have been originally in Chǐ District (34°33′ N, 114°45′ E) but later moved eastward (for the eastward move of Lǔ, see page 3 and 5:11n). Later texts put Syà near the Jōu homeland or its later capital on the Lwò River (Chang **Archaeology** 319). The location currently favored by archaeologists is Aṙlǐtóu (34°42′ N, 112°45′ E), to the west of Kǐ. The whole Syà question is complicated by cultural pride (Thorp **Xia** 36–38).

Jv̀ng Sywǽn, followed in the translation, takes syèn 獻 as syén 賢 "worthies" (oral versus written tradition). The syèn = syén equation occurs in several Shū, all first attested *later than* 3:9. In the Shī, syèn means "presented to the ruler," and wv́n-syèn 文獻 may thus in fact be simply "written records" of sacrifices.

This wish for ancient documents (compare 11:23 on contemporary ones) ends in a conscientious admission that none are available. The demand will shortly be met, with less scruple, by a whole series of *forged* ancient documents.

> 3:10. The Master said, The dì sacrifice from the libation onward – I simply do not wish to see it.

This angry passage (as the arrow > indicates) is from the final protest addenda. Its point of attachment was the dì 禘 sacrifice mentioned in the following 3:11, and its interpolation isolates 3:9 (which had been originally paired with 3:11). It contradicts the uncertainty of 3:9 and 3:11 by implying that "Confucius" knew that part of this rite was inauthentic, and thus knew the rite itself.

Chinese dislikes long object phrases, and often preposes them, as here, to topic position, resuming them by a pronoun ("it") in the sentence proper.

⌐ 3:11. Someone asked for an explanation of the dì sacrifice. The Master said, I do not know. The relation of one who *did* know to All Under Heaven would be like holding something here. And he pointed to his palm.⌐

One who understood, and could perform, the dì rite (etymologically related to the dì 帝 divinely sanctioned rulers of the Shāng dynasty) would be able to rule the world (tyēn-syà 天下, "[all] Under Heaven," in its cosmological sense; for the older, merely diplomatic sense of the term, see 4:10): to be a universal king. Note the rationalizing assumption that rites *have* explanations.

Before the insertion of the confident 3:10, 3:11 had paired with 3:9 as showing *ignorance* of ancient rites. With sufficient anger comes certitude.

∟ 3:12. "Sacrifice as though present: sacrifice to spirits as though the spirits were present." The Master said, If I do not take part in the sacrifice, it is as though I did not sacrifice.⌐

The quoted maxim (perhaps based on a rhyme between jì 祭 "offer libation" and dzài 在 "be present") required belief in the spirit that was sacrificed to. The Master replies with a seemingly compatible but different idea: one must be directly present at a sacrifice; it may not be delegated or performed in absentia. The shift of emphasis is from outward belief to inner sincerity (compare 7:35).

⌐ 3:13. Wángsūn Jyǎ asked, "Than beseech the alcove, rather beseech the stove," what does this mean? The Master said, It is not true. One who has incurred guilt with Heaven has no one to whom he can pray.⌐

The original pairing is with the other folk maxim in 3:12; the 3:13/14 pairing enforced by the insertion of 3:10 lacks substance. The saying here contrasts the efficacy of offerings to the spirits of departed family members, whose shrine was at a corner of the house, with offerings to the stove or kitchen god; it means that the living are more help to you than the dead. The Master rises to this "cynical piece of peasant-lore" (Waley) by rejecting it outright (compare 3:12). Though withholding *assent* toward the otherworld, he forbade *disrespect*.

∟ 3:14. The Master said, Jōu could look back upon the Two Dynasties. How splendid was its culture! And we follow Jōu.⌐

Here, echoing the section-initial 3:9, is the idea that rites accumulate, each age succeeding the last. The lost Syà and Yīn (Shāng) rites thus do not matter; they are subsumed in Jōu, *and Lǔ succeeds Jōu*. Chí, whose ruling lineage had been ended by the Tyén assassination, was not a successor to anything. Liturgically, Lǔ had the better credentials. The Chí usurpation of the Jōu title King in 0342 must thus have infuriated the Lǔ people beyond endurance.

[C. Adjustments to Ritual]

⌐ 3:15. The Master entered the Great Shrine, and at every stage asked questions. Someone said, Who says this son of a man of Dzōu knows ritual? At every stage he asks questions. The Master said, *That* is the ritual.

> The extreme meanings of lǐ 禮, "ritual" versus "courtesy," here alternate to make the pun on which the saying turns. The Master knows the ritual (for the assumption that rituals had meanings, see 3:11). But it would be discourteous for him, as a spectator, to display superior knowledge. You may, indeed must, admire your hosts's prize Monet, but you should refrain from launching into a discourse on Impressionism. Note the subtle acceptance of expertise in this passage, contrasting with its scornful rejection as recently as 9:2. We are here in the age of the thaumaturge, a technician of ritual or master of ceremonies.
>
> For the first time since 5:1–2, we get incidental biographical data about Confucius: his father was from Dzōu, 25 km south of the Lǔ capital. This seems intrinsically plausible, since it reverses the aggrandizement process (Dzōu is clearly a town of low prestige), and we are inclined to accept it as true.

└ 3:16. The Master said, In archery one does not emphasize the hide, because strengths may not be at the same level. This was the old way.

> The hide is the leather covering the archery target: piercing it was of military importance, since the enemy at this period would be wearing leather armor. Confucius here claims an "older" principle which emphasized aim, not force. We venture to doubt this, as simply another example of attributing virtue, even ritual virtue, to some distant past. Archery (see 3:7), despite the civilizing intent which is evident in LY 3, was still a weapon at this period.

⌐ 3:17. Dž-gùng wanted to do away with the sacrificial lamb at the Announcement of the New Moon. The Master said, Sż, you grudge the lamb; I grudge the ritual.

> Aì 愛 "love" is here "feel sorry for, be solicitous toward," thus "grudge." For "grudging" versus "feeling sorry for" a sacrificial ox, see the famous MC 1A7.
>
> We doubt the usual explanation of this ritual: that the announcement is to the *ancestors*. Announcements to ancestors (see the Sùng section of the Shī) were of the doings and needs of the descendants. Calendrological information (like the announcement of intercalary months; CC sv 0621; Legge **Ch'un** 243) was essential guidance for the rural population, and it seems likely that this, while perhaps *invoking* an ancestor, was a public ceremony (as in MC 1A7). The theoretical point of 3:17 is that some elements of ritual cannot be adapted or reinterpreted: a valid sacrifice requires the sacrifice *of* something.

└ 3:18. The Master said, If one served one's ruler by observing every last detail of propriety, people would regard it as obsequious.

> In contrast to the paired 3:17 (the pairing in this section is not dislocated by the addition of protest passages), there are some observances that can and should be mitigated. The implication is that the old court propriety involved greater elaborateness than the newer style. This can be disputed (the likely direction of ritual evolution would seem to be toward elaboration), but may be noted as the view of the period. In terms of that view, note that the sort of changes that were resisted in 9:3 as disrespectful are now, 60 years later, being accepted.

⌐ 3:19. Dìng-gūng asked, When a ruler employs a minister, when a minister serves a ruler – how should it be? Confucius answered, The ruler employs the minister with propriety; the minister serves the ruler with loyalty.

> This seems old-fashioned and even feudal, but it is instead progressive: it seeks to impose on the ruler's treatment of his ministers a restraint symmetrical to that which loyalty had always imposed on the minister's service to the ruler.

L 3:20. The Master said, The Gwān-jyw̄: happy but not licentious; sad but not wounded.

> This refers to Shī 1, the first of the Lǔ poems in that anthology, and describes its emotional message. It supposedly depicts the courtship of King Wv́n of Jōu, ending with his marriage. The question of personal feeling in the ruler, whose every act is of state consequence, was a delicate one. Here, the royal suitor feels passionate longing for a proper outcome, and experiences the loneliness of the quest without prejudice to the joys of its completion. See Waley **Songs** #87 (note that Waley rearranges the Shī topically) or Legge **She** 1.

[D. Praise and Blame of Ancient Rituals]

⌐ 3:21. Aī-gūng asked about the shv̀ from Dzǎi Wǒ. Dzǎi Wǒ replied, The Syàhòu lineage used a pine, the Yīn people used a cypress, the Jōu people used a chestnut, saying it would make the populace be in fear and trembling. The Master heard of it and said, What is over one does not analyze, what is done with one does not reprove, what has passed away one does not blame.

> The question is what sort of tree is planted to mark the shv̀ 社 or altar of the soil (for the associated phallic fertility cult, see Karlgren **Fecundity** 10–21). The first two involve puns (the gūng 公 phonetic of sūng 松 "pine" means "father" in archaic usage; the phonetic of bwó 柏 "cypress" occurs in pwò 魄 "soul"), and Dzǎi Wǒ suggests a pun on lì 栗 "chestnut" and lì 慄 "fear" for the third. He goes wrong not with his punning exegesis (these were standard practice), but with its critical character. Jōu is no longer in the grammatical present tense (see 3:14 for the politically important statement "We follow [*after*] Jōu"), and our criticism, unlike a remonstrance against current practice, cannot reach it.
>
> Dzǎi Wǒ is rebuked, but at a high level, as ritual expert to the Prince of Lǔ. His rehabilitation from the unpromising beginning of 5:10a/b (compare his insolent pun in 6:26), which was complete in 11:3, is here carried even further.

> L 3:22. The Master said, Gwǎn Jùng's capacity was small indeed! Someone said, Was Gwǎn Jùng frugal? He said, Gwǎn had three wives; among his officers there were no concurrent duties; how could *he* be frugal? If so, then did Gwǎn Jùng understand ritual? He said, Rulers of states have a gate screen; Gwǎn also had a gate screen. When rulers of states celebrate the amity between two rulers, they have a cup stand; Gwǎn also had a cup stand. If Gwǎn understood ritual, who does *not* understand ritual?

> This is the last use of chì 器 "vessel" to mean "capacity for office" (see 13:25). Technical knowledge (as in 5:18) does not excuse arrogation; *it makes it worse.* Gwǎn Jùng, minister to Hwán-gūng of Chí (reigned 0685–0643), here stands for the expert but misguided ritual advisors of the usurping Chí "King."

⌐ 3:23. The Master, in discussing music with the Lǔ Grand Preceptor, said, The art of music, or the part of it that may be understood, is that when it first begins, it is tentative, but as it continues along, it settles down, it brightens up, it opens out; and so it comes to an end.⌐

This is music minus the part that only musicians know (interval theory and instrumental technique, which by the rule of 3:15 would infringe the province of the expert), namely, a listener's-ear impression of the progress of a piece of court-orchestra music. The passage can be better understood after a year of playing lead drum in a Japanese gagaku ensemble, gagaku being the nearest extant analogue of classic Chinese music; next best is exposure to recordings. These pieces are at first unfocused rhythmically and melodically, but as they procede, they gradually become more metrically defined, coloristically rich, and thematically intense. There is also a brief ending phase, called lwàn 亂, when, after the culmination of the gradual climax (typically at 5 to 7 minutes), the elements again dissolve. Ravel's tour-de-force coloristic crescendo Bolero, though longer (14 minutes), has similar constructional features: repetition of a strophic melody, increasing tension as the basic principle of form, and an ending in disarray. For an appreciation of the Lǔ court orchestra's performance of Shr̄ 1 (the Gwān-jyw̄ piece mentioned in 3:20), see *8:15[14].

Lǔ here claims for itself the court and public splendors that in the 05c had been available only in Chí (see 7:14). The later custodians of the Analects did not fail to notice this modest implication, and the head of the school, Dž-shv̀n, interpolated a passage (*18:9[18]) which offers an aggrandizing rationalization: Chí court music had actually been previously established by refugees from Lǔ.

∟ 3:25. The Master said of the Sháu that it was wholly beautiful and wholly good. He said of the Wǔ that it was wholly beautiful, but not wholly good.⌐

See again 7:14, where the Sháu 韶 or "Summons" was first mentioned; it is supposed to have accompanied a mime of King Wv́n. The Wǔ 武 "Martial" was a mime of the exploits of King Wǔ, necessarily symbolizing his forcible conquest. It is this that the Master finds less estimable. The Confucians at this juncture were, and to the end of their court prominence (LY 15) with various qualifications remained, the antimilitary party at the Lǔ court. This involved a considerable shift of position for a group with an ultimately military origin. The theoretical issue is between cultural hegemony leading imperceptibly to political dominion (symbolized by King Wv́n) and straight military conquest (King Wǔ). Mencius, who was a student in the school at this time, would further develop the contrast in his own political theory (see MC 1A6).

In the original (if incomplete) version of LY 3, this piece served as the envoi. With the intrusion of the anti-Chí 3:22, enforcing the pairing 3:21/22 and 3:23/25, a new envoi was added to round the chapter out at 24 sayings:

> ∟ 3:26. The Master said, Occupying high position without magnanimity, performing rituals without assiduousness, attending funerals without grief – how can I look on at such things?

This is the last of the intruded protest passages. It returns to several earlier themes, and at bottom concerns governmental inappropriateness and ritual insincerity. The added third point, *emotional* insincerity, is no doubt strained, but it is consistent in the only way that propaganda needs to be consistent.

Interpolations

LY 3 resumes the LY 7 interest in music, as well as developing the LY 10 interest in all aspects of ritual. We thus place here certain interpolations in those chapters which seem to reflect those emphases, but which seem to be later in date than those we conclude were added following LY 10.

For a complete finding list of interpolated passages, see page 329.

Added to LY 7

*7:31. The Sheriff of Chv́n asked, Did Jāu-gūng know ritual? Confucius said, He knew ritual. Confucius withdrew, and he beckoned Wūmǎ Chí to come forward, and said, I have heard that the gentleman is not partisan. Is the gentleman after all partisan? Your ruler took a wife in Wú who was of the same surname, and called her the Eldest Daughter from Wú. If your ruler knew ritual, who does not know ritual? Wūmǎ Chí reported this. The Master said, Chyōu is fortunate: if by chance he makes a mistake, others are sure to find out about it. [7:30]

> This wonderful bit of sarcasm shares a phrase with 3:15 (see also 3:22), and the basic idea that the display of ritual knowledge may not be ritually correct (Confucius could not have criticized his own ruler while in another state). It also changes the politics of Confucius: if we are right, the actual Confucius was loyal to Jāu-gūng as the legitimate Prince, whereas now that the legitimacy issue has faded, Jāu-gūng is criticizable. And it gives Confucius a grander life, replacing the vague wanderings of 7:23 and 9:5 with a diplomatic visit.

*7:36. The Master said, If he is lavish, he will grow improvident; if he is frugal, he will grow rigid. Than improvident, be rather rigid. [7:35]

> This is the point of 3:4 (with which Waley **Analects** 131n4 also compares it). It recognizes that qualities have their characteristic mode of excess, and that excess is bad, but also insists that there is a preferable, *least worst* excess. These sayings, and several in LY 3, show a Confucian discomfort with ministerial wealth in the new state, and a nostalgia for sterner, more frugal times of old.

*7:37. The Master said, The gentleman is poised and unruffled; the little man is always in a dither. [7:36]

> Again we have the gentleman / little man contrast. The Lǔ Confucians were beginning to compete with such humble-origin groups as the Micians at court; the same was occurring in Chí, as a Mician strain in some early GZ passages shows (see GZ 3:6–9; Rickett **Guanzi** 92–93). This passage contrasts old status, which is accustomed to the court ethos and its conventions, and new status, which displays the anxious striving of the noninitiate. The implication is that those with a courtly background (or an intensive course in LY 10?) will always be better prepared to function in a court role than those without.

*7:38. The Master was warm but strict, imposing but not aggressive, respectful but calm. [7:37]

> Whereas, by implication, the "little people" violate the guidelines of propriety in seeking expedient friendships, intimidate others when they are in authority, and grovel obsequiously before superiors when they are *not* in authority.

Added to LY 10

*10:15. When he enters the Great Shrine, at every stage he asks questions. [10:14]

Perhaps the students had been taking too literally the misguided criticism of Confucius in 3:15. Adding just *this line* of 3:15 to the reference manual LY 10 sets up a context which assures that 3:15 will have its intended, sarcastic effect.

Note the implication, here and in 3:15, explicit in 3:9 and 3:21, that rituals, and indeed their separate performance stages, had historical or sacrificial "explanations." LY 3 is above all a *rationalizing* chapter.

Reflections

The skewed parallelism of LY 3 suggests a research project: did a similar afterthought give rise to the double parallelism of LY 5?

Note the creation of the historical anecdote in *7:31. A key technical advance is the narrative change of scene implied in 3:15 and 3:21, and overt in *7:31. The anecdote was perfected in the later DJ (Watson Tso passim).

LY 3 raises a recurring question: is Confucianism a religion? This arises from the modern definition, that religion is anything held in common by a community. The old view, that religion requires a supernatural belief, seems to be the line that is drawn in the Analects itself. On that basis, earlier readers (Creel **Confucius** 113–122, Mote **Foundations** 18–19) have concluded that Confucianism operates on the secular side of that line, acknowledging spiritual entities and sacrificing to ancestral spirits, but remaining philosophically aloof from the spirit realm. Future term papers on this theme should distinguish acknowledgement and belief. To respect prayer is not the same as to pray.

Another LY 3 question is the Confucian view of the individual. The old one-directional feudal ethic of LY 4 has greatly evolved by LY 3: the ruler is in principle liable to the same standards, and criticisms, as the officer. Aesthetic sensibility adds an interior note; so does the insistence on inner feeling as the basis of ritual. The value of ritual as incipiently constitutional for society has been noticed by de Bary **Rights** 196 and Ames **Rites** 201, 209. A careful reader may be able to find more of this in LY 3.

Aī-gūng's direct tax of 0490 marked the end of indirect sovereignty and thus of feudalism. So did William the Conqueror's compiling the Domesday Book, in 1085 (Cross **England** 81f). Henry I's establishment of the "curia regis" (King's Council), a working bureaucracy rather than a personal retinue, comes 45 years after Domesday (**England** 97f); 45 years after 0490 brings us to LY 7, where Confucius is seen *as someone with a policy* (a Jōu-derived Lǔ cultural hegemony), an initiative unlikely from the passive, dutiful Confucius of LY 4. Under John, the English barons gained legal rights (Magna Carta, 1214; **England** 141f). There is no precisely parallel Chinese event in the analogous year 0361, but the hint of bilaterality in 3:19 (c0342), noted above, is only off by some 19 years, perhaps close enough for a cross-cultural parallel.

Myths tend to accumulate around major figures, but we may distinguish between spontaneous (Lincoln; Lewis **Myths**) and managed mythification (Lee; Connelly **Marble**). The Confucius of LY 3 seems to be of the latter type, less biographically developed than emblematically emphasized. What we have here is perhaps a myth of Confucianism rather than of Confucius himself.

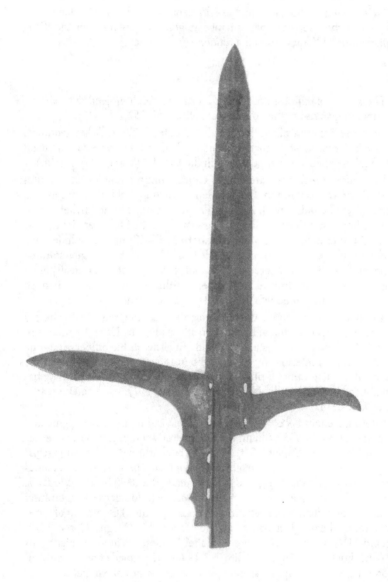

Bronze Halberd (see LY 12:7)

Height 44 cm (17·3 in). 05c/04c. Courtesy Freer Gallery of Art (80·208)
Gift of General and Mrs. Albert Wedemeyer

12

c0326

This is the age of the Hundred Schools, when rival theorists argue their views not only before rulers, but against each other. New topics of interest to the Confucians and other schools include the inner life of the individual, the role of the common people in the state, and the logic of definition. Older interests such as ritualism are also developed. This gives LY 12 a quality of turbulent excitement, quite different from the impassioned consistency of LY 3.

Mencius was probably with the Lǔ Confucian school at this time; he would begin his public career in 0320. His ideas as preserved in MC 1 are close to some found in LY 12, and suggest that he may have had a role in the chapter. Other parts of LY 12 seem anti-Mencian, and are probably attributable to the school head, Dž-jīng. This mixture might imply that Dž-jīng had come to the headship as a minor, creating an interim and giving Mencius limited scope. We may thus have here not only a jumble of ideas, but a tussle of personalities.

The numbering of passages is identical in the Legge text.

[A. Cryptic Answers]

12:1. Yén Ywæn asked about rʻn. The Master said, To overcome the self and turn to propriety is rʻn. If one day he can overcome himself and turn to rʻn, the world will turn to rʻn along with him. To be rʻn comes from the self; does it then come from others? Yén Ywæn said, I beg to ask for the details. The Master said, If it is improper, do not look at it. If it is improper, do not listen to it. If it is improper, do not speak of it. If it is improper, do not do it. Yén Ywæn said, Though Hwéɪ is not quick, he begs to devote himself to this saying.

Yén Hwéɪ is linked with rʻn from LY 6:7, but whereas from 5:9 through 11:4 Hwéɪ is the great inferrer, in 12:1 he abjectly begs for details (mù 目). This rebukes "Hwéɪ" (though the advice – to overcome the self – evokes meditation technique; Mencius, as seen in MC 2A2, was also an adept), and reflects a more formal style between teacher and pupil. The four "details" (trivialized in the Three Monkeys of later art) make two pairs: do not promote impropriety either passively (by seeing or hearing it) or actively (by saying or doing it).

The passage turns on the relation between rʻn and lǐ, and the sense of the verb gwēɪ 歸 "[re]turn" (compare Kieschnick **Analects**). It says that: (1) rʻn is something to which one "goes" (it is voluntary) after overcoming the self (it is not innate); (2) it is conformity to lǐ "propriety" and has no content apart from lǐ; and (3) as in 3:9, it is a virtue not of the minister but of the ruler, and through him affects the whole populace. Gwēɪ "go to, give assent to" (the putative "ascribe [it] to him," as in Lau and Dawson, is here inappropriate), is used in DDJ 14, 16, and 22 of a "return" to a primal inner state of stillness; DDJ 22 adds that such a person influences the world. This mystical idea is thus here assimilated to a lǐ framework. The dàu of LY 4 was the way politics *ought* to be, but lǐ in the middle Analects is the ideal human and social condition. Such translations of rʻn as "manhood" (Pound **Analects** 23) or "manhood at its best" (Ware **Sayings** 18) owe much to this and the following passages.

∟ 12:2. Jùng-gūng asked about rʹn. The Master said, He leaves the gate as though he were meeting an important visitor, he uses the people as though he were assisting at a great sacrifice. What he himself does not want, let him not do it to others. In the state he will have no resentment, in the family he will have no resentment. Jùng-gūng said, Though Yūng is not quick, he begs to devote himself to this saying.

> This ends with the same obsequious formula as 12:1. The denial of one's "quickness" seems to be a gesture of respect to the teacher, who controls every stage of the learning process; Confucius used to ask more. This passage tells us that Jùng-gūng is actually [Rǎn] Yūng; on whom see 5:5, 6:1, and 11:3. 12:2 emphasizes respect for the gravity of one's task: the attitudes proper to court ceremony are the model for the secular bureaucratic and personnel functions. As in 12:1, rʹn dissolves into lǐ, but here still retaining the "otherness" of rʹn.
>
> This Golden Rule (compare 5:12) is identical with Tobit 4:15 (c0175, the era of the Hàn silk route; Pfeiffer **Times** 274). As ascribed to Hillel (c040; Johnson **Jews** 127), it stands for the intuitive in religion, against the ritualism of Hillel's rival Shammai. 12:2 too, despite the sacrificial images, is at bottom a prescription for every aspect of life and work: a lateral maxim and not a hierarchical injunction; an "otherness" self-corrective for society.

⌐ 12:3. Szmǎ Nyóu asked about rʹn. The Master said, As to rʹn, one should speak hesitantly. He said, If one speaks hesitantly, is he rʹn? The Master said, Doing it is difficult; in speaking of it, how can one but hesitate?

> Nyóu (for attempts to identify him, see Leslie **Notes** 2–26), unlike the polite 11:3 figures revisited in 12:1/2, is *really* dumb. He confuses modal chí 其 "should [speak]," which was intended, with pronoun chí "his [speaking]," thus coming out with the notion that a rʹn man is one who speaks circumspectly. The reply, in contrast to 12:2, is in the older tradition of "rʹn." See also 12:4.

∟ 12:4. Szmǎ Nyóu asked about the gentleman. The Master said, The gentleman does not grieve and does not fear. He said, If one does not grieve and does not fear, does that mean he is a gentleman? The Master said, On examining within he finds no flaw; why then should he grieve or fear?

> As in 12:3, Nyóu takes the Master's *description* of a term as a *definition*; the Master then supplies an explanation of the description. As in 12:1, the idea of the gentleman as one possessing inner perfection suggests the meditation view. This passage is thus "progressive," whereas the paired 12:3 is "traditional."

Ŀ 12:5. Szmǎ Nyóu, grieving, said, Other men all have brothers, I alone have none. Dž-syà said, Shāng has heard that death and life have their appointed limits, wealth and honor rest with heaven. If a gentleman is assiduous and omits nothing, is respectful to others and displays decorum, then within the Four Seas, all are his brothers. Why should a gentleman worry that he has no brothers?

> Dž-syà's comments on fate and universal brotherhood sound like proverbs, and both are still proverbial in Chinese (Smith **Proverbs** 41). Leslie **Notes** 5–6 doubts the authenticity of 12:5, partly because Dž-syà appears in it, but Dž-syà in 3:8 was already a hero of the ritualist tradition. His appearance here seems consistent with that LY 3 trend, which here merges with the new populism.

[B. Open Answers]

⌐ 12:6. Dž-jāng asked about "perceptive." The Master said, Insidious slanders and wounding accusations: if he does not act because of them, he can be called perceptive. Insidious slanders and wounding accusations: if he does not act because of them, he can be called detached.

> These queries are handled more straightforwardly than those preceding: no humbling of the questioner, and no puns in the answer. But the sequence is the same, starting with description but leading to something like a definition. The essence of *this* definition is the parallel between míng 明 "clarity, insight" (for a link with the rise of written culture see Turner **Progress**) and ywěn 遠 "distant, remote." The perceptive person is detached: perceiving the irritations, but not distracted by them. True perception is keeping the mind on the main point. Compare DDJ 16 (c0340): "To know the constant is called perceptive."

∟ 12:7. Dž-gùng asked about government. The Master said, Enough food; enough weapons; the people having confidence in him. Dž-gùng said, If he could not help but let something go, of these three, which would be first? He said, Let the weapons go. Dž-gùng said, If he could not help but let something go, of these two, which would be first? He said, Let the food go. Since antiquity there has always been death, but if the people lack confidence, he cannot stand.

> This, the first Analects definition of government, locates it in the confidence (syìn 信) of the people, not (GZ 3:18; Rickett **Guanzi** 95; Brooks **Gwǎndž** 3), in the government's ability to feed or protect them or the credibility (syìn 信) of its threat of punishment. This is the core of what we may call Confucian populism. Later passages will argue that the social requisites of food and defense follow from this basis. All rests on the need to gain the allegiance, and military service, of the newly important lower orders. A problem much argued at this time is how to get the conscript soldier to die for the state (GZ 1:3, Rickett **Guanzi** 54). The elite warrior had been trained from birth in an ethic of self-sacrifice; not so the jade carver, who tended to take a "little man" view of the value of his own life (Orwell **McGill** 120). The answer here proposed is a sense of identification with the state (Orwell **England** 266f).
>
> The line about death is proverbial (Smith **Proverbs** 41), the third such passage in this chapter, and a suggestive index of its overall populist leaning. Whether such lines are *folk* proverbs (see Leslie **Notes** 6) is another matter.

⌐ 12:8. Jí Dž-chvíng said, The gentleman is simply substance; what is the point of style? Dž-gùng said, Regrettable is His Excellency's definition of the gentleman; a team of horses cannot overtake the tongue. Style is as important as substance, substance is as important as style. The hide of a tiger or leopard is indistinguishable from the hide of a dog or sheep.

> "Team of horses" is yet another proverb, though not noted as such by Smith. Dž-gùng worries about the eminence of the questioner, a Wèi statesman, whose remark will get attention that no later refutation can counter. His own refutation affirms the style/substance dictum in 6:18, and insists that culture (the figured pelt of a game animal) is better than vulgarity (the utility hair of a domestic animal), even though they can be reduced to the same terms.

⌐ 12:9. Aī-gūng asked of Yŏu Rwò, It is a year of scarcity, and there is not enough for my needs; what is to be done? Yŏu Rwò replied, Why not tithe? He said, With *two* tithes, I still have not enough: how should I tithe? He replied, If the Hundred Families have enough, what ruler will not also have enough? But if the Hundred Families do *not* have enough, what ruler can expect to have enough?

> The current tax rate was obviously two tithes (20%) of the harvest; Aī-gūng is disposed to increase this to cover needs (as later dynasties also discovered, it is in hard times that claims on the government granary, to relieve hardship, are greater). Yŏu Rwò (not, we may note, called "Yŏudž") suggests not merely contentment with the 20% (yielding a smaller amount since the total harvest is smaller), but a reduction to 10%, halving an already too-small revenue. This can only be a part of a current dialogue with the Chí theorists (GZ 3:11, 7:10; Rickett **Guanzi** 93f, 142), who felt that government apparatus was primary. Here, as in 12:7, the Analects holds that the *people* are primary: government wealth is a luxury that hard times may not permit. The ideal governmental food distribution system is to leave the food with the people in the first place.
>
> Superimposed on the basic pairing, in this section, is an ABAB secondary pairing: 12:7 and 12:9 are parallel statements about statecraft.

[C. The State and the People]

⌐ 12:10. Dž-jāng asked about exalting virtue and deciding contradictions. The Master said, To put first loyalty and fidelity, and to follow what is right, is to exalt virtue. When you love someone to wish them life, and when you hate someone to wish them death, first wishing life and then wishing death: this is a contradiction. "Truly it was not for her wealth / But only for the difference."

> This has a complex background in contemporary discourse. Exalting the role of the virtuous and discriminating in cases of logical contrariety were topics of concern to the Micians. Rather than discuss them in Mician terms, the Master restates classic positions on loyalty (9:25) and right (4:10). He seems to give ground by citing a case of inconsistency (from Shr 188; Waley **Songs** #105, first loving and then hating the same person), but on reflection we see that the contradiction is purely a matter of inconsistency *within oneself*, and that such cases never arise if one's own dedication stays constant. The utility of virtue is that it obviates ethical legerdemain. This passage is not so much a reflection, as a contemptuous rejection, of contemporary logical sophistication.

⌐ 12:11. Chí Jǐng-gūng asked Confucius about government. Confucius replied, The ruler is a ruler, the minister is a minister, the father is a father, the son is a son. The Prince said, Good indeed! Truly, if the ruler is not a ruler, the minister is not a minister, the father is not a father, and the son is not a son, even if I have millet, will I be able to eat it?

> All social roles contribute: if they do not function, the resulting chaos threatens the state's survival. Note that the ruler's safety, as in 12:9, is an outcome and not a precondition of social stability: the people come first. This vivid statement of social interdependence (responding to GZ 2:45–46, Rickett **Guanzi** 78–79) is famous in Chinese tradition, and has been used (Rosemont **Mirror** 70–74) as a basis for evading the solipsism typical of most Western social philosophy.

┌ 12:12a. The Master said, One who from a single word could decide litigations – that would be Yóu, would it not?

> Dž-lù's persona was redefined in 11:13b as daring and hasty. The idea is that he is prepared to hear only one side of a case, but this is *not enough*; it appears that contemporary jurisprudence required testimony from both sides. Yw̌ 獄 "cases" later means "prisons," further supporting the possibility of incarceration punishments noted in 5:1n. There is ample evidence for 03c penal *servitude* (Brooks **Slavery**), and probably the mechanism for imposing such punishments existed by LY 12 (see the contemporary MZ 9 and 12; Mei **Ethical** 37 and 63).

└ 12:13. The Master said, In hearing lawsuits, I am no better than anybody else; what is required is to bring it about that there *are no* lawsuits.

> Here is another kind of proceeding: sùng 訟 "lawsuits." On the evidence of the Shr̄ (see Waley **Songs** 63–65), which may be projected from about this period, they were initiated as complaints of wronged individuals to local elders (or the prince himself? gūng 公 "prince" is phonetic in sùng 訟 "suit"). The yw̌ of 12:12a may be contrasted as governmental proceedings, based on public prohibitions. This implies two levels: a common law allowing complaints of social wrong, administered by local elders, and looking to social reparations; and a penal law, defined by government proclamation, enforced by magistrates and leading to punishment by the state. The latter is a feature of what we now call Legalism, a governmental theory that arose in the 04c. Chí Legalism seems to have provided for appeals from local to central government courts (GZ 3:16, Rickett **Guanzi** 95). This connected the two social strata, as part of the process of making one nation out of a stratified society: the population had access to central justice, and were liable to court-proclaimed law. Like the relation between ruler and minister in 3:9, that between ruler and populace is now not only *direct* (the early 05c innovation), but *reciprocal* (the mid 04c revolution). 12:13 is unimpressed; yóu 猶 "as bad as; no better than" is pejorative, implying that even a good man is only so good as a judge: judging is *intrinsically* flawed.

┌ 12:14. Dž-jāng asked about government. The Master said, Be occupied with it unwearyingly, carry it out loyally.

> A precept for the bureaucrat rather than the ruler; this is the period when the bureaucratic state is being worked out in detail. It has already been found that administration takes both time and energy, and centers on national purpose. The comparable Chí Legalist maxim is GZ 2:42 (Rickett **Guanzi** 77).

└ 12:15. The Master said, If he learns widely in culture but limits it by ritual, he will surely manage not to overstep its proper boundary.

> Identical with 6:27 except that it lacks the explicit subject "the gentleman," and that the meaning of lǐ has shifted from "propriety" to "ritual." It balances the progressive 12:14 by affirming that the old maxims are as good as the new concepts. The new concepts also claim to give new depth to the old maxims, and juxtapoxing the old maxims may help to emphasize this.

└ 12:16. The Master said, The gentleman completes the good in others, and does not complete their evil. The little man does the opposite of this.

> An echo of the 12:14/15 contrast; compare also 4:7, which fits not too badly into the new, benevolent definition of rv́n which LY 12 suddenly advances.

[D. The Theory of Rule]

╭ 12:17. Jì Kāngdž asked Confucius about government. Confucius replied,
Government is correcting. If you lead on a correct basis, who will dare *not* to be
correct?

> This is a pun on jv̀ng 正 "correct" and jv̀ng 政 "government," understood as
> exemplary rather than coercive. If (as in 12:1) the ruler has the right qualities,
> those below will *spontaneously* acquire those qualities. We might call this the
> *assent* of the governed; their capacity to respond to good influence. The effect
> of an exemplary ruler is later called the transformation (hwà 化) of society; the
> term occurs in DDJ 37 (c0309) and in DDJ 57 (c0280), and often in Mencius.
> It is opposed to the *compulsion* theory, which "corrects" by force and fear.

╰ 12:18. Jì Kāngdž was worried about robbers, and asked Confucius. Confucius
replied, If somehow *you* had no desires, then even if you offered them rewards, they
would not steal.

> This complements 12:17 as a maxim of *preventive* government: the ruler's lack
> of desire will cause desire to vanish from the people. The suppression of desire,
> central for the meditation adept, occurs in DDJ 12 and 19. Worry about
> robbers, implying increased wealth, is typical of this period; see DDJ 9 and 3.

╭ 12:19. Jì Kāngdž asked Confucius about government, saying, If I kill those who
have not the Way in order to uphold those who have the Way, how would that be?
Confucius replied, You are there to *govern*; what use have you for *killing*? If you
desire the good, the people will be good. The virtue of the gentleman is the wind;
the virtue of the little people is the grass. The wind on the grass will surely bend it.

> The temptation to achieve public order by public massacre is always with us.
> "Confucius" will have none of it, and instead reverts to the exemplar theory of
> 12:17/18, and adds a nature metaphor to show that the people are intrinsically
> malleable, and will conform themselves to the ruler (for a Mician parallel, see
> MZ 16, Mei **Ethical** 95–97; for a Legalist one, GZ 3:10, Rickett **Guanzi** 93).
> Note that appeal to nature has now entered the repertoire of argument.

╰ 12:20. Dž-jāng asked, What must an officer do that he may be called successful?
The Master said, What is it you mean by successful? Dž-jāng replied, In the state
sure to be known, in the family sure to be known. The Master said, This is being
known, it is not being successful. Now, as for successful: His character is straight
and he loves the right; he inquires into words and observes appearances; he is
considerate of those below him – in the state he is sure to be successful, in the
family he is sure to be successful. Whereas, being known: his appearance adopts rv́n
but his conduct departs from it, and he can so continue without self-doubt – in the
state he is sure to be known; in the family he is sure to be known.

> The theory of ruler influence as it applies to lower strata of government and
> other leadership. Dž-jāng asks about dá 達 "reaching the goal, accomplished"
> but he *describes* it as wv̀n 聞 "be heard of, be known." The contrast is between
> achieving an ethical goal and advancing a personal reputation. The diagnostic
> mark of the result-oriented officer is his wider ethical horizon; his otherness.
> The charisma of the self-confident phony is also acknowledged.

⌐ 12:21. Fán Chŕ was going along on an excursion below the dance altar, and said, I venture to ask about exalting virtue, improving shortcomings, and deciding contradictions. The Master said, Good indeed is this question! To first serve and later attain, is that not exalting virtue? To attack one's evils, but never attack the evils of others, is that not improving shortcomings? "For the anger of a morning, to forget one's self and even one's kin," is that not a contradiction?

> The list of topics is that of 12:10 with an extra one in the middle, and it is fair to compare the answers. Exalting virtue is here put in terms of motive: one acts for the result and not the reward. As to shortcomings, Fán Chŕ is reminded that his *own* shortcomings, not those of others, are his concern; another classic idea. For the third, the Master follows 12:10 by giving an example, not of deciding, but of contradiction itself. In 12:10 the temptation was fickle love; here, it is the distraction of anger. In both cases the passions are seen as enemies of the faculty of judgement. The implicit point (perhaps in opposition to the Micians, who emphasized logical consistency) is that there *are* no contradictions: when two desiderata seem to conflict, it is always intuitively obvious which is right.

> With these similarities of theme, why is this passage not in section 12B?

└ 12:22. Fán Chŕ asked about rν́n. The Master said, Loving others. He asked about knowledge. The Master said, Knowing others. Fán Chŕ did not understand. The Master said, If you raise the straight and put them over the crooked, you make the crooked straight. Fán Chŕ withdrew. He saw Dž-syà and said, Just now I saw the Master and asked about knowledge, and the Master said, "If you raise the straight and put them over the crooked, you make the crooked straight." What does this mean? Dž-syà said, Rich indeed is this saying! When Shùn possessed All Under Heaven, he searched among the many and raised up Gāu-yáu, and those who were not rν́n drew away. When Tāng possessed All Under Heaven, he searched among the many and raised up Yī Yĭn, and those who were not rν́n drew away.

> As though in answer to our preceding query, we get a rulership theory which shows that seeming personal-cultivation advice may have statecraft overtones.

> In the complications of the second question, it is easy to miss the first, but it is momentous: rν́n is defined not as in LY 4, as a code which its possessor honors in all circumstances, but as the Mician principle of loving all others (this was the Mician answer to war; see MZ 14, Mei **Ethical** 78f). Together with the shifting of rν́n from a subject virtue to a ruler virtue (12:1), this implies the "compassionate government" (rν́n jν̀ng) theory which Mencius later made his own (MC 1A5; Graham **Disputers** 113 notes that only "by the time of Mencius" does rν́n mean "benevolence," and here we have the corresponding, proto-Mencian, stage in the Analects). Next comes knowledge: not the ruler's administrative skill, but his capacity to recognize that skill in others. It is at this point that Fán Chŕ goes astray. He expects the ruler to *act* (compare 12:19), and finds instead that the ruler must *delegate*. The ruler's virtue is compassion, and precisely that compassion leads him to seek out – and, be it noted, from the multitude and not the from the civil list, another Mician touch – those with the skill to *implement* his compassion in practical administration.

> The awkward question of where, in a universalist state, the not-rν́n are to draw away *to*, is not here raised; the answer tends to favor Legalist theories.

[E. Envoi: Friendship]

⌐ 12:23. Dž-gùng asked about friends. The Master said, Inform them with loyalty and guide them with goodness, but if that does not suffice, then stop. Do not cause yourself embarrassment.

> Having previously (at 12:20) made the transition from rulership to assistantship, we next have the question of lateral linkages among the assistants. 12:23 asserts that one should use leadership and influence among associates, and desist if the effort is unsuccessful. This is a major modification of the classic principle of being concerned only with *one's own* shortcomings (see 4:14). It means that the new ethics is not mere group solidarity, but gives wider scope to the power of positive example. Note that the extension does not go so far as to require the denunciation of erring associates, a requirement that the contemporary Chí Legalists did make (see most dramatically 13:18). As 12:19 might have put it, you are there to influence, not to denounce. With the explicit understanding, in 12:23, that if your influence does not avail, you may validly distance yourself from what, in the end, can only be a perilous association.

∟ 12:24. Dzv̄ngdž said, The gentleman with his culture gathers friends, and with his friends supports rv́n.

> The previous saying tells us how to distance ourselves from friends, and we may next wonder how to attract them, and what does the circle of friends, once it comes into being by attraction, accomplish in the state? The answer is that friends are attracted by sharing the same cultural values, and, once attracted, become a strong social force in support of those values. Friends do not develop an agenda: they serve the agenda that brought them together in the first place. With this maxim, the solitary 05c warrior code of LY 4 is adapted to the needs and awarenesses of the new 04c society. What we learn here is that society is not *somewhere else*: every interaction, among colleagues as well as on the street, and more consequentially among colleagues than on the street, shapes society. Hence the importance, newly recognized in this period, of right interactions.

Interpolations

As of this writing, we have not found interpolated passages which suggest an association with LY 12. This finding is subject to reconsideration in the light of further study, but it is consistent with our inference about LY 12: that it was put together during the minority of the school head Dž-jīng, possibly with a contribution from Mencius, and presumably with general oversight by the Kŭng elders. One can readily imagine the latter authorizing the composition of new material to keep the school abreast of Chí Legalism and other novelties, but stopping short of allowing creative access to the older layers of the text.

Mencius, whose adjusted traditional dates are 0387–0303, was over 60 as of our hypothesized completion date for LY 12 (c0326). We know from the genuine interviews in MC 1 that Mencius was ambitious and proud (he is even more ambitious and proud in the later *additions* to MC 1). It is conceivable that he had hoped to head the Lŭ school himself, and that his contribution to LY 12, if such it was, represented a bid for local ideological significance.

For a complete finding list of interpolated passages, see page 329.

Reflections

Among the excitements of LY 12 are its evident contact with Dàuist and Legalist ideas, in the DDJ and GZ, respectively. Dàuist ideas tend to be *sources* of Analects doctrine, whereas Legalist ones cause reactions and reformulation, but both are important. So are those from Mician sources. A few LY 12 Mician themes may be mentioned here. One is reliance on ancient, *pre-Jōu* rulers as models of administrative perfection (Tāng in 12:22 is the founder of Shāng; Shùn is supposed to have been a pre-Shāng ruler). This antiquarian device, which is soon adopted by later Confucianism, is here a novelty. Contemporary Mician writings refer to a whole string of these ancient rulers; the Analects seems to be using the tactic in self-defense. Mician influence is also seen in the meritocratic motif in 12:22 ("Esteem for Ability," MZ 8–10, Mei **Ethical** 30f, is a central Mician tenet). The characteristic Mician term shàn 善 "good" (12:19, compare the more tentative 11:19a), and above all the definition of Confucian řn as Mician ài in 12:22, attest a Mician philosophic presence.

LY 12 contains at least two theories of government. One is authoritarian (if beneficent in method), and is based on the Dàuist idea of the transforming sage (section 12C). The other, more participative and upward-determined, may be Mician (12D). In one, the ruler produces a benign society through direct, almost magical, influence; in the other, he produces it by feeling keenly the need for it, and using others to achieve the actual result. Thus 12C and 12D. What then of 12A and 12B? Has the chapter an overall theory, as LY 3 did? Does the envoi summarize the end, or return symmetrically to the beginning? All these questions make practicable weekend exercises.

Another question is the Mencian one. Our conclusion, from rhetorical and linguistic evidence, is that only the following Mencius passages are actual transcripts: 1A1, 1A3a (only through the phrase "the beginning of royal government"), 1A5, 1A6, 1B1, 1B9, 1B10, and 1B12–16. The ideas and assumptions they contain are not many. All seem to us to be prefigured in this chapter and in LY 13. MC 1B1, for instance, where the ruler's tenderness of heart is claimed to be a sufficient beginning for the reform of society and the dominion of the world, seems to reflect LY 12:22. It is probably fruitful to regard LY 12–13 as constituting evidence of the early Mencius before the onset of his formal career in MC 1A1 (0320). We rarely have the chance to examine a Chinese thinker up close; the "Confucius" of most of the Analects is a mere figment of convenience, emblematic of continuity while receptive to novelty. But here, possibly, is a real person. The LY 12–13 and early MC 1 material would probably repay serious study.

Much of the technical and social change we have noted for this period is discovered by observing the appearance of new words for new objects: silk, tailored clothing, the practice of medicine, and many others. More difficult is the detection of differences despite use of the *same* term. Consider friendship. In 5:25 and 8:5, it implies mere friendly feelings, while 9:25 ("do not befriend moral inferiors") suggests a more permanent association. Something like a mutual moral pressure group, supporting the redefined virtue řn, has emerged by 12:23/24. This, notably, is a lateral and not a vertical social institution. This recognition of the validity of lateral social institutions is one more instance of the widening horizon for the individual in 04c society.

Bronze Mirror (see p106 and p108)
Diameter 11·7 cm (4·6 in). 04c. Courtesy Freer Gallery of Art (74·120)

13

c0322

LY 13 is a twin of LY 12, and gives us a slightly later cross-section of the Hundred Schools debate. The proportion of possibly Mencian ideas seems smaller than in LY 12, and Dž-jīng may thus have had a relatively larger role in its composition. The theory of government has here evolved since LY 12, but in a practical direction distinct from the more idealistic Mencian view.

The numbering of passages is identical in the Legge text.

[A. Ends and Means of Government]

┌ 13:1. Dž-lù asked about government. The Master said, Lead them, work them. He requested more. He said, Do not weary them.

Dž-lù in 13:1 parallels Yén Hwéi in 12:1; for the Yén Hwéi / Dž-lù schematic opposition see Waley **Analects** 20 and the Interpolations, below. The last line is "Do not (wú 毋) grow weary" in the received text; we here adopt the Lǔ reading vùt 勿 (Jyèshàu 60), implying a pronoun object and a causative verb, giving a better grammatical parallel with the previous line, and adding an intelligible final caution: one should not be *too* efficient in working the people. The motif of "leaving something undone" is also prominent in the paired 13:2.

└ 13:2. Jùng-gūng was Steward of the Jì. He asked about government. The Master said, Lead the responsible officers, pardon small faults, advance worthy talents. He said, How shall I recognize the worthy talents so that I can advance them? He said, Advance the ones you know. The ones you do *not* know: will others reject them?

Jùng-gūng (Rǎn Yūng) also appears in the parallel 12:2. The 12:1/2 topic of rv́n has become the 13:1/2 topic of government; the two together make up Mencius's rv́n (compassionate) government. We have here some practical advice about delegating, priorities (not picking at details), and promotion. The "responsible officers" are the subordinate specialists. Overlooking small faults keeps personnel procedures simple. The need for new talent exceeds what one man's acquaintance can supply, hence the delegating of selection, contrasting with the older single-channel system (see 4:1). Promotion by merit is also a major theme of the contemporary Chí Legalists (GZ 7:6, Rickett **Guanzi** 140) and the Micians (MZ 9; Mei **Ethical** 36f).

┌ 13:4. Fán Chŕ asked to study agriculture. The Master said, I am not as good for that as some old farmer. He asked to study gardening. He said, I am not as good for that as some old gardener. Fán Chŕ went out. The Master said, A little man indeed is Fán Syw̄! If the superiors love ritual, then among the people none will dare but be assiduous. If the superiors love right, then among the people none will dare but be submissive. If the superiors love fidelity, then among the people none will dare but respect the facts. If these conditions obtain, the people of the four quarters will come with their children on their backs. What use has he for *agriculture*?

A rejection of the Legalistic love of subject specialization within government. If you can attract the people (see 13:16) by doing *your* job, you won't need to know *their* job. For "four quarters" (the world), see at left, and 13:20 below.

└ 13:5. The Master said, If he can recite the 300 Poems, but in applying them to government he gets nowhere, or being sent to the four quarters he cannot make an apposite response, then, many though they be, what are they good for?

> This is the first suggestion that the Shī had reached 300 poems, essentially its present size. The idea is that the Shī give advice for government, and are a repertoire of allusion for diplomatic discourse. DJ examples of the latter (see Wýn 4 [for the year 0623]; Legge **Ch'un** 239b) are numerous but probably retrospective; one may doubt whether even in 0322 the Shī were that widely known (it is surely suggestive that the authentic Mencius, from 0320 onward, never quotes Shī poems to the rulers he addresses). The utilitarian view of the Shī here is notable; by the 03c (17:8a/b) it will have dwindled in Analects esteem to something nearer a mere school textbook. Note that "four quarters" here includes foreign states; in the 03c (20:1[19]) it will mean the domain of the universal ruler. The late 04c proved to be the end of an open phase of Warring States intellectual life, and the onset of a more closed, proto-Imperial phase.

┌ 13:6. The Master said, If his person is correct, then without his giving an order it will be carried out; if his person is not correct, even though he does give an order, it will not be obeyed.

> Among late 04c rulership theorists was Shvn Dàu, later a member of the Jì-syà circle in Chí (SJ 74, 5/2346; Nienhauser **Records** 7/183), who is said to have developed the idea that it is not the ruler's character, but the potential inherent in his position (shì 勢), which explains his efficacy (Mote **Foundations** 107). 13:6 insists instead that a ruler's power comes from his actual character (compare 12:17 on correctness, 12:18 on charisma), but it also notices the resonance of that character with the executive staff around the ruler; something or other forms a medium in which orders get carried out and things get done. We may call this the *coherence*, rather than the *charisma*, theory of the ruler.

└ 13:9. The Master went to Wèi, and Rǎn Yǒu was his equerry. The Master said, How numerous they are! Rǎn Yǒu said, Once they are numerous, what should be added to that? He said, Enrich them. He said, Once they are rich, what should be added to that? He said, Teach them.

> This additive saying (starting with a first stage, and adding two later ones) contrasts with the subtractive 12:7 (where a system is reduced to its basis; here, ideology is the *last* of the three ingredients. The primacy of the people's stomachs was a tenet of Chí Legalism (GZ 3:18, Rickett **Guanzi** 95) and also of Lǔ Dàuism: DDJ 12, which we date to c0324, may be the proximate source of the 13:9 formula. We will see below (13:29/30) that "teaching" the people means military or premilitary training. A vital problem for the new-style state (see 12:7) was how to induce the little people who now largely made up its armies to fight and die for it. 13:9 theorizes that they must first be numerous enough to draw on, and prosperous enough to feel grateful, before they can be called on for such sacrifices. This differs from the 12:7 "trust" theory. It is instead transactional, resting on gifts between the state and its people, not directly on the people's elementary confidence in the ruler. It is thus a step less feudal than 12:7. It is a theory of the populace from the vantage point of war and not of peace. Together with the paired 13:8, it implies an objectively based resonance or coherence theory of the whole society.

[B. The Role of Ministers]

⌐ 13:10. The Master said, If only there were one who would use me, within a month it should be viable, and in three years it would be finished.

> For the civilization of the masses, see 13:9. The ministerial timetable is an end to disorder in three months, and a fully functional society in three years.

⌐ 13:11. The Master said, If good men ran the state for a hundred years, one could finally rise above cruelty and abolish killing – true indeed is this saying!

> A 97-year difference (in 13:10/11) in the schedule for abolishing mutilations (one gloss has "robbers") and executions invites comment. Punishments may have been among the methods envisioned in 13:10, whereas the ideal society of 13:11 (note the assimilation of the Mician term "good"), which can dispense with deterrents, would require a century of social preparation to achieve.

⌐ 13:13. The Master said, If once he can correct his person, what problem would there be in his serving in government? If he cannot correct his own person, how can he be good enough to correct others?

> This punning definition of government (j̀vng 政) as correctness (j̀vng 正) echoes 13:6 (compare 12:17), but applies to the officer rather than the ruler.

└ 13:14. Master Răn withdrew from court. The Master said, Why are you so late? He replied, There was government. The Master said, I expect it was business. If there had been government, though I am not employed, I expect that I would have heard about it.

> A sardonic gloss on "government business" (see 11:3), contrasting [personal] business with [public] government. Even as a private citizen, "Confucius" would have been aware of any overtime devotion to the good of the state. Few lines in the Analects are more quotable by those *not* employed, as a comment on those who *are*. It may have expressed contempt for the self-seeking Micians; if 13:11 is also anti-Mician, then we must recognize a secondary ABAB pairing.

└ 13:15. Dìng-gūng asked, One saying that could prosper a state: is there such a thing? Confucius replied, No saying could be as efficacious as that. But people have a saying, "To be a ruler is hard; to be a minister is not easy." If one understands the difficulty of being a ruler, would not this be one saying that could prosper a state? He said, One saying that could destroy a state: is there such a thing? Confucius replied, No saying could be as efficacious as that. But people have a saying, "I have no joy in being a ruler save in being able to speak and have no one disobey." If he is good and no one disobeys, is that not good? But if he is *not* good and no one disobeys, would this not be one saying that could destroy a state?

> The chief danger to the state is not an external enemy, but *its own ruler*, and the right of protest thus becomes part of the defensive structure of the state. This is one of several Analects passages defining the idea of the censorate, an institutionalized internal criticism that is the most recognizably Confucian of Imperial government forms (Hucker **Censorial** 194–198). It is also the first Analects passage to acknowledge the need for a comprehensive maxim rather than many particular ones; compare *15:3[15a], *15:24[15a], and *4:15[1]. Yẃ 予 "I" (compare 7:23n) here here appears in its original sense as a royal pronoun.

[C. The Basis of Government]

┌ 13:16. The Prince of Shv̀ asked about government. The Master said, When the near are happy, and the distant come.

> The Prince, mentioned in 7:19, is revived to make a point that was incidental in 13:4: the test of government is the happiness of its people, and the wish of others to *become* its people. This is the primary formulation of the Confucian populists; it was criticized by the Lǔ Micians (MZ 46:10, Mei **Ethical** 216), but adopted, with cosmological embellishments, by the Chí Legalists (GZ 1:1, Rickett **Guanzi** 52). The weakness of the immigration test is that it can only be applied in a competitive situation, with more than one state to choose from. This option vanished, for China, in the Chín unification of 0221.

└ 13:17. Dž-syà was Steward of Jyw̌-fù. He asked about government. The Master said, Do not be in a flurry, do not pay attention to petty advantages. If you are in a flurry, you will not get there. If you pay attention to petty advantages, then the great affairs will not come to completion.

> This pairs with 13:16 as goal with method. One should not be distracted by impatience or greed from the larger tasks. There is no philosophy here, but practicality has its place. The ability to see the point (Churchill **Allance** 24), or to prioritize around it (Barnett **Generals** 268–269), is exceedingly rare.
>
> The Chí dialect word sù 速 "flurry" (see Fāng-yén 2:34) occurs in none of the contact GZ passages, and is thus independent evidence of close relations with Chí at this period. These seem to have been both political and economic.

┌ 13:18. The Prince of Shv̀ was speaking to Confucius, and said, In our county there is one Upright Gǔng; his father stole a sheep and the son gave evidence against him. Confucius said, The upright ones in our county are different from this; a son will screen a father, and a father will screen a son. A sort of uprightness is involved in this also.

> This passage rejects the Legalist coercion state, where order is kept from above, and other social structures such as the family simply vanish. The issue is whether lower structures articulate with, or yield to, higher ones. 13:18 opts for articulation, which emphasizes honoring, not betraying, these local obligations (the seemingly apologetic 在 其 中 "is involved in" is sarcastic). The contrast between different states (Lǔ and Shv̀) points to the contemporary problem of nonuniversal social values, for which see also the paired 13:19.

└ 13:19. Fán Chí asked about rv́n. The Master said, In his dwelling, respectful; in his responsibilities, assiduous; toward others, loyal – though one go even to the Yí or Dí, this cannot be cast away.

> The feudal value rv́n is here (see 13:18) reinterpreted as a *multilevel* standard: the familial has its place, the governmental has its place, and loyalty within the newly important relation of friendship has its place. The claim of universality despite cultural variants addresses the challenge of cultural relativism in 13:18, and responds to the Mician position on the sensitive subject of funeral customs (MZ 25, Mei **Ethical** 132–133), which had compared non-Chinese practices (hence the "Yí and Dí" peoples mentioned here). MZ 25, on our view, was compiled somewhat before the present passage was written (Brooks **Triplets**).

⊾ 13:20. Dž-gùng asked, What must he be like before one can call him an officer? The Master said, In carrying out his own purposes he has a sense of shame; in being sent on missions to the four quarters, be does not disgrace his ruler's command – *he* may be called an officer. He said, I venture to ask what is next best. He said, His lineage and clan esteem him as filial to them; his county council esteems him as fraternal to them. He said, I venture to ask what is next best. He said, In word he is sure to be faithful, in deed he is sure to be effective: he is a pertinacious little man, but we may still regard him as being next. He said, Those who are now taking part in government; what about them? The Master, said, Ugh! Those dipper-and-scoop people: how are *they* worth calculating?

> One difficulty in understanding the Analects is the varied value given to what look like the same terms. Loyalty and fidelity, honored in other sayings, here rank low on the list of public virtues. One must look beyond inconsistency (Syẃndž criticized fluctuating use of terminology; under Syẃndzian pressure an interpolated *13:3[19] on consistency of terms was added to LY 13 in c0253) to the intent of each saying. Here, the top grade (with duties abroad; for the symbolism of sž-fāng 四方 "four quarters," see the mirror on page 98, with four schematic mountains surrounding the center area) has inner compunctions and outer adroitness, the next is functional in a more limited (community) sphere, and the next in a still more limited (individual) sphere. 13:20 attempts to harmonize insights recorded in various passages earlier in this section.

> At about this time, Chí had decimalized its old system of measures, but Lǔ seems to have kept a nondecimal system, with different units for different commodities, hence constant conversion between units was needed to monitor government inventories. It seems to be the pettifogging of these accountants that triggers the scorn here expressed (the dǒu 斗 "dipper" and shāu 筲 "scoop" held 16 and 12 handfuls respectively; the same ratio as that between English avoirdupois and troy pounds). The Lǔ government evidently employed such clerks, so that opposition to the accountancy theory of the state in LY 12–13 may be not merely theoretical, but a practical matter of Lǔ court politics.

[D. The Official in the New Society]

⌐ 13:23. The Master said, The gentleman is harmonious but not conformist. The little man is conformist but not harmonious.

> Compare *7:38[3]. The little man emphasizes his likeness to colleagues; the gentleman has a higher principle in view, and relates to colleagues in terms of that principle. This may be a criticism of the Mician principle of conformity (túng 同; MZ 11-13, Mei **Ethical** 56–77). The implication is that the principled and the sycophant do not mix, and only the principled are safely employable. Virtue, as the interpolated *4:25[2] will presently note, must have neighbors. Thus we have Gresham's law of ethics: the group low disables the group high.

⌐ 13:24. Dž-gùng asked, If his countrymen all like him, what about it? The Master said, You cannot yet act. [He asked], If his countrymen all hate him, what about it? The Master said, You cannot yet act. It is not as good as if the good among his countrymen like him, and the not good hate him.

> Again emphasizing a theoretical limitation on the validity of peer judgements.

˹ 13:25. The Master said, The gentleman is easy to serve but hard to please. If you try to please him otherwise than in accordance with the Way, he will *not* be pleased. When he employs others, he uses them as implements. The little man is hard to serve but easy to please. If you try to please him, even other than in accordance with the Way, he *will* be pleased. When he employs others, he seeks to get everything out of them.

> Personalistic rather than principled conduct downplays results and emphasizes favors. Chì 器 in earlier passages (see 3:22n) always means "vessel" (and, as a metaphor, the "capacity" of a man for office), but from this point on in the text it has the meaning of "edged tool." The implication is that well before c0325 the Lǔ metal trades were turning out chiefly tools and weapons (things with sharp edges) rather than vessels (things with volumes). We may be witnessing the conversion of the state and its people to a war footing (metal plowshares and chisels being as much implements of war as swords and knives). The foreground meaning is that the right kind of officer uses people appropriately, whereas the little man is indiscriminate in his use of men, and, so to speak, uses the screwdriver to open the paint can, thus spoiling it as a screwdriver.
>
> The slightly later DDJ 28 (c0313) objects to just this "use" of men.

˺ 13:26. The Master said, The gentleman is dignified but not arrogant; the little man is arrogant but not dignified.

> This saying (compare 13:23) is so profound as to leave little room for comment. Arrogance is the refuge of those without anything of which they can be proud.

˹ 13:27. The Master said, Steady, solid, quaint, quiet: near to rν́n.

> For "steady," see "steadfast" in 5:11; for "quiet," see "hesitant" in 12:3. It is easier to see that the *opposites* of these qualities are little-people traits.

˺ 13:28. Dž-lù asked, What must he be like to be called an officer? The Master said, Particular, punctilious, agreeable – *him* one can call an officer. With friends, particular and punctilious; with brothers, agreeable.

> This surprisingly unofficial description (compare 13:20) needs reflection in the light of earlier passages. 13:27/28 may be seen as personal finishing touches on the more official, conduct-based earlier sayings. There is no implication (13:20 *forbids* the implication) that mere domestic virtue makes one a proper officer. We have seen that a gentleman is strict with his friends (12:23) but makes a special category for his family (13:18), an exemption which 13:28 preserves.

[E. Envoi: Preparation for War]

˹ 13:29. The Master said, When good men have taught the people for seven years, one may then have recourse to arms.

> This glosses the "teaching" of 13:9 as military training, or social indoctrination leading up to it. The goal of state organization, as seen in LY 13, is war.

˺ 13:30. The Master said, To do battle without instructing the people – this is called throwing them away.

> This warning complements 13:29: the schedule for integrating the people into society and the army cannot be rushed. Convincement is necessary.

Interpolations

LY 13 is stiffer than LY 12, but maintains its interest in new ideas. There are interpolations elsewhere in the text that seem close in theme to LY 13, and may thus date from that period. This suggests that Dž-jīng, as he approached maturity, was taking a stronger role in this chapter, not only changing its tone from that of LY 12, but adjusting the earlier text to be consistent with it.

For a complete finding list of interpolated passages, see page 329.

Added to LY 5

*5:16. The Master said of Dž-chǎn, Of the Ways of the Gentleman, he possessed four: his personal conduct was respectful, his serving his superiors was assiduous, his nourishing the people was kind, and his using the people was appropriate. [5:15]

> Dž-chǎn was an 06c statesman of Jvng. He figures in the DJ as a (mostly) adroit manager of a state of the second military rank. Note the two aspects of governing the people: providing for their welfare (in which the gentleman is generous rather than harsh) and deploying them as a labor force (in which he observes factors like seasonability). Yì 義 "appropriate" means "what is proper, what is their due" in 6:22. In 4:16, and in Dž-jīng's first solo chapter at 2:24, it means "what is right." One should not rush to equate this with the modern concept of "human rights," but there is a parallel: not a *law*, human or divine, but a *societal expectation* of proper treatment by others.

Added to LY 6

*6:24. The Master said, Chí with one change would reach to Lǔ, and Lǔ with one change would reach to the Way. [6:22]

> This political statement, however condescending, is in Lǔ terms friendly to Chí, and seems to suggest that the alignment with "Wèi" (see 9:15) was at an end. The literal Wèi had been eclipsed during the 04c by the post-Jìn state Ngwèi, which in 0365 had moved its capital east to Lyáng, near to Wèi. In c0330 Wèi had moved its capital to Pú-yáng; its territory was little more than that city, and it scarcely existed as a state. A Lǔ rapprochement with Chí is suggested by evidences of intellectual contact, faint in LY 11 (c0360) and clear in LY 12 (c0326). The LY 3 kingship quarrel seems to have been made up.

Added to LY 9

*9:14. The Master wanted to dwell among the Nine Yí. Someone said, They are crude; how will you manage? The Master said, If a gentleman dwelt among them, what crudity would there be? [9:13]

> This seems to follow after *5:7[11] (the Master's intention to take a raft out to sea, leaving behind his own familiar culture); it asks how the gentleman could function without "this [defining] culture" (see 9:5). The answer is that the gentleman has his own civilizing influence, and can make culture around him. Compare "all men are brothers" (12:5) and the universally valid rvn (13:19). Such thoughts sustained many a Táng-dynasty official exiled to a remote area.

*9:26. The Master said, The Three Armies can be deprived of their leader, but a common man cannot be deprived of his will. [9:25]

> If correctly placed (it agrees with the background assumptions of 13:29–30, and the note of popular appropriateness in *5:16, above), this is the first Analects reference to the Three Armies, whose wings had separate commanders and could execute combined maneuvers, and whose general was the brains of the campaign. The parallel between the "mind" of an army (see the contemporary SBF 7; Griffith **Sun** 108) and the "will" of an individual is suggestive. This affirmation, that even a humble fellow's "will" is inalienable, is the strongest statement so far of what a modern reader might call individual rights.

Added to LY 12

*12:12b. Dž-lù never slept over an agreement. [12:12b]

> This remark, part of the myth of the rashness of Dž-lù, seems too slight for a passage, but also nonconsecutive as a final sentence in 12:12. It may be a comment to 12:12 which was later merged with it. For a humorous example of an incorporated comment in the Mencius, see Kennedy **Literary** 493.
>
> The presumption is that the extra words were added in small characters beside the original text, on the same bamboo strip. Full interpolation (untying the roll, inserting new strips, and writing the new text on them) would not have been called for (for the form of these bamboo strips, see Tsien **Written** 95 and Tsien **Paper** 31, the latter of Hàn date). The introduction of writing on silk will shortly transform the whole textual situation.

Reflections

> The LY 13 interpolations, though presumably the work of Dž-jīng, strongly support such typical Mencian populist ideas as the importance (see *5:16[13]) and even the individual integrity (see *9:26[13]) of the commoners. Their role as both the tax base and the military conscript base made it urgent for states to succeed in attracting them. This market advantage of the people did not survive the competitive Warring States period, into the unitary Empire.
>
> LY 13 proper (which Mencius may have influenced) *implies* intellectual relations with Chí; the interpolated *6:24[13] (probably by Dž-jīng) *expresses* that situation openly. Greater literary freedom may have obtained in interpolations.
>
> The Yí in *9:14[13] must be foreign, since the indigenous non-Chinese peoples (Lattimore **Frontiers** 345) had by now been absorbed. Among foreign peoples at this period were the Altai tribe attested at Pazyryk (51°30′ N, 86° E) on the upper Ob. The radiocarbon date for Tomb 2 at this site is c0390, from which dendrochronology gives dates of c0377 for Tomb 4, c0353 for Tomb 3, and c0331 for the similar Tombs 5 and 6 (Hiebert **Pazyryk** 120f). Tombs 3, 5, and 6 contained Chinese artifacts: silk fabric, lacquered wood (middle Warring States lacquer used a light wood or fabric core, better adapted to long-range export; Wang **Han** 81), and a bronze mirror (Rudenko **Frozen** 319f) like that on p98 above, a type for which molds have been found at the later capital of Yén (Lawton **Art** 86f, So **Traders** 147f, page 108 below). The Altai horsemen rode astride, like the customers of the silk trade which is implied by *5:22[11].

No Chinese artifacts have been found in later Altai tombs. The span of *contact* implied would be a few years earlier than the respective *burial* dates, or c0355–c0333. 0355 closely follows the 0357 accession of the Chí ruler who in 0342 proclaimed himself King Wēi. It may represent an economic initiative by this evidently vigorous leader, expanding earlier trade with the Scythians, or with other areas liable to secondary trading or raiding by the Scythians.

We observe in this period the rise of the mass army of maneuver, a development with profound consequences for society. It made it necessary to implant elite motivations in the the lower orders, so that they would identify with the state and become willing to risk death in its service (compare 12:7). This chapter focuses on this need in 13:29/30. Mencius was consulted as late as c0312 by a local ruler about troops who had fled from battle (MC 1B12), hence we know that this project had its failures, but it was obviously attempted.

As a counterpart to this acculturation of the lower orders, LY 13 also proposes an identity of culture between the ministers and the ruler (13:15). This effort too would later continue. One thing that hampered Imperial Confucianism as a political force may have been the fact that this culture gap between the palace and the mandarinate never closed, but rather widened.

A further consequence of the military changes was the militarization of civil office: where the early Analects uses only the term jywndž "gentleman" for its ideal minister, the text at this point begins to use the military term "officer" (shr 士) in this same sense, as in 13:20 and 13:28.

Pú 僕, the "equerry" of 13:9, occurs nowhere else in the Analects. Legge notes that it means "servant," but still translates "acted as his driver" (thus Waley "drove him," Lau "drove for him," Dawson "drove his carriage"). But in 2:5, from almost the same period, the word for driving a chariot is yẁ 御, and the point of the sardonic 9:2 is that driving (yẁ) is a highly developed skill, not to be expected of a menial (DJ sv Jàu 7; Legge **Ch'un** 616a, lists ten social strata, the last five being menial; pú is ninth). The Shr̄ uses pú in four poems. In one (Shr̄ 247GH; Legge **She** 478) it is a verb meaning "attached," in one (Shr̄ 192J; Legge **She** 319) it implies one walking beside (in attachment to?) the draft animal of a fully loaded cart, and in one (Shr̄ 3D; Legge **She** 9) it suggests an outrider for a military chariot. We conjecture that here and in 13:9 pú may mean a mounted escort rather than a driver.

Riding, a Bedouin informant tells us, is not required for horse breeding, and so need not be inferred from the stables of Lǔ (*10:11[11], c0360) or the tailoring of what may have been mere export clothing (*5:22[11], c0360). But archaeology (So **Traders** 29) attests Chinese riding near the northern border. SJ 15 (2/735, compare JGT #239–242; Crump **Ts'e** 296f) claims that the first elite cavalry force was formed in Jàu in 0307, despite resistance to the "barbarian [tailored] clothes" required by riding astride. This attests the foreign *associations* of riding in the late 04c. The clothing of low-status persons, not robes but a loincloth wrap (Rudolph **Han** #9 "servant," compare p46), would not have inhibited riding astride, which may have been first adopted at a lower social level (note the children playing horse in MZ 46:11; Mei **Ethical** 216). Elite adoption of riding in 0307 would then amount in part to low-to-high acculturation, such as is condemned by the "Confucius" of 13:4. Given these bits of social history, it is possible that the word pú in 13:9 constitutes an early, perhaps inadvertent, reference to the new and still unprestigious art of riding.

Clay Mirror Mold (see p98 and p106)
Diameter 11·7 cm (4·6 in). 04c. Courtesy Freer Gallery of Art (FSC-P200)

2

c0317

LY 2 continues the statecraft interest of LY 12–13, but with new elements: science, family virtues, and a renewed interest in teaching. It abandons the tolerance of war shown in 13:29–30 and adopts a civilian, even familial, stance. We place it in the period after Dž-jīng had assumed control of the Lǔ school. This probably occurred in 0321, and reduced Mencius's role, precipitating his departure in 0320. LY 2 may have been a summary and update of LY 12–13, on the occasion of the first year of Píng-gūng of Lǔ, in 0317. Mencius was then in Lǔ, on leave from Chí for his mother's funeral. Píng-gūng wanted to see him, but was dissuaded from doing so by one of his retinue (MC 1B16). It would seem that Mencius, however impractical his advice, did have the gift of attracting the notice of rulers. Under Dž-jīng's leadership, on the other hand, the Lǔ school later found itself on the losing side at court. Firmly as the hereditary Kǔng line was now established, there must have been those in the Lǔ school who felt it had been a mistake to let the more worldly Mencius go.

The numbering of passages is identical in the Legge text.

[A. Virtuous Government]

⌐ 2:1. The Master said, To conduct government by virtue can be compared to the North Star: it occupies its place, and the many stars bow before it.

The idea of the influence of the virtuous ruler appeared in 12:17, and that of a permanent maxim in 13:15; here they are joined with a new astronomical symbolism, the first time the physical world has served as a prototype, not a metaphor (compare 6:23), for the human world. This may reflect the theories of Dzōu Yěn 鄒衍, who apparently flourished in Chí at this time. Among ideas associated with him are the yīn/yáng duality, the Five Planets (wǔ-syíng 五行 "five walkers" or movable stars) cyclic dominance theory (Brooks **Earliest**), and a correspondence theory linking astral and terrestrial events, and offering a scientific way to predict the future and recover the past. All these ideas appear in the DJ (c0312). Dzōu Yěn's geography seems to have been based on nested 3×3 square arrays, of which the Nine Yí of *9:14[13] may be a schematic echo.

There was in this period no literal pole star, the immediate circumpolar region being essentially empty until much later times (Pankenier **Astrology**). Whether we imagine a polar void or (as the text seems to require) a polar star, the thrust of the saying is the magical power of inactivity. Bauer **Happiness** 21 notes the moral and physical force of the pivot-star's "powerful calm."

∟ 2:2. The Master said, The 300 Poems: if with one saying I should epitomize them, it would be "In your thoughts, be without depravity."

The idea of an epitome further develops the "basis" concept of 3:4 and the "constant maxim" concept of 13:15. This particular line (which, Waley argues, originally meant "Ah, without a flaw!") is from Shī 297, the first poem in the Lǔ Sùng (Shī 297–300), meant as a "last word" on the Shī from its then-last section (the Shāng Sùng, Shī 301–305, came later). This cultural sanction for virtuous *thought* parallels the natural metaphor for virtuous *influence* in 2:1.

⌐ 2:3. The Master said, Lead them with government and regulate them by punishments, and the people will evade them with no sense of shame. Lead them with virtue and regulate them by ritual, and they will acquire a sense of shame – and moreover, they will be orderly.

> The Legalist government by deterrent (chí 齊 is "to regulate, bring into line") *will not work*; order can only be produced by strengthening internal motivation (compare 12:7). Eberhard **Guilt** 122 speculates that shame, as the inverse of honor, is more natural for the elite; here is an attempt to extend it downward. The focus on education is typical of LY 2. For reciprocity in ritual, see 3:19n.

└ 2:4. The Master said, At fifteen I was determined on learning, at thirty I was established, at forty I had no doubts, at fifty I understood the commands of Heaven, at sixty my ears were obedient, and at seventy I may follow what my heart desires without transgressing the limits.

> The internalization of ethical ideals: (1) will to learn, (2) vision of the ideal, (3) resolving contradictions of principle, (4) grasping the *cosmic structure* of virtue, as in 2:1, a contemporary wrinkle which interrupts the psychological sequence, (5) overcoming inner resistance to ethical imperatives, and (6) transfiguring the inner impulse itself. The final state is like what the Buddhists call isvara 自在, the capacity to act without doing harm, which characterizes the Bodhisattva. If Confucius did not survive into his 71st year, as 03c evidence still suggests (see page 266), this would have been seen as from the very end of his life.
>
> A precursor saying may have been, and the first two stages are still often taken, in terms of career progress. So interpreted, it defines a midlife career crisis for Analects readers. Hán Yẁ, in his 31st year, writing to a friend in 698, notes that he is now behind schedule for "establishing himself" with posterity (Hán **Jāng Jì**; translated up to the quotation in Hartman **Han** 161f).

[B. Filiality]

⌐ 2:5. Mv̀ng Yídž asked about filiality. The Master said, Never disobey. Fán Chř was driving, and the Master told him, The descendant of the Mv̀ng asked me about filiality, and I replied, Never disobey. Fán Chř said, What does that mean? The Master said, When they are alive, serve them with propriety; when they are dead, inter them with propriety, and sacrifice to them with propriety.

> Lǐ, the basis of rv́n in 12:1, here becomes the theoretical basis of filial piety. The noble questioner does not query the Master's cryptic saying (compare 12:1/2), but takes it in its obvious sense "never disobey *parents*." The Master provokes a clarifying question to show that what one should not disobey is not parents, but principles. See also 3:9, where ritual gives a constitutional context for relations that are liable to monopoly from the command end. This passage, like 13:15, asserts a right to judge, and even refuse, the demands of the ruler.

└ 2:6. Mv̀ng Wǔ-bwó asked about filiality. The Master said, When his father and mother are anxious only lest he may fall ill.

> A good son does not cause his parents worry about his conduct, and he is so assiduous in caring for them that they fear that he may injure his own health. Wǔ-bwó, the son of Yídž, gets more traditional advice than his father in 2:5.

⌐ 2:7. Dž-yóu asked about filiality. The Master said, The filiality of the present day: it is merely what one might call being able to provide nourishment. But if we consider the dogs and horses, they all get their nourishment. If there is no respect, where is the difference?

> The internalizing of values here affects not only filiality, which becomes an attitude rather than a set of actions, but also the word denoting the attitude. Jìng 敬, in earlier passages mostly "assiduous" (in the performance of duties), somewhere in this vicinity acquires the later standard meaning "respectful" (previously rendered by gūng 恭). Note the distaste for the unfeeling manners of the "present," which also comes through in 13:20.

└ 2:8. Dž-syà asked about filiality. The Master said, The *demeanor* is difficult. If there is work, the younger bear the toil of it; if there are wine and food, the elder get the best portions – did *this* ever count as filiality?

> Again the Master shows contempt for outward observances, and fixes on a different crux: not the inward feeling of 2:7, but its expression in the demeanor. Mere considerate actions do not suffice.

[C. Higher and Lower Consistencies]

⌐ 2:9. The Master said, I can talk all day with Hwéı, and he never disagrees with me; he seems to be stupid. But if, after he has withdrawn, I observe his personal conduct, it is adequate to serve as an illustration. *Hwéı* is not stupid.

> The implication (compare 5:12) is that *the Master* is stupid, to have mistaken Hwéı's ready inner assent for mere superficial acceptance (note the expectation that a good student will *challenge* the teacher). DDJ 20 (c0320) praises the seeming unworldly "stupidity" of the meditation adept.

└ 2:10. The Master said, See what he bases himself on, observe what he follows, find out what he is comfortable with. Where can the man hide? Where can the man hide?

> The art of judging from incomplete evidence. As in 2:9, judgement of future performance is based on observation of present performance. This does not mean that the possession of one good quality guarantees other good qualities (a dangerous error which beginners frequently make), but, more subtly, that the *sources* and *influences* of action are a useful *predictor* of action.

⌐ 2:11. The Master said, Warming up the old so as to understand the new: such a one can be a teacher.

> We take ár 而 as resultative ("so as") rather than connective ("and") between the two clauses describing a teacher; compare MZ 46:17 (Mei **Ethical** 219), criticizing LY 7:1, to which this is a rejoinder. It reflects the position of a school head in charge of a body of received doctrine, but continually adapting it ("warming it up") to make it applicable to new political and cultural needs.

└ 2:12. The Master said, The gentleman is not used as an implement.

> For the deployment of lower staff according to their specific skills, see 13:25. This (like DDJ 28) objects to its application to people of the better sort, repeating the idea (see 9:2) that the gentleman is not a specialist, but needs scope for generality, as against the standard bureaucratic limitation of function.

⌐ 2:13. Dž-gùng asked about the gentleman. The Master said, First he carries out his words, and then he remains consistent with them.

> The keeping of promises has been a virtue from the beginning of the text; here, a new dimension is added: a *consistency of position* in the promises. The old loyalty concept included continuity in the object of loyalty, typically a person. As the state detaches itself from its ruler, a different basis of personal consistency is needed: an internalized loyalty, or integrity.

> Waley's interpretation, followed by Dawson and Leys, in effect "first tests his words in practice and only then recommends them as guidelines," seems to us a forced reading of the final words, 從之 "follows them."

∟ 2:14. The Master said, The gentleman is broad and not partial; the little man is partial and not broad.

> The gentleman is consistent at the level of large principles; the little man, at that of precise loyalties. If we see this saying as associated with the foregoing, it seems to support our reading of the foregoing.

⌐ 2:15. The Master said, If he studies and does not reflect, he will be rigid. If he reflects but does not study, he will be shaky.

> This can quite satisfactorily be taken as asserting the need for both personal thought and attention to tradition, in maintaining the tradition (compare 2:11). With an eye to hints in earlier passages, we are inclined to see in "reflection" a specifically meditational component (compare *4:25 below).

∟ 2:16. The Master said, If someone attacks from another end, he will do harm.

> For the technical meaning of dwān 端 "end" in induction, compare 9:8. In the context of the paired 2:15, this passage may be aimed not at heterodox *ideas* (the usual explanation) but at other *ways of reasoning*. This rules out syncretic tendencies like the openness to Mician values such as "love," which in 12:22 was equated with Confucian rvn. The limited acceptance of meditative insights in the paired 2:15 will, in a similar way, be reduced in the later 15:31[15a]. The Confucian stance hardens, as the Hundred Schools debate leads its participants to define themselves more rigorously *as against each other*.

⌐ 2:17. The Master said, Yóu, shall I teach you about knowing? To regard knowing it as knowing it; to regard *not* knowing it as *not* knowing it – *this* is knowing.

> This famous advice to Dž-lù (for "not knowing *it*," we follow the Lǔ text, which has explicitly 弗知; **Shř-wvn** 50) warns against overconfidence in knowledge. True wisdom 知 includes awareness 知 of the limits of knowledge 知.

∟ 2:18. Dž-jāng was studying for a salaried position. The Master said, Hear much but omit what is doubtful, and speak circumspectly of the rest, and you will have few problems. See much but omit what is shaky, and act circumspectly on the rest, and you will have few regrets. If in your words you have few problems, and in your actions you have few regrets, salary will come along in due course.

> A paired saying on the topic of doubtful knowledge. The seeming moral is not to base yourself on what you don't know, or don't *securely* know. We suspect that a prototype maxim may have recommended mere bureaucratic caution: an emphasis on the *avoidance of mistakes*. It is the unobjectionable, not the outstanding, who succeed. LY 2 here steps back from the bolder LY 12–13.

[D. Influencing the People]

⌐ 2:19. Aī-gūng asked, What must I do so that the people will be submissive? Confucius replied, Raise up the straight and put them over the crooked, and the people will be submissive. Raise up the crooked and put them over the straight, and the people will not be submissive.

> The Legalists recommended force, based on proclaimed law, as a means of securing public order. This response requires that those in charge of the people must themselves be models of behavior (see 2:3), and not mere enforcers.

∟ 2:20. Jì Kāngdž asked, To make the people be respectful, loyal, and motivated, what should one do? The Master said, Regard them with austerity, and they will be respectful. Be filial and kind, and they will be loyal. Raise up the good to teach their deficiencies, and they will be motivated.

> The phrase "filial and kind" is common in the Mician writings. The final phrase echoes 2:19 by stressing that officials should evoke self-motivation rather than compel obedience. The teaching aspect of public influence is again stressed, as in 13:29–30, but here in a civil, not a military, context. This saying marks a step in the evolution of the population toward something like citizens. The pairing of Aī-gūng and Jì Kāngdž reminds us (compare LY 5–6) that they no longer define sides in a legitimacy struggle, but are simply alternate spokesmen for rulership. The state has become *an entity in itself*, detached from the personality, and even the pedigree, of its ruler.

⌐ 2:21. Someone said to Confucius, Why are you not in government? The Master said, The Shū says, "Be ye filial, only filial, be friendly toward your brothers, and you will contribute to the government." This too, then, is being in government. Why should you speak of being "in government?"

> As Legge notes, the use of the formal designation Confucius (Kŭngdž 孔子) implies a high-ranking questioner. This defense of being out of government feels like an anticipation of the retrenchment theory of LY 1, from a period when the Confucians, we infer, had in fact lost their position at the Lŭ court. Their court position, as of LY 2, may already be growing uncomfortable.
>
> Shū 49 (Legge **Shoo** 535) contains the quoted line, but this text as we now have it is a later forgery, and whatever text 2:21 originally quoted from is lost. It evidently linked domestic and public virtue, a contemporary innovation. There is no point in discussing it as though it were an actual ancient record.

∟ 2:22. The Master said, A man, but without fidelity: I don't know if that can be. A large cart with no yoke, a small cart with no collar: how shall one make them go?

> The form of this saying derives from the punning 3:3. A man assiduous in his personal duties is still playing a public part (2:21), but one who is unreliable at the personal level is hardly a man at all. The implication is that some things cannot be produced by education (compare 2:19/20), but must be present on their own. 2:22 approaches a definition of what is ethically human, but in active rather than descriptive terms: fidelity is something you *do*, not something you *are*. Note that in this nongovernmental saying (compare 2:21) the essential virtue is the lateral "fidelity" rather than the vertical "loyalty." Society has its own structure; it is not simply an object of influence from above.

[E. Envoi: Guidelines for the Future]

⌐ 2:23. Dž-jāng asked whether ten generations hence could be foreknown. The Master said, In the Yīn's continuing with the Syà rituals, what they subtracted and added can be known. In the Jōu's continuing with the Yīn rituals, what they subtracted and added can be known. And if someone should carry on after the Jōu, even though it were a hundred generations, it can be known.

> The Confucians saw Lǔ as the inheritor of Jōu. This required that its rituals, said as recently as 3:9 to lack tradition, should be authentic. Authenticity is here supplied by a scientific extrapolation theory like that of Dzōu Yěn (2:1), which let *historical* changes be calculated with the same precision as *eclipses*. This highly positivistic confidence underlies the predictive historiography of the Dzwǒ Jwàn, and also led to an era of scientific forgery, in which many purportedly "ancient" texts were produced and, with rare exceptions, accepted.

L 2:24. The Master said, If it is not his own spirit but he sacrifices to it, he is presumptuous. If he sees what is right but does not do it, he lacks courage.

> This recalls the Quaker advice to shun the spiritual duty of *another* (the "spirit" in 2:24 is ancestral), but also enjoins one's *own* duty. Here, as in Plato's Laches (see Brooks **Courage**), military courage first evolves into moral courage.
>
> The pairing is based on formal change (2:23) versus ethical permanency (2:24). Both are knowable, and thus constant, to the perceptive observer.

Interpolations

Whereas LY 12 and 13 were added to the end of the text, Dž-jīng preposed this chapter, as the angry LY 3 had been preposed. This had the effect of giving great structural prominence to the novel LY 2 emphasis on filiality. There was however little precedent for this idea in the classic Analects. Dž-jīng then did an even more outrageous thing, adding to the arch-classic LY 4 enough extra sayings (their relation to LY 2 ideas will be clear from the commentary below) to expand it from 16 to the standard 24, including *a whole series* on filiality.

For a complete finding list of interpolated passages, see page 329.

Added to LY 4

⌐ *4:18. The Master said, In serving his father and mother, he remonstrates gently. If he sees that his ideas are not followed, then he again becomes dutiful without disobedience, and energetic without resentment. [4:18]

> This extends into the private realm the principle of remonstrance earlier enunciated in 13:15 and later developed in 14:7. It also limits that principle by the ultimate authority of the parents, right or wrong.

L *4:19. The Master said, While his father and mother are alive, he does not travel far; if he *does* travel, he must have a definite destination. [4:19]

> It must always be possible to summon the son to fulfil overriding filial duties. There is a social bias in the maxim: official errands to definite places would have been allowed, but not open-ended speculative commercial excursions.

⌐ *4:20. The Master said, If for three years he does not change from the ways of his father, he may be called filial. [4:20]

True filiality is shown only *after* the lifetime of the parents, by inner submission to their example. This is the first hint of a three-year period, not yet explicitly a mourning period, in the death of a parent. A dispute later broke out between Confucians and Micians over the attempt of the former to claim a three-year mourning period as ancient practice (compare MC 3A2). Some would-be royal lineages at this time probably had a tradition of extended observance of the death of a previous king. *4:20 emphasizes inner feeling in what might be called sentimental matters. It is incorporated as a guideline in the later 1:11.

L *4:21. The Master said, The ages of one's father and mother cannot but be known. In the one case, he will be happy; in the other, he will be anxious. [4:21]

Again the note of appropriate feeling. The seemingly intimate matter of the parents' ages is of valid interest to the son in the proper exercise of filial responsibility; aged parents require extra watchfulness.

⌐ *4:22. The Master said, If the words of those of old did not readily issue forth, it was that they were ashamed lest they should not come up to them. [4:22]

Their reluctance in making promises was out of concern at the difficulty of fulfilling them. See the governmental 12:3, and note that we are now in a section on the new, public virtue of fidelity (see 2:22, above).

L *4:23. The Master said, Those who err on the side of strictness are few. [4:23]

This contrasts loose modern practice with the ancient scruple of 4:22.

L *4:24. The Master said, The gentleman wants to be slow in giving his word, but quick in carrying it out. [4:24]

This gives an envoi to both the preceding sayings, balancing care in making promises with expeditiousness in carrying them out. Note that this virtue is exemplified by Dž-lù in *12:12b[13]. His new image as a man in an ethical hurry may thus not be entirely negative.

L *4:25. The Master said, Virtue is not solitary; it must have neighbors. [4:25]

This is meant as a chapter envoi, echoing the "neighborhood" motif in 4:1. The point of this gnomic but beautiful saying is the social character of virtue: it may not be practiced in isolation. It may also be aimed at the contemporary Lǔ meditation school, who by the nature of their technique were prone to pursue "virtue" in isolation. This criticism gradually increased. 2:15 notes that the results of meditation ("thought") must be subjected to conscious processes ("study"). This is followed, in *15:31[15a] (from later in the headship of Dž-jīng), by a rejection of meditation as wholly inferior to study. From LY 12 through LY 15 we see a progressive rejection of the meditation art which from LY 7 through LY 11 had clearly fascinated the Analects people, and at a certain level continued to do so afterward.

This saying was recognized as a quote from Confucius by no less than Nero Wolfe (Stout **Second** 116); a second Analectism (9:22) was spotted by Archie Goodwin (**Second** 160). The influence of the Analects, in reducing the early thuggish characterization of Archie, and establishing a "family" ambience in Stout's later novels, has been unaccountably ignored by literary historians.

Added to LY 13

*13:12. [The Master said, If there were one who could be a King, it would surely be only a generation until everyone was rv́n]. [13:12]

> The distinctive usage wàng-jv̌ 王者 "one who functions as a [true] King" or, in the context of the times, "one who could bring all the world under one rule," occurs nowhere else in the Analects. Since in the present LY 13 it falls between two pairs of sayings (see p101), it must be an interpolation, but exactly when was it added? We append here a plausible but (in our view) ultimately incorrect argument, to show the difficulty of such determinations.
>
> The term wàngjv̌ occurs in Mencius. One might regard it as "Mencian," and date *13:12 to the time of LY 2, after Mencius's departure from Lǔ, and several years after his first interviews (0320 and later) with rulers of other states, on the assumption that the new term had by then reached Lǔ. But analysis of the Mencius interviews in MC 1 (Brooks **Interviews**; compare 12r) shows that half of them are interpolations. Eliminating these, we find that Mencius never uses this term in his interviews with two successive Kings of Lyáng (MC 1A1, most of 1A3, 15, and 1A6), covering the period 0320–0319, nor in his first interview with the King of Chí (MC 1B1, c0318). Mencius visited Lǔ at the beginning of Píng-gūng's reign (MC 1B16), but since the term wàngjv̌ was not yet in his repertoire, this is irrelevant. The term is absent from later Mencian interviews, through Dzōu Mù-gūng (MC 1B12, c0312). It first occurs in the second interview with Tv́ng Wv́n-gūng (MC 1B14, c0307). Mencius thus does not seem to have used this term until a decade later than the composition of LY 2. We have therefore dated *13:12 to shortly after LY 15 (c0305); see p138.

⌐ *13:22a. The Master said, The men of the south have a saying: "A man without stability cannot be made into a diviner or a physician." Good! "If he does not stabilize his virtue, he may well incur shame." [13:22a]

> Folk sayings are also cited in contemporary Mician and Dàuist texts. For the stabilizing of omens, see Waley **Changes** 136f; the quote from Yì hexagram 32:3 (Wilhelm **I** 1/137) is the first Analects evidence for the existence of the Yì. This praise of ethical persistence echoes the educability motif of *13:21, above.
>
> By a fortunate coincidence, we are able to demonstrate that divination of the Yì type was known in the south at exactly this period, namely c0317. The recently excavated tomb of a Chǔ official at present-day Bāushān (Weld **Cases**) contains a series of state documents spanning the years 0322–0316 and a more personal divination record apparently covering the tomb occupant's last illness. It may not be improper to note the association, in that tomb and in this saying, between divination and medicine.

L *13:22b. The Master said, One does not simply inquire of the oracle and then stop. [13:22b]

> *13:22a hinted that virtue needs continuous action (hv́ng 恆 "stabilization"); we here learn that a favorable prospect needs to be furthered by one's own efforts. The emphasis on *continued human input,* to reach and maintain a desired condition, suggests the continuous ethical intensity of Dzv̄ngdž (8:3). It is also reminiscent of the linguistic repetition psychology of the Hopi culture (Whorf **Reality** 148f). Such devices here acquire an almost moral dimension. Virtue, like chance, as Pasteur would say, "favors the prepared mind."

Reflections

We may note here some elements in LY 2 not found in LY 12–13, which perhaps reflect the school head Dž-jīng, who was now operating (as we infer) without the input of Mencius, who had left the school to begin his own career.

Conspicuous among these is the fact that LY 2 was preposed, rather than added to the tail of the previous Analects. This has a precedent in LY 3 but it is nevertheless a strong move; it probably sought to change the context of the older material. Second comes the skillful insertion of new ideas in the old material of LY 4:18–25. These include the filial piety emphasis, which would be consistent with Dž-jīng's hereditary position (as against his meritocratic challenger Mencius), and the teaching emphasis, which would be appropriate to his position as school head (note the strong policy orientation of LY 12–13). There is a certain tension here: the role of the hereditary and unquestioned leader of a school is different from that of one advisor among many at an essentially meritocratic court. We shall later see that under Dž-jīng's guidance the Lǔ Confucians fared badly at Píng-gūng's court.

On the policy or theory level itself, the development is more continuous with LY 12–13, though articulated with an intangibly greater rigidity. It may be interesting to see what ideas in LY 2 can be traced to prototypes in LY 12–13.

The third salient LY 2 emphasis is its faint but unmistakable interest in science, or what at that time leaned in that direction (2:1). This brings up some large comparative issues. Western readers tend to see their own early history in what might be called Galilean terms: a war between the church (representing arbitrary authority) and science (representing freedom of thought based on appeal to objective fact: "Eppur si muove"). From that viewpoint, it is tempting to see ritual as oppressive, and science as a bulwark of freedom. The alignment in early China seems different. Ritual had a potentially constitutional function, establishing limits of civility and mutuality between (3:19) and within (3:7), political strata, in both Sùng (de Bary **Rights** 187) and modern Confucianism (Ames **Rites** 209), whereas science in its Chinese form developed no tradition of its own, and tended to authenticate the divine and thus undiscussable authenticity claims of later-model emperors. The prophecy of Orwell (**1984**), not the plea of Feynman (**Joking** 338f), thus proved true. The moral for comparative history is that elements of culture such as astronomy may interact *in more than one way* with the other elements in the same culture.

The same caution applies with law. The Western model conceives of law as partaking of the regularity of nature (the dàu) and thus above the ruler. Some late Warring States texts take this view of the dàu (Turner **Theory** 74, Peerenboom **Law** 92–95), but they are theories and not invocable sanctions. The concept of dàu was like that of the sage-king: a recommendation not grounded in any social reality. The fact seems to be that early Chinese laws were issued by rulers to keep the lower orders in line (Orwell **England** 261), and not framed by barons to keep the King in check (Cross **England** 141f).

Meanwhile, as of this chapter (c0317), Chín faced a strategic choice. In 0316 it chose to expand, not east, but south into Shǔ (Sage **Sichuan** 107–117). This doubled its area by other means than the benevolent policy urged in 13:4. Chǔ was thus induced to shift its efforts east, upsetting the balance of power. This had an effect on Lǔ politics which we will presently encounter in LY 15.

Jade Archer's Ring (see LY 14:5)
Height 4·5 cm (1·8 in). 04c/03c. Courtesy Freer Gallery of Art (39·25, reverse)

14
c0310

LY 14 continues developments that are first visible in LY 2: the importance of writing, the rise of cosmology, and the militarization of policy. Píng-gūng apparently wanted to make Lǔ a major player in the game of war; an alliance with Chín was considered, and Chǔ eventually intervened. The Confucians urged their vision of a cultural rather than a political role for Lǔ in the east, and a protected position for the criticism of the officer in the new state. They also held a rational rather than mystical version of the theory of ruler influence. In these areas they seem to have lost ground to the Micians, Dàuists, and military theorists. LY 14 finds the Lǔ Confucians in an embattled condition.

LY 14 follows the DJ of c0312 (see 14:15n), and includes some sharp comments on that work; we have thus dated the chapter to shortly after c0312. Dž-jīng would at this time still have been the head of the Lǔ school.

Reference numbers to Legge are given at the end of each passage.

[A. The Officer and the State]

⌐ 14:1a. Syèn asked about the shameful. The Master said, When the state has the Way, to be paid, and when the state has *not* the Way, to be *still* paid – *that* is shameful. [14:1]

> Syèn is Ywǽn Sz̄ (see 6:5). In the bureaucratized state, honor is increasingly seen in terms of money (compare 4:5 and 5:21). 14:1a notes that even honor is shameful if it comes from an improper connection. Compare 14:3, below.

∟ 14:2. The Master said, To be an officer, and yet fond of ease, is not good enough to count as being an officer at all. [14:3]

> The same point made a different way: it is the responsibilities of office, and not the perquisites of office, that are the point of office.

⌐ 14:3. The Master said, When the state has the Way, he speaks boldly and acts boldly. When the state has not the Way, he acts boldly but his words are conciliatory. [14:4]

> When the state is functioning, officers can be candid in opinion and vigorous in action. When it is not, action is still needed, but advocacy must be indirect. The test of not having the "Way" is thus a ruler's unwillingness to hear advice. 14:3 implies that candor is crucial to the state, and the ruler its chief enemy.

∟ 14:5. Námgūng Kwò asked Confucius, Yì was good at archery; Aù labored with the boat; neither died a natural death. Yw̌ and Jí personally farmed, and came to possess All Under Heaven. Our Respected Master did not reply. Námgūng Kwò went out. The Master said, A gentleman indeed is that man! A respecter of virtue indeed is that man! [14:6].

> The arts of peace, not war, are the basis of the state; compare DDJ 42 (c0300) and the popular agrarian movements noted in Graham **Tillers**. Yw̌ and Jí figure in Shū 55; a Mician version of it is quoted in MZ 9 (c0320; Mei **Ethical** 46). The elegant surname Námgūng 南宮 is still met with in Korea.

⌐ 14:7. The Master said, If he loves them, can he but exact toil from them? If he is loyal to him, can he but offer criticism of him? [14:8]

> The people do not like toil, but in their own interest the ruler must induce them to toil at farming. The ruler does not like criticism, but for the good of the state (on which loyalty now focuses), the officer must sometimes criticize. This goes beyond the "propriety" argument of 13:19 to a "duty" argument; it is another basic precept of the censorial idea (Hucker **Censorial** 188f).

└ 14:8. The Master said, When they prepared an edict, Pí Chv́n made the rough copy, Shř-shú criticized it, the diplomat Dž-yw̌ polished it, and Dž-chǎn of Dūnglǐ added ornament to it. [14:9]

> The point of this seeming bit of trivia is that the ruler's message actually comes from the officials, and the ruler only addresses the people in their voice.
>
> Those mentioned are from late 06c Jv̀ng. The idea that early society was administered by documents is also found in the DJ, but there too it is an anachronism: not until the 04c would public pronouncements have been functional. 14:8 shows the importance of state documents *as of c0310*, and the disposition to ascribe the documentary mode of government to earlier periods. The Shū documents are an extreme instance of this disposition; see 2:21n.

[B. Historical Models for the Officer]

⌐ 14:9. Someone asked about Dž-chǎn. The Master said, A kindly man. They asked about Dž-syī. He said, That one! That one! They asked about Gwǎn Jùng. He said, That man took away the three hundred towns of Pyén from the head of the Bwó clan, and caused him to eat coarse food, but until his teeth fell out he had not a resentful word to say. [14:10]

> The first of these ministers, Dž-chǎn of Jv̀ng, is criticized for being kindly rather than firm (compare the positive view of *5:16[13]). The second, an 05c Chǔ minister, is also disapproved of (Chǔ was Lǔ's major enemy at this time; compare the more positive view in the contemporary Chí text DJ). Gwǎn Jùng is here a model of the conciliatory use of force, inducing local barons to yield their privileges to the government (compare the more hostile 3:22). There is no consistency, with other texts or with the earlier Analects, in the view here taken of these figures; they are simply emblems of policy. The policy here being recommended seemingly favored consolidation of factions within Lǔ.

└ 14:11. The Master said, Mùng Gūng-chwò would have been overqualified as an elder in Jàu or Ngwèi, but he could not have been a great dignitary even in Tv́ng or Sywē. [14:12]

> Jàu and Ngwèi were Jìn successor states after 0403 (note the anachronism); Tv́ng and Sywē were tiny statelets south of Lǔ. The implication is that Mv̀ng Gūng-chwò (said to have been head of the Mv̀ng clan in Confucius's time) was a minor talent, unfit for high office, who deserved to lose his local power.
>
> Mencius, also surnamed Mv̀ng, left Chí in 0313 after giving bad advice to its King on intervening in Yēn. By 0310 he may already have become advisor to the future Prince of tiny Tv́ng. Is the Lǔ school, perhaps envying his big-state early career, here metaphorically jeering at the small-state end to that career?

⌐ 14:12a. Dž-lù asked about the perfect man. The Master said, The knowledge of Dzàng Wŭ-jùng, the desirelessness of Gūng-chwò, the courage of Jwāngdž of Byèn, the accomplishments of Rǎn Chyóu – if one added culture in the form of ritual and music, that would do as a perfect man. [14:13a]

> Waley wonders at the mention of Rǎn Chyóu, but the whole list is suspect. Wŭ-jùng, praised for practical savvy in the DJ, is deflated in 14:14; Gūng-chwò was belittled in 14:11; no one knows anything about Jwāngdž of Byèn. Even the term "perfect [or complete] man" (chv́ng-rv́n 成 人) is Dàuist (see JZ 20:4, Watson **Chuang** 214), not Confucian (it never recurs in the Analects). It is perhaps best to take the passage as sardonic, disapproving of its ostensible ideal (the perfect man) and exemplifying that "ideal" in recognizably negative terms. The "desirelessness" of Gūng-chwò may reflect that of Mencius (see MC 2A2); This meditative "ideal" masks power politics (Wŭ-jùng), riotousness (Jwāngdž), and corruption (Rǎn Chyóu). For the real views of the text, see rather 14:12b.

└ 14:12b. He said, As for a perfect man in the present day, why must he be thus? To see profit but think of right; to see danger but accept orders; despite constant pressure, not to forget his lifelong words – that too could be a perfect man. [14:13b]

> The "said" marks the original independence of the now joined 14:12a and 12b. For "making do with less" in a corrupt world, see 7:12 and 7:16. This passage celebrates the LY 4 virtues of honor, courage, and fidelity.

⌐ 14:13. The Master asked Gūngmíng Jyǎ about Gūngshú Wv́ndž, Is it true that his excellency did not speak, did not laugh, and did not take? Gūngmíng Jyǎ replied, Whoever said that has exaggerated. His excellency spoke only when it was timely, and others did not weary of his speaking. He laughed only when he was happy, and others did not weary of his laughing. He took only when it was right, and others did not weary of his taking. The Master said, Could it have been so? How could it have been so? [14:14]

> Confucius here doubts the praise of a "complete man" by one of his adherents. We may compare, and in the light of 14:12a/b we may doubt the sincerity of, the "taking without causing resentment" attributed to Gwǎn Jùng in 14:9.

└ 14:14. The Master said, Dzàng Wŭ-jùng from his base in Fáng asked of Lŭ that Wéi should succeed him. Though they say he did not compel his ruler, I do not believe it. [14:15]

> The pairing is based on distrust of a historical claim (for this one, see the DJ sv Syāng 23, Legge **Ch'un** 503; this criticism is acknowledged in a "Jùng-ní" comment later added to the DJ, Legge 504b). The question of how we know what we know in history greatly interested the late 04c. Claims of ancient precedent gave an advantage in debate. Confucian willingness to challenge the historical claims of other parties reaches its apex in MC 7B3 (c0252).

└ 14:15. The Master said, Jìn Wv́n-gūng was artful but not correct. Chí Hwán-gūng was correct but not artful. [14:16]

> The two heroes of the DJ, whose historiography 14:15 attacks. Wv́n-gūng's *state* of Jìn was tripartitioned in 0403, Hwán-gūng's *line* was brought to an end in Chí by the Tyén assassins. Note the implied praise of balance: neither quality alone is enough to safeguard a rulership over time.

[C. Larger Historical Principles]

⌐ 14:16. Dž-lù said, Hwán-gūng killed Prince Jyōu, and Sháu Hū died for him, but Gwǎn Jùng did not die. Would one say that he was not rv́n? The Master said, That Hwán-gūng nine times assembled the several Lords without using arms or chariots was Gwǎn Jùng's doing. But as to his rv́n, as to his rv́n. . . ! [14:17]

> Gwǎn Jùng, the minister of Chí Hwán-gūng (see Rosen **Kuan**) treacherously abandoned his original master, to make his second master the leader or bà 霸 "hegemon" of the Lords (Rosen **Hegemon**). He raises the issue of new versus old loyalty, and that of the new functional state versus the old personalistic state (see Wang **Loyalty**). 14:16 classically disapproves of this, but compare 14:17.

∟ 14:17. Dž-gùng said, Gwǎn Jùng was not rv́n, was he? When Hwán-gūng killed Prince Jyōu, he could not bring himself to die, and even served him as minister. The Master said, Hwán-gūng was leader of the lords, and united All Under Heaven; the people down to the present receive the benefit of it. Without Gwǎn Jùng, we would be wearing our hair long and lapping our robes to the left. How can this be compared to the consistency of some common man or common woman, to cut his own throat in some ditch or drain, and no one would ever know it? [14:17]

> This refutes 14:16; which is right? The Analects often pairs conflicting sayings, sometimes to suggest nuances, sometimes to balance new and old ideas. The new idea here is a pragmatic, postfeudal, view of Gwǎn Jùng as saving Chinese culture from being overrun by barbarians. 14:16 respects chivalric "honor," but for 14:17, results count. "Nine times assembled the Lords" (14:16) and "united All Under Heaven" (14:17) are echoed in GZ 20, which (Rickett **Guanzi** 318) disputes the DJ estimate of Gwǎn Jùng; GZ 20 was in turn a source of GY 6, from c0304 (Brooks **Prospects** 50). These varying estimates of Gwǎn Jùng show the competition to annex exemplary figures. The late 04c war of ideas was carried on in part as a war of symbolic personages.

⌐ 14:18. Gūngshú Wv́ndž's minister and great officer Jwàn was promoted with Wv́ndž. The Master heard of it, and said, He may well be called Wv́n. [14:19]

> A classic touch; the epithet (here, the name) Wv́n "Cultured" is consistently used in the Analects in the contrary sense of "open to humble ways" (5:15). This is so traditional that we might anticipate a reversal in the paired 14:19.

∟ 14:19. The Master had spoken of Wèi Líng-gūng's lack of the Way. Kāngdž said, If so, why was he not destroyed? Confucius said, Jùngshú Yw̌ had charge of visitors and guests, Invocator Twó had charge of the ancestral shrine, Wángsūn Jyǎ had charge of military strategy. That being so, how should he be destroyed? [14:20]

> Jūngshú Yw̌ is the Kǔng Wv́ndž of 5:15. This defines the state not in terms of its ruler (the bad Prince Líng of Wèi) but *of its functions*: the ruler's character no longer matters. This illuminates the Gwǎn Jùng comment in 14:17 (results count). This trend of thought is best identified as Legalist; it derives from the new-style, directly ruled postfeudal state which emerged in the 05c in Lǔ and especially Chí, where discontinuity in the ruling line made the state receptive to innovation. Personal virtue still matters (section 14B), but the Analects in 14C concedes that it also matters whether the state wins or loses. The mention of a court military officer may reflect growing militarization in Lǔ at this time.

[D. The Confucians in Office]

⌐ 14:21. Chv́n Chv́ngdž had killed Jyěn-gūng. Confucius bathed and went to court. He reported to Aī-gūng, Chv́n Hwán has killed his ruler. I ask to punish him. The Prince said, Report it to the Three Masters. Confucius said, As I follow after the Great Dignitaries, I did not dare not to report; and my sovereign says to report it to the Three Masters. He went to the Three Masters and reported, but was not given permission. Confucius said, As I follow after the Great Dignitaries, I did not dare not to report. [14:22]

> This refers to the 0481 Tyén (Chv́n) usurpation in Chí. In the DJ (Aī 14; Legge **Ch'un** 840), Confucius argues that the people would side with a Lǔ invasion, and refuses to consult the Three Clans. There may be a parallel with Mencius's advising Chí to invade disordered Yēn in 0314 (MC 1B10). 14:21 also absolves the Lǔ Confucians of any complicity in the Chí usurpation.

└ 14:22. Dž-lù asked about serving a ruler. The Master said, Do not deceive him; rather, oppose him. [14:21]

> Loyalty requires candor, and precludes sabotage; this "loyal opposition" saying is another foundational statement for the later censorial system.

⌐ 14:32. Wēishv́ng Mǒu said to Confucius, Why is Chyōu so skittish? Is it not for the sake of displaying his eloquence? Confucius said, I would not dare be eloquent, but I deprecate stubbornness. [14:34]

> This assumes that "Confucius" has been flitting from court to court (compare DJ Aī 11, Legge **Ch'un** 826b) making speeches in search of a ministership; the charge of disloyalty is phrased as vanity. Confucius denies that he is vain, and belittles consistency itself as stubbornness: loyalty is to principle, and it matters little where it is realized. The itinerant Mencius was also criticized as disloyal, and 14:32 (like 14:21) may be a defense of a brother Confucian.

└ 14:36. Gūngbwó Lyáu accused Dž-lù to the Jì clan. Džfú Jǐng-bwó reported it, and said, Our Respected Master must have some animus against Gūngbwó Lyáu. My influence is still sufficient to have him exposed in the marketplace. The Master said, Is the Way about to be implemented? It is Fate. Is the Way about to be discarded? It is Fate. What will Gūngbwó Lyáu be able to do against Fate? [14:38]

> The plaza (shr̀ 市) of 10:6c is here an execution ground. Confucius refuses secular help, and appeals to the higher sanctions of 7:23 and 9:5. The Micians hated this Confucian reliance on Fate; see MZ 35–37 (Mei **Ethical** 182–199).

╘ 14:40. Dž-jāng said, The Shū says, "When Gāu-dzūng was in the mourning hut, for three years he did not speak." What does it mean? The Master said, Why just Gāu-dzūng? All the men of old were like this. When the ruler passed away, the hundred officials continued in office, and took orders from the Steward of the Tomb, for three years. [14:43]

> The Shū 43 quote refers to a Shāng ruler; it is the first statement of a three-year mourning rule (*4:20² was a harbinger). MC 3A2 (03c) says that Mencius urged that a Prince of Tv́ng observe it, but the Tv́ng elders argued that neither they nor the parent Lǔ line had ever done so. 14:40 does not join this dispute; its point is that government does not stop for the death of a ruler: *it continues.*

[E. Envoi: The Welfare of the People]

⌐ 14:41. The Master said, When the superiors love propriety, the people are easy to employ. [14:44]

> The employment here meant is in forced labor projects, not government office. For this now familiar populist tenet, see the earlier 13:1 and 13:4.

∟ 14:42. Dž-lù asked about the gentleman. The Master said, He cultivates himself so as to produce assiduousness. He said, If he achieves this, is that all? He said, He cultivates himself so as to ease the lot of others. He said, If he achieves this, is that all? He said, He cultivates himself so as to ease the lot of the Hundred Families. If he cultivates himself so as to ease the lot of the Hundred Families, could even Yáu or Shùn criticize him? [14:45]

> The "so as to" reflects the incipient aspect of the verbs: "labors toward a result" (see Whorf **Reality** 151 and *13:22b², p116 above). The ruler sets an example; in 14:42 that example reaches the people at large (the "Hundred Families"), and he thus ranks with Yáu and Shùn. This is the first Analects mention of these supposed ancient rulers, who had appeared earlier in the Mician writings. Cultivating the self to benefit others is at bottom a Dàuist idea; compare 15:5.

Interpolations

The sayings in the first concentric layer added to the small Dzvngdž core of LY 8 (the 8B layer; for 8C, see LY 18) have many affinities with LY 12–15, such as a new but subordinate role for rvn. They also lack such devices as numerical groupings, which are typical of LY 16. We append them here, with some sayings that may have been added at about this time to other chapters.

For a complete finding list of interpolated passages, see page 329.

Added to LY 7

*7:11. The Master said to Yén Ywǣn, When they use him, he acts; when they cast him aside, he waits – it is only me and you that have this, is it not? Dž-lù said, If the Master were running the Three Armies, who would he have as an associate? The Master said, One who would rush a tiger or breast a river, who would die with no regret – I would *not* associate with. What I would require is someone who oversees affairs with trepidation, and prefers to succeed by consultation. [7:10]

> Yén Hwéi wins praise for his submissiveness. Rash Dž-lù, jealous, thinks he would fare better in a military setting, but his recklessness (the allusion is to Shr̄ 195, Legge **She** 333; for 04c man/animal combat, see Lewis **Violence** 153) only loses out to cautious strategy. See also SBF 3:10 (c0312), Griffith **Sun** 79, for the new-style general's preference for victories that minimize losses.

*7:13. What the Master was careful about were abstinence, war, and illness. [7:12]

> The bureaucratic virtue of carefulness, shvn 慎, first appears at 2:18 (c0317); next are this and *8:2a, below; compare 1:9, 1:14, and 19:25. All subjects mentioned here seem to have involved the state temple: abstinence precedes sacrifice, which might be occasioned by the illness of rulers. For the planning of military campaigns in the temple precincts, see SBF 1:28 (Griffith **Sun** 71).

*7:15. Răn Yŏu said, Is our Respected Master for the Ruler of Wèi? Dž-gùng said, Right; I shall ask him. He went in and said, Bwó-yí and Shú-chí: what sort of men were they? He said, Worthy men of old. He said, Were they resentful? He said, They sought rvn and they got rvn; what should they resent? He went out, and said, Our Respected Master is not for him. [7:14]

> The father was trying to oust, from the rulership of Wèi, the son in whose favor he had abdicated. The ancient rulers Bwó-yí and Shú-chí had abandoned their states out of principle, and thus make a diplomatically adroit way of asking a question which, within Wèi itself, could not be framed directly. As in *7:11 above, Confucius favors impassiveness rather than insistence on formal rights, and deplores violent contention. In 0314 the King of Yēn had abdicated in favor of his minister Dž-jī; civil chaos ensued, and Mencius (MC 1B10) had recommended that Chí intervene. This piece seems to question the wisdom of that advice (Chí was expelled from Yēn by a group of other states in 0313).

*7:21. The Master did not speak of freaks of nature, feats of strength, disorders, or spirits. [7:20]

> Freaks of nature (birds flying backward, falling stars) were recorded as baleful portents in the CC, and the DJ commentary of c0312 abounds in fulfilled predictions as well as feats of strength and uncanny events (Watson **Tso** 139f and 120f; the hero of the former is Confucius's father, which must have been intensely embarrassing to the newly pacific Lǔ Confucians). Distaste for military prowess appears as early as 11:13b in the changed image of Dž-lù (compare *5:7[11] and 3:16) and is further developed in *7:11, above. For the Mician belief in supernatural retribution, see MZ 29–31 (Mei **Ethical** 160f).
>
> Lists like this and the next can be very evocative literarily; they are the ancestor of those in Sei Shōnagon (Waley **Pillow** 22–24, 93, 123f, 131f).

*7:25. The Master based his teaching on four things: culture, conduct, loyalty, and fidelity. [7:24]

> This positive parallel to *7:21, above, reaffirms the 05c range of Confucius's teachings, and pulls back at least momentarily from the new 04c terrain.

Added to LY 8

⌈   *8:2a. The Master said, If he is respectful without propriety, he becomes wearisome. If he is careful without propriety, he becomes finicky. If he is brave without propriety, he becomes disruptive. If he is upright without propriety, he becomes censorious. [8:2a]

> Jyǎu 絞 "tangled" means "censorious" also in the DJ (Jāu 1, Legge **Ch'un** 576b "sharp"). For lǐ "propriety" as a moderating principle, see 12:1; for moderation, and tact in particular, rather than the old extremism, see *7:11, above.

⌊   *8:2b. If the gentleman is dependable toward his kin, the people will be inspired to be rvn. If his old friends are not cast off, the people will not be unstable. [8:2b]

> Dú 篤 "dependable" (translated as "sound" in 11:19b) here for the first time acquires moral import. The exemplary ruler concept is typical of the late 04c, but this particular saying evidently helps define the sort of rvn which it was hoped to induce in the populace. Rvn here can only be something like "trust."

⌐ *8:8. The Master said, He is inspired by the Shř, given a foundation by Ritual, and completed by Music. [8:8]

> These were probably texts rather than merely values, hence the capital letters. Some ritual writings of the period are included in later collections. The Music canon seems to have comprised accompaniments to the Shř poems and some separate court dances; it has not survived. Pedagogically, the beginner is motivated by ideals of conduct in the Shř, learns to embody them in behavior by ritual, and in some Platonic sense given a broad social vision by the study of music, including actual performance. There was a hint of music in 11:15, and we first see Confucius himself playing an instrument in *14:39[18].

∟ *8:9. The Master said, The people can be made to follow it; they cannot be made to understand it. [8:9]

> The people can respond to a higher-level example, but they cannot themselves generate that example, or even understand what it is they are responding to; they have moral susceptibility without moral instinct. This retreats from the degree of educability asserted in LY 12–13 (see 12:19), which, with MZ 16 (Mei **Ethical** 96f) are the high-water mark of Warring States populist theory.

⌐ *8:10. The Master said, If people love valor and are suffering from poverty, there will be disorder. And if people are merely not rv́n and are suffering excessively, there will be disorder. [8:10]

> This echoes the 8:2b fear of the people, whose refusal of military service imperils the state, and whose love of martial qualities also imperils the state, but it is also a warning that a state which tolerates popular suffering will be in danger even from those who are not by nature fractious. Suffering is bad policy.

∟ *8:11. The Master said, If one had all the abilities and excellences of the Prince of Jōu, and were at the same time arrogant and stingy, then the rest would not be worth looking at. [8:11]

> The essence of the new-style ruler is modesty and generosity. The people must not be made to feel the lowliness of their situation, or be subjected to want. This and *8:10 are paired on the basis of the implied policies of the ruler.

⌐ *8:12. The Master said, One who would study for three years without aiming at wealth is not easy to find. [8:12]

> The school course evidently lasted three years (compare the tripartite subject matter of *8:8, above), and qualified students for profitable positions. 8:12 deplores the lack of any higher motive in its students than the pursuit of profit.

∟ *8:13. The Master said, He is dependable, faithful, and loves study; he will hold unto death to the Way of the Good. Into a precarious state he will not enter; in a disordered state he will not remain. When All Under Heaven has the Way, he is seen; when it does not have the Way, he is invisible. When the state has the Way, to be poor and humble in it is shameful; when the state has not the Way, to be wealthy and honored in it is shameful. [8:13]

> Notice the portability of the gentleman (compare 14:32), who like the people (13:4) will leave a bad situation for a better one. The Mician "Good," resisted in 11:19a, has been assimilated since 13:11. The last line of *8:13 echoes 14:1.

⌐ *8:14. The Master said, If he does not occupy the position, he does not give counsel for the policies. [8:14]

> The idea that the gentleman does not comment on things that are not his business goes back to the limited duty of the old-style warrior, and recurs in *14:26a[15b] as glossed in *14:26b[15b]. The new context for this principle in c0310 was the emergence of advisorships as distinct from ministerships. We are told in SJ 74 (5/2344–2346) that, in the wake of Mencius's departure from Chí, its ruler established a number of high-profile stipendiaries at Jì-syà. These had government *rank* but not government *duties*; instead, they wrote long treatises. LY *8:14 may be disapproving this separation of ability and accountability. Churchill too, at a not less militarily dire moment, recognized the anomaly of the "exalted brooding over affairs" which is the lot of the minister without a department, and thus without the power to affect outcomes (**Storm** 409).

∟ *8:15. The Master said, When Preceptor Jř began the Gwān-jyw̄ coda, how impressively it filled the ears! [8:15]

> A technical approval of how one music-master conducted the coda of Shř 1 (see 3:20, 3:23). Music-masters were blind (15:42), and must have learned the repertoire by rote. If the Canon of Music contained notation (*8:8c, opposite), it was probably an elite transcript of expert practice, not an expert handbook. The pairing is based on this expert/layman contrast.

⌐ *8:16. The Master said, Wild but not upright, unschooled but not eager, simple but not candid – I do not recognize them. [8:16]

> The quality kwáng 狂 "mad," here "wild," is in many cultures allowed direct expression without incurring offence (see 18:5). But such privileged behavior ought at least to be straightforward. The other two clauses have the same logic: students should have virtues proper to their shortcomings (compare 4:7).

∟ *8:17. The Master said, Learn as though you would never get there, as though you were afraid of losing it. [8:17]

> This paired saying seems to confirm students as the focus of *8:16. It is also a cousin to the ardent 9:11, and the strenuous Dzv̄ngdzian fervor of 8:3.

Added to LY 3

*3:5. The Master said, The Yí and Dí *with* rulers are not the equal of the several Syà states *without* them. [3:5]

> However well ordered politically, foreigners are inferior. This view is new in 14:17, and reverses the inclusive 12:5; it has thus provoked commentary. Waley (ap 5:7) sees *all* mentions of other cultures as examples of a "noble savage" motif; Leys notes that interpretations of *3:5 have varied with the political relation of China to the steppe peoples. Analects comments on foreign peoples occur within a 50-year span, and evolve from *5:7[11] (c0360) and 12:5 (c0326, positive) through 13:19 and *9:14[13] (c0322, moderate) to 14:17 and *3:5 (c0310, hostile). This change may reflect the aggressions of the Syūngnú, which inspired defensive walls (0324, in Chín; Yü **Hsiung-nu** 118) and the use of cavalry (0307, in Jàu; page 117 above). The DJ (Jāu 10; Legge **Ch'un** 668a) approves of learning from other cultures; the Analects here disagrees.

Added to LY 13

*13:8. The Master said that Jīng, son of the the Prince of Wèi, knew how to live in his house. When he first began to have something, he said, They will somehow suffice. When he came to have a little more, he said, They will be more or less complete. When he had a great deal, he said, They will be rather beautiful. [13:8]

> The two elliptical expressions "have [wealth]" and "they [ancestral rites]" show how well established were private wealth and ancestral piety at this time, though in the Analects they are something of a new note at this point. There is nothing in LY 10, an extended survey of the daily manners of a high officer as of c0380, that implies an important place for domestic ancestral rituals. Other evidence suggests that these were an 04c extension of the established ancestral observances of the ruling line. A metaphorical portrait of Confucius's palatial mansion in 19:23 does mention an ancestral shrine, with hundreds of menials in attendance, though by that time the Confucius myth had developed to the point where he is seen as virtually a state institution, so that remarks about his residence are not evidence for private wealth. Nevertheless, private households do seem in the 04c to have acquired the means of enjoyment, and even of splendor, that had once belonged exclusively to the ruler.

*13:21. The Master said, If he cannot get those of moderate conduct to associate with, he will surely have to make do with the wild or the timid, will he not? The wild will go ahead and do *something*, and the timid will have some things that they will *not* do. [13:21]

> "Wild" (compare *8:16[14] above) and timid are clearly a viable second-best. Possible interpretations range from Waley, who sees both as representing a single preferable extreme (the "impetuous and hasty" versus the timid and conscientious), to Lau, who sees them rather as naming opposite extremes ("undisciplined" versus "overscrupulous") which are equally workable. Which is right? Most of the commentators agree with Lau. It is not decisive that some glosses on the second character, jywǣn 狷, give the meaning "urgent," since others give "timid," and the word is rare in any case (this is its only Analects occurrence). The explanations *in the passage*, relied on by Legge, tend to imply opposites (going ahead versus leaving out). Since the earliest dictionaries were not studies of meaning but repositories of commentary, glosses do not have an authority greater than the passage itself. Legge thus seems justified in abandoning the dictionary, and trusting instead the implications of the passage.
>
> The phrase "moderate conduct" implies a "mean" theory of virtue, in which the right amount is between two extremes. This notion, like some others which come into view at about this time, is very Greek in feeling; the older view (see 5:21, 8:3) was that virtue lay *at one extreme*. We may have here the difference between the warrior's code and the bureaucrat's job description.
>
> Waley (following Legge) cites MC 7B37, which expounds this passage in terms of mid 03c thought, including that of a text called the Jūng Yūng "Doctrine of the Mean," apparently then in process of compilation (see below, in the commentary to *6:29[18]). Legge also refers to *8:16 (above), which we assign to this same group of interpolations. That saying made the point that "bluntness" without uprightness is intolerable. This saying gives the corollary: as long as they are sincere, the impetuous are not only tolerable but educable.

Reflections

We sense in LY 14 a swirl of conflicting opinion. One refuge from the uncertainty of debate was the precision of science, one of whose forms in this period was an astronomically based yīn/yáng 陰 陽 theory, which explained normal seasonal events and predicted baleful ones. The computed rituals of 2:23 (c0317), the predictions of the DJ (c0312), and the cyclical theory of the Mencians (MC 2B13), attacked by Syẃndž in SZ 6:7 (Knoblock **Xunzi** 1/224), bypassed debate by controlling history itself.

There was also Heaven. Eno **Heaven** 79f devotes a chapter to analyzing all occurrences of tyēn 天 "Heaven" in the Analects, and finds two modes: the descriptive and the prescriptive. It is a fruitful exercise to arrange these passages in the order assigned them in the present work, to see if a sharp transition between the two modes occurred, and if so, at what date.

Debate itself could be *sharpened* by the logic of statement, developed from the late 04c onward by the Micians (see Graham **Later**). This is echoed in the Analects tendency to define rather than merely state in LY 12, and especially (as Van Norden **Mencius** points out) in LY 13.

Texts counted too. The Shŕ is complete; in DJ (Legge **Ch'un** 549f) it comprises all but the Shāng Sùng, or the 300 poems it is said to have in 13:5, and a Shū corpus begins, imitating genuine inscriptions (MZ 16 cites records "engraved on bronze and stone," Mei **Ethical** 92; see page 130). The Analects hesitates to credit them (for intentional forgery, see McPhee **Hovings** 24 and the MZ 48:4 jeer, "*Your* antiquity is not old enough," Mei **Ethical** 233), but was gradually drawn into the race to create a citable antiquity. The DJ itself is a reconstructed past, the ancestor of both Chinese history and Chinese fiction. For chivalry, see Watson **Tso**; for spicier passages like the career of Lady Syà, a sermon on the evil influence of women, see Legge (**Ch'un** 305b, 308a, 347–348, and 527a). The DJ was the Gone with the Wind of c0312 (compare Connelly **Marble** 131f), weaving romance into the fabric of cultural nostalgia. As noted above, the Analects disagreed with the political agenda of the DJ, while conceding that the state had needs which political theory should address.

Another authority was tradition as embodied in lineage. This is the age of invented ruler genealogies (Chí, in an inscription, and Ngwèi, in the spurious Bamboo Annals, both claimed descent from the mythical Yellow Emperor). Allan **Heir** explores the contrast between lineage and merit; the Yēn incident of 0314 focused this "hot" issue. Politically, LY 14 emphasizes the continuity of ministers rather than rulers, a "constitutional" tendency, creating, with the ruler and the state, a third locus of political identity.

Finally, there is exoticism, especially that of far places. An imaginary journey to west Asia is implicit in the Tale of Emperor Mù (Cheng **Mu**). Meditation (inner rather than outer wandering) and the uncanny but practical divination of the Yì, unknown to the historical Confucius (Dubs **Changes**) but attested in this period (*13:22a²n), were analogous fascinations. In a context of frantic change, the Yì or "Changes" gave a rationale for seeing *within* change an underlying principle of hvng: an achievable stability.

In politics, there were two major options for the state: the new bureaucracy being newly *developed* in Chí, or the imagined classic Jōu monarchy being *revived*, also in Chí. As of LY 14, the choice between them is still open.

Inscription on a Jōu Bronze Vessel (see p129)
Height 8·5 cm (3·3 in). Early 010c. Courtesy Freer Gallery of Art (33·2, detail)

15
c0305

The LY 14 Confucians had gone a certain way with the Lǔ policy of military buildup. LY 15 marks a break. It shows an increasing distance from what were probably by now common assumptions: that unification was inevitable, and that sovereignty in the resulting state would be based on the model of the supposed emperors of antiquity (a myth being constructed at this period), rather than the bureaucratic model favored by the Gwǎndž thinkers in Chí, and to an extent by the Analects group in Lǔ. LY 15 marks the moment when the course of intellectual history decisively got away from the Lǔ Confucians, leaving them viable but not dominant. Lǔ had come under the de facto control of Chǔ, and, if we accept a Shř Jì hint, the Lǔ ruler who succeeded in 0302 was called not Prince but Lord (Hóu), symbolizing his subordination to Chǔ. The continuity of LY 15 with LY 14 suggests Dž-jīng's continuing headship. Its content also appears to attest his increasing frustration.

Reference numbers to Legge are given at the end of each passage.

[A. Critique of Rulers]

⌐ 15:1. Wèi Líng-gūng asked Confucius about tactics. Confucius replied, If it is matters of stemdish and stand, I have heard of them; if it is matters of armies and campaigns, I have never studied them. Next day he resumed his travels. [15:1a]

> Ritual, not conquest (the allusions are to sacrificial offering vessels and the contemporary military handbook Sūndž), are the true concern of government. This passage and 14:32 are combined in a late addition to the DJ (under Aī 11 [0484], Legge **Ch'un** 826b), which weaves them into a precisely dated version of the growing myth of the international Confucius.

L 15:2. In Chýn he ran out of supplies, and his followers became so weak that they could not stand up. Dž-lù angrily presented himself, and said, May a gentleman too find himself in want? The Master said, A gentleman may assuredly find himself in want. When a *little* man finds himself in want, he caves in. [15:1b]

> There is always somebody who thinks that being good guarantees a good life. The real difference between the good people and the little people is how they take hardship. The little people lose their interest in good; the good stay firm. This is an evocation of the classic 4:5, balancing the nonclassic 15:1.

⌐ 15:5. The Master said, One who did not act but produced order: that would be Shùn, would it not? For what did he do? He maintained a respectful stance, and faced toward the south, and nothing more. [15:4]

> Here is the Confucian version of the inactive (wú-wéi 無 爲) ruler, whose classic Dàuist form is given in DDJ 2–3 (the restatement of this mystical ideal in DDJ 39, we argue, is contemporary with 15:5). The Confucian version combines the idea of moral example (12:19, 2:1) and the bureaucratic notion of a ruler who symbolizes the identity of the state, while leaving its policies to its managers. This division of function between charisma and power was not, for better or worse, the plan on which the later Imperial state was constructed.

[B. The Gentleman and His Colleagues]

┌ 15:6. Dž-jāng asked about being successful. The Master said, If his words are loyal and faithful, and his actions sincere and respectful, then even in the states of the Mán and Mwò he will be successful. If his words are not loyal and faithful, and his actions not sincere and respectful, then even in his own region and village, will he be successful? When he stands, he should see this before him; when riding in his carriage, he should see it on the crossbar. If he does this, he will be successful. Dž-jāng wrote it on his sash. [15:5]

> This is the earliest Analects reference to writing on silk. Contemporary Mician texts refer to archival documents as "written on bamboo *and silk*" (Mei **Ethical** 92, 147, 167). Not only was this practice common enough in c0305 to be assumed for earlier periods, the literate seem to have carried brush and ink around with them as a matter of course. Compare, from a less literate period, the jibe at book learning in 11:23 and the oral presumption behind *5:14[11].
>
> The verb syíng 行 "act, succeed" and its noun syìng 行 "action, success" imply an action reaching its intended end. Dž-jāng's utilitarian question, reminiscent of the Micians and Legalists, here gets an ethical twist.
>
> The names Mán and Mwò (conventionally defined as the tribes of south and north, respectively) are here used in a general sense. Despite increasing hostility at this time to non-Chinese peoples, this saying assumes an underlying level of common humanity, where ethical precepts hold universally true.

└ 15:7. The Master said, Upright indeed was Archivist Yẃ! If the state had the Way, he was like an arrow; if the state had not the Way, he was like an arrow. A gentleman indeed was Chyẃ Bwó-yẁ! If the state had the Way, he served; if the state had not the Way, he rolled it up and hid it in his bosom. [15:6]

> This saying praises alternative ideals of conduct: the rigid and the flexible (compare 17:8). The unbending model is the "stupid" Níng Wǔdž (5:21), from the classic warrior code; the second, also classic, but civil and flexible, is the ideal to which later political theory increasingly inclines. Ethics has not grown a new foot, but may here be glimpsed in the process of shifting from one to the other of its two classic feet. The 04c search is not only for a new state structure, but for a "survivable" individual code of conduct within that structure.

┌ 15:8. The Master said, If he can be talked to and you do not talk to him, you waste the man. If he cannot be talked to and you talk to him, you waste your talk. The knowledgeable will not waste a man, but will also not waste his talk. [15:7]

> Waley (**Three** 13f, PB x–xi, ap JZ 26:8b, Watson **Chuang** 302, which is based on this passage) notes the difficulty of keeping the play on the verb and noun senses of yén 言 "talk." Rendering the noun as "words" does spoil the wit. But the question is: what is the "talk" *about?* 15:8 develops 12:24 on friends, here colleagues to persuade. An officer may validly oppose a ruler (14:22), and be joined in that stand by others. Officers have not only a group *ethos*, as before, but a group *interest*. Here is part of the classic charter for elite politics.

└ 15:9. The Master said, The dedicated officer and rín man; he will never seek life by harming rín, and he may even bring about his own death in realizing rín. [15:8]

> And here are the *hazards* of politics, which the rín or principled man accepts.

⌐ 15:12. The Master said, If a man has no worries about what is far off, he will assuredly have troubles that are near at hand. [15:11]

> Note the need to plan, to anticipate, indeed to worry; once the responsibility of the ruler but now that of the managerial elite. It relates strongly to the new virtue of carefulness seen in 2:18 and *7:13[14].

∟ 15:15. The Master said, If he makes his own duties heavy, and asks less of others, he will keep resentment at a distance. [15:14]

> This is the classic leadership maxim: being harder on oneself than on others (4:17, 12:16; a leader should *lead*, not watch). Unlike the paired 15:12, this saying seems to disapprove of the new bureaucratic virtue of delegation. The balancing of new and old in these chapters (as with Gwǎn Jùng in 14:16/17) makes it difficult to give a coherent account of their philosophy, but it does illustrate their strategy of wary, even covert, doctrinal evolution.

⌐ 15:16. The Master said, One who does not say, "What is to be done, what is to be done" – I don't know *what* is to be done with him! [15:15]

> This is a pun, and a pun on an idiom at that (for the same idiom, see 9:24); no successful English rendition can be other than a variant of Waley's solution. The "blunt" students of *8:16[14] (or 9:24) lacked the ethical impulse that would have made them educable. These officers lack the concern for the evil times that might have made them partners in *improving* the evil times.

∟ 15:17. The Master said, Those with whom one can be together all the day long, but who never speak of what is right, or who love to carry out little acts of kindness: they are difficult indeed! [15:16]

> Another type of incorrigible: concerned, but *on a miniature level,* with no interest in larger issues of right. A miniscule impulse is not expected to grow into a larger one; a man's *scope,* in LY 15 political theory, is a fixed quantity.

[C. The Gentleman in Power]

⌐ 15:25. The Master said, In my relationship to others, who have I blamed? Who have I praised? But if there be any I have praised, there is a way they may be tested. This people is the same as that with which the Three Dynasties proceeded along their upright way. [15:24]

> The "others" are contemporary rulers and ministers. Note the empirical test of their efficacy, and the idea of the people as that out of which the state is fashioned. As in *8:9[14] (and in Plato's Laws; Schwartz **World** 308), the people cannot evolve order themselves; their order mirrors the ruler's order. The idea that Syà, Shāng, and Jōu had an identical art of ruling is new (compare 3:21). This *single antiquity* is typical of late 04c linear-integrationist political theory.

∟ 15:26. The Master said, I still go back to when scribes left blanks, and those with horses assigned others to drive them. Now all that is gone. [15:25]

> Scrupulous care of a text one is copying, or a horse one owns. The error is to intrude your own inexpertise: guessing the doubtful character (note the praise of Archivist Yẃ in 15:7) or taking the reins. The Confucians saw themselves in this period as defenders of cultural integrity: keeping the record straight.

Γ 15:27. The Master said, Clever words confuse virtue. If in small things he cannot forbear, then he will confuse great plans. [15:26]

> The clauses are not verbally parallel, and are probably a maxim and a codicil, rather than two maxims. The basic warning is against rhetoric, which confuses the issue being discussed. The codicil warns that specious juniors will not be cured by promoting them (compare 15:16/17). Most sayings in this section bear on personnel procurement and promotion.

L 15:28. The Master said, When the many hate him, one must always look into it; when the many love him, one must always look into it. [15:27]

> This digs a little deeper into 13:24, implying that a unanimous opinion is always suspect (13:24 as good as says that a *non*unanimous opinion is normal). Note that those in charge of the people are being monitored by their superiors.

Γ 15:32. The Master said, The gentleman takes thought for the Way; he does not take thought for his own livelihood. If one farms, subsistence will come in the course of it; if one studies, a stipend will come in the course of it. The gentleman worries about the Way; he does not worry about poverty. [15.31]

> The ABBA parallelism of this saying is unusual, but presents no interpretative difficulties. One can do what *leads* to salary, but not *because* it leads to salary.

L 15:33. The Master said, If your knowledge reaches it, but your r̆n cannot maintain it, then though you may get it, you will surely lose it. If your knowledge reaches it and your r̆n can maintain it, but you approach them without dignity, then the people will not be respectful. If your knowledge reaches it and your r̆n can maintain it and you approach them with dignity, but you motivate them with anything other than propriety, it is still not good enough. [15:32]

> For the elements of the polity, compare 12:7, 13:5, and 14:5. The know-how which gains you the state in the first place may be military (this, as is seen also in the contemporary stratum of the Mencius, is the age of conquest theory), but it can only be maintained with civil virtues. Then comes demeanor (compare 15:5), to evoke an answering sobriety in the people, and last of all propriety in dealing with the people. This may refer to the ordering of rural tasks according to the calendar: a Monthly Ordinances text (Ywè Lìng) probably existed in the 04c; a later version is in HNZ 5 (Major **Heaven** 217f), and a still later one in the Lǐ Jì (LJ 4; Legge **Li** 1/249f). The late 04c is the period when many of the central culture-hero myths were first invented, and the ordering, even the ritualizing, of the annual cycle is part of that trend.

Γ 15:34. The Master said, The gentleman cannot know little things, but can accept great responsibilities. The little man cannot accept great responsibilities, but can know little things. [15:33]

> A more classic view (compare 13:4) of the generalist and the specialist.

L 15:35. The Master said, The relation of the people to r̆n is nearer than to water or fire. As for water or fire, I have seen those who trod on them and died; I have never seen anyone who trod on r̆n and died. [15:34]

> Water is essential to life, and fire to civilization, but neither partakes as closely of the nature of humanity itself as does r̆n (here equivalent to "humaneness").

[D. Official Careers]

⌐ 15:37. The Master said, The gentleman is steadfast but not stubborn. [15:36]

> This retreats from the Níng Wǔdž position of 5:21, in the direction of the flexibility of 14:32, and so helps clarify the choice left hanging in 15:7.

└ 15:38. The Master said, In serving his ruler, he is attentive to his duty and negligent of his livelihood. [15:37]

> Except for the atypically direct mention of livelihood (compare 5:32), this is traditional, reasserting the idea (4:5) that duty and career may be in conflict.

╘ 15:40. The Master said, If their Way is not the same, one cannot take counsel together with them. [15:39]

> Compare 9:30 and the similar but more metaphoric 2:16. All these sayings emphasize the importance of dedication to right, and deprecate any lesser, or more self-interested, consistency. This too is probably anti-Mician.

[E. Envoi: Courtly Practices]

⌐ 15:41. The Master said, The words should reach their goal, and nothing more. [15:40]

> The only virtue of an official communication is *that it communicate.* This has many parallels as a maxim, not excluding Matthew Arnold ("Have something to say and say it as clearly as you can; that is the only secret of style"). This commonsense view of language is perhaps being asserted here in opposition to the contemporary, especially Mician, *analytical* interest in language.

└ 15:42. Preceptor Myěn came for an interview. When he reached the steps, the Master said, Here are the steps. When he reached the mat, the Master said, Here is the mat. When all had been seated, the Master informed him, So-and-so is here; So-and-so is here. When Preceptor Myěn had gone out, Dž-jāng asked, When one is speaking with a Preceptor, is this the way? The Master said, Yes, this is assuredly the way to assist a Preceptor. [15:42]

> The Preceptor (we would say, Conductor) is a blind man, and teaches by rote and repetition, not by book. As custodian of the court musical tradition, he is a person of consequence, and thus deserves respect. It seems that Confucius, in receiving his visitor, guides him up the steps and to his place (sitting-mat), and names those present, none of which is part of the normal LY 10 protocol. Dž-jāng questions this extra solicitude, which seems to sacrifice Confucius's dignity as host, but which is explained as situationally appropriate.
>
> The previous saying deplores excessive ornament in literary style; this one advocates simple directness in reception-protocol. They do not appear to sum up, but rather to form a codicil to, the chapter proper. They partake however of the utilitarian simplicity that is characteristic of the chapter.
>
> Confucius himself continues to be pictured as a person of consequence, who receives guests like a ruler. The word for coming into his presence is jyèn (perhaps better syèn) 見 "appear, be seen [have an interview with]," which occurs with a disciple in 15:2 and with a dignitary in 15:42. It is also the technical term used in the Mencius text for formal audiences with kings.

Interpolations Series A: c0301/c0300

LY 14 and LY 15 are smothered in interpolations which swell them to twice the size of the usual chapter. Why were these not simply put into two separate chapters? We infer (see Appendix 3) that the Analects functioned in this period in part as a record of things said at court. From the overt 15:1/2, and the hint of failed criticism in 15:12, we assume a rupture between the Confucians and the court. It seems from LY 14 that Confucians supported a strong Lǔ cultural initiative, but only a frugal use of force (with emphasis on strategy). They probably supported the apparent Lǔ policy: an alliance with distant Chín against nearby and aggressive Chǔ. In 0302, a new ruler succeeded in Lǔ, posthumously called Wv́n-hóu ("Lord") rather than Wv́n-gūng ("Prince," implying independence), perhaps because of pressure from Chǔ. Chǔ itself was beset in the west by Chín in 0301–0300, perhaps interrupting its eastern expansion. We infer these stages: (1) Chǔ forced Lǔ into underlordship in 0302 at the succession of Wv́n-hóu, and the Confucians left the court. With no court connection, and no court diary, no further chapter modules were begun. (2) Chín distracted Chǔ in 0301–0300, creating a situation in which the Confucians may have hoped to return to power; in this period they added hopeful afterthoughts to their latest court record, LY 15. (3) With renewed Chǔ pressure in 0299 through Dž-jīng's death in 0296, the school added to LY 15, and to LY 13–14, material of a more pessimistic and indeed recriminatory kind.

Whether or not this scenario is precisely correct, there seem to be two distinct groups of LY 14/15 interpolations, and we give them separately here. Immediately below are the 0301–0300 series; the 0299–0296 addenda follow.

For a complete finding list of interpolated passages, see page 329.

Added to LY 15

⌈ *15:3. The Master said, Sž, you regard me as one who has studied a lot and remembers it, do you not? He replied, Yes. Is that wrong? He said, It is wrong. I have one thing by which I string it all together. [15:2]

> Its expression in a body of miscellaneous maxims gave Confucianism a useful evolutionary flexibility, but hampered it in competing against the Micians with their ten principles, which, however ill-assorted (Waley **Three** 164; PB 122), probably had at the time the persuasiveness of any Decalogue. *15:3 asserts that Confucianism has a structure too (its esoteric nature is implied by the use of the sacral pronoun yw 予 "I," see 3:8), and tops the Micians with a *unitary* principle (compare 13:15; for its content, see *15:24[15a]). Interpolation, of which art Dž-jīng was a bold practitioner, lets one impose this kind of unity on the past. The unity here is *conceptual*: all sayings are ultimately one doctrine. This philosophic rigor, like the cosmic unity of 2:1 and the historiographic unity of 15:25, attests something like a scientific mindset in this period.

∟ *15:4. The Master said, Yóu, those who know virtue are few. [15:3]

> Notice the pairing: two sayings addressed to disciples (Dž-gùng and Dž-lù), one defending the home school, and the other disparaging the competition. Though thematically intrusive as placed in LY 15, this pair fits in smoothly between the earlier pairs; *formally*, Dž-jīng is not trashing his own chapter.

⌐ *15:10. Dž-gùng asked about being rʹn. The Master said, If an artisan wants to do his job well, he must first sharpen his tools. When dwelling in some country, serve the worthy among its dignitaries; befriend the rʹn among its officers. [15:9]

> This makes explicit a practical point about friends which was less obvious in earlier sayings (12:24): friends, and indeed associations too high-ranking for friendship ("serve" implies relationships of sponsorship and clientship at the level of real power), are to be cultivated for the purpose of bringing about the right political result, that result being the aim, or agenda, or definition, of rʹn.

∟ *15:11. Yén Ywæn asked about running a state. The Master said, Follow the calendar of Syà, ride in the carriage of Yīn, wear the garments of Jōu. For music, the Sháu and Wǔ. Get rid of the songs of Jʋ̀ng and banish flatterers: the songs of Jʋ̀ng are lewd, and flatterers are dangerous. [15:10]

> This summarizes earlier recommendations: the Three Dynasties (3:21; for the Babylonian chariot of Yīn, see Shaughnessy **Chariot**) and the old court dances (3:25); the ritual concept of the state is now established. Except in 6:16, the Analects opposes artful talkers, now including the logic-wielding Micians.
>
> We identify the Jʋ̀ng songs with the Jʋ̀ng folk-poems of Shī 75–96. Dž-syà's idea of the Shī, visible in the DJ (Legge **Ch'un** 549f), is that it documents the culture of the several states, to predict which would succeed politically. The Analects sees the Shī as moral exempla, meant to be imitated. Is Shī 87, they ask, with its floozyish inconstancy, what you want your daughter to be like?

> > If you love me tenderly,
> > Lift your robe and cross the Dzv̄n;
> > If you love me not at all,
> > Are you then the only one?
> >   – The craziest of crazy lads, is all you are!
> > If you love me tenderly,
> > Lift your robe and cross the Wàı;
> > If you love me not at all,
> > Are you then the only guy?
> >   –The craziest of crazy lads, is all you are!

⌐ *15:23. The Master said, A gentleman does not promote a man because of his sayings, or reject a saying because of the man. [15:22]

> That judgements of worth should be based on more than words goes back to the 05c (5:10b); the plea that *advice* should also stand on its merits is new.

∟ *15:24. Dž-gùng asked, is there one saying that one can put in practice in all circumstances? The Master said, That would be empathy, would it not? What he himself does not want, let him not do it to others. [15:23]

> The Golden Rule from 12:2 is here given a name (shù 恕 "empathy," also rendered "reciprocity") and a status as a central saying, in line with the promise of *15:3 (compare the later *4:15[1]). The pairing with *15:23 hints that this saying was liable to rejection because of its source (probably non-Confucian; see 5:12n). For the analogous concept in contemporary Micianism (which school however never calls it by the name shù), see MZ 16 (Mei **Ethical** 90). Its acceptance here shows the Lǔ Confucians, fortified by the *15:23 principle, in an assimilating as well as a systematizing mood.

⌐ *15:29. The Master said, A man can broaden a Way; it is not the Way that broadens a man. [15:28]

> This is probably a swipe at the Dàuists, whose ineffable Way was certainly impressive to the Lǔ government, offering, as it seemed to do, a method by which the individual, or the small state, could almost magically become more effective than they really were. Dàuism is the power politics of the powerless.

L *15:31. The Master said, I once went all day without eating, and all night without sleeping, in order to think. I gained nothing. It is not as good as studying. [15:30]

> Mencius, easily the most visible Confucian of his day, was not someone the Lǔ group cared to attack publicly. He had been (if we credit the seeming personal reminiscence in MC 2A2) himself an adherent of the Lǔ meditationist group whose text was the DDJ, and whose crossover hero was the reflective Yén Hwéi (note the wary treatment of Hwéi in MC 2A2). Dž-jīng's 2:15 had accepted meditation as a complementary way of knowledge, and as late as 15:5 he even accepted the Dáuist idea of the ruler. Now, with Mencius only recently dead, comes the break. Here and in the paired *15:29, the Dàuist art of meditation is rejected. Like the systematic pulling together of earlier sayings, above, this cleansing of tradition was surely meant to clarify and strengthen Confucianism. Compare *13:12 and *14:1b, immediately below.

Interpolations Series B: c0299/c0296

See the prefatory note to the preceding group of interpolations. These are the later, more bitter additions which we assume Dž-jīng made to LY 14–15 after the hope of Confucian return to court prominence had proved vain, and regrets and recriminations, some of them aimed at the ruler, were in order.

Added to LY 13

*13:7. The Master said, The governments of Lǔ and Wèi are still brothers. [13:7]

> They had been granted as territories to literal brothers, in early Jōu times. Since Wèi by this time has been reduced by Ngwèi to almost zero territory, this may be a wry comment on the near-extinction of Lǔ sovereignty by Chǔ.

*13:12. The Master said, If there were one who could be a King, it would surely be only a generation until everyone was rv́n. [13:12]

> A complaint of the Lǔ ruler, in the terms used by Mencius to Tv́ng Wv́n-gūng (MC 1B12; see page 116, above), perhaps inserted in LY 13 in his memory.

Added to LY 14

*14:1b. "Overcoming pride, resentment, and desire so that they no longer occur: can this be regarded as rv́n?" The Master said, It can be regarded as difficult. As for its being rv́n, I wouldn't know. [14:2]

> This rejects the Dàuist suppression of desire to achieve special mental states. It follows on *15:29/31, in the previous group, but goes beyond them to dismantle the use of the Dàuist term "overcome," used in 12:1. Confucianism is not merely *distancing itself* from a rival; it is *dismantling part of its former self*.

*14:4. The Master said, Those with virtue will always have something to say, but those with things to say are not always virtuous. Those with rv́n are always brave, but those who do brave things are not always rv́n. [14:5]

> The old contrast between virtue and well-spokenness, to which is added a new link between rv́n and courage. Courage has been revived as a moral quality.

*14:6. The Master said, A gentleman who was *not* also rv́n: such things have been. But there never was a little man who *was* rv́n. [14:7]

> An admission (we Confucians have had our share of failures) and a complaint (but the nobodies who took our places at court lacked our special qualities).

*14:10. The Master said, To be poor and without resentment is difficult. To be rich and without pride is easy. [14:11]

> The virtues of success are disparaged, and those of failure are extolled.

*14:20. The Master said, If his words are incautious, he will find it difficult to carry them out. [14:21]

> Legge instances *4:22[2], with which we cannot but agree, since we ascribe both sayings to Dž-jīng. The advice is obvious; perhaps the emotional point of it is to justify an advocacy which, in retrospect, may have seemed *too* cautious.

*14:23. The Master said, The gentleman is successful at a high level; the little man is successful at a low level. [14:24]

> This can be read as a division-of-labor generalism, and such is certainly its value for later Confucianism; the Mencian school's classic formulation is in MC 3A4 (mid 03c). In the historical context we assume for it, it can also be read as a sour-grapes retrospection, impugning the quality of successful rivals.

⌐ *14:24. The Master said, The studies of the ancients were for themselves; the studies of the moderns are for others. [14:25]

> We follow the commentators in taking this as critical of the moderns: the ancients studied to improve themselves *to be worthy of public service*, whereas the moderns study *to gain the good opinion of others*. This criticism may have in view the Mician branch school in Lŭ, which by this period was turning out students of its own; see MZ 46:5 (Mei **Ethical** 214) and note its pro-Chŭ focus.

∟ *14:25. Chyẃ Bwó-yẁ sent a messenger to Confucius. Confucius sat down with him, and inquired of him, How is your Respected Master doing? He replied, My Respected Master wishes to reduce the number of his errors, but has not yet been able to. When the messenger went out, the Master said, This is a messenger? This is a messenger? [14:26]

> It is improper (compare *7:31[3]) to criticize one's leader before others. We thus agree with Waley against Legge that Confucius's final remark is disapproving. Legge assumes that Bwó-yẁ was a disciple of Confucius, but though he has his place in the modern Temple of Confucius, 15:7 does not treat him so, and the protocol of *14:25 (Confucius is called Kŭngdž in the presence of his envoy) makes him a respected superior. If he were a disciple, Confucius's praise of the messenger's candor would be praise for Bwó-yẁ's wish to improve himself, and the passage would be an incitement to self-cultivation. Since he is not, *14:25, like the paired *14:24, is a sarcastic denunciation of the vulgar ways of the age.

⌐ *14:26a. The Master said, If he does not occupy the position, he does not take council for the policies. [14:27]

> This is identical with *8:14[14], and is probably just an idea Dž-jīng used twice. Of the two paired sayings, *14:26b, following, is the more consecutive.

└ *14:26b. Dzv̄ngdž said, The gentleman's thoughts do not go beyond his own responsibilities. [14:28]

> Dzv̄ngdž had been on Dž-jīng's mind since he wrote the LY 8 interpolations. This is not yet the filial paragon Dzv̄ngdž of LY 1 (the next later chapter), and thus seems to belong here. In that context, the pair of sayings may perhaps be validly read as an unemployed but worthy speaker disdaining comment on the nonentities who do at the moment hold office, rather in the manner of 13:14, composed either by the young Dž-jīng or with his knowledge during his minority. We noted that 13:14 may be anti-Mician, and that suggestion seems not less appropriate here. The very fastidiousness and punctilio of the bystander somehow condemn the officeholder.

⌐ *14:27. The Master said, The gentleman is ashamed to have his words run beyond his deeds. [14:29]

> Another maxim, echoing *14:10 above, and perhaps, like it, critical of those in power, though the pairing here suggests a different nuance. See next.

└ *14:28. The Master said, The ways of the gentleman are three, and I am not capable of them. The rv́n man is never anxious, the wise man is never in doubt, the brave man is never afraid. Dž-gùng said, This is our Respected Master's own Way! [14:30]

> The three "ways" are identical with those of 9:29, but the Master's confession of inadequacy is new. This and *14:27 pair readily enough, as respectively praising and exemplifying understatement. As part of this group of resentful sayings, they may be a justification for earlier cautious posture in office, and a balancing praise of "Confucius's" own virtues; that is, a self-criticism by the head of the LY 15 school, Dž-jīng, amounting in the end to a self-vindication.

⌐ *14:29. Dž-gùng liked to compare himself with others. The Master said, Sż must certainly be a worthy man. I myself have not the time. [14:31]

> An echo of the Dž-gùng criticisms in LY 5, and, like the next, nostalgic.

└ *14:30. The Master said, He does not worry about others not knowing him; he worries about whether he is capable. [14:32]

> An echo of the real Confucius's 4:14. Having in the previous pair found his own conduct defensible and his character admirable, Dž-jīng now turns to the question of recriminations, deploring them in *14:29, and here evoking the old feudal principle that one is *not responsible for outcomes*. As head of a failed court faction, Dž-jīng was very much in Confucius's own historic position.

┕ *14:31. The Master said, He does not anticipate betrayal; he does not assume infidelity. Compared to one who knew it all beforehand, is he not worthier? [14:33]

> Like *14:27, a justification of a policy which, by hindsight, might have been wiser. But how virtuous is such cynical wisdom? Compare Churchill's verdict on Chamberlain (**Storm** 325–326 "good faith," **Hour** 550–551 "worthy").

⌐ *14:33. The Master said, A Jì is not praised for its strength; it is praised for its character. [14:35]

> Jì seems to be the name of an individual horse. Late Hàn commentaries, and the Shwō-wv́n dictionary, agree, and add that Jì could go "a thousand leagues a day" (300 American miles: a good Arabian can negotiate with style the modern endurance race of 100 miles; 300 miles is virtually impossible). Horses bred for strength are no good for distance. The gentleman is not to be prized for his utility in doing the heavy chores (compare 2:12), but for his "heart" ("character" or dv́ 德, elsewhere "virtue") that lets him stay the long course. Like the paired *14:35, this a complaint of being wrongly used at court.

> A chariot horse good for a thousand leagues would be ineffective if yoked with one good for five hundred leagues. "Jì" thus seems to be a rider's mount, not a charioteer's horse. If so (compare JGT #92, translated in Crump Ts'e 100 in the latter sense), here is another hint of the new art of riding astride.

L *14:35. The Master said, No one knows me, do they. Dž-gùng said, Why is it that no one knows the Master? The Master said, I do not resent Heaven; I do not fault men. I study at a humble level, that I may succeed at a high level. The one who knows me: will it not be Heaven? [14:37]

> "Knows," here and in several of the above sayings, is "recognizes the ability of." The passage is a rumination on failure, balanced by a sense of compensatory recognition higher up. It has the metaphysics if not the Heavenly-sponsorship assurance of 9:5. The Lǔ court may have failed to recognize the value of the Confucian group, but the Confucians feel sure they will be vindicated.

Added to LY 15

⌐ *15:13. The Master said, It is all over! I have not seen anyone who loves virtue as much as he loves beauty. [15:12]

> The almost identical 9:18 was a criticism of unworthy student material. This seems, in the context of the stratum, to be instead a criticism of the ruler of Lǔ, for disdaining substantial virtues and prizing instead more superficial qualities, like those of the glib Micians and mystical Dàuists who were currently in favor.

L *15:14. The Master said, Dzàng Wv́n-jùng was a stealer of positions, was he not? He knew the worth of Lyǒusyà Hwèi but would not take his stand with him. [15:13]

> A jibe at Lǔ courtiers for favoring the like-minded. Preferring compatibility to quality is a classic personnel problem (Caplow **Marketplace** 107, 137–139); here (compare Parkinson **Law** 80–81) is the classic diagnosis.

⌐ *15:19. The Master said, The gentleman takes it as a fault if he is incapable of something; he does not take it as a fault if others do not know him. [15:18]

> Similar, except for its verb (here, "regard as a fault"), to *14:30, opposite.

L *15:20. The Master said, The gentleman is concerned lest he leave the world when his reputation is not yet established. [15:19]

> Along with the implied duty to contribute to the public good, this evokes 4:5 by acknowledging the only allowable ambition of the gentleman: not power, but the chance to make a name for himself in his own lifetime.

⌐ *15:21. The Master said, The gentleman seeks it in himself; the small man seeks it in others. [15:20]

Similar to 15:15, in the main chapter, but with a possible further nuance, which might offer guidance to the disappointed disciples: the small man requires ratification of worth in the approval of others; the gentleman is self-sufficient in his sense of worth. We might consider here not only the classic Dzv̄ngdzian statement 8:3, but its contemporary update in 12:4.

L *15:22. The Master said, The gentleman strives, but he does not contend; he associates, but he is not partisan. [15:21]

By keeping principle first in his mind, he avoids the smaller temptations to *jealousy* of colleagues, and also to excessive *solidarity* with colleagues. These maxims can be seen in context as criticisms of the Lǔ courtiers for their mutual validation (*15:21) and contentious partisanship (*15:22).

Ŀ *15:30. The Master said, To make a mistake and not change: this is what one calls making a mistake. [15:29].

On its face, a mere intensification of part of 9:25; in context, a complaint of the Lǔ government for not correcting its error in excluding the Confucians.

Reflections

The reader should by now have a sense of the complex interplay, in this period, between competing court factions and their ideologies. The span from c0325 through c0300, which ends (in the Analects) with LY 15, is the Hundred Schools phase of Chinese intellectual history, a high point comparable in vigor, variety, and significance to the Athenian one before and after Socrates.

The sort of tact required in the fruitful comparison of cultures is one of the 72 needful things not taught in schools, but with due caution the reader may note some striking similarities between early Greece and early China. One is that both are characterized by a *multiple polity*, literally at war with itself (one scholarly volume is titled The Warring States of Greece). Greek public debate had a background of fluid alliances and military threats. War has an urgency, a way of concentrating human attention, that is hard to replicate in softer times. William James sought its moral equivalent (Kallen **James** 341–347), though he admits that his solution runs to Tolstoyan sentimentality. From the viewpoint of world philosophy, we must put this question among the unsolved.

It is notable that LY 14–15 not only refine LY 12–13, but as their troubles increase, revisit the classic LY 4–9 as well. And it is touching that, having left the Lǔ court over their antiwar stand (15:1), the Confucians in their isolation reasserted the virtue of courage (15:8/9, *14:4[15]). Many Confucians in later centuries abundantly showed this physical courage in pursuit of ethical ideals.

It is not so surprising that the Confucians with their military origins evolved into ceremonialists and managers; note the parallel of the Japanese samurai under Tokugawa peace (1615–1867) and Meiji internationalism (1868–1912). A reflective reader will find many resonances in such a work as Fukuzawa's **Autobiography**. Some upper samurai, like the Analects Confucians, went into administration; some lower ones (Fukuzawa's own group) drifted into trade.

Fukuzawa's book gives us the cultural feel of such a transition. His father's contempt for money, mingled with his responsibility as overseer of his lord's treasury (p1–2), has the same tension we saw in LY 5. And the father's anger upon finding that his children were being taught multiplication, a tool of the vulgar merchants, has exactly the tone of classic disdain with which 13:20 regards the absurd unit-conversions of the treasury scriveners of Lǔ.

Among the things the Analects is trying to work out in this period are the nature of rulership and the proper relation between the ruler and the ministers (or the bureaucracy). There is also much interest in how the bureaucracy works: in running things. One stimulus to this was probably the increasing size of government, with the department heads needing to delegate, supervise, and plan ahead. Study of military procurement, or of strategy as a function of military procurement, in World War 2, will show that these skills are vital to national survival, and thus perhaps valuable. If philosophy is knowing how to live life well, the art of managing public life belongs somewhere in the mix.

It does not belong to "philosophy" as defined by modern departments of that name. Western philosophy, with its quaint preoccupation with ontology, epistemology, and logic, is largely a residue of religious questions involving statements about the existence of, knowledge of, and valid deductions about, the ultimately unknowable. The tradition represented by the Analects has no enduring interest in any of this. It spends time instead on such practical matters as how to get along in office, how to be in charge of things effectively, how to lead, how to wait, how to dare. For light on these subjects, vital for individual success and national survival, the student of Western philosophy waits in vain.

The efforts of Lǔ thinkers in the Hundred Schools days went partly into opposing each other. So what emerged from all this? Were there winners? Metzger **Roots** 112 notes that *society* was the winner; that both the Confucians and the Micians contributed to the collective institutional expertise which preserved the Chinese Empire, despite the folly of Chinese Emperors (14:19), for more than two thousand years.

It is tempting to suggest that the student make an outline of the Confucian idea of the state as of LY 15, as a way of updating a project mentioned in 9r. But it is difficult to say what data should be included. We can see, most easily in the group of revisionist interpolations above, how closely balanced was the Lǔ Confucian school between acceptance and rejection of given ideas, such as that of meditation and its implications for government. The pairs of pro and con statements which are a characteristic of Analects rhetoric (the classic case is 14:16/17) are in our view not mere ambivalence; they reflect the vagueness of the boundary, *at the time*, between hostile ideas and adaptable ideas. And the classic ideas of the school *were still there*, in the earlier Analects chapters to which, as is proved by the fact that it was worth interpolating in them, the school still referred. Keeping its doctrinal identity intact, while at the same time keeping its controversial interface viable, was an impossible challenge. We need not be surprised if the Analects repeats itself, and contradicts itself, and then *homogenizes* itself, as part of the process of extending itself in time.

For all the effort that went into these kinds of boundary maintenance, we find in the end that Dž-jīng does not, in his final interpolations, go much beyond oscillating on familiar ground. For a breakthrough into new territory, we will have to turn to his son and successor Dž-gāu, in LY 1.

Jade Hair Ornament (see LY 1:13)

Height 6·6 cm (2·6 in). 04/03c. Courtesy Freer Gallery of Art (30·28)

1

c0294

Dž-jīng died at 56 in c0295, and his son Dž-gāu succeeded him in c0294. It probably seemed, at that time, that the loss of court influence was permanent. As the LY 15 interpolations show, Dž-jīng had both scolded and encouraged the members, but without improving their morale. Dž-gāu came to the rescue by redefining the school and the Confucian enterprise, displacing the goal of state service on which its thoughts and efforts had previously been focused.

In its place, the chapter offers what one might call a citizen ethic, which holds that virtue is valuable even **without** public service. Learning (1:1, 1:4), the family (1:2, 1:6, 1:11), and the public worth of family piety (1:2, 1:9) are its chief points; it is here that the value system noted by Lattimore **Frontiers** 398 as postfeudal actually first appears. It was to be central, a millennium later, in the emergence of neo-Confucianism. Here, however, it is all new, and the chapter begins by reassuring those to whom the new way must at first have seemed insufficient and unsatisfying.

LY 1 lacks thematic divisions; it is a single continuous dialogue between old and new ideas. The numbering of passages is identical in the Legge text.

⌐ 1:1. The Master said, To learn and in due time rehearse it: is this not also pleasurable? To have friends coming from far places: is this not also delightful? If others do not recognize him but he is not disheartened, is he not also a gentleman?

> This "also" (acknowledging that these are not the standard pleasures of the gentleman) invites comparison with 4:1, once the head of the text, with its hope of recognition. Here, learning is its own end. Notwithstanding Kennedy **Fenollosa** 462, learning is here rote memorization and repetition: not "putting into practice" (sỳing 行) but syí 習, the musician's "practice," the "rehearse" of the translation. Discussion with colleagues from distant states such as Chí must have been a solace in the absence of a current political role in Lǔ.
>
> 1:1 is now the first Analects saying learned by students, and thus the best remembered. Even today, a traveler in Japan can elicit a certain response by reciting it in the traditional "kambun" reading: "Shi iwaku, Manabite, toki ni kore o narau, mata ["also"] yorokobashikarazu ya? Tomo ari, empō yori kitaru, mata tanoshikarazu ya? Hito shirazu shite, ikarazu, mata kunshi narazu ya?"

∟ 1:2. Yŏudž said, One whose deportment is filial and fraternal but loves to oppose his superiors, is rare. One who does not love to oppose his superiors but does love to foment disorder, has never existed. The gentleman works on the basis; when the basis is set, then the Way comes to exist. Filiality and fraternity are the basis of rýn, are they not?

> Yŏu Rwò, who first appeared in 12:9, is here quoted as Yŏudž "Master Yŏu," the headship role we infer he had in LY 6. He extends the analytical approach, applied in 3:4 to ritual, not to virtues, but to something larger – the way in which private and individual virtues underlie the public Way, the ideal social order. Being barred from *government* service, the Confucians here take on a duty of *public* service.

⌐ 1:3. The Master said, Artful words and an impressive appearance: seldom are they rv́n.

Like 1:2, this saying centers on rv́n, but returns to a sense of it that Confucius (see 4:8) would have recognized. The exact words are from 5:25; they will recur in 17:15. Fittingly, "Confucius" is here again the speaker. The saying in context probably expresses contempt for those who, more fortunate than the isolated Confucians, have the ear of the Prince of Lǔ. Like the structurally parallel saying 4:3, it evokes the faculty of disliking.

└ 1:4. Dzv̄ngdž said, I daily examine myself in three ways. In planning on behalf of others, have I been disloyal? In associating with friends, have I been unfaithful? What has been transmitted to me, have I not rehearsed?

The strenuously self-critical Dzv̄ngdž of 8:3 is a superb choice as the speaker of this self-examination saying. The modest jūng/syìn virtues (an important trait of this chapter is that it exalts qualities earlier identified as ordinary) appeared in the self-cultivation saying 5:28. The novelty comes at the end, where the 5:28 verb sywé/syàu 學 "learn by imitation" becomes "learn by memorizing texts." The verb syí 習 ("practice" as distinct from "performance") appeared in passing in 1:1, but here it forms the crux, and indeed the climax, of the saying. Book memorization is not *preparatory* to action, it is itself a sufficing action.

⌐ 1:6. The Master said, A student when at home should be filial, when away from home should be fraternal. He should be circumspect but faithful, should love all the multitude but be intimate only with the rv́n. If after doing this he has any strength left over, he can use that to study culture.

Here, *both members* of the rù/chū 入 / 出 home/away dichotomy are limited to the family virtues of 1:2, respect for parents and deference to elder brothers (compare 9:16, where "away" is public versus domestic life). Reinforcing this, the subject is dìdž "disciple," not jyv̄ndž "gentleman." These students are destined for roles not in government but in society. The Lǔ group, being out of power, was seemingly marketing Confucianism to a wider audience. Note again, in 1:4 above, that the daily ethical checklist included no public conduct. In addition, 1:6 echoes the classic 7:6 on arts as recreation, and the recent 12:3 (glossed as a lower virtue by 13:20) on caution in making promises, and *4:22[2], by its LY 4 position a classic saying ever since its interpolation in c0317.

└ 1:7. Dž-syà said, He sees the worthy as worthy; he makes light of beauty. If in serving father and mother he can exhaust his strength; if in serving his ruler he can bring all his faculties to bear; if in associating with friends he always keeps his word – though one might say he has not "studied," I would certainly call him a scholar.

Yì sv̀ 易 色 in the first clause can mean "change countenance," or like 9:18 and *15:13[15] it can be read "as much as [others value] beauty." With Durrant **Translating** 119 (citing Chv́n Dzǔ-fàn, c1750), we construe in parallel clauses VO/VO (note the putative verb shift "worthy > regard as worthy"). The energy of desire is *rechanneled into* (not merely equaled by) the emulation of virtue.

The "I" here (wú 吾; compare wǒ 我 in 4:6) is unemphatic, but the logic of the saying itself implies a contrast. Study (personal self-cultivation) is here separated from a "scholarship" which was perhaps identified with the court; compare the paired 1:6 and the unifying final saying 1:15.

⌐ 1:8. The Master said, If he is not solid, he will not be held in awe; if he studies, he will not be rigid. Let him put first loyalty and fidelity, let him not make friends of those who are not at the same level as himself, and if he makes a mistake, then let him not be afraid to change it.

> Commentators differ (Lyóu **Jv̀ng-yì**) over whether gù 固 is positive or negative. The fact that all Analects uses with ethical nuances are negative seems to decide the matter. For the flexible virtue of the 03c, with its dislike of rigidity, see 9:4[18]. Chan **Source** 20 notes that the friendship maxim in the second part conflicts with 8:5 on learning from inferiors. This part is quoted almost exactly from the equally early 9:25, where it contrasts with 8:5 as official advice versus self-cultivation advice. In the self-cultivational context of LY 1, it recommends not perfection (*no* mistakes), but improvement (learning *from* mistakes).

> The Japanese kambun equivalent of the last phrase (Yoshikawa **Rongo** 1/12, 1/295) is: "ayamateba, sunawachi aratamuru ni *habakaru koto nakare*." This habakaru koto nakare, "let him not be afraid," was the occasion of the most hilarious misfired allusion in all Oriental literature. The Japanese court lady Sei Shōnagon tells in §45 of her Pillow Book how she once quoted LY 1:8 ("do not be afraid . . . "), c998, to a visitor, Yukinari, expecting him to complete the quotation and ". . . change" [his conduct]. Instead, he took "do not be afraid" as an invitation to intimacy (Waley **Pillow** 65, Morris **Pillow** 1/54, Kaneko **Makura** 271). Such are the hazards of erudition in exotic languages.

└ 1:9. Dzv̄ngdž said, When concern for the departed continues until they are far away, the virtue of the people will have become substantial.

> The idea here is lingering rather than perfunctory funerary observances. The Confucians at this time were advocating a protracted mourning period, reaching into the third year, which had for some time been observed at court. A dispute developed with the Micians (see 17:19), who held that the practice was wasteful and untraditional; as late as MC 3A2 (mid 03c) it was argued in Tv̀ng that their kinsmen, the earlier rulers of Lǔ, had not practiced it.

> This passage makes Dzv̄ngdž a spokesman for filial piety, a role at odds with the Dzv̄ngdž of LY 8 but close to the emblematic Dzv̄ngdž of later legend (Waley **Analects** 20; Hsiao **Role**). This marks a stage in his evolving myth.

⌐ 1:11. The Master said, When his father is living, watch his intentions; when his father is deceased, watch his actions. If for three years he has not changed from the ways of his father, he can be called filial.

> This, like 1:6, features the Master as speaker, and draws on a saying added by Dž-jīng to LY 4 (*4:20[2]). The new context is a domestic reduction of the official skill (2:10) of judging character by actions. Refraining from change for three years shows a seemly, internalized submission to the father's ways during the psychological "distancing" process after his death.

└ 1:13. Yŏudž said, If his promises are close to what is right, his word can be relied on. If his respect is close to propriety, he will avoid shame and disgrace. If he marries one who has not wronged her own kin, she can be part of his clan.

> Not one promise, but a pattern of reliability. A girl (following Waley) who is devoted to her own clan can best become a dutiful member of another clan. 1:13 (compare 14:18) is the first mention of a *specifically* feminine virtue.

[Envoi: Education]

⌐ 1:14. The Master said, If a gentleman in his eating does not seek to be filled and in his dwelling does not seek comfort, if he is assiduous in deed and cautious in word, if he associates with those who possess the Way and so is corrected by them, he can be said to love learning.

As in the final sections of LY 4–6, we end with the self-improvement idea in its empirical version: things that any sincere learner-from-experience can master.

∟ 1:15. Dž-gùng said, "Poor but does not flatter, rich but does not sneer" – how would that do? The Master said, It would do. But it is not as good as "Poor but happy, rich but loving propriety." Dž-gùng said, The Poem says, "As though cut, as though ground, as though smoothed, as though polished" – Is this what it means? The Master said, Sž can at last be talked with about the Poetry: I tell him things in terms of the past, and he knows what is to come.

The praise of skill in inference goes back to 7:8, the ideal of happiness (rather than mere lack of complaint) in poverty to 6:11, and the Shr̄ analysis to 3:8, where the questioner is Dž-syà rather than Dž-gùng. This passage, like the paired 1:14, is thus a mosaic of familiar exhortations to practical virtue.

It contrasts with 1:14 in balancing empirical ethics with the higher life: the ethics of wealth, and the greater sophistications of literary exposition. The moral of the quote from Shr̄ 55 seems to be the idea of a gradual approach (here, in jade-working) to perfection. Like 1:14, it enjoins continuous effort, but in the different context of wealth and refinement.

Together, these sayings conclude the chapter by defining a sphere of action that may be excluded from the previous goal of high government office, but retains all the validity, and the cultural elegance, of the court ethic.

Interpolations

Dž-jīng, who came to the headship as a youth, became the master interpolator: who *wrote* more of the text, and *interpolated* more into it, than anybody else. Counting as his the chapters (LY 12–13) in which he may have had outside assistance, we find him to have been responsible for 120 main sayings and 67 interpolations, a total of 187, or 35% of the 530 sayings into which we divide the text. Especially in his last years, when he was adding to his own LY 14–15, he will have been watched by his heir Dž-gāu. The concept of interpolating sayings (and, with LY 2, even preposing chapters) will thus have been familiar to Dž-gāu. In terms of content, Dž-gāu obeys his own rule in 1:11 (derived from his father's *4:20²) by following his father's opening (see LY 2) toward domestic virtue. But Dž-gāu's style, as a writer and interpolator, is distinctive. His own LY 1 varies in several ways (briefer, and lacking a fourfold thematic division) from what we may call the standard Analects chapter. His interpolations are also distinctive: whereas the late Dž-jīng liked to interpolate paired sayings, Dž-gāu, in what is plausibly assignable to him, preferred singles. The true filial piety (see *4:20², and compare LY 9 vis-à-vis LY 7) is not fixity, but change with a meaningful relation to precedent.

For a complete finding list of interpolated passages, see page 329.

Added to LY 4

It was probably still recognized in the school that LY 4 was the original, literally Confucian, chapter. Dž-gāu may well have known that it was his father who had extended LY 4 to the standard 24 sayings. It will not have been unfilial for Dž-gāu to have further added to LY 4 (the example of augmenting Dž-jīng's material had been set by Dž-jīng himself), but as usual, his style is different. Where Dž-jīng had so closely imitated the spare style of the original that the present authors were deceived by his LY 4 addenda until 15 October 1993, and even then only detected them by close linguistic analysis, Dž-gāu here brings his own style, and his predilection for disciple sayings, into his interpolations.

*4:15. The Master said, Shv̄m! My Way: by one thing I link it together. Dzv̄ngdž said, Yes. The Master went out, and the disciples asked, What did he mean? Dzv̄ngdž said, Our Respected Master's Way is simply loyalty and empathy. [4:15]

> This respectfully combines Dž-jīng's claim of an underlying doctrinal unity (see *15:3[15a]) with his own doctrine of empathy (see *15:24[15a]).

*4:26. Dž-yóu said, If in serving his prince he is accusatory, he will be disgraced. If with friends he is accusatory, he will become estranged from them. [4:26]

> The basic maxim of low-profile conduct. Accusation (shù 數, "telling off" the mistakes of another) will alienate both superiors and associates. Notice the dual focus both here (loyalty and empathy) and in *4:15 (superiors and associates).

Added to LY 5

*5:26. Yén Ywǣn and Jì-lù were in attendance. The Master said, Why does not each of you tell your wish? Dž-lù said, I should like carriage and horse, and light mantles to wear, to share them with my friends, and not mind if they ruined them. Yén Ywǣn said, I should like not to parade my good deeds, or to cause others trouble. Dž-lù said, I should like to hear the Master's wish. The Master said, The old, I would comfort; friends, I would trust; the young, I would cherish. [5:25].

> Jì-lù (Lù the Youngest) and Dž-lù (with Dž- "Young Master" replacing the birth-sequence prefix) are equivalent. The random alternation here was noted by Tswēi Shù as a feature of the less organized LY 16–20. Dž-lù wants wealth enough not to mind if his rowdy friends spoil something valuable. Virtuous Yén Hwéi jabs at Dž-lù's wish to "parade his good deeds" and himself wishes to be "no trouble to others" (his parents; see 2:6). This filiality wins the round. Dž-lù, making a last try, asks the Master's wish. The answer is a masterpiece of reconciliation. He rebukes Yén Hwéi (better than mere untroublesomeness is a *positive* wish to care for parents). He acknowledges Dž-lù (it is *right* to trust one's friends). Having thus redressed the balance, he expresses his affection for both: "cherish the young (and guide them in improving)." It is very touching. It also symbolically resolves the rivalry between action and meditation.
>
> This "sweet" Confucius (see also *11:24[1], below) is highly attractive to modern readers; see the tribute in Lin **Wisdom** 28–31, which is based also on Lǐ Jì anecdotes from the same 03c as LY 1 and its interpolations. In many ways, including the psychological, the 03c comes across to later posterity as very familiar territory indeed (compare Waley **Three** 12, PB [ix]).

Added to LY 9

LY 9 is another chapter which, as the above notes have shown, Dž-gāu paid particular attention to. As with LY 4, he may also have added to it:

*9:30b.   Flowers of the cherry-tree:
                           Daintily their petals sway;
                           How do I not think of you?
                           But your home is far away.

The Master said, He did not really think of her. If he had, what "far away" would there have been? [9:30]

> This poem, not now in the Shŕ but perhaps from the lost "White Flowers," is a courtship-song, or as Confucius remarks, an excuse-for-noncourtship song. The element of sympathy for the female half of courtship incidents is very strong in the Shŕ, but this is the first time it has been incorporated into the Analects; it thus relates in terms of ideological focus to Dž-gāu's 1:13.

Added to LY 11

*11:24. Dž-lù, Dzvng Syī, Rǎn Yóu, and Gūngsyī Hwá were sitting in attendance. The Master said, You consider me as a day older than you, but don't so consider me. As you are at leisure, you say, They don't know me. But if someone *did* know you, what would you? Dž-lù, taking the lead, answered, A thousand-chariot state, situated between larger states: add to that military maneuvers, in consequence of which it was suffering famine; if Yóu ran it, in three years it could be made to have courage, and to know what to do. Our Respected Master smiled at him. Chyóu, what about you? He answered, An area of sixty or seventy, or fifty or sixty: if Chyóu ran it, in three years it could be made to have enough populace. As to the rituals and music, I would rely on a gentleman. Chŕ, what about you? He answered, I do not say I would be capable of it, but I should like to study to that end. The services in the ancestral shrine, such as diplomatic conferences: dressed in robe and cap, I should like to be a junior minister at them. Dyěn, what about you? His thrumming of his psaltery grew faint, and as it echoed away, he put the psaltery aside and rose. He replied, It is different from the choices of the other three. The Master said, What is the harm? It is just each telling his wish. He said, At the end of spring, when the spring clothes have been finished, with capped youths five or six, and boys six or seven, to go swimming in the Yí, take the air by the dance platform, and go home singing. Our Respected Master sighed deeply and said, I am with Dyěn.

When the other three had gone, Dzvng Syī stayed behind. Dzvng Syī said, Now, what was it about the words of the other three? The Master said, It was just each telling his wish; that was all. He said, Why did the Respected Master smile at Yóu? The Master said, One runs a country by propriety. His words were not deferential, so I smiled at him. [He asked], Then Chyóu did not want a state? [He answered], When did you see an area of sixty or seventy, or fifty or sixty, that was not a state? [He asked],Then Chŕ did not want a state? [He answered],The conference at the ancestral shrine: if it does not involve the Lords, then what? And if Chŕ were officiating in a *junior* capacity, who could officiate in a *senior* capacity? [11:25]

The disciples are "at leisure" in the sense of being out of office; no one "knows them" in the 4:2 sense of recognizing their potential for office. *11:24[1] tests their ability to accept this situation. Dzvng Syī is the father of Dzvngdž (compare Yén Lù's cameo in 11:8). The psaltery (sv̀ 瑟) was a larger cithern (chín 琴); both were flat hollow rectangles with strings stretched lengthwise (Rudolph **Han** 77), rare in Warring States orchestras (von Falkenhausen **Suspended** 334, 344) and used rather for the expression of personal feelings. Playing one implied taste, which Dzvng Syī shows in his indifference to office. The Master gently disapproves of the desire for office shown by the other three.

If (with Waley) we take "five or six" as "five times six" or thirty, and so on, we get 72 pre- and post-pubertal young men on Dzvng Syī's spring outing, a number later associated with the disciples of Confucius, but here excessive. The dozen men and boys recalls early Plato, and the idyllic outing echoes the Phaedrus, the Yí River corresponding to the Ilissus. This is the longest, and the most beautiful, of Analects passages. Its tranquil resignation recalls 1:1, its gently reproving Confucius links it to *5:26[1], and its outdoor air anticipates the even more famous Mencius Bull Mountain allegory (MC 6A8, c0265).

Reflections

The chapter eliminates the political aspect of Confucianism (except as a deferred aspiration) and focuses on the personal. The LY 12 debate among courts is here attenuated to a dialogue among individuals.

An imposing personal manner (wēi 威 "awe-inspiring") is stressed for the first time in 1:8. It may have been a trait that those not born to power found it difficult to simulate (Hazlitt **Look** 183; Barnett **Generals** 319).

The LY 1 themes of personal development and domestic virtue had first appeared in LY 2. The mechanism of habit inculcation (rote reiteration) is a natural secondary emphasis. James noted the role of habit in the formation of character, and of character in the formation of society (Kallen **James** 269–280).

The Analects/DDJ relation has been close from LY 12 on. The span of the DDJ seems to be c0340–c0249 (Brooks **Prospects** 63f, 70f); it begins with a mystical focus in DDJ 14 and later turns to statecraft (Creel **Aspects** 43–45). No critical scholar defends the attribution of the DDJ to Lǎudž, and in any case its long timespan precludes a single author. But it is possible that Lǎudž was associated with the *part* of the DDJ that was written in parallel with LY 1. (1) The Lǐ family genealogy quoted in SJ 63 goes back to Lǐ Dǎn, the Lǎu Dǎn of the DDJ. If each name on this list is the son of the preceding (one is said to be a great-great-grandson, probably to backdate Lǐ Dǎn), then at 25 years per birth generation, Dǎn died in c0275. (2) The most plausible Lǎudž story in the JZ text is JZ 3:4 (Watson **Chuang** 52f), where he is criticized for inspiring affection in others (the JZ enjoins emotional detachment). The DDJ chapters from around the turn of the century (40 on weakness, 42 on sympathy, 49 on returning good for evil, 51 on the parentship of the Way) attest just this sort of gentle and solicitous personality, and might be his work. It is then just conceivable that Dž-gāu's Dàuist opposite number was the original Lǎu Dǎn.

LY 1, like the contemporary DDJ, is pacific, detached, and familial. Its withdrawal from politics is atypical of the Analects as a whole, but it established a vital psychological option for later Confucians forced out of politics.

Jade Figure of a Tiger (see LY 16:1)
Length 14·8 cm (5·8 in). 04c/03c. Courtesy Freer Gallery of Art (32·43)

16
c0285

In 0286, Chí conquered Sùng, adding 50% to its area and almost surrounding Lǔ. 16:1–3 protest this outrage, in a style reminiscent of 3:1–3. A coalition of major states soon (0285) intervened, forcing the Chí armies back out of Sùng and driving its ruler, King Mǐn, to exile and death (in 0284).

The chapter which was being compiled before this dramatic interruption featured numerical groupings (the Three This and Nine That), a device imitated from the Gwǎndž and Mwòdž, and noted by Tswēi Shù as typical of the later Analects, LY 16–20. LY 16 as it finally took shape has a palindromic 1-2-6-2-1 pattern in its four thematic sections, unlike the alternating-speaker device of LY 1 but attesting a cognate sensibility. LY 1 and 16 both consist of 12 sayings, and were probably meant to frame the Analects as it then was, emphasizing the new domestic and personal themes. We are thus inclined to attribute both of them to the same school head, Dž-gāu.

The numbering of passages is identical in the Legge text.

[A. Against Impending Conquest]

16:1. The Jì were going to attack Jwān-yẃ. Rǎn Yǒu and Jì-lù were received by Confucius, and said, The Jì are going to do something about Jwān-yẃ. Confucius said, Chyóu, is this not your own fault? Now, as to Jwān-yẃ, in antiquity the former kings made it responsible for Dūng-mv́ng, and now, moreover, it is within the boundaries of the state; it is the servant of the altars of the soil and the harvest. Why should one attack it? Rǎn Yǒu said, Our Respected Master wishes it; neither of us two ministers wishes it. Confucius said, Chyóu, Jōu Rv̀n has a saying, "Let those with strength step into line, let those without desist." If he wavers and they do not support him, if he stumbles and they do not sustain him, what use are they as ministers? And moreover, if one speaks of fault: if a tiger or rhinoceros gets out of its cage, or a piece of horn or jade is broken in its container, whose fault is it?

Rǎn Yǒu said, Well, but as for Jwān-yẃ: it is strong, and it is near to Bì. If he does not take it now, it will be a worry to his sons and grandsons in later ages. Confucius said, Chyóu, a gentleman scorns to refuse to admit he wants something, and yet persist in arguing in favor of it. Chyōu has heard that those in charge of a nation or a family do not worry that they have little, but worry that the little they have is unevenly distributed; that they do not worry about poverty, but worry about discontent. In a word, if things are equitable, there is no "poverty," if things are harmonious, there is no "little," if there is content, there is no fear of overthrow. If all is thus, and should the distant still not submit, he will cultivate civil virtues to induce them to come, and once they have come, he will make them content. Now you, Yóu and Chyóu, are ministers to your Respected Master, and though the distant do not submit, he is unable to induce them to come; though the state is divided and partitioned, he is unable to safeguard it; he is even planning to loose shield and spear within the state. I fear that the worries of the Jì are not in Jwān-yẃ, but are instead to be found within his own walls.

This protest should properly be read after the calmer and earlier portion of the chapter, 16:4–10, and we urge the reader to make this detour.

In c0287, Chí spread anti-Sùng propaganda (JGT #478f, Crump **Ts'e** 565f; note the reference to LY *13:22b[2] at the end of JGT #479; Waley **Three** 137f, PB 100f) to prepare its conquest of Sùng; this passage reacts to such excuses. Cities were sometimes dedicated to the support of sacrifices, and "Confucius" cites "Jwān-yw's" support of the "Dūng-mv́ng Mountain" rite (Sùng, we recall, preserved Shāng sacrifices). Jōu Rv̀n is a military authority quoted in the DJ (Yǐn 6, Jāu 5; Legge **Ch'un** 21b, 604a). Gān/gv̄ 干 戈 is more precisely "shield and poleax" (in this period perhaps a halberd; see page 88), but the point of the phrase is alliteration ("shield and spear") rather than denotation. The argument that the impending war is "within the state" shows how far Shāng was accepted as part of a unitary China. The final moral is that war will not prevent disorder: only an egalitarian policy – a peace in the functional sense – can achieve this.

After *11:24[1], also by Dž-gāu, this impassioned denunciation is the longest consecutive piece of prose in the Analects. Given that the Chí threat to Sùng is its true subject, it was then really addressed to the Confucians in Chí, who may have gained high rank in that state, but at the cost of all principle.

[B. Dynastic Curses]

┌ 16:2. Confucius said, When All Under Heaven has the Way, rituals and music and military campaigns derive from the Son of Heaven. When All Under Heaven has not the Way, rituals and music and military campaigns derive from the Lords. When they derive from the Lords, it will be rare that all is not lost after ten generations; when they derive from the great officers, it will be rare that all is not lost after five generations. When subordinate officers are in charge of the mandates of state, it will be rare that all is not lost after three generations. When All Under Heaven has the Way, government does not rest with the great officers. When All Under Heaven has the Way, the ordinary people do not confer among themselves.

> One usurpation (of executive impulse by ministers) leads to another (plotting among the people). This passage assumes a theory of Spring and Autumn history in which the loss of ruler initiative led to wars and the destruction of states. The DJ embodies such a theory (Hsu **Ancient** 25f); its appearance here testifies to the influence of the DJ shortly after its appearance in Chí. The point here is to threaten Chí with disaster if it persists with its plan to invade Sùng.

└ 16:3. Confucius said, It has been five generations since salaries departed from the princely house, and four generations since government devolved upon the great officers. Hence it is that the descendants of the Three Hwán are so reduced.

> This links with 16:2, which predicted the downfall of the Jì (the state of Chí) if it carried out its military adventure, by exulting in that downfall. In 0286 Chí carried out its intended attack on Sùng, and in 0285 a coalition of rival states, alarmed that Chí had increased its area and thus upset the balance of power, combined to attack Chí. Mǐn-wáng was driven from his state, was refused refuge by several cities, and finally died in a border village. The 16:2–3 curses thus came true: Chí never recovered its military strength, and from this date was not a major player in the game of unification (Maspero **Antiquity** 263).

[C. Numerical Listings]

┌ 16:4. Confucius said, What is helpful is Three Befriendings, and what is harmful is Three Befriendings. To befriend the upright, to befriend the candid, to befriend those who have heard much: these are helpful. To befriend the partisan, to befriend those who prize weakness, to befriend the glib: these are harmful.

> Here begins the calm, or pre-Sùng, part of the chapter. The wrong friends are those snared in petty advocacy, the low-profile "weakness" Dàuists of DDJ 43, and the specious talkers. All in their way emphasize indirection, and are thus hateful to the temperamentally steadfast Confucians. Notice that the contrast is phrased in terms of profit: an almost Mician type of moral accountancy.

└ 16:5. Confucius said, What is helpful is Three Joys, and what is harmful is Three Joys. To joy in seasonal ritual and music, to joy in the goodness of men of the Way, to joy in having many worthy friends: these are helpful. To joy in arrogant pleasures, to joy in dissipated adventures, to joy in feasting and music: these are harmful.

> The formal parallel with 16:4 is obvious. The three good joys are an ordered culture, past exemplars of conduct, and the association of the like-minded. This last looks like the mere friendliness of 1:1, but much passion for right can smoulder amid such innocuousness. In 16:1 it bursts into flame. The friends from Chí and elsewhere implied in 1:1n are ratified by the clear links in LY 16 with Chí and Mencian influences. The Confucians, whatever their role in Lǔ, were active in what we may call the *international* Confucianism of the period.
>
> There is a pun in both sets: "joy in" (yàu) and "music" (ywè) are written with the same character, 樂. The Micians opposed music as wasteful (MZ 32, Mei **Ethical** 175f). The Sywndzians would later produce a reasoned defense of music (SZ 20), whose first line (Knoblock **Xunzi** 3/80) uses the same pun, defending music as intrinsically appropriate to the human spirit.

┌ 16:6. Confucius said, In attending a gentleman there are Three Errors. To speak when he has not yet mentioned something, we may call this assertive. *Not* to speak when he *has* mentioned something, we may call this secretive. To speak without watching his countenance and expression, we may call this blind.

> A renascent Confucian art of the courtier. It updates the balancing of speaking and not speaking in 14:3, but also recognizes a need for timeliness of speech in a subordinate role. The advice is the same, but one waits for an occasion.

└ 16:7. Confucius said, The gentleman has Three Bewares. When he is young, and his blood and breath are not yet fixed, he bewares of lust. When he is mature, and his blood and breath are firm, he bewares of temper. When he is old, and his blood and breath are feeble, he bewares of acquisitiveness.

> The idea of characteristic temptations at different ages (see 2:4) here takes a physiological turn. The "blood and breath" theory (also mentioned in DJ) posited separate circulation of blood and breath, jointly determining the vitality of an organism. The same (erroneous) idea was held in Greece at this time (Hammond **Classical** sv Anatomy). Both cultures later realized that there is only one circulation, and this "vital humors" theory was abandoned. A curious coincidence (Greece and China were at opposite ends of the silk trade, and Aristotle notes attempts to make local silk in Cos; Hammond **Classical** sv Silk).

┌ 16:8. Confucius said, The gentleman has three things he is in awe of. He is in awe of the commands of Heaven, he is in awe of great men, and he is in awe of the words of the Sages. The little man does not know the commands of Heaven, and so is not in awe of them; he disdains great men, and jeers at the words of the Sages.

> We may again think of 2:4, in the phrase "commands of Heaven." The concept of Heaven was in this period becoming part of the standard discourse of all the philosophical schools. The areas of concern here have much the same map as those in 16:5 – the natural order, the political order, the wisdom of tradition. The energy of these last few sayings is developing in the direction of court partisanship, and the last line is especially bitter at the jeerings of what is probably DDJ 53, at the grandly robed and overfed officials who "lead the people into brigandage." The targets of this satire seem to be Confucian, and there may have been, in c0285, at least some Confucians at the Lǔ court.

└ 16:10. Confucius said, The gentleman has Nine Thoughts. In seeing he thinks of being clear, in hearing he thinks of being perceptive, in expressing he thinks of being warm, in appearance he thinks of being respectful, in word he thinks of being loyal, in deed he thinks of being assiduous, in doubt he thinks of inquiring, in anger he thinks of consequences, and seeing a chance of gain he thinks whether it is right.

> For several of these "think of" phrases we could more idiomatically say "is concerned to, takes care to." All but the last are paired. Seeing and hearing are the basic learning methods; one tries to use them effectively. Expression and demeanor are basic behavior, and a balance of affability and courtesy cover the ground. Then come the old pair of word and deed, with fidelity and duty uppermost. The next pair are relatively new, and seem to give counsel for bureaucratic position: if you don't know, ask, and if you are angry, forbear. Finally, the set ends with an unpaired and thus somewhat emphasized saying (that clause, having an extra word, is also not tightly parallel to the other eight). For love of gain as a failing of age, see 16:7.
>
> This series of Threes thus culminates in a courtier's grand Nine. It may be relevant that Dzōu Yěn's astral/terrestrial correspondence theory (of which we seemed to see echoes in LY 2, c0317) later gave way to a vogue for mapping terrestrial phenomena on each other. These groupings are a further extension into the realm of ethics. The number nine appears to have been a major element in Dzōu Yěn's nested ninefold geography (Needham **Science** 2/236). If this fact is being alluded to here, then 16:10 may have been intended as something like a map for the courtier.

[D. Disapproval of Actions]

┌ 16:11. Confucius said, When he sees the good it is as though he could not catch up to it; when he sees the not-good it is as though he had put his hand into scalding water – I have seen such men, and I have heard such words. He dwells in retirement in order to realize his intention; he does right in order to advance his Way – I have heard such words, but I have not seen such men.

> These are Confucian (8:17[14]) versus Dàuist ideals. The Dàuists recommended an indirect courtiership and art of diplomacy (DDJ 54–56) to the ruler of Lǔ. 16:11 dismisses these Dàuist claims as unreal and unsubstantiated.

˪ 16:12. Prince Jǐng of Chí had a thousand teams of horses, but on the day he died, the people could find nothing to praise in him. Bwó-yí and Shú-chí starved to death at the foot of Shǒu-yáng, but the people down to the present praise them. Is this not an example?

> It is an example of the principle in the closely paired 16:11. It is not cast as a Confucius saying, a trait that we will find increasingly common in these late chapters. Chí Jǐng-gūng may symbolize the fate of Chí Mǐn-wáng (see 16:2c), who died not only despised but rejected by the common people (note the role of the common people, in contemporary Confucian political theory, as judges of the past). He sought to expand his state by war, whereas Bwó-yí and Shú-chí left their states out of principle. It seems that the Analects Confucians are here, circa 0285, enjoying the triumph of their principles in real life.

[E. Envoi: Education]

16:13. Chýn Kàng asked Bwó-yẃ, Do you have, besides, something special that you have heard? He replied, I do not. He was once standing alone, and Lǐ with hurrying steps was crossing the courtyard. He said, Have you studied the Shī? I replied, I have not. He said, If you do not study the Shī, you will be unable to carry on conversation. Lǐ withdrew and studied the Shī. Another day he was again standing alone, and Lǐ with hurrying steps was crossing the courtyard. He said, Have you studied the rituals? I replied, I have not. He said, If you don't study the rituals, you will have nothing on which to take your stand. Lǐ withdrew and studied the rituals. I heard these two things. Chýn Kàng withdrew and happily said, I asked one thing and I got three. I heard about the Shī. I heard about the rituals. And I also heard that the gentleman keeps distant from his son.

> This passage imagines the jealousy aroused by the Master's own son, who by his position as the presumptive successor is suspected by the other students of getting special, private teaching "besides" that which was available to all. The invented disciple Chýn Kàng threatens him unless he reveals these secrets (is this a memory of Dž-gāu's, from his days as the predesignated successor of the then school head?). The efforts of the son to deny favoritism on his father's part, and his own lack of gumption, give the anecdote a slightly comical air. Its ostensible purpose is to make an educational point, which is the one paraded by Chýn Kàng at the end: the father keeps distant from his son. This is interesting as typical of 03c practice, whereas in earlier and poorer times, a father would presumably have taken more personal pains with his son. It is also interesting in that it shows the Shī/Rituals/Music of *8:8[14] reduced to two elements, Music being absent. It will take 25 years before this Shī/Lǐ grouping is replaced by the Shī/Shū one which remained canonical in later tradition.

> We should also not overlook the literary realism of this anecdote, another of Dž-gāu's masterpieces. It is the most fully realized picture the Analects gives us of the Confucian-school courtyard, with the the nervous heir (coming to life from his scant prior mention in 11:8) and the belligerent older student. The setting is doubtless that of the actual Confucian school as of c0285. To imagine that courtyard peopled with the Master and his circle must have heartened the LY 16 Confucians, trapped in their all too post-Confucian century.

Interpolations

These pieces reverse previous doctrine, and by Dž-gāu's rule of filiality in 1:11, they should thus follow the end of the three-year mourning for Dž-jīng, giving a terminus a quo of c0292. Our best guess is a date nearer to LY 16 (c0285).

For a complete finding list of interpolated passages, see page 329.

Added to LY 8

*8:4. When Dzv̄ngdž fell ill, Mv̀ng Jìngdž inquired of him. Dzv̄ngdž said, When a bird is about to die, its song is sad; when a man is about to die, his words are good. What the gentleman prizes in the Way are three things. From the movements of his demeanor, he bans cruelty and arrogance. To the expressions of his countenance, he summons fidelity. From the words he utters, he bans coarseness and vulgarity. As to the ordering of splintbox and stand, there are specialists available. [8:4]

> This redo of 8:3 honors Dzv̄ngdž (also prominent in LY 1) by a visit from the head of the Mv̀ng clan, and makes his last words a wisdom precept rather than a personal summary. Its triple structure recalls the triples of 16:4–10. The use of "bans" in both clauses 1 and 3 may look like a misprint, but the ABA form of "bans/summons/bans" (literally, "distances/nears/distances" 遠 / 近 / 遠) is like Dž-gāu's symmetrical LY 16 chapter structure, and thus may be original.
>
> The stunner is the concluding allusion to the climax line of 15:1, where Confucius himself is made to claim just such expertise in ritual arrangements. It would seem that Dž-gāu is decisively turning from the school's previous ritual emphasis to his own more inward, personal-cultivation agenda.

Added to LY 11

*11:12. Jì-lù asked about serving ghosts and spirits. The Master said, You cannot yet serve men, how could you serve the ghosts? He said, I venture to ask about the dead. He said, You do not yet know the living, how could you know the dead? [11:11]

> This is one of the classic passages against, or at any rate disclaiming the importance of knowledge about, the world of spirits. In historical context, it represents a rejection of the belief in the unseen world on which the validity of sacrifice rests, and which the mid 04c Analects had in fact acknowledged. We have here something like agnostic humanism, bent on life, not on death.

Reflections

Dž-jīng and Dž-gāu present us with our most interesting father/son authorial pair since Dzv̄ngdž and Dzv̄ng Ywæn (LY 7 and LY 8/9). The same pattern of respect and divergence applies, and may be investigated at term paper length. We may here ask: why was it that the father, who had annexed domestic virtue in his LY 2, failed to see it as the answer to the doctrinal dilemma of c0302? In large perspective, this is not at all surprising. It is familiar in the sciences that discoverers and developers tend to be different people, and that the mind has great difficulty in taking a second step in the same direction, so that it is hard to follow up even one's own first breakthrough with a second.

As the Confucian school resumes contact with the Lǔ court, in LY 16, it seems that the Mician enmities which occupied Dž-jīng have been replaced by Dàuist ones. The ten basic tenets of the Micians were fixed by the early 03c, and, being thus canonized, tended not to grow further in later years. The Micians remained politically visible, and attacked the Confucians on cultural issues such as the three-year mourning (see LY 17), but their ethical push was over, and that school had instead turned to the logic of statement (Hu **Logical**, Graham **Later**). The Confucians had been affected by several Mician ideas: the popular welfare, mutuality, moral accountancy. There was no merger, but that front was quiet. Not so the Dàuists. Their distinctively pacific statecraft was being exerted on behalf of Lǔ (which beleaguered state the country envisioned in the later DDJ greatly resembles), and, practical or not, it was evidently getting a hearing at court. The bickering at the DDJ (see 16:4 and 16:8) suggests that this group was the chief policy rival to the Analects Confucians. The Micians may also have served as defensive-warfare experts, a low-profile tactic consistent with the soft DDJ line.

Readers of the speculation on Lǐ or Lǎu Dǎn (lǎu 老 is the epithet "old") in 1r (page 151) may wonder how far back his gentle antiwar philosophy goes in the DDJ. We see a break at DDJ 26, earlier chapters having a mystical context. If so, then Lǐ Dǎn's term as group head will have been c0314–c0275, very close to the standard 40-year term of a transmission genealogy.

The DDJ relationship (like all the other Analects connections) ran in two directions. For all the brusque dismissal of "weakness" as a policy in LY 16, the self-cultivation agenda of LY 1 was in all probability Dàuist-influenced.

As for the Micians, it would be a violation of tact to compare them with John Stuart Mill merely because both explored logic and stressed "utility." Such microcorrespondences are rarely fruitful. But the societies of 04c Lǔ and 19c England do have points in common, among them the industrial advances which, in Lǔ, permitted large-volume production of silk and iron, an expansion of trade to exploit those surpluses, a simultaneous growth of wealth and squalor (domestic slavery advancing at the same pace as domestic freedom), and the rise of aspirations to happiness among the little people. There was in 04c Lǔ also a discovery of psychological interiority: an interest in feelings and their origins which will lead to a debate on human nature (LY 17). The recasting of personal ethics from a feudal-duty basis in Confucius to a reciprocity basis in the late 04c Analects, symbolized in the concept shù 恕 "empathy," attests this trend. This term occurs only twice in the Analects: Dž-jīng's interpolated *15:24[15a] and Dž-gāu's interpolated *4:15[l]. But a close reading of LY 15–1 will show that these passages merely exemplify a general conceptual shift that seems to have been occurring at about this time. The mystical inwardness of the DDJ (Waley **Way** 32–33) is another example.

It seems that by this time the interpolation had become a literary medium in its own right, distinct from the saying, and with different rules of propriety. More invention was allowed (the much-loved Yén Hwéi / Dž-lù stories are both interpolations), and more space was available (all the longest Analects passages are interpolations or, like 16:1, intrusions). This freedom gives scope to certain literary predilections. Dž-gāu, whose primary chapters have a style of their own (the mapping of LY 16 on LY 1 is a nice study in compositional proclivity), seems to have enjoyed the different options available in the interpolation.

Archaizing Bronze Bell (see LY 17:9)
Height 36·8 cm (14·5 in). 04c. Courtesy Arthur M. Sackler Gallery (V-124)

17
c0270

A new Lǔ Prince, Chǐng-gūng, succeeded in 0279 as a virtual puppet of Chǔ. An effort was apparently made to tempt the Confucians into higher office, which as legitimists they at first indignantly refused. At last, however, they seem to have agreed, and 17:1, which stands structurally apart from the rest of LY 17, seems to symbolize that acceptance. The school head was Dž-shv̀n, who would hold that position until the dissolution of the school itself in 0249.

Reference numbers to Legge are given at the end of each passage.

⊢ 17:1. Yáng Hwò wanted to see Confucius. Confucius would not see him. He sent Confucius a pig. Confucius, timing it so that he would be out, went to pay his respects, but met him on the way. He said to Confucius, "Come, I would say something to you. One who cherishes his treasure and thereby lets his state go astray, can he be called rv́n?" He said, He cannot. "One who would like to serve in government, but keeps missing his chance, can he be called sensible?" He said, He cannot. "Days and months are passing away, and years will not be given to us." Confucius said, Very well, I am going to take office. [17:1]

> Yáng Hwò, the usurping minister of the Jì clan, should represent an illegitimate regime, but since he speaks with the authority of the royal yv́ 予 "I" (see 13:15), Confucius's capitulation is presumably sincere. The image of "cherishing a treasure" (placing it in the bosom of one's robe) also occurs in DDJ 70 (c0274).

[A. On Human Nature]

⌐ 17:2a. The Master said, By nature they are near each other; by habitual action they become farther apart. [17:2]

> In the 03c debate on human nature (syìng 性), the old view (12:19; compare MC 6A7) was a *convergence* theory: the ruler transforms society, thus reducing individual differences. Later come *divergence* theories like 17:2a. The Mencian variant (MC 6A8) holds that people are good, but brutalized by experience. Syv́ndž (SZ 23) responds that people are bad, but may be bettered by teaching.

∟ 17:2b. The Master said, It is the highest wisdom and the lowest stupidity that do not change. [17:3]

> This modifies the harsh *8:9[14] to make most people amenable to improvement.

⊢ 17:3. The Master went to Wǔ-chv́ng and heard sounds of strings and song. Our Respected Master smiled in amusement and said, In trimming a chicken, where would you use an ox knife? Dž-yóu replied, In earlier days Yěn heard it from his Respected Master: if gentlemen study the Way, they will come to love others, and if little people study the Way, they will be easy to employ. The Master said, You disciples, what Yěn says is right. My previous words were merely teasing him. [17:4]

> Confucius here assumes the old two-layer view of society, according to which teaching the people classical music is absurd. Dž-yóu, defending the new inclusive view (compare MC 1B1, Legge **Mencius** 150f), makes him recant.

[B. The Temptation to Serve]

⌐ 17:4. Gūngshān Fú-ràu headed a revolt in Bì. He sent an invitation, and the Master wanted to go. Dž-lù was not pleased, and said, When at last you go, why must it be Gūngshān that you go to? The Master said, Well, he has invited me, and how should it be for nothing? If there were one who would use me, could I not make a Jōu in the East? [17:5]

> The contrary-to-fact use of the term "Jōu in the East" refutes the now-popular name "Eastern Jōu" for the period 0771–0221. The goal of each eastern state was to become a power in the east, symmetrical to the Jōu remnant in the west. Despite the unsavory credentials of the rebel, Confucius is tempted. Note the implication: a valid government can be established despite a tarnished ruler.

∟ 17:6. Bì Syì sent an invitation, and the Master wanted to go. Dž-lù said, In earlier days Yóu heard it from his Respected Master: "One who in his own person does what is not good, the gentleman will not join." Bì Syì is in revolt, with a base in Jūng-mǒu. If now the Master were to go, what would it look like? The Master said, Yes, there was such a remark. But is it not said, "Is a thing hard? Then it can be ground but will not wear. Is a thing white? Then it can be dyed but will not stain." Do you think I am a bottle-gourd? How can I be hung up and never eaten? [17:7]

> Confucius's anguish at being constrained by the old legitimacy theory (Bì Syì is supposed to have been a Jìn officer, but the story is a mere parallel to 17:4) tells us that this theory is becoming untenable in the eyes of the school of Lǔ. See 17:1, above, and the ultimate affirmation of the same point in 18:6.
>
> The bottle-gourd was dried as a container, not eaten like other melons. Being eaten symbolizes having one's value absorbed into the community.

[C. An Educational Crisis]

⌐ 17:8a. The Master said, Little ones, why do you not study the Shī? With the Shī you can inspire, you can observe, you can be congenial, you can express resentment. Applying them to what is near, you can serve your father; applying them to what is far, you can serve your ruler. And you will become acquainted with the names of birds and beasts, plants and trees. [17:9]

> This begins with diplomatic uses (13:5), continues with the identity of public and personal realms (9:16), and ends with the vocabulary argument beloved of bad textbook writers. Legge's rueful comment on this last line ("We do indeed learn *names* enow," She 3) never fails to draw a laugh from Shī students.
>
> Resentment and other emotions occur *in* the Shī, but here we have the official gentleman obliquely expressing his own emotions *by quoting* the Shī: he is evidently entitled to display, and thus in the first place to feel, resentment. This marks a revolution in feelings, and in social attitudes toward feelings.

∟ 17:8b. The Master said to Bwó-yw, Have you done the Jōu-nán and Shàu-nán? If a man has not done the Jōu-nán and Shàu-nán, he will be like one who stands facing the wall, will he not? [17:10]

> This fills in the background for 16:13, giving for it only the practical motives cited in 17:8a. The Shī was a trademark text of the Syẃndž school; see below.

⌐ 17:9. The Master said, "*Ritual, ritual*" – does it mean no more than jade and silk? "*Music, music*" – does it mean no more than bells and drums? [17:11]

For jade in ritual, see 10:4. We have dealt with the Shī in 17:8a/b, and now turn to the other two parts of the *8:8[14] curriculum (p126). The point seems to be that ritual and music are understood only superficially by contemporaries.

∟ 17:10. The Master said, Stern of aspect but soft within – I would compare it to a little man; it is like a thief boring through a wall. [17:12]

Here again, the externals (demeanor, a part of ritual) conceal inner falsity. Sternness is a desirable quality since 1:8, but should imply inner firmness.

⌐ 17:11. The Master said, Country magnates are thieves of virtue. [17:13]

This centrist saying has occasioned much philological ingenuity over the years. Waley, relying on MC 7B37, makes it out to be complimentary, but see next.

∟ 17:12. The Master said, To hear it on the highway and tell it on the footpath is a waste of virtue. [17:14]

Pearls before swine, the negativity confirming 17:11 as negative. These four sayings may refer to Sywndž, the rising Confucian star of the early 03c (as Mencius had been in the late 04c). He was born in Jàu, and perhaps studied Confucianism in Ngwèi. His non-Lǔ origin may be the target of these rustic aspersions. He emphasized ritual (SZ 19) and music (SZ 20), the subjects of 17:9/10, and studied the hard words in the Shī (Karlgren **History** 32f finds that most Hàn glosses on the Shī are Sywndzian). 17:9–12 thus make sense as a sarcastic criticism of Sywndž. The last line in the otherwise positive 17:8a, above (which is problematic; Lau suspects a text corruption) may anticipate the 17:9–12 critique of Sywndž's philological approach to the Shī.

[D. Denunciations]

⌐ 17:13. The Master.said, Can a common man take part in the service of a ruler? When he has not yet got it, he worries about getting it; once he has got it, he worries lest he lose it. And once he becomes worried lest he lose it, there is no extreme he will not go to. [17:15]

... to keep it. The lack of aplomb, the greed for power as such, that affects the wrong sort of person in or out of office. A comment on the competition.

∟ 17:14. The Master said, In earlier times the people had three shortcomings, but at present it seems that they have lost them. The wild ones of old were impetuous; the wild ones of today are violent. The proud ones of old were principled; the proud ones of today are arrogant. The stupid ones of old were upright; the stupid ones of today are no more than specious. [17:16]

Not mitigations but exacerbations (see *8:16[14]); "people" means "subjects." One thinks of old Nǐng Wǔdž's "stupidity" (5:21) concealing his inner loyalty; the modern postures here listed lack this "shortcoming" of inner principle.

The vices are those of officials. 17:13/14 thus criticize rivals, perhaps the "wild" Dàuists. Note that the classic DDJ 20 had amiably called *itself* "stupid," whereas stupidifying the *people*, as was proposed by the more recent DDJ 65, is opposed to the educationist policy of 17:3.

┌ 17:15. The Master said, Clever words and beguiling looks – seldom are they rv́n. [17:17]

> A similar pronouncement had first appeared in 5:25; it was given exactly this pithier form in 1:3. Its repetition may show a distaste for current controversy.

└ 17:16. The Master said, I hate the purple encroaching on the crimson. I hate the Songs of Jv̀ng disturbing the classical music. I hate the sharp mouths overthrowing states and families. [17:18]

> Purple (see 10:5a) may have been a new and expensive dye, displacing the old standard vegetable reds. For the "Songs of Jv̀ng" (Shī 75–95) and the enmity they aroused among the Confucians, see *15:11[15a]; the tunes associated with them were evidently popular at this period (for popular music among the elite, see also MC 1B1). The accusation is of vulgarity (compare 7:11/12 above), which as in 17:14 is more likely to be the wrong behavior of the mighty than the normal behavior of the literally vulgar. 17:16 hates it that good old ways are replaced by tasteless new ways, and that the political order is imperiled by it. "Sharp mouths" echoes the "clever words" of the paired 17:15. Someone must be preaching new doctrines that threaten the old order. As in 7:9–12, it is hard not to think of Syv́ndž, who wanted to follow "the later kings" rather than the mythical ancient sages who were invented to symbolize certain values. Syv́ndž was on easy terms with power: in SZ 15 (Knoblock **Xunzi** 2/211f), for example, he argues military strategy before the King of Jàu. His pupil Lǐ Sz̄ was the chief minister of Chín at the time of its conquest of the Empire in 0221.
>
> We now take up Waley's challenge (17:11 above) to read MC 7B37. It is based on a whole cluster of Analects sayings and phrases, among them 17:16. It must therefore be later than all of them, but not necessarily *very much* later. An unbiased reading of MC 7B37 shows that it can be construed as criticism of a rival rather than a villager. For that rival, Syv́ndž is the obvious candidate. From MC 6A and SZ 23, with their directly opposing views of human nature, we know that Syv́ndž *was* a foe of the Mencians. Who more plausible?
>
> 17:16 for various reasons must precede at some distance the 0255 Chǔ partial conquest of Lǔ, and the arrival of Syv́ndž as Director of southern Lǔ. If so, then the war between Syv́ndž and the Lǔ Confucians dates from before the conquest of Lǔ, and perhaps from his years in Chí, an important finding.

┌ 17:17. The Master said, I wish not to say anything. Dž-gùng said, If the Master does not speak, then what will we little ones have to transmit? The Master said, What does *Heaven* say? The four seasons go their way, and the hundred entities are produced withal. What does *Heaven* say? [17:19]

> The solemn pronoun yẃ 予 "I" (compare *15:3[15a]) implies a serious echo of DDJ 73 and the proto-Hwáng/Lǎu nature concept (Peerenboom **Law** 64).

└ 17:18. Rú Bēi wanted to see Confucius. Confucius excused himself on account of illness. When the bearer of the message was going out the door, he took up his psaltery and sang, letting him hear it. [17:20]

> Letting him know that his request for an audience (a technical term; note the formal name "Confucius") is unwelcome. Who does Rú Bēi represent? One thinks of the would-be employers of 17:4/6, but the tone of collegial courtesy and the hint of doctrinal differences in 17:16 suggest rather a doctrinal rival.

⌐ 17:19. Dzăı Wŏ asked, Is the three-year mourning period not too long? If
gentlemen for three years do not do ceremonies, ceremonies are sure to be lost. If
gentlemen for three years do not do music, music is sure to vanish. When the old
grain is gone, and the new grain has been piled high; when once bow and tinder
have changed the fire – that period should suffice. The Master said, If you were to
eat your rice, and wear your brocades, would you feel comfortable with yourself? He
said, I would feel comfortable. [The Master said], If you would feel comfortable,
then do it. But as to the gentleman's way of being in mourning: if he ate dainties
he would not find them sweet; if he heard music he would not find it enjoyable; if
he abode in his usual place he would not be comfortable; therefore he does not do
them. But if now you would be comfortable, then do them. Dzăı Wŏ went out, and
the Master said, Such is Yẃ's lack of rν́n! Only when Yẃ had been alive for three
years did he finally leave the bosom of his father and his mother. Now, a three-year
mourning is the universal mourning custom of the world. Did Yẃ receive three
years of love from his father and mother? [17:21]

> The "bow and tinder" fire drill is used to rekindle fires in the new year. As early
> as the late 04c (*4:20², 14:40), the Confucians had advocated the three-year
> mourning concept; MC 3A2 shows Mencius urging it in Tv́ng. The frugal
> Micians wrote treatises (MZ 25; Mei **Ethical** 123f) denouncing it; 17:19 rebuts
> them. It was answered in its turn (MZ 48:12, Mei **Ethical** 236f), with an
> anecdote quoting and ridiculing this symmetry theory of mourning. Whether
> they are winning it is too soon to tell, but no one can say that the Confucians
> are not at least holding up their end of the contemporary culture wars.

└ 17:20. The Master said, One who eats his fill all day long, and never uses his
mind on anything, is a difficult case. Are there not such things as gammon and
chess? Would it not be better to play them? [17:22]

> Gammon (Yang **Game**) and chess suggest the growth of wealth, leisure, and
> thus boredom (Maugham **Cakes** 37–38). MC 6A9 hilariously improves on the
> chess image in criticizing a ruler, but the 17:19 pair suggests a lower object of
> this intellectual scorn; perhaps the primitivists of JZ 9 (Watson **Chuang** 106).

⌐ 17:21. Dž-lù said, Should a gentleman prize courage? The Master said, With the
gentleman, right comes before all else. If a gentleman has courage but lacks a sense
of right, he will make a rebellion. If a little man has courage but lacks a sense of
right, he will become a thief. [17:23]

> The old military virtue of courage is now a danger unless tempered by right.
> For the prevalence of thieves in the age of wealth, see 12:18 and DDJ 53, 57.

└ 17:22. Dž-gùng said, Does the gentleman too have his hates? The Master said,
He has his hates. He hates those who speak of the bad points of others, he hates
those who dwell downstream and criticize those above, he hates those who are
brave without propriety, he hates those who are daring but violent. He said, Does
Sż too have his hates? [He said], He hates weakness passing for wisdom, he hates
impudence passing for courage, he hates slander passing for uprightness. [17:24]

> Hatred, like courage, is a classic virtue (see 4:3/4), here directed at rivals such
> as the Dàuists (for "downstream" see DDJ 61), but mostly the standard crowd:
> carpers, whiners, swaggerers, bullies; the specious, pushy, and insinuating.

[E. Envoi: Again on Human Nature]

⌐ 17:23. The Master said, Women and little people are hard to handle. If you let them get close, they presume; if you keep them at a distance, they resent it. [17:25]

Our Chinese correspondents report (1995) a movement to eliminate this remark on women (no one has so far arisen to defend the "little people") by reading nwdž 女子 "women" as rǔ dž 汝子 "your children." Nw *may* stand for rǔ in early texts, but that emendation would give a second-person form atypical of Analects maxims. No doubt the saying somewhat lacks gallantry as it stands, but transferring it to children seems ungallant too.

What then does the unamended line mean? Women figure incidentally as wives in 05/04c Analects passages, but not until 1:13 do we hear of a standard of conduct *applicable* to a future wife. This seems to imply increased ethical stature. Greater wealth is changing households, leading to grander houses, more formal living arrangements, and social distance between family members (including children; 16:13). As earlier noted, more respect is now given to personal feelings: an empathy ethic is emerging. 17:23 implies a situation of rising emotional expectations, and acknowledges the resentment that arises when expectations are denied. Admitting resentment as a discussable part of social situations is a major social advance, paralleling the new admissibility of courtier resentment in 17:8a. *Women are becoming more visible.*

Women of court rank were noted in the DJ, and now also in the Analects (*6:28, below). They raise the specter of harem influence on politics, which the Confucians consistently deplored; this may be the thrust of 17:23. Slave women also existed: slaves of both sexes wearing iron collars, slaughtered to accompany their masters, have been found in 03c tombs (Wagner **Iron** 170f).

L 17:24. The Master said, If he is forty and is still hated, he will probably be so until the end. [17:26]

17:23 does not envision change in women or little people; this paired saying finds equal inflexibility within the male elite. Forty seems to have been seen as the terminus of personality development (compare 9:23, 2:4); by then, the mix is presumed to be set. The chapter returns to its 17:2 beginning, but on an ethically pessimistic note. The final verdict is that only a segment of society, and not all of *them*, are capable of enough virtue to be usable in office.

Interpolations

The resumption of involvement with the court led to renewed activity in interpolation (compare the slight output of Dž-gāu during the period of exile, LY 1 and 16). Subjects range from court protocol to doctrinal points, in the spirit of the feistily combative main chapter. The principal one, however, is the saying preposed as 17:1, which changes the stance of LY 17 from principled refusal to reluctant acceptance of high office under a tainted Lǔ regime.

Also of interest are the "junk" interpolations: the seemingly irrelevant bits of lore which Tswēi Shù used as another criterion for his late chapter group, the first sample being *16:14[17] below. On examination, these turn out to make more Analects sense than at first appears.

For a complete finding list of interpolated passages, see page 329.

Added to LY 5

*5:13. Dž-gùng said, Our Respected Master's cultural accomplishments we can contrive to hear about, but our Respected Master's explanation of nature and the Way of Heaven, we cannot in any way contrive to hear about. [5:12]

> Wvn 文 "culture" we have met before; the present term wvn-jāng 文章 occurs otherwise only in *8:19[18], where it describes the cultural splendor of Yáu. Confucius is not an emperor with a culture of his own, and we must thus take it here as "his *teaching of* culture." The complaint is that "Confucius" has not discoursed on fashionable topics: human nature (see 17:2a) and the cosmos as a model for earthly society (see 17:17 and the phrase 天 之 道 "the Way of Heaven" from DDJ 73, of this same period). *5:13 leaves open the possibility that the Master *has* views on these subjects, which are merely difficult for the disciples to find out about. The strain, for the mid 03c Lǔ Confucian school, of having nothing canonical to say on major contemporary issues is palpable in this passage. For Szmǎ Chyēn's agonized failure to find fairness in the rational historical cosmos of the "Way of Heaven," see Durrrant **Mirror** 23f.

Added to LY 6

*6:28. The Master saw Nándž. Dž-lù was not pleased. Our Respected Master took an oath about it, saying, Whatever wrong I have done, may Heaven reject it! May Heaven reject it! [6:26]

> The situation, like that in 17:4/6, implies a questionable political contact. Nándž was the dissolute consort of Líng-gūng of Wèi (see *7:15[14] and 15:1). Confucius is supposed to have seen her privately, presumably seeking support for a ministership; his oath denying any wrongdoing uses the sacral yw 予, "I." The implication of wrongful feminine political influence is an important cultural sign of the times (the 03c times; compare 17:23n, above).

Added to LY 7

*7:18. What the Master pronounced in classical speech were the Shī, the Shū, and the Instructions for Ritual. [7:17]

> Special pronunciation (the term used is yǎ yén 雅 言, "elegant" or perhaps "court" speech) implies special veneration, and perhaps some linguistic time depth, for these evidently canonical works. As in *8:8[14], there are three subjects, but here the Music is replaced by the Shū; the fact that the Music has dropped out perhaps reflects the fact that this classic was lost before the Hàn dynasty. The Analects only twice quotes individual Shū (12:21, 14:40); the DJ and MZ of that same late 04c period quote a wider range. By c0270, half a century later, there seems to be a collection. The school of Sywndž quotes only one Shū outside the set of 28 or 29 that made up the early Hàn Confucian inventory (Shaughnessy **Shu** 377, 380), and it seems that in about this period the canonization processes were far advanced; the text situation increasingly resembles the one that we know from Hàn bibliographies. Again (see 17:9–12), we seem to have evidence of the intellectual influence of Sywndž in 03c Lǔ. For an original composition in the archaic Shū mode by the Lǔ Confucians (coming late to this particular species of literature), see 20:1[19].

Added to LY 11

*11:20. Dž-lù asked, When I hear something, shall I put it into practice? The Master said, You have father and elder brother living; how should you hear something and put it into practice? Rǎn Yǒu asked, When I hear something, shall I put it into practice? The Master said, When you hear something, put it into practice. Gūngsyī Hwá said, When Yǒu asked, "When I hear something, shall I put it into practice?" the Master said, "You have father and elder brother living." When Chyóu asked, "When I hear something, shall I put it into practice?" the Master said, "When you hear something, put it into practice." Chr̄ is confused, and ventures to ask about it. The Master said, Chyóu tends to hold back, so I pushed him forward; Yǒu tends to go ahead of others, so I held him back. [11:21]

> This recalls 2:5, where the meaning of a seemingly simple statement is elicited only by a second questioner. Pedagogically, it establishes the idea of advice adjusted to the individual student. The existence of different answers to the same question refutes the idea that the question itself has a constant answer. Constancy was an ideal of the late 04c, which wanted a maxim valid in all circumstances (*15:24[15a]), or including all other maxims (*4:15[1]). The situationality of *11:20 destroys this hope. It also undercuts Mician logic, since a statement with many sequels cannot be a link in a deductive chain.

> From 4:3/4 to 14:17/18 and beyond, some Analects paired sayings seem to be opposite in meaning, causing interpretational cruxes: which is right? This story allows the answer: both, for different people at different times. Such situational fluidity is the bane of philology, but the soul of hermeneutics (see Henderson **Scripture** ch4). There was already a focus on "tradition" in 1:4, and *11:20 seems to show the Analects itself in the process of becoming canonical.

Added to LY 14

*14:34. Someone said, Requite malice with kindness: how about that? The Master said, With what then will you requite kindness? Requite malice with uprightness; requite kindness with kindness. [14:36]

> This objects to the niceness principle of DDJ 49 and 63, and wants an ethic that distinguishes good and bad. "Malice" is ywæn 怨, usually "resentment." "Kindness" (dv́ 德), usually "virtue," shades into "character, latency," Waley's "power." The 03c is in part an age of niceness (its "sweet" Confucius persona may have been defensively adapted from the affable early 03c Lǎu Dǎn). The DDJ 63 idea recurs in Luke 6:27, near the (perhaps Mician?) Golden Rule in its post-Hillel or *6:30[18] form at Luke 6:31 (widely separated in the earlier Matthew 5:44, 7:12. As Christianity evolves toward its final international form, it homes more consistently on its Oriental heritage). The scorn of *14:34 thus does not seem to have harmed the long-range viability of DDJ 63.

> The word "requite" (bàu 報) has the technical sense of reciprocating a deed or a gift (Yang **Basis**); it occurs in folk-courtship contexts in the Shr̄ (Waley **Songs** 31 notes the parallel with English pastoral poetry); the classic example is Shr̄ 64 (Waley #18). The DDJ use of this transactional term puts even wrongdoers within the group of those with whom one has social relations. The LY 17 Confucians (compare 12:19) refuse to open the gate that wide.

⌐ *14:43. Ywǽn Ràng sat asprawl in the Master's presence. The Master said, In youth not lineal or fraternal, in maturity with nothing to pass on, growing older without dying – this is a brigand! He struck him on the shin with his staff. [14:46]

12:1 saw an increase in student/teacher formality; this piece laments its lapse. The basic sitting posture (still standard on formal Japanese occasions) is that illustrated in Rudolph Han #65; the Japanese verb kuzusu denotes shifting to a less tiring, more "open" position, with lower legs crossed and knees apart. "Confucius" stigmatizes this implied disrespect for tradition as a lack of lineality (sywn 孫; read 遜) or respect for one's heritage (see *15:18n below), and a sign of future worthlessness, having nothing to pass on to one's own heirs. Note the reference to brigands as a symbol of the breakdown of civilization.

After this physical assault on a student, the mere *impatience* of 5:10a, from two hundred years earlier, is almost idyllic. The 03c was not an age of niceness; it was an age of mingled niceness and cruelty – an age of extended extremes.

∟ *14:44. A youth from Chywè Association came bearing an order. Someone asked, Is he one who is improving? The Master said, I have seen how he stands informally in his place, I have seen how he walks side by side with his elders. He is not one who is in search of improvement; he is one who wants to get ahead quickly. [14:47]

Another vignette of cultural decline in the young: not a desire to improve by associating with his moral superiors, but an eagerness to get ahead by hanging around the powerful. Note the presence of adolescents, túng 童 (the "lads" of Shř 87, page 137), in the school of *11:24[1] and in this official messenger role. One of the extremes to which the 03c goes is extending adult functions to younger ages; this culminates in the cult of the prodigy in early Hàn, as represented by the career of Jyǎ Yì (Brooks **Prospects** 3). The fault here is not slovenly disrespect, as in the paired *14:43, but an assumption of equality with official superiors, as walking *with* them rather than respectfully *behind* them (note that some of the conversations in the 05c Analects chapters seem to require the assumption that the speakers are walking essentially together, not in file). Chywè 闕 is said to have been Confucius's own residential league or locality; the "order" may have been from the court. If this bright neighbor lad is serving as a court page, the upward social mobility that we conjectured as of LY 7 seems to be still present and flourishing, two hundred years later.

Added to LY 15

*15:18. The Master said, If a gentleman has right as his substance, and puts it in practice with propriety, promulgates it with lineality, and brings it to a conclusion with fidelity, he is a gentleman indeed! [15:17]

Here is the new virtue of "lineality" which also occurred in *14:43 above. It suggests an emphasis on maintaining the position of the newly wealthy families by emphasizing the duty of children not to other individuals *in* the family, but to family continuity itself: honoring one's pedigree. The aspects incumbent on an adult, in this saying, given "right" as personal equipment, are to practice that right courteously in his own deeds, transmit it lineally to his children in private life, and carry it out faithfully with his associates in public life. For all the novel family focus, here, the *public* expression of right is still the ultimate goal.

Added to LY 1

*1:5. The Master said, To lead a state of a thousand chariots, be assiduous in administration and keep faith; make expenditures frugally and be solicitous of others; and employ the people according to the season. [1:5]

A thousand chariots might (by MC 1A1) be the private army of a great clan in a myriad-chariot state like Ngwèi. On that basis, schematic as it clearly is, Lǔ at the time of Mencius's remark (c0320) might have had three or four thousand chariots. MC 5B7 envisions Lǔ before Mù-gūng (c0400) to have been a thousand-chariot state; this might have been the force available to the palace proper. LY 16:12 mentions that a ruler of the larger state of Chí in c0500 personally disposed of a thousand teams of horses; the resources of the entire state would therefore have been larger. All this is consistent enough that we may conclude that the "state of a thousand chariots" mentioned in this saying is 05c Lǔ as a writer of the 03c might retrospectively have imagined it.

The description does not imply a minister "leading" that state, but a middle administrator: dutiful toward his superiors, thoughtful of his junior colleagues, and appropriate in his demands on the subject population.

*1:10. Dž-chín asked Dž-gùng, When our Respected Master arrives in some country, he always manages to hear about its government. Does he seek this, or does he wait until they give it to him? Dž-gùng said, Our Respected Master is warm, genial, respectful, restrained, and deferential; in this way he gets it. Our Respected Master's "seeking" is perhaps different from other people's seeking, is it not? [1:10]

Other people poke and pry; "Confucius" by his open manner invites (does not simply await) confidences. Inside information about who is really who in administration is probably being acted on in the visit to Nándž, *6:28 above. Apart from the literal "warm up" of 2:11 (c0317), "warmness" as a personal quality first occurs in *7:38[3] (general demeanor) and thereafter in the 03c passages 16:10 (of facial expression) and 19:9 (general manner). The next adjective, lyáng 良, is unique in the text. In Mencius it occurs in "goodman" (husband, MC 4B33) and in "goodmind" (conscience, MC 6A8). Since the qualities urged in *1:10 need to be directly apparent to an observer, we should imagine it here as meaning "projecting an air of good intention" or "genial." The complex art of geniality may be seen in action in Parker **Taming** 83–85.

The modal chí 其 "expect" is here replaced by chí-jū 其諸, otherwise found only in the Gūngyáng Jwàn, an early Hàn commentary on the CC. Waley notes this without drawing the inference that this passage has early Hàn linguistic affinities, and so might be nearer the 03c than the mid 04c to which he ascribes most of the Analects (Waley **Analects** 21–22). His observation that Dzvngdž in LY 1 is later than Dzvngdž in LY 8, suggesting a link to the Hàn myth of Dzvngdž (**Analects** 20), put another piece of the puzzle into his hands. In both myth *and* language, LY 1 displays what look like 03c relations.

This missed opportunity is noted not in derogation of Waley, one of the heroes of our field, but to show how hard it is to have ideas, or recognize them when they turn up. What makes a new idea hard to recognize is the old idea you already have (Beveridge **Art** 102f, PB 142f). Dzvngdž's daily effort (1:4) was to *advance* in virtue. Continual effort is also required in the intellectual sphere, but it consists in being at all times ready to *retreat* from previous gains.

*1:16. The Master said, He does not worry that others do not know him; he worries that he does not know others. [1:16]

> This evokes three similar sayings (4:14, *14:30[15b], and *15:19[15b]) but differs from them importantly: instead of striving in the second clause to further prepare himself for possible recognition, the gentleman exerts himself outward, on behalf of others of even lower rank. It thus implies a "niceness" period, when empathy is accepted as central to the value system.

Reflections

The extremeness of 03c conditions (see *14:43[17]n, above) makes itself felt in many ways, among them the alienation of ordinary people. The Jwāngdž (JZ), with which the Analects spars directly in LY 18:5–7, is the great champion of these leftover people: the poor, the crippled, the ugly, the socially deprived. As a parallel tendency, we note in LY 17 (indeed, from LY 1 on) an emphasis on personal feelings. In the Mencian school, the feelings are the ground for reasserting human universality; see the Bull Mountain allegory in MC 6A8 (Waley **Three** 115–118, PB 83–86; and, poignantly, Blacker **Intent** 26–27).

Waley's comments on this passage note the breath-control aspect in Mencius's thinking. MC 6A8 is not by Mencius, but the perhaps authentic MC 2A2 (Legge **Mencius** 185f) does establish his use of this technique; it tallies with the Analects evidence (11:8b) for an 04c Lǔ meditation group with Yén Hwéi as its cult figure. In MC 2A2 we notice Mencius's disciples pushing to get Mencius to admit a special devotion to Yén Hwéi, and Mencius himself refusing to be identified with what may by then have been a Dàuist heresy.

Mencius's doctrines enraged other Confucians, including those of Chí and Ngwèi, who were becoming increasingly more important. Sywndž was the most energetic of these rivals; his counterattack on the Mencian theory of human nature (SZ 23, Knoblock **Xunzi** 3/150f; actually a counter to MC 6A2, Legge **Mencius** 395) is worth reading for a sense of the acrimony of the period. The Lǔ school by tradition expressed its ideas in the aphoristic medium of Confucius's sayings, and could not use the Sywndzian longer forms (though some 03c Analects passages are dialogues stretched almost to essay length). This may have been something of a tactical handicap in the war of ideas.

The 03c debate on human nature is still vigorous today. For a series of arguments within Sinology, and with an eye to contemporary relevance, see Graham **Background**, Ames **Conception**, and Bloom **Arguments** (readers are reminded that these essays assume a different relative chronology of the Analects and other texts than the one expounded in the present book).

There *is* something Warring States-ish about the 20c (Waley **Three** 11–12, PB ix; Mote **Foundations** 99). That does not refute our earlier suggestion that Aī-gūng may be the William the Conqueror of Lǔ: historical situations may have more than one parallel, each with its own sequences and its own timescales. Coulborn **Feudalism** begins by defining feudalism descriptively, but ends by insisting on position within a historical sequence as essential to the concept. Such programmatic expectations keep one from noticing cases of acceleration (such as Trotsky's law of combined development) or divergence. Comparative history consists not in mapping one history on another history, but in discovering factors that tend to cohere, or not, in analogous situations.

Phoenix Design on Bronze Mirror (see LY 18:6)
Height 2·0 cm (0·8 in). 03c. Courtesy Freer Gallery of Art (44·6)

18

c0262

LY 18 continues under the same head, Dž-shv̀n, and in the same context of philosophical disputation, as LY 17. It is a short chapter, and was probably compiled more as a controversial position than as a calm, inner-determined repertoire of sayings. The controversy in question is the classic one: whether to serve an illegitimate ruler (which at this juncture would likely have been the Chŭ-dominated Prince of Lŭ), to which the classic answer (see 4:5) was "No." On that question, LY 18 takes a brilliantly nonclassical position (see 18:6), consistent with the more recent line of political theory: now that the state can be conceived separately from the ruler, as something with its own needs and loyalty focus, the ruler's credentials, still decisive in 17:4/6, no longer count. The larger needs of human society are the determining concern.

This chapter, and associated interpolations in other chapters, was written before the partial Chŭ conquest of Lŭ brought Syw̆ndž directly on the scene as the military governor of occupied Lŭ, and the intellectual nemesis of Lŭ. Though much of interest can be detected in the covert sayings of LY 19–20, it has to be read between the lines. LY 18 is the last free Analects chapter.

The numbering of passages is identical in the Legge text.

⌐ 18:3. Chí Jǐng-gūng was awaiting a visit from Confucius. He said, To treat him like the head of the Jì clan – *that* I cannot do. I shall treat him as between the Jì and the Mv̀ng. He said, I am old, and cannot use you. Confucius went on his way.

> The two "he said" both refer to Jǐng-gūng, before and during Confucius's visit; the repetition here signals a narrative lapse of time. This is a redo of the 15:1 story of a visit to Wèi (with the same concluding verb syíng 行 "went his way"), upgraded to the more powerful Chí. The major new detail is the implication that Confucius should have been treated with the ceremonies due the head of the Jì; in other words, as a virtual head of state. The highest position previously claimed for him was that of prime minister to the Prince of Lŭ, in 14:21.
>
> For a Mician expansion of this story, see MZ 47:3 (Mei **Ethical** 223).

└ 18:4. Chí presented female musicians. Jì Hwándž accepted them, and for three days did not hold court. Confucius went on his way.

> Evidently Dž-shv̀n is also thinking of Confucius's days in Lŭ, since he here adds an anecdote explaining the rupture *between* Confucius and Lŭ. There is absolutely no warrant for accepting this as historical. It is in the pattern of ruler encounters established by the historical Mencius, and here grafted onto the evolving myth of Confucius. It must not be forgotten by analysts of the Analects that the Mencians were a rival school, and the prominence of their founder set a standard *for Confucians* that the Lŭ group could not afford to ignore. The departure of Confucius in 18:4 (compare 15:1/2) may be seen as imitating that of Mencius from Chí following the Yēn incident, the propriety of which is debated endlessly throughout the Mencius text (for example MC 2B11–12; Legge **Mencius** 228f). This defense had apparently confirmed departure as the seemly response. In any case, Confucius here does it too.

⌐ 18:5. Jyē-yẃ, the Madman of Chǔ, passed by Confucius singing,

>   Phoenix, ho! Phoenix, ho!
>   How is your virtue now brought low!
>   You cannot now reprove a past mistake;
>   You still can overtake a future woe.
>   Have done, oh! Have done, oh!
>   Those who now serve, at their own risk do so!

Confucius descended, and wanted to talk with him, but he quickened his steps and evaded him, and he was not able to talk with him.

> This is a rebuttal to the almost identical scene in the Jwāngdž (JZ 4:7; Watson **Chuang** 66), which cryptically censures Confucius for persisting in office in difficult times. It changes a detail at the end of the otherwise identically quoted anecdote. The new detail is Confucius's attempt *to refute the criticism,* and the unwillingness of the critic to stand his ground; its implied meaning is the Madman's lack of courage. Those who are only looking to save their own skins are of no use to others, or to the state. What Confucius probably wanted to say was what Frederick the Great *did* say to his troops at Cologne on 18 June 1757: "You wretches, do you want to live forever?"

> 18:6. Tall-in-the-Mud and Bold-in-the-Mire were plowing as a team. Confucius passed by, and sent Dž-lù to ask them about the ford. Tall-in-the-Mud said, Who is that driving? Dž-lù said, It is Kǔng Chyōu. He said, Would that be Kǔng Chyōu of Lǔ? He said, It would. He said, Oh, *he* knows the ford.

He asked of Bold-in-the-Mire. Bold-in-the-Mire said, Who are *you?* He said, Jùng Yóu. He said, Would that be the follower of Kǔng Chyōu of Lǔ? He replied, Yes. He said, A thing overflowing – All Under Heaven is such, and who is going to change it? Besides, than follow one who only withdraws from *men,* why not rather follow one who withdraws from the *age?* He went on plowing without further pause.

Dž-lù went and reported it. Our Respected Master said consolingly, Birds and beasts cannot be flocked together with. Were I not a follower of other men, with whom should I take part? If the world possessed the Way, Chyōu would not be doing his part to change it.

> For the symbol >, see 18:7n below. This counter-anecdote uses phrases from JZ 9:1, 12:5 and 12:9b (Watson **Chuang** 105, 131 "proceeded with work," 134f) and inspires a rejoinder in JZ 20:4, where Confucius is depicted as giving up his principles and living happily with birds and beasts (Watson 213f). The names of the primitivist hermits (compare MC 3A4 and Graham **Tillers**) exaggerate those given to Jwāngdž characters. The point of 18:6 is that it is precisely the danger that creates the obligation. Humankind, such as it is, is all that human beings can validly labor for. That this eloquent appeal was not lost on the JZ 4 people is shown by the fact that later parts of that chapter advocate *rejoining* the dangerous world (Brooks **Jwāngdž 4**; see also page 258 below).

> The covert meaning of "ask about the ford" is "seek for a way out of the chaos of the times." The literary hermit Táu Chyén (372–427) ended his famous "Peachblossom Fountain Preface" allegory with the line, "Since then, there has been no one to ask about the ford." This is a twinge of conscience; a sense that his own hermit life in evil times fell short of this imperative.

└ 18:7. Dž-lù was following, but fell behind. He met an old man who was carrying a basket on a staff. Dž-lù asked, Have you seen my Respected Master? The old man said, His four limbs he does not bestir, the five grains he cannot distinguish – who is your "Respected Master?" He planted his stick in the earth and began weeding. Dž-lù joined his hands respectfully, and stood there, waiting. He gave Dž-lù shelter for the night, killed a chicken and made a soup to feed him, and presented his two sons to him. Next day, Dž-lù went and reported it. The Master said, He is a hermit, and had Dž-lù go back and see him, but when he got there, he had gone. Dž-lù said, Not to serve is to have no sense of duty. Distinctions of age and youth may not be set aside; how can duties of ruler and subject be set aside? He wants to keep his person pure, and in the process disorders higher relations. The gentleman's serving is merely doing his duty. That the Way does not obtain: *this* he knows already.

> Unlike the invented 18:6, which ridicules the hermits from the beginning, 18:7 reads at first as favorable to the hermit, from whom Dž-lù respectfully seeks enlightenment. Only at the end, when the hermit is found to have run away, do our sympathies turn. The parallel with 18:5 suggests an outside source, which (or an analogue of which; not all the Jwāngdž has come down to us) may be JZ 25:6 (Watson **Chuang** 285f). The peroration, and thus the moral, is a more spelled-out version of the one in 18:6.
>
> The 18:5–7 series consists of what we may call a split pair, with 18:5 and 18:7 parallel stories based on Jwāngdž originals, separated (split) by a freely invented story on the same theme, but not as close to either of the flanking stories as they are to each other. This would suggest that the middle piece is an interpolation, and in previous chapters such a situation has been so interpreted. We note, however, that once the ABA interpolated triplet (examples include 3:4–6, with *3:5[14] splitting a Lín Fàng pair 3:4/6, or the very recent 17:4/6, on improper offers, which are to be split by the self-interpolated *17:5[18] passage grouped with this chapter) has become familiar through memorization and repetition, it is only a question of time before the ABA structure, like the AA structure of the basic pairing pattern, comes to be seen as valid in its own right. We assume that this stage has been reached with this triplet, directly inspired by Dž-shv̀n's own prior interpolation of the ministerial *17:5[18] between the anti-ministerial 17:4/6. It seems to us that the ABA framing structure here gives, and was meant to give, an architectural prominence to the central 18:6.

Interpolations

The LY 18 breakthrough from the old rigid concept of the state was echoed in interpolations placed in other Analects chapters; Dž-shv̀n seems indeed to have concentrated on these rather than on completing the 24-saying plan for LY 18. These political passages are probably of the same date as LY 18 itself, or c0262.

Some other interpolations (and all those added to LY 8) are not Confucian sayings, but bits of historic lore, imitating the Shū documents in constructing a new heritage to replace the obsolete feudal one. The idea that one can make direct contact with the past and future by mental effort, first stated in 2:23, is here adopted as a method. These lore passages are probably slightly later than the chapter proper and its associated political interpolations, or c0260.

For a complete finding list of interpolated passages, see page 329.

Added to LY 6

┌ *6:29. The Master said, The efficacy of the Middle Method, is it not the
ultimate? But among the people it has long indeed been rare! [6:27]

> The Jūng Yūng ("Middle Method") must refer to the text of that name, known
> in English since Legge as the "Doctrine of the Mean," which as Waley notes
> (**Analects** 241) has early 03c affinities but refers also to the Chín unification.
> It is thus an accretional text, whose early segments existed by LY 18, and whose
> late ones fall after 0221. JY 4 (Legge **Analects** 387) seems to be the core; a line
> in it is identical to one in LY 18:7. JY 5 is a variant (the Way is not practiced).
> JY 6 brings in Shùn, who figures in the present set of interpolations. There are
> several phrases in common with earlier Analects passages, and also links with
> various parts of the Mencius. With JY 3, probably added to the core at the same
> time as JY 7, we encounter the phrase here duplicated as LY *6:29. This shows
> a strong affinity between the nascent JY text and the Analects, though the fact
> that the JY apparently continued to be compiled into the Chín dynasty, while
> the Analects did not, suggests that they were sponsored by different groups.
> *6:29 thus gives a tantalizing hint of the activities of the Jūng Yūng group.

└ *6:30. Dž-gùng said, If there were one who bestowed benefits widely among the
people, and could relieve the condition of the multitude, how would that be?
Could he be called rv́n? The Master said, Why need one bother with "rv́n" – he
would surely be a sage; could even Yáu and Shùn find fault with him? As for rv́n:
You yourself want position, so you give position to others; you yourself want to
advance, so you advance others. To be able to *take one's example from near at hand*
– that can be said to be the method of rv́n. [6:28]

> The classic Golden Rule in its positive form as a basis for ethical extrapolation
> (the "near at hand" is one's own directly experienced character) here balances
> the novel technique of the middle course in *6:29. Note that the sage ruler is
> a *populist* ruler, who benefits the people in good times and saves them from
> disaster in bad. Disasters as a test of government derive from the 04c Micians
> (see MZ 16, Mei **Ethical** 87) and are also typical of the 03c (notice the image
> of the times as engulfed by calamity, like a flood, in 18:6). Yáu and Shùn,
> unknown in the early Analects, figure also in the LY 8 interpolations, below.

Added to LY 8

> These LY 8 additions, many of them containing ancient-ruler lore, enclose that
> chapter as previously augmented, with *8:1 at the head, and *8:18–21 at the
> tail. Like the LY 18 interpolations, below, they expand doctrine by constructing
> a validating antiquity; we date both to c0260, slightly later than LY 18 proper.

*8:1. The Master said, Tài-bwó is one who may be called perfectly virtuous. Thrice
he renounced the dominion of All Under Heaven, and the people had no chance
to praise him for it. [8:1]

> Tài-bwó relinquished the succession in favor of his nephew, the Jōu "cultural"
> founder Wv́n-wáng (see Nivison **Paradox** 35; the theory of sacrificing lineage
> to merit continues to develop). The people could not praise him because it was
> long before they directly benefited (compare *6:30 above) from his selflessness.

⌐ *8:18. The Master said, Impressive indeed was the way in which Shùn and Yw̌ possessed All Under Heaven, yet did not take part in it. [8:18]

> The last predicate means "were not involved in it, kept aloof from it," as the counterpart virtue to giving it away altogether (*8:1); Shùn and Yw̌ came to power by merit, not inheritance. Compare the earlier DDJ 10: the Way gives birth but does not possess (yǒu 有, as here). The DDJ image is maternal: the mother bears the child, but does not own the child; the child is its own person. Both the mother and the sage stand somewhat aside from their creations.

∟ *8:19. The Master said, Great indeed was Yáu's acting as a ruler. Impressive! It was Heaven that was great; it was Yáu that patterned on it. Pervasive was he, and the people were unable to give it a name. Impressive was his bringing things to completion; dazzling was his possession of cultural splendor. [8:19]

> The phrase wv́n-jāng (here "cultural splendor") occurs also in *5:13[17], where it is equally hard to define; we must infer that the perfection of social order under Yáu had its appropriate cultural perfection. The motif of not receiving praise from the people whom one benefits is common in these interpolations, and also in the Dàuism of the DDJ, by which (while it resists the nihilistic Dàuism of the Jwāngdž) the Analects of the period is evidently much affected. Another motif is modeling society on a cosmic order, implied in LY 2 (c0317). There is an 03c tussle between Heaven and man as the type of human virtue.

⌐ *8:20a. Shùn had five servitors, and all under Heaven was governed. [8:20a]

∟ *8:20b. King Wǔ said, I have ten ordering servitors. [8:20b]

> These bits of lore are like those added to LY 16 and 18 (see below); Legge (and Tswēi Shù before him) had already noted their strangeness. King Wǔ uses the pronoun yẃ 予 "I" in its historically accurate sense as a ruler's self-reference. The word translated "ordering" (lwàn 亂) normally means "disordering," as when the rhythmic pulse dissolves in the coda of a piece of Warring States music (see 3:23n), but these passages involve antique or supposedly antique usages, and whatever will confer an archaic tone is admissible. By context the word must here mean "able, order-producing," and so we assume that it does.
>
> Five (Parkinson **Law** 34f) or perhaps six (Beveridge **Art** 63, PB 86) are the maximum viable executive committee for a small project, or a large state.

⌐ *8:20c. Confucius said, "Talent is difficult," is it not so? The age of Táng and Yẃ, in just this point was successful. [In King Wǔ's ten] there was a woman; they were only nine men. Of three parts of All Under Heaven they held two, and with them submissively served Yīn – the virtue of Jōu can be said to be perfect virtue! [8:20c]

> A phrase seems to have dropped out of this two-part comment on *8:20a/b, and is here supplied in brackets. The first comment (Táng and Yẃ are the dynastic names for Yáu and Shùn, respectively) approves Parkinson's view that it is impossible to find more than five able people at one time. In the second part, the usually inclusive term rv́n 人 "man" is taken in its exclusive sense "male," a footnote on 17:23. Whether the woman of the ten was the wife or mother of Wv́n-wáng is much debated; this particular myth was obviously still evolving. Opinions differed as to whether the coming unification would be by force. Some traditions emphasize the violence of the Shāng/Jōu transition (Yīn is the dynastic name of late Shāng); this passage, optimistically, takes a pacific view.

└ *8:21. The Master said, In Yw̌, I have no fault to find. He had simple drink and food, but used the utmost devotion toward the ghosts and spirits. He had bad clothes and robes, but displayed the utmost beauty in his headdress and surplice. He had a lowly hall and chamber, but put forth all his strength on ditching and draining. In Yw̌, I have no fault to find. [8:21]

> Yw̌ was first associated with farming (Brooks **Myth**; see 14:5). Later he became a hero who drained the waters of a great flood, thus fixing the watercourses. This myth is attested as early as the late 04c; the Analects is slow to assimilate this and other aspects of the new antiquity. The selflessness of Yw̌ in laboring for the common good is given ritual expression: ignoring his personal comfort, he puts his effort into ritual observances. Compare the "beautiful" of *13:8[14].

Added to LY 9

*9:4. The Master avoided four things: no wish, no will, no set, no self. [9:4]

> This cryptic line is explained by Lyóu Jv̌ng-yì in the light of the political fluidity of *18:8b[18] ("no may, no may not"), which we refer to this same period. Its third predicate, the adverb bì 必 "invariably," is with difficulty nominalized in English. All invite intellectual interpretation: no fixed opinions, no foregone conclusions, no stubbornness, no self-absorption. This can equally well evoke the supple art of the 03c courtier or the intellectual ethos of modern research (Beveridge **Art** 115, PB 160). It would have shocked Confucius, who sacrificed office for principle (see 4:10), but it suits the 03c. Only Ware and Lau render the prohibitive force of the repeated verb wú 毋 "do not." *9:4 may have been originally a self-cultivation rule, here imperfectly adapted to a political context.

*9:9. The Master said, The phoenix does not come; the River puts forth no diagram. I am finished! [9:8]

> This despair is symbolized by late images: the phoenix omen (for this motif, surprisingly rare in Warring States art, see page 172), and the River Diagram (the reference is to the Yellow River). The latter is not interpreted as the magic square of order three until Hàn times (we are grateful to Nathan Sivin for this clarification); in the late 04c it may have been a 3 × 3 array representing the nine parts of China in Dzōu Yěn's geography; a symbol of universal dominion. The meaning is then, I shall not live to see the achievement of the new order.
>
> Yoshikawa **Zakki**, an essay by a specialist for the (Japanese) general reader, contains a meditation on this passage.

Added to LY 3

*3:24. The borderman of Yí asked to be presented; he said, Whenever a gentleman comes to this place, I have never failed to be presented to him. The followers presented him. When he came out, he said, You disciples, why do you worry about failure? That All Under Heaven has not had the Way has long indeed been true. Heaven is going to make of your Respected Master a wooden gong. [3:24]

> The frontier guard as spokesman is a Dàuist device; see JZ 12:4 (Watson **Chuang** 130), where Yáu is chastened by one. The prediction here is benign: the Master will sound the public note of a new and better age.

Added to LY 14

⌐ *14:37a. The Master said, The worthy withdraw from the age, the next withdraw from a place, the next withdraw at a look, the next withdraw at a word. [14:39]

> The "withdraw" (bì 辟) is exactly the term used by the hermit of 18:6, above, and expresses the same prickly scrupulosity as that shown by Mencius in his departure from Chí. This may seem to contradict 18:6, but see next.

∟ *14:37b. The Master said, Those who rose up were seven. [14:40]

> But for the paired comment, this would look like a bit of ancient lore randomly added to the text. Waley interprets dzwò 作 "arose" as "invented," implying culture heroes; Lyóu Jvng-yì 324) takes it instead as "rose and departed," and lists seven or so political recluses, among them those of 18:5–7 above, and, more plausibly, Bwó-yí and Shú-chí from 5:23 (compare *18:8a, below).
>
> This sentiment might better fit the period of withdrawal, LY 1 and 16. We note however the similarity of wording in *14:37a and 18:6, and the similarity of manner in *14:37b and the various lore interpolations, in dating them here. We take these passages as an assertion of ancient principle which balances, and does not refute, the LY 18 assertion of relative freedom within that principle. Compare the following pair.

⌐ *14:38. Dž-lù passed the night at Stone Gate. The gate watchman said, Where are you from? Dž-lù said, I am from Mr. Kŭng. He said, Isn't that the one who knows it can't be done, but goes on doing it? [14:41]

> Perhaps an echo of JZ 25:6 (Watson **Chuang** 285), where Confucius himself stays overnight on a journey and is gawked at disapprovingly by the locals. The question, which the gatekeeper intends as derisory ("he does not see the futility of his efforts"), will be taken by Analects readers as adulatory, in just the sense of 18:6 ("he is not deterred by the hopelessness of his task from pursuing it"). In its miniature way, it achieves the same reversal of expectation as 18:6.

∟ *14:39. The Master was playing the chimes in Wèi. Someone with a basket on his back passed by Mr. Kŭng's gate, and said, Has he not something in mind, he who plays the chimes? After a time, he said, Vulgar! If nobody recognizes you, there is an end of it: "If it is deep, plunge in: if shallow, lift your skirt." The Master said, How consistent! From that point of view, there is indeed no difficulty. [14:42]

> The quote is from Shr 34 (Waley **Songs** #54), and recommends adapting to circumstances. The only difficulty in reading such anecdotes is the layers of irony they contain. The "consistency" of the rustic recluse, which he demands that Confucius should adopt, is in fact expediency: a *lack* of fixed principle that equally tolerates good and bad situations. Confucius, as his playing shows (the chimes are an orchestral and not a private instrument, as witness *18:9 below; his house in Wèi must have been lavishly furnished), has instead a principle. He is not feudally bound to lineal loyalty, or even to a code of personal purity. That is what the basketman keeps, and LY 18 sacrifices. What LY 18 retains, as reaffirmed in 14:37a/b and upheld here, is a commitment to good order (see *6:30). This more difficult kind of consistency lies beyond prudence, or even rigid principle: a resolute intention that is responsive to the particular situation. It may be such a conflictive consistency that *9:4 above is defining.

Added to LY 16

*16:9. Confucius said, Those who know it from birth are the highest, those who know it from study are next, those who despite difficulties study it are next after that. Those who in difficulties do *not* study: these are the lowest. [16:9]

> Confucius disclaims innate knowledge in 7:20, but now the Mencians are claiming that anyone can be a Yáu or a Shùn (MC 6B2). This saying is echoed in JY 20 (Legge **Analects** 407), but there the fourth category is dropped, and the other three are grades of intelligence, all of which eventually reach the goal. In LY *16:9, kùn 困 "difficulties" must refer to outward circumstances; the last two types are then those in difficult circumstances who have, or lack, the will to learn. It is in the middle levels that progress due to effort is possible, as in 17:2b. The Analects group, while widening the range within which they used to posit educability, are not prepared to go *all* the way with the Mencians.
>
> This saying, like *17:5 below, splits a previous pair. Once in place, it is a model of the ABA form which we have assumed (see 18:7n above) is used intentionally and originally in 18:5–7.

*16:14. The wife of the sovereign of a state: when the sovereign refers to her, he says "The Distinguished One," when the Distinguished One refers to herself, she says "This small youth," when the people of the same state refer to her, they say "The Sovereign's Distinguished One," when he refers to her in another state, he says "The Orphaned One's Little Sovereign," and when the people of the other state refer to her, they also say "The Sovereign's Distinguished One." [16:14]

> This (compare *8:20b above) gives reference conventions for women of rank. One suspects that their prominence outside the palace circle is new, and that this protocol was invented to meet the new need. As Waley notes, none of the terms is specifically female, though fū-rv́n 夫人 "Distinguished One" is always translated, and is now probably felt, as feminine. It is a twin of dàifū 大夫, which in Spring and Autumn meant court dignitaries, including husbands of the Prince's daughters. The "youth" (túng 童) is the "lad" of the song quoted at *15:11[15], and seems also to be a term of normally masculine reference.

Added to LY 17

*17:5. Dž-jāng asked Confucius about rv́n. Confucius said, One who can practice the Five everywhere under Heaven would be rv́n. He begged to ask about them. He said, Respect, magnanimity, fidelity, diligence, kindness. If he is respectful, he will not be snubbed. If he is magnanimous, he will win the multitude. If he is faithful, others will do their duty for him. If he is diligent, he will have success. If he is kindly, he will be able to employ others. [17:6]

> The rv́n person is here seen as a ruler or a high minister deputizing for a ruler. Only the first and fourth are personal; the rest are recipes for getting and using power: attracting a popular following, motivating subordinates, and inducing major talents to work for him. Note the presence of the "kindliness" scorned as a virtue in 14:9, but in the present kindly century accepted in the list of Five. *17:5 may be an afterthought definition of the ideal ruler envisioned in the original chapter's 17:4/6; compare 13:10/11.

Added to LY 18

These lore passages encapsulate LY 18 as the concentric additions to LY 8, above, surrounded *that* chapter. They are probably close in date to the LY 8 lore passages; at the least, all must follow rather than precede the LY 18 core. Such equations might be used to divide these interpolations into multiple strata (compare the interpolations in LY 15). As a beginning in this direction we have tentatively dated the LY 18 and other lore passages to c0260 rather than c0262.

⌐ *18:1a. The Master of Wēi left him, the Master of Jī became his slave, Bĭ-gān remonstrated and died. [18:1a]

> For the lore/comment pair, see 14:37a/b, above. The "him" is the bad last ruler of the Shāng or Yīn period. This approval of suicidal remonstrance against a depraved ruler had an enormous effect in inspiring individuals to feats of personal courage in later, despotic centuries.

ᒪ *18:1b. Confucius said, The Yīn in them had three rv́n men. [18:1b]

> The "in them" refers to the paired *18:1a. Here is another case where rv́n can be said to mean "dedicated to principle in the discharge of official duties."

Ŀ *18:2. When Lyŏusyà Hwèi was Leader of the Officers, he was thrice dismissed. People said, Can you not bring yourself to go elsewhere? He said, If I should serve others with an upright Way, where can I go that I would not be thrice dismissed? And if I am going to serve others with a crooked Way, why need I leave the country of my father and mother? [18:2]

> The criticism of Hwèi is that he lacks dignity; he retorts that he has principle, or (wryly), if not principle, at least a proper sentiment toward his native place. Wryness tends to get lost over the millennia, but this passage holds up nicely; it remains one of the retorts most beloved of latter-day Analects followers.

⌐ *18:8a. Subjects who went into seclusion were Bwó-yí, Shú-chí, Yẃ Jùng, Yí Yì, Jū Jāng, Lyŏusyà Hwèi, Shàu-lyén. [18:8a]

> There is some difficulty about one of the names (see below), but otherwise these might be the mysterious "seven" of *14:37b, above.

ᒪ *18:8b. The Master said, They did not bend their wills, they did not disgrace their persons: these were Bwó-yí and Shú-chí, were they not? One might say of Lyŏusyà Hwèi and Shàu-lyén that they bent their wills and disgraced their persons; their words matched their station and their deeds matched their concerns; this and no more. One might say of Yẃ Jùng and Yí Yì that they dwelt in seclusion and were unrestrained in speech; in their persons they showed purity, and in their retirement they showed flexibility. As for me, I am different from these: I have no "may" and no "may not." [18:8b]

> Only six of the *18:8a names appear here. The Táng scholiast Lù Dv́-míng suspects that the seventh, Jū Jāng, is a corruption in *18:8a. This makes it agree with *18:8b, but at the cost of any light *18:18a might have shed on *14:37b.
>
> The Master's concluding remark rejects all these models in favor of a more flexible standard; compare *9:4 above (and the simplified version in MC 5B1, Legge **Mencius** 369). The recurring problem of service versus exit from service has remained vexatious for Confucians down to the present time.

┌ *18:9. Grand Preceptor Jŕ went to Chí, second course Gān went to Chŭ, third course Lyáu went to Tsài, fourth course Chywē went to Chín, drummer Fāng-shú went to the River, taborer Wŭ went to the Hàn, and Lesser Preceptor Yáng and chime-player Syāng went to the sea. [18:9]

> Master Jŕ we met in *8:15[14]; the next few were leaders (lead wind-players?) at different courses of banquets (or different meals?). The dispersal of the court musicians implies a disaster; Waley suggests the exile of Jāu-gūng in 0517. The River is the Yellow River, the Hàn is a tributary of the Yángdž, the sea is the Eastern Sea (compare *5:7[11]). The scattering extends over the entire map.

> This probably exaggerates Lŭ music in Confucius's time (in 7:14, c0450, it was outclassed by Chí). Lŭ court music *is* however implicit in the interview with a Lŭ Grand Preceptor, 3:23 (c0342); these two passages attest musical growth in Lŭ over the period c0450–c0342. But a pious school head, referring both *to the time of Confucius*, might have thought to reconcile 3:23 (implying court music in Lŭ) and 7:14 (attesting it in Chí) by creating a link in *18:9 (where a Lŭ musician goes to Chí, establishing Chí music *from a Lŭ source*).

> *18:10. The Prince of Jōu said to the Prince of Lŭ, The gentleman does not favor relatives; he does not make great ministers resent not being used. Old associates he does not without reason cast off; he does not look for everything in one man. [18:10]

> For the symbol >, see *18:11n, below. The Jōu regent Jōu-gūng (see 7:5) speaks to his heir, the first Prince of Lŭ. No statecraft rule (in Lŭ, at any rate: Chí theorists used Gwăn Jùng) could have higher authority. It recommends a rational bureaucracy, where nepotism is resisted and officers are given proper scope. Claims of acquaintance are admitted, but dismissal for cause is retained. In assigning men to tasks, the ruler will use them according to their skills, as in 13:25 (without making the 2:12 exception for gentlemen). The new issue (depending on the meaning of shī 施 "put forward," which some authorities, citing JY, define as "replace") is that of nepotism. It was perhaps raised by the increased prominence of the ruler's wife in this period (see *16:14n above).

└ *18:11. Jōu had eight officers: Bwó-dát and Bwó-gwāt, Jùng-tūt and Jùng-hūt, Shú-yà and Shú-syà, and Jì-swéi and Jì-gwéi. [18:11]

> The point of this list seems to be its rhyming pairs of names, here phonetically antiqued to give an idea of the impression they may have conveyed at the time. The prefixes are the standard sequential ones for sons in the same family: Bwó "elder," Shú "younger," Jùng "next," and Jì "least." Nothing useful is known of these people, who are thus as obscure to us as those in *18:9.

> Here, as in 18:5–7, with its middle member marked by >, is an original split pair, or triplet: *18:9/11 resonate, while *18:10 introduces a policy statement. It may be that this bit of structure is a stylistic trademark of Dž-shvn.

Reflections

None of the core LY 18 passages are sayings; all of them are anecdotes. This form was introduced in the DJ, developed in the Mencius (note the virtual short story in MC 4B33), and became the medium of choice for the mob of Jwāngdž writers. By thus keeping up with the latest literary techniques, the Analects people showed themselves worthy of a continued part in the fray.

There was a tactical dilemma facing the Analects writers at this period. Direct rebuttals to Jwāngdž (as in 18:5–7) violated the historical convention of the Analects, and like any rebuttal gave the attacker more visibility. A safer tactic was to avoid contemporary polemic and put the argument beyond debate by basing it on ancient history, as is done in the bits of lore attached to LY 18 and other 03c chapters (noticed by Tswēı Shù as one trait of these chapters). But rival schools could make up lore too, leading to the taunt of the Micians to the Confucians, in the race to forge speeches of ever more ancient kings, "Your antiquity isn't old enough" (MZ 48:4, from c0285; Mei **Ethical** 233).

Schneider (**Madman** 17f and 42f) observes that the emblematic figures of Bwó-yí and Shú-chí figure in an aristocratic framework, whereas the Madman of Chŭ in 18:5 is from the world of the minister. The transition in the Analects is from 16:7, where Bwó-yí and Shú-chí are still revered, via the agonizing reappraisal of LY 17, to *18:8b, where Confucius distances himself from them. But the principled recluses of *18:8a continued as a type; see the early Hàn Four Ancients of SJ 55 (4/2044–2047; Watson **Records** 1/146–149). For an overview of the tension between service and reclusion, see Mote **Eremitism**.

There is another side to Confucius's undaunted resolve in 18:6, and that is the truly daunting conditions from which the recluses were retreating. One gets in a number of contemporary texts a picture of a society which had virtually dissolved. Slavery had become widespread, and is often mentioned (Brooks **Slavery**): the convict laborers swarm in JZ 11:3 (Watson **Chuang** 118) and MC 7A2 (Legge **Mencius** 450). Besides the brigands already noticed above, there were the wandering armed men who gravitated to the estates of the rich as private retainers (JGT 154, Crump **Ts'e** 189; for further examples compare Liu **Knight** 13f). The sale of wife and children into slavery was a recourse for at least one noble in debt (JGT #153, Crump **Ts'e** 188), and Kinney **Infant** 117 notes the abandonment of children by starving commoners (MC 1A7, Legge **Mencius** 148, and MZ 5, Mei **Ethical** 21). Even apart from the endemic warfare, times were hard.

Waley (**Analects** 21) sees 18:5–7 as from "a world hostile to Confucius." We can follow him, up to a point. We can see the Dàuists sneaking up to Confucian headquarters in the dead of night. We can see them jimmying open a window. We can see them taking the Analects manuscript out of its drawer in the office desk. We can see them writing anti-Confucian anecdotes into it. We can hear them chortling as they vanish into the night. What we *can't* see is the scene next morning, where Dž-shv̀n comes in, opens the book, finds the Dàuist stories, scratches his head, mumbles, Well, yeah; I guess I *must* have, and calls the students in to memorize them. We envision an earthier reaction.

If Waley's theory does not hold, then these stories are *not* intrusive, but reflect a creative engagement of the Analects partisans with the Jwāngdž partisans. *This part of the text* must then be post-Jwāngdzian, and the Analects as a whole must cover a long time period. In this way (see also Appendix 1), one arrives at something like the present theory of the text.

What did the Confucians do, once back in office? DDJ 70–75, from this period, complain of Legalistic policies, and it may then be that the Analects Confucians were already adopting this outlook, a convergence anticipating the one that Hsiao **Political** 456f notes for Confucians in general during the Hàn. We may thus wish to be alert for hints of Legalism in the next layer, LY 19.

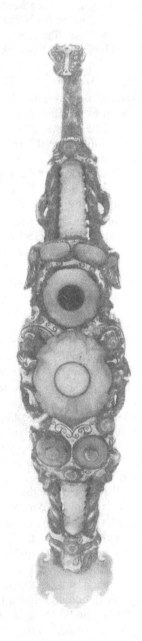

Ornate Bronze Belt Hook (see LY 19:7)

Length 22 cm (8·7 in). 03c. Courtesy Freer Gallery of Art (54·121)

19
c0253

In the winter of 0255/0254, Chŭ armies occupied the southern part of Lŭ. To oversee the newly conquered territory, they set up a Directorship in Lán-líng (34°42′ N, 117°49′ E), and as Director they picked Sywn Chīng. For three years (0257–0255) he had been the oldest member and ex officio libationer at the revived Jì-syà establishment in Chí, but his position there had become difficult, perhaps due to friction with colleagues representing earlier Chí thought (SJ 74, Nienhauser **Records** 7/184). He thus moved to Lán-líng, and established a school that would last until his Chŭ patron died in 0238, and would exert a profound influence on Confucianism well into the Hàn dynasty.

Northern Lŭ was not occupied, but its affairs were effectively controlled from Lán-líng. The Analects, with Dž-shvn continuing as head, responds to Sywndž with defiance (the main chapter) but also interest (the interpolations made at that time in other chapters). LY 19 has a subtly satirical dimension, and, like all underground literature, can be hard to decode in later ages. It is made up of sayings by five disciples, three of them criticized by the others. Those three disapprove errors that may be emphases of the Sywndzian school, and their squabbling may be a caricature of Sywndž's own contentiousness: attacks on other viewpoints fill substantial stretches of the Sywndzian writings.

The numbering of passages is identical in the Legge text.

[A. Dž-jāng]

⌐ 19:1. Dž-jāng said, If an officer when faced with danger carries out his orders, if when faced with profit he thinks of right, if when sacrificing he thinks of humility, and if when in mourning he thinks of his grief, I expect that he will do.

This is the first appearance of Dž-jāng as a primary speaker. He shows courage, useful for a threatened country. All his points have earlier Analects precedents; for profit versus right, see 16:10.

∟ 19:2. Dž-jāng said, If his hold on virtue is not wide, if his trust in the Way is not sincere, how can one say he is there? And how can one say he is *not* there?

Ardor has always been demanded (4:9, 5:10a, 6:12); for wideness, see *15:29[15a]. This may deplore Sywndzian adaptability (SZ 3:5, Knoblock **Xunzi** 1/175f): "These semi-Confucians are neither quite with us nor wholly against us."

∟ 19:3. Dž-syà's disciples asked Dž-jāng about personal relationships. Dž-jāng said, What does Dž-syà say? They replied, Dž-syà says, Those whom you can, you associate with; those whom you can't, you rebuff. Dž-jāng said, That is different from what I have heard. The gentleman respects the worthy but countenances the many. He esteems the good but pities the incapable. Am I a great worthy? Then among others, whom should I not countenance? Am I unworthy? Then the others will rebuff *me*; what need have I to rebuff the others?

This plea for inclusiveness and against arrogance wryly notes the superfluity of hauteur: it labels you as an uncomprehensive and thus unworthy person, who (like the contentious Sywndž) is unlikely to receive attentions requiring rebuff.

[B. Dž-syà]

⌐ 19:4. Dž-syà said, Though they may be little Ways, there will surely be something in them worth seeing, yet if carried too far, there is the danger of being distracted. For this reason the gentleman does not do them.

This may be aimed at the Syẃndzian emphasis on text study. "Distracted" is literally ní 泥 "mud," in the present context perhaps "bogged down."

L 19:5. Dž-syà said, If day by day he is aware of what he lacks, and if month by month he does not forget what he can do, one can call him fond of learning.

A favorite passage of teachers; more than one book title has borrowed from it. Note the emphasis on skill over information: what one has learned *to do.*

⌐ 19:6. Dž-syà said, To be of wide learning and sincere intent, to question incisively and reflect on what is close at hand – rv́n will be found in this.

For jìn 近 "at hand, nearby," compare *6:30[18]. Notice that learning is by questioning followed by personal reflection (the classic method), rather than by memorization of texts (more recent), and that its practice is, or leads to, rv́n. Another passage that has generated its share of book titles in later ages.

L 19:7. Dž-syà said, The hundred artisans dwell in their shops to perfect their specialty, and the gentleman studies to realize his Way.

The apprenticeship motif is socially suggestive. The end of the gentleman's effort of skill development is the Way, not here political but personal. Skill cultivation is a major motif in the Jwāngdž (JZ 19:9–10, Watson **Chuang** 204f), often as a symbol for meditational expertise.

⌐ 19:8. Dž-syà said, The mistakes of the little people will always be in the direction of culture.

Or, as an interpretative translation would say, of superficial elaboration.

L 19:9. Dž-syà said, The gentleman has three aspects. When you view him from afar, he is awe-inspiring. When you get close to him, he is warm. When you listen to his words, he is severe.

Formal in demeanor, affable in personal contact, incisive in counsel.

⌐ 19:10. Dž-syà said, The gentleman is faithful, and only then exacts toil from his people. If there were not trust, then they would think he was oppressing them. He is faithful, and only then remonstrates. If there were not trust, he would think he was slandering him.

Establishing trust is vital, in directing the populace ("they" in the first clause) or in chiding the sovereign ("he" in the second). Here is a more complete blueprint for the postfeudal state than before, with the sovereign limited to an advice-taking role and the minister ("gentleman") operationally in charge.

L 19:11. Dž-syà said, With greater virtue, one does not cross the lines. With lesser virtue, it is all right to come and go.

This ethical latitude offends Legge ("very questionable"); Waley takes "greater virtue" as "undertakings of greater moral import." If so, then "virtue" becomes "internalized *sense* of virtue," or what the Mencians mean by conscience.

⌐ 19:12. Dž-yóu said, Dž-syà's disciples: if it is sprinkling and sweeping, responding and replying, or advancing and retreating, they are satisfactory. They look to the details. But if you get them onto the basics, they have nothing. What is to be done? Dž-syà heard this, and said, No, Yén Yóu is wrong. The Way of the Gentleman is:

> He to whom 'tis early told
> Will weary of it ere he's old

I would compare it to grass and trees; each one is different from the rest. The Way of the Gentleman: how can it be criticized? The one who has a beginning, and who has an end, will he not be a Sagely Man?

This defends a teaching sequence beginning with details: theory encountered too early can be overwhelming or unintelligible. This is pedagogically sound (too much of education is answers to questions the student has not yet asked), and perhaps also a criticism of a theory-first trend in the Sywndzian school.

The last piece in each section so far *criticizes another disciple*: Dž-jāng reproved Dž-syà in 19:3, and Dž-syà here refutes Dž-yóu. Who will be next?

[C. Dž-yóu]

⌐ 19:14. Dž-yóu said, In mourning, go to the point of grief and stop.

The form should not outrun the feeling (compare *7:9[10] and 3:4). Is it not the Sywndzians who are championing excessively elaborate mourning customs?

∟ 19:15. Dž-yóu said, My friend Jāng: when it comes to doing what is difficult, he is capable. But he is not yet rvn.

"What is difficult" seems to be the demeanor and not the mere duty (see 2:8). What is granted to Dž-jāng was recommended by Dž-yóu in the paired saying.

This criticism eliminates Dž-jāng as a possible winner. All persons quoted so far have also been criticized. We are at a formal crux.

∟ 19:16. Dzvngdž said, Pompous indeed is Jāng. It is hard to be rvn alongside him.

To finish off Dž-jāng, we have Dzvngdž chiming in; it is *in rvn* that Dž-jāng falls short. Dzvngdž himself is now in the running as the undefeated candidate.

[D. Dzvngdž]

⌐ 19:17. Dzvngdž said, I have heard from our Respected Master, A man who has not had occasion to exert himself to the full will surely do so in mourning his parents.

Continuing the sequence (begun in 19:14) on mourning, and displaying Dzvngdž in the filial piety phase for which he is mythically renowned in Hàn.

∟ 19:18. Dzvngdž said, I have heard from our Respected Master, As for the filiality of Mvng Jwāngdž, the rest one might manage, but his not changing his father's ministers and his father's government – *this* is difficult to manage.

This is still firmly within the filiality vein, but it extends the reach of the interpolated *4:20[2], which first enjoined restraint in making changes even after a parent's death, to the "government" sphere (one gathers, the policy sphere).

⌊ 19:19. The head of the Mvng made Yáng Fū the Leader of the Officers. He asked Dzvngdž about it. Dzvngdž said, That those on high have lost the Way, and that the people have scattered, is of long standing. If you find evidences of it, then feel grief and pity; do not rejoice over it.

> It is Yáng Fū, not the head of the Mvng, who inquires. Shř Shī 士 師 "Leader of the Officers" is the post Confucius might have held (Waley **Analects** 15). The legal term chíng 情 "circumstances, evidences" appears in 13:4 as "facts." Dzvngdž feels that the culture of Lǔ (*postconquest* Lǔ?) is not what it was.

[E. Dž-gùng]

> Now it is Dž-gùng's turn. Will he attack Dzvngdž? Or do something else, now that the circle of criticisms has been closed (19:15–16) and not reopened?

⌐ 19:20. Dž-gùng said, The evils of Jòu cannot have been as extreme as that. For this reason, the gentleman hates to dwell in the lower reaches, since all the world's evils tend to accumulate there.

> Jòu 紂 (not the dynasty, which is Jōu 周 in the level tone) was the bad last ruler of the Shāng dynasty, conquered by King Wǔ of Jōu. The atrocities told of him are typical of the "bad last ruler" historical paradigm, used to justify an end or transfer of sovereignty. For "lower reaches," see DDJ 66 (compare the reaction in 17:22 to DDJ 61). Like MC 7B3 (Legge **Mencius** 479), 19:20 is a major Warring States expression of distrust in other people's forged ancient texts.

⌊ 19:21. Dž-gùng said, The gentleman's mistakes are like eclipses of sun or moon. If he makes a mistake, everyone sees him; if he changes, everyone looks up to him.

> Just as rulers get extra blame (19:20), they also get extra credit for reforming. The use of eclipses as a not wholly baneful symbol, here, bears on the question of whether several *spurious* eclipses might have been interpolated into the CC to honor the birthdates of Confucius and his forbears (see page 266).

⌐ 19:22. Gūngsūn Cháu of Wèi asked Dž-gùng, From whom did Jùng-ní learn? Dž-gùng said, The culture of Wvn and Wǔ has not fallen to the ground: it exists among men. The worthy know its larger aspects; the unworthy know its smaller aspects – no one *does not* possess the Way of Wvn and Wǔ. From whom did our Respected Master *not* learn? But equally, what *regular* preceptor did he have?

> Dž-gùng here returns to the question he muffed in 9:6, and handles it nicely, making a virtue rather than an embarrassment of Confucius's eclectic youth, and in the process implicitly damning Sywndž's "regular" type of school.
>
> The social implications are important: even the unworthy (bù-syén 不 賢) are part of society, with a unique role in embodying and preserving its values.

⌊ 19:23. Shúsūn Wǔ-shú, talking with the great officers at court, said, Dž-gùng is worthier than Jùng-ní. Džfú Jǐng-bwó reported this to Dž-gùng. Dž-gùng said, I would compare it to the wall of a mansion. Sž's wall comes up to your shoulder, and you can see how attractive the house is. Our Respected Master's wall is several rods high, and if you cannot find a gate to go in by, you do not see the elegance of the ancestral shrine, or the splendor of the hundred officials, and those who find that gate are few indeed. So then, is not the Respected Master's remark appropriate?

The second "Respected Master" refers to Shúsūn Wŭ-shú. This again deals with those who would disparage Confucius; here, their tactic is not to attack Confucius, but to praise Dž-gùng (Sž), who, as we have seen in 11:18b, was reputed to be rich. The reply is that Dž-gùng's virtues are obvious to all, but the higher virtues of Confucius are visible only to those who "find the gate" by understanding his teachings. That only his intimates appreciate Confucius's virtues implies that those virtues are not public, and the sacrificial touches in the comparison further support the implication that they are rather mystical.

Syŵndž did not possess the lineal *tradition* of Confucius, but specialized instead in the learned explication of texts which had come to be *associated* with Confucius. He rarely quotes Confucius, but regularly quotes the Shī and Shū. The gibe at Confucius in 19:22 may be Syŵndzian ridicule of the Lŭ lack of a transmitted *text* "tradition." The Lŭ response is that the culture, as preserved by its own people, is their tradition. This is followed in 19:23 by the crusher "Few indeed are those who find that gate." So much for Syŵndž.

┌ 19:24. Shúsūn Wŭ-shú had tried to disparage Jùng-ní. Dž-gùng said, It cannot be done; Jùng-ní cannot be disparaged. The worthiness of others is a hill or mound; one can walk up them. Jùng-ní is the sun and moon; there is no way one could walk up them. Though a man should want to cut himself off, what harm would that do to the sun and moon? It would merely show that he lacked a sense of proportion.

The word "disparage" at the beginning of this saying is incipient rather than indicative in aspect ("made as though to disparage," not "did disparage"). Incipient aspect is covert rather than overt, linguistically speaking: there is no inflection or auxiliary word to signal it. The sense of the sentence is the only guide. As to the designation "Jùng-ní," it is new in this chapter, though met with in the 03c works of other schools. Conventions vary somewhat from text to text, but often "Jùng-ní" is relation-neutral, unlike "Confucius" ("Master Kŭng"), which acknowledges his status as an authority figure. This may imply that we have here a debate *among* schools, not a question *within* one school.

A final pair refuting a disparagement of Confucius which may represent the criticism of the Syŵndž school. Their "dropping out" of the doctrinal lineage is compared to a man's seceding from the sun and moon: merely ridiculous.

└ 19:25. Chýn Dž-chín said to Dž-gùng, You are being polite; how could Jùng-ní be worthier than you? Dž-gùng said, A gentleman for one word is seen to be wise, or for one word is seen to be unwise: of words one cannot but take care. Jùng-ní's being unsurpassable is like Heaven's being unclimbable by stairs. When our Respected Master got control of a state or a family, it was what one calls "If he caused them to stand, they stood; if he showed them the Way, they went; if he invited them, they came; if he moved them, they were harmonious." In life, honored; in death, lamented – how could it be that anyone should surpass him?

Claiming for Confucius not merely capacity, but actual achievement, in both the state and the family; a late stage of Confucian myth. His "achievements" figure among those attributed in LY 12–13 to the ideal ruler. The phrase "climbing to Heaven" occurs in MC 7A41 (Legge **Mencius** 474).

The ambition of LY 17, to have some ministership, *any* ministership, is here calmly taken as a long-accomplished fact. The myth is growing rapidly.

Interpolations

These Sywndzian interpolations are too few to be plausible as appeasement, and may represent genuine borrowings. They include an addition to LY 19 itself, and may be slightly later than the chapter date; we put them all at c0252.

For a complete finding list of interpolated passages, see page 329.

Added to LY 13

*13:3. Dž-lù said, If the Ruler of Wèi were waiting for the Master to run his government, what would the Master do first? The Master said, It would certainly be to rectify names, would it not? Dž-lù said, Is there such a thing? The Master is off the track. What is this about rectifying? The Master said, Boorish indeed is Yóu! The gentleman, with respect to what he does not understand, should maintain an abashed silence. If names are not rectified, speech will not be representative. If speech is not representative, things will not get done. If things do not get done, rites and music will not flourish. If rites and music do not flourish, punishments and penalties will not be just. And if punishments and penalties are not just, the people will have nowhere to put hand or foot. Therefore, as to the gentleman: if he names something, it must be sayable, and if he says something, it must be doable. The gentleman's relation to words is to leave nothing whatever to chance. [13:3]

> This "chain argument" was noticed by Waley (**Analects** 22) as Sywndzian, and the doctrine of "rectifying names" forms a whole chapter in that text (SZ 22; Knoblock **Xunzi** 3/113f). Waley notes the astonishment of Dž-lù as betraying the novelty of the idea, an insight which we have applied to similar passages.
>
> This Sywndzian idea has precedents in 12:11 ("let the father be a father") and elsewhere (Makeham **Name** 39f), but whereas 12:11 can be read as social role fulfilment, *13:3 is about the chain of command. These interpolations, then, do not satirize, but *adapt from*, Sywndž. Given Sywndž's Legalist leaning, the question asked in 18r perhaps begins to be answered.
>
> Waley mentions a historical "language crisis," which he dates to the late 04c or early 03c (**Way** 59). The precision of naming here enjoined does relate to a general interest, much developed in the Mician school (Graham **Later**; compare Graham **Three**), in the logic of precise statement and valid inference.

Added to LY 15

*15:36. The Master said, With rýn, one need not defer to one's teacher. [15:35]

> However it was originally meant, the Sywndzian or post-Sywndzian saying "Blue [dye] comes from indigo [plants], but it is bluer than indigo" (SZ 1:1; Knoblock **Xunzi** 1/135) is later taken to refer to students surpassing teachers. Deference to *teachers* limits the success of *students*, not to mention the *school*.

*15:39. The Master said, There is teaching, but there are no kinds. [15:38]

> Lèi 類, logical or social class, otherwise unknown in the Analects, is common in Sywndž (Knoblock **Xunzi** 1/252). *15:39 agrees with Mencius (MC 2B2, 3A1, 4B32): the sages and ourselves are of one kind; any difference is in degree of cultivation. Thus, "There are *teaching* differences, but no *class* differences."

Added to LY 1

*1:12. Yŏudž said, In the practice of ritual, harmony is to be esteemed. The Way of the Former Kings was beautiful in this: in small things and great they followed it. If there is something that does not go right, one should recognize the principle of harmony, and then it will become harmonious. But if it is not moderated by ritual itself, it still won't go right. [1:12]

> "Way of the Former Kings" is Sywńdzian (SZ4:10, Knoblock **Xunzi** 1/192f). SZ 2:2 (**Xunzi** 1/152f) unites harmony and ritual. *1:12 accepts the "harmony" insight as showing the end which a given observance is "trying to reach to" (we do not follow Mao **Suggestions** 283, who punctuates differently, requiring an elucidation of the square-bracket type). But it also insists (compare 19:12) that ritual precedent itself exerts a necessary limiting effect on its application.

Added to LY 17

*17:7. The Master said, Yóu, Have you heard the Six Maxims and the Six Distortions? He replied, I have not. [He said], Be at ease; I will tell you. To love rv́n but not to love study; its distortion is stupidity. To love wisdom but not to love study; its distortion is diffuseness. To love fidelity but not to love study; its distortion is banditry. To love uprightness but not to love study; its distortion is censoriousness. To love courage but not to love study; its distortion is riotousness. To love firmness but not to love study; its distortion is wildness. [17:8]

> "Be at ease" suggests an invitation to assume a less formal posture, to facilitate relaxed and thus effective listening (for a Japanese parallel, see *14:43[17]n).
>
> These six are partly derived from the four of *8:2a[14]. The chief difference is that study, not ritual, is the moderating force which directs impulses into proper channels. The idea of distortion (bì 蔽 "abuse") is developed in SZ 21 ("Explaining Distortions," Knoblock **Xunzi** 3/88 has "Dispelling Blindness"). Sywńdž is the great advocate of an intellectually tidy universe.

Added to LY 19

*19:13. Dž-syà said, If he is underoccupied in service, he may study. If he is underoccupied in study, he may serve. [19:13]

> "Underoccupied" (yōu 優; in 14:11 "overqualified") is having more capacity than the task at hand calls for. The interplay of study and office fits Sywńdž, who was a producer of talent for all the states. One pupil came from Tsài, earlier absorbed by Chǔ (Lǐ Sž), and another from Hán (Hán Fēi); both went to the highest bidder (Chín). His school was free of the one-state connection that limited the Lǔ Confucians. Not being committed to an aphoristic style let Sywńdž produce the extended essays that are the hallmark of his school. His career (born in Jàu, studied in Ngwèi, honored in Chí, employed in Chǔ) had a multinational character, in higher posts than proto-multinational Mencius. He thought and discoursed to a later generation, on a wider scale.
>
> The service/exit equilibrium (*18:8a/b[18]) is here resolved in a practical way, or at least without reference to any awkward questions of personal principle. Sywńdž tends to get on with the job; the Lǔ Confucians agonize a little more.

Added as LY 20

The following piece was a chapter by itself (LY 20) in the copy of the Analects concealed in the schoolroom wall in 0249, and rediscovered in c0154; in the present text it is combined with 20:2–3, which were originally a fragmentary 21st chapter. It owes nothing to previous Analects chapter form, but is instead in the style of the Shū; its archaic diction, lapsing from the purported words of sage rulers into historical summary, ornaments and gives sonority to a plan for the state, whose ruler is accountable to Heaven for his administration of justice, encouragement of trade, and solicitude for the people. What seems a jumble is actually a landmark document. Its date of composition might be c0251.

*20:1. Yáu said, Oh, you Shùn! Heaven's order of succession, upon your person comes to rest / Unto the Mean do you hold fast! / And within the Four Seas vast / Heaven's favor long will last.

Shùn also in this way commanded Yw̌.

[Tāng] said, I, the little child Lw̌, venture to sacrifice a black bull, and to announce openly to the most eminent Lord God: The guilty I will not venture to pardon, God's servitors I will not mislead; the determination lies with the heart of God. If I in my own person incur guilt, do not visit it upon the myriad places; if the myriad places should incur guilt, let that guilt lie upon my own person.

Jōu had great beneficence; the good men, these it enriched. "Though there be relatives of Jōu, they shall not equal the rv́n men. If the Hundred Families should incur a fault, let it lie upon me, the One Man."

He attended to weights and measures, examined rules and standards, restored disused offices, and a government of the Four Quarters put them in practice withal. He revived extinguished states, continued interrupted successions, promoted subjects in seclusion, and the people Under Heaven gave their hearts to him. What he emphasized was the people, food, mourning, and sacrifice. He was generous, and thus won over the multitude. He was faithful, and thus the people trusted him. He was diligent, and thus had success. He was fair, and thus made others happy.

The archaic pronoun yw̌ 予 "I" (see 7:23) here resumes its original context.

The Yáu charge to Shùn (and from Shùn to Yw̌) implies a meritocratic, not a lineal successor. It invokes the Jūng Yūng ("Mean") as a balancing principle, and as a condition of retaining the mandate to rule.

Next is Tāng ("He"), founder of Shāng. Behind the sacrifices, invoked from old inscriptions, is a bureaucratic concern for due process: the guilty will not be protected nor law officers deceived; any guilt the people incur will be considered the ruler's fault. This is the corollary of the magic-efficacy theory of rule: the people, even if nominally guilty, are what the ruler has made them.

The Jōu are the ideal: meritocracy (see *18:10[18]), responsibility alike for the people's livelihood (see 12:9) and misdeeds, and for a rational bureaucracy (contrast 13:20), reconciling the secluded (*18:8a[18]), generosity (see *6:30[18]), faith (12:7, *17:5[18]), and above all fairness. This word, gūng 公, originally "Prince," in 6:14 already "public" (see the early DDJ 16), is now "fair" – having the equitable character on which alone a public culture can rest.

Reflections

We may begin our examination of *20:1 by asking, where does it fit into the context of its time? Like Mencius, it envisions a universal ("Four Quarters") sovereignty, but looks to the continuance rather than the extirpation of local ruler lineages. This is not a revived feudalism, but rather a unified federalism (compare 13:18, which had sheltered families from the law). Along with these concessions to Legalism, we find a strong distaste for punishment, particularly punishment of the people, for whose errors the ruler is ultimately responsible. The Lǔ Confucians may have wanted the extirpation of Sùng to be reversed, but they did not want virtue itself to be locally confined.

Our search for LY 19 Legalisms (see 18r) found only *13:3, *19:13, and *20:1. The first is merely bureaucratic, the second unclear, the third benign. The hostility to Legalistic punishments is very like that of DDJ 72–75, which implies that both may be reacting to a third, Legalist presence at the Lǔ court. We thus infer the existence of a court Legalist faction in Lǔ, prior to 0255. After 0254, direct Syẃndzian influence on the LY 19 theories becomes the likeliest hypothesis. Evidence for the Confucian/Legalist convergence noted by Hsiao for Hàn is thus best sought in the school of Syẃndž, but the LY 19–20 lean toward universalism may constitute a footnote to that tendency.

Syẃndž too must be seen in context. Warring States thought from c0320 on was collectively engaged in designing the universal political state which the Warring States technologies of war and peace were making inevitable. One item in the technology of peace, the technology of governing, is the know-how involved in controlling more than a local area. It was apparently gained from experience in administering conquered territory (see Creel **Beginnings**). The experience being acquired by Chǔ, in the LY 19 year c0253, in administering its annexed but not yet absorbed territory of southern Lǔ, must itself have been part of that process of refining a new technology of rule.

The Dàuists, who were seemingly high enough at the Lǔ court to be held accountable for the 0254 loss of half its territory and population, justified it as a desirable outcome in DDJ 80 ("Make the state small, make the people few," Henricks **Te** 36, 156). This apologia anticipates the "inactivity" of a 4c Dàuist minister (Waley **Lo-yang** 48–53). As for the defensive-war Micians, MZ 50 (c0254; Mei **Ethical** 257), which relocates Mwòdž from Lǔ to Chí, suggests that an ungrateful Lǔ government had dismissed them.

All the LY 19 disciples can be seen as in some way criticizing Syẃndž, but only the three whose mutual wrangling *caricatured* him drew a response from Lán-líng: an addendum to the earlier diatribe SZ 6 (Knoblock **Xunzi** 1/229) vilifies precisely Dž-jāng, Dž-syà, and Dž-yóu. As for Yén Hwéi, whom we have not seen in any uninterpolated passage since 12:1, he has found a new home among the Dàuists (JZ 6:7, 20:7, 22:11, Watson **Chuang** 90f, 217f, 246f), toward whom he had from the first shown a certain predilection (see 6:23n), and with whom he is living happily ever after.

On the long-term viability of the LY 19–20 political proposals, de Bary (**Trouble** 2; compare Wakeman **Remarks** 21) notes that their sanctions, based on paradigms of antiquity, later proved "susceptible of appropriation" by rulers. The Lǔ Confucians, to borrow a metaphor from JZ 4:3 (Watson **Chuang** 62), are here philosophizing to a steamroller.

Gold Inlaid Crossbow Fittings (see p195)
Length 25·6 cm (10·4 in). 04c/03c. Courtesy Freer Gallery of Art (32·15–16)

20
c0249

The Chŭ conquest of southern Lŭ in 0255/0254 was completed in 0249 by absorbing the north (the crossbow, the decisive weapon of the 03c, had been pioneered by Chŭ). This ended Lŭ sovereignty and added its territory to Chŭ (for a cup from which a victory toast might have been drunk, see page198). This brought to an end five schools of thought which had been associated with the Lŭ court: the Dàuists of the DDJ (whose text ended with DDJ 81), the northern and southern Mencians (MC 7, MC 3), the Lŭ Micians (MZ 50), and the Analects group, whose last fragment we shall now examine (for 20:1, the 20th chapter of the text as divided by the school itself, see under LY 19; this truncated chapter was in their terms the 21st). It consists of two sayings, both featuring Dž-jāng, with whose remark LY 19 had also opened. It was written, like everything else from LY 17 on, by the last head of the school, Dž-shvn.

The numbering of passages is identical in the Legge text.

⌐ 20:2. Dž-jāng asked Confucius, What must one be like before he may serve in government? The Master said, If he honor the Five Beauties and shun the Four Evils, he may serve in government. Dž-jāng said, What are the Five Beauties? The Master said, The gentleman is kind but not extravagant, toils them but does not cause resentment, desires but does not covet, is serene but not haughty, is impressive but not alarming. Dž-jāng said, What does "kindly but not extravagant" mean? The Master said, To use what the people find profitable to profit them, is this not "kindly but not extravagant?" If he choose what can be toiled at and makes them toil at it, who would be resentful? If he desires rvn and gets rvn, what should he covet? If the gentleman does not distinguish between many and few, between small and great, if he dares not be dismissive, is he not "serene but not haughty?" And if the gentleman puts in order robe and cap, and conveys elevation in gaze and glance, so that men seeing him in his dignity from afar will regard him with awe, is he not "impressive but not alarming?"

Dž-jāng said, What are the Four Evils? The Master said, To kill without instructing: one calls that cruel. To expect completion without giving warning: one calls that oppressive. To enforce timeliness though late in commanding: one calls that robbery. In associating with others, to grudge rewards: one calls that officious.

> This portrait of the ideal minister complements the ideal ruler of 20:1[19]. It does not reject punishments, but states conditions for their being valid: no exaction without prior notice, no assumption of motive without inculcation of motive, no payment in excess or payment withheld. Only the first Beauty and the last Evil deal with rewards rather than punishments, but the whole outline explores the Legalist technology of rule by positive and negative reinforcements. The two mingle clearly in the last of the Beauties: the imposing manner necessary for one in authority (compare Vreeland D. V. 126 on de Gaulle).
>
> There are precedents in LY 12–13, but the catalogue of abuses of power is so knowledgeable that one assumes it is prompted by contact with the court Legalists of Lŭ, whom we infer the Dàuists had earlier opposed (DDJ 72–75).

˪ 20:3. Confucius said, If he does not know fate, he has no way to be a gentleman. If he does not know the rites, he has no way to take his stand. If he does not know words, he has no way to understand others.

To know what can and cannot be done in present circumstances, to know the limits and possibilities of the times, what might be called the protocol of Heaven, is to "know fate," and qualifies him for high public responsibilities. To know the protocol of earth, ceremonies and courtesies, the procedural side of life, the guiding of civic intercourse that precedent and usage can provide, is to "know the rites," and qualifies him for a functional role in government. To know the protocol of men, the way they reveal themselves and collaborate through language, is to "know words," and qualifies him as a colleague.

These requisites, the counterpart of the guidelines in the paired 20:2, give a carefully considered view of the qualifications of the 03c government official. As contrasted with 4:1, the oldest saying in the book, they show a functional, even lateral, approach to staff procurement, not the patient and dutiful stance of the 05c elite aspirant hoping to be noticed by the ruler. The topic is the same, but the change wrought by 230 years of political evolution is enormous.

Interpolations

For a complete finding list of interpolated passages, see page 329.

Reflections

As the Chǔ army approached, it seems that Dž-shv̀n hid the Analects, and some other stray jottings, in the wall of the school headquarters, and plastered them over. Some members of the school escaped to Chí and wrote down the text from memory on their arrival, it was added to and rearranged over the next 28 years until Chí too was conquered (by Chín, in 0221), and that version also ceased to be actively maintained.

Dž-shv̀n himself, according to family tradition (SJ 43), went to Ngwèi, where he became a minister of state and died in c0237 at the age of 57. The departure of the leader suggests that there was no major presence of Analects Confucians in Lǔ after 0249. Lǔ Confucianism as we know it from the history of Hàn scholarship (SJ 121) is largely Syẃndzian Confucianism, with its ritual emphasis, its text philology tradition, and its eye on the unified political state, not deeply concerned for the feudal past whether literal or romanticized.

In early Hàn, when the 0213 Chín ban on Confucian texts was lifted, the Lǔ and Chí Analects were transcribed from the memory of Lǔ and Chí scholars, these becoming the "Lǔ" and "Chí" versions of the work. Quite naturally, the Lǔ version was regarded as more authoritative by Hàn scholars. In c0157 a Hàn prince was given the former Lǔ as his domain. He tore down the old palace and a nearby building to erect a proper mansion, and in the wall of the adjacent building, apparently the old Confucian headquarters, Dž-shv̀n's hidden copy of the Analects came to light. It varied from the "Lǔ" text largely in sentence particles and minor points of orthography. This is called the "Old" text, from the Warring States script in which, before the Chín standardization of writing, it had been written. The "Old" text gradually replaced the "Lǔ" text in scholarly favor, and is at most points the basis for our present Analects.

One Lǔ/Old difference is that the final saying, 20:3, appears only in the Old text (written) and not in the generally similar Lǔ text (oral; the Dìng-syèn Analects has written 20:3 *in small characters* after 20:2, showing the increasing influence of the Gǔ text by c055; **Shr̄-wv́n** 54). This can only mean that this passage was first written down, with a view (precluded by the 0249 conquest) to being later given out for memorization. This text-based memory is the opposite of the situation in the LY 4 core, which on our view was rather a memory-based text. The transition from oral to written society was noticed in 15:6 (late 04c). The changing nature of the Analects itself, oral at its beginning and written at its end, shows that it lies on both sides of that transition.

We add here a final cautionary tale. In 1922 (Chan **Way** 35, 45, 68), Lyáng Chǐ-chāu began a controversy with Hú Shr̄ (Hu Shih) on the date of the DDJ, arguing inter alia that (following Gù Jyé-gāng) the use of gūng "fair" is late, thus ruling out the traditional c0500 date for the DDJ, which uses that term. Hú (**Recent** 385f) cited in rebuttal the Analects use of gūng "fair"as proving the c0500 date, and went on (as does Chan **Way** 70–71) to assert that ideas do not evolve, and that all such claims are therefore groundless. He would have done better to consider that the Analects use of gūng "fair" is in *20:1[19], in a chapter which Tswēi Shù had argued is in the late group LY 16–20. Hú himself (Hummel **Eminent** 2/776) had in 1923 called attention to Tswēi's discoveries by a paper on "Tswēi Shù as a Scientific Historian." This was admirable work. Alas, that the revival of "scientific history" should have been so fragile!

No critical scholar now believes in the 06c DDJ, but what can students learn from this episode? First, that reason will not always triumph in a contest with something else. Hú and others delayed the acceptance of the 03c DDJ by 60 years. Second, scholars are not divided into Column A and Column B; anybody, including an eminent person like Hú, can and does make a mistake. Third, when you find yourself, in an argument, rejecting the whole proposition that evidence leads to conclusions, you too are possibly making a mistake.

As to the Analects itself, we note in the last LY 20 sayings that, though the *20:1[19] word gūng 公 does not recur, fairness is still prominent as a concept. The virtue rv́n had come to be used in the last years of the Analects text for a variety of gentlemanly qualities, and was displaced from the focus of attention as the school concentrated instead on the inner workings of government. Ritual too, though it figures in the LY 19 satire, had seemingly lost its old centrality. If the Lǔ Confucians at the end organized their views under any one concept, it was perhaps instead fairness. That concept can be recognized in the forgiving rulership of 12:17–22 and the teaching maxims of 13:29–30. The final position of Analects Confucianism thus appears to be based on its Mencian phase.

The word gūng "fair, impartial" goes back further, to DDJ 16, in the Dàuist text that evolved beside the Analects. This adds dimensions to LY 20: not only is it Mencian at its roots, but those roots lie in Dàuist/populistic soil. They also reach into other areas: the enigmatic 05c Golden Rule maxim, 5:12, and the Mician definition of rv́n as "love for others" in 12:22. Thus have many sources, both known and unknown, contributed their share to the final Analects.

From first to last, the Analects never strays from the furious integrity of Confucius, but it takes it into areas that would have amazed him, transmuting his code of honor into a code of public obligation, and his vertical loyalty into a vision of a reciprocal society, accepting not only of its rulers, but of itself.

Lacquer Drinking Cup from Chŭ (see 20h)

Height 23·5 cm (9·3 in). 05c/04c. Courtesy Freer Gallery of Art (49·1)

Appendices

Fragment of the Lǔ Analects Text (LY 4:1)
"To dwell in rv́n . . ." (里仁 . . .)
*Engraved on stone in 175/183. Original size. After Mǎ **Shŕ Jīng** (fragment 481)*

Appendix 1
The Accretion Theory of the Analects

Inconsistencies within the Analects have usually been explained in such a way as to allow all parts of the text to be regarded as close to Confucius, and thus as valid sources for his life and thought. A typical theory is that different chapters were compiled by different disciples, variations in content being attributed to individual disciple interests or levels of understanding. Jvng Sywæn (died c200) suggested Rǎn Yūng, Dž-yóu, and Dž-syà;[1] other versions exist. Such *monolithic* theories keep the compilation of the text within living memory of Confucius. Lyǒu Dzūng-ywæn (773–819) noted that Dzvng Shvm[2] is called Dzvngdž "Master Dzvng" in the work, implying that his disciples had a role in its compilation, and placing it the second, not the first, disciple generation.[3]

Later scholars have gone on to suggest what amounts to an evolutionary view of the text.[4] The first such suggestion was made by Hú Yín (1098–1156),[5] who noted that the last ten chapters, LY 11–20, are formally less well organized than the first ten, LY 1–10. This sets up an "upper and lower" division of the Analects, and at least leaves open the possibility of a time lag between them.

Itō Jinsai (1627–1705) further argued that LY 10 (presumed to be a portrait of Confucius) was meant to end the work, and that LY 11–20, with longer narratives and frequent use of numerical categories (such as the "Three Dangers" of LY 16:7), which are not found in LY 1–10, was a later continuation.[6]

Tswēi Shù (1740–1816) noticed that some of the traits characterizing LY 11–20 are concentrated in the last half of that span: LY 16–20.[7] In his later writings,[8] he pointed out further features of this later Analects style, including inconsistencies, improbabilities, and an excessive degree of formality between Confucius and his followers. Tswēi thus in effect distinguishes a *very* late layer, LY 16–20, within the previously identified Hú/Itō *late* layer, LY 11–20.

[1]Jvng Syw 421. It may be relevant that these are the only disciples who have the last word in an Analects debate with the Master; see LY 6:2, 17:3, and 3:8. LY 1:15 is a literary reworking of 3:8, and not (at any rate from our point of view) a fourth case.

[2]曾 參; the -m distinguishes him from his second son Dzvng Shvn 曾 申.

[3]Lyǒu **Byèn** 1/68–69. This brief essay by a member of the Hán Yw circle might be said to mark the beginning of critical Analects scholarship.

[4]Fung **History** 1/19f (compare Nivison **Chang** 119–120), Taam **Studies** 165, Pokora **Pre-Han** 30, and Cheng **Lun Yü** 314; contrast Schwartz **World** 61–62.

[5]The "Hú" cited in Jū **Jí Jù** ap LY 16:11 is frequently construed as the much better known Hú Aň-gwó 胡 安 國 (1074–1138), but is unambiguously identified as his nephew Hú Yín 胡 寅 in Jū **Yw-lèi** 19:9r (2/705); for Yín's career, see **Sùng Shř** 435 (6/24201).

[6]Itō **Kogi** 2, Spae Itō 178–179. The upper/lower distinction is acknowledged as cogent in Yang **Note** 313–314 (1957), and underlies the discussion in Hú **Byèn-jvng** (1978). Itō's disciple Dazai Shundai, however (**Kokun** 5/3r ap LY 9:7, 7/8 ap LY 14:1; **Gaiden** 1/2rv), reverted to a two-compiler theory, featuring Chín Jāng and Ywæn Syèn.

[7]Tswēi **Yw Shwō** 21–24.

[8]Tswēi **Byèn Yí** 25–33, collecting material from Tswēi's **Kǎu-syìn** studies. For other summaries, see Hummel **Eminent** sv Ts'ui Shu; Lau **Analects** 264–268.

Arthur Waley (1889–1966) agreed that the Tswēi Shù layer, LY 16–20, was late. Within the Hú/Itō "upper" Analects, LY 1–10, he saw LY 10 as irrelevant, and noted that Dzv̄ngdž is quite differently characterized in LY 1 and LY 8. Waley concluded that LY 3–9 were the earliest portion of the text.[9]

As noticed by Pokora,[10] these theories are not mutually exclusive, but will *combine to form a single conjecture.* To Waley's LY 3–9 core, we add LY 1–2 and 10 to get the Hú/Itō early layer LY 1–10, then the middle layer LY 11–15 distinguished by Tswēi, and finally his latest layer, LY 16–20, to make up the Hú/Itō "lower" Analects, and the entire work. In schematic form, with chapter numbers in **bold** marking the new additions at each stage, we would have:

```
        03 04 05 06 07 08 09
  01 02 03 04 05 06 07 08 09 10
  01 02 03 04 05 06 07 08 09 10 11 12 13 14 15
  01 02 03 04 05 06 07 08 09 10 11 12 13 14 16 16 17 18 19 20
```

This four-stratum theory brings us to the verge of an *accretion hypothesis* for the text.

Another Route

We may also begin with the three Analects texts listed in the Hàn palace library catalogue, HS 30. These were the Lǔ and Chí texts (presumably transcribed from the memory of Lǔ and Chí scholars after the 0191 Hàn lifting of the 0213 Chín ban on Confucian writings), with 20 and 22 chapters,[11] and the Gǔ or old-script text, on which our present text is based, supposedly recovered in the c0154 demolition of a building near the former Lǔ palace which may have housed the Lǔ school.[12] This had 21 chapters, with "two Dž-jāng [chapters]." That is, besides LY 19, which begins with "Dž-jāng asked," *another* chapter had that initial phrase. This would be true of our present text if LY 20:1, a composition in Shū style, were separate, and LY 21 began with 20:2, a Dž-jāng question. We infer that this *was* the case, and that the difference is merely one of division: Lǔ and Gǔ *contained the same material.*

HS 30 names the two extra Chí chapters: Asking About Kingship 問王[13] and Knowing the Way 知道. These suggest nothing in the present text, and imply new material; that is, the Chí text *has grown beyond* the Lǔ text.[14] If the Lǔ Confucians were quiescent after the 0249 conquest of Lǔ,[15] but the Chí Confucians remained active until the 0221 conquest of Chí, then the longer period of activity in Chí, plus an assumption of continuous growth, will explain the greater length of the Chí text.

[9]Waley **Analects** 21.

[10]Pokora **Pre-Han** 30.

[11]A damaged copy of a pre-055 Hàn bamboo text close to the Lǔ version was found in a tomb in Dìng-syèn (Jyěn-bàu 10; sample transcriptions in **Shř-wv́n**); it is currently (1997) being translated by Roger G. Ames and Henry Rosemont, Jr. A more eclectic Lǔ text was engraved on stone in 175–183; extant fragments are collected in Ma **Shř Jīng**.

[12]Pelliot **Chou King** discredits this story as involved with the old-script Shū forgery; Brooks **Controversies** argues that the Analects aspect rests on a basis of fact.

[13]Or, Asking About the Jade 問玉; JSWD 15 (30v) has "Kingship."

[14]The Chí Analects also had additional material in the portion corresponding to the 20 (or 21) chapters of the Gǔ version; see again JDSW 15 (30v).

[15]As is implied by the departure of the Lǔ school head to Ngwèi; see 20r, above.

This latter hypothesis implies a *rate* of growth, for the late 03c Chí Analects, of two chapters in 28 years, or about 14 years per chapter. Assuming constant growth at that rate, the 19 full chapters of the Lǔ Analects imply a beginning 266 years *before* 0249. This would reach back to 0515: within the lifetime of Confucius.

This rough initial projection can be refined by considering other evidence. Nothing in the Analects is spoken directly by Confucius (his sayings are introduced by the third-person formula "The Master said" 子曰), hence none of these sayings can have been written down before his death in 0479.[16] Taking that as the earliest date for the core chapter, the other 18 chapters to be distributed over the 230 years until 0249 give an average time span of 12·7 years per chapter, or half the average 25-year *birth* generation (*transmission* generations average 40 years). That is, the Lǔ Analects seems to have accumulated at an average rate of 2 chapters per generation. This version of the hypothesis thus implies that the beginnings of the Analects may indeed go back to a point of contact with the historical Confucius (a possibility doubted by several recent scholars),[17] and that the *typical* leader of the school, whether later leaders succeeded by birth or were designated by their predecessors, contributed not one, but more than one, chapter module to the accumulating text.

Combining the Theories

It is common to both versions of the theory, and to many other such theories not here mentioned,[18] that the chapter, either singly or in clusters, is the basic unit of accretion. The Pokora synthesis suggests that the natural attachment point for accretions is at the tail of the text, with a few chapters also being placed in front of previous material. And the inference from the HS 30 entries is that the time depth of the text may be considerable: on the order of centuries rather than years.

These suggestions together define the hypothesis that there is an earliest core of the work, perhaps a single chapter, going back to just after the death of Confucius in 0479, and (if the Pokora synthesis is in the right general direction) within the Waley early layer LY 3–9; specifically, at or near the beginning of that layer. This directs attention to the first two Waley chapters, LY 3 and 4.

Of them, LY 4 has several seemingly early features. The LY 4 sayings are the shortest in any Analects chapter (they average 19 words, against 30 for the text as a whole, and 123 for the seemingly late LY 20 fragment). All but two of them begin with a "The Master said" incipit, a simplicity unique in the work. Literary devices found in other chapters (disciple questions, dialogues, narrative settings, transitions) are lacking in LY 4. And, except for two passages (which also have other anomalies), no other persons are named in LY 4:[19] the focus is exclusively on the Master.

---

[16]The traditional date. Maspero **Antique** 376n1 / **Antiquity** 449n1, approved by Waley (**Analects** 16n2, 79) and Riegel (**Review** 791), argues for c0450. One difficulty which this addresses (too few descendants of Confucius are listed in SJ 47 to cover the school headship from 0479 to Hàn) is otherwise resolved by the present theory, which recognizes *disciples rather than descendants* as the early leaders of the movement.

[17]For example, Waley **Analects** 25; Tsuda **Rongo** 240–291.

[18]For example, Kimura **Kōshi** 473f, Takeuchi **Rongo** 192f, Lau **Analects** 273f.

[19]Tsuda **Rongo** 272f notes that LY 4 uniquely lacks ancient-sage references and similar anachronisms, though he does not himself draw the indicated inference.

The idea of a memorial, occasioned by Confucius's death in 0479, gives a likely motive for the nucleus. Its literary technique is little removed from the forms of writing that would have been known as of that year: bronze inscriptions and bamboo-slip chronicle entries. This makes LY 4 not only unique in the Analects, but unique *in a way that would be plausible for an early 05c core text.*

Some linguistic details support this identification. Lǔ dialect sž 斯 "then" occurs (but along with the standard dzv́ 則 "then"), as would be expected in sayings of Confucius, who by tradition was born in the Lǔ capital area. Very striking is the occurrence of the full verb yẃ 於 "be in relation to" (4:5), whereas other chapters have only the coverb yẃ "in relation to." Coverbs in general derive from full verbs, thus yóu 由 "follow" > yóu "from." An original verb may continue in use along with its derived coverb, but verbal yẃ is virtually unknown in Warring States texts.[20] Notable too is verbal chǔ 處 "take one's place in" (4:1–2, 4:5): the rest of the text uses the noun chù 處 "place," but replaces the verb with jyw̄ 居 "dwell."

Thus, not only is LY 4 *distinctive* within the text, but some of its features imply *greater linguistic age* than the rest of the text, in agreement with the idea that these sayings were spoken to, and remembered by, Confucius's protégés. These points support the conclusion that LY 4 is, or contains within it, the original core of the Analects compilation, around which the remaining portions of the text were added by a process of accretion over time.

Later Material in LY 4

All the *formal* exceptions to the above descriptions cluster in two sayings. One is 4:15, which not only names Dzv̄ngdž but *features him as a speaker.* This is so unusual in LY 4 that it is very likely an interpolation. And LY 4:26 not only features, but *is a saying of,* Dž-yóu; this too is is presumably a later addition.[21]

It emerges from further study that the early *linguistic* features cited above occur *only in the area 4:1–17,* never in 4:18–25. Also, the standard word dzv́ 則 "then" in 4:21 conflicts dialectically with the Lǔ usage sž 斯 "then" in 4:7. We may then conservatively suspect that 4:18–25 are an extended later addition.

Finally, LY 4:1–17 and 4:18–25 appear to belong to different stages within the long-term shift from postverbal (F) to preverbal (B) position for various types of adverbial expression (a linguistic process which is still not quite complete at the present time), and the induced shift toward verbs instead of nouns as sentence final elements. Of the 48 predicates in 4:1–17, a total of 39 end with a verb object or other noun element (81% *nominal endings*), while the 15 predicates of 4:18–25 have 40% *nominal endings*. This tends to confirm a later date for 4:18–25, leaving the sixteen sayings of 4:1–14 plus 4:16–17 as the probable nucleus.

---

[20]Nivison **Hampers** notes an inscription on lacquer from the tomb of the Lord of Dzv̄ng (closed after 0443), one line of which reads 日辰於維 "the sun's [zodiacal space] *is in* the [winter-spring] corner." It is possible that this seeming prayer was cast in an archaic style, and that full verbal 於 was obsolete in the west also by the mid 05c.

[21]Given the Dzv̄ngdž interpolation *4:15, one wonders if Dž-yóu was also esteemed as a leader of the school. LJ 2 supports this; see page 210 below. That interpolations might be added without disturbing previous text is implied by the format of the Hàn copy of the Lǔ Analects, which tends to begin a strip with the *first* words of a passage, and leave the rest of the slip blank after the *last* words of a passage (see **Shr̀-wv́n** 49).

The Overall Chronology of the Analects

We now have a theory that the LY 4 core dates from 0479 and LY 20 from 0249, and that all other chapters, including the three which now precede LY 4, are from intermediate dates. We next ask whether any of these chapters can plausibly be dated *within that time span*. The following details deserve consideration:

• LY 6:3 first uses the posthumous epithet of Āi-gūng (d 0469), and so must have been written **after 0469**, whereas LY 4 and 5 might still be before 0469.

• LY 8:3 portrays the death of Dzv̄ngdž (d 0436); it cannot be earlier than, and was probably written **in or shortly after 0436**. LY 7 should then be before 0436.

• LY 9:15 (cf 7:14) turns from Chí to Wèi for ceremonial models, and may reflect a diplomatic shift which might have been motivated by the battles between Chí and Lǔ in 0412, 0411, and 0408. Allowing some time to establish this new alliance, a plausible date for at least those portions of LY 9 might be c0405.

• LY 12–13 articulate values close to those urged by Mencius in the interviews recorded in MC 1. Mencius studied in the Lǔ Confucian school; these chapters look like a source, or an early school version, of his ideas. Since his career outside Lǔ began in c0320,[22] his last date in Lǔ would be c0321. LY 12 might moderately, and LY 13 closely, precede this year, perhaps c0326 and c0322.

• LY 16:1 protests a pending outrage (nominally, a Jì clan attack on the nearby town of Jwān-yẃ) which suggests the Chí destruction of Sùng in 0286; it thus might be from c0287. LY 16:2–3 seem to be dynastic curses whose logic is based on the number of generations since the usurpation of power by the Tyén clan in Chí; they may plausibly be seen as Lǔ denunciations following the actual Chí conquest of 0286. This portion of the chapter might therefore date from c0285.

• LY 17:4 and 17:6 are about service under an illegitimate ruler. There are no known usurpations in the Lǔ line, but it can be inferred[23] that in 0272 the King of Chǔ reduced the status of the Lǔ ruler (from Prince/gūng to Lord/hóu), giving Chǔ a dominant role in Lǔ internal affairs. This could easily raise a legitimacy issue for Lǔ officials. LY 17 might then be from shortly afterward, c0270.

• LY 18:5–7 resemble, and probably respond to, passages in the Jwāngdž anthology, regarded as being generally of mid-03c date. In content, LY 18 resolves the LY 17 service dilemma, and probably follows LY 17 at no very great interval. We may tentatively assign it to a point halfway between LY 17 and 19, or c0262.

• LY 19 seems to include veiled criticism of Sywndž, and may follow the Chǔ partial conquest of Lǔ in 0255, and Sywndž's installation as Director (Lìng 令) in Lán-líng (in southern, occupied Lǔ) in 0254. It may thus be from c0253.

• LY 20 appears to have been interrupted in mid-compilation; one plausible interruption would be the Chǔ conquest and absorption of northern Lǔ in 0249.

No one of these implied dates is decisive, but together they are surely suggestive: whether based on absolute "outside" events or on relative "internal" relations, they occur *in consecutive chronological order* as they stand in the chapter sequence of the present text, supporting the hypothesis that chapters from LY 4 through LY 20 represent a linear growth process in which each chapter is a separate accretion unit: a module of growth.

---

[22]Lau **Mencius** Appendix 1.

[23]From details which seem to survive embedded in SJ 15 and 33 (Brooks **Princes**).

The Preposed Chapters, LY 1–3

Of this parallel set of accretions, which by hypothesis were added in the order LY 3–2–1, we may similarly note the following:

• LY 3 is on the subject of public ritual, a seeming advance over the rules of personal protocol in LY 10 (further developed in LY 11); it may thus follow both. Several passages (3:1–3, 3:6, 3:10) denounce the usurpation of royal usages in public ritual. An event which might have provoked this sense of outrage is the Chí ruler's usurpation of the Jōu title "King" (wáng 王). The SJ chronology is known to be defective in this area, and the BA gives no direct information. Interpreting the SJ claim of a *rulership* change in 0342 as instead a *reign* change, and noting that this is the year after Chí's victory in the battle of Mǎ-líng (given by BA as 0343), we may assign the Chí kingship to 0342. The date of those passages in LY 3 which seem to respond to this event would then most plausibly also be c0342.

• LY 2 contains (in 2:1) astral symbolism of a type usually associated with Chí thought (it is found also in seemingly early parts of the Gwǎndž), and implies Chí influence of the sort noted above in LY 12–13. Since such cosmological symbols are not found in LY 12–13, LY 2 must postdate the later of them (LY 13, c0321). In content, LY 2 may be described as in part a development of the Mencian or proto-Mencian populism of LY 12–13. The rulership symbol in 2:1 suggests a summary prepared, sometime after c0321, for a ruler of Lǔ. One plausible occasion for such a presentation would be the accession of Lǔ Píng-gūng in 0317.

• LY 1 reflects a Confucian group *out of power* (1:1) and thus emphasizes the social, rather than the governmental, utility of its doctrines (1:2, 1:6, 1:8). It thus probably follows the politically engaged chapters LY 14–15. Since it does not show the formal traits of the Tswēi Shù late layer, it must precede the earliest Tswēi Shù chapter, LY 16 (c0287–0285). The exit of the Confucians from power in Lǔ may well have been a result of court changes imposed after the reduction of Lǔ to vassalage under Chǔ after the death of Píng-gūng (0303) and the establishment of the puppet ruler Wýn-hóu in 0302. This would imply for LY 1 an *earliest* date (terminus a quo) of c0302, the actual chapter, allowing some time to establish the new basis of the school, being perhaps somewhat later: c0294.

Like those suggested above for LY 4–20, none of these proposed dates is inevitable, but the fact that all appear *in reverse sequence* supports the hypothesis of an outward accretion, in the order LY 3–2–1, from the presumed LY 4 core.

The Final Hypothesis

The two chapter sequences can now be interleaved to give a detailed accretion hypothesis. Beginning with the LY 4 core (c0479), we would have: LY 5-6 (the latter c0460), 7-8 (the latter c0436), 9 (c0405), 10–11–3 (the last c0342), 12 (c0326) 13 (c0322), 2 (c0317), 14–15–1 (the last perhaps c0294), 16 (some passages from c0287–0285), 17 (c0270), 18 (c0262), 19 (c0253), and 20 (0249). Dates for the remaining chapters can be proposed by interpolation in the above scheme: LY 5 at c0473, LY 7 at c0450 (toward the middle of Dzv̄ngdž's headship), LY 10 at c0380 and 11 at c0360, spacing them out evenly over the early 04c, and LY 14 and 15 at c0310 and c0305, leading to the end of Píng-gūng's reign.

This hypothesis not only *incorporates* but *explains* Waley's remark about changes in the Dzv̄ngdž persona between LY 8 (early) and LY 1 (mythically late) and Tswēi Shù's observations of formal irregularities in the last five chapters, which on this view turn out to be from the 03c. It will be assumed as true in what follows.

Text Additions

Since accretions are most easily made at the *end* of a text, *preposed* chapters are exceptional. These seem to come at points of external (the Chí kingship; LY 3) or internal *stress* (the accessions of Lǔ Píng-gūng and Wv́n-hóu; LY 2 and 1), which might well have evoked a special statement or reaction from the Lǔ Confucians. This external logic may be behind the front placement of LY 1–3, which may have been topical manifestoes rather than routine evolutions. We will presently find that several interpolated *passages* seem also to have a high-profile intent.

The Pairing of Sayings

Earlier commentators have noted close relations between specific pairs of Analects sayings, though it has not been appreciated that such pairing, admittedly often based on trivial features, characterizes *the entire text*, giving a background against which disruptive interpolated sayings can be relatively easily recognized. Thus LY 4:15, already suspect as featuring a speaker other than Confucius, becomes further suspect in that *it separates two closely paired sayings*:

4:14 Confucius: Care not for office, but **only whether you deserve it**
4:15.   (Dzv̄ngdž explains a cryptic saying of Confucius)
4:16 Confucius: Emphasize not advantage, but **only what is right**

The rhetorical parallel between 4:14 and 4:16 is obvious.[24] So is the substantive parallel: both express an ethic of obligation rather than a systematic philosophy, whereas 4:15 purports to give a basic principle linking *all* Confucius's sayings.

Complementing the pairing principle is the section principle: pairs of sayings (sometimes ending with a single unpaired saying) tend to be arranged in sections with a thematic or other coherent unity.[25] This unity also has value as an aid in the detection of extraneous material. Interpretatively, it helps us to see into the mind of the chapter compiler, and to discern the common tendency that the sayings were felt to possess at the time of their composition.

We now turn to a detailed analysis of each chapter, to develop the still-rough hypothesis which we have reached by the above argument.

The Organization of Analects Chapters

In the following pages, each chapter is taken up in turn, interpolations are identified, and any indications of date noted. Relying in part on Appendix 4, suggestions are made about the compiler of the chapter, who, we assume, will normally have been the current head of the Confucian school. On each right-hand page, the layout of the chapter material (minus interpolations) – its sectional divisions and pairing patterns – will be shown schematically in an overview or *conspectus*. These explanations will serve to develop the accretion theory, and also to show how the selection of sayings in the main translation was arrived at.

[24]Symmetrical pairing and twinning also recur constantly as structural principles in Warring States art, as may be seen in the illustrations on pages 20, 50, and 78.

[25]This sectioning principle has been noticed in LY 4 by Lau **Analects** 269f, and in other places by earlier commentators. As far as we know, we are the first to propose that sectioning, like the pairing of sayings, is a *pervasive structural device* in the Analects.

LY 4

Chapter Inventory. The concordance text has **26 passages** for LY 4, none of which suggest subdivision.

Interpolations. All but two of the 26 passages are introduced by a "The Master said" (Dž ywē 子曰) formula, a spareness of style (and absence of narrative rhetoric) unparalleled in any other chapter. This leads to the inference that this is the oldest chapter, and also to the suspicion that the few exceptional passages are intrusive. The exceptions include the only speeches by named persons. One of them (4:26) is actually *attributed* to another speaker, Dž-yóu, and 4:15 is in effect also a disciple saying: it ends with Dzv̄ngdž interpreting a cryptic saying of the Master. 4:26 is in the chapter-final position, a likely place to attach an interpolation. 4:15 betrays itself by interrupting an evidently intentional pair of sayings emphasizing deserving rather than getting. On these independent formal grounds, 4:15 and 4:26 should be excluded as interpolations. Another series of interpolations is identified below.

Language and Form. LY 4 contains several unique or (in the case of the verb yẃ 於) archaic usages, which independently suggest that it is early within the text. But these usages are confined to the range 4:1–17; they are absent, and at points contradicted, in the following 4:18–25. It thus seems that 4:18–25 are also an interpolation, albeit a carefully crafted one keeping the *formal*, if not the *linguistic*, features of 4:1–17 (minus *4:15): relative brevity, narrative simplicity, and the invariable Dž ywē incipit. The 4:18–25 sayings emphasize domestic and personal virtues, in sharp contrast with the official focus of 4:1–17, and were presumably added to legitimize a later doctrinal shift in that direction. Removing them leaves an original chapter comprising **16 passages**, which readily fall into four topical groupings: a first section (4:1–7) on the virtue rʹn, and less well defined ones on dàu (the Way; 4:8–10), rival value systems (4:11–13), and the effort to acquire the sort of virtue that is a qualification for office (4:14–17).[26]

Pairing of sayings is sometimes based merely on repeated words (chǔ 處 "abide" in 4:1–2; wù 惡 "hate" in 4:3–4) and sometimes on parallel ideas (the dedicated man's superiority to death and shame in 4:8/9; the emphasis on deserving in 4:14/16). Unpaired single passages at the end of thematic sections tend to have a summative or envoi function. The logic of this design might not convince a modern editor, but it seems to be present in the material. It quite possibly influenced the arrangement, and perhaps even the selection, of the chapter materials.

Date. Archaic traits in some sayings suggests that LY 4 is not merely the Analects nucleus, but that it may preserve Confucius's own literal words, as remembered by his followers. If so, the most readily imaginable occasion for its compilation will have been early in the mourning period after his death in 0479.

Compiler. No organized "school" is implied by the LY 4 sayings (compare the bickering in LY 5); Confucius would then have left behind simply his individual protégés. MC 3A4 says that Dž-gùng mourned for Confucius for six years, not the conventional three. This role among the disciples, though perhaps mythically elaborated, suggests **Dž-gùng** 子貢 as the compiler of the LY 4 memorial, which subsequently grew, by repeated extension, into our Analects.

---

[26]Lau **Analects** 269–270 agrees with the first grouping but diverges thereafter; his sections are 4:1–7, 4:8–9, 4:10–17, 4:18–21, and the remainder, 4:22–26.

[Original Chapter]

[A. The Cardinal Virtue Rŕn 仁]

1 It is good to **abide** in rŕn
2 Only the rŕn man can **abide** extreme situations
3 The rŕn man knows what to **hate**
4 The rŕn man will not **hate** anybody
5 One must put rŕn above **desire**
6 Nobody now loves rŕn with **passion**
7 One notes faults only to recognize the associated type of rŕn

[B. The Public Context: Dàu 道]

8 One who hears that the dàu obtains **will not mind death**
9 One who is set upon the dàu **will be superior to shame**
10 The gentleman in relation to the tyēn-syà

[C. The Gentleman and His Opposite]

11 Preference for **local or special situations** marks the unworthy man
12 Official actions based on **personal advantage** will arouse resentment
13 Government based on **propriety and deference** is the only option

[D. Preparation for Office]

14 Care not whether you get office, but whether you **deserve** it
16 Emphasize not advantage, but only **what is right**
17 Learn from both the worthy and the unworthy

[Later Extension]

[Filial Duty]

18 One may differ with parents **but must accept their judgement**
19 One may travel away from parents **but must not go far**
20 One should maintain a father's ways for three **years** (nyén) of mourning
21 One should be aware, either way, of the **ages** (nyén) of parents

[Keeping One's Word]

22 The old-timers **said little** lest fulfilment should not match promise
23 Few now err in **too strict** an adherence to their given word
24 A gentleman will be slow to promise but diligent to perform

[Chapter Envoi]

25 Virtue is not solitary; it must have neighbors

LY 4 Conspectus
(Including the 4:18–25 addendum)

LY 5

Chapter Inventory. The concordance text contains 28 sayings, of which two can be subdivided: 5:10 with its second "The Master said" formula, and 5:19 with its parallel internal structure. It is easy to see why these closely related sayings were later combined as one, but it is more fruitful to recognize them here as paired rather than single elements. Dividing them (as 5:10a/10b and 5:19a/19b) gives a total of **30 passages** in the received text of the chapter.

Interpolations. The use of pairing to detect interpolations is complicated by the fact that LY 5 turns out to employ, in its middle two sections, a *double* pairing structure, where each saying relates through one link to the *preceding* saying, and through another to the *following* saying.[27] 5:7, however, evidently interrupts 5:6/8, 5:16 interrupts 5:15/17, 5:22 interrupts 5:21/23, and 5:26 interrupts 5:25/27. The closeness of the pairing that results when these passages are removed confirms their intrusiveness. For the consecutive 5:13–14, we rely on content: they are respectively a saying of Dž-gùng rather than Confucius (note that both the intrusive passages in LY 4 were also disciple sayings), and a description rather than a quotation (again violating the otherwise consistent literary texture of this chapter and of LY 4). Removing these six doubtful sayings leaves **24 passages** to be accounted for as presumptively original material.

Language and Form. Thematically, these cluster into a symmetrical structure of 3-9-9-3 sayings, analogous to the elaborate double pairing already noted. The chapter is concerned throughout with judgements of persons, and the principle of thematic division seems to be by the category of persons judged: (A) relatives and outsiders, (B) protégés, (C) historical figures, and (D) Confucius himself. LY 5D emphasizes self-cultivation; it may have been intended as structurally parallel to the last section of the original LY 4, where a similar note was sounded.

Date. There is no direct evidence. The atmosphere of a school for *aspirants* implies a stage somewhere between LY 4 (advice to *individuals*) and LY 6 (advice to *officeholders*). If Dž-gùng was the leading figure in the period immediately after Confucius's death, then the late MC 3A4 (see above), which gives him that role for six years, may reflect historical fact. The Dž-gùng interlude might then occupy 0479–0474, the next phase would begin c0473, and LY 5 can be dated at c0470.

Compiler. Criticism of Dž-gùng (5:4, 5:9, 5:12) eliminates him as the compiler of LY 5 (the implied tension makes sense if he was the *previous* leader of the group). Candidates for the headship of the first organized group are few. Those whose names occur in LY with the suffix -dž "Master," like Dzv̄ngdž and Yŏudž, suggest a somewhat more formalized stage. Among other possibilities, **Dž-yóu** 子游 stands out: a saying of his (4:26) was interpolated (with one of Dzv̄ngdž's, 4:15) in LY 4, which if still remembered as the text core would have been a place of honor. The first head of the organized school would need official experience, and of protégés credited in the next layer (LY 6) with official experience, Dž-yóu is the only one praised for his conduct in office. Finally, this office was in Wǔ-chv́ng, which was controlled by the legitimate Prince, so that Dž-yóu would presumably have been acceptable to the legitimist LY 5 group.

---

[27]The two series are separately listed at the left and right of the conspectus opposite. We are indebted to Dennis Grafflin (**Structure**) for sharing his findings on LY linking.

[A. Confucius's Family and Rival Mentors]

Gūngyĕ Cháng	1	⌈ is unlucky but blameless
Nán Rúng	2	⌊ is circumspect but worthy
Dž-jyèn	3	⌶ is cultivated

[B. The Original Protégés]

Dž-gùng	4	⌈ is at least elegant
Rǎn Yūng, though **not rv́n enough** ⌝	5	⌊ is at least straightforward
Chīdyāu Kāi, though **not syìn enough** ⌟	6	⌈ is allowed to take office
Dž-lù, though **said not to be rv́n** ⌝	8	⌊ is recommended for office
Dž-gùng is **said not to be quick** ⌟	9	⌈ and implicitly scolded
Indolent **Dzǎı Yv́** ⌝	10a	⌊ is not worth scolding
Specious **Dzǎı Yv́** ⌟	10b	⌈ did not live up to his promise
Shv̄n Chv́ng, **claimed to be steadfast** ⌝	11	⌊ did not justify his reputation
Dž-gùng is **vain of his empathy** ⌟	12	⌶ and cannot live up to his ideal

[C. Exemplary Personages]

Kǔng Wv́ndž is cultured	15	⌈ despite vulgar experience
Yèn Píng-**jùng** is punctilious ⌝	17	⌊ despite long acquaintance
Dzàng Wv́n-**jùng**'s knowledge ⌟	18	⌈ does not guarantee propriety
[**Triple**] detachment ⌝	19a	⌊ does not attest rv́n
[**Triple**] departure ⌟	19b	⌈ does not qualify Chv́n **Wv́ndž**
Excessive circumspection ⌝	20	⌊ does not avail Jì **Wv́ndž**
Foolish fidelity ⌟	21	⌈ is shown in **extreme crisis**
Proverbial loyalty ⌝	23	⌊ is shown in **ultimate suffering**
Proverbial honesty ⌟	24	⌶ is not after all flawless

[D. Confucius on Self-Improvement]

Confucius emulates	25	⌈ others' virtues
Confucius finds none correcting	27	⌊ their own faults
Confucius is eminent	28	⌶ only in self-improvement

LY 5 Conspectus
(Showing double pairing)

LY 6

Chapter Inventory. The concordance text of LY 6 contains **30 passages**, none of them seeming to require subdivision.

Interpolations. Of the 30, 6:17 interrupts a pair of sayings about external qualities, 6:15 (on modesty) falls thematically between 6:14 (summing up a series of sayings on official fitness) and 6:18 (one of a pair on surface qualities), and 6:24 falls between the closely linked pairs 6:22/23 (contrasting rv́n and jĭ) and 6:25/26 (based on verbal puns). 6:27 (on acquiring the qualities of a jyūndž) seems to end a series on that topic, implying a final section like those noted in LY 4 and LY 5. On formal grounds, then, 6:15, 6:17, and 6:24 appear to be interpolations. The last three sayings, 6:28–30, relate neither to the final-section theme of acquiring virtues nor very obviously to each other. They are placed at the vulnerable chapter end, and are thus also intrinsically suspect by position. 6:28 is on a meeting between Confucius and a Wèi princess, 6:29 refers to the Jūng Yūng, a text with Mencian affinities and thus probably of 03c date, and 6:30 refers to Yáu and Shùn, otherwise unknown in what seem to be early texts. Eliminating these six passages leaves a total of **24 passages** in LY 6, the same as in LY 5 (and the number to which LY 4 was brought up by the 4:18f extension). The 24-passage form was to become standard for later Analects chapters. What, if anything, the number 24 may have symbolized we must leave as a subject for speculation.

Form. The four thematic sections partly parallel those in LY 5: (A) fitness for office, (B) judgements of the original protégés, (C) the harmony of virtues, and (D) the acquisition of virtues. These in turn form two clusters, A/B and C/D, the first section of each containing 3 sayings (the overall form is 3-11-3-7). The elaborate type of double-pairing which we observed in LY 5 does not seem present in LY 6, so that a different authorial hand may be suspected.

Date. LY 6 deals with problems encountered in office and not merely with the acquisition of office, and so may reflect an advanced stage of the Analects school. A notable feature of LY 6 is its larger self-cultivation section: LY 4 and LY 5 devoted their last 3 sayings to this subject, which in LY 6 takes up the last 7 sayings. There is an implied terminus post quem: 6:3 quotes Aī-gūng by that posthumous name, and therefore must date from after his death in 0469. There is nothing in LY 6 (such as systematic hostility to Dž-yóu or to any other plausible previous head of the school) to imply an abrupt transition from LY 5, and the LY 6 hint of responsible positions held by certain disciples suggests a significant passage of time since LY 5. A dating in the vicinity of c0460 would be consistent with these considerations.

Compiler. It was noted above that the honorific names Yŏudž and Dzv̄ngdž may imply a position as heads of the school in the period *after* LY 5. Of the two, Dzv̄ngdž is shown surrounded by disciples in LY 8, and was thus probably head as of the preceding LY 7. This leaves LY 6 as the possible province of Yŏu Rwò 有若 or Yŏudž 有子. Later tradition implies that Yŏudž was either disliked or resented.[28] This would explain the few sayings attributed to him in the text, and the lack of an interpolated saying in LY 4 (an honor accorded to both Dž-yóu and Dzv̄ngdž). Like the hostility toward Dž-gùng in LY 5, this suggests a headship either stormy in itself, or later disavowed by the school tradition.

---

[28]For a positive reading of some of the later evidence, see Lau **Analects** 260–261.

[A. Fitness for High Office]

1 Confucius feels that **Răn Yūng** could hold a responsible position
2 Confucius agrees with **Răn Yūng** about laxness in a leader
3 Only dead **Yén Hwèi** really had the will to improve himself (< 5:28)

[B. Judgements In and Out of Office]

4 Răn Chyóu **improperly grants** excessive travel allowance
5 Ywæn Sz̄ **improperly refuses** unneeded salary allowance
6 Răn Yūng described as **worthy though humble**
7 Yén Hwèi said to be **rv́n though poor**
8 **Jì Kāngdž** inquires about employability of three disciples (< 5:8)
9 **Jì clan** rejected as an employer by Mǐn Dž-chyēn (< 5:5)
10 **Tragic illness** of worthy Răn Gv̄ng
11 **Lyrical poverty** of worthy Yén Hwèi
12 **Faint-hearted Răn Chyóu** gives up without exerting himself
13 **Vulgar Dž-syà** expends energy on the wrong subject
14 Dž-yóu discovers a punctilious official subordinate

[C. The Balance of Qualities]

16 **Showy qualities** necessary in practical life (reverses 5:25)
18 **Showy qualities** must however be balanced by inner substance
19 Inner integrity is the very life of man

[D. Acquiring the Qualities of the Gentleman]

20 Taking pleasure in truth is the **highest** of three stages
21 Openness to the appeal of virtue is the **higher** of two types of men
22 **Jì and rv́n contrasted:** questions of Fán Chŕ
23 **Jì and rv́n contrasted:** metaphor of mountains and rivers
25 **Pun** (gū versus bùgū) on things which lack their proper nature
26 **Pun** (rv́n versus rv́n) on degree to which good men can be deceived
27 Wide learning moderated by ritual propriety is enough for the gentleman

LY 6 Conspectus

LY 7

Chapter Inventory. The concordance text of LY 7 contains 38 passages, of which 7:26 contains a second "The Master said" formula, and is probably two closely related sayings which have been later combined. Dividing it (as 7:26a/26b) gives a total of **39 passages** in the received text of the chapter.

Interpolations. Eleven of these are descriptions rather than quotations, and thus depart from the norm of the book so far. Of them, 7:4, 13, and 21 interrupt pairs of sayings (see opposite), and 7:15, 25, and 27 fall *between* pairs of sayings. These six are thus formally intrusive as well as typologically anomalous; we conclude that all eleven (the other five are 7:9–10, 18, 32, and 38) are interpolations. Two passages, 7:11 and 31, are anecdotes with narrative changes of scene, for which there is no earlier precedent. With the removal of the descriptive passages, both fall between two well-defined pairs of sayings. This anomaly of placement confirms the doubt raised by their novelty of structure, and we conclude that both are interpolations. Finally, 7:36–37, coming (given the elimination of 7:38) at the end of the chapter, do not pair with each other, nor does 7:36 pair with 7:35. 7:35 itself describes the last hours of Confucius. LY 7 as a whole, in contrast with LY 5–6, which teem with disciples, focuses largely on Confucius. It seems to have been meant as a portrait of the founder, with the 7:35 death scene, summing up his life retrospectively, as its final element. We thus conclude that 7:36–37 are later additions. Removing these fifteen passages gives a total inventory of **24 passages**, the same as in LY 5–6.

Language and Form. LY 7:5 recalls Confucius's dreams of Jōu-gūng. Probably that part of the chapter is meant to characterize Confucius in his youth, just as 7:35 (an unpaired envoi to 7:33–34) evidently looks back on his life from its end. The pairing pattern isolates 7:6, 19, and 30 as *internal* unpaired envois, presumably marking thematic divisions (as in LY 4–6). We might expect to find these devoted to early (7:7–19) versus late (7:20–30) teaching periods. There is support for this in the youthful enthusiasm of 7:14 (on music), and the world-weary despair of 7:26a/b. In 7:23 occurs the distinctive, probably archaizing pronoun yw 予 (we are grateful to David Keightley for defining its archaic use as a first-person *singular* form), which also occurs in LY 8, and in both chapters occurs in contexts featuring death or the supernatural. This usage was probably based on a mistaken inference from the occurrence of the pronoun in inscriptions on preserved ritual bronze vessels, with their supernatural context. That nuance is developed further in later chapters.

Date. There are no direct indications. By its position, LY 7 follows LY 6 (c0460) and precedes LY 8 (which is dated by the portrayed death of Dzv̄ngdž to c0436). We may reasonably assign it to c0450, in approximately the middle of that span.

Compiler. The death of **Dzv̄ngdž**, portrayed in the following LY 8, makes it a first hypothesis that he was school head as of the compilation of LY 7. The LY 7 portrait of Confucius contains many novel features, and its implied date, more than a generation after his death, suggests that these novel features are inventions; their recurrence in the LY 8 Dzv̄ngdž sayings also points to Dzv̄ngdž as the likely author. The aesthetic sensibility attributed to "Confucius" in 7:14 is compatible with Dzv̄ngdž's quotation of a poem on his deathbed in 8:3, the sacral pronoun in the supernatural protection claim of 7:23 recurs in Dzv̄ngdž's 8:3, and the same mixture of moral strenuousness and ultimate moral confidence characterizes the two death scenes, Confucius's in 7:35 and Dzv̄ngdž's in 8:3. On the whole, then, the attribution of LY 7 to Dzv̄ngdž seems relatively well founded.

[A. Personal Character]

1 Confucius succeeds **as a transmitter**; he does not make up anything
2 Confucius succeeds **as a learner and teacher**; he does not weary
3 Confucius falls short **in learning from the good** and reforming the evil
5 Confucius falls short **of his early dream visions** of Jōu-gūng
6 Confucius's advice to beginners: Way, virtue, r̆n, cultural expertise

[B. Early Teaching]

7   Confucius has never turned away **a poor student**
8   Confucius will not put up with **an indolent student**
12 Confucius is **not distracted** from principle by chance of improper gain
14 Confucius is **distracted** from eating by beauty of Chí ritual dances
16 Confucius is **indifferent** to temptations of wealth and position
17 Confucius is **intent** on continuing his studies
19 Confucius refuses illegitimate office in favor of learning and teaching

[C. Late Teaching]

20 Confucius is **not a sage**: he loves the past and learns from it
22 Confucius is **not a snob**: he can learn from anybody in the street
23 Confucius **claims Heavenly invulnerability** to threat of brigand
24 Confucius **disclaims esoteric teaching** against doubts of disciples
26a Confucius despairs of meeting **a sage**
26b Confucius despairs of meeting **a worthy man**
28 Confucius is **not a sage**: he uses lower methods
29 Confucius is **not a snob**: he will accept any questioner
30 If you truly want r̆n, then r̆n is right there beside you

[D. Retrospection and Death]

33 Confucius **though energetic** has had no chance to show his talent
34 Confucius **though not a sage** has been unwearying in his teaching
35 Confucius's life has been in itself a sufficient prayer

LY 7 Conspectus

LY 8

Chapter Inventory. The concordance text of LY 8 has 21 passages, of which 8:2 has a second "The Master said" formula, and may be divided as 8:2a/b. 8:20 has a triple form (two lore statements followed by a "Confucius said" formula), and may be divided as 8:20a/b/c. These divisions give a chapter total of **24 passages**.

Form and Interpolations. By the LY 5–7 precedent, 24 sayings is the full complement of a standard chapter, seemingly leaving no room for interpolations. But the five sayings 8:3–7, attributed to Dzv̄ngdž, stand out from the rest of the chapter. The first two, 8:3–4, are deathbed scenes, of which the more impressive, 8:4, in which Dzv̄ngdž is visited by the head of the Mv̀ng clan, is suspect as an aggrandizing interpolation. The other **4 passages** then form a plausible core.

8:2a/b pair *with each other*. 8:1, on the Jōu ancestor Tài-bwó, is thus isolated in its immediate context, but has affinities with the ancient figures (Yáu, Shùn, Yw̌, the early Jōu kings) in 8:18–21. It seems that 8:1 and 8:18–21 are an *encapsulating* addendum, most of it appended, with one passage placed at the chapter head to legitimize the rest. Between this and the Dzv̄ngdž core (8:3–7) is a middle stratum comprising 8:2a/b and 8:8–17, which is also self-consistent, though different from the Dzv̄ngdž core and the outer layer. The linking idea is emphasis on ritual (8:2a) and subordination of rv́n (8:2b, 8:10). This suggests that the Dzv̄ngdž material (8:3–7 less 8:4) is the original chapter, which we may call 8A, that 8:2a/b and 8:8–17 are a first addendum, which we may call 8B, and that 8:1 and 8:18–21 are a second addendum, which we may call 8C. The late date of 8C is supported by the fact that *no earlier figure than Jōu-gūng*, the first ruler of Lǔ, is mentioned in the Analects through LY 7. The motive for 8C, besides filling out the chapter to standard length, may have been to create a Confucian pedigree for these mythical figures.[29]

The contempt of 8:4 for the "ordering of ritual vessels" contradicts the ritual emphasis in 8B, and is thus later than 8B, but it also lacks the 8C antiquarianism, and since 8C seems to have completed the 24-passage form, it must predate 8C, as a single-passage interpolation added sometime between the two layer additions.

Language. The Dzv̄ngdž sayings include the sacral pronoun yw̌ 予 replacing wú 吾 as the first-person pronoun. This usage links the 8A core with LY 7, where the same usage first occurs, not contradicting the natural inference that LY 7 was compiled by Dzv̄ngdž during his lifetime, as head of the Lǔ Confucian school.

Date. The 8A core may be a memorial compilation for Dzv̄ngdž (its 4 *sayings* paralleling the 4 *sections* of the Confucius memorial, LY 4). It may in any case plausibly be dated to the year of his death, traditionally **0436**.

Compiler. Dzv̄ngdž's elder son **Dzv̄ng Ywæn** 曾 元 was presumably his chief mourner, and is thus also the likeliest compiler of the 8A memorial sayings.

---

[29]Kimura Kōshi 322–329 agrees that the concentric 8:1, 8:18–21 is the latest layer. He sees 8:2b as Dzv̄ngdž's comment on Confucius's 2a, and 8:1 and 8:2a/b as duplicated in several strata – (a) 8:1, 8:18–21, (b) 8:1–2, (c) 8:2–7, (d) 8:2, 8:8–17 – handed down in *both* the schools of Confucius and of Dzv̄ngdž before being combined in the later school of Dzv̄ngdž. Eno **Sources** proposes a complex variant of the Kimura hypothesis. We feel that a one-school accretion hypothesis adequately explains the Analects material, but note the need for further study of the Dzv̄ngdž school both in and before Hàn.

8A   8B   ?   8C

[Antiquity Addendum, 8C]
┌ 1   virtuous Tài-bwó

[Ritual Addendum, 8B]
2a   Ritual **limits** on behavior
┌ 2b   Gentleman as **models**

[Dzv̄ngdž Memorial, 8A]   [Dzv̄ngdž Aggrandizement]
3 Dzv̄ngdž **dies**

                < 4 Dzv̄ngdž dies; Mv̀ng head visits

5 Dzv̄ngdž's **deceased** friend Yén Hwéı
6 Dzv̄ngdž on competence of the **gentleman**
7 Dzv̄ngdž on moral duty of the **gentleman**

└ 8   Three-stage curriculum for **gentlemen**
  9   Culture cannot be understood by **commoners**
10   Hardships make most people **lawless**
11   Arrogance in a gentleman is a **defect**
12   Most three-year students aspire to **office**
13   Advice to future **officials**
14   Prohibition against **outsiders** discussing policy
15   Appreciation of **court** musician J̇r's performance
16   **Disapproval** of the insincere and dishonest
17   **Anxiety** about even sincere learners

└ 18   **Virtue** of Shùn and Yw̌
  19   **Virtue** of Yáu

20a   Shùn's five **ministers**
20b   Wǔ's ten **ministers**

20c   Comment on Tāng and Yw̌
21   Comment on **Yw̌**

LY 8 Conspectus
(Including later concentric additions 8B and 8C and single interpolation 8:4)

LY 9

Chapter Inventory. The concordance text of LY 9 contains 30 passages, of which 9:30 has a second, internal "The Master said" formula, and may be divided as 9:30a/b. This division gives a total of **31 passages.**

Interpolations. As in LY 7, several passages (9:1, 4, and 10) are descriptions rather than quotations. The first of these precedes a pair of sayings, and thus is also formally extraneous. Other suspect passages interrupt pairs (9:9, 26) or fail to pair with an envoi (9:14, 30b); these four passages, making seven in all, should be considered interpolations. Removing them leaves **24 passages** in the chapter.

Language and Form. Thematic divisions are formally signaled by unpaired envois at 9:5 (the end of a section of three sayings on culture) and 9:30a (the chapter end). Study of content suggests another thematic break at 9:16, ending a series depicting Confucius's life, and preceding one on the pursuit of virtue. A final section, 9:28–30a, is concerned with rivalries and intrigues in office, and how to judge colleagues.[30] Several LY 9 passages have counterparts in LY 7 or LY 8, most dramatically the Confucius death scene in 9:12 (relating to 7:35).[31] The thematic division at 9:16/17 is paralleled by an indebtedness pattern: 9:16 is the last passage with an LY 7 counterpart, while 9:17 is the first passage based on LY 8. The resulting sectional pattern, 3-8-10-3, contains a formal innovation:

LY 4	7- 3	3- 3	16 passages
LY 5	3- 9	9- 3	24 passages
LY 6	3-11	3- 7	24 passages
LY 7	5- 7	9- 3	24 passages
LY 8	2- 2		4 passages
LY 9	3- 8	10- 3	24 passages

it is the first *full-length* chapter in which some sections have an even number of passages, and thus do not conclude with the finishing device of an unpaired envoi.

Date. The statement in 9:15 that a reform of Lǔ court music occurred after "Confucius's" return from Wèi contrasts with 7:14, in which "Confucius" finds that Chí court music surpassed his previous experience. A Lǔ political shift from Chí to Wèi may be implied. If the Chí attacks on Lǔ territory in 0412, 0411, and 0408 motivated Lǔ to make a new alliance with Wèi, then negotiations might have occurred in 0407/0406, and the new cultural alignment might have had time to be reflected in the elite culture of Lǔ, and thus mirrored in LY 9, by c0405.

Compiler. The close relation of LY 9 to LY 7–8, respectively the chapter and some individual sayings of Dzvngdž, has a parallel in the fact that the use of the pronoun yŵ 予 in solemn contexts also occurs in LY 9. Dzvng Ywæn 曾元, the most likely scribe for LY 8, is by the same token the most likely inheritor of Dzvngdž's role as school head. LY 9 would then reflect his tenure, which would cover the years from 0436 (Dzvngdž's death) to slightly after c0405.

---

[30]Kimura Kōshi 329f divides the chapter into three sections by content: manners (9:1–15), love of learning (9:16–23, with 9:16 distinctive), and teaching (9:24–30). We use formal factors in reaching our slightly different segmentation of the material.

[31]Kimura Kōshi 339f notes this same similarity, and suggests that LY 9 "may have used material left over by the LY 7 compiler."

[A. On Culture]

2   Culture is **more than** mastery of specific skills
3   Culture is **not mere** retention of older usages
5   Confucius has a divine mandate to preserve Jōu culture (< 7:5, 7:23)

[B. Confucius's Life and Teaching]

6   Confucius stresses his **humble beginnings** (< 7:19, 7:34)
7   Variant of preceding: **humble circumstances**
8   **Among beginners,** Confucius will talk with anybody (< 7:7, 7:29)
11 **As an adept,** Yén Hwéi despairs of exhausting Confucius's example
12 Confucius renounces **sham** retinue at death (< 7:35)
13 Confucius awaits **proper** office during life
15 Confucius reforms **court poetry** after return from Wèi (< 7:14)
16 Confucius satisfied with **court and family** duties (< 7:2)

[C. The Pursuit of Virtue]

17 Stream as **model of unremitting progress** (< 8:3)
18 Sexual desire as **paradigm of intense concentration** (< 8:3)
19 Confucius will help any who **make an effort** on their own
20 Yén Hwéi as an example of **assiduousness** in lessons (< 8:5)
21 Confucius **laments** Yén Hwéi's death (< 8:5)
22 Confucius **alludes** to Yén Hwéi's death (< 8:5)
23 Men deserve no respect **if they fail to realize early promise**
24 Maxims are fine only **if they succeed in inspiring better conduct**
25 **Don't be afraid** to change if you are wrong
27 **Don't be ashamed** of being poorly dressed

[D. Intrigues in Office]

28 Pine as an emblem of **fidelity in hard times** (< 8:6)
29 One with true virtue can **withstand adversities and dangers** (< 8:6)
30a Distinction among low-level and high-level colleagues

LY 9 Conspectus
(Showing affinities with LY 7 and LY 8)

LY 10

Chapter Inventory. The material of LY 10, unlike that of every other Analects chapter, consists of descriptions of behavior rather than of quotations from Confucius. Editors differ widely in the way they divide it into passages. The Hv́ Yèn commentary as preserved with the notes of Hwáng Kǎn (488–545), a copy of which was recovered in Japan, specifies that the entire chapter is to be regarded as a single section. Later editors note this "old" tradition, but subdivide the material in various ways: Jū Syī (1130–1200) into 17 passages, Lyóu Bǎu-nán (1791–1855) into 15, Legge (1861) into 18, the 1929 concordance into 21, Waley (1938) into 18, and Lau (1979) into 27. Its thematic consistency makes it a virtual treatise, as the "old" tradition recognizes; on the other hand, with the formal precedent of LY 4–9 in mind, the compilers of LY 10 may well have construed their treatise as falling into paragraphs, as later commentators implicitly suggest. We find the following subdivisions of the 21 concordance sections to be both convenient and meaningful: 1a/b, 5a/b/c, 6a/b/c/d/e, 7a/b, 12a/b, and 16a/b. These divisions give 31 passages. Recombining 10:6e/7a into one (both deal with behavior during meals) yields a final chapter total of **30 passages**.

Interpolations. Waley[32] has pointed out that the main material was originally descriptive of the "gentleman" (jyw̄ndž 君子), preserved as the subject of 10:5a, and that the substitution of the grammatical subject Kǔngdž 孔子 "Confucius" is an overlay. The situation is thus the reverse of that in LY 7 or LY 9, where the descriptive passages were exceptional; here, description is the norm, and passages which report conversations of Confucius or mention his disciples or other figures (10:10 Jì Kāngdž, 10:11 and 10:15 implicitly Confucius, 10:21 Dž-lù) should be excised as later Confucianizations. With 10:21 goes 10:20, a possibly related and in any case cryptic fragment. 10:9 is out of place thematically, and presumably later. Eliminating these interpolations reduces the chapter total from 30 to **24 passages**.

Form and Language. This presumptively original material can be seen as grouped under four distinct headings: Court etiquette (10:1a–4), rules concerning clothing and food (10:5a–6e/7a), visits and gifts (10:7b–14), and private behavior (10:16a–19). Pairing is detectable as a principle of arrangement (see the conspectus at right). The layout (5-8-6-5) recalls that of LY 9, in which also the first and last sections are of the same size, and both middle sections (of which the first is one pair longer than the second) lack an envoi passage. There is a thematic progression from courtly to private protocol. Linguistically, the chapter is rich in reduplicative expressions (affectives) used, as in the Shr̄, to describe manner or attitude.

Date and Compiler. The SJ 47 list of Kǔng descendants ends with datable Hàn figures. Counting back from these at 25 years per succession-generation, they reach to c0400, implying a period of Kǔng leadership following the disciple phase which began with the death of Confucius and ended with Dzv̄ngdž's son Dzv̄ng Ywǽn in c0400. SJ 47 then gives us the names of the Kǔng heads of the school, from c0400 to the end of Lǔ in 0249. The first of them, Dž-sz̄ 子思, would occupy the first quarter of the 04c,[33] and LY 10, which as a unique production is probably his only chapter, may plausibly be dated to the end of that span, c0380.

---

[32]Waley **Analects** 146n1 and 147n3.

[33]For a more detailed conjecture on the Kǔng lineage, see Appendix 4.

[A. Public Occasions]

1a Speaks hesitantly in the village but readily at court (**slow/fast**)
1b At court, is casual with lower officers, circumspect with ruler (**fast/slow**)
2   Etiquette for receiving a court guest (**another**)
3   Etiquette for entering as a court guest (**oneself**)
4   Etiquette for acting as a symbolic presenter

[B. Clothing and Food]

5a **Formal** wear
5b **Informal** wear
5c Sacrificial **dress**
6a Sacrificial **food**
6b Prohibitions **against** certain tainted food
6c Limits **allowed** on meat, wine, and spices
6d **Handling** and eating of sacrificial-offering food gifts
6e/7a **Posture** while eating sacrificial-offering food

[C. Visits and Gifts]

7b Does not remain at local banquet after elders leave (**going**)
8   Is only an observer at local ritual celebrations (**staying**)
12a Etiquette for receiving gifts of food from ruler (**receiving favor**)
12b Etiquette of attending prince at meals (**returning favor**)
13 Receiving visit from prince while ill (**receiving**)
14 Responding to summons from prince (**returning**)

[D. Private Behavior]

16a Funeral of impoverished friend (**giving**)
16b Receiving presents from friend (**receiving**)
17 Posture during sleep (**avoiding death**)
18 Respect to those in mourning (**accepting death**)
19 Mounting and driving chariot

LY 10 Conspectus

LY 11

Chapter Inventory. The concordance text of LY 11 contains 24 passages, of which three (11:13, 18, and 19) either have, or as Waley points out in the case of 11:13, clearly imply, a second "The Master said" incipit. Each should be divided (into 11:13a/b, 18a/b, and 19a/b), giving a total of **27 passages.**

Interpolations. Three of these are structurally anomalous. 11:12 is on the afterlife, perhaps prompted by the funeral topic of 11:8–11, but itself a general statement alien to the chapter ethos, which is wholly concerned with judgements of disciples.[34] It is thus implausible as an envoi to 11:8–11. 11:20 and 21 do not pair with each other, but are followed by the pair 11:22/23; they thus compete for the role of envoi to 11:19a/b. The aspirational 11:21 is akin to the aspirational 11:19a/b, whereas the longer 11:20 is about adjusting advice to the individual, and hence, however interesting, thematically irrelevant and presumably late. Finally, the long and beautiful 11:24 follows the pair 11:22/23, and structurally can only be an envoi to them, but its theme (that a elegant seclusion is preferable to office) is opposed to the service ethos of the chapter, and its literary devices (descriptions of feelings, descriptions of nature, sheer length) are unprecedented in the Analects up to this point. These three, 11:12, 20, and 24, may thus be construed as interpolations. Eliminating them leaves the chapter with a total of **24 passages.**

Form. The pairing pattern shows two envois, 11:3 (defining 11:1–3 as a first section, which is thematically devoted to evaluations of *groups* of disciples) and 11:21 (marking the end of a self-cultivation group that includes only 11:19a/b; a final thematic section on self-cultivation has appeared in many earlier chapters). The four highly emotional sayings on Yén Hwéı's death (11:8–11) follow four sayings in praise of disciples including Yén Hwéı (11:4–7), and seem to be a series of positive evaluations, whereas 11:13a–18b alternate praise and denunciation, and focus especially on Dž-lù. These would then constitute the two inner sections.

The final pair, 11:22/23, are a novelty: not a single-saying *section* envoi (like 11:21, preceding), but a paired-section *chapter* envoi. Such concluding doublets become a standard structural feature in almost all subsequent chapters. This one resumes the hostility to Dž-lù which was thematic in 11C, and so is not a true chapter summary, but more precisely a retrospective highlight.

Date and Authorship. The chief feature of LY 11, besides its focus on disciple evaluations, is its strident tone, which shifts from what 11:10 admits is exaggerated mourning for Yén Hwéı to criticism of Dž-lù, a note formally emphasized by the new chapter envoi. This contrasts with the neutral prescriptive tone of LY 10, and must represent a different author, presumably one within the Kŭng family (veneration of Yén Hwéı, a kinsman of Confucius, and opposition to other disciples, would be intelligible for Kŭng family members). The only available candidate is the next name of the SJ 47 list, **Dž-shàng** 子上. As to date, in the absence of internal evidence we may provisionally conjecture c0360, halfway between the conjectural c0380 of LY 10, preceding, and the more closely datable 0342 of LY 3, following.

---

[34]Lau **Analects** 270, astonishingly, says that LY 11 is "entirely devoted to Confucius." Soothill's title for LY 11 is "Chiefly Concerning the Disciples." Waley **Analects** 142n4 further construes LY 11:19, which does not mention disciples by name, as a remark on Confucius's additude toward those "in different stages of progress."

[A. The Disciple Pantheon]

1   Confucius **prefers** his earlier disciples
2   Confucius **misses** his Chv́n and Tsàɪ disciples
3   Pantheon of ten distinguished disciples

[B. Praise of Disciples: Yén Hwéɪ]

4   Yén Hwéɪ "no help," **he accepted all Confucius's sayings**
5   Mǐn Dž-chyēn a good son, **his actions confirm his relatives' praise**
6   Nán Rúng assiduous in **repeating an exemplary poem stanza**
7   Yén Hwéɪ had an unmatched **dedication to learning**
8   Confucius **refuses his chariot** for Yén Hwéɪ's burial
9   Confucius **mourns for Hwéɪ's death** as ending his Heavenly mission
10 Confucius resists suggestion that he is **mourning excessively** for Hwéɪ
11 Confucius criticizes disciples for giving Hwéɪ **too grand** a funeral

[C. Praise and Blame of Disciples: Dž-lú]

13a Confucius pleased with dutiful attitudes of **Mǐn Dž-chyēn** and others
13b Confucius implicitly displeased with **Dž-lù's** rashness
14   Confucius pleased with conservative remark of **Mǐn Dž-chyēn**
15   Confucius criticizes conduct of **Dž-lù**
16   Confucius **balances shortcomings** of Dž-jāng and Dž-syà
17   Confucius **denounces** extortionate conduct of Rǎn Chyóu
18a Confucius distributes **criticism** of four disciples
18b Confucius balances **praise** of Yén Hwéɪ and (sardonically) Dž-gùng

[D. Self-Cultivation]

19a Must follow proper path to **reach esoteric goal**
19b Cannot tell if outward finesse **implies a true gentleman**
21   Yén Hwéɪ "cannot die" while there is a chance to learn from Confucius

[E. Envoi: Final Denunciations]

22   Confucius **belittles** official capacity of Dž-lù and Rǎn Chyóu
23   Confucius **resents** Dž-lù's glib defense of his conduct

LY 11 Conspectus

LY 3

Chapter Inventory. The concordance text of LY 3 contains **26 passages**, none of them seeming to require subdivision.

Interpolations. As will be seen, the chapter was apparently distorted in the final stages of compilation, and its pairing pattern is thus not a simple guide to the detection of interpolations. We may rely instead, initially, on the evident fact that virtually the whole chapter is on the subject of ritual.[35] The two sayings 3:5 and 3:24 deal more directly with the subject of political forms and proprieties, and are thus suspect as interpolations. We may then notice that 3:4, a contrast between Chinese and non-Chinese political forms, interrupts two closely parallel sayings, 3:4/6, both of which mention Lín Fàng,[36] and that 3:24, a prediction of better political times to come, similarly interrupts two closely parallel sayings, 3:23/25, both dealing with court music. Eliminating 3:5 and 3:24 leaves **24 passages**.

Form. Most of the chapter sayings are about the theory and practice of public ritual; several are however exercised about the usurpation of higher-level ritual forms. This note is sounded in the opening 3:1–3, where the usurpation is of the royal dance and poetic repertoire, and is also seen in the sarcastic 3:6 mention of Lín Fàng (compare the harmless question of Lín Fàng himself, in 3:4), 3:10 on the dì sacrifice (compare the simple exposition of the dì sacrifice, in 3:11), and the angry dismissal of the knowledge of Gwǎn Jùng in 3:22, who knows everything about ritual except that he is not entitled to practice certain parts of it. The final cry of pain in 3:26 concludes this subset of sayings. It is manifest that the compilers of LY 3 are reacting against some ritual abuse in Lǔ (symbolized by the Jì clan, 3:1–2 or in Chí (symbolized by Gwǎn Jùng, 3:22). These protest passages, though they technically complete the 24-saying chapter form, at some places produce skewed parallel structures (notably the dì sacrifice pieces, 3:10 and 11), and hence do not fulfill, but violate, a chapter structure presumably partly complete at the time they were added. LY 3 then seems to have begun in retrospective calm, and ended in contemporary rage. For the flawed structure, including three protest passages which form a sort of extra prologue at the head of the chapter, see the conspectus at right.

Date. The ritual outrage which is by far the likeliest target of the protest passages is the Chí usurpation of the royal title King (wáng 王) in 0342, some years before the same title was adopted by the ruler of Ngwèi (in 0335). These passages, and thus the completion of the chapter as a whole, would then date from **0342**.

Compiler. This dating puts us in the probable headship of the third figure on the SJ 47 Kǔng descendant list, **Dž-jyā 子家**. Nothing is known of him from SJ 47 except that he died at the relatively early age of 45.

---

[35]Lau **Analects** 269 claims that this general trait is "without any exception," but this holds for the chapter as it stands only if one views all government and social functions as aspects of ritual. Compare n35, following. LY 3, like all Kǔng family chapters so far, does nevertheless remain strongly monothematic.

[36]Lau **Analects** ap 3:6 himself refers to 3:4, as does virtually every commentator of any standing since the semi-anonymous Hàn scholar Bāu 包 (see Lyóu Jv̀ng-yì ap 3:6). This may well count as one of the great missed opportunities in Analects scholarship. The Lín Fàng pair, though ultimately complex, is still probably the easiest place to begin to observe the separation of closely related sayings by the intrusion of later material.

[Prologue: The Usurpation of Ritual]

1 Confucius **cannot bear** usurpatious Jì rituals
2 Confucius **sardonic about** Jì use of Shī ceremonial poem
3 One who is not rv́n has nothing to do with ritual or music

[A. Basic Principles of Ritual]

4 **Lín Fàng** asks about guidelines for ritual
6 Jì know no more about the mountain sacrifice than **Lín Fàng**
7 **Courtesy underlies** seeming competition in archery (cf 16)
8 **Ritual maxim hidden** in seeming description in Shī poem

[B. Explanations of Ritual Traditions]

9 Evolution of ritual allows prediction of future rituals (cf 14)
10 Confucius cannot bear to watch the usurped **dì sacrifice**
11 Confucius **explains dì** sacrifice implies political domination
12 Confucius **rejects gloss on jì** "offering" as dzài "be present"
13 Confucius **disapproves** folk maxim valuing food over sacrifices
14 Confucius **exults** in the richness of the Jōu heritage (cf 9)

[C. Adjustments to Ritual]

15 Confucius asks **politely** about each step of Grand Shrine service
16 Old way was **not to count** piercing the hide in archery (cf 7)
17 Dž-gùng wants to abolish **old ways**; Confucius prefers them
18 Serving ruler by **older protocol** would now seem sycophantic
19 Confucius analyzes ritual as framework for **minister/ruler relation**
20 Confucius expounds Shī poem as ideal of **husband/wife relation**

[D. Praise and Blame of Ancient Rituals]

21 Dzǎi Wǒ rebuked for **criticizing** Jōu grave customs to Aī-gūng
22 Confucius **belittles** the ritual expertise of Gwǎn Jùng
23 Talk with Lǔ music master about **orchestral** performance practice
25 Pacific Shàu **dance** beautiful; martial Wǔ **dance** not completely so
26 Confucius cannot bear insincerity in sacrifice

LY 3 Conspectus

(The passages comprising the final protest layer are indented)

LY 12

Chapter Inventory and Interpolations. The concordance text of LY 12 contains 24 passages, of which 12:12 ends with a seeming editorial comment. Dividing it as 12:12a/b gives **25 passages.** Leslie questions 12:5 as possibly interpolated,[37] but it fits the pattern of the chapter, which is on now-familiar lines. Retaining it, and eliminating only 12:12b, yields a final chapter total of **24 passages.**

Form. Lau notes that almost every saying in LY 12 is a question.[38] We may further observe that the chapter seems to be divided by the content of the question, or, in the first two sections, by the degree of indirectness in the answer. The first section in particular emphasizes that the questioners (including the once notably acute Yén Hwéi) do not fully understand the answer or grasp its consequences, thus centering the learning process wholly in the teacher. This may reflect a new contemporary formality in the relations between teacher and student (see GZ 59); it also suits the ritual emphasis of the Kŭng heads as seen in LY 10–11 and LY 3.

The profile of the chapter, determined by pairing and confirmed by thematic grouping, is 5-4-7-6-2. The first four sections follow the LY 9–11 model in having sections with and without envois; however, it alternates these, rather than confining the sections without envois to the middle of the chapter. The LY 11 innovation of a chapter envoi, or concluding pair of sayings, is resumed (it had been dropped in LY 3, perhaps to make LY 3 resemble the earlier chapters, and thus seem plausible in its role as a preposed chapter). The last few chapter profiles are:

LY 9	3-8	10- 3	24 passages
LY 10	5-8	6- 5	24 passages
LY 11	3-8	8- 3 -2	24 passages including envoi
LY 3	[3] 4-6	6- 5	24 passages including prologue
LY 12	5-4	7- 6 -2	24 passages including envoi

A remarkable feature of the chapter is its frequent echoes of contemporary texts, implying an interschool dialogue which it seems not inappropriate to identify as a sign of the onset of the so-called Hundred Schools period. Some echoes of chapters of the Chí Legalist compilation Gwăndž (GZ) which seem to be themselves early, or to reflect early ideas, are indicated in the conspectus, opposite. Apart from the GZ connection, LY 12 ventures into new ground in discussing the theory of the state and of rulership; topics which were never mentioned by Confucius.

Date. The benevolent populism of LY 12 is close to that expressed in the interviews of Mencius (MC 1). To a lesser extent, this is also true of LY 13. Both presumably represent the Analects-school heritage of Mencius, and may be dated shortly before his public career in 0320. LY 12 might thus be assigned to c0326.

Compiler. This date would fall within the early years of the fourth SJ 47 figure, Dž-jīng 子京. Given the early deaths of several Kŭngs, at least some must have succeeded to the headship as minors, before age 20. A transitional stewardship may have occurred on such occasions. If Dž-jīng was an early successor, and Mencius was still in the school as a senior student, Mencius himself may have been included on Dž-jīng's transition team, and thus had an opportunity to influence LY 12.

[37]Leslie **Notes** 2–27, especially the suggestion in 5–6.
[38]Lau **Analects** 270–271.

[A. Cryptic Answers]

1   Yén Hwéı asks about rʹvn; **promises to practice** maxim
2   Răn Yūng asks about rʹvn; **promises to practice** maxim (< GZ 3:5–6)
3   Szmă Nyóu asks about rʹvn; **misses the point** of the answer
4   Szmă Nyóu asks about the jywῆndz̆; **misses the point** of the answer
5   Szmă Nyóu grieves about fate; is rebuked by Dž-syà (< GZ 2:10)

[B. Open Answers]

6   Dž-jāng asks about wisdom; gets **straight** answer
7   Dž-gùng asks about government; gets **consecutive** answer (< GZ 1:3)
8   Statesman belittles culture; is **rebuked** by Dž-gùng
9   Prince unsatisfied with taxes; is **rebuked** by Yŏudž (< GZ 3:11, 7:10)

[C. The State and the People]

10 Dž-jāng asks about inconsistency; gets **poem**
11 Prince asks about government: gets **cryptic prose** (< GZ 2:45–46)
12a Confucius remarks that Dž-lù is **efficient in judging**
13 Confucius remarks that it is better to **have no trials** (< GZ 3:16)
14 Dž-jāng gets advice on **diligence** in public business (< GZ 2:42)
15 Confucius remarks about role of **ritual** in public business (> GZ 1:2)
16 Confucius contrasts gentleman and little man

[D. The Theory of Rule]

17 Jì Kāngdž gets **punning definition** of administration (< GZ 3:10)
18 Jì Kāngdž gets **inverse advice** about reducing crime (< GZ 3:10)
19 Jì Kāngdž gets distinction between **ruling and killing** (< GZ 1:3, 7:7)
20 Dž-jāng gets distinction between **fame and influence**
21 Confucius **uses poem** to answer Fán Chŕ question
22 Confucius **uses pun** to answer Fán Chŕ question (< GZ 3:9, 7:7)

[E. Envoi: Friendship]

23 Dž-gùng asks about **friends**
24 Dzv̄ngdž comments about **friends** in propagating rʹvn

LY 12 Conspectus
(Influence from < and on > the Gwăndž is noted in parentheses)

LY 13

Chapter Inventory. The concordance text of LY 13 contains 30 passages, of which 13:22 has a second "The Master said" incipit, and should be divided as 13:22a/b, giving a chapter total of **31 passages.**

Interpolations. Seven of these are in one way or another formally anomalous, and thus suspect as possible interpolations. 13:3 and 13:12 fall between pairs of sayings which seem to be on the same theme, and should be in the same section; 13:3 and 13:12 therefore do not suggest themselves as section envois. 13:7–8, not themselves an obvious pair (one is governmental, and the other ritualistic, in content), interrupt the plausible pair 13:6/9. And 13:21 and 13:22a/b both come between the plausible envoi saying 13:20 (which seems to relate to the preceding passages without pairing with the last of them) and the plausible pair 13:23/24, the latter of which seems to begin a new theme, and thus a probably marks a new thematic section. All of these are thus presumptively interpolations. Eliminating them leaves the chapter with a total of **24 passages.**

Form and Content. As thus clarified, the thematic tenor of the entire chapter is the theory of government; specifically, an opposition to what are recognizable as Legalist theories of government, some of which have counterparts in seemingly early chapters of the Gwǎndž. Within that general theme, there are four sections developing subtopics such as the nature of government and the character of the ruler and his ministers.[39] The formal ground plan is 6-5-5-6-2, a symmetrical chapter followed by the two-passage envoi which has been standard practice since LY 11. Like previous examples, the envoi is a thematic footnote to the chapter, rather than an epitome of it as a whole, or an echo of its beginning passage.

Within sections, there is, in addition to the basic AABB successive-pairing pattern, a seemingly intentional use of *alternating* pairing: ABAB (as in 13:16–19, which alternate general and specific rules of administration), and also of *palindromic* pairing: ABBA (as in 13:25–28), the latter echoing the palindromic layout of the main chapter (6-5-5-6), and bringing the main chapter to a formal close. This formal wit has precedents in earlier chapters, but it is new in LY 13 as compared to LY 12. The content, like that of LY 12, is close to the position of Mencius in MC 1, but perhaps less conspicuously so than LY 12 itself.

Date. For the reason cited under LY 12, LY 13 should precede the beginning of Mencius's career in 0320, and by position it should also follow LY 12. The arbitrary date c0322 is an initial hypothesis that satisifies both these conditions.

Compiler. The closeness of LY 13 to LY 12 in time suggests the same compiler, Dž-jīng. The differences in the style and to a lesser extent in the thematic emphasis of LY 13 imply either that his character is developing, or that it is being given fuller scope. If, as conjectured above, he was a minor as of the composition of LY 12, these differences might be explained by his having reached an age of independent discretion as of the composition of LY 13. This inference has affected the solution proposed in Appendix 4 (page 287) to the chronology of the Kǔng school heads.

---

[39]Lau **Analects** 271 sees a main thematic break between 13:17 (ending a series on government) and 13:18 (beginning a series on the gentleman). We rely on the envoi function of 13:15 and 13:21 as section dividers in reaching our different conclusion.

[A. Ends and Means of Government]

1   Dž-lù asks about **government**
2   Rǎn Yūng asks about **government** (< GZ 3:15, 7:6, 7:19)

4   The **peasant skill of husbandry** is not needed by ministers
5   The **elegant accomplishment of the Poems** is worthless if not practical

6   The upright ruler's orders will be obeyed **without asking** (< GZ 7:10)
9   The ruler must **enrich and teach** the people (> GZ 1:3, 3:29, 7:7)

[B. The Role of Ministers]

10   If I had power, **in only 3 years** I could finish the job
11   It is true that **only after 100 years** could one abolish executions

13   **A private person** who governs himself can govern others (< GZ 3:19)
14   **A private person** is still concerned with government policy
15   The ruler must not govern for private purposes

[C. The Basis of Government]

16   **Test of government** is approval of its people (< GZ 1:1, 3:7)
17   **Technique of government** is delegation (< GZ 2:35)

18   Family loyalties **vary** in different places
19   The principle of loyalty is **universal** in all places
20   On official scrupulousness and adroitness

[D. The Official in the New Society]

23   Little man and gentleman **have opposite character**
24   Good man and bad man **have opposite opinions**

25   Gentleman is **easy to work for;** little man is easy to please
26   Gentleman is **dignified;** little man is arrogant

27   Steadiness and solidity are **near to** ŕ́n
28   Precision and scruple are **the attributes of** the officer

[E. Envoi: Preparation for War]

29   The people **are ready** for war after seven years' indoctrination
30   To lead **an untrained** people into war is to cast them away

LY 13 Conspectus

(Influence from < and on > the Gwǎndž is noted in parentheses)

LY 2

Chapter Inventory. The concordance text of LY 2 contains **24 passages**, none of them seeming to require subdivision.

Interpolations. The 24 passages of the concordance text exactly meet the now familiar expectation for the standard Analects chapter, and none of them seems to interrupt, or be otherwise misplaced in, the also familiar pattern of four thematic sections (plus chapter envoi), each composed of paired sayings with or without a final envoi saying. It would thus seem that there are no interpolations, and that the original chapter contained these same **24 passages**. This agrees with, but is even more pronounced than, the small number of interpolations found in the also preposed chapter LY 3, which had only two. It would seem that text-initial position gave a prominence which not only exerted a powerful influence on perceptions of the rest of the work, but conferred a visibility which to some extent protected it from interpolations. There has so far been no clear indication in the text itself that the Analects was memorized by students in the Lǔ school (LY 13:5 suggests that at least portions of the Shī corpus were being memorized by those in office), and even if it were, it is a familiar truth that the beginning of a text is the part that sits firmest in memory. Compare the discussions of LY 14–15 and LY 1, following.

Form and Content. Like the preceding LY 12–13, LY 2 considers questions of government, but unlike them it is not solely on that theme.[40] It also discusses, and devotes its second section to, the domestic virtue of filiality, relating it to earlier values by the unifying principle of ritual propriety (12:5). There is no sense that filiality replaces public virtues; rather, the chapter invites the inference that it completes the personal virtues of the gentleman. This inclusion also resolves a conflict between family and state loyalty that was raised by 13:18 (Upright Gǔng). It will be further worked into the system in the later LY 1.

Formally, LY 2 uses the ABAB pairing variants which were also noted in LY 13. It departs from earlier precedent in having no section-final envoi passages; unlike every previous chapter, all its sections contain an even number of sayings. The profiles of the last few chapters are:

LY 12	5-4	7-6	-2	24 passages
LY 13	6-5	5-6	-2	24 passages
LY 2	4-4	10-4	-2	24 passages

Date. LY 2 is in part compatible with, but in part moves beyond, LY 12–13; it is notably less Mencian than LY 12–13. This implies a time after, but probably not *long* after, the departure of Mencius in or shortly prior to 0320. Its initial section strikes the new cosmological note, with the ruler seen as the still point at the center of the turning universe. This flattery, and the summative nature of the chapter, would be appropriate for a presentation to Lǔ Píng-gūng, and a highly suitable time for such a presentation would be the year of his accession, 0317.

Compiler. That year would put the chapter still within the probable lifetime of Dž-jīng, whose independent ideological and stylistic tendencies, free of any immediate Mencian presence, it may thus represent.

---

[40]Lau **Analects** 269 however seems to go too far in saying that the chapter "lacks any obvious principle of organization."

[A. Virtuous Government]

1 Governing by virtue is a **fixed star** for the people (~ GZ 3:29–35)
2   The culture of the 300 Shī is **without a flaw** (> GZ 3:29)
3 Governing by virtue will **produce order** among the people (> GZ 3:35)
4   Confucius describes process of **perfecting virtue**

[B. Filiality]

5 Mv̀ng Yìdž asks about filiality: is told about ritual as **outer** guideline
6   Mv̀ng Wǔ-bwó asks about filiality; is told to be **assiduous**
7 Dž-yóu asks about filiality; is reminded of **inner** emotional basis
8   Dž-syà asks about filiality; is told that **more than deeds** is required

[C. Higher and Lower Consistencies]

9 Yén Hwéı seems stupid but **on inquiry** is not stupid
10 Men's nature is revealed by **observation** of their behavior (< GZ 3:17)
11 A teacher must adapt, not **merely repeat the old**
12 A gentleman must use judgement, not be **merely a tool**
13 A gentleman considers things from **the other person's viewpoint**
14 A gentleman sees things from **a wide perspective**
15 Meditative insights **are risky** unless moderated by study
16 Analogous values **are harmful** if not derived from the same postulates
17 Know **when you do not know** something
18 Be **skeptical** of what you hear, cautious in what you say

[D. Influencing the People]

19 Promote the honest **to get popular support** (~ GZ 3:37–38)
20 Display filiality **to get the loyalty of the people** (~ GZ 3:37–38)
21 Confucius's life **is a contribution** to government
22 An untrustworthy man **is absolutely useless**

[E. Envoi: Guidelines for the Future]

23 **Change**: nature of the eventual successor of Jōu (> GZ 2:62)
24 **Permanency**: refrain from the improper and do the needful

LY 2 Conspectus

(Influence from <, on >, and with ~ the Gwǎndž is noted in parentheses)
(ABAB pairs are indented)

LY 14

Chapter Inventory. The concordance text of LY 14 contains 44 passages, of which four suggest subdivision due to their internal parallel structure. These are 14:1 (two parallel comments), 14:12 (very similar), 14:26 (two similar sayings credited to different speakers), and 14:37 (a second "The Master said" incipit). All but 14:12 are also divided in the traditional text used by Legge. Separating them as 14:1a/b, 14:12a/b. 14:27a/b, and 14:37a/b brings the chapter total to **48 passages**.

Form and Interpolations. LY 14 and 15, exceptionally, are twice the size of the average 24-passage Analects chapter. Either they have been composed from the beginning as a double of the usual form, which the thematic structure does not suggest,[41] or they are massively interpolated. If the latter, then the interpolations are intended for these chapters in particular, and are not random later intrusions. In that case, it seems likely that the interpolations come from shortly after the chapters themselves, and constitute extensions rather than interpolations in the usual sense. This makes errors in identifying interpolations less costly, since the time differential may be small, but it also makes such errors more likely, due to the difficulty of discovering the original structure, overlaid as it seems to be by intrusions.

On the precedent established by the preceding chapters, LY 14 might be expected to have an overall thematic direction, to be divided into four thematic sections with a final envoi, and to consist of **24 passages**. As to the overall theme, impressions vary: Lau finds it to be "how to be a man,"[42] Soothill sees the chapter as governmental.[43] Our own impression favors the latter view. Our conclusions as to the chapter structure are set forth in the conspectus at right; the argument for identifying the interpolations is implicit in this positive structure.

Date. LY 14 opens by criticizing the propriety of accepting salary whether or not a government is behaving in an orderly fashion ("possesses the Way," 14:1a), noting that an officer must be geographically portable (14:2), wary in bad times (14:3), support agriculture over military policy (14:5), and tirelessly admonish the ruler (14:7); it ends by applying a populist test to governments, and noting that the ruler's love of lǐ ("propriety, due process") is vital to meeting that test. This situation will reach an apparent crisis in 15:1–2. Unfortunately, we know little of Lǔ court politics except from the Analects itself. The political theory of LY 14 agrees with that implied by LY 12–13 (c0326–0322), and may be a further development of it. The emphasis on the niceties of departure may reflect the controversy (MC, passim) over Mencius's departure from Chí after the Yēn debacle of 0314 (itself reliably attested by the BA). LY 14 also seems to follow the Dzwǒ Jwàn, which from internal evidence was compiled in c0312. All this suggests an LY 14 date of c0310.

Compiler. Such a date would make LY 14 available as a source for the court politics of Píng-gūng's later reign, and suggest the continued headship of **Dž-jǐng**.

---

[41]Waley **Analects** 21 finds that parts of LY 14 "are not Confucian in their origin;" Lau **Analects** 271 notes that the chapter is "at first sight somewhat mixed in content."

[42]Lau **Analects** 271. In terms of the later scholastic view of the text, which sees it as emphasizing individual self-realization, every Analects chapter could be so characterized (for an analysis of LY 1–4 from this point of view, see Appendix 5).

[43]Soothill **Analects** supplies for LY 14 the title "Chiefly Concerning Government and Certain Rulers."

[A. The Officer and the State]

1a It is shameful to **accept** pay equally from **good and bad** governments
2   Service is the true **duty** of an officer

3   The proper conduct of the officer in **good and bad** times
5   Agriculture is the right **basis** for the country

7   Officers must **faithfully admonish** superiors
8   Scribes must **skillfully transmit** communications

[B. Historical Models for the Officer]

9   Gwǎn Jùng able to act without incurring **resentment**
11 It is difficult not to **resent** poverty

12a Past figures combine to define the **historical ideal**
12b On a more practical **present-day standard**

13 Confucius **questions** the description of an ideal figure
14 Confucius **doubts** the reputed lack of pressure in a dispossession

15 Contrasted achievements and shortcomings of two historical figures

[C. Larger Historical Principles]

16 Gwǎn Jùng is **criticized** for his misuse of ritual knowledge
17 Gwǎn Jùng is **vindicated** as contributing more than ordinary men

18 Gūngshú Wv́ndž is praised for **advancing a subordinate**
19 Wèi Líng-gūng was sustained by **able subordinates**

[D. The Confucians in Office]

21 Duty of an officer to **openly denounce** an outside atrocity
22 Duty of an officer to **openly oppose** his own ruler

32 Confucius was flexibly willing to **leave** Lǔ
36 Intrigues of enemies against Confucius **within** Lǔ

40 Procedure of officials during dynastic transition

[E. Envoi: The Welfare of the People]

41 If the ruler loves propriety, the people can be **used**
42 A minister who **benefits** the people is better than Yáu or Shùn

LY 14 Conspectus
(ABAB pairs are indented)

LY 15

Chapter Inventory. The concordance text of LY 15 contains **42 passages**, none of which immediately invites subdivision.

Form and Interpolations. The situation of LY 14 recurs in LY 15; the chapter has apparently been overlaid with an almost equal number of interpolations, in which circumstances the distinguishing of the original chapter format, and thus the objective identification of interpolations, is exceptionally difficult. On the model of LY 14, we assume that there is some version of the usual **24-passage** chapter pattern, probably in four thematic sections with a two-passage envoi, and that we have to identify a total of 18 passages which do not fit such a pattern as convincingly as those which are conjectured to constitute it.

The overall theme continues, as in LY 14 and for that matter in all chapters from LY 12 onward, to be governmental, and the strained court situation implied in LY 14 would appear, from the break implied or envisioned in 15:1, to have reached the point of crisis; the final saying in the unsorted material, 15:42, seems to complain that giving guidance under current conditions is like leading a blind man. Against this general background, there seem to emerge recognizable thematic sections on the risks (section B) and responsibilities (section C) of the honest courtier, and his specific tasks in troubled times (section D). ABAB pairing, noted on the LY 14 conspectus, seems to occur here in the two middle sections, giving palindromic symmetry to the design, which appears to be reflected also in the sizes of the sections, the profile (apart from the envoi) being apparently 3-8-8-3. This internal consistency of design is matched by the external continuity of elements of that design with earlier chapters, especially LY 13:

LY 12	5-4	7-6	-2	24 passages
LY 13	6-5	5-6	-2	24 passages
LY 2	6-4	10-4	-2	24 passages
LY 14	6-7	4-5	-2	24 passages
LY 15	3-8	8-3	-2	24 passages

Due to the number of interpolations, the arguments in individual cases must be the implicit ones contained in the statement of the pattern which the chapter makes when they are removed, as shown schematically in the conspectus, opposite. As noted under LY 14, and as developed in the detailed commentary to the passages appended in the main translation of LY 15, the time lag for most of these interpolations seems relatively small, which at least reduces the import of the almost inevitable errors in distinguishing original from added material.

Date. As an apparent later stage in the tense political situation implied by LY 14 (note the amplification, in 15:1, of the motif of principled political departure that was introduced in 14:32), we may plausibly assign LY 15 a hypothetical date shortly afterward, but still within the same reign, perhaps c0305. The evidently urgent situation itself is the best explanation of the remarkable number of what seem most likely to be afterthought self-interpolations in these two chapters.

Compiler. The closeness in apparent time again favors the inference that the chapter was produced under the continuing headship of **Dž-jīng**. If so, then the sectional profiles given above are a record of his formal choices as a compiler of Analects chapters (that in LY 12 is perhaps compromised by its origin under a transition arrangement). On present inferences, his is the largest contribution to the Analects, and this portion of the text might thus repay authorial analysis.

[A. Critique of Rulers]

1 Confucius in Wèi **criticizes** war-oriented policy
2 Confucius in Chv́n **maintains balance** despite hardship
5 The ideal inactive ruler will leave policy to ministers

[B. The Gentleman and His Superiors]

6 Maxim for **morally advancing oneself**
7   **Surviving** in changed circumstances

8 Waste neither words nor the chance of **convincing others**
9   **Danger to life** may result from following rv́n

12 The minister **must plan for what is far off**
15 The minister must **keep resentment at a distance**

16 Students who **lack a sense of urgency** are hopeless
17 Colleagues who **never speak of the right** are difficult

[C. The Gentleman in Power]

25 Ruler's virtue is **revealed** by the condition of the people
26   **Scribal honesty** requires leaving uncertain passages blank

27 Gentleman's virtue is **obstructed** by concern for small things
28   **Judicial proceedings** must beware of unanimity

32 The gentleman is concerned for **principle**, not livelihood
33   Sequence of **establishing relations with the people** in a state

34 The gentleman is concerned for **great issues**, not small tasks
35   Importance of **rv́n as a basic reliance of the people** in a state

[D. Official Colleagues]

37 An officer should be **faithful but not supine**
38 An officer should be **dedicted and not avaricious**

40 There is no compromise with those who disagree on fundamentals

[E. Envoi: Courtly Practices]

41 The only virtue of an official communication is **that it communicate**
42 The proper way to help a blind man is **to guide him step by step**

LY 15 Conspectus
(ABAB pairs are indented)

LY 1

Chapter Inventory. The concordance text of LY 1 contains **16 passages**, none of which immediately invites subdivision.

Form and Interpolations. It is clear that the usual 24-saying chapter model does not apply. Lau finds "a lack of internal organization" in LY 1, but notes that (with LY 8, and he might have added LY 19) it contains many disciple sayings.[44] These very disciple sayings may be the key to the chapter organization, since there is an obvious tendency for them to occur in alternation with sayings of Confucius. The inventory (the chapter number 1 has been suppressed in these formulas) is:

Confucius:	1,	3,	5–6,	8,	11,	14,	16
Disciples:	2,	4,	7,	9–10,	12–13,	15	

Evidently, if one saying were removed from each group of two, the remaining sayings would alternate between the Confucius and disciple sets. In content, the groups themselves split between governmental and personal-cultivation maxims:

Government:	5,	10,	12
Personal:	6,	9,	13

If one of these themes were inconsistent with the theme of the rest of the material, we would have a principle of elimination. Given the governmental focus of the five preceding chapters (LY 12–13, 2, 14–15), it might be expected that LY 1 would also be predominantly governmental. Instead, the only clearly governmental sayings are the three listed above (1:5, 10, 12) plus Confucius's final 1:16. LY 1 thus breaks with its precursors. Since the chapter itself has been (conspicuously) preposed rather than (routinely) postposed in the book, it would seem that the compilers also recognized this. On the double criterion of formal and thematic fit, we may thus identify as interpolations the four sayings 1:5, 10, 12, and 16, leaving 12 original sayings, exactly half the normal complement, in which Confucian and disciple sayings systematically alternate. Once we reach this point, we may then notice that the disciples in the latter series form a probably intentional palindromic pattern:

Yŏudž / Dzv̄ngdž / Dž-syà / Dzv̄ngdž / Yŏudž / [Envoi: Dž-gùng]

Date. Of these three disciples, Waley has observed that the Dzv̄ngdž of this chapter is very different from that of LY 8, being much closer to the filial paragon Dzv̄ngdž of later times.[45] We may add that his colleague and predecessor Yŏudž is here also revived from earlier obscurity, as a spokesman for domestic virtues. In its context following LY 15, this abandonment of government seems to imply the withdrawal from court that was threatened in 15:1. This might have happened at the beginning of the new reign of Wv́n-hóu, who succeeded in 0302, his lower title hóu "Lord"[46] being a sign of outward domination (presumably by Chǔ, which was at this period expanding as an eastern power) which may also have affected the Confucians' influence at the Lǔ court. Allowing time to recenter the Lǔ school on a personal rather than governmental basis, we might date LY 1 to c0294.

Compiler. This would bring us to the probable headship of the next name on the SJ 47 list, Dž-jīng's son **Dž-gāu** 子高.

---

[44]Lau **Analects** 273.

[45]Waley **Analects** 20.

[46]This nomenclature is preserved in SJ 15 sv 0295 (Brooks **Princes**).

1   Confucius: It is the part of a gentleman not to resent **unemployment**
2   Yŏudž: Domestic virtues are the basis of **public** virtues
3   Confucius: Clever speech is **incompatible** with rv́n
4   Dzv̄ngdž: On constant self-examination for **complance** with virtue

6   Confucius: Cultivate domestic virtues, **then** polite accomplishments
7   Dž-syà: The domestically virtuous do not **need** polite accomplishments

8   Confucius: Basic qualities are the foundation of **political** culture
9   Dzv̄ngdž: Proper respect at funerals shows health of **popular** culture

11   Confucius: True filiality only shows after the death of **one's** father
13   Yŏudž: A dutiful daughter will be the best wife (in **another** clan)

[Envoi: Education]

14   Confucius: The assiduous man has the true **love** of learning
15   Dž-gùng: The ability to draw inferences is the **height** of learning

LY 1 Conspectus
(Note the ABAB pattern of speakers, superimposed on the AABB pairing pattern)

LY 16

Chapter Inventory. The concordance text of LY 16 contains **14 passages**, none of which (including the double statement 16:11 and 16:12, which seem to be meant as literarily single units) insistently suggests subdivision.

Form and Interpolations. As with LY 1, it is obvious that the 24-passage chapter module is not relevant to LY 16, which must therefore be analyzed de novo.

LY 16:1, which after *11:24[1] is the longest passage in the Analects, denounces two disciples who have failed to dissuade their ruler from his plan to attack a small neighbor state. As with LY 3, this vehemence suggests a reaction to a contemporary event. It is followed by two dynastic curses, predicting extinction for an evil state, which are emotionally if not formally compatible with 16:1. Next come several sayings organized by numerical category (the Three This and Nine That), a device which does not occur in earlier chapters, and is one criterion used by Tswēi Shù[47] to distinguish LY 16–20 as later than the rest of the book. These comprise 16:4–10, within which 16:9, though it can be *analyzed* as about three levels of learning ability, does not begin, as the others do, with a *label* to that effect. Eliminating it as formally inconsistent leaves six sayings in three formally well-defined pairs. Of the remainder, the last piece, 16:14, is a handlist of nomenclatural terms for the wives of rulers, and has nothing to do with the rest of the chapter (such bits of stray data are another of Tswēi's criteria for LY 16–20). For this reason, and given its suspicious position at the end of the chapter, we exclude it also. The remaining three group as 16:11–12 (on public virtues) and 16:13 (on the educational process). The latter cannot be an envoi to the preceding pair, and must be taken as a *chapter* envoi (unique in that previous chapter envois have had *two* passages).

The resulting layout then has five thematic sections, arranged in a palindromic 1-2-6-2-1 pattern, and totaling **12 passages**.

Date. The impending conquest which animates 16:1 may be the intended Chí conquest of Sùng, which took place in 0286; the 16:2–3 curses would then be responses to the *actual* conquest. It is implied by JGT #479, which purports to be a sample of it, that Chí prepared the conquest by portraying the King of Sùng as a monster of depravity.[48] Such a conquest would have nearly surrounded Lǔ, and threatened its own later absorption. In 0285, an alliance of states, responding to this change in the balance of power, attacked Chí, whose King Mǐn died as a fugitive. We may then plausibly assign the middle of the chapter to before 0287, 16:1 to the preconquest year 0287 itself, and 16:2–3 and any other finishing touches to c0285.

Compiler. This date implies the continued headship of Dž-gāu. Several features of this chapter resemble those of his LY 1, among them the use of a 12-passage rather than 24-passage form, a palindromic ground plan, and an envoi of one or two sayings on education. This recalls the self-cultivation theme of the final sections of the "classic" 05c Analects chapters. So does the reappearance of the 05c heads Yŏudž and Dzvngdž, previously ignored or castigated by the Kǔng school. We note that in c0285, these two chapters, LY 1 and LY 16, one at its head and one at its tail, would have framed the entire Analects as it existed at that time.

---

[47]So Lau **Analects** 264–268. Takeuchi **Rongo** 13 and 192–195 argues that LY 16–18 are late, but LY 19–20 are less so. Our results tend to support Tswēi and Lau.

[48]Crump **Ts'e** #479; compare Waley **Three** 137–141 (PB 100–105).

[A. Against Impending Conquest]

1   Confucius assails Răn Chyóu and Dž-lù for not preventing it

[B. Dynastic Curses]

2   When **ministers usurp**, doom will come in five generations
3   Since the **princely line lost power**, four generations have passed

[C. Numerical Listings]

4   Three profitable **and three unprofitable** friendships
5   Three profitable **and three harmful** pleasures

6   **Three missteps** of those who serve rulers
7   **Three avoidances** of the gentleman

8   Three things the gentleman **fears**
10   Three things the gentleman **takes thought for**

[D. Disapproval of Actions]

11   **There are none** who labor in obscurity to advance the Way
12   **There were none** to praise Chí Jǐng-gūng at his death

[E. Envoi: Education]

13   Chv́n Kàng extracts three principles from Confucius's son Bwó-yv́

LY 16 Conspectus

(Compare the form of LY 1, preceding, which also has 12 passages)

LY 17

Chapter Inventory. The concordance text of LY 17 contains 24 passages, of which two (17:2, 17:8) have an internal "The Master said" incipit, and should be divided (as 17:2a/b and 17:8a/b), making **26 passages** in all.

Interpolations. The changes introduced into the standard Analects chapter form since it was established with LY 5 (c0470) have in turn complicated the task of detecting interpolations, functionally defined as passages which interrupt that form. Thus, 9:1 was identified as an interpolation in the first instance because it preceded the pair 9:2/3, creating a 1+2 pattern for which there was *at that time* no formal precedent, but the special form of LY 16 (see above), in which 16:1–3 as part of a palindromic ground plan have the pattern 1+2, has now created just this precedent. Earlier interpolations themselves, having become established in the experience *of later readers* as normal, may in principle sooner or later serve as precedents. Thus a passage interpolated between a pair, such as 3:5 (which we date to c0310), in the Lín Fàng pair 3:4/6 (originally c0342) might eventually establish the "split pair" as a valid, and compositionally available, formal device.

In the present chapter, it is formally likely, on the old criteria, that 17:5, which splits a verbally close pair, 17:4/6, on refusing office, is an interpolation, and that 17:7, which comes between that pair and the next without seeming to serve as an envoi to the former, is also an interpolation. Eliminating them leaves **24 passages** with familiar subpatterns of paired-saying sections ending with optional unpaired envois, together with a two-passage final envoi which, like those of LY 1 and 16, is on the general subject of education and educability. The overall character of this chapter is angry: it denounces those in office, darkly disapproves of what look like rival claims to virtue and textual expertise, and is glumly unoptimistic about the capacity of certain types of people for self-improvement. This conclusion is novel in that it echoes the theme of the pair 17:2a/b, and the echo in turn suggests that these two pairs were at one time the intended beginning and end of the chapter.

The most striking passages in the chapter are 17:4/6, in which Confucius *refuses* office under unsavory rulers, but with evident reluctance. Despite the formal completeness of the thematic layout as described above, it is hard not to compare this with 17:1, in which Confucius, equally reluctantly, is *persuaded* to serve. Quite apart from the fact that LY 18 will soon eloquently defend service under evil regimes as not only allowable but politically imperative, it seems that 17:1 records an acceptance of what was reluctantly refused in 17:4/6, and that it does so not as a later interpolation but as an afterthought to the chapter, one for which LY 16 has provided a formal precedent. We thus treat 17:1 as part of the chapter design, though a part which *stands outside* the original thematic groups.

Date. It is substantively obvious that LY 17 reflects a Confucian return to power under disreputable conditions. This might reflect the nominal downgrading of the new ruler Chǐng-gūng (who had succeeded in 0279) from Prince (gūng 公) to Lord (hóu 侯), again presumably under Chǔ pressure, thus creating a virtual satellite government in Lǔ which the culturalist and nationalist Confucians might well have regarded with distaste. If so, we may plausibly date LY 17 slightly later, to c0270.

Compiler. This date would put us in the second quarter of the 03c, and thus into the period of the probable headship of **Dž-shv̀n** 子慎, who would presumably have held that position until the dissolution of the Lǔ school, a consequence of the dissolution of the state of Lǔ itself, at the middle of the century.

1 Yáng Hwò persuades reluctant Confucius to take office

[A. On Human Nature]

2a People start out close together and only later **diverge**
2b Only the wisest and the stupidest cannot **change**
3 Confucius concedes that educating the public is valid

[B. The Temptation to Serve]

4 Confucius **tempted by rebel** Gūngshān Fú-ràu to serve; refuses
6 Confucius **tempted by rebel** Bì Syì to serve; protests the need to refuse

[C. An Educational Crisis]

8a Disciples urged to study **the Shī**
8b Disciples urged to study **the first section of the Shī**
9 Ritual and music are more than **their outward implements**
10 The dishonest lack the inward reality but have **the outward manner**
11 The **rural magnates** are the thieves of virtue
12 Telling higher truths **in the byways** is a waste of virtue

[D. Denunciations]

13 Criticism of those **currently in office**
14 Decline in character of **the common people**
15 **Cleverness and beauty** seldom betoken rv́n (*repeated from 1:3*)
16 **Garish new usages** are replacing classic ones
17 Confucius would rather give his message **without words**
18 Confucius gives the bearer of an unwanted gift **a nonverbal reply**
19 Defense against **selfish economic objections** to three-year mourning
20 Complaint of **sensuous and lazy** students
21 **Criticizes to Dž-lù** an overemphasis on courage
22 **Complains with Dž-gùng** about various sorts of depraved conduct

[E. Envoi: Again on Human Nature]

23 Women and little people **are hard to deal with**
24 One disliked in maturity **will always be so**

LY 17 Conspectus
(17:1 is a formal afterthought, and stands outside the original chapter design)

LY 18

Chapter Inventory. The concordance text of LY 18 contains 11 passages, of which 18:1 and 18:8 both contain an internal "The Master said" (18:1 has more precisely "Confucius said" 孔 子 曰). This seems to warrant their subdivision as 18:1a/b and 18:8a/b, bringing the chapter total to **13 passages.**

Interpolations. Seemingly analogous to 16:14, the piece of extraneous lore that was at some point appended to LY 16, are 18:1a (a list of virtuous Shāng dynasty personages), 18:2 (featuring a remark by Lyǒusyà Hwèi), 18:8a (a list of various ancient worthies), 18:9 (a list of musicians who went from Lǔ to other states), 18:10 (a quotation from Jōu-gūng), and 8:11a (a rhyming list of Jōu dynasty personages), which crop up at both ends of LY 18. Like 16:14, these do not mention Confucius, and might be dismissed as stray matter lodged in the text due to lax housekeeping at Confucian headquarters. However, 18:1a and 18:11a are both followed by closely associated comments of Confucius, in 18:1b and 18:11b. This would seem to rule out any theory of adventitious addition, either here or (by symmetry) in LY 16. These passages must thus be part of the Analects, and since they are very close to each other in type, and equally distant from the remaining LY 18 passages in theme, we may regard them as a single group of concentric additions to LY 18. That interpretation reduces the original chapter to the **5 passages** 18:3–7.[49]

Form and Content. 18:3–4 pair as vignettes from Confucius's political career (showing him in even more exalted company than 15:1, though still ultimately unsuccessful). The remaining three pieces, 18:5–7, are all criticisms of Confucius by recluses of a type familiar from the Jwāngdž. Of them, 18:5 has a counterpart in JZ 4:7 that is verbally identical except for the ending, and 18:7 has a close parallel in JZ 25:6.[50] The longer 18:6, which falls between them, has no equally close Jwāngdž counterpart. By earlier precedent, it would for that reason be suspected of being intrusive in the closely related 18:5/7 *pair*, but given its common theme, it can also be argued that it serves as the animating centerpiece in the 18:5–7 *trio*. This would mean that the compiler is using as a compositional model the split pair that arose from interpolations like that in the Lín Fàng area (3:4–6) of LY 3. A yet more relevant model, for this series and the whole chapter, is LY 8 as its central Dzēngdž portion would have looked (8:3–5, 8:6–7) after the addition of the second deathbed scene, *8:4[16]. By our theory of LY 8 (see above), there was never a time when the chapter *as a whole* had that aspect (we date the 8B[14] concentric accretions earlier than *8:4[16]), but it is plausible that for later compilers, as for modern readers, the Dzēngdž core remained visible as such.

Date. There are no seeming references to contemporary events, and in the absence of an established dating for the different parts of the Jwāngdž, the close relations of LY 18 with JZ 4 and JZ 25, among other segments, do not yield a date. We may provisionally date LY 18 halfway between LY 17 and LY 19, or c0262.

Compiler. This falls in the quarter-century which is likely to have been that of the headship of Dž-shv̀n, and since SJ 47 tells us that Dž-shv̀n continued his career in Ngwèi, it would seem that he was himself displaced by the Chǔ conquest of Lǔ, and thus that he continued as Lǔ school head as of this *and all succeeding* chapters.

---

[49]Kimura Kōshi 449f identifies these same passages as later additions.

[50]Waley **Analects** 21 and Lau **Analects** 268–269 note this series as Dàuist in tone.

18A   18B

[Ancient Lore Addendum]
  1a Virtuous Shāng dynasty personages
  1b Confucius **comments** on the 18:1a personages
⌐ 2 Remark of the scrupulous Lyŏusyà Hwèi

[Original Chapter]
3 Chí Jǐng-gūng cannot use Confucius; Confucius **leaves Chí**
4 Chí distracts Lǔ ruler with dancing girls; Confucius **leaves Lǔ**
5 Madman Jyé-yẃ berates Confucius for serving; **flees** when confronted
6 Confucius **eloquently affirms** to hermit farmers his duty to humankind
7 Old farmer derides Confucius for unnatural life; **flees** when confronted

  ∟ 8a Virtuous ancient personages from various periods
    8b Confucius **comments** on the 8a personages
     9 Exodus of **Lǔ** court musicians to various places
    10 Remark of Jōu-gūng to **Lǔ-gūng**
    11 Rhyming list of Jōu personages

LY 18 Conspectus
(Compare the LY 8 conspectus, above, and note here the primary triplet 18:5–7)

LY 19

Chapter Inventory. The concordance text of LY 19 contains **25 passages**, none of which suggests subdivision.

Form and Interpolations. As we approach the end of the text, there is very little time left between the date of the chapter and the cutoff date for the Analects as a whole. The total number of 25 passages suggests that we have here to deal with the standard 24-passage model, and at the same time, fortunately, that we are to suspect only one potential interpolation within that model.

It does not help to notice that there are disciple sayings, since it turns out that the entire chapter consists of nothing but disciple sayings. We next turn to the formal layout of the chapter, which is generally organized by the disciples. Thus, 19:1–3 are sayings of Dž-jāng, and 19:4–13 are sayings of Dž-syà; so also Dž-yóu in 19:14–16, Dzv̄ngdž in 19:17–19, and Dž-gùng in 19:20–25. It will be seen that this more precise rule also yields no exceptions. Finally, we may notice that the Dž-jāng section ends with a criticism of Dž-syà (19:3), who is the disciple featured in the following section. This would also be true of the Dž-syà section if it ended with 19:12 (which criticizes Dž-yóu, whose section follows). Instead, it ends with 19:13, which is about the balance of study and official employment. 19:13 thus interrupts this sectional linking device (which ends with 19:15–16, where Dzv̄ngdž closes the circle by criticizing Dž-jāng; later sections are not linked in this way), and is the needed interpolation. Eliminating it yields the expected **24 passages**.

Content. The three circularly interlocked sections have a palindromic 3-9-3 ground plan. The next section, that featuring Dzv̄ngdž, ends (in 19:19) by asking for forbearance about the evidences of cultural decay in Lǔ, a theme which is picked up by the first Dž-gùng saying (19:20), where it is also noted that the myths of ancient depravities are also greatly exaggerated. The Dž-gùng section reaches, and ends on, a plateau of eulogy for Confucius as beyond all cavil and comparison the greatest of sages, an all but heavenly personage. It seems evident that the last two sections are intended to lead out of the mutual disparagements of the circular set of the first three sections, into an affirmation that Confucius is the answer to both doctrinal and larger social questions.

Date. Disciple sayings have been part of the Analects repertoire since LY 1, which featured them structurally, but this exclusive *focus* on disciples is remarkable. It is further to be suspected that the mutual wrangling portrayed in the first three sections is somehow symbolic of inter-Confucian disputes, and that the exit from that wrangling into a renewed centering on Confucius, in the last two sections, amounts to a recommendation of harmony for all factions. The three wrangling sections seem to criticize emphases that were characteristic of the school of Syẃndž, and the chapter may thus be an appeal for unity against the divisive stance of Syẃndž, who in SZ 6 (Knoblock **Xunzi** 224 and 303n48 argues against this reading) had severely criticized "Dž-sz̄ and Mencius," that is, the Analectal and Mencian schools, and whose intolerance for what he called partial or divergent views is abundantly reflected throughout the preserved writings of the Syẃndzian school. In the wake of the 0255/0254 Chǔ partial conquest, Syẃndž had became Director of Lán-líng, in southern Lǔ, presumably with influence over unoccupied northern Lǔ, including the capital where the Analects school was located. As a response to this new intellectual overlordship, LY 19 may plausibly be dated to c0253.

Compiler. As argued above, this must still have been **Dž-shv̀n**.

[A. Dž-jāng]

1 The **true officer** is brave, honest, and reverent in mourning
2 Those **partly committed** to virtue are neither with you nor against you
3 Dž-jāng criticizes Dž-syà [see next section] on how to treat outsiders

[B. Dž-syà]

4 A **superfluity of knowledge** only hinders the gentleman
5 He who knows **what he lacks** is the true lover of learning
6 The **reflective** student will incidentally achieve rə́n
7 The **assiduous** gentleman will perfect himself in the dàu
8 The **little man** tends to overelaborate
9 The **gentleman** has three outer aspects
10 The gentleman toward **subordinates and superiors**
11 The gentleman toward **major and minor matters**
12 Dž-syà criticizes Dž-yóu [see next section] on sequence in teaching

[C. Dž-yóu]

14 Mourning should not be carried **beyond the point of grief**
15 Doing "what is difficult" does not **reach as far as rə́n**
16 Dzv̄ngdž criticizes Dž-jāng [see first section] for his pomposity

[D. Dzv̄ngdž]

17 Has heard Confucius speak of the moral dimension of **mourning**
18 Has heard Confucius praise **posthumous respect for father**
19 Dzv̄ngdž urges compassion for evidences of cultural decay

[E. Dž-gùng]

20 Defends ancient ruler against **exaggerated atrocity myths**
21 Notes that shortcomings of gentleman **will be widely known**
22 Extols Confucius's learning as **too subtle for ordinary perceptions**
23 Extols Confucius's character as **too profound for ordinary eyes**
24 Disparagement of Confucius **only reflects badly on the critic**
25 Disparagement of Confucius **makes the critic look like a fool**

LY 19 Conspectus
(Note the cyclic linkages at 19:3, 19:12, and 19:16)

LY 20

Chapter Inventory. The concordance text of LY 20 contains **3 passages.** It is well known that the Lǔ text (the one largely favored by scholars during Hàn, and chosen to be engraved on stone at the end of Hàn) lacked the third of these,[51] which is included in our present text on the authority of the Gǔ or old-script text, supposedly recovered in early Hàn from the wall of "Confucius's house" (in our view, rather the headquarters of the late Lǔ school, near to the Lǔ palace complex). The HS 30 description of the Gǔ text notes that it had not 20 but 21 chapters, with "two Dž-jāng." That is, besides the present LY 19, which begins with a Dž-jāng saying, there must have been another chapter division with that incipit. 20:1 is an archaizing piece in the style of a Shū document. By quotes from and descriptions of ancient rulers it presents the evolution of the ideal model of civil government; it does not mention Confucius, and has been felt to be more or less extraneous to the Analects by several scholars.[52] We see it as an essential statement of late Confucian political theory, which, like the lore passages in LY 16 and 18, is part of the text, but if it originally formed a separate division (in effect, LY 20) *within* the text, then the remaining 20:2–3 would have been a chapter of their own. That chapter would have had a Dž-jāng incipit, since he is the interlocutor in the first passage.[53]

On the authority of this presumably original copy of the work, we should then regard 20:1 as constituting "LY 20" and 20:2–3 as "LY 21." We have been dissuaded from numbering the passages this way by our decision to keep the chapter numbers of the received text. Instead, we have adopted the anomalous solution of treating 20:1 as an addendum to LY 19. As an interpolation, it thus has the formula 20:1[19], for whose illogical aspect we apologize herewith. As a gesture to the other solution, these sequences appear as "LY 20" and "LY 21" on the conspectus, opposite.

Interpolations. Within the meaning of the chapter-division problem discussed above, none of the concordance passages are *later* interpolations, giving the received LY 20 a complement of **3 passages.** LY 20:1, anomalously but consistently, has been treated as an *interpolation after* (it is more precisely a *sequel to*) LY 19.

Form. LY 20:1 is a single, separate, pseudo-archaic document. The barely begun next chapter is represented by LY 20:2–3. For present purposes these can be regarded as paired (they discuss the minister and the gentleman), but they are of enormously different length, and were more likely raw material which the compiler had begun to accumulate, and would eventually have arranged more convincingly. As they stand, these passages are *preliminary to* the intended chapter form.

Date. The manifest interruption of LY 20 (or, if one follows Gǔ, LY 21) early in its process of accumulation implies a catastrophe. By far the likeliest catastrophe is the final conquest and absorption of northern Lǔ by Chǔ, in **0249.**

Compiler. By earlier argument, this was Dž-shv̀n. The SJ 47 report of his Ngwèi ministership, relied upon above to infer that he was head *until* 0249, also implies that he left Lǔ *after* 0249, and that the school ceased to function as an organization. Its heritage after that date will thus have been in the care of individuals in Lǔ.

---

[51]For the end of the Lǔ text at 20:2, see Mǎ **Shŕ Jīng** fragment 513.

[52]Waley **Analects** 21, Lau **Analects** 201 n1, 268.

[53]Waley **Analects** 252 also notes the separation of 20:1 and 20:2–3 in Gǔ.

[The Original LY 20; Complete as a Unit]
1 [Treatise on government in the form of an archaic document]

[The Original LY 21: Preliminary Sketches]
2 Dž-jāng asks about the characteristics of a **minister**; gets long reply
3 Confucius briefly characterizes the **gentleman**

LY 20 Conspectus
(Shown here, according to the Gǔ text, as a finished LY 20 and an incipient LY 21)

A Final Note on Form

This concludes our survey and analysis of the individual Analects chapters. It demonstrates that the rough hypothesis developed at the beginning of this Appendix can be developed in detail without manifest inconsistency, and to that extent lends support to that hypothesis.

As a by-product, the demonstration seems also to establish that there is a structure to Analects chapters, in which a set of formal elements like pairing and sectional division, some of them present from the beginning and others developed during the life of the text, are combined in different ways, and with what look like different personal predilections, to produce a standard chapter form and a number of variants on that form, as well as some highly individual departures from it, typically at moments of external challenge. The fact that the discovery procedures for these chapter forms do not give identical results for all chapters would seem to show that the reported forms are not analytically imposed, and at the same time that devices of form were used imaginatively and not routinely by the several compilers or authors. The possibility of statements being made through the medium of form is also open. One might regard the four *passages* of the LY 8 Dzv̄ngdž memorial as a respectful allusion to the four *sections* of the LY 4 Confucius memorial. Similarly, the 12-passage chapters LY 1 and 16 are of interest in that they may well have been from the same hand, and were together meant to frame and recontext the entire preceding Analects. Beyond this, their 12-passage form may be an intentional halving of the then normal 24-passage form, saying in effect (of the domestic focus which in them replaces the previous courtly focus) that in isolation from politics, a virtue of merely domestic scope is humanly incomplete.

We may here recapitulate the chapter profiles arrived at by this analysis:

Chapter				c-number	Name	Passages
LY 4	7- 3	3- 3		c0479	Dž-gùng	16 passages
LY 5	3- 9	9- 3		c0470	Dž-yóu	24 passages
LY 6	3-11	3- 7		c0460	Yǒudž	24 passages
LY 7	5- 7	9- 3		c0450	Dzv̄ngdž	24 passages
LY 8	2- 2			c0436	Dzv̄ng Ywæn	4 passages
LY 9	3- 8	10- 3		c0405	"	24 passages
LY 10	5- 8	6- 5		c0380	Dž-sz̄	24 passages
LY 11	3- 8	8- 3	-2	c0360	Dž-shàng	24 passages
> LY 3	3- 4	6- 6	-5	c0342	Dž-jyā	24 passages
LY 12	5- 4	7- 6	-2	c0326	Dž-jīng	24 passages
LY 13	6- 5	5- 6	-2	c0322	"	24 passages
> LY 2	4- 4	10- 4	-2	c0317	"	24 passages
LY 14	6- 7	4- 5	-2	c0310	"	24 passages
LY 15	3- 8	8- 3	-2	c0305	"	24 passages
> LY 1		10	-2	c0294	Dž-gāu	12 passages
LY 16	1- 2	6- 2	-1	c0285	"	12 passages
LY 17	1- 3- 2	6-10	-2	c0270	Dž-shv̀n	24 passages
LY 18	2- 3			c0262	"	5 passages
LY 19	3- 9	3- 3	-6	c0253	"	24 passages
LY 20	1 2			c0249	"	3 passages

The total number of passages in these original structures is 388. Together with the 142 interpolations distinguished by the above argument, this gives 530 passages for the Analects as a whole, the interpolations thus comprising 27% of that whole.

Appendix 2
Developmental Patterns in the Analects

The essence of an accretional theory for any text is that it assigns different dates to different portions of the text, thus accounting for otherwise problematic variations in language, form, or content. In the previous Appendix, apart from a presumption about the progressive aggrandizement of Confucius himself, we have relied on *formal* criteria in defining an accretional theory for the Analects. It is thus an independent test of that theory to explore its implications for *content*. Specifically, we wish to see if the Analects material, arranged as in Appendix 1, implies the developmental picture that we would expect from chronologically ordered evidence covering a 230-year span during a period known to be one of rapid technological and political change. In this Appendix, we apply that test by noting the distribution of terms and ideas in the basic chapter material, largely ignoring passages identified as interpolations. This is meant to show that the proposed chapter sequence is essentially sound, and superior to the integral theory in accounting for what we actually find in the text. For this purpose, we will limit ourselves to items of intellectual or material culture whose developmental direction is either intrinsically plausible or archaeologically attested. Once the developmental character of the text has been confirmed, it will also be useful to go on to examine a few developmental sequences whose outcome *cannot* be assumed. That is, at some point it becomes valid to look to the accretional Analects for new information about the period. Among topics of special interest for Analects readers are the implied histories of the supposedly ancient classics Shī, Shū, and Yì, which turn out to enter the awareness of the Lǔ Confucians later than the orthodox account of these texts would require, thus challenging the orthodox account itself.

An Overview

Before proceeding to specifics, we may notice a single, impressive feature of the distribution patterns. This is the occurrence of words and concepts which are proved by the respective school texts to have been associated with such rival trends of thought as the Dàuist, Legalist, and Mician movements. As the commentary to the main translation will show, we find in the 05c layers of the text persistent hints that the Lǔ Confucians were aware of a technique of meditation. There are also 05c indications of material progress, an interest in the ethics of salary, and of what might be called a popular morality of reciprocal responsibility. But there are no signs of any *organized advocacy groups* based on those or other concerns. If we draw, across our proposed Analects chapter sequence, a line after LY 3 and before LY 2 –

LY 4-5-6-7-8-9-10-11-3 / 12-13-2-14-15-1-16-17-18-19-20

– then *every* specific Analects textual resemblance to lines in the Dàu/Dv́ Jīng, the Gwǎndž, or the Mwòdž, and *every* unambiguous echo of the cosmological ideas now associated with Dzōu Yěn, or the military tactics of the mass army expounded in the Sūndž, falls *after* that line. There could be no neater demonstration that the age of philosophical interaction, the so-called Hundred Schools period, some at least of whose participants are agreed to be of 04c date, has *a definite point of onset* in the Analects. This pattern is very hard to explain on the theory that differences between the several Analects chapters are due to their having been compiled by different 05c disciples, with different 05c philosophical interests.

Confucius

We may begin by reviewing our initial assumptions, to see how consistently our expectation of gradual Confucian aggrandizement is fulfilled in the final theory.

Confucius's Rank. It is clear from the tone of LY 4 that Confucius was in real life steadfast in principle (4:6) but frustrated in practice (4:5); this is not the voice of a successful statesman. Later chapters never quite lose sight of this career failure, but they place it, so to speak, at increasingly higher levels:

4:5	Prefers integrity to success
5:21	Praises integrity over survival
5:8	Recommends disciples to the head of the Mvng clan
6:8	Recommends disciples to the de facto ruler of Lǔ, Jì Kāngdž
6:3	Recommends disciples to the official ruler of Lǔ, Aī-gūng
7:14	Portrayed as observing ritual practice in Chí
9:15	Portrayed as transmitting ritual expertise from Wèi
11:8	Claims to rank just behind the Great Dignitaries
14:21	Urges Aī-gūng to invade Chí in response to assassination of its ruler
14:32	Criticized as going from place to place in search of a ministership
15:1	Leaves Wèi in a huff after its ruler asks the wrong question
17:4	Refuses office under a rebel leader
17:6	Tempted by office under a rebel leader
18:3	Received in Chí on a par with heads of Jì and Mvng clans
18:4	Resigns Lǔ ministership in a huff after ruler becomes distracted

The transition from no rank to modest rank comes before LY 11, and the further promotion to a virtually ministerial rank comes before LY 14. Neither coincides with the "Hundred Schools" dividing line, which is before LY 12. This data set thus does not support the idea of a layer-type theory of the text with a break before LY 12. It implies two *additional* breaks. Still other breaks will be implicit in other data sets. The ultimate implication of *all* the data sets is the continuous-accretion theory.

Confucius's Travels. This development generally parallels that described above:

6:4	[Disciple makes chariot journey to Chí]
7:14	Confucius journeys [presumably by chariot] to Chí
7:19	[Disciple is present in Shv (south of Lǔ)]
7:23	Confucius unafraid of enemy [in unspecified location]
9:5	Confucius unafraid of enemy in Kwáng [south of Lǔ]
9:15	Confucius returns [presumptively by chariot] from Wèi
11:2	Confucius is in Chvn [well south of Lǔ]
11:21	Confucius is alarmed in Kwáng [presumably en route to Chvn]
15:1	Confucius interviews the ruler of Wèi
15:2	Confucius undergoes hardship in Chvn

We note that travel both north and south is specified for disciples [in the passages bracketed above] before it is attributed to Confucius, and it would be possible to argue that Confucius himself never left Lǔ during his lifetime. In Appendix 4 we argue instead that Confucius visited Chí and Jìn in the period of Jāu-gūng's exile, and Sùng in the late years of Dìng-gūng, and feel that this modest core of fact better explains the particular form taken by the subsequent aggrandizing myth. The data here cited document the gradual expansion of the Chvn/Tsài journey, with details being added to it, and previous claims being fitted in around it. By the 03c, this perilous episode was part of the public myth of Confucius, taken for granted both by his votaries (JZ 28:15, Watson 318f) and his detractors (JZ 20:4, Watson 213f).

Confucius's Chariot. Here again, it is probably a false clue that Confucius is initially portrayed as walking rather than driving; the likely situation is that the chariot was reserved for ceremonial or long-distance use:

7:22	Confucius portrayed as walking
7:14	Confucius journeys [presumably by chariot] to Chí
9:15	Confucius returns [presumably by chariot] from Wèi
9:2	Confucius sarcastically undertakes to perfect himself in chariot driving
[10:18f	Chariot etiquette is now now part of the gentleman's standard image]
11:8	Confucius owns, and by protocol cannot give up, a chariot
13:9	Confucius is [outridden?] in his chariot by Răn Yŏu
2:5	Confucius is driven in his chariot by Fán Chŕ
2:22	Confucius uses chariot metaphor
15:6	Confucius uses chariot metaphor
18:5	Confucius descends from chariot to talk to Madman

The only developmental aspect in the data is then an increased tendency to portray Confucius in his official role, which involves the chariot as an incident of that role.

Confucius's House. The data also show an increasing splendor of residence, starting with zero (in LY 4–6 he is seen at the homes of *others*, never at his own). Again, a grand house is credited to disciples before it is asserted of Confucius:

4:1–17	Confucius addresses individual disciples; no setting mentioned
5:1–28	Confucius sometimes addresses multiple disciples; no setting mentioned
6:10	Confucius visits a disciple at *the disciple's* house
6:11	Confucius describes a disciple's life in *the disciple's* house
7:29	Confucius receives a visitor while himself away from home
8:3	Dzv̄ngdž has disciples who frequent his "gate"
9:2	Confucius answers a criticism made on the criticizer's turf
[10:12f	Domestic etiquette prescribed for the ideal gentleman]
11:2	Confucius (cf 8:3) has disciples who frequent his "gate"
11:15	Contrast between outer hall and inner chamber
16:13	Confucius's house has a courtyard in which disciples meet
19:23	Confucius's palatial residence, complete with ancestral shrine, in Lŭ

What Confucius as a chariot warrior's heir probably did *not* have was a town house; it seems likely that the disciples who headed the posthumous school first achieved this degree of affluence, which was then projected back onto Confucius himself.

Confucius's School. The format in which the Master's teachings are inculcated also changes systematically over time, in parallel with their architectural context:

4:1f	No implied contact among disciples; all maxims envision action
5:1f	Group contact among disciples, all aiming at public office
6:12	Răn Chyóu not strong enough to follow "the Master's Way"
7:1	First hint of transmitted rather than original content of teaching
7:5	Emphasizes continuity with Jōu dynasty
7:7	Tuition payments, open admissions; public office goal minimized
8:3	Dzv̄ngdž evidently presides over an organized, residential school
9:12	Confucius dies in the arms of his disciples; residential school implied
12:1f	Highly formal master/disciple format
1:1	Memorization of texts emphasized
16:13	Schoolyard portrayed; study of Shr̄ and ritual enjoined

The general picture is one of increasing formality, an increasing claim to base the school's teachings not on Confucius's wisdom but on a heritage from antiquity, and, finally, an increasing curricularization of that antiquity.

Material and Social Developments

Before further exploring the history of the Confucian school, we take up some topics whose probable developmental trajectory is known from archaeological or other evidence, and can thus confirm or refute the proposed chapter sequence.

Hunting and Animals. It is known that an older hunting culture was replaced in this millennium by a farming culture. The Analects shows evidence of this change in the replacement of fur by woven cloth for clothing and of game animals by domestic animals for food, and in the increasing rarity of wild or game animals:

6:4	Disciple wears fur robes on diplomatic errand
9:27	Poor disciple wears hemp robe; rich colleagues wear furs
10:5a	Last mention of fur as normal clothing for gentlemen, c0380
10:5c	Plant-fiber robe prescribed for sacrifice, probably for traditional reasons
11:14	Enlarging of government storehouse, implying central grain reserves
11:17	Increase in the rate of the government tax on the harvest
3:7	Highly ritualized (and thus perhaps partly symbolic?) archery contest
12:9	Proposal to go beyond a 20% tax rate on the harvest
13:4	State interest in the arts of plant husbandry
13:9	Population increase, presumably based on improved agriculture
15:6	Disciple writes saying on sash (necessarily of silk, not fur)
16:1	Reference to wild animals in zoos

The stylization or loss of the *skills* of the hunt (archery) and of *trophies* of the hunt (fur clothing) is counterpointed by an increase in farm production, and in state *concern* for efficient farm production and the revenues it produces. No single watershed date probably exists for this comprehensive change, but the above data suggest that the center of gravity shifted somewhere near the beginning of the 04c.

Silk has replaced older types of plant-fiber cloth even for ritual purposes in 9:3. To have made such inroads on ritual usage, silk production with its specialized mulberry-growing and weaving, and thus the displacement of hunting by farming, must have been advanced by the end of the 05c, thus refining the above conjecture.

Chì 器. Despite scholarly debate on details, there is no doubt that the Warring States increasingly used metal for utilitarian rather than ritual purposes. This change is reflected in the word chì, which in the early part of the text refers to a ritual vessel, either in itself or as a metaphor for the "capacity" of a minister. Later, the primary or default meaning of the word is instead an edged tool or weapon:

5:4	"You are a *vessel* [an elegant ritual vessel]," c0470
3:22	Gwǎn Jùng's *capacity* [as a minister] was small indeed," c0342
13:25	"He [the supervisor] takes account of their *capacity* [or *ability*]," c0322
2:12	"A gentleman is not to be used as an *implement*," c0317
*15:10	"Must first sharpen his *tools*," c0301 (terminus a quo, c0305)

There is little doubt that the first two usages have in mind a vessel, and that the last two intend a special-purpose edged tool such as a knife or chisel; the association of such specific function with lower-status persons, in contrast to the general ability of the minister, confirms this. 13:25, in the middle, might be taken either way; in view of the other examples, it is more likely to reflect the later usage. We thus have a change in denotation paralleling a development in material culture. From these examples, the linguistic shift might date from c0330. Given the innate conservatism of language, this might place the prior culture change in the early 04c or late 05c. All these developments thus cohere into a single, general material-culture change.

The Army. Here again, experts differ over the exact timetable, but it seems not to be in doubt that the millennium saw a shift from an elite, chivalric warfare based on long-range archery and the horse-drawn chariot, in effect a warfare of encounter, to a mass army of maneuver, still with chariots but based on infantry and close-order weapons such as the sword. The latter phase is also characterized by the production of handbooks of strategy such as the Sūndž Bīng-fǎ, which themselves stress not only the power but the costs of the newer style warfare. Among the key phrases is sān-jywn 三軍 "the three armies," which, whatever its meaning in earlier times, seems in the Warring States to denote a force trained to carry out simultaneous operations such as flank attacks or encirclement; unfortunately, all Analects occurrences of this term are in interpolated passages. Perhaps the central problem of the new army was how to get its low-status conscripts to die in its service:

13:29   Right government must precede leading the people to war, c0322
13:30   Must teach people before taking them to war
14:19   Refers to a commander of the armies 軍旅
15:1   Confucius refuses to discuss army 軍旅 matters

If we consult the contemporary Gwǎndž (see page 257), we find that this part of the Analects is in the middle of a wider debate on the place of the people in the state, particularly as respects their legal and military obligations. So far as it goes, the Analects evidence attests the new-style army as of the third quarter of the 04c.

The People. References to the mín 民 "populace" in the Analects do not always have the same sense; so also with jùng 眾 "masses." A third term, bǎi-syìng 百姓 "the Hundred [many] Families/Surnames" has a more limited distribution. In the list below, these terms are given in **bold** when they seem to evoke the new society:

6:2   Indulgence toward the mín
9:3   Jùng in the sense of a majority of the courtiers
10:7b–8 Village rituals are apart from, though witnessed by, the elite
11:23   The mín and their sacrifices are apart from those of the elite
3:21   Criticizes the overawing of the **mín** by funeral customs in ancient times
12:2   Treat the **mín** as though presiding at a sacrifice
12:7   The trust of the **mín** in the ruler is vital to government
12:9   Concern for the tax-paying **bǎi-syìng**
12:19   If the ruler loves what is good, the **mín** will be easy to govern
12:22   **Jùng** as a source of promotion to ministerships
13:4   The ruler influences the **mín** by the example of his own desires
14:41   If the ruler loves ritual, the **mín** will be docile
14:42   Ruler cultivates himself so as to ease the lot of the **bǎi-syìng**
15:28   Approval of the **jùng** is a factor in official evaluations
19:3   Esteem the talented, but include the **jùng**
20:1   If any of the **bǎi-syìng** do wrong, the ruler will take the blame

LY 4 already gave a vivid impression of a society in which court office had become newly available to a lower-status group, the "little people" of that chapter and the next. The text thus opens upon a society already in transition. The absence of this term in LY 7–9 suggests that the disdain which it implies later moderated. What the above data add to this impression is that by LY 3 (c0342), that is, by the mid 04c, the people at large had come to be more thoroughly integrated into society, with the ruler acknowledging an interest in, and in time even a responsibility for, their welfare and behavior. With allowances for the probable reluctance of the Analects to report military matters, it would seem that the transition to this new civil role closely parallels the separately attested transition to the new-style mass army.

Unpredictable Developments

These examples show that between the Analects chapters we have designated as early and those we have designated as late, there occur changes in material and social culture which are abundantly documented outside the text, and which on grounds of general historical plausibility could not in any case be conceived of as occurring *in the opposite direction*. Moreover, those changes themselves are easily seen as part of a single inclusive transition from one type of society and economy to another. Such changes carry their own conviction, and at some point the number of such historically plausible sequences will amount to a confirmation of the present accretion hypothesis. It will then be permissible to use the accretional Analects as a historical source in its own right, and to ask it questions to which we do not know the precise answers in advance. This section includes a few such questions, centering on the evolution of the teachings of the Confucian school itself.

Rvn vs Li. The dispute over which of these values is central to the Analects is of long standing. The data show a pattern which is not linear, but still intelligible:

4:1–7	Rvn is central to Confucius's own idea of his value system
4:13	Mention of li and ràng (deference) as intrinsic to government
5:19	Rvn is misunderstood by a disciple as meaning bureaucratic scruple
6:22	Disciple question about rvn
6:23	Poetic but cryptic contrast between rvn and jr (knowledge)
7:6	Rvn is described in instrumental terms
8:7	Rvn is described by Dzvngdž as a burden
9:29	Rvn is said to be inimical to sorrow
10:1–19	Ritual conduct manual; rvn is never mentioned
11:1–23	Rvn is never mentioned
3:1–26	Ritual theory treatise
3:3	Rvn is reintroduced as a sort of prerequisite to valid ritual practice
12:1–2	Rvn is literally redefined as conformity to ritual
12:22	Rvn in the ruler is equated with love (ài) of the people

We have here not an either/or situation, but a developmental sequence in which rvn, central to Confucius, was unclear to his earliest successors, and by the end of the 05c had become sentimental and obsolescent. In the 04c (it helps to know, on grounds explained in Appendix 4, that this is the start of the Kŭng family headship) an entirely new ethos, based on li, suddenly supervenes, and rvn is at first banished, and later reintroduced as a detail in the li system. It is then (in 12:22, which again, it is useful to know, shows Mician influence) once more redefined, and thereafter (and in the Mencian school, which splits off at this point from the Analects) has a number of meanings vaguely centering on the concept of "benevolence." The clear implication is that rvn in its original, stalwart sense was central to Confucius, whereas li later replaced it as the central concept of Lŭ Confucianism.

Courage. Another martial value that fares ill in the later Analects is yŭng 勇 "courage." Suggestive landmarks in its evolution are:

9:29	The brave are never afraid (only positive mention in primary sense)
2:24	To see the right and not do it is to lack courage (moral reinterpretation)
14:12	Yŭng (presumably in new sense) is part of a gentleman's equipment
17:21	A gentleman will not approve of yŭng (in the sense of rowdyism)

We seem to have here a military virtue (05c) reinterpreted in moral terms (04c), and finally abandoned (03c). The first two phases parallel the case of rvn. The last, which may reflect the rise of "free sword" desperadoes in the 03c, is unique.

We may here go back to the point reached on page 251, and explore some less predictable aspects of the Confucian curriculum.

The Shr̄. No text is cited or mentioned in the original sayings of LY 4, or in those of LY 5–6, which have some claim to have been written within living memory of Confucius. Furthermore, the pedagogical focus in those chapters is on listening and reflecting, not reading or memorizing; neither of which terms occurs. There is thus no support in the Analects for the Hàn view that Confucius compiled or commented on any of the texts which became canonical in Hàn. Of the three "classic" texts quoted in the later Analects, the Shr̄ has the longest pedigree:

6:13	Dž-syà should not attend to the learning of the little people (Fv̄ng?)
8:3	Dzv̄ngdž quotes something like Shr̄ 196 (Yǎ)
9:15	Yǎ and Sùng sections of the Shr̄ are mentioned as now properly placed
9:27	Dž-lù quotes Shr̄ 33 (Fv̄ng)
10:1f	No mention; Shr̄ apparently had no role in ordinary court proceedings
11:6	Quotes Shr̄ 256 (Yǎ) in a seemingly appropriate moral sense
3:8	Forced ritual reinterpretation of Shr̄ 57 (Fv̄ng) by Dž-syà
12:10	Confucius quotes from Shr̄ 188 (Yǎ) to conclude a comment
13:5	Shr̄ corpus mentioned as containing 300 poems
2:2	Shr̄ 297 cited in forced interpretation as an epitome of all 300 poems
1:15	Remake of 3:8: Dž-gùng replaces Dž-syà as the ideal Shr̄ interpreter
16:13	Shr̄ study recommended to the young
17:16	Complains of the immorality of the Jv̄ng Fv̄ng (Shr̄ 75–95)
17:8a	Gives a pedestrian rationale for Shr̄ study

In effect the Shr̄ is disapproved of at the beginning (6:13) and the end (17:16) of its association with the Analects. In the middle it becomes something of an authority, but the tension between its manifest meaning and most of the uses made of it in the Analects is suggestive. It would seem that the Shr̄ gradually took shape between c0460 (LY 6:13) and c0322 (LY 13:5), close to, but not within, the Analects group.

The Shū. Apart from interpolated passages, nothing is heard of anything like the present Shū until c0317:

2:21	Confucius quotes (as "the Shū") from something like Shū 49
14:40	Disciple quotes (as "the Shū") from the present Shū 43
20:1	[Composition in the style of a Shū document]

The Micians seem to have been the first to use the device of citing supposedly ancient documents. The one accepted as an authority in LY 2:21 is evidently from this Mician repertoire; in the present inventory it is an "old script" piece, all of which are now agreed to be later forgeries (Shaughnessy **Shu** 377). It is uncertain who produced the first of the Confucian counter-Shū, such as that quoted seven years later in LY 14:40. It is not until c0250 (LY 20:1) that we find the Analects itself composing texts in the Shū style.

The Yì. All undisputed Analects mentions of or quotations from the Yì are interpolations, a privileged level of the book which seems to have been a haven for new material which for whatever reason could not readily be accommodated in the main text. The Yì, like the Shū, is absent from the Analects horizon until c0317, when a pair of sayings which we date to that period refer to it:

*13:22a	Approves (quoting Yì 32) of folk saying about diviners needing stability
*13:22b	Advises active, not passive, consultation of the oracle

Like the Shū, but even more completely, the Yì vanishes from the Analects after this lone late 04c quotation. It never becomes part of the Analects expository ethos.

Orality vs Literacy. There is little doubt that there is a general Warring States trend from oral toward written modes of text retention and transmission, but it is of interest to ask whether a transition from one to the other can be observed in the Analects. Nothing in the character of the original LY 4 core sayings suggests that they were recorded when first delivered; hence our assumption of a posthumous compilation. The parallelistic, mnemonic form of these sayings (see pages 17–18) supports this inference. By contrast, at the other end of the text, the final saying in the book (20:3) is known only in the Gǔ written text, and not in the Lǔ version which supposedly represents a memorized version. It would appear that, in c0249, the school head would first *write* a new saying, and only later assign it for memory by students. In between must come an indication that writing had begun to be the primary mode of retention. One such sign is:

15:6   Disciple writes just-heard saying on the sash of his robe, c0305

but mention of the completed Shī in 13:5, and Mician citation of supposed ancient documents from about that period, would seem to push the transition further back. It seems safest to suppose that the shift took place nearer to the mid 04c.

Philosophical Maturity. As a final exploration, this time including evidence from interpolations, we note a change in how the Analects tradition viewed itself.

4:1f	Collection of apparently ad hoc maxims, but thematically arranged
11:23	Confucius resents literalistic disciple application of a former remark
3:4	Disciple asks for an underlying explanatory principle of ritual
12:1–4	First definitions of terms
13:15	Ruler asks for a saying that could compass the rise or fall of the state
*15:3[15a]	Disciple asks for a maxim applicable in all circumstances
*15:24[15a]	Disciple told that Confucius's sayings have a linking principle
*4:15[1]	Disciple reveals the linking principle as jūng 忠 and shū 恕
17:6	Confucius protests being trapped by his former remark
*11:20[17]	Confucius insists on the situational relativity of his maxims

Apart from the implicit systematizing impulse latent in the thematic arrangement of the core LY 4 sayings, there does not seem to be a conscious push toward viewing doctrine as coherent until 11:23, a protest against consistency, implies the issue. The idea that a doctrine is the better for having fundamental (3:4) or well-defined (12:1f) or uniquely efficacious (13:15) or nonsituational (*15:3) or linking (*15:24, *4:15) principles becomes evident in the middle and late 04c, at about the literacy transition, but then once more subsides, and is replaced by an impatience with consistency (17:6, *11:20). As with the brief flirtation with the Shū and Yì in the same period, or the even briefer dalliance with cosmology in 2:1, one feels that philosophical rigor is another Analects enthusiasm that in the end did not "take." The genius of Confucianism, as perceived by itself, seems ultimately to have been in situational flexibility: scope for applying general principles to specific cases.

Summary. Like many of the observations made in the foregoing pages, there is nothing new in this conclusion. That should perhaps be seen as a recommendation for the validity of the present theory, not as a failure in its application. It was not to be expected that later tradition would be wholly wrong in its estimation of the character of the Confucian movement, or that if it *should* be in error at some particular points, that critical scholars would not have raised questions about just those points. We would then claim, as the main contribution of these conclusions, not that they are surprising, but that they put the unsurprising in a more precise, and thus a more historically actionable, chronological framework.

Appendix 3
A Window on the Hundred Schools

Appendix 1 tested the consistency of the accretion theory of the Analects, and Appendix 2 explored the capacity of that theory to generate a developmental picture of the Warring States. As a third test, we here inquire whether confronting the accretional Analects with other texts yields historically meaningful conjunctions.

The Gwǎndž. GZ 3 (dated by Rickett to the 04c) deals with the question of the role of the people, but its view of that role varies within the chapter. GZ 3:2–3 says that the supply of food and armaments is crucial to survival, and recommends the use of rewards and penalties. GZ 3:8 and 3:10 sharpen this to the use of rewards and *punishments*, and 3:18 repeats that the food supply is basic.[1] To this LY 12:7 retorts that there are three basics, not two, and that more basic than food and weapons is the confidence of the people. As to capital punishment, LY 12:19 responds that government is there to govern, not to kill, and that if government sets an example, people will follow it. To this LY 13:9 and 13:29–30 add that before people can be called on for military service, they must be taught: not merely advised of their obligations, but motivated to accept them. So far we have a disagreement between GZ and the Analects. But the later passage GZ 3:29–35 *adopts the position of LY 13*, in a section devoted to the inculcation of virtues, including the new Confucian virtue of propriety (lǐ 禮) which is emphasized in LY 12–13. It is impossible not to feel that the last paragraphs of GZ 3 are later than the first, and that, in the interim, GZ 3 has accepted some Analects criticisms of its early theories. Schematically:

GZ 3:2–3   Basis of society is food and arms; use rewards and penalties
GZ 3:8, 10   Use rewards and punishments
GZ 3:18   Basis of society is food
     LY 12:1   Makes lǐ (propriety) the chief virtue
     LY 12:7   Basis of society is food, arms, *and trust*
     LY 12:19   Government has no business killing
     LY 13:9, 29–30   Education of people is fundamental
GZ 3:29–35   Inculcate virtues, including lǐ, among the people

The Dzwǒ Jwàn (c0312) generally approves of Dzàng Wǔ-jùng, an 06c Lǔ magnate. Under Syāng 23 (0550) it tells how, fleeing from intrigue, he offers to give up his city Fáng and leave Lǔ if his brother Wéi is made head of the Dzàng family, an offer which the Lǔ Prince accepts.[2] Wǔ-jùng in this story is a victim of intrigue. LY 14:14 ("I do not believe it") doubts this. Acknowledging this suspicion, a comment appended to the DJ passage under the name of Jùng-ní [Confucius] says of Wǔ-jùng, "There was cause for it; he was disobedient, and showed lack of empathy (shù 恕)." These Jùng-ní comments are suspected of being later additions to the DJ. In this case, it seems clear that an original DJ judgement was modified, in response not to criticism from Confucius, but more literally from the Analects:

DJ Syāng 23   Portrays Dzàng Wǔ-jùng as wronged (c0312)
     LY 14:14   Suspects Wǔ-jùng of bringing pressure (c0310)
DJ addendum   Admits some wrong on Wǔ-jùng's part (after c0310)

---

[1]GZ references are to paragraph in Rickett **Guanzi**; compare Brooks **Gwǎndž 3**.
[2]See Legge **Ch'un** 503a/b; the following Jùng-ní comment is at 504b.

The Mwòdž. A point of difference between the Confucian and Mician schools was the three-year mourning period for a parent, which the Confucians claimed as ancient, and the Micians condemned as wasteful in a trio of tracts (MZ 23–25) of which only the last survives; MZ 25 takes the line that mourners should resume their livelihood immediately on returning from the funeral. More specifically, in MZ 48:8 "Mwòdž" objects to extended mourning on the grounds that it interrupts not only the work of the people, but the official duties of the elite.[3] In LY 17:19, the renegade disciple Dzǎı Wǒ is made to urge a natural-year mourning, arguing in very similar vein that a longer period is too long an interruption of the gentleman's work of maintaining the cultural tradition, and that culture itself will suffer. "Confucius" in response deplores Dzǎı Wǒ's lack of feeling for his parents, noting, as an opposing natural sanction, the parallel between the three years that an infant is carried in its parents' arms, and the balancing three years it mourns for a parent. In MZ 48:12, a few lines below the inciting 48:8, this psychological rationalism is ridiculed as "the ultimate in stupidity" – a baby knowing it cannot get its parents back, yet crying for them unceasingly. "How is the wisdom of the Confucians worth more than that of a baby?" Though the Micians in this case end up unconvinced, there is no doubt that a two-way dialogue is taking place:

MZ 48:8	Mwòdž deplores damage to culture by extended mourning
LY 17:19	Disciple rebuked for urging a similar position
LY 17:19	Confucius cites parents' nurture of infant
MZ 48:12	Mwòdž ridicules Confucians as "no wiser than a baby"

The Jwāngdž. JZ 4 has several images of uselessness: the tree which is not cut down because there is nothing it can be made into (JZ 4:4–5) or the cripple whose disability protects him from military service (JZ 4:6). That these symbolize avoiding government service is apparent in 4:7, a denunciation of Confucius by the Madman of Chǔ, who berates him for his dangerous inclination to hold office in evil times. This episode is repeated almost identically in LY 18:5, with the telling difference that the end is changed to have Confucius attempt to address the Madman, who flees. The implication is that such criticisms, and such critics, are cowardly. This point is made directly in LY 18:6, which rejects the prudent device of camouflage and knowingly risks danger for the sake of making the world itself less dangerous. This imputation of cowardice seems to have come home to the JZ 4 group, and in a stunning series of anecdotes, JZ 4:1–3, proposed at the beginning of JZ 4 as though to signal the change, they explore – in two cases with Confucius as the mentor – a new Way of remaining safe while accepting the call to government service under dangerous conditions.[4] A similar change of orientation, presumably a fruit of this encounter between the two texts, can be found in each of JZ 3–7, but this instance will sufficiently show the dispute, *and the fact that the Confucians win*:

JZ 4:4–6	Images of uselessness
JZ 4:7	Madman of Chǔ denounces Confucius for office-seeking
LY 18:5	Confucius questions Madman, who flees
LY 18:6	Urges the duty to serve in perilous times
JZ 4:1–3	Confucius and others show how to serve in perilous times

---

[3]See Mei **Ethical** 234–237 for the two MZ 48 passages quoted here and below; the translations given are our own.

[4]Brooks **Jwāngdž** 4.

An Extended Instance

Examples of more extended dialogue include the Analects/DDJ relationship, treated elsewhere,[5] and the Mician series MZ 46–50, which we examine here. The link between MZ 48:8/12 and LY 17:19 (c0270) establishes one contact point; the MZ 46:10 criticism of LY 13:16 (c0322) defines another. Putting *all* of MZ 46–50 beside the Analects reveals a pattern of contact over about a century, sporadic at both ends, but continuous for the middle 50 years. To get a sense of the relationship from the Mician side, we here list all MZ 46–50 passages and the related Analects ones. Directional symbols denote influence from (<) or to (>) another passage; unclear influences or similarities are indicated by (~):

	LY			MZ	
11:16	too much is as bad as too little				
			>	46:1	faster is better than slower
3:9	Confucius confesses ignorance of ancient rituals				
			>	46:2	spirits know ancient rituals
12:11	each has proper role	~	46:3		division of labor in urging virtue
	(Both these passages may be influenced by GZ 2:45–46)				
12:22	rýn defined as love (ài)	<	46:4		love is right even if unsuccessful
12:8	appearances deceptive	<	46:5		poor disciple is after all successful
				46:6	dedication is not wrong
12:8	animal skin simile	>	46:7		criticizes animal metaphors
13:15	need for remonstrance	>	46:8		criticizes dispraise of "early kings"
				46:9	state regalia are worthless
13:16	answers Shv̀-gūng	>	46:10		criticizes Confucius's answer
			>	46:11	war both disruptive and childish
13:5	Shī must be applicable	~	46:12		doctrines must be applicable
				46:13	leaving office [anticipates LY *8:13[14]]
				46:14	men accept unjustified praise
				46:15	disputes claim of three early models
	(MC 1A3: example of soldiers who ran away, but not as far as others, c0320)				
			>	46:16	rejects "late desertion" excuse
				46:17	attacks LY 7:1, defends innovation
13:18	defends family partialism	>	46:18		attacks family partialism
13:29	training people for war	>	46:19		irrationality of war; harms people
				46:20	oaths are ridiculous
2:24	advocates moral courage	>	46:21		condemns physical courage

With the material in MZ sequence, as here, some LY items (12:8, 13:5) are out of order; we infer that the above is the *order of composition* for both sides, and that the LY passages were rearranged when compiled into final chapter format. Besides the Analects, MZ responds to the Gwǎndž and the speeches of Mencius. For some MZ passages we cannot suggest an extant inciting text; MZ 46:9 and 20 may oppose the general Confucian ritual ethos, and not any specific Analects formulation of it. Except at the beginning, when it *contributes* ideas, the MZ seems largely defensive; hence, perhaps, the early appearance of the exit theme (MZ 46:13, before 0320) which appears slightly later (LY *8:13[14], c0310) on the Confucian side.

---

[5]Brooks **Prospects** 63–66 and 70–73.

LY		MZ
14:12b men will die for principle ~	47:1	men will die for principle
14:32 advocacy while in disfavor ~	47:2	advocacy while in isolation
	47:3	ideas good though of humble origin
	47:4	ancient kings should be followed
	47:5	theories must be applicable

(unknown source for numerical-category formulations)

	47:6	against the Six Partialities

(the Analects will not adopt this device until LY 16:4, c0290)

	47:7	failures do not impugn the standard

(MC 1B9: there is a specific qualfication that ministers possess, c0309)

15:34	gentlemen are generalists	~	47:8	ministers need a specific skill
15:42	courtesy to blind man	~	47:9	passing example of blind man
15:38	should ignore livelihood	~	47:10	gentlemen are careless of selves
15:40	despise low colleagues	>	47:11	gentlemen refuse humble help
15:26	suspicious of old writings	>	47:12	sages recorded wisdom in writings
		>	47:13	defends reading many writings

(MC 1B13: "Tv́ng is a small state . . ," c0307)

	>	47:14	"Wèi is a small state . . ."

(MC 1B13: recommends defensive measures)

15:1	Confucius despises war	~	47:15	recommends defense, not luxury
15:1	Confucius leaves Wèi	>	47:15	gentlemen leave because of low pay

(this is surely among the cattiest of all the Mician rejoinders)

15:25	scope same as early kings	<	47:16	gentlemen deny the early kings
15:16	despair of teachability	>	47:17	gentlemen refuse to teach virtue

(unknown source for directional fortune-telling)

	>	47:18	such predictions are impractical

(Sūndž B īng-fǎ 5: simile of rock breaking egg)

	>	47:19	simile of rock breaking egg

As observed in this second series of correspondences, the Mwòdž text exhibits many of the qualities found in the previous series. It is largely reactive to other points of view, perhaps suggesting that the Micians may have held a relatively low position at the Lǔ court; some nonreactive passages seem to be encouragements of the perhaps disheartened Mician followers. The Mician stance is also conspicuously obdurate in its tone, sometimes borrowing phrases or illustrations from other texts, but virtually never adopting an idea or a value, and never acknowledging a defeat. This doctrinal self-identity is functional for a group contending for favor at court; conviction as such is impressive. There is also tactical flexibility. MZ 46:11 and 19 articulate a pure anti-war position, based on the classic MZ 17, against Confucian willingness to train the people for war (LY 13:39). MZ 47:1 instead draws on the also classic but later MZ 18–19, acknowledging just wars and showing how the people can be induced to die fighting in them, and MZ 47:15 urges defensive precautions which the LY 15:1 Confucians refuse to discuss. The Micians thus consistently *maximize their differences* with the Confucians, who in the end (as we infer) lose their influence at court. After final sparring with the defeated Confucians (MZ 47:16–17), the Micians drop them as opponents, and turn to other matters. Among the other matters is reading Sūndž, the contemporary handbook on strategy. It is known that at some point the Micians became specialists in defensive war, compiling their own tactical handbook (MZ 51f). This may have been the point.

	LY			MZ
	(impending Chí conquest of Sùng, c0286)			
16:1	protest to ruler's advisors	~	48:1	urges need to protest to ruler
			48:2	defends exhorting the people
	(Confucians are circulating texts representing Jōu antiquity)			
		>	48:3	unimportance of correct dress
*7:18[17]	use of antique speech	>	48:4	unimportance of antique speech
*7:18[17]	... for Shī, Shū, ritual	>	48:5	Confucius knows Shī, Shū, ritual
[14:36 on fate, 1:1 on study]		>	48:6	fate and study are contradictory
*11:12[16]	against spirits	>	48:7	argues spiritual retribution
17:19	rational mourning ...	<	48:8	rational theory of mourning
		>	48:9	sacrifice implies belief in spirits
		>	48:10	defends shorter mourning period
			48:11	wisdom not relative
17:19	... is rejected with simile	>	48:12	ridicules "infant" simile of LY 17:19
17:9	music has meaning	<	48:13	denies "music for music's sake"
		>	48:14	against music and funerals
			48:15	defends attack on Confucius
			48:16	defends citing Confucius
			48:17	defends learning as desirable
			48:18	defends untraditional students
			48:19	deflects expectation of blessing
[7:35 ill Confucius; no prayer]		>	48:20	illness does not refute spirits
			48:21	refuses to teach archery
	(MC 6A1–4 features philosophical opponent Gàudž)			
		~	48:22	refuses to denounce Gàudž
		~	48:23	belittles Gàudž's supposed virtue
		~	48:24	cites LY 13:13 against Gàudž

The close interplay between MZ 46–47 and the parallel Analects breaks down in MZ 48. There still occur what look like a few contacts with especially outspoken positions (LY 16:1), but much of the ongoing opposition between the two schools is expressed by the citing of previous Analects passages by the Mwòdž. There is a positive citation of a Confucian saying in MZ 48:24, preceded by a general defense of using such appropriated wisdom in 48:16, implying that such appropriation had occurred (and been challenged) in the Mician *school* before an actual specimen of it happened to be recorded in the Mician school *text*. Such a practice is evidence that Confucius was in this period no longer a monopoly of his own school, but to some extent public property; his appropriation by the partly contemporary Jwāngdž is further evidence for this development. Confucius *had become a public figure*, identified with a certain position (based on a dedication to public service and emphasizing ritual and the now all-but-classic texts Shī and Shū), but also capable of being made the spokesman of a different position in the text of a rival school.

The parallel Mician school itself seems to have developed by this time into a major enterprise. The MZ 46–47 references to disciples imply only a few pupils trained for public office; the MZ 48:15f series suggests a larger school, not so closely linked to success in an official career, but increasingly to learning "for its own sake." The attack on this "cultural" position as respects music in MZ 48:13 is an anti-ritual stand, not an exception. LY 17:8a/b and 16 imply a similar development of cultural, rather than exclusively professional, education on the Confucian side.

LY		MZ

(DDJ 61 advises being subordinate to the larger states)

	~ 49:1	serve a larger state for protection

(MC 6B4, anti-war persuasion)
(JZ 25:5, anti-war persuasion)

	~ 49:2	Mwòdž argues against attacking Lǔ
	~ 49:3	Mwòdž argues against weapons
	~ 49:4	Mwòdž argues against an attack
	~ 49:5	Mwòdž refutes "just war" concept
[earlier MZ 47:12]	> 49:6	rulers wrongly brag of conquest
[earlier MZ 17]	> 49:7	gentlemen are confused in values
	49:8	Chinese worse than cannibals
	49:9	denunciation of obituaries
	49:10	denunciation of ritual etiquette
	49:11	observe results, not just intentions
	49:12	Mician student dies in battle

(MC 3A4 disputes with agrarian primitivist spokesman)

	~ 49:13	against agrarian primitivism
*18:2[18] why leave native state?	~ 49:14	why leave one's native state?
[earlier MZ 8–37]	> 49:15	urges Ten Mician Doctrines
	49:16	explains misfortune of pupil
	49:17	criticizes greedy sacrifice
	49:18	future can be predicted
	49:19	brave but not wise
	49:20	treachery of Mician student
	49:21	battle of Chǔ and Ywè
	49:22	against useless technology
	49:23	dissuades attack on Sùng

(Chǔ conquers southern Lǔ, 0255)
(DDJ 80 represents loss of half the state as an improvement)

	50:1	no gratitude for saving Sùng

The terrain here is utterly different. The Micians are in a position to advise on policy, and in that position they focus on the issue of war. They are not closely engaged with the Confucians, who probably had little power at this period, and from whose text they pick up only a turn of phrase, but speak in their own voice. In MZ 46 they had gone back to dispute early Analects sayings; here, they invoke their own text, not only the primary anti-war statement MZ 17 (the earliest Mician tract) but the whole mass of now-canonical ethical pronouncements. They do not debate the Mencians or the Jwāngdž groups; they address the topics these groups address. Their chief opponents are the makers of war; the agrarian primitivists (MZ 49:13), the deluded makers of peace, are a second concern.

The turn toward military theory in MZ 47 leads in MZ 49 to the creation of a school for defensive warfare, as attested by the complaint of the father of a student who had died in that service (49:12). By comparison with this relevant energy, the absorption of the contemporary Analects in its doctrinal differences with Sywndž must seem beside the point, however fertile for reflection under the unified state, once the Micians had lost their last-ditch struggle to stabilize the multi-state system.

Here, then, is another interlocking piece of the Warring States dialogue.

Appendix 4
Confucius and His Circle

We here attempt[1] to derive, from the earliest Analects and compatible sources, a picture of Confucius, his ancestors, his disciples, and his Kŭng-family successors.

Confucius's Dates

Death. The earliest statement of the date of Confucius's death (a jĭ/chŏu 己丑 day, #26 in the 60-day calendrical cycle, in the 4th month of Aĭ-gūng's 16th year of reign, 0479) is found in the part of the Dzwŏ Jwàn (DJ) which extends beyond the cutoff date of 0481 observed by the Gūngyáng (GYJ) and Gŭlyáng (GLJ) texts.[2] It has been challenged by Maspero, but his proposed date of a generation later, or c0454, raises new problems,[3] and the old ones it addresses can be solved in other ways. Thus, the reference to Aĭ-gūng (d 0469) by his posthumous title in LY 6 does not mean that *Confucius* lived past 0469, merely that *this chapter* was written after 0469. Again, the SJ 47 list of Confucius's descendants is too short (at 25 years per birth generation) to reach from a datable Chín figure[4] back to Confucius, but this is unproblematic if, as LY 8 implies, there had been a preceding period of disciple headship. There is no competing tradition, early or late, and the death date in DJ is compatible with all indications in the earliest Analects. We thus accept it.

Birth.[5] The version of CC associated with DJ (no *independent* CC text exists) has no entry for the birth of Confucius, or for anyone not a son of the Lŭ Prince. Birth entries exist under 0552 (21st year of Syāng-gūng) in the CC associated with the GYJ and GLJ commentaries. The former runs: 十有一月、庚子、孔子生 "in the 11th month, on the day ḡng/dž (#37 of the 60-day cycle), Master Kŭng was born." The GLJ entry is identical except that it omits the month, thus implicitly dating the birth to the 10th month, the last mentioned in earlier CC entries. The first day of the 9th month in both texts (recorded in connection with a solar eclipse) is ḡng/syw̌ 庚戌 (cycle #47); that of the 10th month, another solar eclipse, is ḡng/chv́n 庚辰 (#17), 30 days later. Then a ḡng/dž day (cycle #37) *could have occurred* 20 days after the second eclipse, in the 10th month, or 60 days after that, in the 12th month, but a ḡng/dž day in the 11th month is *arithmetically impossible*. It would seem that, with Dubs,[6] we should simply ignore GYJ, and adopt GLJ.

---

[1]This summary is abridged from the fuller treatment in Brooks **Life**.

[2]It is repeated at SJ 15 (2/680; year only) and SJ 47 (4/1945; Yang **Records** 26).

[3]Maspero **Antique** 376n1 / **Antiquity** 449n1, Waley **Analects** 16n2, 79, and Riegel **Review** 791. There is no evidence that Confucius lived, let alone spent his last 14 years, under Lŭ Dàu-gūng (r 0468–0432). See further Creel **Confucius** 296–297.

[4]Confucius's son Bwó-yẃ predeceased him (LY 11:8); his presumptive successor is Dž-sž, next on the SJ 47 list. But six generations after *him* is Kŭng Fù. Fù died in 0208, the end of the reign of the rebel Chv́n Shv̀, at the stated age of 57. This implies a c0265 birthdate. If Dž-sž was born 150 years earlier (6 birth generations, at 25 years), or c0415, then he *cannot have been* the son of Bwó-yẃ, who had died at least 65 years earlier.

[5]Readers not caring to follow the detailed birthdate argument may skip to page 267.

[6]Dubs **Date** 146.

But there are difficulties. (1) By scholarly consensus GYJ is earlier than GLJ,[7] thus GYJ is not garbling an earlier *correct* entry; instead, GLJ is rationalizing an earlier *absurd* entry. (2) The absurdity in GYJ is its specification of "11th month," despite the resulting inconsistency. It is not a slip of the brush, but intentional. What was the intent? (3) The 10th-month eclipse entry is itself spurious: no eclipse occurred on or near that date[8] (in general, successive-month eclipses *are not visible* from a single location).[9] This suggests that the second eclipse entry was an addition, made to honor the month of Confucius's birth. Such supernatural conjunctions are intrinsically suspect. (4) The Shř Jì follows the *historiography* of GYJ,[10] yet SJ 47, the chapter on Confucius, *does not give* the GYJ birthdate; just the year Syāng 22 (0551). Since no month or day is given, this cannot be based on a ritual record. GLJ did not yet exist. Both SJ compilers were court astronomers, and would have recognized the absurdity of GYJ. In this dilemma, the material used for SJ 47, some of it at least probably assembled by Szmǎ Tán, a student of the Yì, may have abandoned GYJ and substituted the birthdate 0551, which allows a numerologically significant age of 72 at death, a datum which, as we shall see below, is associated with the entry of the originally heterodox Yì tradition into Confucianism.

The CC Eclipses. It would then seem that when Szmǎ Chyén in c0107 wrote up the SJ 47 chapter on Confucius,[11] he had before him only the GYJ birth record (0552), flawed because of its calendrical absurdity, and Tán's 0551, which he adopted, though calculating Confucius's age at death as 73 rather than 72. No other pre-SJ source for Confucius's birthdate is known to exist. If there *is* a birth record, it then presumably lies behind GYJ, distorted by its association with a false eclipse. To determine the nature of the distortion, we here consider CC eclipses in general. They are reliable,[12] recording eclipses on days when modern astronomy says they occurred. Not all visible eclipses are recorded,[13] but those recorded were visible.

The exceptions are four entries for which no plausible eclipses exist, and which therefore can only be invented.[14] These are:

CC Year	Intl Yr	Mo	Cyclical Day		Notable Coincidence
Syī 15	0645	05	[none given]		nothing
Sywæn 17	0592	06	癸卯	(#40)	nothing
Syāng 21	0552	10	庚辰	(#17)	month before Confucius's birth
Syāng 24	0549	08	癸巳	(#30)	nothing

[7]Pokora **Pre-Han** 26. GYJ was the text of the 02c Hàn Modernizers, while GLJ was the text of the 01c Reformists, who were dominant from c070 on (Loewe **Crisis** 11–13).

[8]Stephenson **Atlas** xv, noting, in all, *four* impossible CC eclipses (see further below).

[9]Dubs **Date** 142.

[10]Watson **Ssu-ma** 78f; note the connection with Dǔng Jùng-shū (84).

[11]Brooks **Shř Jì** 10. For Tán's pro-Dàuist tract of c0138, see Watson **Ssu-ma** 43–48.

[12]The recent Stephenson **Atlas** shows closer agreement than Chalmers **Appendix**.

[13]Some of the omissions may have political implications; see further in Brooks **Life**.

[14]Stephenson and Chalmers, despite small differences in their calculations, agree that these are problematic. Dubs **Date** 142 explains one as due to a good-faith copying error; Stephenson **Atlas** xv attributes all four to "false sightings or possibly abortive predictions." Given the general accuracy of the CC, these courteous conjectures fail to convince.

It is likely that these are not *four separate and independent plans* to tamper with the CC eclipses, but have a single agenda. The agenda with which the third is clearly involved is the highlighting of Confucius's birth. Thus the others probably relate to other members of his lineage. The second is 40 years (a long generation?) before the third; the first is 53 years (two normal generations) before the second. A plausible hypothesis for these three eclipses is then that they were added to the CC to highlight the births of Confucius's great-grandfather, his father, and himself.

Plausibility. Apart from omitting Confucius's grandfather, it may be objected that this theory claims that false eclipses *celebrate* the births of Confucius and his forebears, whereas eclipses are *bad* omens in the CC and in Hàn portentology.[15] This may make it unlikely that the false entries were made by court astronomers. But the calendrical absurdity of GYJ already implies the hand of an amateur. When did amateurs have access to the CC? The CC had been in non-court hands since at least the compilation of the DJ in Chí, in c0312, and the DJ-associated CC indeed contains all four false eclipses. However, presumably in line with its general Chí strategy of downplaying the Lǔ sage Confucius, there is nothing in the DJ about his birth. That is, the false eclipses are *in* the CC, but they are *symbolically inactive* – no narrative use is made of them. This suggests that they were present in the version of CC that was brought to Chí from Lǔ, and were made earlier by Lǔ Confucians. The obvious candidate among Lǔ Confucians is the Analects school. As will be argued in detail below, it had since c0400 been led by a hereditary series of Kǔng descendants of Confucius. As LY 11:3 shows, in c0360 the Kǔngs were actively concerned to revise and re-establish the tradition of the disciples. It would be consistent for the calendrically inexpert Kǔngs to have added entries to their CC, to honor the births of Confucius and his Lǔ ancestors.

The DJ compilers presumably knew the Kǔng lore of Confucius's birth, and toned it down as part of a policy not to emphasize Lǔ connections in addressing a Chí royal audience. But knowledge of that lore may easily have persisted in Chí, and it is to Chí that the GYJ in particular traced its tradition of interpretation.[16] There is thus a possible link between the Kǔng Analects school, the false eclipses in the DJ text of CC, and the GYJ school of CC interpretation in Hàn. The false CC *birth entry* for Confucius may have been present in the Chí text of CC used by the DJ compilers (and excised by them for diplomatic reasons), or it may have been added by those who possessed that copy after c0312. Either possibility will serve.

The Kǔng Interpolation Theory. It is then to the Kǔng family that we would look for a tradition glorifying Confucius and his Lǔ ancestors. According to family tradition as preserved in KZJY, it was Confucius's great-grandfather, a refugee from Sùng, who established the Kǔng line in Lǔ. Our theory is then that the CC false eclipses were added to the CC by the Kǔngs of Lǔ, in their copy of the CC, sometime around the middle of the 04c.

---

[15]For traditional versions of this objection, see Legge **Ch'un** 492.

[16]SJ 121, written in c060 after Sžmǎ Chyēn's death, mentions a Master Húwú 胡毋 of Chí as a CC expert in the time of Hàn Jǐng-dì (r 0156–0141). The GYJ tradition as stated by Hv Syōu 何休 (123–182) is that Húwú was a pupil of one Gūngyáng; still later tradition gives *a whole line* of Gūngyáng transmitters, reaching back to Dž-syà. The evidence suggests that *what later became* the GYJ tradition was in Jǐng-dì's time an undifferentiated CC tradition, which had been handed down in Chí rather than in Lǔ.

We may note, with Dubs, the fact that the CC birth entry for Confucius is in the month *after* an eclipse, even though insistence on this fact is what produces the famous GYJ absurdity. This must have been how the relation of birth to eclipse was remembered in the family. Though the *onset* of an eclipse was baleful (the one in the 6th month of 0612 was met, according to the CC, with drums and sacrifices),[17] an individual might well take pride in being born just *after* one.[18] If Confucius's grandfather lacks such a record, the likely reason is that he was *actually born* in the month after an eclipse, so that no interpolated eclipse was necessary. This model[19] was then generalized to other Lǔ Kǔngs, Confucius's birth being further honored by having a *second* eclipse added in the *same* month. For the grandfather's eclipse, there are two options, the likelier being the one in 0612: it was conspicuous in Lǔ, and suggests a later age at marriage (the 33rd rather than 18th year) for Confucius's great-grandfather, consistent with typical military-family career patterns.[20]

The fourth false eclipse in 0549, three years after the third, cannot be a later generation. It is more likely a shadow entry for Confucius himself: an original location from which the present birth entry has been moved, leaving the spurious eclipse entry in place. It is generally assumed by students of this problem that Confucius's age at death is mythically linked with the claimed number of his disciples. A slight increase *in the number of claimed disciples* could then have led to a backward adjustment in his birthdate. It will be argued below that the relevant change is from a claimed 70 disciples (the old tradition, known to Mencius when he left Lǔ in c0321 and retained in the writings of his school, MC 2A3 and 4B31) to 72 (the new one, claimed in the title of the Kǔng family disciple list in KZJY 38). The adjustment is imperfect: Confucius was 70 at his death, agreeing with the Mencian tradition, if born in the year of the fourth false eclipse, but 73 (not 72) if born in the year of the third. Presumably the real 0552 eclipse was the best available (there was no eclipse in 0551) as a peg on which to hang the false eclipse.

Conclusion. Moving the birth entry to the month after *two* eclipses in 0549 still leaves a problem: the genuine 0549 eclipse was on the 1st day of the 7th month (jyǎ/dž 甲子, cycle #01) and the spurious one on the 1st day of the 8th month (gwěi/sž 癸巳, cycle #30). The interpolated birth entry would then have specified a gв̄ng/dž 庚子-day, cycle #37, *in the 9th month*; again an impossibility. The real month must have been the 2nd, 4th, 6th, 8th, 10th, or 12th. Surviving tradition seems to favor the 8th month.[21] If so, Confucius, like his grandfather, really *was* born in the month after an eclipse, a coincidence that invited mythic elaboration. We conclude that Confucius was born on a gв̄ng/dž day in the 8th month of 0549.

---

[17]Legge **Ch'un** 270.

[18]Old men in Ohio have been known to brag that they were born in the year of an especially hard winter. Compare also 19:21n, above; the operative point may be that the period *after* an eclipse or other disaster can function as a rebirth or revitalization symbol.

[19]Possibly reinforced, it will presently appear, by a similar pattern at Confucius's birth.

[20]The other eclipse is 0626 (Wv́n 1). The average age at marriage of 18 of Churchill's WW2 generals was 36 years (data from Keegan **Generals**). War is a jealous mistress.

[21]Sacrifices at the Confucian temple in Lǔ were in the 2nd and 8th months (Legge **Analects** Prolegomena 91); the rationale is that by the Syà calendar (recommended in LY *15:11[15a]), the equivalent to the CC date is the 8th month, 27th day. The Republic proclaimed the 27th of the 8th *Western* month (August) as the birth month of Confucius.

Confucius's Ancestors

KZJY 39 gives a series of notable ancestors in Sùng, and a series of less eminent Lŭ-connected ones. The former, intrinsically suspect as a mythic elaboration, are already referred to (under the year 0535)[22] in the DJ of 0312. We may here consider the more plausible traditions concerning the later, or Lŭ, ancestors. The KZJY 39 account seems to be the earliest; some of its details are also present, if undeveloped, in the DJ, and it is embroidered, not always in a friendly sense, in SJ 47.[23]

Great-Grandfather. By the eclipse hypothesis, Kŭng Fáng-shú 防叔 of Sùng was born in the 6th month of 0645 (Syī 15), married not later than the middle of 0613, and produced a son in the 7th month of 0612. We may now test this guess by comparing it with the sound parts of the remaining evidence.[24] KZJY 39 says that Fáng-shú "fled to Lŭ to avoid the Hwà 華 disaster." From the CC we may identify Hwà as Hwà Ywǽn 華元, who figured in Sùng affairs in the late 07c and early 06c. Several crises stand out in his career, but given Fáng-shú's name (fáng 防 means "defend"), and the military exploits of his grandson, Confucius's father, the relevant one is a battle with Jv̀ng in the 2nd month of 0607, in which Hwà Ywǽn, the leader, was captured and later ransomed; blame for this defeat is in the DJ ascribed to a resentful charioteer, a typical DJ narrative topos, but may in fact have rested on his subordinate commanders, giving them a motive to seek refuge in Lŭ.[25] Fáng-shú would have been in his 38th year at the time of the battle; a plausible age for responsible command. No deeds are recorded for Fáng-shú in Lŭ, and it is possible that he was denied a position to avoid offending Hwà Ywǽn,[26] who was prominent in Sùng down to 0576[27] and made diplomatic visits to Lŭ in 0587 and 0583.[28]

[22]Legge **Ch'un** 618bf. If born in the 8th month of 0549, Confucius would in 0535 have just begun his 15th year, the point at which (by LY 2:4) he had "determined upon study." It is just possible that the placement of this DJ story confirms the 0549 birthdate.

[23]Ariel **K'ung** 65–69 considers KZJY a forgery, but it and the forged Kŭng Tsúngdž (KTZ) relate differently to Wáng Sù (195–256). KZJY is annotated by Wáng (which would tend to exculpate him; Graham **Reflections** 283); KTZ is not. KTZ reinterprets Gūngsūn Lúng; KZJY does not. Ariel's data (and Kramers **K'ung**, and the fact that the life spans of Kŭng successors are less plausible in KTZ) make sense if Wáng *annotated* KZJY, but he or his daughter later *wrote* KTZ; see Kramers **Chia Yü**. In any case, KZJY (present text 42 chapters) has expanded beyond its HS 30 (27 chapter) form; it needs to be evaluated chapter by chapter, not as an integral work. On KZJY 38, see further below.

[24]"Guess" and "plausible" are standard heuristic in mathematics (Polya **Induction** v), physics (Feynman **Law** 143), and biology (Beveridge **Art** 46; PB 63).

[25]CC sv Sywǽn 2 and the associated DJ expansion; Legge **Ch'un** 289, which notes that the supposed architect of defeat, Hwà Ywǽn's resentful charioteer Yáng Jv̄n 羊斟, fled to Lŭ after confronting the ransomed and returned Hwà Ywǽn.

[26]The protocol is that the state of refuge may harbor the individual, but cannot show him conspicuous favor in the presence of ranking representatives of the state of origin.

[27]CC sv Chv́ng 15 (Legge **Ch'un** 387–389). Hwà Ywǽn's insistence (in the DJ story) that he would return from Jin to Sùng only if given the right to punish the leaders of the other side bespeaks a vindictive nature, and sheds further light on this supposition.

[28]CC sv Chv́ng 4 (Legge **Ch'un** 354) and Chv́ng 8 (Legge **Ch'un** 366, 367a). The purpose of the former visit is not stated; the latter was to arrange a marriage between the son of the Prince of Sùng and the eldest daughter of the Prince of Lŭ. The Lŭ court would have gone out of its way to avoid offending the Sùng envoy on the latter occasion.

Grandfather. By hypothesis, Kŭng Bwó-syà 伯夏 was born in Sùng in the 7th month of 0612. His name alludes to the dynasty supposed to have preceded the Shāng, whose traditions were kept in Sùng; compare the personal (Shāng 商) and formal (Dž-syà 子夏) names of Confucius's disciple. He would have been in his 5th year when the family fled to Lŭ in 0607. Nothing is recorded for him in Lŭ, due perhaps to the enmity of Hwà Ywæn, whose prominence in Sùng extended to 0576, when Bwó-syà would have been already 36, too late to be launching a career.

Father. By hypothesis, he was born in the 6th month of 0592, and was thus 16 in 0576, when Hwà Ywæn's continuing prominence in Sùng still boded ill for his career prospects as a scion of the Lŭ Kŭngs. It has been too little noted[29] that Confucius's father, Shú or Shúlyáng Hv̀ 叔梁紇, *did not bear* the Kŭng surname. Also, by LY 3:15, Confucius was the "son of a man from Dzōu 郰," south of the Lŭ capital, whereas his Kŭng ancestors had settled in Fáng-shān 防山, eastward of it.[30] This looks like an intentional renunciation of the family surname and a seeking of new fortunes in Dzōu. According to the DJ, in the 5th month of 0563, Dzōu Hv̀ ("Hv̀ from Dzōu") held up the portcullis at the small southern fortress of Bì-yáng while his Lŭ comrades escaped.[31] By our hypothesis, Hv̀ was then in his 29th year. This seems late for an exploit of sheer strength, but is consistent with career profiles of modern weight lifters.[32] In the autumn of 0556, Chí besieged Táu, northwest of the Lŭ capital, while a second Chí force attacked Dzàng Hv̀ in Fáng, to the east; Dzōu Shú Hv̀ ("Shú Hv̀ of Dzōu") and two others led a party of 300 in an attack to extricate Dzàng Hv̀ from Fáng.[33] Autumn means the 7th month or later, so Hv̀ was now 37, being just *past* his birthday in that year. This is a plausible age at which to have advanced in a career to the point of commanding a task force on a mission within a campaign.[34] The new surname Shú may imply patronage by the Shú clan, one of whom was the chief minister in Lŭ at this period, following the first exploit.

[29]An exception is Kennedy **Butterfly** 318. Creel's claim (**Confucius** 297–298n3–4) that Shúlyáng Hv̀ has nothing to do with Confucius is unconvincing. The fact that in his appearances in the DJ he is not identified as Confucius's father is not decisive: Yŏu Rwò, on his one DJ appearance, is not identified as a future disciple of Confucius either, though DJ often makes, for civilians as well as rulers, predictions of future achievements.

[30]Implicit in KZJY 39; more overt in SJ 47 (4/1906, Yang **Records** 1) as the place where Shúlyáng Hv̀ was buried; the SJ commentary locates it 25 leagues (8 miles) east of the capital Chyw̄-fù, not unreachable from, but not adjacent to, Dzōu, which is some 45 leagues (15 miles) *south* of the capital, a total journey of perhaps 35 actual road miles.

[31]CC sv Syāng 10 (Legge **Ch'un** 445–446). The allied attack was led by Jìn; the Lŭ party was commanded by a member of the Mv̀ng clan. Entry to the gate of Bì-yáng was gained by a ruse involving a cart, which, once admitted, was followed by concealed shock troops. It is this raiding party which Hv̀'s feat of strength saved from capture.

[32]Body mass is required for these feats. Best performances of weight lifters come late, eg John Davis, career 1938–1952, best lift 1951, aged 30. Averaging four careers (Davis, Tommy Kono, Vasily Alexeyev, David Rigert, but excluding the exceptional Norbert Schemansky, 1948–1964, best 1961 at 37 years 10 months) gives an average peak age of 30 years 3 months. Hv̀ was 28 years 11 months by Western count at the time of his lift.

[33]CC sv Syāng 17 (Legge **Ch'un** 474). The two co-commanders were named Dzàng.

[34]Orde Wingate was, by Chinese reckoning, in his 38th year when he led the guerrilla force that for four months assisted regular British army units in the Ethiopian campaign, ending in their entry into Addis Ababa on 5 May 1941 (Keegan **Generals** 284–285).

Mother. KZJY 39 tells how Hv̀ got a wife from the Yén family. Some details are exaggerated but early, such as the claim that the no-longer-young suitor came of Sùng royal stock (a motif already present in DJ). Others are folkloric and late, such as the availability of *three* Yén daughters, and Hv̀'s *nine* daughters by a former wife. We may assume an unmarried, mature Hv̀. The bride's name was Jv̄ng-dzài 徵在 or "summoned to be present," an unusual name for a female, implying as it does an order to attend the court. This way of enshrining the summons attests its rarity, hence the Yéns were not in court service, but to be summoned at all they must have been *court-connected*, and hence may have been artisans, traders, or other suppliers to the palace. The likely occasion for receiving such persons is the first year of a reign; the only possible candidate for Jv̄ng-dzài's birth is Syāng 1, 0572. Hv̀ did not enter that social range until he moved to the capital, evidently after his 0556 victory, or at earliest 0555; he may have come courting in c0554. In that year, Hv̀ was 38, twice the average age of marriage for males, not prime material despite future prospects based on his Shú connections; Jv̄ng-dzài was 18, half his age, and near the standard marriage age for females. To make this mismatch socially intelligible, we may conjecture (with support from the tradition of Yén Hwéi's poverty) that the Yén family were then down on their luck. The marriage[35] may be assigned to c0553.

Brother. By LY 5:2, Confucius had an older brother who could not himself arrange his daughter's marriage. By the above inferences, he would have been born in c0552. KZJY 39 gives his name as Mv̀ng-pí, perhaps implying a skin condition (pí 皮 means "skin"), and says that he was a cripple, which would explain LY 5:2. Such a condition would also disqualify him from inheriting in a military family, and the family thus urgently required a second son.

Summary. The above conjectures are here recapitulated in a table:

CC Year	Intl Yr	Mo	Cycl Day	Event
Syī 15	0645	05		[spurious CC eclipse]
Syī 15	0645	06		Kǔng Fáng-shú born in Sùng
Wv́n 15	0612	07	#38	**genuine CC eclipse**; 93% totality
Wv́n 15	0612	08		Kǔng Bwó-syà born in Sùng
Sywǣn 2	0607	02		Sùng army of Hwà Ywǣn defeated
	0607?			Kǔng Fáng-shú flees to Lǔ
Sywǣn 17	0592	06	#17	[spurious CC eclipse]
Sywǣn 17	0592	05		Hv̀ born to Kǔng family in Lǔ
Sywǣn 31	0576			Hwà Ywǣn still influential in Sùng
	0575?			Hv̀ relocates to Dzōu
Syāng 1	0572			Yén Jv̄ng-dzài born in Lǔ capital
Syāng 10	0563	05	#31	Hv̀ "of Dzōu" lifts portcullis
	0562?			Hv̀ is patronized by Shú clan?
Syāng 17	0556	07		"Shú" Hv̀ of Dzōu leads mission
Syāng 18	0555?			Hv̀ relocates to Lǔ capital
Syāng 20	0553?			Hv̀ marries bride from Yén family
Syāng 21	0552			Hv̀'s first son Mv̀ng-pí born

[35]KZJY 39 emphasizes that the bride had to be persuaded to accept the groom; the present hypothesis is consistent with KZJY 39, where age disparity is the chief crux; the marriage was irregular in that sense. SJ 47 cattily calls it an "illicit union" (yě hv́ 野合), thus setting off centuries of steamy speculation and heated defense.

Confucius's Life

Youth. KZJY 39 says that the couple prayed at Ní-shān 尼山, southeast of the capital,[36] and that Confucius was born afterward, by the above hypothesis perhaps in the 8th month of 0549, three years after his brother, his given name Chyōu 丘 "Hill" and style -ní 尼 both deriving from the prayer for his birth at Ní-shān.[37] When he was in his third year, c0546, his father, now called Shú-lyáng 叔梁 Hv̀, died, by our hypothesis at age c46. Hv̀ will have had, to support his chariot, a landholding near the capital; if this fact is reflected in the new element -lyáng "weir" in his surname, it may have been distinctive in including a pond for irrigation and for fish cultivation. Its management will in any case have been beyond the powers of a child of three and his crippled brother of six, and Confucius's youth must thus have been spent in eking out a living by means not customary for the son and heir of a warrior. This implication is supported by 05c Analects references to his early hardship and makeshift livelihood (see LY 9:6; this element is played down in the later Analects). At 19 he married a daughter of the Jyēn-gwān 开官 family of Sùng. This may seem a suspiciously exalted match (-gwān means "office"), but no other holder of this surname seems to have been identified,[38] and we may plausibly assume that the bride, like Confucius himself, was from a family of exiles from Sùng living in Lǔ. This does not necessarily imply a reconciliation between Confucius and the Kǔngs of Fáng-shān; it will be argued below that Confucius had inherited from his father a circle of acquaintance based in part on such exile families in Lǔ, and one of these may have helped to arrange the marriage.[39]

Son. The next year (at 20, c0530), a son was born, and Jāu-gūng sent a present of carp, the baby being named Lǐ 鯉 "Carp" or Bwó-yẃ 伯魚 "Fish" in response. This is plausible enough: as heir to a military landholding, Confucius was liable for military service, and a gift of fish (by LY 10:12a, live ones would have been bred, not eaten) would reflect concern for his livelihood and that of his heir. By LY 11:8, Bwó-yẃ predeceased his father; KZJY 39 says that he died in his 50th year, or c0481. Confucius did not long survive this disappointment, himself dying in early 0479.

Service. A DJ story[40] has Confucius known at 17 to the Mv̀ng clan as learned in ritual; SJ 47 tops this with tales of foreign travel in his twenties. This is out of the question for an impoverished youth. More likely, delayed by hardship, he took up his military duties as a member of Jāu-gūng's guard only in his c30th year, c0520, and even then (LY 9:2) was none too expert in the use of bow and chariot.

---

[36]For the fertility rite that may have been involved, see Jensen **Wise** 421f.

[37]SJ 47 repeats the KZJY 39 data that lead to this inference, and superadds a claim that "hill" referred to the shape of his head. This second explanation reflects Hàn physiognomy, and would appear to be a typical mythical elaboration.

[38]Some texts of KZJY 39 emend the surname to the well-known Shànggwān 上官, but the more obscure form is clearly the source of all variants in this family of texts.

[39]Confucius's mother may have died earlier. KZJY 39 does not mention her death; in SJ 47 it precedes a story in which he is said to be 17. She may have died when he was c15, or in c0535, she being c37; Legge **Analects** Prolegomena 61 gives "0527" [0528]. LJ (Tán-gūng A10; Legge **Li** 124f) claims he did not know the site of his father's grave; this may preserve a memory that he was not at this time in touch with the Kǔngs.

[40]DJ Jāu 7 (0535) 9th month, Legge **Ch'un** 618bf, assuming the 0551 birthdate.

Jāu-gūng's Exile occurred in 0517, following his botched coup against the Jì. Confucius's natural course (consistent with the steadfastness which, from LY 4:5, was his *self-perceived* central quality) would have been to continue as a member of his personal guard. SJ 47, ignoring Confucius's political legitimism as expressed in LY 4:7, and the animus of LY 5–6 against those who served the Jì, has him taking service under the Jì clan, and traveling on his own account to Chí, where he is interviewed by Chí Jǐng-gūng. The two possibilities are not wholly antithetical, but the likeliest relation between them is that the second is a mythic exaggeration of the first. Jāu-gūng in exile was supported by the Prince of Chí, who twice in 0515 received him in the Chí capital. On those occasions, Confucius, as a member of Jāu-gūng's escort, would have been in Jǐng-gūng's presence, might have exchanged words with him, and would have witnessed the musical performance which inspired LY 7:14, the earliest and most plausible Analects claim of Confucius's travels.

The CC tells us that Chí conquered the border town of Ywn 鄆 and in 0516 gave it to Jāu-gūng as a residence; the Chí visits followed in 0515. In 0514 Jāu-gūng visited Gān-hóu 乾 侯 on the Lǔ/Jìn border, went back to Ywn, and returned to Gān-hóu. In 0513 the residents of Ywn, doubtless weary of the burden of the exile court, simply abandoned the town, and Jāu-gūng stayed in Gān-hóu until his death in 0510. Military challenges were few, and service at the exile establishment may have exposed Confucius to the civil side of court life for which his military background had not trained him; the late LY 19:22 emphasizes that he had no regular teacher in cultural matters, and picked up his knowledge as he could; the theme of learning from all and sundry is constant throughout the early LY 5–9.

Dìng-gūng. The Jì clan let Jāu-gūng's younger brother, known as Dìng-gūng, succeed in 0509; Jāu-gūng loyalists like Confucius were probably at first excluded from positions at court. For his daughter, perhaps born c0527 (three years after Bwó-yw) and by now a marriageable 19, Confucius could find no better husband than the jailbird Gūngyě Cháng (LY 5:1). Presumably he simply occupied his landholding in the early years of Dìng-gūng's reign, 0509–0495 (SJ 47 describes that period as one of retirement and teaching). A new note appears with the CC record of the razing of Jì and Shú clan-stronghold walls in 0498, a centrist policy which might have given Confucius more scope (though surely not at the ministerial level claimed by DJ and SJ 47). The 05c Analects (7:23 and 9:5) hints at a trip to Sùng and possibly the states south of it, which might have been a semiofficial effort to win support for the centrist initiative (later myth dates this trip or its beginning to 0496 and makes it part of Confucius's principled exit from his mythical Lǔ ministership). The date itself is plausible; in that year Lǔ walled some cities for defense against Jìn.

Āi-gūng succeeded in 0494, and showed energy in continuing centrist policies, culminating in an apparent direct land tax imposed in 0483, which converted the previous endowed military elite into a salaried civilian elite; he also displayed enterprise in rallying foreign support for the legitimate line against the other clans. He might well have offered a post to the loyalist Confucius from c0494. It will then have been between c0494 and his withdrawal from court in 0481, after his son's death, that Confucius, who doubtless had friends and associates under Dìng-gūng, probably first attracted a significant number of official court protégés.

In all of the above, we find that the most frugal inferences from outside tradition best fit the implications of the early Analects, and indicate a core of probable fact from which the mighty Confucius persona of the DJ, the late Analects, and SJ 47 might rationally have evolved in response to school needs and family pressures.

The Analects Disciples

We now come to the part of Confucius's life for which the Analects gives direct, though still tantalizingly scanty, evidence.

Roster. Statements of the number of Confucius's disciples cluster in the 70s: the 70 of MC 2A3 and 4B31 (early to mid 03c; retained in SJ 121), the perhaps original 70 but nominal 72 (actually 77) of KZJY 38, the claimed inner circle of 72 in SJ 47 (c0107, but based on earlier notes), and the 77 of SJ 67 (also c0107). These look like an expanding, but generally stable, tradition.[41] As Waley (**Analects** 19) notes, the plausible Analects names number about 20;[42] those mentioned *as disciples* in the *early* Analects, before direct memory seems to fade out with Dzv̄ngdž in LY 7, are even fewer. If to those who figure in the second section of LY 5, and those employed or rated as employable in LY 6, we add Yŏudž ("Master Yŏu") on the probability that he was a pre-Dzv̄ngdž head of the school, we get just 16, namely:

*Dž-gùng (5:4, 9, 12, 6:8)	Shv̄n Chv́ng (5:11)
*Rǎn Yūng (5:5, 6:1, 6:6)	Dž-sāng Bwódž (6:2)
Chīdyāu Kāı (5:6)	Ywǽn Sz̄ (6:5)
*Dž-lù (5:8, 6:8)	*Mǐn Dž-chyēn (6:9)
*[Rǎn] Chyóu (5:8, 6:4, 6:8, 6:12)	*Rǎn Gv̄ng (6:10)
[Gūngsyī] Chⅰ̀ (5:8, 6:4)	*Dž-syà (6:13)
*[Yén] Hwéı (5:9, 6:3, 6:7, 6:11)	*Dž-yóu (6:14)
*Dzǎı Yẃ (5:10ab)	[Yŏudž]

On the Analects evidence, these are the certain members of the original circle of official protégés. Among near misses are the mere questioners Dž-jāng in 5:19a/b and Fán Chⅰ̀ in 6:22, and the later school head Dzv̄ngdž in 8:3–7. The enigmatic Láu of LY 9:7 (identified by commentators with Chín Jāng) seems to claim memory of Confucius, but at that late date (c0405) it can only be an indirect memory.

The ten asterisked names on this list are those comprising the later LY 11:3 disciple pantheon (c0360).[43] Of the other six, four (Chīdyāu Kāı, Gūngsyī Chⅰ̀, Shv̄n Chv́ng, and Dž-sāng Bwódž) vanish altogether in the later Analects, Ywǽn Sz̄ recurs just once, in 14:1a, and the problematic Yŏudž is *first* mentioned in 12:9.

Disciple Names. In the KZJY and SJ disciple inventories, all these people have a personal name (míng 名) and an often semantically related social or formal name (dž 字), the formal name being usually preceded by the honorific Dž- 子 prefix. In the Analects itself a different pattern obtains, in which the use of the Dž- prefix is restricted to a small and definite group. The Dž- group are often known by just their Dž- name (as Dž-gùng, whose surname is never given), whereas the non-Dž- group are usually known by surname plus personal or formal name (most conspicuously Yén Hwéı, who is sometimes Yén Hwéı, sometimes Yén Ywān, but *never* Dž-ywǽn). This pattern of name usage seems to preserve a distinction later lost or normalized. What was it?

[41]The SJ 47 (4/1938) claim of an outer circle of 3,000 beyond the inner circle of 72 may be dismissed as a bit of numerical fantasizing, akin to the claim that Confucius chose the 305 Shⅰ̄ poems from an original corpus of 3,000 (SJ 47, 4/1936).

[42]Morohashi **Jimbutsu** gets 30, but by including relatives and other doubtful persons.

[43]For the place of this grouping in the history of the disciples, see page 290 below.

Money. One factor is wealth, sometimes symbolized by possession of a chariot:

Dž-	Non-Dž-
Dž-lù (chariot, *5:26[1])	Yén Hwéi (poor, 6:11; no chariot, 11:8)
Dž-hwá (chariot, rich, 6:4)	
Dž-gùng (rich, 11:18b)	

But not all who are rich (such as Ywæn Sz̄, who in 6:5 can afford to return his salary to the court) has the Dž- prefix, and some Dž- protégés appear more as cultured than as specifically rich: Dž-gùng is described as a ritual vessel in 5:4, and Dž-syà is chided in 6:13 for failing to uphold the higher culture as against the lower.

Social Origins. Another factor which correlates with Dž- status is social origin, as reflected in palace-lineage or occupational surnames. The one disciple clearly of ruling-group origin is Dž-lù, whose surname Jùng 仲 (18:6, short for Shújùng) links him with the Shú clan. Dž-syà's surname Bŭ 卜 "omen" suggests divination specialists, and thus a tradition of palace association, and Dž-yóu's surname Yén 言 "words" might indicate palace ritual invocators. At the other end of the scale is the surname Răn (冉 = 染 "Dyer"), providing three of the sixteen undoubted protégés, none of whom ever evinces a Dž- usage, though Răn Chyóu appears in 6:8 as equally employable with Dž-lù, and in 16:1 as his actual colleague. In this list of possible occupational surnames, those that may have been purveyors to the palace, as distinct from merchants to a wider commercial public, are given in **bold**:

Dž-gùng	Dwānmù 端木 "Stump"	Timber purveyor?[44]
Dž-hwá	Gūngsyī 宮西 "West of Palace"	Potter?[45]
Răn Chyóu	Răn 冉 = 染 "Dye"	Dyer
Răn Gv̄ng	"	"
Răn Yūng	"	"
Chīdyāu Kāı	Chīdyāu 漆雕 "Lacquer Carver"	Lacquer carver
Dzăı Yẃ	Dzăı 宰 "Sty-ward = Steward"	Butcher
Dž-sāng Bwódž	Dž-sāng 子桑 "Master of Mulberry"	Grover
Yén Hwéı	Yén 顏 "Face"	Cosmetics maker?[46]
Ywæn Sz̄	Ywæn 原 "Plain, Meadow?"	Shepherd?

Shv̄n Chv́ng's surname is apparently not occupational but geographical (see 5:11n). The correlation of Dž- with the presumption of close palace connection is evident.

This makes sense if we posit three statuses (ruler-related, palace-connected, and outside), a real but ignored factor (wealth), and an acknowledged factor (culture): (1) the ruler-related (Dž-lù) use Dž- regardless of wealth, (2) the palace-connected (Dž-gùng) use Dž- if wealthy, but (3) the outside do not automatically acquire Dž- along with wealth (Ywæn Sz̄), lack of culture (Yén Hwéı) being one factor, just as betrayal of culture by its possessors (Dž-syà) is a major lapse for the Dž- group.

[44]The court would be the major buyer of architectural-quality timber; see LY 5:18.

[45]The potters were located west of the Lŭ palace; see Needham v5 pt6 p297. Smelly occupations (dyeing, lacquer, meatcutting) seem not to have been sited near the palace.

[46]See discussion of this possibility above and at 10n23. The hypothesis would be that Confucius's mother came from palace-connected official purveyors, whereas Yén Hwéı's branch (note his father's name, Lù 路 "journey," and his own, Hwéı 回 "return") were engaged in outside trading in cosmetics, and would thus have been a step lower socially. Note Hwéı's gratitude for being taught "culture" by the Master in 9:11.

Lǔ Society. This picture gives us a hint of the forces shaping 05c Lǔ society. The overall impression is of a palace-centered culture which is becoming accessible not only to its associated artisan providers, but also to more distant entrepreneurs. Money from these non-court (and apparently also not *court-controlled*) enterprises was convertible into access, but social acceptance (symbolized by the Dž- prefix) was withheld until that access was confirmed by acquisition of the higher culture. The implication is that not only can wealth and social status be acquired (LY 4:5), but the higher culture can also be acquired (9:11). It will therefore not be wrong to characterize this as an open society. Such a newly open palace society, with its sometimes vulgar new members retaining their original profit ethos, and not yet having absorbed the traditional others-first ethos, is compatible with what we sense behind the LY 4–5 complaints about the "little people."

The KZJY Disciples

The Longer Lists. For further evidence on the social placement and nature of the Confucius circle, we must turn to the "disciple" lists. There are two of these, which are similar in length and organization. Both begin with a group of names for which more detail is given, and to which more or less anecdotal material is attached, and both continue with a second group of names for which only surname, personal name, and formal name are given. This division is implicit in KZJY 38, and explicitly noted in SJ 67. A few difficulties notwithstanding, the 77 names of the KZJY 38 list ("Explanation of the 72 Disciples," 七十二弟子解) can be matched one for one with the 77 names of the SJ 67 list ("Notice of the Disciples of Jùng-ní," 仲尼弟子列傳). Unexpectedly, most of the names on the lists are not high-profile Analects personalities such as the clan heir Mv`ng Yìdž of LY 2:5, who we might expect would be claimed as a disciple, but who does not appear. Instead, many of them are totally unknown, could serve no readily imaginable aggrandizing agenda, and, since no other hypothesis suggests itself, may be an actual inventory of the larger Confucius circle, of which we only see the employable tip in the Analects. Before proceeding, however, we must ascertain whether KZJY 38 or SJ 67 is earlier, and how reliable the earlier list itself may be.[47]

---

[47]This preliminary demonstration is called a lemma in mathematics; humanistic scholars might well borrow this useful term. Readers who are prepared to take on faith the relative validity of the KZJY 38 disciple list may skip directly to page 282.

For the widespread scholarly impression that the KZJY is a forgery by Wáng Sù, see the brief counter-argument in n23, above, which argues among other things that our KZJY has grown between the 27-chapter version recorded in the HS 30 palace library catalogue and the 44-chapter version which we possess today. It is easy to demonstrate that KZJY 38, the disciple list, is among the chapters added to the work after Hàn, and the demonstration at the same time proves that the list is not itself a post-Hàn forgery, but was known *as an independent document* in Hàn times. It is obvious that KZJY 38 or its precursor has a close relation to the structurally identical SJ 67, and SJ 67 explicitly states that it has used (and improved on) an earlier text, which it calls a Register of Disciples (弟子籍) and describes as "an old [pre-Chín] writing of the Kǔng family." A text which is clearly close to our KZJY 38 is cited by Jv`ng Sywæn (127–200) in his commentary to SJ 67 #2, not as the Jyā Yw̌ or Kǔngdž Jyā-yw̌ (as do all later commentators) but as the List of Confucius's Disciples (孔子弟子目錄). It is only after Wáng Sù's time that this second tradition is cited by commentators *as the KZJY*. The inference must be that the list in question circulated separately throughout Hàn and most of Latter Hàn, and was only combined with the Kǔngdž Jyā-yw̌ at the time of, and most likely by, Wáng Sù.

KZJY vs SJ. Several points suggest that the KZJY 38 list is anterior to SJ 67, though in its present form it has suffered some scribal corruption. Among them are:

• SJ 67 in effect says so: it mentions using, and improving upon, an old (pre-Chín script) text of the Kǔng clan called Disciple Register 弟子籍.

• SJ 67 claims to have improved on this work by supplementing it from the Analects. KZJY 38 in general avoids citing Analects stories in its first, or anecdote-containing, half of the list. SJ 67 also claims to have improved on this work by getting rid of doubtful data. Stories attached in KZJY 38 to four persons not mentioned in the Analects are in SJ 67 eliminated, and the four persons are demoted to the non-anecdote-containing half of the list.

• KZJY 38 mentions 72 disciples in its title, but actually has 77. SJ 67 has, and claims, 77 disciples. It would seem that the KZJY list grew after its first compilation, and that SJ took that expanded list as a starting point.

• Both lists begin with the ten LY 11:3 disciples, but whereas KZJY 38 keeps the Analects order, SJ 67 switches two pairs, #5–6 and #7–8. The Analects order is authoritative, hence KZJY 38 is earlier, and the SJ variant, whose effect is to list the three Rǎns in succession, is a revision.

• Both lists give ages (in number of years younger than Confucius) for disciples in the first section (though in the present KZJY 38 those for the first ten disciples are missing). The disciple ages vary between the two lists. Boodberg **Zoographic** 445–447 suggests that some disciple names derive from the animal associated with the cyclical year of their birth. His best example is Lyáng Jān, whose personal (鱣) and formal (魚) names both involve fish; by SJ 67 #30, Jān was 29 years younger than Confucius, and hence was born in a dragon (symbolically, fish) year. But the cycle of sixty was not applied to years earlier than the 03c, so this theory is untenable for the 06c, and any agreement of disciple ages with that theory is suspect. KZJY 38 #32 gives Lyáng Jān as 39 years younger than Confucius. It would seem that SJ has altered this to agree with a theory of the Boodberg type. KZJY is then primary.

• The two lists have largely the same names, but in different order, some KZJY names in the first section being placed later in the SJ list, as though an SJ copyist had omitted a KZJY entry, and then, on realizing the error, added it *at the point he had then reached*. The opposite scenario, with a KZJY copyist repeatedly *anticipating* SJ, is a less typical scribal error.

• Divergences in the second section are more drastic, but on collating the lists, we find that KZJY 38 #51 Sywē Bāng 薛邦 matches SJ 67 #63 Jvng Gwó 鄭國. The latter appears to respect the Hàn taboo on the name Bāng 邦 of the first Hàn emperor; the usual Hàn substitution was gwó 國. The pre-Chín KZJY (see above), would not have come under this taboo.

We may thus take the sequence KZJY 38 > SJ 67 as established. But KZJY 38 has undergone scribal corruption since its prototype served as the source for SJ 67:

• As comparison with SJ 67 shows, the present KZJY 38 represents a later stage in the spread of the honorific Dž- prefix, and

• The present KZJY 38 displays an Analectizing tendency, so that the original entry Chín Rǎn 秦冉, an unknown figure preserved only in SJ 67, is in the present KZJY 38 replaced by the known Chín Láu 琴牢 (LY 9:7)

so that it cannot be simply substituted for the SJ 67 list, or taken uncritically as the source for that list. Instead, the proto-KZJY 38 must be reconstructed from the combined testimony of that list and SJ 67 in their present form.

Reconstruction Guidelines. In reconstructing the source text which SJ 67 calls the Register of Disciples 弟子籍 from the derived texts SJ 67 and KZJY 38, the woodblock Bwó-nà 百納 edition of SJ has been used to avoid later typesetting errors, and KZJY citations in early SJ commentaries have been substituted, where different, for the reading of the SBTK Sùng woodblock or other extant editions of KZJY. Basic principles are that elements found in both derived texts are attributed to the source, and where readings differ, the "more difficult" (such as SJ tú 徒 for the graphically and semantically similar, but less learned, KZJY tsúng 從) are to be preferred. There are also some visible traits and preferences of the respective texts and their copyists, which have been used as further guidelines:

• The stated SJ Analectizing tendency is seen in its substituting, for the unknown KZJY Shv̄n Lyáu 申繚 (a commentary reading), the known Gūngbwó Lyáu 公伯僚 (LY 14:36), an enemy of Dž-lù who cannot have been a disciple. In general, non-Analectizing readings are followed.

• SJ variations from the KZJY order seem sometimes inadvertent (see above) but also sometimes purposive; one tendency is to group similar surnames, such as KZJY #46 and 48, both Gūngsyī 公西 > SJ 67 #76–77. In all cases, explainable or not, the KZJY order is followed.

• Having grouped the two Gūngsyī, SJ assimilates the second formal name (KZJY 子尚) to the homophonous first (子上, both Dž-shàng). In such phonetic substitutions (as KZJY #64 守 ~ SJ #49 首), KZJY is followed.

• The KZJY #52 surname Shŕ 石 appears in SJ #47 as Hòu 后, where the difference amounts to adding a stroke in SJ. This seems to be a misreading of the extra dot often added to 石. KZJY is followed.

• For KZJY #45 Jyé 潔, SJ #70 has Syé 絜. The source text undoubtedly lacked the reformed-script "water" determinative, and *calligraphically*, SJ better reflects it, but the *word* is more adequately conveyed to modern readers by the form with determinative. Where SJ and KZJY have *different* determinatives, SJ, as the earlier transcription, is followed.

• Where either text provides a formal name without the Dž- prefix, , or where one text has prefix 子 and the other the apparently elegant suffix 之 (as in KZJY #52 里之 ~ SJ #47 子里), the unaffixed form is followed.

• KZJY #49 has surname Rángsż 穰駟; SJ #42 has Răngsż 壤駟. The KZJY form 穰 "stalk of grain" may be a semantic amelioration of the cruder 壤 "loam." For the KZJY #55 name Jv́ 哲 "wise" SJ #73 has Jv́ 晢 "bright," better balancing the personal name Hēı 黑 "black." For KZJY #34 Rú 儒 "Confucian," SJ #32 has rú 孺 "child." Both the latter look like instances of intellectual aggrandization. In all cases, the humbler form is followed.

• In the same entry with KZJY #40 (corresponding to SJ #71) is #41, Kŭng Sywǽn 孔璇, one of two Kŭngs in KZJY and the only anecdotally elaborated one. His presence is probably a Kŭng aggrandizement. SJ #72, Yén Hv́, which corresponds with it by default, has been substituted.

• The KZJY 38 #42 surname Syī 奚 is given as Syīrúng 奚容 in SJ 67 #50, similarly KZJY 38 #54 Dzwŏ 左 ~ SJ 67 #61 Dzwŏrv́n 左人. In these and other cases, a character appears to have dropped out of the KZJY list, and the fuller SJ readings are followed.

In the outline of the reconstruction at right, it has not been possible to indicate which readings rely on SJ, an SJ commentary, or a variant text of KZJY. In addition to surname, personal name, and formal name, we also give the age (number of years younger than Confucius), when that datum is supplied in the better sources.

01	Yén Hwéı	顏回	子淵		40	Shújùng Hwèı	叔仲會	子期	54
02	Mǐn Sǔn	閔損	子騫	29	41	Yén Hv́	顏何	稱	
03	Rǎn Gv̄ng	冉耕	伯牛		42	Chín Dzǔ	秦祖	子南	
04	Rǎn Yūng	冉雍	仲弓		43	Syīrúng Jv̄n	奚容箴	子晳	
05	Dzǎı Yv́	宰予	子我		44	Gūngdzǔ Gōudz̄	公祖句兹	子之	
06	Dwānmù Sz̀	端木賜	子貢		45	Lyén Jyé	廉潔	曹	
07	Rǎn Chyóu	冉求	子有		46	Gūngsyī Yv́-rú	公西輿如	子上	
08	Jùng Yóu	仲由	子路		47	Hǎnfù Hēı	罕父黑	索	
09	Yén Yěn	言偃	子游	35	48	Gūngsyī Jv̄n	公西箴	子尚	
10	Bǔ Shāng	卜商	子夏		49	Rǎngsz̀ Chr̀	壤駟赤	子徒	
11	Jwānsūn Shr̄	顓孫師	子張	48	50	Rǎn Jì	冉季	子產	
12	Dzv̄ng Shv̄m	曾參	子輿	46	51	Sywē Bāng	薛邦	子徒	
13	Tántáı Myè-míng	澹臺滅明	子羽	49	52	Shŕ Chǔ	石處	里	
14	Gāu Cháı	高柴	子羔	40	53	Chyāu Shàn	鄡單	子家	
15	Mì Bù-chí	密不齊	子賤	49	54	Dzwǒrv́n Yǐng	左人郢	行	
16	Fán Syv̄	樊須	子遲	46	55	Dí Hēı	狄黑	晳	
17	Yǒu Rwò	有若	有	36	56	Shāng Dzv́	商澤	子秀	
18	Gūngsyī Chr̀	公西赤	子華	42	57	Rv̀n Bù-chí	任不齊	選	
19	Ywǽn Syèn	原憲	子思	36	58	Rúng Chí	榮祈	子祺	
20	Gūngyě Cháng	公冶長	子長		59	Yén Kwàı	顏噲	子聲	
21	Námgūng Tāu	南宮綯	子容		60	Ywǽn Táu	原桃	籍	
22	Gūngsyī Kv̀	公析克	季沉		61	Gūngjyēn Dìng	公肩定	中	
23	Dzv̄ng Dyěn	曾點	子晳		62	Chín Fēı	秦非	子之	
24	Yén Yóu	顏由	路	6	63	Chīdyāu Tú	漆雕徒	文	
25	Shāng Jyv̀	商瞿	子木	29	64	Yēn Jí	燕級	思	
26	Chīdyāu Kāı	漆雕開	子若	11	65	Gūngsyà Shǒu	公夏守	乘	
27	Gūnglyáng Rú	公良孺	子正		66	Gōujǐng Jyāng	句井疆	子界	
28	Chín Shāng	秦商	丕兹	4	67	Bùshú Chv́ng	步叔乘	子車	
29	Yén Gāu	顏高	子驕	50	68	Shŕ Dzwò-shǔ	石作蜀	子明	
30	Sz̄mǎ Lí-gv̄ng	司馬黎耕	子牛		69	Gwēı Sywǽn	邽選	子斂	
31	Wūmǎ Shr̄	巫馬施	子旗	30	70	Shŕ Jŕ-cháng	施之常	子恒	
32	Lyáng Jān	梁鱣	叔魚	39	71	Shv̄n Lyáu	申繚	子周	
33	Chín Rǎn	秦冉	開		72	Ywè Kàı	樂欬	子聲	
34	Rǎn Rú	冉孺	子魚	50	73	Yén Jŕ-pú	顏之僕	子叔	
35	Yén Syīn	顏辛	子柳	46	74	Kǔng Fú	孔弗	子蔑	
36	Bwó Chyén	伯虔	楷	50	75	Chīdyāu Chr̀	漆雕哆	子斂	
37	Gūngsūn Chǔng	公孫寵	子石	53	76	Sywǽn Chv́ng	懸成	子橫	
38	Tsáu Syv̀	曹卹	子循	50	77	Yén Dzǔ	顏祖	襄	
39	Shv̄n Chv́ng	申樘	周						

弟子籍

The Disciple Register (DZJ)

The Prototype of KZJY̌ 38 as a Source for SJ 67, c0107

Refinements. The resulting document, which we may call Disciple Register (Dìdž Jì, or DZJ) to distinguish it from its later KZJY 38 form, still needs to be purged of one or two layers of accretions: a probable two names raising it from a conjectured initial 70 (the tradition reported by the Mencius) to the 72 of the title, and an undoubted increment of five names raising that nominal 72 to an actual, and unacknowledged, 77. We have seen that both the SJ 67 and KZJY 38 later versions are subject to Analectizing tendencies, so that we may not assume that congruity with the Analects is a touchstone for this list, which seems to have been made and/or maintained at a certain distance from the Analects. But there are a few suggestions that may be made toward identifying incremental strata.

One concerns #25 (Shāng Jyẁ), who seems to be present in the text simply as an expert in the Yì. The SJ 67 version supplies an entire transmission-genealogy of the Yì; since this goes down to Yáng Hv́ 楊何, and notes that he was given a post under Hàn Wǔ-dì due to his Yì expertise in c0125,[48] not long before SJ 67 itself was written, this SJ genealogy is a Hàn product, and cannot be attributed to the source document DZJ (KZJY 38 simply states that Jyẁ received the Yì from Confucius). He recurs at greater length in #32 (Lyáng Jān), where he successfully predicts that the childless Jān (who is about to put away his wife) will shortly have an heir. There is nothing in #32 but this story. Neither figure is known to the Analects, the Lǐ Jì, or para-Confucian writings in general (Shāng Jyẁ does figure in the Yì apocrypha, a set of writings handed down not in Confucian but in a separate Yì tradition). It would seem that Lyáng Jān is present in this list merely to validate Shāng Jyẁ, and that Shāng Jyẁ is present merely to validate the Yì in the Confucian tradition. Here, then, are two spurious names with a clear agenda, as a candidate for the conjectured two-name increment. When might they have been added? LY *13:22b[2] (c0317) has Confucius approving of the Yì as a wisdom book and not a divination manual, hence the probability is before c0317. The acceptance of the Yì as a discussable text,[49] and the induced raising of the disciple number to 72, must have followed Mencius's departure in c0321, since neither development was known to Mencius, whose school ignores the Yì and always mentions 70 disciples. The range is thus c0320/c0318. These changes also presumably produced the shift of Confucius's official birthdate from 0549 to 0552 in the Kŭng-controlled copy of the CC, hence this copy must have been transmitted to Chí after the period c0320/c0318. This agrees with our date of c0312 for the final Chí DJ, and leaves open the possibility that the Lǔ DJ was taken to Chí by a member of the retinue of Mencius himself, who in c0317 visited Lǔ for his mother's funeral, subsequently returning to Chí.

---

[48]SJ 67 specificies the period Ywǽn-shwò 元朔, or 0128/0124, which we transcribe as c0125. The later SJ 121 6/3127 (Watson **Records** 2/409), a chapter begun by Sz̄mǎ Chyēn but finished only in c060 by his nephew Yáng Yŭn, and which disagrees at many points with SJ 67, gives an earlier date: the first year of Ywǽn-gwāng 元光 or 0134. The parallel genealogy in HS 88 7/3597 has a number of changes from that in SJ 67, the effect of which is to emphasize the Lǔ connections of the Yì, and minimize the southern ones; it is obvious from LY *13:22a[2] that when it first came into the orbit of the Analects, the Yì had southern associations.

[49]Never a canonical one as far as the Analects is concerned; the Yì is never mentioned or alluded to later in the text, nor does it figure in the Syẃndzian canon; it gradually gained official status during Hàn. For a document which may represent an early, internal Confucian apologia for the Yì, structured as a dialogue between Confucius and Dž-gùng, see the Mǎwáng Dwēi text called Yàu or Essentials, Shaughnessy I 235–243.

The Second Increment. Since there will have been no emblematic value in adding names to the nonanecdotal half of the list, the unacknowledged five entries made after the "72 Disciple" title was attached to it[50] are probably to be found in the anecdotal entries of the first half. One possibility is Gūnglyáng Rú (#27), a brave man who is said to have escorted Confucius on his travels, or Chín Shāng (#28), whose father is said to have been renowned with Confucius's father Shúlyáng Hv̀ as a strong man. But the bravery of the former, and the strength of the latter, are both qualities played down in the later Analects. They thus seem to be in the opposite direction to the main trend of the Confucius myth, and for that reason less likely to be part of it. They seem more plausibly construed as family memories. More promising are possible Analectizing updates, keeping the list current with highlights of the later Analects. Persons mentioned in the Analects, or associated with Analects tendencies, whose first occurrence in that text is after LY 11, are:

31	Wūmǎ Shī	(companion in Chvn)	*7:31[3]	(c0342)
30	Szmǎ Lí-gvng	(notably problematic)	12:3–5	(c0326)
22	Gūngsyī Kv̀	(a hermit figure; see next)	*11:24[1]	(c0294)
23	Dzvng Dyěn	(a hermit apologist)	*11:24[1]	(c0294)
29	Yén Gāu	(driver in Wèi; story of Nándž)	*6:28[18]	(c0270)

Yǒudž, who first appears in 12:9, was on previous inferences remembered as a disciple, though taboo in LY 11. We suggest, then, that the above five are the second level of additions to the text. Four keep up with later-Analects innovations.[51] One, the recluse Gūngsyī Kv̀, whom Confucius is said to have singled out for special praise, expands on a late Analects theme: the advocacy of a nonservice position in LY 1 and *11:24[1]. Here, as with the Yì addenda above, the relation between the list and the Analects is not that the list mirrors the Analects, but that it records in detail some movements that are barely visible in the Analects itself.

Date of the List of 70. The list is based on LY 11:3 and cannot be earlier than c0360. The first disciple mentioned after LY 11:3 in LY 11 who is not included in 11:3 itself is Dž-jāng (11:16); next are Dzvngdž and Gāu Chái (11:18a). These (with the enigmatic Tántái Myè-míng) are also the next names in the list, comprising its #11–14. This close relation between chapter and list suggests that the list is also a product of c0360. As to its validity, we note that it contains the obscure Shvn Chvng of 5:11[52] and Dž-sāng Bwódž of 6:2,[53] and (assuming the presence of Yǒudž) is thus complete for the sixteen 05c disciples, even those not developed in 04c tradition.

---

[50]Szmǎ Chyēn's reference to it as the Dìdž Jì may be merely a tactical convenience; quoting the number 72 would cast doubt on the validity of his own 77-name list.

[51]Not all: among later Analects figures who were *not* added to this list are Bwó-yv̆'s classmate Chvn Kàng (16:13, c0285) and the sprawling Ywæn Răng (*14:43, c0270).

[52]Already detected by the Táng SJ commentator Szmǎ Jvn, who simply equated the LY name Chvng 根 with the SJ name Táng 堂 (the present SJ text has Dǎng 黨) as phonetically compatible. The actual process of corruption may have been: (1) the LY form Chvng 根 "prop," (2) the phonetically similar Chvng 樘, also "prop," which we reconstruct for the DZJ, (3a) the graphically similar SJ Dǎng 黨, and separately (3b) whatever KZJY form was displaced by the Analectizing substitution of Chvn Kàng at #39.

[53]If we take the odd Dž-sāng as an epithet rather than a surname, and analyze the atypical name Bwódž 伯子 normally as "Master Bwó," Bwó becoming then the surname, we may equate him with the Bwó Chyén 伯虔 of #36.

The Original List. On that basis, the actual list put together by the Kŭng family in c0360 would have been that shown at right (the seven names argued above as having been later Kŭng additions are eliminated from the previous reconstruction, but, for reader convenience, without changing the numbering of the list).

Further Purifications. But the Kŭngs in c0360, as their dismissive treatment of the important figure Dzv̄ngdž in LY 11 makes clear, were obviously concerned to standardize and reshape the disciple tradition, not simply to record it, and the list of 70 must itself be scrutinized for problematic data: names which cannot in fact have been part of Confucius's circle, however that circle may be defined.

We should eliminate Dž-jyèn (#15, LY 5:3) who figures in the 05c Analects, but is mentioned there not as a member of Confucius's circle, but as a worthy member of someone *else's*. His presence on the list is in all probability appropriative; an implicit claim that Confucius was virtually the only teacher in the 05c. Again, Confucius's and his brother's sons-in-law (#20–21; LY 5:1–2) are doubtful, since the daughters married to them will have thenceforth become part of *their* circles, and no longer part of Confucius's circle. On the other hand, Yén Hwéi's father Yén Lù (#24, LY 11:8) cannot have been a *doctrinal disciple*, but as the head of a poor family with a link to Confucius through his son, he may have been a *dependent* (11:8 shows him relying on Confucius for help with his son's funeral).

Entries #11–13 are a special case. It is clear in LY 5 that Dž-jāng, though a questioner, is not himself a protégé; he is reputed to be from Chýn. Dzv̄ng Shv̄m, said to be from Wŭ-chýng and pictured as living there in MC 4B31, cannot have passed his years of protégéship under Confucius; the lack of protégé acquaintance in his LY 7–8 also argues against his having been a member of the original circle; he is rather a latecomer, whose connection to the Confucian school was probably Dž-yóu, said in 6:14 to have been Steward of Wŭ-chýng. Tántái Myè-míng, the supposed protégé mentioned in 6:14, may be a kenning for Dzv̄ngdž: Dzv̄ng 曾 is cognate with dzv̄ng 增 "layer," while -tái 臺 means "raised platform." Similarly the personal name Shv̄m 參 is the name of a constellation (not identical with the Western constellation Orion, but centering on the star astronomers call ζ Orionis); the disyllabic personal name Myè-míng 滅明 "dim and brighten" might refer to the flickering of stars. In the pun-infested early Analects, this name may be a way of *mentioning* Dzv̄ngdž (perhaps the golden hopeful of the school at that point) without actually *naming* him. These entries suggest that the early school, including its LY 9 phase under Dzv̄ng Ywǽn, had a strongly southern focus, and that the Kŭng takeover in the 04c was in part a northern recapture. They are thus part of the history of the *school*, but do not represent persons actually in the Confucius *circle*, and need to be eliminated from the list to reveal that circle.

Disciples first mentioned in LY 11, such as Gāu Chái, may be allowed to stand; he is not sufficiently exemplary to be suspicious. Of names unknown to the Analects but having stories in the KZJY 38 list, Shújùng Hwèi (apparently of the same clan as Dž-lù) is dubious; he is seemingly mentioned (#40) only for his extreme youth. He is, as has been noted above, the peg on which an equally extravagant invention, the youthful Kŭng Sywǽn, is later hung. It will be safer to eliminate him.

What is left? Yén Lù in the upper half of the list, and all the unknowns on the lower half, are not plausible as future officials. They are more likely to be people who looked to Confucius for support, leadership, and perhaps social advancement. In short, we seem to have here an inventory of Confucius's *client circle*.

01	Yén Hwéɪ	顏回	子淵		40	Shújùng Hwèɪ	叔仲會	子期	54
02	Mǐn Sǔn	閔損	子騫	29	41	Yén Hv́	顏何	稱	
03	Rǎn Gv̄ng	冉耕	伯牛		42	Chín Dzǔ	秦祖	子南	
04	Rǎn Yūng	冉雍	仲弓		43	Syīrúng Jv̄n	奚容箴	子皙	
05	Dzǎɪ Yv́	宰予	子我		44	Gūngdzǔ Gōudz̄	公祖句茲	子之	
06	Dwānmù Sz̀	端木賜	子貢		45	Lyén Jyé	廉潔	曹	
07	Rǎn Chyóu	冉求	子有		46	Gūngsyī Yv́-rú	公西輿如	子上	
08	Jùng Yóu	仲由	子路		47	Hǎnfù Hēɪ	罕父黑	索	
09	Yén Yěn	言偃	子游	35	48	Gūngsyī Jv̄n	公西箴	子尚	
10	Bǔ Shāng	卜商	子夏		49	Rǎngsz̀ Chř	壤駟赤	子徒	
11	Jwānsūn Shř	顓孫師	子張	48	50	Rǎn Jì	冉季	子產	
12	Dzv̄ng Shv̄m	曾參	子輿	46	51	Sywē Bāng	薛邦	子徒	
13	Tántái Myè-míng	澹臺滅明	子羽	49	52	Shŕ Chǔ	石處	里	
14	Gāu Chái	高柴	子羔	40	53	Chyāu Shàn	鄡單	子家	
15	Mì Bù-chí	密不齊	子賤	49	54	Dzwǒrv́n Yǐng	左人郢	行	
16	Fán Syv̄	樊須	子遲	46	55	Dí Hēɪ	狄黑	皙	
17	Yǒu Rwò	有若	有	36	56	Shāng Dzv́	商澤	子秀	
18	Gūngsyī Chř	公西赤	子華	42	57	Rv̀n Bù-chí	任不齊	選	
19	Ywén Syèn	原憲	子思	36	58	Rúng Chí	榮祈	子祺	
20	Gūngyě Cháng	公冶長	子長		59	Yén Kwàɪ	顏噲	子聲	
21	Námgūng Tāu	南宮紹	子容		60	Ywén Táu	原桃	籍	
					61	Gūngjyēn Dìng	公肩定	中	
					62	Chín Fēɪ	秦非	子之	
24	Yén Yóu	顏由	路	6	63	Chīdyāu Tú	漆雕徒	文	
					64	Yēn Jí	燕級	思	
26	Chīdyāu Kāɪ	漆雕開	子若	11	65	Gūngsyà Shǒu	公夏守	乘	
27	Gūnglyáng Rú	公良孺	子正		66	Gōujǐng Jyāng	句井疆	子界	
28	Chín Shāng	秦商	丕茲	4	67	Bùshú Chv́ng	步叔乘	子車	
					68	Shŕ Dzwò-shǔ	石作蜀	子明	
					69	Gwēɪ Sywǎn	邦選	子斂	
					70	Shŕ Jř-cháng	施之常	子恒	
					71	Shv̄n Lyáu	申繚	子周	
33	Chín Rǎn	秦冉	開		72	Ywè Kàɪ	樂欬	子聲	
34	Rǎn Rú	冉孺	子魚	50	73	Yén Jř-pú	顏之僕	子叔	
35	Yén Syīn	顏辛	子柳	46	74	Kǔng Fú	孔弗	子蔑	
36	Bwó Chyén	伯虔	楷	50	75	Chīdyāu Chř	漆雕哆	子斂	
37	Gūngsūn Chǔng	公孫寵	子石	53	76	Sywǎn Chv́ng	懸成	子橫	
38	Tsáu Syv̀	曹卹	子循	50	77	Yén Dzǔ	顏祖	襄	
39	Shv̄n Chv̄ng	申樘	周						

弟子元籍
The Original 70-Member Register
As Compiled by the Kǔng Family in c0360 (7 names eliminated from DZJ)

The Client Circle. If we make the changes argued for above, and continue to retain Yŏu Rwò, very probably an early head of the school but still apparently under a ban as of c0360,[54] we arrive at the list of 63 shown opposite, as all that we are entitled to rely on for early information about the actual circle of Confucius. It carries more than conjectural conviction due to the presence on it of all sixteen Analects-documented original protégés, including (very probably) Shv́n Chv́ng and (less surely but still plausibly) Dž-sāng Bwódž. If these names were in exactly their Analects form, or were arranged in an Analects-based order (as are the 11:3 names), they could be simply an Analects extract, which could easily have been done in Hàn. As it is, the divergence from Analects form separates the list from the Analects, and gives it independent evidentiary value.

Our first impression of the list is that its surnames tend to repeat, and that the known protégés such as the three Rǎns tend to bring in their wake other bearers of that surname; in this case another two Rǎns. Similarly, behind the known protégés of that surname, we have another seven Yéns, two Gūngsyīs, two Chīdyāus, one Ywæn, and one Shv̄n. Surname clusters without a known protégé and which, like most of the above, are clearly of artisan origin, are two Shŕ 石 ("stone," grindstone maker? jadeworker?) and one Ywè 樂 "musician"). These artisan-origin persons and groups doubtless hoped for a court career, with its associated affluence (LY 4:5, 6:5), or at the very least for help with a contract to supply the court. The conclusion that suggests itself from the clustering of surnames is that a place in the protégé circle seems to have represented in many cases not the official aspiration of an individual, but the livelihood hope of a group.

Another class of entries represent relationship. The eight Yéns are probably a connection of Confucius's mother, the KZJY version of the list tells us that Chín Shāng (#28), one of four Chíns, was the son of an associate of Confucius's father, and the single Kǔng on the list (#74) is said in a late but plausible commentary to have been the son of Confucius's crippled elder brother.[55] It may be relevant that Confucius, once past his early struggles, was the proprietor of a landholding, and thus, besides the court contact which a landholding implies, able to feed people from his own resources. A poor man undergoing starvation can prolong the process by weekly visits to the table of a gentleman farmer.

The third systematic category, overlapping with the other two, is surnames of geographical origin: the four Chíns and two Shv̄ns mentioned above plus one each of Tsáu 曹, Sywē 薛, Chyāu 鄡, Shāng 商 (that is, Sùng), Yēn 燕, and Gwēi 邽. These together comprise twelve persons, or 19% of the entire list. They probably represent what has been called the exile community in which Confucius's father is conjectured, above, to have moved.

---

[54]We may note in passing that, with Dž-jāng and Dzv̄ngdž, he seems to be part of the southern group whose center was Dž-yóu. In the DJ under 0487 (Legge **Ch'un** 816a) he is represented as one of 300 footsoldiers picked for an assault on the camp of an invading Wú force. His service on the southern frontier might have brought him to the attention of Dž-yóu, who could have recommended him to Confucius (then still alive and with a mentor function in Lǔ). That this same passage also mentions Tántái Myè-míng reminds us that DJ is not a history, but the record of a stage in the evolution of a myth.

[55]For what it may be worth in a list which has passed through Kǔng hands, the use of this surname tends to suggest that Confucius and his brother had resumed the Kǔng surname in their lifetimes, most likely not later than the beginning of Dìng-gūng's reign.

01	Yén Hwéi	顏回	子淵					
02	Mǐn Sǔn	閔損	子騫	29	41	Yén Hŕ	顏何	稱
03	Rǎn Gvng	冉耕	伯牛		42	Chín Dzǔ	秦祖	子南
04	Rǎn Yūng	冉雍	仲弓		43	Syīrúng Jvn	奚容箴 子晢
05	Dzǎi Yŕ	宰予	子我		44	Gūngdzǔ Gōudž	公祖句茲 子之
06	Dwānmù Sž	端木賜	子貢		45	Lyén Jyé	廉潔	曹
07	Rǎn Chyóu	冉求	子有		46	Gūngsyī Yŕ-rú	公西輿如 子上
08	Jùng Yóu	仲由	子路		47	Hǎnfǔ Hēi	罕父黑	索
09	Yén Yěn	言偃	子游	35	48	Gūngsyī Jvn	公西箴	子尚
10	Bǔ Shāng	卜商	子夏		49	Rǎngsž Chŕ	壤駟赤 子徒
					50	Rǎn Jì	冉季	子產
					51	Sywē Bāng	薛邦	子徒
					52	Shŕ Chǔ	石處	里
14	Gāu Chái	高柴	子羔	40	53	Chyāu Shàn	鄡單	子家
					54	Dzwŏrŕn Yǐng	左人郢	行
16	Fán Syŵ	樊須	子遲	46	55	Dí Hēi	狄黑	晢
17	Yǒu Rwò	有若	有	36	56	Shāng Dzŕ	商澤	子秀
18	Gūngsyī Chŕ	公西赤	子華	42	57	Rvn Bù-chí	任不齊	選
19	Ywǽn Syèn	原憲	子思	36	58	Rúng Chí	榮祈	子祺
					59	Yén Kwài	顏噲	子聲
					60	Ywǽn Táu	原桃	籍
					61	Gūngjyēn Dìng	公肩定	中
					62	Chín Fēi	秦非	子之
24	Yén Yóu	顏由	路	6	63	Chīdyāu Tú	漆雕徒	文
					64	Yēn Jí	燕級	思
26	Chīdyāu Kāi	漆雕開	子若	11	65	Gūngsyà Shǒu	公夏守	乘
27	Gūnglyáng Rú	公良孺	子正		66	Gōujǐng Jyāng	句井疆	子界
28	Chín Shāng	秦商	丕茲	4	67	Bùshú Chvng	步叔乘	子車
					68	Shŕ Dzwò-shú	石作蜀	子明
					69	Gwēi Sywǎn	邽選	子斂
					70	Shŕ Jĭ-cháng	施之常	子恒
					71	Shvn Lyáu	申繚	子周
33	Chín Rǎn	秦冉	開		72	Ywè Kài	樂欬	子聲
34	Rǎn Rú	冉孺	子魚	50	73	Yén Jĭ-pú	顏之僕	子叔
35	Yén Syīn	顏辛	子柳	46	74	Kǔng Fú	孔弗	子蔑
36	Bwó Chyén	伯虔	楷	50	75	Chīdyāu Chŕ	漆雕哆	子斂
37	Gūngsūn Chǔng	公孫龍	子石	53	76	Sywǽn Chvng	懸成	子橫
38	Tsáu Syŵ	曹卹	子循	50	77	Yén Dzǔ	顏祖	襄
39	Shvn Chvng	申樘	周					

The Confucius Client Circle
As Derived from the Kǔng Family "Disciple" List of c0360 (Total: 63 Names)

Mentorship. We may now consider the age data on this list. If Confucius was born in the 8th month of 0549, he would have reached his 20th year, the transition to adulthood and eligibility to become a protégé, in the 8th month of 0530. But the list is presumably skewed by the Kǔng family's relocation of Confucius's birth year to 0552, which would put his year of matriculation back to 0533. Then to find the calendar year in which a protégé was seen *by the Kǔng list* as reaching the age of protégéship, we subtract the age from 0533. We excise Yén Lù and Chín Shāng, Confucius's same-generation contemporaries, and also eliminate Chīdyāu Kāi.[56] We then get the following distribution, by year, of 12 protégéship inceptions:

```
                                                          x
                    x                          x          x
    x               x    x          x    x     x          x          x
  0504    0501    0498    0495    0492    0489    0486    0483    0480
```

In other words, a third of these protégéships begin under Dìng-gūng, most of them in the last four years of his reign (beginning precisely in 0498, the year of the Lǔ walling initiative which was earlier suggested as a probable index that Confucius might have been acceptable at court), another third in the early years of Aī-gūng, and a final third stacked up in the years 0483 and after, most of them precisely in that year (that of the new tax policy, which probably increased the importance of office relative to landholding, and thus put new pressure on the protégé system). We may note that there is no support in these figures[57] for the idea that Confucius increased his teaching after withdrawing from court; on the contrary, his teaching, or rather mentorship, seems to be coordinated with his holding a position at court. On the other hand, there is a much support in them for the general career trajectory which was conjectured above: obscurity in the early part of Dìng-gūng's reign, access in the last part of that reign, full visibility in the early years of Aī-gūng, and a special impetus given to the protégé system as a whole in 0483.

Confucius's function as a mentor was then a by-product of his court career, and we cannot validly envision him as a teacher in his early years, or after his retirement in 0481. His function as a leader in the circle which the client list reveals to us will have been earlier, and must have played its role in his Dìng-gūng period.

It remains to say, of Confucius as a teacher, that the respectful Chinese term Kǔng Fūdž 孔夫子, which supposedly lies behind the missionary Latinization "Confucius," is not a native term, but itself an invention of Western missionaries.[58]

---

[56]Whose given age differential is the unlikely 11. SJ 67 does not give an age for Chīdyāu Kāi, so influence from this text is eliminated as a factor. The content of the KZJY 38 entry tells us that Kāi declined office not, as in LY 5:6 because he was not yet perfected in good faith, but because he was absorbed in the study of the Shàng-shū (the Shū Jīng). This can only be a post-04c story, and we must assume that the curious age also reflects some late notion of the life history of Confucius. We ignore it here.

[57]Such as they are; the key first ten are missing from KZJY. Of the SJ figures, which Wáng Sù apparently copied into his edition of KZJY, Wáng himself notes that they are self-contradictory, that for Yén Hwéi being inconsistent with the LY 11:8 claim that he postdeceased Bwó-yw̌. The reason for their excision may be precisely that they could not be reconciled with the internally inconsistent later myth of Confucius and his disciples.

[58]Jensen **Invention**.

The Kŭng Family Successors

Presumption. The list of Kŭng descendants at the end of SJ 47 begins with Confucius's son Bwó-yẃ, who predeceased him. Next is Dž-sz̄, said to be Bwó-yẃ's son and the author of the Jūng Yūng: both a lineal and a doctrinal successor. When Syẃndž attacks "Dž-sz̄ and Mencius," he presumably means the school of Lŭ, with Dž-sz̄ its chief posthumous leader and Mencius its most prominent later product.[59] The Mencius text contains vignettes of Dž-sz̄,[60] presumably reflecting Mencius's own impressions,[61] which depict Dž-sz̄ as on familiar terms with the Lŭ Prince.

This implied direct-succession picture collapses upon examination. If Dž-sz̄ had directly succeeded Confucius, the Prince who showed him such favor would have been Āi-gūng (r 0494–0469), but the Mencian material shows him as minister to Mù-gūng (r 0410–0378), a gap of at least sixty years, or about two generations.

The same discrepancy is latent in the SJ list itself. The names, formal names, and ages at death (here listed as "aet") of these Kŭngs, counting Confucius as generation 1 and Bwó-yẃ as generation 2, appear in SJ 47 as follows:

3. Kŭng Jí 伋	Dž-sz̄ 子思		aet 62
4. Kŭng Bwó 白	Dž-shàng 子上		aet 47
5. Kŭng Chyóu 求	Dž-jyā 子家		aet 45
6. Kŭng Jī 箕	Dž-jīng 子京		aet 46
7. Kŭng Chwān 穿	Dž-gāu 子高		aet 51
8. [no personal name]	Dž-shv̀n 子慎	minister in Ngwèi	aet 57
9. Kŭng Fù 鮒		erudite of Chv́n Shv̀	aet 57

Later generations are in Hàn, and do not concern us here. #9, Fù, is said to have died with Chv́n Shv̀, whose reign of less than a year ended in 0208. Assuming that Fù had not yet reached his birthday in that year, his lifespan is then c0265–0208. Fù could not have succeeded as school head before his 20th year, 0246. By then, Lŭ was extinct and his father, the previous school head, had emigrated to Ngwèi.

At 25 years per birth generation, Dž-sz̄'s birthdate will be 6 generations or 150 years before Fù's birthdate c0265, or c0415. Then Dž-sz̄ reached adulthood in 0396, and could have served Mù-gūng as Mencius implies, but never Āi-gūng. Therefore, Dž-sz̄ was neither the grandson of Confucius nor his direct successor. But he could have succeeded Dzv̄ng Ywǽn, whose LY 9 we have dated to c0405, and with slight adjustments in the dates, this is what we assume actually happened.

[59]SZ 6:7, Knoblock **Xunzi** 1/224. This attack has been a problem for later Confucians (see Knoblock 1/214f and 1/245f), but it rings true as a piece of Warring States polemic. Syẃndž deplored the influence of the Lŭ school, and on the evidence of LY 17 and 19, the feeling was mutual. The Mencians and the Syẃndž school had a separate debate on human nature (MC 6A1–8 versus SZ 23); the Analects weighs in with LY 17:2, supporting the Mencian side of that debate. The Jūng Yūng, credited to Dž-sz̄, has echoes in LY *6:28 (citing the name Jūng Yūng) and in the Mencius, again emphasizing their closeness. It is this polarity between the Analects and Mencius on the one hand, and Syẃndž on the other, to which the irascible SZ 6:7 remark evidently refers.

[60]Dž-sz̄ in his role as a person of consequence in Lŭ is mentioned in MC 2B11, 5B6, 5B7, and 6B6 (he appears in other connections in MC 4B31 and 5B3).

[61]Mencius himself (c0387–c0303) can hardly have known Dž-sz̄ directly, but he was probably a student in the Lŭ school at a time when memories of him were still current.

It is notable that all Kŭngs in the SJ list who may be presumed to have served as Lŭ school heads have the Dž- prefix on their formal names, whereas Fù, who could not have done so, lacks that prefix. The distinction is not one of office, since Fù held office under a ruler. The prefix thus confirms the implication of the dates.

Wáng Sù repeats the SJ list in his postface to KZJY, with some variants:

3. Kŭng Jí 伋	Dž-sž 子思		aet 62
4. Kŭng Bwó 白	Dž-shàng 子上		aet 47
5. Kŭng Aù 傲	Dž-jyā 子家		aet 45
later named Chyóu 求			
6. Kŭng Kv̆ 槾	Dž-jŕ 子直		aet 46
7. Kŭng Chwān 穿	Dž-gāu 子高		aet 57
8. Kŭng Wŭ 武	Dž-shùn 子順	minister in Ngwèi	aet 57
named Wēı 微, later named Bīn 斌			
9. Kŭng Fù 鮒	Dž-yw̆ 子魚	erudite of Chv̆n Shv̀	–
later named Jyǎ 甲			

Besides the changes, and the addition of a personal name in generation 8, this list moves the two "aet 57" up a generation, leaving generation 9 blank. It extends the Dž- prefix to Fù. In SJ 47, Fù dies without issue, and the line continues through his younger brother; the KZJY preface assigns Fù a son, and a grandson who served Hàn Gāu-dzŭ and was present at the battle of Gāı-syà (0202). If we conveniently forget the date of Chv̆n Shv̀'s (and Fù's) death, this effectively adds two additional generations to the pre-Hàn Kŭng succession, thus implicitly filling the Dž-sž gap.

The Kŭng Tsúngdž (KTZ) fills it a different way, by attributing to Dž-sž himself an age at death of 78, and assigning the following lifespans,[62]

2. Kŭng Lĭ 鯉	Bwó-yw̆ 伯魚	–0483	
3. Kŭng Jí 伋	Dž-sž 子思	0479–0402	[aet 78]
4. Kŭng Bwó 白	Dž-shàng 子上	0429–0383	[aet 47]
5. Kŭng Chyóu 求	Dž-jyā 子家	0390–0346	[aet 45]
6. Kŭng Kv̆ 槾	Dž-jŕ 子直	0351–0306	[aet 46]
7. Kŭng Chwān 穿	Dž-gāu 子高	0312–0262	[aet 51]
8. Kŭng Wŭ 武	Dž-shùn 子順	0293–0237	[aet 57]
9. Kŭng Fù 鮒	Dž-yw̆ 子魚	0264–0208	[aet 57]

still leaving four years between Bwó-yw̆'s death and the birth of his supposed son Dž-sž.[63] These KTZ and KZJY preface variants are labored rather than convincing, and in the present book we have followed SJ 47 as the earliest evidence.

The Kŭng Lineage of the Analects is reconstructed at right from SJ 47, from the arithmetical fact that at least one of the Kŭng heads must have succeeded as a minor, and from the observed fact that LY 12–13 seem to reflect such a situation, LY 12 being strikingly Mencian, and LY 13 less so. The known date of Mencius's departure from Lŭ (c0321) establishes a historically fixed point for these inferences. These limits taken together do not uniquely determine a chronology, but rather a family of generally similar chronologies; our suggestion represents one of these.

---

[62]As extracted from KTZ by Ariel **K'ung** 8.

[63]Which, with divergences as to whether Fù or his brother hid the wall texts and other matters, Ariel **K'ung** 13f tries to reconcile. He does *not* try to rationalize the KTZ 5 dialogues between Confucius (KTZ deathdate 0479) and Dž-sž (KTZ birthdate 0479).

0439   [Kŭng Dž-sž born]
0436 Death of Dzv̄ngdž   LY 8
0435 Dzv̄ng Ywǽn succeeds as school head
0408   [**Last of several Chí attacks on Lŭ border**]
0405 Dzv̄ng Ywǽn aet 68?   LY 9
0404 Dzv̄ng Ywǽn dies (aet c69?); succession possibly uncertain

Kŭng Succession Begins

0402 Dž-sž becomes school head, aet 38
0399   [Kŭng Dž-shàng born]
0387   [Mencius born]
0380 Dž-sž aet 60   LY 10
0378 Dž-sž dies, aet 62
0377 Dž-shàng succeeds, aet 24
0372   [Kŭng Dž-jyā born]
0360 Dž-shàng aet 40   LY 11
0354 Dž-shàng dies, aet 46
0353 Dž-jyā succeeds, aet 20
0342   [Chí Kingship proclaimed]
0342 Dž-jyā aet 31   LY 3
0340   [Kŭng Dž-jīng born]
0328 Dž-jyā dies, aet 45
0327 Dž-jīng aet 14; Mencius among interim supervisors
0326 Dž-jīng aet 15, relatively compliant; much Mencian input   LY 12
0322 Dž-jīng aet 19, more assertive; less Mencian input   LY 13
0321 Dž-jīng succeeds, aet 20; Mencius leaves Lŭ
0321   [Kŭng Dž-gāu born]
0320   [Mencius begins public career, aet c66]
0317 Dž-jīng aet 24, Lŭ Píng-gūng 1st year   LY 2
0310 Dž-jīng aet 31   LY 14
0305 Dž-jīng aet 36   LY 15
0295 Dž-jīng dies, aet 46
0294 Dž-gāu succeeds, aet 28   LY 1
0293   [Kŭng Dž-shv̀n born]
0285   [Chí conquest of Sùng]
0285 Dž-gāu aet 37   LY 16
0271 Dž-gāu dies, aet 51
0270 Dž-shv̀n succeeds, aet 24   LY 17
0265   [Kŭng Fù born]
0262 Dž-shv̀n aet 32   LY 18
0255   [Chŭ conquest of southern Lŭ]
0254   [Syẃndž becomes Director in Lán-líng]
0253 Dž-shv̀n aet 41   LY 19
0251 Dž-shv̀n aet 43   LY 20:1
0250 Dž-shv̀n aet 44   LY 20:2–3
0249   [Chŭ extinguishes Lŭ]
0249 Dž-shv̀n aet 45; goes to Ngwèı
0243   [Ngwèı minister Syı̀n-líng Jyẃn dies]
0242 Dž-shv̀n **becomes minister in Ngwèı**
0237 Dž-shv̀n **dies in Ngwèı, aet 57**
0209 **Fù takes office as erudite under Chv́n Shv̀**
0208 **Fù dies in the fall of Chv́n, aet 57**

Chronology of the Kŭng Succession
Data known from SJ 67 or other sources in **bold**

The Fate of the Major Disciples

It will be obvious that there is tension between the 05c protégés and the Kŭng lineage, with the Kŭngs first attempting (LY 11) to discredit the disciples, and then (with Wáng Sù and the KTZ) to deny their existence altogether. It is against this background of rival legitimacies that the evolution of the disciples must be seen. One milestone in this evolution is LY 5–6 (c0460). From a century later, we have:

The LY 11:3 Ten (c0360), whose members are often valued for other qualities than they were praised for, or for just the qualities they *lacked*, in the earlier LY 5–6:

Name	LY 5–6 (c0470–0460)	LY 11:3 (c0360)
Yén Hwéi	intent on virtue	virtuous conduct
Mǐn Dž-chyēn	politically scrupulous	virtuous conduct
Rǎn Gvng	vaguely esteemed	virtuous conduct
Rǎn Yūng	rv́n, not glib; able to govern	virtuous conduct
Dzǎi Wǒ	lazy, uncommitted, punning	skill in language
Dž-gùng	elegant but overrates himself	skill in language
Rǎn Chyóu	corrupt in office	administration
Dž-lù	adequate for recruiting	administration
Dž-yóu	good administrator	culture
Dž-syà	betrays the higher culture	culture

Except for Dž-yóu, the last six were largely dispraised in LY 5–6, but are here given an honorable place; the reversal of 05c opinion is fairly comprehensive. It is simplest to take 11:3 as a revision, rather than a summary, of the earlier Analects. The almost obsessive emphasis on Yén Hwéi in LY 11, like his top listing here, is probably the nearest the Kŭngs could come to insisting on a family connection, or at any rate to blaming the school's problems on the *lack* of a family connection.[64]

The LY 19 Five (c0253, from a century later) shows a drastic realignment from the 11:3 pantheon. The first five of the 11:3 ten do not appear at all. Two of the last five do appear, but are merely sacrificed to a controversialist tactic, being used to emblematize Sývndzian school heresies (as such, all three are disavowed in SZ 6). Of the two positive spokesmen for the chapter, one was not listed at all in 11:3:

Name	Place in LY 11:3	Role in LY 19
Dž-jāng	not listed	negative emblem
Dž-syà	#10, praised for culture	negative emblem
Dž-yóu	#9, praised for culture	negative emblem
Dzvngdž	not listed	chapter spokesman
Dž-gùng	#6, praised for eloquence	chapter spokesman

Whereas the first three (Dž-syà and Dž-yóu probably because of their identification with the Shī, the chief Sývndzian text) *represent* excesses of the Sývndzian school, the last two more directly *condemn* the Sývndzian age, with its fixed curriculum, its emphasis on depraved later cultural traditions, and its lack of reliance on the personal authority of Confucius. Here too, it seems to be only contemporary need, and not any documentary interest in historical truth as such, that drives the chapter.

---

[64]Note the power of accretion to affect the text's message. No Analects reader but has wondered what would have happened had insightful Yén Hwéi outlived stuffy Dzvngdž and so "influenced the subsequent development of the school" (Waley **Analects** 20).

We now attempt to summarize, from the viewpoint of the above argument, the origins, character, and later histories of the sixteen certain protégés, the two major posthumous Dzv̄ngdž and Dž-jāng, and the more shadowy Fán Chř.

Mǐn Dž-chyēn. By DZJ (assuming that it is using the relocated Confucius birthdate), he is the oldest protégé, born c0523. His Analects mentions are civilian, and he may have begun a protégéship at the civilian age of adulthood, in c0503 (Dìng-gūng 7). His surname suggests no occupation; his Dž- prefix implies social acceptance. His scrupulousness is noted in 6:9 and elaborated in 11:3 and 11:13. He is said to deserve his family's good opinion in 11:5, an early instance of the filiality motif, but he does not continue as emblematic of filiality, being replaced in that role by Dzv̄ngdž. He vanishes from the text after his LY 11 appearances.

Dž-yóu appears in 6:14 as a judicious administrator. As we read the DJ evidence, he was Steward of Wǔ-chv́ng by the 0487 (Āi-gūng 8) campaign in which Yǒu Rwò took part. Since this may not have been his first year in that post, and since the post itself cannot have been a first assignment, his protégéship under Confucius would seem to go back to Dìng-gūng, possibly c0497, after the walling initiative and near the time of Confucius's trip to Sùng. He must have had military credentials to be assigned to Wǔ-chv́ng, and so might have been among Confucius's escort in Sùng. By other evidence, he may have been the author of LY 5, and thus the leader of what can for the first time be called a school rather than a circle, though a less organized one than it became under Yǒudž. After his 6:14 mention he is enshrined in 11:3 (for culture, not administration; not wholly irrelevant given the artistic expertise implied by the form of LY 5), and recast as an apprentice of filiality in 2:7. His political stature is not forgotten: he gives a warning on remonstrance in *4:26[1] (c0294) and reappears as Wǔ-chv́ng Steward in a potshot at Syv́ndž in 17:3; he is also a negative emblem in LY 19. Though thus expended in symbolic controversy in the 03c Analects, he appears frequently and positively in the ritual collections such as the Lǐ Jì, thus completing the evolution begun in LY 2:7. He would appear to have been notable in both the early military and late civilian stages of the typical 05c career, and thus an ideal choice to head the first Confucian school in c0470, but to have been developed in later centuries only in the latter aspect.

Youdž. By DZJ, he was born c0516. As a military man, his apprenticeship may have been relatively late, and by the Wú campaign of 0487, when he was 28, he may not yet have had contact with Confucius, hence the suggestion that he owed his introduction to the senior protégé Dž-yóu, whom he may have met in 0487 at Wǔ-chv́ng. His surname suggests no occupation, but his lack of the Dž- prefix implies a modest background, as does the homely character of LY 6, which we assign to his authorship. His -dž suffix labels him as a head of the school, and if, as we infer, he was Dž-yóu's successor, his contact with Dž-yóu in 0487 may have paved the way; he praises Dž-yóu in 6:14. Despite being head in c0460, he is never mentioned in the early Analects (though Dzv̄ngdž at least must have known him) or the 11:3 pantheon, and does not appear at all until LY 12 (c0326). In 12:9 he is shown as advising Āi-gūng, implying the ministerial role that (according to the Mencius) Dž-sz̄ later had, and suggesting a considerable status for the school under his headship. He seems to have been the first to bear the -dž suffix, and thus the first to be head of an organized school; perhaps tensions associated with that change left a hostile legacy. In *1:12[19] (c0253) he appears as a ritual specialist, reflecting the nature of the 03c school and displaying the same evolution that we see with Dž-yóu, but not necessarily providing evidence for the historical Yǒu Rwò.

Dž-gùng. From his surname, he was from a palace-supplier background, and from his Dž- prefix, he was accepted in his time as having mastered the high culture. His role in later legend as the most devoted of Confucius's mourners suggests that he was the chief figure among whatever group of followers thought of themselves as constituting the immediate posthumous circle, and thus the most likely compiler of the LY 4 core sayings. The attempt of the next chapter, LY 5, to disabuse him of his impression of his own competence, may easily be a senior figure (Dž-yóu) putting in his place a younger whippersnapper who has temporarily and by default lucked into a role of influence. He fades out of view in the last half of the 05c, is enshrined for eloquence in the 11:3 pantheon, and then regains prominence as Dž-lù loses it; one or the other of the two functions narratively, at any given point, as the companion of Confucius and the counterfoil to Yén Hwéɩ. By LY 19, partly by the attrition of some rival figures, he has become the chief spokesman for the movement, and specifically for its stance of centering on the person of Confucius; his Analects trajectory attests the durability of the supporting role. 11:18a hints at wealth gained through trade, and SJ 67 (in which list his is by far the longest entry) recounts in the style of the Jàn-gwó Tsv̀ his diplomatic triumph on behalf of Chí, and notes that he died in Chí. He seems to have been ahead of his time in the 05c, but to have perfectly suited the mercantile culture of the 04c and 03c, thus enabling him to become an icon in Chí without at the same time being abandoned by Lǔ. He is also a frequent figure in the later Confucian ritual texts.

Dž-syà by his surname came by inherited palace connection to the same cultural expertise that Dž-gùng probably won through contact. From his first (and disapproving) appearance in 6:13 he is frequently associated with the Shī, thus doubtless explaining his place in the transmission genealogy of that text; in LY 19 he is the negative emblem of a fussy sort of ritualism associated (as the Shī itself had by then become associated) with the Syẃndž school. He may be said to symbolize both the pro and the con sides of the curricularizing tendency within the Analects. He figures occasionally in the later ritual compilations.

Chīdyāu Kāɩ is the visible member of three Chīdyāus in DZJ, all of artisan origin, and in the Analects lacking the accolade of the Dž- prefix. He appears only once (in 5:6, owning himself not ready for office), a fact which will astonish many Analects readers, since that appearance is an indelible one. An outside tradition also exists. HFZ 50 (c0150) mentions a Chīdyāu branch of Confucianism, emphasizing integrity in the face of danger; such a view is criticized in SZ 4:4 as the courage of the "little man," perhaps a gibe at its artisan origins, and MZ 39 (also 03c) notes Chīdyāu's "menacing" (tsán 殘) appearance as a sign of potential rebelliousness. Courage in the fractious sense is disapproved in the late Analects, and the eclipse of Kāɩ may be due to his becoming identified with it (Analects disapproval is aimed instead at Dž-lù, who also tends to vanish). HS 30 lists a Chīdyāudž in 13 chapters, which it attributes to a descendant (Chīdyāu Chǐ 啟) of the disciple.[65] Kāɩ's low age differential (11) in DZJ may be an attempt to bring both disciple and descendant within the client circle, as was done with the fathers of Yén Hwéɩ and Dzv̄ngdž; if so, the text (we cannot tell if it advised bellicosity) may have been of 03c date.

---

[65]Chǐ 啟 was the personal name of the pre-SJ Hàn Emperor Jǐng, and one would thus expect this name to be converted in HS 30 to the usual substitution Kāɩ 開, and in that form to court confusion with the disciple Kāɩ.

Shvn Chvng, whose instant of fame is in LY 5:11, is represented, though in a scribally garbled form, in the DZJ list, where he serves as one guarantor of the reality of that list. His forebears were apparently from the extinct state of Shvn, and he shows traits perhaps intelligible in a member of the Lǔ exile community: a firm determination to make good which, as "Confucius" makes clear in 5:11, is different from the poised equanimity required of the successful and ponderable gentleman.

Dž-sāng Bwódž has a much more positive instant of fame in LY 6:2 and a much more garbled survival as (perhaps) the Bwó Chyén of the DZJ list. As a grove proprietor, he will have had an economic fallback option, and his "laxity" in 6:2 agrees with the situation of someone who can afford to fail in the search for office.

Ywǽn Sz̄. His surname is not unequivocally informative; from 6:5 we know that he was in easy financial circumstances (able to decline an official salary, which it was the goal of many of the client group to obtain) but not socially certified by the Dž- prefix; socially, he seems to be a more successful version of Dž-sāng Bwódž. Confucius in 6:5 criticizes him for a lack of social imagination, a lesson more appropriate for the thoughtless rich (who regard money in symbolic rather than subsistence terms) than for the poor. His recurrence in 14:1a, where the issue is the propriety of service, including receipt of salary, is wholly in character. What Legge calls his "carelessness of worldly advantages" is literarily exaggerated as extreme poverty in JZ 28:11, where his principled answer abashes his rich and arrogant caller, none other than Dž-gùng. Ywǽn Sz̄ belongs with those Analects characters, of whom the best-known example is Yén Hwéi, who vanish from that text in the 03c and are absorbed instead into the literary repertoire of the Jwāngdž.

Dzǎi Yẃ has a possibly artisanal surname (it could also be derived from the "steward" or official sense of the word) and lacks the Dž- prefix; as with the three preceding figures, it is his shortcomings, chiefly energy and dedication, that dominate his 05c Analects appearances (in 5:10a/b and 6:26, the latter being a satire on the concept of rv́n). He is embraced by the Kǔngs and enshrined for his eloquence (6:26 involves a pun) in 11:3. In keeping with this new dignity he appears in 3:21 as a ritual expounder to Āī-gūng, but faithful to his 05c persona he is again criticized by "Confucius" for an inappropriate pun. In 17:19 he is brought back to symbolize the wrong (in this case, the Mician) side of a ritual question: the validity of the three-year mourning practice. He is thus literarily stable in the Analects, and does not migrate to the Jwāngdž. His pairing with Dž-gùng in 11:3 as "eloquent" may reflect an outside tradition of a career in diplomacy that existed already at that time (c0360); SJ 67 suggests such a development by claiming that he held office in Chí, was involved in a rebellion, and was executed with his family; even in myth he seems to have been an embarrassment to the school.

Rǎn Gv̄ng, like his two Analects kinsman seemingly of artisan stock, and without a Dž- prefix, dies regretted by Confucius in 6:10, is enshrined in the 11:3 pantheon (in the "virtue" category, perhaps implying the poverty which is suggested in 6:10), and is never heard from again, in the Analects or elsewhere.

Rǎn Yūng is defended by Confucius in 5:5 for lack of eloquence, and praised by him as having rulership capacity in 6:1, qualified by a 6:6 remark suggesting that his parentage rendered him socially ineligible for such a position. The Kǔngs in 11:3 pair him with Rǎn Gv̄ng as virtuous. He is a questioner in 12:2 (in close parallel with Yén Hwéi in 12:1), and breaks into office in 12:2 (under the Jì, but in the 04c that no longer carried an imputation of treachery). He vanishes thereafter.

Răn Chyóu, who *does* achieve office, is the success story of the Răn clan, but he is disapproved of (faintly in 5:8 and the parallel 6:8; openly in 6:4 and 6:12) for his conduct in office; even more than the lazy Dzăi Ýw or the presumptuous Dž-gùng, he is the villain of the 05c school. Apart from his enshrinment (for executive ability, in parallel with Dž-lù) in 11:3, he keeps this character even in the same chapter's 11:17 (compare the similar, and nearby, disapproval of Dž-lù in 11:15) and 11:22 (Dž-lù is faulted in the same passage), and through 3:6 and 13:14 to the last failure, and the last co-denunciation with Dž-lù, in the eloquent 16:1. Like some of his erring colleagues, Chyóu exits from the Analects only to reappear in the Jwāngdž (JZ 22:10), where he questions a Dàuized Confucius on "the time before Heaven and Earth existed," such cosmic speculations being only hinted at (17:17, c0270) or altogether interdicted (*5:13, also c0270) in the contemporary Analects.

Dž-lù is of ruler-connected stock, specifically the Shú clan who may have been the patrons of Confucius's father; his presence in the circle may thus be hereditary rather than meritocratic. In the 05c Analects he is faintly praised (5:8, 6:8) or chided (for his impostures at Confucius's death, 7:35; reworked in 9:12) but never shown in office; he once (7:19) intermediates between Confucius and a petty ruler. His parallelism with Răn Chyóu (from 11:3 and 11:15 to its climax in 16:1) may thus be a literary fiction. His literary symbiosis with Yén Hwéi, with his wrong answer the perfect counterfoil to Hwéi's right one, is another literary fiction, played out in just two interpolated passages (*5:26, c0294, and *7:11, c0310), a fact which will surprise many readers, for whom these anecdotes loom large. For the 05c, one gets the impression of a weak candidate whom the text, very understandably, is reluctant to criticize. In LY 11 he acquires a rash, even swashbuckling, persona (11:13b, reinforced by the interpolated *5:7 and *7:11), perhaps as a way of criticizing the Chīdyāu movement, which retained or exaggerated the military aspect of early Confucianism which the ritualistic Kŭngs were trying to replace. By the DJ (c0312), this has become a full-blown story of Dž-lù's death in a duel, defending his Wèi patron (Legge Ch'un 843). In real life (and in the scholarly rather than romantic tradition preserved in SJ 121) Dž-lù survived the Master; by LY 7–8 he was one of three disciples whom the posthumous Dzvngdž may have known. He switches roles with the Confucius of 7:19 in 17:4 and 6, disapproving of unsavory offices which Confucius is tempted to take, and alternates with Dž-gùng in the later Analects as the escort of Confucius; his last primary Analects appearance is in that role (18:6). Shortly thereafter, he is appropriated by the Jwāngdž in his basic late role as Confucius's companion, but once (JZ 28:15) as a swordsman, doing a sword dance.

Yén Hwéi, of probable artisan origin and without a Dž- prefix, was related to Confucius on his mother's side, and enjoys an unassailable narrative position in the early Analects (5:9, 6:3, 6:7, 6:11). Alone of the early circle, he is praised for his skill in mental concentration, and for his love of "study" (which in this precurricular age means mental self-cultivation); by 9:11 that study takes on a clearly transcendent character, and in 11:18b he is described as often "empty," a frequent codeword for meditative practices. Beginning in 12:1 he is treated with unwonted roughness and appears stupid rather than clever; in this same period the text first admits meditation as a second way of knowledge (2:15; in the nearby 2:9, Hwéi is defended against the imputation of stupidity) and later rejects it altogether (*15:31[15a], c0301; compare Hwéi's question about government in *15:11[15a]). Thereafter Hwéi vanishes from the Analects, but reappears in the Jwāngdž, in one case (JZ 6:7) as a meditative adept. He is the prime example of narrative obsolescence in the Analects.

Myths of Early Death. As with Dž-lù, but beginning earlier, there attaches to Yén Hwéı a myth that he predeceased Confucius. With Dž-lù, there is a double tradition (both parts of which figure in Hàn tradition, the romantic one in SJ 67 and the more plausible scholarly one in SJ 121). Yén Hwéı is treated as alive in 5:9 (c0470) and first treated as deceased in the probably retrospective 6:11 (c0460); the natural inference is that he died in c0465. Since Dzv̄ngdž alludes to him as dead but also as a friend in 8:5 (a recollected saying from before c0436), and since Dzv̄ngdž himself, on any reading of the evidence, came late to the school, the probability from this direct testimony also is that Yén Hwéı survived Confucius. The motif of his early death continues to be developed in the Analects as a great loss to the school, and reaches a peak of lamentation in LY 11, which would perfectly suit the agenda of the Kŭng linealists as against the Dzv̄ngdž meritocrats, but the utility of the myth merely explains the myth. In its final form it seems likely to be a thematic transfer from the fact of the early death of Confucius's son Bwó-yẃ. Conceivably the appearance of a parallel myth of Dž-lù is affected by the fact that he had in the meantime become narratively involved with Yén Hwéı.

Gūngsyī Hwá, possibly of artisan background, and (in 6:4) with an honorific Dž- prefix. He is mentioned with Dž-lù and Răn Chyóu as employable in 5:8, and shown on an official mission to Chí in 6:4; the dispute over the allowance granted his family by his colleague Răn Chyóu turns on the fact that Dž-hwá is wealthy. He is thus an upwardly mobile success story, but also an example of what Confucius in LY 4 dislikes about the culture of upward mobility. His DZJ age differential would give him a birthdate of c0510, reaching adulthood in c0490. Consistently with this, his 7:34 mention by Dzv̄ngdž (which does *not* use his Dž- prefix; the only Analects instance of variation in this usage) suggests he may have been known to Dzv̄ngdž. Interpolations apart, he vanishes from the text after LY 11, along with the vital 05c issues of legitimacy and corruption in office which he symbolized.

Dzv̄ngdž. His surname (there was a state of Dzv̄ng) suggests a member of the exile community in Lŭ; by tradition he was a resident not of the capital but of the southern fortress town of Wŭ-chv́ng. His dying credo in 8:3 suggests the energy of the outsider (compare Shv̄n Chv́ng). If, as suggested above (page 282), the odd name Tántáı Myè-míng in 6:14 is a kenning rubric for Dzv̄ngdž, under which he can be referred to, and praised, without violating contemporary literary convention, his scrupulousness in office may also be a trait of the meritocratic social newcomer. With Dž-yóu and Dž-jāng, he represents the southern focus which is conspicuous in the 05c school. Unless we are prepared to accept the possibility of random or hostile interpolations in the text, we must take LY 8:3–7 as proving that at the time of his death (0436) Dzv̄ngdž was the head of the Lŭ school. Given the thematic features common to those sayings and LY 7, he was the author of LY 7 and thus the architect of a major change in the perception of Confucius. As the chief figure in 05c Confucianism, he is damned by omission and innuendo in LY 11:3 and 11:18a, respectively, but is later rehabilitated in a domestic (12:24, 1:4) and increasingly ritualized (1:9, c0294) mode, more compatible with the Kŭng agenda. He is a ritual spokesman, apparently in a positive sense, in his last bow in 19:16–18. At some point after his death he acquired, if not his own school, at any rate his own text. This is recorded in the HS 30 Palace library catalogue as having 18 chapters, and seems to have been included, perhaps entire, in Dà Dàı Lĭ 49–58; it was still extant in early Táng. Dzv̄ngdž is also frequently quoted in the Hàn ritual compilations. This late, "outside" (non-Analectal) Dzv̄ngdž tradition still awaits systematic study.

Dž-jāng, said to be from Chv́n, is unlikely as a protégé of Confucius in Lŭ. His DZJ-implied birth year is 0503 (two years younger than Dzv̄ngdž), so that he came of age in 0485. He is a bystander in LY 5–6 and does not make the 11:3 pantheon. We infer that like Dzv̄ngdž he is one of Dž-yóu's coterie of southern-connected people. His literary role in the early text is the neutral questioner, who exists to elicit a wise comment from Confucius. His role expands in the late chapters; at the end, he is the sole survivor: the only disciple who appears in LY 20.

Fán Chŕ is also a questioner rather than a candidate on his earliest appearance (6:22), but, unlike Dž-jāng, he does not develop into a major figure; he is still a questioner (not a notably perceptive one) in the late 04c, and vanishes thereafter.

The Dubious Disciples, those who appear first in the Kŭng period, are suspect as literary inventions. It is notable, for instance, that the plausible Lín Fàng, who appears only in LY 3:4 and 3:6, is not claimed as a disciple on any of the later lists. We assume, however, that those first mentioned in LY 11 are probably sound, since it was evidently the intention of that chapter not to create a new disciple tradition but to revise a known one. For Gāu Chái, the decisive passage is not his patronage by Dž-lù (11:23), since this might be a case of second-order clientship, but 11:18a, where he is plonked with the chapter enemy Dzv̄ngdž, and where it would serve no literary purpose to introduce an unfamiliar personage. In general, no later tradition or text ascription attaches to later-mentioned people, while Dž-jyèn, manifestly not a disciple in 5:3 but nevertheless *appearing* in 5:3, has a Mìdž 宓子 attributed to him in the HS 30 catalogue, along with an associated work, the Jǐngdž 景子, which is said to comment on the Mìdž sayings and to be (seemingly) by a Dž-jyèn disciple. It would seem that, whether genuine protégés or not, the 05c names had a market value denied to those of later appearance, and thus lesser pedigree. It follows that the later centuries *still knew* what in the Analects went back to the earlier centuries. This awareness may affect the placing of interpolations, only the early school heads, for example, being honored with sayings interpolated into the LY 4 core.

The Nobodies. DZJ #34–38 are persons who, except for Bwó Chyén (#36, if he is rightly identified with Dž-sāng Bwódž), are unknown to the Analects but also not obvious myths. They have age differentials of 46 (Yén Syīn), 50 (Rǎn Rú, Tsáu Syẁ), and 53 (Gūngsūn Chǔng). Yén Syīn would have come of age in 0487, and Bwó Chyén, Rǎn Rú and Tsáu Syẁ in 0483, Confucius being still active at court; Gūngsūn Chǔng would have come of age in 0480, the year after his retirement. It seems that even these late arrivals expected, and in Bwódž's case actually got, counsel pursuant to a career, but also that the people Confucius attracted in those last years were not of the same quality or status as his earliest protégés, and that his degree of real or anticipated court influence, not his reputation as a philosopher, was the key factor in his attraction of protégés. The youngest, Gūngsūn Chǔng, would appear to be an aspirant to office who gambled on Confucius's continued longevity, and lost. For him, the LY 4 maxims as remembered by older colleagues would have had a real-life function as a surrogate mentor.

Summing Up. We note in conclusion that nowhere in the above discussion does post-05c data plausibly augment 05c data; in many cases it clearly reflects a later agenda. The inference is that a picture based solely on early data, even though (as with Yén Hwéi's death) sometimes shocking to readers schooled in the integral Analects, is truer than one contaminated by late data. The line between the two is probably to be located after LY 6, with LY 7–9 still containing usable impressions, and the Kŭng period from LY 10 on being increasingly revisionist and mythological.

Appendix 5
A Reading of LY 1–4 in Text Order

Analects 1–4 are here presented, not in their historical order, but in the order that they have in the text in its presumed final form, which we conclude it had reached as of the Chǔ conquest of 0249, and which it still has in all later versions. Besides reverting to this sequence, we have also restored the interpolated passages which in the main translation were relocated to their approximate chronological position. These four chapters are thus presented here in the sequence in which latter-day readers have always encountered them.

Putting the preposed chapters LY 1–3 *in initial position* before LY 4 makes it possible for readers familiar with the order of the present text to consult those chapters in their familiar places; in that sense, this Appendix serves as a supplement of convenience to the main translation, where only from LY 4 onward do the order of chapter composition and that of chapter sequence coincide. The agreement with the standard text is made yet greater by the presence of the restored interpolations.

What one discovers on thus rearranging the text is that changing the sequence of the text *also significantly changes its meaning.* The principal effect of the change is to give the entire Analects the character of the three preposed chapters, making this originally eccentric material (LY 1, especially, is from an atypical period of disengagement from contemporary politics) decisive in establishing a context for the study and appreciation of the work. Thus, in contrast to the Original Analects which the present book has attempted to rediscover, this Appendix presents a sample of the Final Analects. The versions of LY 1–4 passages given here are therefore not simply repeated from the main translation, but are *different from them* at points where the rearrangement either obscures the original sense or imposes a new one. In addition to its convenience value, this Appendix offers the reader an opportunity to see in detail how the meaning of the earlier parts of the text *at the time they were written* was obscured and uniformized in its final preposed and interpolated form.

The Principal Changes

The first thing that preposing LY 1–3 accomplishes is to emphasize their contents *by having the reader encounter them first,* without any precedents or antecedents, so that they form the reader's first impression of Confucius's teachings, and establish a framework of understanding for everything that follows. The mixing of text strata also blurs the evolutionary aspect of the text. The tension between the feudal value "rýn" and the technician's value "knowledge" vanishes, as does the contrast between the empirical Confucius of LY 4 and the cultural transmitter Confucius of LY 7 and later. These and other developmental differences certainly persist in the work in its mixed-strata form, but when noticed at all, they tend to be reduced by readers to their *historically latest terms.*

Second, the presence of the interpolated passages formally interrupts and obscures the original pattern of paired sayings (which in any case was already weak in some chapters), thus disabling the pairing principle as a factor in interpretation. Except for a few striking instances which commentators have always recognized, this all but *eliminates the microcontexts* and strengthens the uniformizing tendency by releasing the local saying into the context of the entire work.

Third is the loss of chapter *sections*, which like the pairing pattern were already weakly distinguished in some cases, and were further compromised over the life of the text by the addition of interpolations. These interpolations, as we have shown above, were not placed at random, but were inserted at carefully chosen points, to update an early idea by juxtaposing a later form of that idea. This artfulness gives the interpolations an effect even greater than their very considerable number (27% of the text) might suggest. The interpolations did not by any means always achieve their intended purpose for all readers, as the scholarly dispute over the outrageous LY 9:1 illustrates. But on the whole, they did succeed in reducing the perceived historical differences between chapters, and the suggestive original clusterings within chapters, thus largely neutralizing their interpretative importance.

In consequence, the dates assigned to chapters in the main translation do not appear here, the presumption of post-Hàn readers being that all the material is more or less *from*, or, if parts of it are scribally later, still more or less accurately *reflects*, the lifetime of Confucius. This is the fourth difference.

Fifth and last, in the Final Analects there are not perceived to be significant differences between the *authors* of different chapters. That the chapters are *different* no one has ever denied, but once these differences are seen as reflecting only the different limitations of the several original disciples, as all the Hàn and later commentaries assume, they lose analytical interest in a tradition whose sole focus is the Confucius persona. Author names are thus not mentioned in what follows. Confucianism speaks with one voice.

Cautionary Marks

As a warning to readers of convenience, and a guideline to others, the points where the wording of the translation has been changed to fit the new context, or where the old wording has a different impact because of that context, are indicated by **boldface** type. The nature of the difference is explained in the commentary.

Envoi

It would be undersanguine to close with the thought that the changes here discussed irretrievably obscured the original thought and character of Confucius. That character, in part enigmatic as it must always remain, somehow survives as a stalwart dedication, a generous anger, that percolates through the larger mass of the later Analects. We feel in the Analects, as we do not in the partly contemporary Gwǎndž, for example, the enduring presence of a forceful personality.

Nor, philosophically, need the blending of the Final Analects be seen as a loss. We have been at pains to show, in the main commentary, how the successors of Confucius broke new and valuable ground in adjusting their inheritance to the changing needs of postfeudal society; in the process making it of far more than antiquarian interest for other postfeudal societies. The sentimental reader may deplore the diluting of the original historical Confucius; the practical reader will instead welcome the nourishing of an ongoing Confucianism. The question is whether the text as finally configured, with its structural pressure from precisely the atypical, preposed chapters, does sufficient justice to this Final Confucianism. On that point, not to anticipate the results of the small experiment in practical reading which follows, it seems to us that there are plentiful reasons for concern, but also nontrivial grounds for hope.

1

This is the page at which the present-day reader opens the Analects, and these are thus the sayings which define the context of all that follows.

The numbering of passages is identical in the Legge text.

1:1. The Master said, To learn and in due time rehearse it: is this not **indeed** pleasurable? To have friends coming from far places: is this not **indeed** delightful? If others do not recognize him, but he is not disheartened, is he not **indeed** a gentleman?

> The repeated yì 亦, originally "also," are here merely exclamatory ("indeed"); 1:1 is the first saying in the book, and there is nothing with which "also" can contrast. Thus, an *alternate* road to virtue (memorizing texts) has become the *only* road. In our own century, the academic tone of 1:1 has made its first line a favorite for scholarly conference participants to quote to each other.

1:2. Yŏudž said, One whose deportment is filial and fraternal but loves to oppose his superiors, is rare. One who does not love to oppose his superiors but does love to foment disorder, has never existed. The gentleman works on the basis; when the basis is set, then the Way comes to exist. Filiality and fraternity are the basis of rv́n, are they not?

> We first encounter rv́n as underlaid by domestic and hierarchical virtues (respect toward fathers and elder brothers), and itself the basis of public order. A filial citizenry is one schooled in docility, the Way at which 1:2 aims.

1:3. The Master said, Artful words and an impressive appearance: seldom are they rv́n.

> Whatever rv́n is, it is incompatible with artifice and insubstantiality.

1:4. Dzv̄ngdž said, I daily examine myself in three ways: in planning on behalf of **others**, have I been disloyal? In associating with friends, have I been unfaithful? What has been transmitted to me, have I not rehearsed?

> This anxious self-concern becomes our model for personal duty. The domestic limitation on "others" in the original 1:4 is for some readers skewed back into the public-service area by the interpolated 1:5, below; see however 1:6n.

1:5. The Master said, To lead a state of a thousand chariots, be assiduous in administration and keep faith; make expenditures frugally and be solicitous of others; and employ the people according to the season.

This rulership interpolation now helps offset the domestic focus of LY 1.

1:6. The Master said, A student when at home should be filial, when away from home should be fraternal. He should be circumspect but faithful, should love all the multitude but be intimate only with the rv́n. If after doing this he has any strength left over, then he can use that to study culture.

> "Fraternal" weakens the public meaning of "away from home" (Huang glosses it as "at school"), and reinforces the domestic sense of the first line of 1:4.

1:7. Dž-syà said, He sees the worthy as worthy; he makes light of beauty. If in serving father and mother he can exhaust his strength; if in serving his ruler he can bring all his faculties to bear; if in associating with friends he always keeps his word – though one might say that has not "studied," I would certainly call him a scholar.

> This more public original saying in turn aids 1:5 against 1:6. It also helps, as it originally did, to dilute the book-learning focus established in 1:1.

1:8. The Master said, If he is not solid he will not be held in awe; if he studies, he will not be rigid. Let him put first loyalty and fidelity, let him not make friends of those who are not at the same level as himself, and if he makes a mistake, then let him not be afraid to **change**.

> The "it" of the original "change *it*" was in the contraction vùt 勿. But the preposed-object rule no longer held in Hàn, and vùt was seen as a mere variant of the basic negative "do not." Rather than correcting the *error*, the reader was thus instructed to correct the *self*, as in the self-perfection theory of 1:2. This is how Sei Shōnagon understood the passage; see the main translation at 1:8n.

1:9. Dzv̄ngdž said, When concern for the departed continues until they are far away, the virtue of the people will have become substantial.

> The emphasis on the funerary side of domestic piety, linking up with the filial image which Dzv̄ngdž presents in Hàn and later legend.

1:10. Dž-chín asked Dž-gùng, When our respected Master arrives in some country, he always manages to hear about its government. Does he seek this, or does he wait until they give it to him? Dž-gùng said, Our Respected Master is warm, genial, respectful, restrained, and deferential; in this way he gets it. Our Respected Master's "seeking" is perhaps different from other people's seeking, is it not?

> He invites it rather than directly asking it. This diplomatic saying would seem to reinforce the public aspect of the chapter, but late school tradition (Huang refers to "Six Classics") sees an ultimately scholastic focus even here.

1:11. The Master said, When his father is living, watch his intentions; when his father is deceased, watch his actions. If for three years he has not changed from the ways of his father, he can be called filial.

> This uses the the three-year mourning as a touchstone for inferring character. The trait here prized is a willing inner subordination to the father's authority.

1:12. Yǒudž said, In the practice of ritual, harmony is to be esteemed. The Way of the Former Kings was beautiful in this: in small things and great they followed it. If there is something that does not go right, one should recognize the principle of harmony, and then it will become harmonious. But if it is not moderated by ritual itself, it still won't go right.

> This piece of ritual theory was inserted between 1:11 (on mourning) and 1:13 (where the speaker is Yǒudž), giving a seemingly consecutive group of three sayings. It recommends concord as a guiding principle, but notes that this flexibility must be guided by a sense of ritual propriety. The ultimate concord is thus not with circumstances, but with the ritual intent. Compare 2:5, below.

1:13. Yŏudž said, If his promises are close to what is right, his word can be relied on. If his respect is close to propriety, he will avoid shame and disgrace. If he marries one who has not wronged her own kin, she can be part of his clan.

These office and family guidelines are given extra depth by the preceding 1:12 statement of a general ritual principle underlying ordinary human affairs. It is this deeply sacramental view of human life, seen not as a particular stage in the development of Confucianism but as suffusing all of Confucianism from its inception (a perception which the sequence 1:11–13 aims precisely to evoke), that is developed in Fingarette **Sacred**.

1:14. The Master said, If a gentleman in his eating does not seek to be filled and in his dwelling does not seek comfort, if he is assiduous in deed and cautious in word, if he associates with those who possess the Way and is corrected by them, he can be said to love learning.

The general air of personal restraint in this passage raises no problems either with the original chapter or with its highlighted and augmented new message.

1:15. Dž-gùng said, "Poor but does not flatter, rich but does not sneer" – how would that do? The Master said, It would do. But it is not as good as "Poor but happy, rich but loving propriety." Dž-gùng said, The Poem says, "As though cut, as though ground, as though smoothed, as though polished" – is this what it means? The Master said, Sż can at last be talked with about the Poetry: I tell him things in terms of the past, and he knows what is to come.

Further praise of the restrained temperament, with the original "propriety" here liable to interpretation in the stronger sense "ritual propriety" and thus smoothly accepting the impetus given to the whole chapter in 1:12, and giving it in turn the further authority of the now more widely accepted classic Shř.

1:16. The Master said, He does not worry that others do not know him; he worries that he does not know others.

This saying now anticipates, and in the consecutive reader's mind replaces, the prototype 4:14 and its sequels. In 4:14 the paired clauses are both based on verbal puns: wèi 位 "position" and lì 立 "stand," and jř 知 "recognize" in both its active and passive moods. Even as altered from the sonorous and courtly prototype 4:14 (and its largely compatible later sequels *14:30[15a] and *15:19[15a]), this saying preserves something of a classic 05c sense of duty, involving the redirection of resentment into more useful channels, but the elimination of the public political ambience that characterized 4:14 and its successors is still vital. The force of 1:16 is social rather than solipsistic, but the society within which it will be imagined as operating hardly exceeds that implied in the keystone saying 1:1 – a group of like-minded individuals, bent on improving themselves, and qualifying as gentlemen precisely by their lack of resentment (one might almost say lack of concern) toward the outer political world. That is, the old, vertical-ethic saying has here become lateralized. It is a stage in the evolution toward the later, also interpolated *6:30[18], which spells out in detail how reciprocal concern for others is supposed to work. We are in the altruist world of DDJ 49 (compare LY *14:34[17]) and DDJ 63.

In retrospect, we may see that 1:16 was probably fashioned as an intentional echo and reinforcement of 1:1, further emphasizing its keynote function.

Chapter Comment

Though for purposes of this Appendix all Analects sayings form a single mutual context, the chapter divisions are still there, and it is natural to ask, of LY 1, what central principle it implies. The answer might be that it is the ritual concept of appropriateness; the secular lǐ 禮 (see the note to 1:13) which probably derived from the literal sacrificial lǐ expertise developed in the 04c Confucian school. The original sacramental sense of lǐ is also alive in the chapter, as is the tissue of hierarchical and predetermined relationships which occur in both court and family life. What the historical reader will see as interpolations in LY 1 (from a later decade, when the Lǔ Confucians were again in service) help give the scriptural reader a sense of government as an ultimate goal, but on balance that goal seems more remote than the more vividly realized personal context. It looms at a distance, dignifying but not defining the ideal individual which the chapter describes.

What of the mysterious virtue rýn 仁? If we base ourselves only on LY 1 as we here have it, the relevant material is 1:2 (where filial and fraternal behavior are its basis), 1:3 (where the artful and imposing are said to rarely have it), and 1:6 (where intimacy is reserved for those who possess it). This fits the domestic and hierarchical character of the chapter, and there most readers will leave it.

A more patient reader can get a little more out of it. First we have 1:2, which can be seen as saying that rýn is at a higher level than the filiality and fraternity on which it rests. Rýn is a way of interaction with those to whom one's relationship is not fixed by family ties: it is family writ large but *not the same* as family. 1:6 then tells us that rýn is not writ all that large: it is indeed a basis for association outside of kinship groups, but only with a select few. The rest of humanity one loves, but keeps a certain distance from. This realistic precept avoids the Mician inclusive tone of 12:22, where rýn is simply the love of others. Rýn in LY 1 is not a given, in relations beyond the family; it must be recognized in individuals; this adds a nonpredetermined note. We learn in 1:3 that rýn is incompatible with artifice: it has a quality of integrity. And 1:16, without mentioning rýn directly, suggests that right behavior is not merely a possession, which one has and then waits to be rewarded for having; it is a cause of action. One gives the world, or a susceptible part of the world, what one hopes to get from it. Expectation creates a balancing obligation.

A reader may object that this is not Confucius's rýn. But does it matter? Confucius rightly enjoys credit for having set the enterprise in motion; credit for where it goes, or what it may be worth when it gets there, belongs to others. The thinkers (and interpolaters) of LY 1 inhabited a less feudal, less preset world than Confucius; they were, like ourselves, coping with a society in which virtue, if it exists at all, is voluntary. They may have much to say to us.

So much for analyzing gnomic sayings. Readers may find it tedious. The Analects itself tends to abandon the pithy style for something more extended. And yet the gnomic style has its place: there are things in life that cannot be expressed at length (Vreeland **D. V.** 97; two words that transformed a situation) or taught consecutively, but are better apprehended in concentrated bursts of attention. Hazlitt **Genius** 108–109 held that genius is unaware of its powers; this is wrong of genius, but it is right of virtue (JZ 20:9: Watson **Chuang** 220). Too much attention, including too much self-attention, spoils it.

2

LY 2, we must remember, does not have a date of its own in the Analects when the Analects is seen as an integral work; it is simply the next chapter. There is no particular logic that we as readers expect a chapter to have. We merely wait, having had a breathing space at the end of the last one, to see what it will say.

The numbering of passages is identical in the Legge text.

2:1. The Master said, To conduct government by virtue can be compared to the North Star: it occupies its place, and the many stars bow before it.

This rulership maxim, with its striking image, prepares us for an emphasis on statesmanship in subsequent sayings in this chapter, this being presumably the special interest of whichever disciple (on the standard Hàn theory of the text) may have been primarily responsible for it.

2:2. The Master said, The **300 Poems**: if with one word I should epitomize them, it would be "In your thoughts, be without depravity."

Whatever the philological accuracy of the quote (and the average reader will unquestioningly accept whatever meaning the local context makes necessary), the mention of the 300 poems early in the book keeps one from suspecting that the Shī was not part of Confucius's repertoire of authorities. The prohibition of "depravity" gives a puritanical spin to the self-cultivation agenda. As for statecraft, there is none; 2:2 (compare 2:4) has an exclusively inward focus.

2:3. The Master said, Lead them with **government**, regulate them by punishments, and the people will evade them with no sense of shame. Lead them with virtue, regulate them by **ritual**, and they will acquire a sense of shame – and moreover, they will be orderly.

The humane, anti-Legalist character of this saying establishes a kindly public character for Confucianism. It also implies that Confucius himself was not only versed in government, but highly enough placed to discourse on it. There is no question of a hard-luck, marginally successful career. As to the lesson of the passage, beyond its governmental insight it affirms the LY 1 idea of ritual as providing the large context for the rest of life.

2:4. The Master said, At fifteen I was determined on **learning**, at thirty I was established, at forty I had no doubts, at fifty I understood the commands of Heaven, at sixty my ears were obedient, and at seventy I may follow what my heart desires **without transgressing** the limits.

The first seeming statement by Confucius *about himself* is a self-cultivation autobiography, with a moral rather than political context, which like LY 1 gives "learning" and not public effectiveness the foreground position. As in 2:3, the psychological insight of the passage, and its transcendent goal, support the concept of Confucius as a sage, as skilled at inner motivation as he is learned in written texts. This is the Confucius of later ages. No amount of politics in what follows can now dislodge the personal-centered implication of LY 1.

2:5. Mv̀ng Yídž asked about **filiality**. The Master said, Never disobeying. Fán Chŕ was driving, and the Master told him, The descendant of the Mv̀ng asked me about filiality, and I replied, Never disobeying. Fán Chŕ said, What does that mean? The Master said, When they are alive, serve them with propriety; when they are dead, inter them with **propriety**, and sacrifice to them with **propriety**.

> The cleverly put idea of "never disobeying [lǐ]" does several things. It confirms Confucius's cryptic quality, his willingness to risk misunderstanding; a trait consistent with the philological high-handedness of 2:2. It confirms filiality as a major concern, and lǐ as the core of Confucius's worldview. And it supports the view of him as a master pedagogue: the school atmosphere of 1:1 is here reinforced with an anecdote in which two disciples figure successively.

2:6. Mv̀ng Wǔ-bwó asked about filiality. The Master said, When his father and mother are anxious only lest he may fall ill.

> This more conventional formulation might lead, and historically did lead, to monstrosities of filial sacrifice that were only occasionally objected to within the increasingly authoritarian later tradition itself (Waley **Yuan** 13f).

2:7. Dž-yóu asked about filiality. The Master said, The filiality of the present day: it is merely what one might call being able to provide nourishment. But if we consider the dogs and horses, they all receive their nourishment. If there is no respect, where is the **difference**?

> A contrasting, feeling-centered view. A critical reader, discounting the idea that the ancients were more filial, will conclude from 2:7 (against the background of the conventional 2:6) that Confucius was an ethical innovator, emphasizing natural promptings to filiality. Beneath these alternatives is the assumption that filiality was of central concern to Confucius. This impression is now probably proof against any evidence, especially evidence of omission, in later chapters.

2:8. Dž-syà asked about filiality. The Master said, The *demeanor* is difficult. If there is work, the younger bear the toil of it; if there are wine and food, the elder get the best portions – did *this* ever count as filiality?

> Another seemingly inward-revisionist view of filiality, supporting the inference that Confucius's historical importance was as an ethical innovator.

2:9. The Master said, I can talk all day with Hwéi, and he never disagrees with me; he seems to be stupid. But if, after he has withdrawn, I observe his personal conduct, it is adequate to serve as an illustration. **Hwéi** is not stupid.

> Readers not specially instructed are liable to miss the contrastive "Hwéi" at the end, but this is still an attractive saying, which also has the "surprise" element we will find again later in the text: Confucius admits an error. Since earlier passages have established his preternatural insight, this reduces to an expression of the genial modesty appropriate to a literal sage.

2:10. The Master said, See what he bases himself on, observe what he follows, find out what he is comfortable with. Where can the man hide? Where can the man hide?

> A saying seemingly on the general art of judgement; nothing in the immediate context requires the first-time reader to envision a political context for it.

2:11. The Master said, Warming up the old so as to understand the new; such a one can be a **teacher**.

> With 2:2, this confirms Confucius's position as the reinterpreter of a classic text tradition for a later age, and reinforces the authority of the classics themselves.

2:12. The Master said, The **gentleman** is not used as an implement.

> Literate modern readers (jywndž) will agree in rejecting petty treatment for jywndž, but may visualize jywndž as cultured men, rather than as supervisors.

2:13. Dž-gùng asked about the gentleman. The Master said, First he carries out his words and then he remains **consistent** with them.

> This general description does not evoke a government context, and confirms the impression that Confucius was primarily a teacher, not himself an officeholder or a trainer of future officeholders.

2:14. The Master said, The gentleman is **broad** and not partial; the little man is partial and not broad.

> The largeness of mind in 2:12 is here reinforced, and that is about all.

2:15. The Master said, If he **studies** and does not reflect, he will be rigid. If he reflects but does not study, he will be shaky.

> This book-learning sense of sywé "learn/study" will prevent the older meaning "acquire by imitation" from ever establishing itself in the text.

2:16. The Master said, If someone attacks from **another end**, he will do harm.

> However the technical metaphor (see 9:8) is construed, and despite the more inclusive 2:14, a disapproval of heterodox ideas or postulates will somehow emerge. The only thing wrong with this historically is that it places Confucius in an age of already sharply defined and directly competing ideologies.

2:17. The Master said, Yóu, shall I teach you about knowing? To regard knowing it as knowing it, to regard *not* knowing it as *not* knowing it – *this* is **wisdom**.

> Jř 知 here will be taken in its "wisdom" sense, as counseling epistemological modesty, not as a more governmentally focused admonition for the bureaucrat, who needs to be very sure of his sources before he can act on his information. In that larger sense, it unquestionably extends the range of Confucian thought.

2:18. Dž-jāng was studying for a salaried position. The Master said, Hear much but omit what is doubtful, and speak circumspectly of the rest, and you will have few problems. See much but omit what is shaky, and act circumspectly on the rest, and you will have few regrets. If in your words you have few problems, and in your actions you have few regrets, salary will come along in due course.

> Without the pairing, this public maxim no longer codefines the scope of 2:17.

2:19. **Aī-gūng** asked, What must I do so that the people will be submissive? Confucius replied, Raise up the straight and put them over the crooked, and the people will be submissive. Raise up the crooked and put them over the straight, and the people will not be submissive.

> The fact that Aī-gūng on his first appearance asks about *policy* (not, as in 6:3, about *protégés*) tends to establish an image of Confucius as a virtual minister.

2:20. **Jì Kāngdž** asked, To make the people be respectful, loyal, and motivated, what should one do? The Master said, Regard them with austerity, and they will be respectful. Be filial and kind, and they will be loyal. Raise up the good to teach their deficiencies, and they will be motivated.

> The adjacency of this and 2:19 with Aī-gūng does not permit a clear vision of the either/or opposition between the Prince and the Jì clan in Confucius's own time, and instead makes him a high-level advisor welcome at any court.

2:21. Someone said to Confucius, Why are you not in government? The Master said, The Shū says, "Be ye filial, only filial, be friendly toward your brothers, and you will contribute to the government." This too, then, is being in government. Why should you speak of being "in government?"

> Again the primacy of filiality over service. The reader who regards government as unsavory will not, from anything in LY 2, be moved to think better of it. The allusiveness of Confucius (Shū 49; Legge **Shoo** 535) further supports his image as a learned and cryptic speaker, and that of the Shū itself as pre-Confucian.

2:22. The Master said, A man, but without fidelity: I don't know if that can be. A large cart with no yoke, a small cart with no collar: how shall one make them go?

> Fidelity certainly registers as a virtue in this saying, but, again, not in a very strongly implied official context.

2:23. **Dž-jāng** asked whether ten generations hence could be foreknown. The Master said, In the **Yīn**'s continuing with the **Syà rituals**, what they subtracted and added can be known. In the Jōu's continuing with the Yīn rituals, what they subtracted and added can be known. And if someone should carry on after the Jōu, even though it were a hundred **generations**, it can be known.

> The ritual emphasis, the antiquarian emphasis, and the idea of cultural continuity all contribute, long before we reach it in the text, to the image of Confucius as "handing on and not inventing" (7:1) the culture of the past.

2:24. The Master said, If it is not **his own spirit** but he sacrifices to it, he is presumptuous. If he sees what is right and does not do it, he lacks courage.

> The general impression from the Analects is that Confucius kept aloof from the supernatural; this saying, however, which seems to take the sacrificial world seriously, gets the consecutive reader off on the wrong foot on this issue.

Chapter Comment

LY 2, like LY 1, abounds in striking observations and vivid images, and makes a strong impression on the reader. It is that much more likely to impose its special angle on perceptions of the Analects as a philosophy.

It cannot be doubted that the ritual/domestic emphasis of LY 1–2 has deeply influenced all later understanding of the Analects and Confucianism. Recent comments defining the family as the core of Confucianism, or least its only presently valid form, include Yu **Remarks** 32, Yü **Remarks** 28, and, from the government level, Zakaria **Culture** 113–115 (compare Kim **Destiny** 191f). For a modern project to define a future Confucianism in terms of the LY 1–2 self-realization ideal (and the JY text which develops that trend), see Tu **Way**.

3

We now come to LY 3, with its unmistakable ritual emphasis, prefigured by the more subtle indications of ritual principles here and there in LY 1–2. Chinese readers from Hàn onward, who knew the Confucians as real-life experts on ceremonial, would have accepted this image as a matter of course.

The numbering of passages is identical in the Legge text.

3:1. The Master said of the head of the Jì, Eight rows of dancers performing in his courtyard: if this can be borne, what cannot be borne?

> This now seems to criticize the *historical* Jì. "Eight rows" remained a symbol of usurpation; the Japanese chronicle Nihon Shoki sv 642 records such a dance (Cranston **Cup** 114f points out that it is a metaphoric allusion to this passage) as being performed by a pretender to Imperial power.

3:2. The **Three Families** exited to the Yūng. The Master said,

> Assisting Princes standing by,
> And Heaven's Son in majesty –

where in the halls of the **Three Families** was *this* drawn from?

> 3:1–2 establish that Confucius *in his lifetime* ranked high enough to see and comment on these ritual abuses. This is the Confucius of the SJ 47 myth.

3:3. The Master said, A man, but not rv́n, what has he to do with **ritual**? A man, but not rv́n, what has he to do with **music**?

> This supports the 1:2 idea of rv́n as a basis, here not of social order in general but of the embodiment of that order in appropriate ceremonies.

3:4. Lín Fàng asked about the basis of ritual. The Master said, Great indeed is this question! In ceremonies: than lavish, be rather sparing. In **funerals**: than detached, be rather moved.

> The basis (principle) which the question elicits is a frugal one, making the point that even legitimate ceremonies should avoid display.

3:5. The Master said, The Yí and Dí *with* rulers are not the equal of the several Syà states *without* them.

> This Sinocentric (the text says Syà-centric) concept defines a limit to Chinese "culturalism" which would have been intelligible to Hàn readers in their wars with the Syūng-nú peoples; see SJ 110 (Watson **Records** 2/155f). As with the statecraft interpolations in LY 1–2, this political comment lets LY 3 stand out less as a *chapter*, and thus be more convincing as merely a *segment*, of the text.

3:6. The Jì were going to **sacrifice** to Mount Tài. The Master said to Rǎn Yǒu, Can you not save the situation? He replied, I cannot. The Master said, Alas! Who will say that Mount Tài is not as good as Lín Fàng!

> 3:4 and 3:6 together establish Confucius as primarily a font of wisdom about the conduct of ceremonies: a public teacher rather than a leader.

3:7. The Master said, "Gentlemen never compete." Surely the exception will be in **archery**? But they bow and yield as they ascend, and drink a toast as they descend: in their competing, they show themselves gentlemen.

> The elite sport of archery (mocked as a small skill in 9:2) is here legitimized by reinterpreting it as emblematic, not of virtue, but of ritual.

3:8. Dž-syà asked,

> The artful smile so charming, ah,
> The lovely eyes so sparkling, ah,
> *The plain on which to make the painting, ah* –

what does it mean? The Master said, The painting comes *after* the plain. He said, Does **ritual** then come *afterward*? The Master said, The one who takes my hint is Shāng; he begins to be talkable-to about the Poetry.

> The added line implies (as did 2:2) cavalier treatment of the Shī text, and confirms the idea that the Shī existed during the lifetime of Confucius, a claim which is not made in the historical Analects. As for the Lǔ silk industry, reputable Analects commentaries simply do not discuss such vulgar matters.

3:9. The Master said, The ceremonies of Syà: I could discuss them, but Kǐ has not enough evidence. The ceremonies of **Yīn**: I could discuss them, but Sùng has not enough evidence. The reason is that the writings and worthies are not enough. If they *were* enough, I could then give evidence for them.

> Again, the words mean the same, but the historical implication is different. This preoccupation of "Confucius" with early dynasties suggests that Confucianism *is not Confucian*, but a transmission of the wisdom of Ancient Oriental Sages to the present degenerate age. This is still the orthodox view in many parts of the world at the present time.

3:10. The Master said, The dì sacrifice from the libation onward – I simply do not wish to see it.

> The words of an expert, and, as in 3:1–2, also a political critic. It is significant for the image of Confucius, as it emerges from the present Analects, that his only political passions so far occur in ritual, rather than in statecraft, contexts.

3:11. Someone asked for an explanation of the dì sacrifice. The Master said, I do not know. The relation of one who *did* know to All Under Heaven would be like holding something here. And he pointed to his palm.

> An artfully placed later passage (such as 3:10 in the seeming dì-sacrifice pair 3:10/11) has local continuity, and can only be detected by reference to chapter structure. But this is unlikely, since modern scholars (as Schwartz **World** 62 "lack of surface organization") find that Analects chapters *have* no structure.

3:12. "Sacrifice as though present: sacrifice to spirits as though the spirits were present." The Master said, If I do not **take part** in the sacrifice, it is as though I did not sacrifice.

> More evidence, not of attendance at ceremonies (3:1–2), but of conviction about sacrifices. This disables in advance the "distancing" which in subsequent (though in fact earlier) chapters defines Confucius's theory of the spirit world.

3:13. Wángsūn Jyǎ asked, "Than beseech the alcove, rather beseech the stove" – what does this mean? The Master said, It is not true. One who has incurred guilt toward Heaven has no one to whom he can pray.

This too depicts Confucius (contrast 7:35) as a conventionally religious man.

3:14. The Master said, Jōu could look back upon the **Two Dynasties**. How splendid was its culture! And we follow Jōu.

In present context, likelier to be read as antiquarian than as developmental.

3:15. The Master entered the Great Shrine, and at every stage asked questions. Someone said, Who says this son of a man of Dzōu knows ritual? At every stage he asks questions. The Master said, *That* is the ritual.

If the Analects were more widely memorized in our culture, this would serve as an admirable comeback at the overbearing hauteur of some tour guide.

3:16. The Master said, In archery one does not emphasize the hide, because strengths may not be at the same level. This was the old way.

As with the Syà dynasty, above, the lack of an evolutionary Warring States context for these sayings is liable to give them greater credence among readers as a literal picture of "older ways" as seen from Confucius's vantage point.

3:17. Dž-gùng wanted to do away with the sacrificial lamb at the Announcement of the New Moon. The Master said, Sż, you grudge the lamb; I grudge the **ritual**.

We have here Confucius not only as a ritual expert, but as an opponent of ritual evolution. This is challenged by the reasonableness toward change shown in 9:3, but the casual reader may never even get as far as 9:3, and will in any case recall from 3:16–17 that Confucius preferred the ancient ways.

3:18. The Master said, If one served one's ruler observing every last detail of propriety, people would regard it as obsequious.

A reader may miss the "mitigation" function of this originally paired saying. Mitigated or not, the personal acceptance of ritual in 3:17 is undeniable.

3:19. Dìng-gūng asked, When a ruler employs a minister, when a minister serves a ruler – how should it be? Confucius answered, The ruler employs the minister with propriety; the minister serves the ruler with loyalty.

The humanistic potential of this statement will be either lost in the statement about ritual, or, if found, attributed to the time of Confucius or earlier. One of the most vital lessons that the panorama of the original, chronological Analects has for us in modern times is that the elements of an emerging civil polity in China *were not always there*: they were achieved gradually, at a certain time and in a certain historical and even material context. They were, in the end, the hard-won achievement of men and not the gratuitous gift of ancient sages.

3:20. The Master said, The **Gwān-jyw̄**: happy but not licentious; sad but not wounded.

A reader will attribute the subtle psychology of Shr̄ 1 to the early Jōu dynasty, instead of reading it as evidence of Warring States sensibilities. As usually read, the Analects attests the antiquity of the Shr̄, and vice versa.

3:21. Aī-gūng asked about the shv̀ from Dzǎı Wǒ. Dzǎı Wǒ replied, The Syàhòu clan used a pine, the Yīn people used a cypress, the Jōu people used a chestnut, saying it would make the populace be in fear and trembling. The Master heard of it and said, What is over one does not analyze, what is done with one does not reprove, what has passed away one does not blame.

> Even the disciples are loremasters. The dissonance between this Dzǎı Wǒ and the renegade of 5:10a/b will inevitably be resolved in favor of the "earlier" 3:21.

3:22. The Master said, Gwǎn Jùng's capacity was small indeed! Someone said, Was Gwǎn Jùng frugal? He said, Gwǎn had three wives, and among his officers there were no concurrent duties; how could *he* be frugal? If so, then did Gwǎn Jùng understand ritual? He said, Rulers of states have a gate screen; Gwǎn also had a gate screen. When rulers of states celebrate the amity between two rulers, they have a cup stand; Gwǎn also had a cup stand. If Gwǎn understood ritual, who does *not* understand ritual?

> This wonderful retort ranks with the subtler, more arch rejoinder of 3:15.

3:23. The Master, discussing music with the Lǔ Grand Preceptor, said, The art of music, or the part of it that may be understood, is that when it first begins, it is tentative, but as it continues along, it settles down, it brightens up, it opens out; and so it comes to an end.

> One hates to admit it, but readers simply tend to skip this sort of passage.

3:24. The borderman of Yí asked to be presented; he said, Whenever a gentleman comes to this place, I have never failed to be presented to him. The followers presented him. When he came out, he said, You disciples, why do you worry about failure? That All Under Heaven has not had the Way has long indeed been true. Heaven is going to make of your Respected Master a wooden gong.

> This intrusion makes hermits appear early in the text, and to that extent supports the nursery tale idea of Lǎudž as the contemporary of Confucius.

3:25. The Master said of the Sháu that it was wholly beautiful and also wholly good. He said of the Wǔ that it was wholly beautiful, but not wholly good.

> How many readers will see the music link to 3:23, across the interrupting 3:24? Especially when the "wooden gong" tocsin in 3:24 confuses the issue?

3:26. The Master said, Occupying high position without magnanimity, performing rituals without assiduousness, attending funerals without grief – how can I look on at such things?

> Probably to be seen as the end, and not the envoi, of this intricate chapter.

Chapter Summary

> Besides the legitimacy theme (3:1–2), HSWJ extracts from LY 3 only 3:8 (Hightower **Wai** 93), on Shī expertise (HSWJ *teaches* Shī expertise). Only the householder's manual LY 10 affords HSWJ so little moral raw material. LY 3 thus deepens ritual, but without widening the ethical scope of LY 1–2.

4

The preceding three chapters have established a personal/domestic/ritual tone for the Analects, but what if a reader were still paying attention as of LY 4?
The numbering of passages is identical in the Legge text.

4:1. The Master said, It is best to dwell in rýn. If he choose not to abide in rýn, how will he get to be **wise**?

> Wisdom (no longer despised practical "knowledge" but an acknowledged virtue) is now, in the new whole-Analects context, the goal of 4:1.

4:2. The Master said, He who is not rýn cannot for long abide in privation; cannot forever abide in happiness. The rýn are content with rýn; the **wise** turn rýn to their advantage.

> With the shift of jî 知 to a positive value ("wisdom," compare 2:17), there is no sarcasm to keep "advantage" from also becoming a positive term. Scandalous.

4:3. The Master said, It is only the rýn who can like others; who can hate others.

> Waley finds this license for dislike out of order, and harmonizes it with the "niceness" sense of rýn by making 4:3 a maxim Confucius quotes in order to reject it; with Lau, we instead respect the obvious meaning of the text.

4:4. The Master said, If once he sets his mind on rýn, he will **be without evil**.

> Lau, who interprets the passage thus, sacrifices the balancing 4:3 to harmonize instead with the goal of inner self-improvement. This draws strength from the cryptic maxim of 2:2 (whose syé 邪 "depravity" matches the present v̀ 惡 "evil").

4:5. The Master said, Wealth and honor: these are what everyone desires, but if he cannot do so in accordance with his principles, he will not abide in them. Poverty and lowliness: these are what everyone hates, but if he cannot do so in accordance with his principles, he will not avoid them. If the gentleman avoid rýn, how shall he **live up to** that name? A gentleman does not for the space of a meal depart from rýn. In direst straits he cleaves to it; in deepest distress he cleaves to it.

> This uncompromisingly sacrificial loyalty to one's own principles cannot but get at least the temporary attention of the most LY 1–3 preconditioned reader. It leaves a trace with which the end of the chapter can then perhaps resonate.

4:6. The Master said, For my part, I have never seen anyone who loved rýn and hated the not-rýn. One who loved rýn would put nothing else above it. One who hated the not-rýn would already himself be rýn; he would not let the not-rýn come near his person. Is there anyone who for a single day has put forth all his strength on rýn? For my part, I have never seen anyone whose *strength* was not sufficient for it. There may be some, but, for my part, I have never seen one.

> This last-ditch devotion to rýn again strikes a note of seriousness, but exactly what sort of rýn it is that a reader is supposed to be devoted to? The strenuosity of the passage is somehow at odds with the familial rýn of 1:2. One solution is to infer a strenuous filial piety like that of MC 5A1 (Legge **Mencius** 342).

4:7. The Master said, In making mistakes, people stay true to type. If you observe their mistakes, you will be able to tell what sort of rvn they have.

> Legge disapproves the import of this saying, quoting a none-too-relevant line from Goldsmith; Dawson ethicalizes it by making a general "understanding of humaneness" its goal. By this empirical test, at least one early statecraft maxim has been wholly neutralized in the arrangement of the present Analects text.

4:8. The Master said, If in the morning he should hear of the **Way**, and that night he should die, it is enough.

> The "Way" is usually understood as a transcendent (Legge "the right way," Soothill "the truth," Lau "hear about the Way"), not a political, desideratum (Wilhelm "dass die Welt in Ordnung sei," Mao **Suggestions** 284), consistently with the self-cultivation emphasis in LY 1–2. The line itself may feel like the realization of a political goal, but the perceived trend of the book will easily overwhelm the feel of any one line. What then is a reader to do?
>
> Trust the feel. Waley remarks "The appeal, even in philosophical texts, has always been to emotion rather than to logic" (**Notes** 187). Recall Churchill's broadcast to the people of occupied France, quoting Gambetta: "Think of it always, speak of it never," and "For the morning will come" (**Hour** 512).

4:9. The Master said, If an officer is dedicated to the **Way**, but is ashamed of having bad clothes or bad food, he is not worth taking counsel with.

> The mention of taking counsel, with its unavoidable goal of public service, does at last resist absorption in the larger general-ethics context imposed by the preposed chapters. For a Hàn reader, in an age when service was virtually the only aim of learning, there would have been a countervailing service context, but for readers in later, more scholastic periods, LY 1–2 become very cogent.

4:10. The Master said, The gentleman's relation to the world is thus: he has no predilections or prohibitions. When he regards something as right, he sides with it.

> This saying was later influential in inhibiting "factional" combinations of Confucians in support of a particular policy. However honorable in principle, this taboo may in the long run have done more to weaken than strengthen Imperial-period Confucianism.

4:11. The Master said, The gentleman likes virtue; the little man likes partiality. The gentleman likes justice; the little man likes mercy.

> Another sanction against "partiality" and against practical politics, much of which involves groups that are for something and against something else. The disapproval of *permanent* issue-defined groups may however be a sound idea; it is the nature of an issue group to want to make permanent the particular discontent on which it is founded. Modern societies too have had trouble seeing how public life can be organized without becoming polarized.

4:12. The Master said, Those who act with a view to their own personal advantage will arouse much resentment.

> The fairness principle will readily detach itself, for a modern reader, from the LY 1–2 context. Here, historically, is an anticipation of the more inclusive fairness concept reached in LY 19–20. If the modern reader gets that far.

4:13. The Master said, If you *can* run the country with courtesy and deference, what is the obstacle? But if you *cannot* run it with courtesy and deference, what good is courtesy?

> Here lurks the idea of ritual as providing a civil context for cooperation in government, and also the *importance* of civil cooperation in government.

4:14. The Master said, He does not worry that he has no position; he worries about whether he is qualified to hold one. He does not worry that no one recognizes his worth; he seeks to become worthy to be recognized.

> The feudal value of never acting above one's station was an unfortunate idea to build into a system which would later cope with more than feudal pressures. But it is clear that for the last page we have been prescribing *for* a political system, and that is a major gain. Remonstrance will recur later (4:18, 4:26).

4:15. The Master said, Shv̄m! My Way: by one thing I link it together. Dzv̄ngdž said, Yes. When the Master went out, the disciples said, What did he mean? Dzv̄ngdž said, Our Respected Master's Way is simply loyalty and empathy.

> Here is the claim of a unified doctrine, which the reader will regard as original. It states two principles. One is loyalty, which a modern reader will take in the modern (04c/03c) sense of national, not feudal loyalty. It sums up the vertical aspect; shù "empathy, reciprocity" is the lateral aspect. Together, they give a two-axis view of how society holds together. Note, if one can after LY 3, that no divine sanction is involved: the state is the common concern of those who comprise it. As political theory, loyalty and empathy both coincide and suffice.

4:16. The Master said, The gentleman concentrates on right; the little man concentrates on advantage.

> This corrects the above: the narrow self-interest of some people in society is a problem for society. The Analects does not solve the problem of how to handle them. But it is obvious that it is easier to do so in an elite politics, where the microculture of the elite can be required as a condition for entry into the elite.

4:17. The Master said, When he sees a worthy man, let him think how he might come up to him; when he sees an unworthy man, let him examine within himself.

> If not lost in the larger self-cultivation mandate of LY 1–2, this reminds us that even those born into the ruling circle of society need to labor ethically to become *fully functioning* members of that society.

4:18. The Master said, In serving father and mother, he remonstrates gently. If he sees that his ideas are not followed, then he again becomes dutiful without disobedience, and energetic without resentment.

> This passage allows difference of opinion but not denial of duty; it defines a rudimentary "loyal opposition" in the family, and by extension in the polity.

4:19. The Master said, While his father and mother are alive, he does not travel far; if he *does* travel, he must have a definite destination.

> Hampering as a modern practical Mician may find this, it is not all wrong to keep the sensibilities of high government figures in touch with specific needs, and the needs of one's own parents are admirably handy for the purpose.

4:20. The Master said, If for three years he does not change from the ways of his father, he may be called filial.

Even in the rigorous form it took in later periods, the three-year mourning implied here was not as disruptive of public life as the Micians anticipated; see the perceptive comment in Waley **Three** 132–133 (PB 97). As to subordination within the family, it is not forever; time gives everyone their turn.

4:21. The Master said, The ages of one's father and mother cannot but be known. In the one case, he will be happy; in the other, he will be anxious.

Merely domestic, and enforcing LY 1–2, but now compare the following:

4:22. The Master said, If the words of those of old did not readily issue forth, it was that they were ashamed lest they should not come up to them.

The unassuming way of those who take seriously the assuming of public duty.

4:23. The Master said, Those who err on the side of strictness are few.

Balances the above; not adding to it, but structurally emphasizing it.

4:24. The Master said, The gentleman wants to be slow in giving his word, but quick in carrying it out.

And again. What I tell you three times is true.

4:25. The Master said, Virtue is not solitary; it must have neighbors.

The social and public nature of virtue, offseting the domestic-piety emphasis.

4:26. Dž-yóu said, If in serving his ruler he is accusatory, he will be disgraced. If with friends he is accusatory, he will become estranged from them.

The bombshell is that one might *be* accusatory with a ruler. This, if obliquely, annexes the whole "censorial" tradition, as expressed elsewhere in the text. In the light of the 4:15 loyalty/reciprocity key, we see that there is also to be reciprocity *along the vertical axis*. This establishes a final symmetry in the political geometry of the Analects. Given support from the beginning of LY 4, this saying allows a role for opinion, and thus permits *politics from below.*

It may be wise to grant the LY 4 point that partisanship is dangerous. Oppositions tend to become institutionalized, and thus to exert an ongoing structural inhibition on cooperation in government. How to allow opinion without giving it a structure of its own is a major dilemma which the text itself, followed by its present annotators, leave as a final project for the reader.

Chapter Comment

We have only two points, in parting for the last time from the Analects. One is the *overt* power of the preposed chapters to shift the text thematically away from its predominantly political focus to their own largely personal and domestic agenda. The simple device of preposing elements is very effective in practice: first impressions tend to be last impressions. But the second point is the *latent* power of older sayings, represented here by LY 4, notwithstanding these late transpositions, and in part because of the presence of even *later* additions within LY 1–4, to convey the original fire of Confucius, along with the insights of his successors: the almost lost political tradition of the Analects.

Apparatus

Fragment of the Lǔ Analects Text (LY *7:11)
". . . who prefers [to succeed] by consultation." (好謀 . . .)
*Engraved on stone in 174/183. Original size. After Mǎ **Shŕ Jīng** (fragment 490)*

Works Cited

This is not a bibliography of the Analects, merely an expansion of the short citation forms used above. If not otherwise specified, the texts of Chinese works relied on are those in the Harvard-Yenching concordance series. Among listed journals, the Notes (N) and Queries (Q) of the University of Massachusetts Warring States Working Group (WSWG) have circulated only within the Group.

To conserve space, the information given here is the minimum that will permit ready identification and retrieval. The short form Surname **Title** is here expanded to **Surname** Name, Full **Title**, both elements of the short form being given in **bold** for faster recognition. Romanization of Chinese names used in published works is followed; other Chinese names and titles are cited in the convention described on page 2, above. Tones, diacritics, and Wade-Giles aspiration marks are ignored in alphabetizing; numerals precede letters. Surnames are given in Chinese order (surname first) without commas; Chinese compound surnames are joined without hyphens. Joint works are given under the name first listed on the title page; anonymous or collaborative works are listed by title and alphabetized by keyword.

Editions not seen are cited [in brackets]. An equals sign indicates identity of pagination between editions. Place of publication is given (in parentheses) only as needed to distinguish otherwise identical publishers. Publisher names are abridged as far as possible, "X University Press" here becoming, in most cases, simply "X."

Text Abbreviations

BA: Bamboo Annals [Jú-shū Jì-nyén]; *see* Legge **Shoo**
CC: Chūn/Chyōu [Spring and Autumn Annals]
DDJ: Dàu-Dv́ Jīng; Mǎ-wáng Dwēi text as edited in Henricks **Te**
DJ: Dzwǒ Jwàn; *see under* CC
GLJ: Gūnglyáng Jwàn; *see under* CC
GY: Gwó Yw̌ (Gwó-sywé Jībv̌n Tsúngshū)
GYJ: Gūngyáng Jwàn; *see under* CC
GZ: Gwǎndž (Sž-bù Bèi-yàu)
HS: Hàn Shū, Jūng-hwá 1965
HSWJ: Hán Shr̄ Wài-jwàn; *see* Lài **Hán**
JDSW: Jīng/Dyěn Shř-wv́n; *see* Lù **Jīng/Dyěn**
JGT: Jàn-Gwó Tsv̀ (Kokuyaku Kambun Taisei)
JY: Jūng Yūng (Shŕsān Jīng Jīng-wv́n)
JZ: Jwāngdž
KZJY: Kǔngdž Jyā-yw̌ (Sž-bù Tsúngkān)
LJ: Lǐ Jì (Shŕsān Jīng Jīng-wv́n)
LSCC: Lw̌-shř Chūn/Chyōu (Jū Dž Jí-chv́ng)
LY: Lún Yw̌ [Analects]
MC: Mencius [Mv̀ngdž]
MTJ: Mù Tyēndž Jwàn (Sž-bù Bèi-yàu, reproduced in Mathieu **Mu**)
MZ: Mwòdž
HNZ: Hwái-nándž (Jū Dž Jí-chv́ng)
SBF: Sūndž Bīng-fǎ; *see* Gwō **Sūndž**
Shr̄: Shr̄ Jīng [Classic of Poetry]
Shū: Shū Jīng [Classic of Documents]
SJ: Shř Jì, Jūng-hwá 1959
SSSY: Shř-shwō Syīn Yw̌ (Jū Dž Jí-chv́ng)
SZ: Syẃndž
Yì: Yì Jīng [Classic of Changes]

Journal and Series Abbreviations

AM: Asia Major
BAI: Bulletin of the Asia Institute
BIHP: Bulletin of the Institute of History and Philology, Academia Sinica
BMFEA: Bulletin of the Museum of Far Eastern Antiquities
CC: Chinese Culture
CIB: China Institute Bulletin
CLEAR: Chinese Literature: Essays, Articles, Reviews
CRI: China Review International
CSA: Chinese Sociology and Anthropology
EC: Early China
FA: Foreign Affairs
GSB: Gǔ Shř Byèn; see Gù **Gǔ Shř**
HJAS: Harvard Journal of Asiatic Studies
HR: History of Religions
JAOS: Journal of the American Oriental Society
JAS: Journal of Asian Studies
JCP: Journal of Chinese Philosophy
JCR: Journal of Chinese Religions
JHKG: Jyāng/Hàn Kǎugǔ
JJC: Jū Dž Jí-chvng (Shř-jyè, and reprints)
JNCBRAS: Journal of the North China Branch of the Royal Asiatic Society
JRE: Journal of Religious Ethics
KBTK: Kambun Taikei
MAO: Mémoires concernant l'Asie Orientale
MS: Monumenta Serica
PEW: Philosophy East and West
SBBY: Sž-bù Bèı-yàu (Jūng-hwá)
SBE: Sacred Books of the East
SBTK: Sž-bù Tsúng-kān (Shāng-wù)
SPP: Sino-Platonic Papers (University of Pennsylvania)
TP: T'oung Pao
WSWG: Warring States Working Group Notes (N) and Queries (Q)
WW: Wen Wu

Books and Articles

Allan Sarah, The **Heir** and the Sage, Chinese Materials Center 1981
Allinson Robert E., The Confucian **Golden** Rule, JCP v12 (1985)
Ames Roger T., The Art of **Rulership**, Hawaii 1983
Ames Roger T., The Mencian **Conception** of Ren Xing, in: Rosemont **Contexts**
Ames Roger T., **Rites** as Rights: The Confucian Alternative, in: Rouner **Human**
Arbuckle Gary, An Unnoticed Religious **Metaphor**, JCR v21 (1993)
Ariel Yoav, **K'ung** Ts'ung-tzu, Princeton 1989
Atkinson Brooks, The Complete Essays and Other Writings of Ralph Waldo **Emerson**, Modern Library 1940
Barnett Correlli, Hitler's **Generals**, Weidenfeld 1989
Barrie J. M., **Half** Hours, Scribner's [1914]; 1933
Barrie J. M., The **Twelve** Pound Look, in: Barrie **Half**
Bauer Wolfgang, China and the Search for **Happiness** [1971]; Seabury 1976
Beveridge W. I. B., The **Art** of Scientific Investigation, Norton 1950; 3ed 1957 Vintage PB nd

Blacker Carmen, **Intent** of Courtesy, in: Morris **Madly**
Blakeley Barry B., **King**, Clan, and Courtier in Ancient Ch'u, AM ser3 v5 pt2 (1992)
Bloom Irene, Mencian **Arguments** on Human Nature, PEW v44 #1 (1994)
Bodde Derk, **Essays** on Chinese Civilization, Princeton PB 1981
Bodde Derk, **Feudalism** in China, in: Coulborn **Feudalism**
Bodde Derk, **Introduction**, in: Bodde **Essays**
Bodde Derk, A **Perplexing** Passage in the Confucian Analects, JAOS v53 (1933)
Bol Peter K., This **Culture** of Ours, Stanford 1992
Boltz William G., **Lao Tzu** Tao Te Ching, in: Loewe **Texts**
Boltz William G., **Word** and Word History in the Analects, TP v69 (1983)
Boodberg Peter A., **Comments** on "Some Great Books of the Oriental Traditions,"
  in: Cohen **Selected**
Boodberg Peter A., Notes on Chinese **Morphology** and Syntax, in: Cohen **Selected**
Boodberg Peter A., **Sino-Altaica III**, in: Cohen **Selected**
Boodberg Peter A., Chinese **Zoographic** Namers as Chronograms, in: Cohen **Selected**
Brooks A. Taeko, **Divination** and Sacrifice in the Chūn/Chyōu, WSWG N61 (1994)
Brooks A. Taeko, **Earliest** Text Occurrences of Yīn/Yáng, WSWG Q52 (1995)
Brooks A. Taeko, **Gwǎndž 3** and the Analects, WSWG N136 (1997)
Brooks A. Taeko, **Jwāngdž 4**, WSWG N108 (1996)
Brooks A. Taeko, Evolution of the Mician Ethical **Triplets**, WSWG N94 (1996)
Brooks E. Bruce, Two Archaeological **Controversies**, WSWG N80 (1995)
Brooks E. Bruce, **Yǔng**, or **Courage**, WSWG N95 (1996)
Brooks E. Bruce, A **Geometry** of the Shī Pǐn, in: Chow, **Wen-lin**; as Shī Pǐn Jyě-syī,
  in: Mwò **Shýn-nw**
Brooks E. Bruce, Mencius's **Interviews**, WSWG N51 (1993)
Brooks E. Bruce, The **Life** and Mentorship of Confucius, SPP #72 (1996)
Brooks E. Bruce, History and **Myth**, AAS/Amherst (28 October 1995)
Brooks E. Bruce, **Point** and Area in the Psychohistory of Lǔ, WSWG N63 (1994)
Brooks E. Bruce, Chronology of the **Princes** of Lǔ, WSWG N10 (1993)
Brooks E. Bruce, The Present State and Future **Prospects** of Pre-Hàn Text Studies,
  SPP #46 (1994)
Brooks E. Bruce, **Shř Jì** Chronology, WSWG N85 (1995)
Brooks E, Bruce, The Earliest Attested **Shū** Texts, WSWG N86 (1995; rev 1997)
Brooks E. Bruce, Warring States **Slavery**, WSWG N90 (1995)
Caplow Theodore, The Academic **Marketplace** [1958]; Anchor PB 1965
Chalmers John, **Appendix** on the Astronomy of the Ancient Chinese, in: Legge **Shoo**
Chan Wing-tsit, The Evolution of the Confucian Concept **Jen**, PEW v4 (1955)
Chan Wing-tsit, A **Source** Book in Chinese Philosophy [1963]; Princeton PB 1969
Chan Wing-tsit, The **Way** of Lao Tzu, Bobbs-Merrill PB 1963
Chang Kwang-chih, The **Archaeology** of Ancient China [1963]; 4ed Yale PB 1986
Cheng Anne, **Lun Yü**, in: Loewe **Texts**
Cheng Te-k'un, The Travels of Emperor **Mu**, JNCBRAS v64–65 (1934)
Chow Tse-tsung, **Wen-lin**, Wisconsin 1968
Churchill Winston S., The Grand **Alliance**, Houghton 1951
Churchill Winston S., Their Finest **Hour**, Houghton 1949
Churchill Winston S., The Gathering **Storm**, Houghton 1948
Chyén Mù, Syēn-Chín Jū Dž Syì-nyén **Kǎu**, 2ed Hong Kong 2v 1956
Cleary Beverly, Dear Mr. **Henshaw**, Morrow 1983
Cohen Alvin P., **Coercing** the Rain Deities in Ancient China, HR v17 (1978)
Cohen Alvin P., **Selected** Works of Peter A. Boodberg, California 1979
Connelly Thomas L., The **Marble** Man, Louisiana 1977
Cook Constance A., **Defining** Chu, Hawaii (forthcoming)
Coulborn Rushton, **Feudalism** in History, Princeton 1956

Cranston Edwin A., The Gem-Glistening Cup, Stanford 1993
Creel Herrlee G., On Two Aspects in Early Taoism, in: Creel Taoism
Creel Herrlee G., The Beginnings of Bureaucracy in China, in: Creel Taoism
Creel H[errlee] G., Confucius, John Day 1949 = Confucius and the Chinese Way, Harper PB 1960
Creel Herrlee G., What Is Taoism? Chicago 1970
Cross Arthur Lyon, A History of England, Macmillan 1914
Crump J. I. Jr., Chan-Kuo Ts'e, Oxford 1970
Dawson Raymond, Confucius: The Analects, Oxford PB 1993
Dazai Shundai, Rongo Kokun, Sūzan 1739
Dazai Shundai, Rongo Kokun Gaiden, Sūzan nd
de Bary Wm. Theodore, Neo-Confucianism and Human Rights, in: Rouner Human
de Bary Wm. Theodore, The Trouble with Confucianism, Harvard 1991
Dubs Homer H., Did Confucius Study the "Book of Changes"? TP v25 (1975)
Dubs Homer H., The Date of Confucius' Birth, AM v1 (1949–50)
Dubs Homer H., The History of the Former Han Dynasty, Waverly 1935–1955 = Wv́n-syīng 3v nd
Durrant Stephen W., The Cloudy Mirror, SUNY PB 1995
Durrant Stephen W., On Translating Lun Yü, CLEAR v3 (1981)
Eberhard Wolfram, Guilt and Sin in Traditional China, California 1967
Egerod Søren, Studia Serica Bernhard Karlgren Dedicata, Munksgaard 1959
Emerson Ralph Waldo, English Traits, in: Atkinson Emerson
Emerson Ralph Waldo, The Fugitive Slave Law, in: Atkinson Emerson
Eno Robert, The Confucian Creation of Heaven, SUNY PB 1990
Eno Robert, Sources for the LY 8 Layers, WSWG Q88 (1997)
Feynman Richard P., Surely You're Joking, Mr. Feynman, Norton 1985
Feynman Richard [P.], The Character of Physical Law [1964]; Modern Library 1994
Fingarette Herbert, Confucius: The Secular as Sacred, Harper PB 1972
Fukuzawa Yūkichi, Autobiography [1934]; Hokuseido PB 1949
Fung Yu-lan, A History of Chinese Philosophy [1931–1934]; 2v Princeton 1952
Goodspeed Edgar J., The Story of the New Testament, Chicago 1916
Gosse Edmund, Father and Son [1907]; Heinemann 1928
Grafflin Dennis, Literary Form, AAS/Amherst (28 October 1995)
Grafflin Dennis, Dialogue on Analects Structure, WSWG Q4–8 (1993)
Graham A. C., The Background of the Mencian Theory of Human Nature, in: Graham Studies
Graham A. C., Disputers of the Tao, Open Court PB 1989
Graham A. C., Later Mohist Logic Ethics and Science, Chinese University Press 1978
Graham A. C., Mo Tzu, in: Loewe Texts
Graham A. C., Reflections and Replies, in: Rosemont Contexts
Graham A. C., Studies in Chinese Philosophy and Philosophical Literature [Singapore 1986]; SUNY PB 1990
Graham A. C., Three Studies of Kung-sun Lung, in: Graham Studies
Graham A. C., The Nung-chia "School of the Tillers," in: Graham Studies
Griffith Samuel B., Sun Tzu: The Art of War, Oxford 1963
Gù Jyé-gāng, On Ancient History, CIB v3 #3 (December 1938)
Gù Jyé-gāng, Gǔ Shř Byèn [7v 1926–1941]; Tài-píng 7v 1962–1963
Gù Jyé-gāng, Lùn Gǔ Shř, in: GSB v1 p59
Gwō Hwà-rwò, Shř-yī Jyā Jù Sūndž, Jūnghwá 1962
Hammond N. G. L., The Oxford Classical Dictionary, Oxford 2ed 1970
Hartman Charles, Han Yü and the T'ang Search for Unity, Princeton 1986
Hán Yẁ, Dá Jāng Jì Shū, in: Hán Jí ch14
Hán Yẁ, Hán Chāng-lí Jí, Shāng-wù 1964

Hazlitt William, Essays, Walter Scott nd
Hazlitt William, Whether Genius is Conscious of its Powers, in: Hazlitt Essays
Hazlitt William, On the Conduct of Life, in: Hazlitt Essays
Hazlitt William, On the Look of a Gentleman, in: Hazlitt Essays
Henderson John B., Scripture, Canon, and Commentary, Princeton 1991
Henricks Robert G., Lao-tzu Te-Tao Ching, Ballantine 1989
Henry Eric, The Motif of Recognition, HJAS v47 #1 (1987)
Henry Eric, Kuo Yü Summaries, unpublished 1994
Hiebert Fredrik T., Pazyryk Chronology and Early Horse Nomads Reconsidered,
     BAI ns v6 (1992)
Hightower James Robert, Han Shih Wai Chuan, Harvard 1952
Hsiao Harry Hsin-i, Problems Concerning Tseng Tzu's Role in the Promotion of
     Filial Pietism, CC v19 #1 (1978)
Hsiao Kung-chuan, A History of Chinese Political Thought [1945]; Princeton PB 1979
Hsu Cho-yun, Ancient China in Transition [1965]; Stanford PB 1968
Hú J̌-gwēi, Lún Yw̌ Byèn-jv̀ng, Lyén-jīng 1978
Hu Shih, The Development of the Logical Method in China [1922]; 2ed Paragon 1963
Hu Shih, A Criticism of Some Recent Methods Used in Dating Lao Tzu [1933];
     HJAS v3 (1937)
Huang Chichung, The Analects of Confucius, Oxford PB 1997
Hucker Charles O., Confucianism and the Chinese Censorial System, in: Nivison
     Action
Hummel Arthur W., Eminent Chinese of the Ch'ing Period, Library of Congress
     2v 1943
The Interpreter's Bible, Abingdon 12v 1951–1957
Itō Jinsai, Rongo Kogi [1683], in: Seki Shisho
Jàu Jǐ-lín, Lún Yw̌ Syīn Tàn, 3ed Rv́n-mín 1976
Jensen Lionel M., The Invention of Confucius and His Chinese Other, "Kong Fuzi,"
     Positions, v1 #2 (1993)
Jensen Lionel M., Wise Man of the Wilds, EC 20 (1995)
Johnson Paul, A History of the Jews, Harper 1987
Jū Syī, Sž-shū Jí Jù, Táiwān Jūng-hwá 1973
Jū Syī, Jūdž Yw̌-lèi, np nd
Jv̀ng Sywǽn, Lún Yw̌ Syẁ, appended to: Lyóu Jv̀ng-yì
Hv́běi Dìng-syèn 40-hàu Hàn-mù Fāchyw̌ Jyěnbàu, WW 1981 #8
Dìngjōu Syī Hàn Jūngshān Hwái-wáng Mù Jú-jyěn Lún Yw̌ Jyèshàu, WW 1997 #5
Kallen Horace M., The Philosophy of William James, Modern Library 1925
Kaneko Motoomi, Makura no Sōshi Hyōshaku [1925]; rev Meiji Shoin 1931
Karlgren Bernhard, Some Fecundity Symbols in Ancient China, BMFEA v2 (1930)
Karlgren Bernhard, The Early History of the Chou Li and Tso Chuan Texts,
     BMFEA v3 (1931)
Karlgren Bernhard, On the Date of the Piao Bells, BMFEA v6 (1924)
Keegan John, Churchill's Generals, Grove Weidenfeld 1991
Kennedy George A., [Review of] Biographies of Meng Hao-jan, in Li: Selected
Kennedy George A., The Butterfly Case, in: Li Selected
Kennedy George A., Fenollosa, Pound, and the Chinese Character, in: Li Selected
Kennedy George A., [Review of] Literary Chinese by the Inductive Method, in: Li
     Selected
Kennedy George A., A Note on Ode 220, in: [Egerod Studia]; Li Selected
Kennedy George A., A Study of the Particle Yen, in: Li Selected
Kieschnick John, Analects 12.1 and the Commentarial Tradition, JAOS v112 (1992)
Kim Dae Jung, Is Culture Destiny? FA v73 #6 (November/December 1994)
Kimura Eiichi, Kōshi to Rongo, Sōbunsha 1971

Kinney Anne Behnke, **Infant** Abandonment in Early China, EC v18 (1993)

Knoblock John, **Xunzi**, 3v Stanford 1988–1994

Kramers Robert Paul, **K'ung** Tzu Chia Yü, Brill 1949

Kramers R[obert] P[aul], K'ung Tzu **Chia Yü**, in: Loewe **Texts**

LaFargue Michael, **Tao** and Method, SUNY 1994

Làı Yén-ywǽn, **Hán** Shř Wàı-jwàn Jīn-jù Jīn-yì, Táıwān Shāngwù 1972

Lattimore Owen, Inner Asian **Frontiers** of China [1940]; Beacon 1962

Lau D. C., Confucius: The **Analects** [Penguin PB 1979]; Chinese University Press 1983

Lau D. C., **Mencius**, Penguin PB 1970

Laufer B[erthold], **Lun Yü** IX, 1, JAOS v54 (1934)

Lawton Thomas, Chinese **Art** of the Warring States Period, Freer Gallery 1982

Legge James, Confucian **Analects**, as: Legge **Classics** v1

Legge James, The **Ch'un** Ts'ew, as: Legge **Classics** v5

Legge James, The Chinese **Classics**, 7v 1861–1872 = 5v Hong Kong 1960

Legge James, The **Li** Ki, SBE 1885 = 2v Banarsidass 1964

Legge James, The Works of **Mencius**, as: Legge **Classics** v2

Legge James, The **She** King or The Book of Poetry, as: Legge **Classics** v4

Legge James, The **Shoo** King, as: Legge **Classics** v3

Leslie D[aniel], **Notes** on the Analects, TP 49 (1961–1962)

Leslie Donald D., Essays on the **Sources** for Chinese History, South Carolina 1973

Lewis Lloyd, **Myths** After Lincoln, Readers Club 1941

Lewis Mark Edward, Sanctioned **Violence** in Early China, SUNY PB 1990

Leys Simon, The **Analects** of Confucius, Norton 1997

Li T'ien-yi, **Selected** Works of George A. Kennedy, Far Eastern 1964

Li Xueqin, **Eastern** Zhou and Qin Civilizations, Yale 1985

Lin Yü-sheng, The **Evolution** of the Pre-Confucian Meaning of Jen, MS v31 (1975)

Lin Yutang, The **Wisdom** of Confucius, Modern Library 1943

Liu James J. Y., The Chinese **Knight** Errant, Chicago 1967

Loewe Michael, **Crisis** and Conflict in Han China, Allen & Unwin 1974

Loewe Michael, Early Chinese **Texts**, Society for the Study of Early China 1993

Lù Dv́-míng, **Jīng/Dyěn** Shř-wv́n, Dǐng-wv́n 1975

Lyóu Bǎu-nán, Lún Yw̌ **Jv̀ng-yì**, [1866], in: JJC v1

Lyǒu Dzūng-ywǽn, Lún Yw̌ **Byèn**, in: Lyǒu **Jí** 1/68

Lyǒu Dzūng-ywǽn, Lyǒu Hv́-dūng **Jí**, Jūng-hwá 2v 1960

Mǎ Hv́ng, Hàn Shř Jīng **Jí**-tsún, Kv̌sywé 1957

Mair Victor H., Old Sinitic *M'ag, EC #15 (1990)

Mair Victor H., **Tao** Te Ching, Bantam PB 1990

Mair Victor H., **Wandering** on the Way, Bantam PB 1994

Major John, **Heaven** and Earth in Early Han Thought, SUNY PB 1993

Makeham John, **Name** and Actuality in Early Chinese Thought, SUNY 1994

Malmqvist Göran, **What** Did the Master Say, in: Roy **Ancient**

Mao Tzu-shui, Some **Suggestions** for a New Translation of the Confucian Analects, in:
    Thompson **Studia**

Maspero Henri, La Chine **Antique**, [1927]; 2ed, Presses Universitaires 1965

Maspero Henri, China in **Antiquity**, Massachusetts 1971

Mather Richard B., Shih-shuo Hsin **Yü**, Minnesota 1973

Mathieu Rémi, Le **Mu** Tianzi Zhuan, Collège de France 1978

Maugham W. Somerset, **Cakes** and Ale, [1930]; Modern Library 1950

McPhee John, A Roomful of **Hovings**, Farrar Straus 1968

Mei Yi-pao, The **Ethical** and Political Works of Motse, [Probsthain 1929] =
    Hyperion 1973 = Ch'eng-wen 1974

Metzger Thomas A., Some Ancient **Roots** of Modern Chinese Thought, EC v11–12
    (1985–1987)

Morgan Evan, **Tao** The Great Luminant [Kegan Paul 1935] = Paragon 1969
Morohashi Tetsuji, Rongo **Jimbutsu** Kō, Shunyōdō 1937
Morris Ivan, The **Pillow** Book of Sei Shōnagon, 2v Columbia 1967
Morris Ivan, **Madly** Singing in the Mountains, Walker 1970 = Harper PB 1972
Mote Frederick W., Confucian **Eremitism** in the Yüan Period, in: Wright **Persuasion**
Mote Frederick W., Intellectual **Foundations** of China [1971]; 2ed McGraw PB 1989
Mwò Lì-fvng, **Shv́n-nw̌** jr Tàn-syẃn, Shànghǎı Gǔjì 1994
Nán Hwái-jǐn, Lún Yw̌ Byé-tsáı, Fù-dàn 1990
Needham Joseph, **Science** and Civilisation in China, Cambridge 1961–
Nienhauser William H. Jr., The Grand Scribe's **Records**, Indiana 1994–
Nivison David S., Confucianism in **Action**, Stanford 1959
Nivison David S., The Life and Thought of **Chang** Hsüeh-ch'eng, Stanford 1966
Nivison David S., **Golden** Rule Arguments in Chinese Moral Philosophy, in: Nivison
    Ways
Nivison David S., The **Hampers** of Zeng, AOS/Boulder (2 November 1985)
Nivison David S., The **Paradox** of "Virtue," in: Nivison **Ways**
Nivison David S., The **Ways** of Confucianism, Open Court 1996
Nivison David S., **Weakness** of Will in Ancient Chinese Philosophy, in: Nivison **Ways**
Ong Walter J., **Orality** and Literacy [1982]; Routledge PB 1988
Orwell George, **1984** [1949]; various editions
Orwell George, **England** Your England, in: Orwell **Essays**
Orwell George, A Collection of **Essays**, Doubleday PB 1954
Orwell George, The Art of Donald **McGill**, in: Orwell **Essays**
Orwell George, **Shooting** an Elephant, in: Orwell **Essays**
Orwell George, **Such**, Such Were the Joys, in: Orwell **Essays**
Palmer Ruth, Subsistence **Rations** at Pylos and Knossos, Minos v25 (1984)
Pankenier David W., Applied **Astrology** in the Guoyu, WSWG/Amherst (4 May 1996)
Parker Robert B., **Ceremony**, Delacorte 1982
Parker Robert B., **Early** Autumn, Delacorte 1981
Parker Robert B., Promised **Land**, Houghton 1976
Parker Robert B., A Savage **Place**, Delacorte 1981
Parker Robert B., Looking for **Rachel** Wallace, Delacorte 1980
Parker Robert B., **Taming** a Sea-Horse, Delacorte 1986
Parkinson C. Northcote, Parkinson's **Law**, Houghton 1957
Peerenboom R. P., **Law** and Morality in Ancient China, SUNY PB 1993
Pelliot Paul, Le **Chou King** en Caractères Anciens et le Chang Chou Che Wen,
    MAO v2 (1916)
Pfeiffer Robert H., History of New Testament **Times**, Harper 1949
Pokora Timoteus, **Pre-Han** Literature, in: Leslie **Sources**
Polya George, **Induction** and Analogy in Mathematics, Princeton 1954
Pound Ezra, The **Analects**, in: Pound **Confucius**
Pound Ezra, **Confucius**, New Directions PB 1969
Reifler Erwin, The Foot of Chou and the **Span** of Han, MS v30 (1970–1971)
Rickett W. Allyn, **Guanzi**, v1 Princeton 1985
Rickett W. Allyn, **Guanzi Xuekan**, EC v14 (1989)
Ride Lindsay, **Biographical** Note, added to Legge **Analects** [Hong Kong 1960 repr]
Riegel Jeffrey K., [**Review** of Maspero **Antiquity**], JAS v39 (1980)
Roetz Heiner, Confucian Ethics of the **Axial** Age, SUNY PB 1993
Rosemont Henry Jr., Chinese Texts and Philosophical **Contexts**, Open Court PB 1991
Rosemont Henry Jr., A Chinese **Mirror**, Open Court PB 1991
Rosen Sydney, Changing Conceptions of the **Hegemon** in Pre-Ch'in China, in: Roy
    Ancient
Rosen Sydney, In Search of the Historical **Kuan** Chung, JAS v35 (1976)

Roth H[arold] D., **Chuang Tzu**, in: Loewe **Texts**
Roundtable Discussion of *The Trouble with Confucianism*, CRI v1 #1 (1994)
Rouner Leroy S., **Human** Rights and the World's Religions, Notre Dame 1988
Roy David T., **Ancient** China, Chinese University Press 1967
Rudenko Sergei I., **Frozen** Tombs of Siberia, Dent 1970
Rudolph Richard C., **Han** Tomb Art of West China, California 1951
Sage Steven F., Ancient **Sichuan** and the Unification of China, SUNY PB 1992
Sawyer Ralph D., The **Seven** Military Classics of Ancient China, Westview 1993
Schneider Lawrence, A **Madman** of Ch'u, California 1980
Schwartz Benjamin I., The **World** of Thought in Ancient China, Harvard 1985
Seki Gi'ichirō, **Shisho** Chūshaku Zensho, Tōyō Tosho 1922
Shaughnessy Edward L., Historical Perspectives on the Introduction of the **Chariot** in China, HJAS v48 #1 (1988)
Shaughnessy Edward L., **I** Ching, Ballantine 1996
Shaughnessy Edward L., Shang **Shu**, in: Loewe **Texts**
Dìngjōu Syī Hàn Jūngshān Hwái-wáng Mù Jú-jyěn Lún Yǔ **Shř-wśn** Sywěn, WW 1997 #5
Sinor Denis, The Cambridge History of Early **Inner** Asia, Cambridge 1990
Sivin Nathan, **Medicine**, Philosophy, and Religion in Ancient China, Variorum 1995
Sivin Nathan, The Myth of the **Naturalists**, in: Sivin **Medicine**
Smith Arthur H., **Proverbs** and Common Sayings from the Chinese [1914]; Dover PB 1965
Snow C. P., Science and **Government**, Harvard 1961
So Jenny F., **Traders** and Raiders, Washington PB 1995
Soothill William Edward, The **Analects** of Confucius [Oliphant 1910; Oxford 1937]; Dover PB 1995
Spae Joseph John, Itō Jinsai [1948]; Paragon 1967
Stephenson Carl, **Mediaeval** Feudalism, Cornell 1942
Stephenson F. R., **Atlas** of Historical Eclipse Maps: East Asia 1500 BC – AD 1900, Cambridge 1986
Stout Rex, The **Second** Confession, Viking 1949
Strayer Joseph R., The **Idea** of Feudalism, in: Coulborn **Feudalism**
Sùng Shř, Jūng-hwá 1977
Taam Cheuk-woon, On **Studies** of Confucius, PEW v3 (1953)
Takeuchi Yoshio, **Rongo** no Kenkyū, in: Takeuchi **Zenshū**
Takeuchi Yoshio, Takeuchi Yoshio **Zenshū**, Kadogawa 10v 1965–1966
Thompson Laurence G., **Studia** Asiatica, Chinese Materials Center 1975
Thorp Robert L., Erlitou and the Search for the **Xia**, EC v16 (1991)
Tom Chung Yee, A Study on the Land **Communications** of the Han Dynasty, New Asia 1967
Tsien Tsuen-hsuin, **Paper** and Printing, as: Needham **Science** v5 pt1 (1985)
Tsien Tsuen-hsuin, **Written** on Bamboo and Silk, Chicago 1962
Tsuda Sōkichi, **Rongo** to Kōshi no Shisō, Iwanami 1946
Tswēı Shù, Lún Yǔ Pyēn/jāng **Byèn Yí**, in: Tswēı **Yí-shū**
Tswēı Shù, **Kǎu-syìn** Lù, in: Tswēı **Yí-shū**
Tswēı Shù, Tswēı Dūng-bì **Yí-shū**, Shř-jyè 1963
Tswēı Shù, Lún Yǔ **Yǔ-shwō**, in: Tswēı **Yí-shū**
Tu Wei-ming, **Way**, Learning, and Politics, SUNY PB 1993
Turner Karen, Law and "**Progress**" in the Analects, WSWG/Amherst 1995
Turner Karen, The **Theory** of Law in the Ching-fa, EC v14 (1989)
Van Norden Bryan W., Yearley on **Mencius**, JRE v21 #2 (1993)
von Falkenhausen Lothar, **Suspended** Music, California 1993
von **Manstein** Erich, **Lost** Victories [1955; 1958]; Presidio 1982

Vreeland Diana, **D. V.**, Knopf 1984

Wagner Donald B., **Iron** and Steel in Ancient China, Brill 1993

Wakeman Frederic, [**Remarks**], in: **Roundtable**

Waley Arthur, The **Analects** of Confucius, Allen & Unwin 1938 = Modern Library PB nd (omitting Textual Notes) and Vintage PB 1989

Waley Arthur, The Book of **Changes**, BMFEA #5 (1933)

Waley Arthur, **Lo-yang** and its Fall, in: Waley **Secret**

Waley Arthur, **Notes** on Translation, in: Waley **Secret**

Waley Arthur, The **Pillow**-Book of Sei Shōnagon, Allen & Unwin 1928 = Grove PB 1960

Waley Arthur, The **Secret** History of the Mongols, Allen & Unwin 1963

Waley Arthur, The Book of **Songs** [1937]; rev Allen & Unwin 1954 = Grove PB 1960

Waley Arthur, **Three** Ways of Thought in Ancient China, Allen & Unwin 1939; Doubleday PB 1956

Waley Arthur, The **Way** and Its Power [1937]; Grove PB 1958

Waley Arthur, **Yuan** Mei, Allen & Unwin 1956

Wang Gung-wu, Feng Tao: An Essay on Confucian **Loyalty**, in: Wright **Personalities**

Wang Zhongshu, **Han** Civilization, Yale 1982

Ware James R., The **Sayings** of Confucius, Mentor PB 1955

Watson Burton, The Complete Works of **Chuang** Tzu, Columbia 1968

Watson Burton, **Records** of the Grand Historian of China, 2v Columbia 1961

Watson Burton, **Ssu-ma** Ch'ien, Columbia 1958

Watson Burton, The **Tso** Chuan, Columbia 1989

Weld Susan R., Legal Administration: **Cases** from the Provinces, in: Cook **Defining**

Whorf Benjamin Lee, Language, Thought, and **Reality**, MIT PB 1956

Wilhelm Richard, Kungfutse **Gespräche**, Diederichs 1921

Wilhelm Richard, The **I** Ching, Pantheon 2v 1950; 3ed Princeton 1967

Willetts William, Chinese **Art**, Braziller 1958

Wodehouse P. G., Clustering Round Young **Bingo**, in: Wodehouse **Jeeves**

Wodehouse P. G., Unpleasantness at **Bludleigh** Court, in: Wodehouse **Mulliner**

Wodehouse P. G., The World of **Jeeves** [Jenkins 1967]; Harper 1986 = PB 1989

Wodehouse P. G., The World of Mr. **Mulliner**, Taplinger 1974

Wodehouse P. G., Without the **Option**, in: Wodehouse **Jeeves**

Wright Arthur F., Confucian **Personalities**, Stanford 1962

Wright Arthur F., The Confucian **Persuasion**, Stanford 1960

Yang Hsien-yi, **Records** of the Historian, Commercial 1974

Yang Lien-sheng, The Concept of Pao as a **Basis** for Social Relations in China, in: Yang **Excursions**

Yang Lien-sheng, **Excursions** in Sinology, Harvard 1969

Yang Lien-sheng, An Additional Note on the Ancient **Game** Liu-po [1947]; in: Yang **Excursions**

Yang Lien-sheng, A Supplementary **Note** on Mr. Chou Fa-kao's Article on the Final Particle 歟, BIHP v29 (1957)

Yoshikawa Kōjirō, **Hōchō** Fushi, Shinchōsha 1971

Yoshikawa Kōjirō, **Rongo**, Asahi Shimbunsha 2v 1965

Yoshikawa Kōjirō, Rongo **Zakki**, in: Yoshikawa **Hōchō**

Yu Anthony, [**Remarks**], in: **Roundtable**

Yü Ying-shih, The **Hsiung-nu**, in: Sinor **Inner**

Yü Ying-shih, [**Remarks**], in: **Roundtable**

Zakaria Fareed, **Culture** Is Destiny, FA v73 #2 (1994)

Zhang Xinxin, Chinese **Lives**, Pantheon PB 1987

Zhang Xuehai, Conclusions from the Ancient City of the **Lu** State, CSA v19 (1986)

Fragment of the Lǔ Analects Text (LY 11:1)
"I [would go with] . . . " (則 吾 . . .)
Engraved on stone in 174/183. Original size. After Mǎ **Shŕ Jīng** *(fragment 493)*

Romanization Equivalence Table

The spelling used for Chinese words in this book, Common Alphabetic or CA (consonants as in English, vowels as in Italian, plus æ as in "cat," v as in "gut," r as in "fur," z as in "adz," and yw – after l or n simply w – for "umlaut u"), is here compared with other systems encountered by English readers (but not including the one used by Legge). The 401 syllables of modern dictionary Mandarin are given in CA order, with their equivalents in: (1) the Pinyin (PY) system, which employs the letters q, x for sounds which are more readily suggested by chy, shy/sy; and (2) the Wade-Giles (WG) system, based on Spanish spellings enshrined in IPA, and rendering English p/b as p'/p.

CA	PY	WG	CA	PY	WG
a	a	a	chwo	chuo	ch'o
ai	ai	ai	chya	qia	ch'ia
an	an	an	chyang	qiang	ch'iang
ang	ang	ang	chyau	qiao	ch'iao
ar	er	erh	chye	qie	ch'ieh
au	ao	ao	chyen	qian	ch'ien
ba	ba	pa	chyou	qiu	ch'iu
bai	bai	pai	chyung	qiong	ch'iung
ban	ban	pan	chyw	qu	ch'ü
bang	bang	pang	chywæn	quan	ch'üan
bau	bao	pao	chywe	que	ch'üeh
bei	bei	pei	chywn	qun	ch'ün
bi	bi	pi			
bin	bin	pin	da	da	ta
bing	bing	ping	dai	dai	tai
bu	bu	pu	dan	dan	tan
bvn	ben	pen	dang	dang	tang
bvng	beng	peng	dau	dao	tao
bwo	bo	po	dei	dei	tei
byau	biao	piao	di	di	ti
bye	bie	pieh	ding	ding	ting
byen	bian	pien	dou	dou	tou
cha	cha	ch'a	du	du	tu
chai	chai	ch'ai	dun	dun	tun
chan	chan	ch'an	dung	dong	tung
chang	chang	ch'ang	dv	de	te
chau	chao	ch'ao	dvng	deng	teng
chi	qi	ch'i	dwan	duan	tuan
chin	qin	ch'in	dwei	dui	tui
ching	qing	ch'ing	dwo	duo	to
chou	chou	ch'ou	dyau	diao	tiao
chr	chi	ch'ih	dye	die	tieh
chu	chu	ch'u	dyen	dian	tien
chun	chun	ch'un	dyou	diu	tiu
chung	chong	ch'ung	dz	zi	tzu
chv	che	ch'e	dza	za	tsa
chvn	chen	ch'en	dzai	zai	tsai
chvng	cheng	ch'eng	dzan	zan	tsan
chwai	chuai	ch'uai	dzang	zang	tsang
chwan	chuan	ch'uan	dzau	zao	tsao
chwang	chuang	ch'uang	dzei	zei	tsei
chwei	chui	ch'ui	dzou	zou	tsou

CA	PY	WG	CA	PY	WG
dzu	zu	tsu	hwei	hui	hui
dzun	zun	tsun	hwo	huo	huo
dzung	zong	tsung	ja	zha	cha
dzv	ze	tse	jai	zhai	chai
dzvn	zen	tsen	jan	zhan	chan
dzvng	zeng	tseng	jang	zhang	chang
dzwan	zuan	tsuan	jau	zhao	chao
dzwei	zui	tsui	jei	zhei	chei
dzwo	zuo	tso	ji	ji	chi
			jin	jin	chin
fa	fa	fa	jing	jing	ching
fan	fan	fan	jou	zhou	chou
fang	fang	fang	jr	zhi	chih
fei	fei	fei	ju	zhu	chu
fou	fou	fou	jun	zhun	chun
fu	fu	fu	jung	zhong	chung
fvn	fen	fen	jv	zhe	che
fvng	feng	feng	jvn	zhen	chen
fwo	fo	fo	jvng	zheng	cheng
			jwa	zhua	chua
gai	gai	kai	jwai	zhuai	chuai
gan	gan	kan	jwan	zhuan	chuan
gang	gang	kang	jwang	zhuang	chuang
gau	gao	kao	jwei	zhui	chui
gei	gei	kei	jwo	zhuo	cho
gou	gou	kou	jya	jia	chia
gu	gu	ku	jyang	jiang	chiang
gun	gun	kun	jyau	jiao	chiao
gung	gong	kung	jye	jie	chieh
gv	ge	ke	jyen	jian	chien
gvn	gen	ken	jyou	jiu	chiu
gvng	geng	keng	jyung	jiong	chiung
gwa	gua	kua	jyw	ju	chü
gwai	guai	kuai	jywæn	juan	chüan
gwan	guan	kuan	jywe	jue	chüeh
gwang	guang	kuang	jywn	jun	chün
gwei	gui	kuei	ka	ka	k'a
gwo	guo	kuo	kai	kai	k'ai
			kan	kan	k'an
ha	ha	ha	kang	kang	k'ang
hai	hai	hai	kau	kao	k'ao
han	han	han	kou	kou	k'ou
hang	hang	hang	ku	ku	k'u
hau	hao	hao	kun	kun	k'un
hei	hei	hei	kung	kong	k'ung
hou	hou	hou	kv	ke	k'e
hu	hu	hu	kvn	ken	k'en
hun	hun	hun	kvng	keng	k'eng
hung	hong	hung	kwa	kua	k'ua
hv	he	he	kwai	kuai	k'uai
hvn	hen	hen	kwan	kuan	k'uan
hvng	heng	heng	kwang	kuang	k'uang
hwa	hua	hua	kwei	kui	k'uei
hwai	huai	huai	kwo	kuo	k'uo
hwan	huan	huan			
hwang	huang	huang			

CA	PY	WG	CA	PY	WG
la	la	la	nu	nu	nu
lai	lai	lai	nun	nun	nun
lan	lan	lan	nung	nong	nung
lang	lang	lang	nv	ne	ne
lau	lao	lao	nvn	nen	nen
lei	lei	lei	nvng	neng	neng
li	li	li	nw	nyu	nü
lin	lin	lin	nwan	nuan	nuan
ling	ling	ling	nwo	nuo	no
lou	lou	lou	nyang	niang	niang
lu	lu	lu	nyau	niao	niao
lun	lun	lun	nye	nie	nieh
lung	long	lung	nyen	nian	nien
lv	le	le	nyou	niu	niu
lvng	leng	leng	nywe	nüe	nüeh
lw	lyu	lü	ou	ou	ou
lwan	luan	luan	pa	pa	p'a
lwo	luo	lo	pai	pai	p'ai
lya	lia	lia	pan	pan	p'an
lyang	liang	liang	pang	pang	p'ang
lyau	liao	liao	pau	pao	p'ao
lye	lie	lieh	pei	pei	p'ei
lyen	lian	lien	pi	pi	p'i
lyou	liu	liu	pin	pin	p'in
lywe	lüe	lüeh	ping	ping	p'ing
ma	ma	ma	pou	pou	p'ou
mai	mai	mai	pu	pu	p'u
man	man	man	pvn	pen	p'en
mang	mang	mang	pvng	peng	p'eng
mau	mao	mao	pwo	po	p'o
mei	mei	mei	pyau	piao	p'iao
mi	mi	mi	pye	pie	p'ieh
min	min	min	pyen	pian	p'ien
ming	ming	ming	r	ri	jih
mou	mou	mou	ran	ran	jan
mu	mu	mu	rang	rang	jang
mvn	men	men	rau	rao	jao
mvng	meng	meng	rou	rou	jou
mwo	mo	mo	ru	ru	ju
myau	miao	miao	run	run	jun
mye	mie	mieh	rung	rong	jung
myen	mian	mien	rv	re	je
myou	miu	miu	rvn	ren	jen
na	na	na	rvng	reng	jeng
nai	nai	nai	rwa	rua	jua
nan	nan	nan	rwan	ruan	juan
nang	nang	nang	rwei	rui	jui
nau	nao	nao	rwo	ruo	jo
nei	nei	nei	sa	sa	sa
ni	ni	ni	sai	sai	sai
nin	nin	nin	san	san	san
ning	ning	ning	sang	sang	sang
nou	nou	nou	sau	sao	sao

CA	PY	WG	CA	PY	WG
			tsa	ca	ts'a
sha	sha	sha	tsai	cai	ts'ai
shai	shai	shai	tsan	can	ts'an
shan	shan	shan	tsang	cang	ts'ang
shang	shang	shang	tsau	cao	ts'ao
shau	shao	shao	tsou	cou	ts'ou
shei	shei	shei	tsu	cu	ts'u
shou	shou	shou	tsun	cun	ts'un
shr	shi	shih	tsung	cong	ts'ung
shu	shu	shu	tsv	ce	ts'e
shun	shun	shun	tsvn	cen	ts'en
shv	she	she	tsvng	ceng	ts'eng
shvn	shen	shen	tswan	cuan	ts'uan
shvng	sheng	sheng	tswei	cui	ts'ui
shwa	shua	shua	tswo	cuo	ts'o
shwai	shuai	shuai	tsz	ci	tz'u
shwan	shuan	shuan	tu	tu	t'u
shwang	shuang	shuang	tun	tun	t'un
shwei	shui	shui	tung	tong	t'ung
shwo	shuo	shuo	tv	te	t'e
sou	sou	sou	tvng	teng	t'eng
su	su	su	twan	tuan	t'uan
sun	sun	sun	twei	tui	t'ui
sung	song	sung	two	tuo	t'o
sv	se	se	tyau	tiao	t'iao
svn	sen	sen	tye	tie	t'ieh
svng	seng	seng	tyen	tian	t'ien
swan	suan	suan			
swei	sui	sui	v	e	e
swo	suo	so	vn	en	en
sya	xia	hsia	vng	eng	eng
syang	xiang	hsiang	wa	wa	wa
syau	xiao	hsiao	wai	wai	wai
sye	xie	hsieh	wan	wan	wan
syen	xian	hsien	wang	wang	wang
syi	xi	hsi	wei	wei	wei
syin	xin	hsin	wo	wo	wo
sying	xing	hsing	wu	wu	wu
syou	xiu	hsiu	wvn	wen	wen
syung	xiong	hsiung	wvng	weng	weng
syw	xu	hsü	ya	ya	ya
sywæn	xuan	hsüan	yang	yang	yang
sywe	xue	hsüeh	yau	yao	yao
sywn	xun	hsün	ye	ye	yeh
sz	si	ssu	yen	yan	yen
			yi	yi	i
ta	ta	t'a	yin	yin	yin
tai	tai	t'ai	ying	ying	ying
tan	tan	t'an	you	you	yu
tang	tang	t'ang	yung	yong	yung
tau	tao	t'ao	yw	yu	yü
ti	ti	t'i	ywæn	yuan	yüan
ting	ting	t'ing	ywe	yue	yüeh
tou	tou	t'ou	ywn	yun	yün

Interpolations Finding List

The 142 interpolations and the anomalous passage 20:1[19] are here listed by concordance number (the Legge number, if different, is given following a slash), with the number of the chapter to which each has been appended, the date assigned to that chapter or, if followed by a dagger (†), to that passage, and the page on which the translation will be found. The two series of interpolations inferred after LY 15 are distinguished as 15a and 15b. The ranges c0301/0300 for the 15a series, and 0299/0296 for the 15b series, are here more compactly given as c0301 and c0298, respectively.

For the formal evidence relied on in identifying interpolations, see Appendix 1.

LY 1 (c0294)

*1:5	> 17	c0270	p170
*1:10	> 17	c0270	170
*1:12	> 19	c0253	191
*1:16	> 17	c0270	171

LY 2 (c0317)

No interpolations

LY 3 (c0342)

*3:5	> 14	c0310	p127
*3:24	> 18	c0262	178

LY 4 (c0479)

*4:15	> 1	c0294	p149
*4:18	> 2	c0317	114
*4:19	> 2	c0317	114
*4:20	> 2	c0317	115
*4:21	> 2	c0317	115
*4:22	> 2	c0317	115
*4:23	> 2	c0317	115
*4:24	> 2	c0317	115
*4:25	> 2	c0317	115
*4:26	> 1	c0294	149

LY 5 (c0470)

*5:7/6	> 11	c0360	p75
*5:13/12	> 17	c0270	167
*5:14/13	> 11	c0360	75
*5:16/15	> 13	c0322	105
*5:22/21	> 11	c0360	75
*5:26/25	> 1	c0294	149

LY 6 (c0460)

*6:15/13	> 11	c0360	p76
*6:17/15	> 11	c0360	76
*6:24/22	> 13	c0322	105
*6:28/26	> 17	c0270	167
*6:29/27	> 18	c0262	176
*6:30/28	> 18	c0262	176

LY 7 (c0450)

*7:4	> 10	c0370†	p65
*7:9/9a	> 10	c0370†	66
*7:10/9b	> 10	c0370†	66
*7:11/10	> 14	c0310	124
*7:13/12	> 14	c0310	124
*7:15/14	> 14	c0310	125
*7:18/17	> 17	c0270	167
*7:21/20	> 14	c0310	125
*7:25/24	> 14	c0310	125
*7:27/26	> 10	c0370†	66
*7:31/30	> 3	c0342	86
*7:32/31	> 10	c0370†	66
*7:36/35	> 3	c0342	86
*7:37/36	> 3	c0342	86
*7:38/37	> 3	c0342	86

LY 8 (c0436)

*8:1	> 18	c0260†	p176
*8:2a	> 14	c0310	125
*8:2b	> 14	c0310	125
*8:4	> 16	c0285	158
*8:8	> 14	c0310	126
*8:9	> 14	c0310	126
*8:10	> 14	c0310	126
*8:11	> 14	c0310	126
*8:12	> 14	c0310	126
*8:13	> 14	c0310	126
*8:14	> 14	c0310	127
*8:15	> 14	c0310	127
*8:16	> 14	c0310	127
*8:17	> 14	c0310	127
*8:18	> 18	c0260†	177
*8:19	> 18	c0260†	177
*8:20a	> 18	c0260†	177
*8:20b	> 18	c0260†	177
*8:20c	> 18	c0260†	177
*8:21	> 18	c0260†	178

LY 9 (c0405)

*9:1	> 11	c0360	p76
*9:4	> 18	c0262	178
*9:9/8	> 18	c0262	178
*9:10/9	> 10	c0370†	66
*9:14/13	> 13	c0322	105
*9:26/25	> 13	c0322	106
*9:30b/30	> 1	c0294	150

LY 10 (c0380)

*10:9/11a	> 11	c0360	p76
*10:10/11b	> 11	c0360	76
*10:11/12	> 11	c0360	77
*10:15/14	> 3	c0342	87
*10:20/18a	> 11	c0360	77
*10:21/18b	> 11	c0360	77

LY 11 (c0360)

*11:12/11	> 16	c0285	p158
*11:20/21	> 17	c0270	168
*11:24/25	> 1	c0294	150

LY 12 (c0326)

*12:12b	> 13	c0322	p106

LY 13 (c0322)

*13:3	> 19	c0253	p190
*13:7	>15b	c0298†	138
*13:8	> 14	c0310	128
*13:12	>15b	c0298†	138
*13:21	> 14	c0310	128
*13:22a	> 2	c0317	116
*13:22b	> 2	c0317	116

LY 14 (c0310)

*14:1b/2	>15b	c0298†	p138
*14:4/5	>15b	c0298†	139
*14:6/7	>15b	c0298†	139
*14:10/11	>15b	c0298†	139
*14:20/21	>15b	c0298†	139
*14:23/24	>15b	c0298†	139
*14:24/25	>15b	c0298†	139
*14:25/26	>15b	c0298†	139
*14:26a/27	>15b	c0298†	140
*14:26b/28	>15b	c0298†	140
*14:27/29	>15b	c0298†	140
*14:28/30	>15b	c0298†	140
*14:29/31	>15b	c0298†	140
*14:30/32	>15b	c0298†	140
*14:31/33	>15b	c0298†	140
*14:33/35	>15b	c0298†	141
*14:34/36	> 17	c0270	168
*14:35/37	>15b	c0298†	p141
*14:37a/39	> 18	c0262	179
*14:37b/40	> 18	c0262	179
*14:38/41	> 18	c0262	179
*14:39/42	> 18	c0262	179
*14:43/46	> 17	c0270	169
*14:44/47	> 17	c0270	169

LY 15 (c0305)

*15:3/2	>15a	c0301†	p136
*15:4/3	>15a	c0301†	136
*15:10/9	>15a	c0301†	137
*15:11/10	>15a	c0301†	137
*15:13/12	>15b	c0298†	141
*15:14/13	>15b	c0298†	141
*15:18/17	> 17	c0270	169
*15:19/18	>15b	c0298†	141
*15:20/19	>15b	c0298†	141
*15:21/20	>15b	c0298†	142
*15:22/21	>15b	c0298†	142
*15:23/22	>15a	c0301†	137
*15:24/23	>15a	c0301†	137
*15:29/28	>15a	c0301†	138
*15:30/29	>15b	c0298†	142
*15:31/30	>15a	c0301†	138
*15:36/35	> 19	c0253	190
*15:39/38	> 19	c0253	190

LY 16 (c0285)

*16:9	> 18	c0262	p180
*16:14	> 18	c0262	180

LY 17 (c0270)

*17:5/6	> 18	c0262	p180
*17:7/8	> 19	c0253	191

LY 18 (c0262)

*18:1a	> 18	c0260†	p181
*18:1b	> 18	c0260†	181
*18:2	> 18	c0260†	181
*18:8a	> 18	c0260†	181
*18:8b	> 18	c0260†	181
*18:9	> 18	c0260†	182
*18:10	> 18	c0260†	182
*18:11	> 18	c0260†	182

LY 19 (c0253)

*19:13	> 19	c0252†	p191

LY 20 (c0249)

20:1	> 19	c0251†	p192

Index

This Index includes words, names, and major themes in the Analects, as well as general subjects developed in the commentary or Appendices; due to space limitations, authors cited are not listed here. References are to Analects passages (3:4 or the interpolated *3:5¹⁴), or notes to them (3:4n, *3:5¹⁴n), or those passages as repeated in Appendix 5 (3:4A) or *their* notes (3:5An); commentaries not attached to passages are cited as 12h (chapter headnote), 12i (prefatory note to the Interpolations section), or 12r (Reflections). References to Appendices are as A1 (Appendix 1). Page numbers are used otherwise; illustrations are marked by a dagger †; fp 8 is "facing page 8." To save space, English meanings following Chinese characters are here given without quotation marks.

Listings are selective rather than exhaustive; where an entry *is* exhaustively indexed, it is given in **bold**, and will serve as a chronological Analects concordance for that term. Names of persons mentioned in the 05c Analects (LY 4–9) are marked with an asterisk. Alternate names are listed under the most generally familiar form.

The order of entries is alphabetical, ignoring tonemarks but respecting word division; the order of citations within a single entry is chronological rather than numerical, and subdivisions within a series of citations are logical rather than alphabetical. All names, Chinese or other, are given in Chinese (surname-first) order without commas, as in the Works Cited list. For the romanization of Chinese words, see the Introduction, page 2, and the headnote to the conversion table on page 325.

Afterword 後序

In obedience to traditional Chinese practice, we here conclude with a note on the genesis of this book, and on the larger tradition of which it is a part.

Doubts about the orthodox view of the Analects, as compiled within a narrow time span by one or more of Confucius's direct disciples, go back to Hán Yẁ 韓愈 and especially to his protégé Lyǒu Dzūng-ywǽn 柳宗元 in the late Táng dynasty, and reached the point of counterstatement with Hú Yín 胡寅 in the Sùng, who first openly suggested that the work might have more than one layer. Tswēi Shù 崔述 in the Chīng elaborated what amounts to a third-layer theory; his results, largely unpublished in his lifetime, were rediscovered and revived in the present century, and may even be said to have been accepted by recent scholars both Chinese and international, as noted at the beginning of Appendix 1, above. As of 1960, however, they had not displaced the orthodox presumption that the text was put together over a relatively *short* time span, and could thus still plausibly be regarded as reflecting, in its entirety, the thought and career of the historical Confucius.

Following various preparatory researches in 1964–1973, our own work on this and kindred problems with the Warring States texts was catalyzed in 1974 by a question from J. R. Hightower about the authenticity of certain Jwāngdž passages. Study of that text, supported by a 1979 grant from the American Council of Learned Societies with funding from the National Endowment for the Humanities, showed that the Jwāngdž was insoluble without reference to the Warring States text problem as a whole, and that the Analects, with its great time depth, was the key to that problem. The critical discovery, that anomalies in the Analects could be resolved by a hypothesis of accretional growth complicated by a parallel *interpolational* growth, was made on 27 April 1980. It was extended in later years into an integrated chronology embracing most of the major Warring States texts.

Discussions in 1981–1987 with David S. Nivison, Victor Mair, F. W. Mote, and the late Joseph F. Fletcher, Jr., exposed the theory to criticism; several footnotes in David Nivison's 13 February 1984 Evans-Wentz lecture constitute, so far as we know, the first scholarly reference to our findings. Various implications of the work were presented for criticism in annual talks in 1984–1993 to the Colloquium Orientologicum of the University of Massachusetts at Amherst. Conversations at the annual meetings of the New England Symposium on Chinese Thought in 1988–1993 were also fruitful, and a 19 May 1990 paper for the Symposium on the Analects / Dàu/Dv́ Jīng relationship received a helpful response. On 11 June 1993, Dean Lee R. Edwards of the College of Humanities and Fine Arts of the University of Massachusetts authorized, and Professor Alvin P. Cohen has since coordinated, an interuniversity Warring States Working Group, which from its first meeting of sixteen persons on 9–10 October 1993, on three occasions with support from the Committee on China and Inner Asia of the Association for Asian Studies, has provided a semiannual forum for the criticism and development of the chronology and its historical interpretation. Highlights included a presentation to the field, proposed by Paul Ropp and given at the New England regional meeting of the Association for Asian Studies on 15 October 1994 with Kidder Smith as moderator and Karen Turner and David N. Keightley as discussants, and a panel on Developmental Aspects of the Warring States for that body on 28 October 1995 with Dennis Grafflin, Constance A. Cook, and Karen Turner as co-participants. Thanks are herewith extended to all concerned.

Our further study of the linguistic evidence culminated on 15 October 1993 in a revision of what we regarded as the extent of the LY 4 core, and a Warring States Working Group exchange with David Nivison on the date of the Chí kingship led on 14 September 1996 to an adjustment of the date previously assigned to LY 3. Lecture audiences at the Universities of North Carolina and Pennsylvania, Bates College, and Harvard, Brown, Indiana and Columbia Universities in 1993–1997 raised a number of other provocative questions which readers will find addressed, if perhaps not definitively answered, in these pages. A 1996 grant from the National Endowment for the Humanities supported continued research on the larger text chronology; those results, for which, as usual, the authors take full responsibility, have been drawn upon for some of the annotations in the present work.

A partial version of the translation was read and, on 29 October 1995, criticized, by twenty members of the Warring States Working Group; more complete versions were later shared with Alvin P. Cohen, Henry Rosemont, Jr., and several students of David N. Keightley. We accept the responsibility for making final choices among the sometimes opposed suggestions and comments which we received in response, all of which have helped to make the present work more nearly adequate to its task.

It was twice hoped to publish a summary account of our general view of the Warring States texts and the history that they imply, against which background this Analects translation would function as the elaboration of one, albeit crucial, detail. In the event, however, the present work carries the double burden of establishing its foundations even as it builds on them. The patience of readers with the steps taken herein to mitigate this dilemma is much appreciated. Irene Bloom originally suggested the book, and Jennifer Crewe, Publisher for the Humanities at Columbia University Press, and in the last stages Ronald C. Harris, Assistant Managing Editor, have forbearingly guided it to its present completion.

The lively interest of the Analects compilers in the visual and musical arts is symbolized in the present work by a series of images of Warring States objects from the collections of the Freer Gallery of Art and the Arthur M. Sackler Gallery. For gracious hospitality during a one-day visit to Washington, and for expert advice and criticism in the selection of objects to exemplify the material and aesthetic context of the Analects, the authors are grateful to Jenny F. So 蘇芳淑, Curator of Ancient Chinese Art; and for assistance with the details of preparing source photographs, and of arranging for permission to reproduce, to Scott Thompson of the Permissions Department, of the Freer Gallery of Art and the Arthur M. Sackler Gallery of the Smithsonian Institution, Washington, DC. For the calligraphy for the Chinese title on the book jacket, with its allusion to the researches of Gù Jyé-gāng 顧頡剛, we are indebted to our colleague Shen Zhongwei 沈鍾偉 of the Department of Asian Languages and Literatures at the University of Massachusetts at Amherst.

To the thinkers and other combatants of the Warring States, on whose courage we have sometimes been glad to draw, and to our readers in the present age, whose potential interest has been our first motivation, we offer our final acknowledgement, and the hope that the resulting book, for all its inevitable flaws and shortcomings, may provide a foundation for more perfect insights in the years to come.

E. Bruce Brooks
A. Taeko Brooks

22 November 1997

Other Works in the Columbia Asian Studies Series

Translations from the Asian Classics

Courtier and Commoner in Ancient China: Selections from the History of the Former Han by Pan Ku, tr. Burton Watson. Also in paperback ed. 1974

Japanese Literature in Chinese, vol. 1: Poetry and Prose in Chinese by Japanese Writers of the Early Period, tr. Burton Watson 1975

Japanese Literature in Chinese, vol. 2: Poetry and Prose in Chinese by Japanese Writers of the Later Period, tr. Burton Watson 1976

Scripture of the Lotus Blossom of the Fine Dharma, tr. Leon Hurvitz. Also in paperback ed. 1976

Love Song of the Dark Lord: Jayadeva's Gītagovinda, tr. Barbara Stoler Miller. Also in paperback ed. Cloth ed. includes critical text of the Sanskrit. 1977; rev. ed. 1997

Ryōkan: Zen Monk-Poet of Japan, tr. Burton Watson 1977

Calming the Mind and Discerning the Real: From the Lam rim chen mo of Tson-kha-pa, tr. Alex Wayman 1978

The Hermit and the Love-Thief: Sanskrit Poems of Bhartrihari and Bilhaṇa, tr. Barbara Stoler Miller 1978

The Lute: Kao Ming's P'i-p'a chi, tr. Jean Mulligan. Also in paperback ed. 1980

A Chronicle of Gods and Sovereigns: Jinnō Shōtōki of Kitabatake Chikafusa, tr. H. Paul Varley 1980

Among the Flowers: The Hua-chien chi, tr. Lois Fusek 1982

Grass Hill: Poems and Prose by the Japanese Monk Gensei, tr. Burton Watson 1983

Doctors, Diviners, and Magicians of Ancient China: Biographies of Fang-shih, tr. Kenneth J. DeWoskin. Also in paperback ed. 1983

Theater of Memory: The Plays of Kālidāsa, ed. Barbara Stoler Miller. Also in paperback ed. 1984

The Columbia Book of Chinese Poetry: From Early Times to the Thirteenth Century, ed. and tr. Burton Watson. Also in paperback ed. 1984

Poems of Love and War: From the Eight Anthologies and the Ten Long Poems of Classical Tamil, tr. A. K. Ramanujan. Also in paperback ed. 1985

The Bhagavad Gita: Krishna's Counsel in Time of War, tr. Barbara Stoler Miller 1986

The Columbia Book of Later Chinese Poetry, ed. and tr. Jonathan Chaves. Also in paperback ed. 1986

The Tso Chuan: Selections from China's Oldest Narrative History, tr. Burton Watson 1989

Waiting for the Wind: Thirty-six Poets of Japan's Late Medieval Age, tr. Steven Carter 1989

Selected Writings of Nichiren, ed. Philip B. Yampolsky 1990

Saigyō, Poems of a Mountain Home, tr. Burton Watson 1990

The Book of Lieh Tzu: A Classic of the Tao, tr. A. C. Graham. Morningside ed. 1990

The Tale of an Anklet: An Epic of South India — The Cilappatikāram of Iḷaṅkō Aṭikaḷ, tr. R. Parthasarathy 1993

Waiting for the Dawn: A Plan for the Prince, tr. and introduction by Wm. Theodore de Bary 1993

Yoshitsune and the Thousand Cherry Trees: A Masterpiece of the Eighteenth-Century Japanese Puppet Theater, tr., annotated, and with introduction by Stanleigh H. Jones, Jr. 1993

The Lotus Sutra, tr. Burton Watson. Also in paperback ed. 1993

The Classic of Changes: A New Translation of the I Ching as Interpreted by Wang Bi, tr. Richard John Lynn 1994

Beyond Spring: Tz'u Poems of the Sung Dynasty, tr. Julie Landau 1994

The Columbia Anthology of Traditional Chinese Literature, ed. Victor H. Mair 1994

Scenes for Mandarins: The Elite Theater of the Ming, tr. Cyril Birch 1995
Letters of Nichiren, ed. Philip B. Yampolsky; tr. Burton Watson et al. 1996
Unforgotten Dreams: Poems by the Zen Monk Shōtetsu, tr. Steven D. Carter 1997
The Vimalakirti Sutra, tr. Burton Watson 1997
Japanese and Chinese Poems to Sing: The Wakan rōei shū, tr. J. Thomas Rimer and
    Jonathan Chaves 1997
A Tower for the Summer Heat, Li Yu, tr. Patrick Hanan 1998
Traditional Japanese Theater: An Anthology of Plays, Karen Brazell 1998
The Original Analects: Sayings of Confucius and His Successors (0479–0249),
    E. Bruce Brooks and A. Taeko Brooks 1998
The Classic of the Way and Virtue: A New Translation of the Tao-te ching of Laozi
    as Interpreted by Wang Bi, tr. Richard John Lynn 1999
The Four Hundred Songs of War and Wisdom: An Anthology of Poems from Classical
    Tamil, The Puranāṇūru, eds. and trans. George L. Hart and Hank Heifetz 1999
Original Tao: Inward Training (Nei-yeh) and the Foundations of Taoist Mysticism,
    by Harold D. Roth 1999
Lao Tzu's Tao Te Ching: A Translation of the Startling New Documents Found at
    Guodian, Robert G. Henricks 2000
The Shorter Columbia Anthology of Traditional Chinese Literature, ed. Victor H.
    Mair 2000
Mistress and Maid (Jiaohongji) by Meng Chengshun, tr. Cyril Birch 2001
Chikamatsu: Five Late Plays, tr. and ed. C. Andrew Gerstle
The Essential Lotus: Selections from the Lotus Sutra, tr. Burton Watson 2002

Modern Asian Literature

Modern Japanese Drama: An Anthology, ed. and tr. Ted. Takaya. Also in paperback
    ed. 1979
Mask and Sword: Two Plays for the Contemporary Japanese Theater, by Yamazaki
    Masakazu, tr. J. Thomas Rimer 1980
Yokomitsu Riichi, Modernist, Dennis Keene 1980
Nepali Visions, Nepali Dreams: The Poetry of Laxmiprasad Devkota, tr. David
    Rubin 1980
Literature of the Hundred Flowers, vol. 1: Criticism and Polemics, ed. Hualing Nieh
    1981
Literature of the Hundred Flowers, vol. 2: Poetry and Fiction, ed. Hualing Nieh
    1981
Modern Chinese Stories and Novellas, 1919–1949, ed. Joseph S. M. Lau, C. T. Hsia,
    and Leo Ou-fan Lee. Also in paperback ed. 1984
A View by the Sea, by Yasuoka Shōtarō, tr. Kären Wigen Lewis 1984
Other Worlds: Arishima Takeo and the Bounds of Modern Japanese Fiction, by Paul
    Anderer 1984
Selected Poems of Sō Chōngju, tr. with introduction by David R. McCann 1989
The Sting of Life: Four Contemporary Japanese Novelists, by Van C. Gessel 1989
Stories of Osaka Life, by Oda Sakunosuke, tr. Burton Watson 1990
The Bodhisattva, or Samantabhadra, by Ishikawa Jun, tr. with introduction by
    William Jefferson Tyler 1990
The Travels of Lao Ts'an, by Liu T'ieh-yün, tr. Harold Shadick. Morningside ed.
    1990
Three Plays by Kōbō Abe, tr. with introduction by Donald Keene 1993
The Columbia Anthology of Modern Chinese Literature, ed. Joseph S. M. Lau and
    Howard Goldblatt 1995
Modern Japanese Tanka, ed. and tr. by Makoto Ueda 1996

Masaoka Shiki: Selected Poems, ed. and tr. by Burton Watson 1997
Writing Women in Modern China: An Anthology of Women's Literature from the Early Twentieth Century, ed. and tr. by Amy D. Dooling and Kristina M. Torgeson 1998
American Stories, by Nagai Kafū, tr. Mitsuko Iriye 2000
The Paper Door and Other Stories, by Shiga Naoya, tr. Lane Dunlop 2001

Studies in Asian Culture

The Ōnin War: History of Its Origins and Background, with a Selective Translation of the Chronicle of Ōnin, by H. Paul Varley 1967
Chinese Government in Ming Times: Seven Studies, ed. Charles O. Hucker 1969
The Actors' Analects (Yakusha Rongo), ed. and tr. by Charles J. Dunn and Bungō Torigoe 1969
Self and Society in Ming Thought, by Wm. Theodore de Bary and the Conference on Ming Thought. Also in paperback ed. 1970
A History of Islamic Philosophy, by Majid Fakhry, 2d ed. 1983
Phantasies of a Love Thief: The Caurapañatcāśikā Attributed to Bilhaṇa, by Barbara Stoler Miller 1971
Iqbal: Poet-Philosopher of Pakistan, ed. Hafeez Malik 1971
The Golden Tradition: An Anthology of Urdu Poetry, ed. and tr. Ahmed Ali. Also in paperback ed. 1973
Conquerors and Confucians: Aspects of Political Change in Late Yüan China, by John W. Dardess 1973
The Unfolding of Neo-Confucianism, by Wm. Theodore de Bary and the Conference on Seventeenth-Century Chinese Thought. Also in paperback ed. 1975
To Acquire Wisdom: The Way of Wang Yang-ming, by Julia Ching 1976
Gods, Priests, and Warriors: The Bhrgus of the Mahābhārata, by Robert P. Goldman 1977
Mei Yao-ch'en and the Development of Early Sung Poetry, by Jonathan Chaves 1976
The Legend of Semimaru, Blind Musician of Japan, by Susan Matisoff 1977
Sir Sayyid Ahmad Khan and Muslim Modernization in India and Pakistan, by Hafeez Malik 1980
The Khilafat Movement: Religious Symbolism and Political Mobilization in India, by Gail Minault 1982
The World of K'ung Shang-jen: A Man of Letters in Early Ch'ing China, by Richard Strassberg 1983
The Lotus Boat: The Origins of Chinese Tz'u Poetry in T'ang Popular Culture, by Marsha L. Wagner 1984
Expressions of Self in Chinese Literature, ed. Robert E. Hegel and Richard C. Hessney 1985
Songs for the Bride: Women's Voices and Wedding Rites of Rural India, by W. G. Archer; eds. Barbara Stoler Miller and Mildred Archer 1986
The Confucian Kingship in Korea: Yŏngjo and the Politics of Sagacity, by JaHyun Kim Haboush 1988

Companions to Asian Studies

Approaches to the Oriental Classics, ed. Wm. Theodore de Bary 1959
Early Chinese Literature, by Burton Watson. Also in paperback ed. 1962
Approaches to Asian Civilizations, eds. Wm. Theodore de Bary and Ainslie T. Embree 1964

The Classic Chinese Novel: A Critical Introduction, by C. T. Hsia. Also in paperback ed. 1968

Chinese Lyricism: Shih Poetry from the Second to the Twelfth Century, tr. Burton Watson. Also in paperback ed. 1971

A Syllabus of Indian Civilization, by Leonard A. Gordon and Barbara Stoler Miller 1971

Twentieth-Century Chinese Stories, ed. C. T. Hsia and Joseph S. M. Lau. Also in paperback ed. 1971

A Syllabus of Chinese Civilization, by J. Mason Gentzler, 2d ed. 1972

A Syllabus of Japanese Civilization, by H. Paul Varley, 2d ed. 1972

An Introduction to Chinese Civilization, ed. John Meskill, with the assistance of J. Mason Gentzler 1973

An Introduction to Japanese Civilization, ed. Arthur E. Tiedemann 1974

Ukifune: Love in the Tale of Genji, ed. Andrew Pekarik 1982

The Pleasures of Japanese Literature, by Donald Keene 1988

A Guide to Oriental Classics, eds. Wm. Theodore de Bary and Ainslie T. Embree; 3d edition ed. Amy Vladeck Heinrich, 2 vols. 1989

Introduction to Asian Civilizations
Wm. Theodore de Bary, General Editor

Sources of Japanese Tradition, 1958; paperback ed., 2 vols., 1964. 2d ed., vol. 1, 2001, compiled by Wm. Theodore de Bary, Donald Keene, George Tanabe, and Paul Varley

Sources of Indian Tradition, 1958; paperback ed., 2 vols., 1964. 2d ed., 2 vols., 1988

Sources of Chinese Tradition, 1960, paperback ed., 2 vols., 1964. 2d ed., vol. 1, 1999, compiled by Wm. Theodore de Bary and Irene Bloom; vol. 2, 2000, compiled by Wm. Theodore de Bary and Richard Lufrano

Sources of Korean Tradition, 1997; 2 vols., vol. 1, 1997, compiled by Peter H. Lee and Wm. Theodore de Bary; vol. 2, 2001, compiled by Yăngho Ch'oe, Peter H. Lee, and Wm. Theodore de Bary

Neo-Confucian Studies

Instructions for Practical Living and Other Neo-Confucian Writings by Wang Yang-ming, tr. Wing-tsit Chan 1963

Reflections on Things at Hand: The Neo-Confucian Anthology, comp. Chu Hsi and Lü Tsu-ch'ien, tr. Wing-tsit Chan 1967

Self and Society in Ming Thought, by Wm. Theodore de Bary and the Conference on Ming Thought. Also in paperback ed. 1970

The Unfolding of Neo-Confucianism, by Wm. Theodore de Bary and the Conference on Seventeenth-Century Chinese Thought. Also in paperback ed. 1975

Principle and Practicality: Essays in Neo-Confucianism and Practical Learning, eds. Wm. Theodore de Bary and Irene Bloom. Also in paperback ed. 1979

The Syncretic Religion of Lin Chao-en, by Judith A. Berling 1980

The Renewal of Buddhism in China: Chu-hung and the Late Ming Synthesis, by Chün-fang Yü 1981

Neo-Confucian Orthodoxy and the Learning of the Mind-and-Heart, by Wm. Theodore de Bary 1981

Yüan Thought: Chinese Thought and Religion Under the Mongols, eds. Hok-lam Chan and Wm. Theodore de Bary 1982

The Liberal Tradition in China, by Wm. Theodore de Bary 1983

The Development and Decline of Chinese Cosmology, by John B. Henderson 1984

The Rise of Neo-Confucianism in Korea, by Wm. Theodore de Bary and JaHyun Kim Haboush 1985

Chiao Hung and the Restructuring of Neo-Confucianism in Late Ming, by Edward T. Ch'ien 1985

Neo-Confucian Terms Explained: Pei-hsi tzu-i, by Ch'en Ch'un, ed. and trans. Wing-tsit Chan 1986

Knowledge Painfully Acquired: K'un-chih chi, by Lo Ch'in-shun, ed. and trans. Irene Bloom 1987

To Become a Sage: The Ten Diagrams on Sage Learning, by Yi T'oegye, ed. and trans. Michael C. Kalton 1988

The Message of the Mind in Neo-Confucian Thought, by Wm. Theodore de Bary 1989

CPSIA information can be obtained
at www.ICGtesting.com
Printed in the USA
LVHW021828130819
627499LV00013B/762